Western Civilizations I

Western Civilizations I

HIS103

Edited by Anna Biel

Cover image Authored by: Willian West. Located at: https://unsplash.com/photos/YpKiwlvhOpI

Published by SUNY OER Services
Milne Library
State University of New York at Geneseo
Geneseo, NY 14454

Distributed by State University of New York Press

ISBN: 978-1-64176-013-3

This book was produced using Pressbooks.com, and PDF rendering was done by PrinceXML.

Contents

4. Ancient Greece and the Hellenistic World

5. Early Roman Civilization and the Roman Republic

6. The Roman Empire

About This Book

Your Western Civilizations I textbook is a compilation of articles written by instructors for universities around the country. The entire compilation is provided free of charge online through a Creative Commons license. You can access or even copy all the material here, for your own reference, even after the semester ends.

Different Versions

An electronic version is made available via your course at https://courses.lumenlearning.com/suny-fmcc-worldhistory/. You may also purchase a physical copy at the College Bookstore. The electronic version has access to multimedia content including video, slideshows, and interactive activities. The print version will have all the same reading material, but not include the multimedia content.

About the Author

There are many different authors; look to the "Licenses and Attributions" section at the end of each chapter to identify contributors. This compilation was edited by Anya Biel at Fulton-Montgomery Community College.

Attributions

1. The Study of History and the Rise of Civilization

Splitting History

Learning Objective

- Analyze the complications inherent to splitting history for the purpose of academic study

Key Points

- The question of what kind of inquiries historians pose, what knowledge they seek, and how they interpret the evidence that they find remains controversial. Historians draw conclusions from the past approaches to history but in the end, they always write in the context of their own time, current dominant ideas of how to interpret the past, and even subjective viewpoints.

- All events that are remembered and preserved in some original form constitute the historical record. The task of historians is to identify the sources that can most usefully contribute to the production of accurate accounts of the past. These sources, known are primary sources or evidence, were produced at the time under study and constitute the foundation of historical inquiry.

- Periodization is the process of categorizing the past into discrete, quantified named blocks of time in order to facilitate the study and analysis of history. This results in descriptive abstractions that provide convenient terms for periods of time with relatively stable characteristics. All systems of periodization are arbitrary.

- The common general split between prehistory, ancient history, Middle Ages, modern history, and contemporary history is a Western division of the largest blocks of time agreed upon by Western historians. However, even within this largely accepted division the perspective of specific national developments and experiences often divides Western historians, as some periodizing labels will be applicable only to particular regions.

- The study of world history emerged as a distinct academic field in order to examine history from a global perspective rather than a solely national perspective of investigation. However, the field still struggles with an inherently Western periodization.

- World historians use a thematic approach to look for common patterns that emerge across all cultures. World history's periodization, as imperfect and biased as it is, serves as a way to organize and systematize knowledge.

Terms

periodization

The process or study of categorizing the past into discrete, quantified named blocks of time in order to facilitate the study and analysis of history. This results in descriptive abstractions that provide convenient terms for periods of time with relatively stable characteristics. However, determining the precise beginning and ending to any period is usually arbitrary.

primary sources

Original sources of information about a topic. In the study of history as an academic discipline, primary sources include artifact, document, diary, manuscript, autobiography, recording, or other source of information that was created at the time under study.

How Do We Write History?

The word *history* comes ultimately from Ancient Greek *historía*, meaning "inquiry," "knowledge from inquiry," or "judge." However, the question of what kind of inquiries historians pose, what knowledge they seek, and how they interpret the evidence that they find remains controversial. Historians draw conclusions from past approaches to history, but in the end, they always write in the context of their own time, current dominant ideas of how to interpret the past, and even subjective viewpoints. Furthermore, current events and developments often trigger which past events, historical periods, or geographical regions are seen as critical and thus should be investigated. Finally, historical studies are designed to provide specific lessons for societies today. In the words of Benedetto Croce, Italian philosopher and historian, "All history is contemporary history."

All events that are remembered and preserved in some original form constitute the historical record. The task of historians is to identify the sources that can most usefully contribute to the production of accurate accounts of the past. These sources, known are primary sources or evidence, were produced at the time under study and constitute the foundation of historical inquiry. Ideally, a historian will use as many available primary sources as can be accessed, but in practice, sources may have been destroyed or may not be available for research. In some cases, the only eyewitness reports of an event may be memoirs, autobiographies, or oral interviews taken years later. Sometimes, the only evidence relating to an event or person in the distant past was written or copied decades or centuries later. Historians remain cautious when working with evidence recorded years, or even decades or centuries, after an event; this kind of evidence poses the question of to what extent witnesses remember events accurately. However, historians also point out that hardly any historical evidence can be seen as objective, as it is always a product of particular individuals, times, and dominant ideas. This is also why researchers try to find as many records of an event under investigation as possible, and it is not unusual that they find evidence that may present contradictory accounts of the same events.

In general, the sources of historical knowledge can be separated into three categories: what is written, what is said, and what is physically preserved. Historians often consult all three.

Periodization

Periodization is the process of categorizing the past into discrete, quantified, named blocks of time in order to facilitate the study and analysis of history. This results in descriptive abstractions that provide convenient terms for periods of time with relatively stable characteristics.

To the extent that history is continuous and cannot be generalized, all systems of periodization are arbitrary. Moreover, determining the precise beginning and ending to any period is also a matter of arbitrary decisions. Eventually, periodizing labels are a reflection of very particular cultural and geographical perspectives, as well as specific subfields or themes of history (e.g., military history, social history, political history, intellectual history, cultural history, etc.).

Consequently, not only do periodizing blocks inevitably overlap, but they also often seemingly conflict with or contradict one another. Some have a cultural usage (the Gilded Age), others refer to prominent historical events (the inter-war years: 1918–1939), yet others are defined by decimal numbering systems (the 1960s, the 17th century). Other periods are named after influential individuals whose impact may or may not have reached beyond certain geographic regions (the Victorian Era, the Edwardian Era, the Napoleonic Era).

Western Historical Periods

The common general split between prehistory (before written history), ancient history, Middle Ages, modern history, and contemporary history (history within the living memory) is a Western division of the largest blocks of time agreed upon by Western historians and representing the Western point of view. For example, the history of Asia or Africa cannot be neatly categorized following these periods.

However, even within this largely accepted division, the perspective of specific national developments and experiences often divides Western historians, as some periodizing labels will be applicable only to particular regions.

This is especially true of labels derived from individuals or ruling dynasties, such as the Jacksonian Era in the United States, or the Merovingian Period in France. Cultural terms may also have a limited, even if larger, reach. For example, the concept of the Romantic period is largely meaningless outside of Europe and European-influenced cultures; even within those areas, different European regions may mark the beginning and the ending points of Romanticism differently. Likewise, the 1960s, although technically applicable to anywhere in the world according to Common Era numbering, has a certain set of specific cultural connotations in certain countries, including sexual revolution, counterculture, or youth rebellion. However, those never emerged in certain regions (e.g., in Spain under Francisco Franco's authoritarian regime). Some historians have also noted that the 1960s, as a descriptive historical period, actually began in the late 1950s and ended in the early 1970s, because the cultural and economic conditions that define the meaning of the period dominated longer than the actual decade of the 1960s.

DOMINVS FRANCISCHVS PETRARCHA

Petrarch by Andrea del Castagno. Petrarch, Italian poet and thinker, conceived of the idea of a European "Dark Age," which later evolved into the tripartite periodization of Western history into Ancient, Middle Ages and Modern.

While world history (also referred to as global history or transnational history) emerged as a distinct academic field of historical study in the 1980s in order to examine history from a global perspective rather than a solely national perspective of investigation, it still struggles with an inherently Western periodization. The common splits used when designing comprehensive college-level world history courses (and thus also used in history textbooks that are usually divided into volumes covering pre-modern and modern eras) are still a result of certain historical developments presented from the perspective of the Western world and particular national experiences. However, even the split between pre-modern and modern eras is problematic because it is complicated by the question of how history educators, textbook authors, and publishers decide to categorize what is known as the early modern era, which is traditionally a period between Renaissance and the end of the Age of Enlightenment. In the end, whether the early modern era is included in the first or the second part of a world history course frequently offered in U.S. colleges is a subjective decision of history educators. As a result, the same questions and choices apply to history textbooks written and published for the U.S. audience.

World historians use a thematic approach to identify common patterns that emerge across all cultures, with two major focal points: integration (how processes of world history have drawn people of the world together) and difference (how patterns of world history reveal the diversity of the human experiences). The periodization of world history, as imperfect and biased as it is, serves as a way to organize and systematize knowledge.

Without it, history would be nothing more than scattered events without a framework designed to help us understand the past.

Sources

Attributions

CC licensed content, Specific attribution

- Boundless World History. **Authored by**: Boundless. **Located at**: https://courses.lumenlearning.com/boundless-worldhistory/. **License**: *CC BY-SA: Attribution-ShareAlike*

Historical Bias

Learning Objective

- Identify some examples of historical bias

Key Points

- Regardless of whether they are conscious or learned implicitly within cultural contexts, biases have been part of historical investigation since the ancient beginnings of the discipline. As such, history provides an excellent example of how biases change, evolve, and even disappear.

- Early attempts to make history an empirical, objective discipline (most notably by Voltaire) did not find many followers. Throughout the 18th and 19th centuries, European historians only strengthened their biases. As Europe gradually dominated the world through the self-imposed mission to colonize nearly all the other continents, Eurocentrism prevailed in history.

- Even within the Eurocentric perspective, not all Europeans were equal; Western historians largely ignored aspects of history, such as class, gender, or ethnicity. Until the rapid development of social history in the 1960s and 1970s, mainstream Western historical narratives focused on political and military history, while cultural or social history was written mostly from the perspective of the elites.

- The biased approach to history-writing transferred also to history-teaching. From the origins of national mass schooling systems in the 19th century, the teaching of history to promote national sentiment has been a high priority. History textbooks in most countries have been tools to foster nationalism and patriotism and to promote the most favorable version of national history.

- Germany attempts to be an example of how to remove nationalistic narratives from history education. The history curriculum in Germany is characterized by a transnational perspective that emphasizes the all-European heritage, minimizes the idea of national pride, and fosters the notion of civil society centered on democracy, human rights, and peace.

- Despite progress and increased focus on groups that have been traditionally excluded from mainstream historical narratives (people of color, women, the working class, the poor, the disabled, LGBTQI-identified people, etc.), bias remains a component of historical investigation.

TermS

Eurocentrism

The practice of viewing the world from a European or generally Western perspective with an implied belief in the pre-eminence of Western culture. It may also be used to describe a view centered on the history or eminence of white people. The term was coined in the 1980s, referring to the notion of European exceptionalism and other Western equivalents, such as American exceptionalism.

Bias in Historical Writing

Bias is an inclination or outlook to present or hold a partial perspective, often accompanied by a refusal to consider the possible merits of alternative points of view. Regardless of whether conscious or learned implicitly within cultural contexts, biases have been part of historical investigation since the ancient beginnings of the discipline. As such, history provides an excellent example of how biases change, evolve, and even disappear.

History as a modern academic discipline based on empirical methods (in this case, studying primary sources in order to reconstruct the past based on available evidence), rose to prominence during the Age of Enlightenment. Voltaire, a French author and thinker, is credited to have developed a fresh outlook on history that broke from the tradition of narrating diplomatic and military events and emphasized customs, social history (the history of ordinary people) and achievements in the arts and sciences. His *Essay on Customs* traced the progress of world civilization in a universal context, thereby rejecting both nationalism and the traditional Christian frame of reference. Voltaire was also the first scholar to make a serious attempt to write the history of the world, eliminating theological frameworks and emphasizing economics, culture, and political history. He was the first to emphasize the debt of medieval culture to Middle Eastern civilization. Although he repeatedly warned against political bias on the part of the historian, he did not miss many opportunities to expose the intolerance and frauds of the Catholic Church over the ages—
a topic that was Voltaire's life-long intellectual interest.

Voltaire's early attempts to make history an empirical, objective discipline did not find many followers. Throughout the 18th and 19th centuries, European historians only strengthened their biases. As Europe gradually benefited from the ongoing scientific progress and dominated the world in the self-imposed mission to colonize nearly all other continents, Eurocentrism prevailed in history. The practice of viewing and presenting the world from a European or generally Western perspective, with an implied belief in the pre-eminence of Western culture, dominated among European historians who contrasted the progressively mechanized character of European culture with traditional hunting, farming and herding societies in many of the areas of the world being newly conquered and colonized. These included the Americas, Asia, Africa and, later, the Pacific and Australasia. Many European writers of this time construed the history of Europe as paradigmatic for the rest of the world. Other cultures were identified as having reached a stage that Europe itself had already passed: primitive hunter-gatherer, farming, early civilization, feudalism and modern liberal-capitalism. Only Europe was considered to have achieved the last stage. With this assumption, Europeans were also presented as racially superior, and European history as a discipline became essentially the history of the dominance of white peoples.

However, even within the Eurocentric perspective, not all Europeans were equal; Western historians largely ignored aspects of history, such as class, gender, or ethnicity. Until relatively recently (particularly the rapid development of social history in the 1960s and 1970s), mainstream Western historical narratives focused on political and military history, while cultural or social history was written mostly from the perspective of the elites. Consequently, what was in fact an experience of a selected few (usually white males of upper classes, with some occasional mentions of their female counterparts), was typically presented as the illustrative experience of the entire society. In the United States, some of the first to break this approach were African American scholars who at the turn of the 20th century wrote histories of black Americans and called for their inclusion in the mainstream historical narrative.

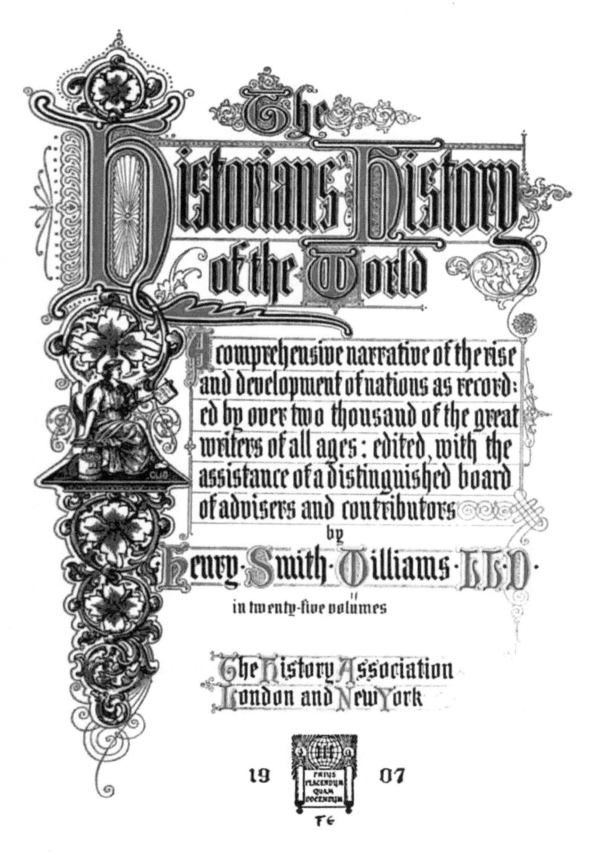

The Historians' History of the World

A comprehensive narrative of the rise and development of nations as recorded by over two thousand of the great writers of all ages: edited, with the assistance of a distinguished board of advisers and contributors

by

Henry Smith Williams LL.D.

in twenty-five volumes

The History Association
London and New York

19   07

TITLE-PAGE DESIGNED AND ENGRAVED
BY TIFFANY & CO., NEW YORK

The title page to The Historians' History of the World: A Comprehensive Narrative of the Rise and Development of Nations as Recorded by over two thousand of the Great Writers of all Ages, 1907. The Historians' History of the World is a 25-volume encyclopedia of world history originally published in English near the beginning of the 20th century. It is quite extensive but its perspective is entirely Western Eurocentric. For example, while four volumes focus on the history of England (with Scotland and Ireland included in one of them), "Poland, the Balkans, Turkey, minor Eastern states, China, Japan" are all described in one volume. It was compiled by Henry Smith Williams, a medical doctor and author, as well as other authorities on history, and published in New York in 1902 by Encyclopædia Britannica and the Outlook Company.

Bias in the Teaching of History

The biased approach to historical writing is present in the teaching of history as well.

From the origins of national mass schooling systems in the 19th century, the teaching of history to promote national sentiment has been a high priority. Until today, in most countries history textbook are tools to foster nationalism and patriotism and promote the most favorable version of national history. In the United States, one of the most striking examples of this approach is the continuous narrative of the United States as a state established on the principles of personal liberty and democracy. Although aspects of U.S. history, such as slavery, genocide of American Indians, or disfranchisement of the large segments of the society for decades after the onset of the American statehood, are now taught in most (yet not all) American schools, they are presented as marginal in the larger narrative of liberty and democracy.

In many countries, history textbooks are sponsored by the national government and are written to put the national heritage in the most favorable light, although academic historians have often fought against the politicization of the textbooks, sometimes with success. Interestingly, the 21st-century Germany attempts to be an example of how to remove nationalistic narratives from history education. As the 20th-century history of Germany is filled with events and processes that are rarely a cause of national pride, the history curriculum in Germany (controlled by the 16 German states) is characterized by a transnational perspective that emphasizes the all-European heritage, minimizes the idea of national pride, and fosters the notion of civil society centered on democracy, human rights, and peace. Yet, even in the rather unusual German case, Eurocentrism continues to dominate.

The challenge to replace national, or even nationalist, perspectives with a more inclusive transnational or global view of human history is also still very present in college-level history curricula. In the United States after World War I, a strong movement emerged at the university level to teach courses in Western Civilization with the aim to give students a common heritage with Europe. After 1980, attention increasingly moved toward teaching world history or requiring students to take courses in non-western cultures. Yet, world history courses still struggle to move beyond the Eurocentric perspective, focusing heavily on the history of Europe and its links to the United States.

Despite all the progress and much more focus on the groups that have been traditionally excluded from mainstream historical narratives (people of color, women, the working class, the poor, the disabled, LGBTQI-identified people, etc.), bias remains a component of historical investigation, whether it is a product of nationalism, author's political views, or an agenda-driven interpretation of sources. It is only appropriate to state that the present world history book, while written in accordance with the most recent scholarly and educational practices, has been written and edited by authors trained in American universities and published in the United States. As such, it is also not free from both national (U.S.) and individual (authors') biases.

Sources

Attributions

CC licensed content, Specific attribution

- Boundless World History. **Authored by**: Boundless. **Located at**: https://courses.lumenlearning.com/boundless-worldhistory/. **License**: *CC BY-SA: Attribution-ShareAlike*

The Imperfect Historical Record

- Explain the consequences of the imperfect historical record

Key Points

- In the study of history as an academic discipline, a primary source is an artifact, document, diary, manuscript, autobiography, recording, or other source of information that was created at the time under study.

- History as an academic discipline is based on primary sources, as evaluated by the community of scholars for whom primary sources are absolutely fundamental to reconstructing the past. Ideally, a historian will use as many primary sources that were created during the time under study as can be accessed. In practice however, some sources have been destroyed, while others are not available for research.

- While some sources are considered more reliable or trustworthy than others, historians point out that hardly any historical evidence can be seen as fully objective since it is always a product of particular individuals, times, and dominant ideas.

- Historical method comprises the techniques and guidelines by which historians use primary sources and other evidence (including the evidence of archaeology) to research and write historical accounts of the past.

- Primary sources may remain in private hands or are located in archives, libraries, museums, historical societies, and special collections. Traditionally, historians attempt to answer historical questions through the study of written documents and oral accounts. They also use such sources as monuments, inscriptions, and pictures. In general, the sources of historical knowledge can be separated into three categories: what is written, what is said, and what is physically preserved. Historians often consult all three.

- Historians use various strategies to reconstruct the past when facing a lack of sources, including collaborating with experts from other academic disciplines, most notably archaeology.

Terms

historical method

A scholarly method that comprises the techniques and guidelines by which historians use primary sources and other evidence (including the evidence of archaeology) to research and write historical accounts of the past.

primary source

In the study of history as an academic discipline, an artifact, document, diary, manuscript, autobiography, recording, or other source of information that was created at the time under study. It serves as an original source of information about the topic.

secondary source

A document or recording that relates or discusses information originally found in a primary source. It contrasts with a primary source, which is an original source of the information being discussed; a primary source can be a person with direct knowledge of a situation, or a document created by such a person. A secondary source involves generalization, analysis, synthesis, interpretation, or evaluation of the original information.

Primary Sources

In the study of history as an academic discipline, a primary source (also called original source or evidence) is an artifact, document, diary, manuscript, autobiography, recording, or other source of information that was created at the time under study. It serves as an original source of information about the topic. Primary sources are distinguished from secondary sources, which cite, comment on, or build upon primary sources. In some cases, a secondary source may also be a primary source, depending on how it is used. For example, a memoir would be considered a primary source in research concerning its author or about his or her friends characterized within it, but the same memoir would be a secondary source if it were used to examine the culture in which its author lived. "Primary" and "secondary" should be understood as relative terms, with sources categorized according to specific historical contexts and what is being studied.

Using Primary Sources: Historical Method

History as an academic discipline is based on primary sources, as evaluated by the community of scholars for whom primary sources are absolutely fundamental to reconstructing the past. Ideally, a historian will use as many primary sources that were created by the people involved at the time under study as can be accessed. In practice however, some sources have been destroyed, while others are not available for research. In some cases, the only eyewitness reports of an event may be memoirs, autobiographies, or oral interviews taken years later. Sometimes, the only evidence relating to an event or person in the distant past was written or copied decades or centuries later. Manuscripts that are sources for classical texts can be copies or fragments of documents. This is a common problem in classical studies, where sometimes only a summary of a book or letter, but not the actual book or letter, has survived. While some sources are considered more reliable or trustworthy than others (e.g., an original government document containing information about an event vs. a recording of a witness recalling the same event years later), historians point out that hardly any historical evidence can be seen as fully objective as it is always a product of particular individuals, times, and dominant ideas. This is also why researchers try to find as many records of an event under investigation as possible, and attempt to resolve evidence that may present contradictory accounts of the same events.

This wall painting (known as The portrait of Paquius Proculo and currently preserved at the Naples National Archaeological Museum) was found in the Roman city of Pompeii and serves as a complex example of a primary source. The fresco would not tell much to historians without corresponding textual and archaeological evidence that helps to establish who the portrayed couple might have been. The man wears a toga, the mark of a Roman citizen, and holds a rotulus, suggesting he is involved in public and/or cultural affairs. The woman holds a stylus and wax tablet, emphasizing that she is educated and literate. It is suspected, based on the physical features of the couple, that they are Samnites, which may explain the desire to show off the status they have reached in Roman society.

Historical method comprises the techniques and guidelines by which historians use primary sources and other evidence (including the evidence of archaeology) to research and write historical accounts of the past. Historians continue to debate what aspects and practices of investigating primary sources should be considered, and what constitutes a primary source when developing the most effective historical method. The question of the nature, and even the possibility, of a sound historical method is so central that it has been continuously raised in the philosophy of history as a question of epistemology.

Finding Primary Sources

Primary sources may remain in private hands or are located in archives, libraries, museums, historical societies, and special collections. These can be public or private. Some are affiliated with universities and colleges, while others are government entities. Materials relating to one area might be spread over a large number of different institutions. These can be distant from the original source of the document. For example, the Huntington Library in California houses a large number of documents from the United Kingdom. While the development of technology has resulted in an increasing number of digitized sources, most primary source materials are not digitized and may only be represented online with a record or finding aid.

Traditionally, historians attempt to answer historical questions through the study of written documents and oral accounts. They also use such sources as monuments, inscriptions, and pictures. In general, the sources of historical knowledge can be separated into three categories: what is written, what is said, and what is physically preserved. Historians often consult all three. However, writing is the marker that separates history from what comes before.

Archaeology is one discipline that is especially helpful to historians. By dealing with buried sites and objects, it contributes to the reconstruction of the past. However, archaeology is constituted by a range of methodologies and approaches that are independent from history. In other words, archaeology does not "fill the gaps" within textual sources but often contrasts its conclusions against those of contemporary textual sources.

Archaeology also provides an illustrative example of how historians can be helped when written records are missing. Unearthing artifacts and working with archaeologists to interpret them based on the expertise of a particular historical era and cultural or geographical area is one effective way to reconstruct the past. If written records are missing, historians often attempt to collect oral accounts of particular events, preferably by eyewitnesses, but sometimes, because of the passage of time, they are forced to work with the following generations. Thus, the question of the reliability of oral history has been widely debated.

When dealing with many government records, historians usually have to wait for a specific period of time before documents are declassified and available to researchers. For political reasons, many sensitive records may be destroyed, withdrawn from collections, or hidden, which may also encourage researchers to rely on oral histories. Missing records of events, or processes that historians believe took place based on very fragmentary evidence, forces historians to seek information in records that may not be a likely sources of information. As archival research is always time-consuming and labor-intensive, this approach poses the risk of never producing desired results, despite the time and effort invested in finding informative and reliable resources. In some cases, historians are forced to speculate (this should be explicitly noted) or simply admit that we do not have sufficient information to reconstruct particular past events or processes.

Sources

Attributions

The Evolution of Humans

Learning Objective

- To understand the process and timeline of human evolution

Key Points

- Humans began to evolve about seven million years ago, and progressed through four stages of evolution. Research shows that the first modern humans appeared 200,000 years ago.
- Neanderthals were a separate species from humans. Although they had larger brain capacity and interbred with humans, they eventually died out.
- A number of theories examine the relationship between environmental conditions and human evolution.
- The main human adaptations have included bipedalism, larger brain size, and reduced sexual dimorphism.

Terms

aridity hypothesis

The theory that the savannah was expanding due to increasingly arid conditions, which then drove hominin adaptation.

turnover pulse hypothesis

The theory that extinctions due to environmental conditions hurt specialist species more than generalist ones, leading to greater evolution among specialists.

Red Queen hypothesis

The theory that species must constantly evolve in order to compete with co-evolving animals around them.

encephalization

An evolutionary increase in the complexity and/or size of the brain.

sexual dimorphism

Differences in size or appearance between the sexes of an animal species.

social brain hypothesis

The theory that improving cognitive capabilities would allow hominins to influence local groups and control resources.

Toba catastrophe theory

The theory that there was a near-extinction event for early humans about 70,000 years ago.

savannah hypothesis

The theory that hominins were forced out of the trees they lived in and onto the expanding savannah; as they did so, they began walking upright on two feet.

hominids

A primate of the family Hominidae that includes humans and their fossil ancestors.

bipedal

Describing an animal that uses only two legs for walking.

Human evolution began with primates. Primate development diverged from other mammals about 85 million years ago. Various divergences among apes, gibbons, orangutans occurred during this period, with *Homini* (including early humans and chimpanzees) separating from *Gorillini* (gorillas) about 8 millions years ago. Humans and chimps then separated about 7.5 million years ago.

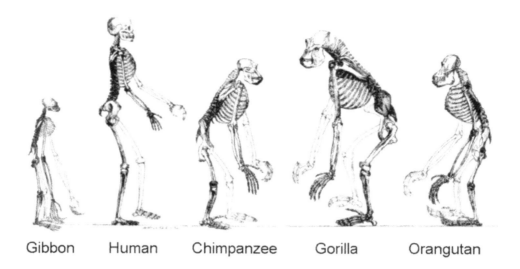

Gibbon   Human   Chimpanzee   Gorilla   Orangutan

Skeletal structure of humans and other primates. A comparison of the skeletal structures of gibbons, humans, chimpanzees, gorillas and orangutans.

Generally, it is believed that hominids first evolved in Africa and then migrated to other areas. There were four main stages of human evolution. The first, between four and seven million years ago, consisted of the proto hominins *Sahelanthropus, Orrorin* and *Ardipithecus.* These humans may have been bipedal, meaning they walked upright on two legs. The second stage, around four million years ago, was marked by the appearance of *Australopithecus,* and the third, around 2.7 million years ago, featured *Paranthropus.*

The fourth stage features the genus *Homo,* which existed between 1.8 and 2.5 million years ago. *Homo habilis,* which used stone tools and had a brain about the size of a chimpanzee, was an early hominin in this period. Coordinating fine hand movements needed for tool use may have led to increasing brain capacity. This was followed by *Homo erectus* and *Homo ergaster,* who had double the brain size and may have been the first to control fire and use more complex tools. *Homo heidelbergensis* appeared about 800,000 years ago, and modern humans, *Homo sapiens,* about 200,000 years ago. Humans acquired symbolic culture and language about 50,000 years ago.

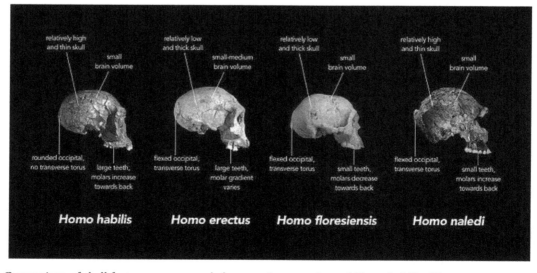

Comparison of skull features among early humans.A comparison of Homo habilis, Homo erectus, Homo floresiensis and Homo naledi skull features.

Neanderthals

A separate species, *Homo neanderthalensis*, had a common ancestor with humans about 660,000 years ago, and engaged in interbreeding with *Homo sapiens* about 45,000 to 80,000 years ago. Although their brains were larger, Neanderthals had fewer social and technological innovations than humans, and they eventually died out.

Theories of Early Human Evolution

The savannah hypothesis states that hominins were forced out of the trees they lived in and onto the expanding savannah; as they did so, they began walking upright on two feet. This idea was expanded in the aridity hypothesis, which posited that the savannah was expanding due to increasingly arid conditions resulting in hominin adaptation. Thus, during periods of intense aridification, hominins also were pushed to evolve and adapt.

The turnover pulse hypothesis states that extinctions due to environmental conditions hurt specialist species more than generalist ones. While generalist species spread out when environmental conditions change, specialist species become more specialized and have a greater rate of evolution. The Red Queen hypothesis states that species must constantly evolve in order to compete with co-evolving animals around them. The social brain hypothesis states that improving cognitive capabilities would allow hominins to influence local groups and control resources. The Toba catastrophe theory states that there was a near-extinction event for early humans about 70,000 years ago.

Human Adaptations

Bipedalism, or walking upright, is one of the main human evolutionary adaptations. Advantages to be found in bipedalism include the freedom of the hands for labor and less physically taxing movement. Walking upright better allows for long distance travel and hunting, for a wider field of vision, a reduction of the amount of skin exposed to the sun, and overall thrives in a savannah environment. Bipedalism resulted in skeletal changes to the legs, knee and ankle joints, spinal vertebrae, toes, and arms. Most significantly, the pelvis became shorter and rounded, with a smaller birth canal, making birth more difficult for humans than other primates. In turn, this resulted in shorter gestation (as babies need to be born before their heads become too large), and more helpless infants who are not fully developed before birth.

Larger brain size, also called encephalization, began in early humans with *Homo habilis* and continued through the Neanderthal line (capacity of 1,200 – 1,900 cm3). The ability of the human brain to continue to grow after birth meant that social learning and language were possible. It is possible that a focus on eating meat, and cooking, allowed for brain growth. Modern humans have a brain volume of 1250 cm3.

Humans have reduced sexual dimorphism, or differences between males and females, and hidden estrus, which means the female is fertile year-round and shows no special sign of fertility. Human sexes still have some differences between them, with males being slightly larger and having more body hair and less body fat. These changes may be related to pair bonding for long-term raising of offspring.

Other adaptations include lessening of body hair, a chin, a descended larynx, and an emphasis on vision instead of smell.

Human Evolution

A video showing evolution from early animals to modern humans: https://youtu.be/hSSzn4bIwZg

Sources

Attributions

CC licensed content, Specific attribution

- Boundless World History. **Authored by**: Boundless. **Located at**: https://courses.lumenlearning.com/boundless-worldhistory/. **License**: *CC BY-SA: Attribution-ShareAlike*

The Neolithic Revolution

Learning Objective

- Explain the significance of the Neolithic Revolution

Key Points

- During the Paleolithic Era, humans grouped together in small societies and subsisted by gathering plants, and fishing, hunting or scavenging wild animals.

- The Neolithic Revolution references a change from a largely nomadic hunter-gatherer way of life to a more settled, agrarian-based one, with the inception of the domestication of various plant and animal species—depending on species locally available and likely also influenced by local culture.

- There are several competing (but not mutually exclusive) theories as to the factors that drove populations to take up agriculture, including the Hilly Flanks hypothesis, the Feasting model, the Demographic theories, the evolutionary/intentionality theory, and the largely discredited Oasis Theory.

- The shift to agricultural food production supported a denser population, which in turn supported larger sedentary communities, the accumulation of goods and tools, and specialization in diverse forms of new labor.

- The nutritional standards of Neolithic populations were generally inferior to that of hunter-gatherers, and they worked longer hours and had shorter life expectancies.

- Life today, including our governments, specialized labor, and trade, is directly related to the advances made in the Neolithic Revolution.

Terms

Hilly Flanks hypothesis

The theory that agriculture began in the hilly flanks of the Taurus and Zagros mountains, where the climate was not drier, and fertile land supported a variety of plants and animals amenable to domestication.

Evolutionary/Intentionality theory

The theory that domestication was part of an evolutionary process between humans and plants.

Neolithic Revolution

The world's first historically verifiable advancement in agriculture. It took place around 12,000 years ago.

Hunter-gatherer

A nomadic lifestyle in which food is obtained from wild plants and animals; in contrast to an agricultural lifestyle, which relies mainly on domesticated species.

Paleolithic Era

A period of history that spans from 2.5 million to 20,000 years ago, during which time humans evolved, used stone tools, and lived as hunter-gatherers.

Oasis Theory

The theory that humans were forced into close association with animals due to changes in climate.

Feasting model

The theory that displays of power through feasting drove agricultural technology.

Specialization

A process where laborers focused on one specialty area rather than creating all needed items.

Demographic theories

Theories about how sedentary populations may have driven agricultural changes.

Before the Rise of Civilization: The Paleolithic Era

The first humans evolved in Africa during the Paleolithic Era, or Stone Age, which spans the period of history from 2.5 million to about 10,000 BCE. During this time, humans lived in small groups as hunter-gatherers, with clear gender divisions for labor. The men hunted animals while the women gathered food, such as fruit, nuts and berries, from the local area. Simple tools made of stone, wood, and bone (such as hand axes, flints and spearheads) were used throughout the period. Fire was controlled, which created heat and light, and allowed for cooking.Humankind gradually evolved from early members of the genus *Homo*—such as *Homo habilis*, who used simple stone tools— into fully behaviorally and anatomically modern humans (*Homo sapiens*) during the Paleolithic era. During the end of the Paleolithic, specifically the Middle and or Upper Paleolithic, humans began to produce the earliest works of art and engage in religious and spiritual behavior, such as burial and ritual. Paleolithic humans were nomads, who often moved their settlements as food became scarce. This eventually resulted in humans spreading out from Africa (beginning roughly 60,000 years ago) and into Eurasia, Southeast Asia, and Australia. By about 40,000 years ago, they had entered Europe, and by about 15,000 years ago, they had reached North America followed by South America.

Stone ball from a set of Paleolithic bolas. Paleoliths (artifacts from the Paleolithic), such as this stone ball, demonstrate some of the stone technologies that the early humans used as tools and weapons.

During about 10,000 BCE, a major change occurred in the way humans lived; this would have a cascading effect on every part of human society and culture. That change was the Neolithic Revolution.

The Neolithic Revolution: From Hunter-Gatherer to Agriculturalist

The beginning of the Neolithic Revolution in different regions has been dated from perhaps 8,000 BCE in the Kuk Early Agricultural Site of Melanesia Kuk to 2,500 BCE in Subsaharan Africa, with some considering the developments of 9,000-7,000 BCE in the Fertile Crescent to be the most important. This transition everywhere is associated with the change from a largely nomadic hunter-gatherer way of life to a more settled, agrarian-based one, due to the inception of the domestication of various plant and animal species—depending on the species locally available, and probably also influenced by local culture.It is not known why humans decided to begin cultivating plants and domesticating animals. While more labor-intensive, the people must have seen the relationship between cultivation of grains and an increase in population. The domestication of animals provided a new source of protein, through meat and milk, along with hides and wool, which allowed for the production of clothing and other objects.There are several competing (but not mutually exclusive) theories about the factors that drove populations to take up agriculture. The most prominent of these are:

- The Oasis Theory, originally proposed by Raphael Pumpelly in 1908, and popularized by V. Gordon Childe in 1928, suggests as the climate got drier due to the Atlantic depressions shifting northward, communities contracted to oases where they were forced into close association with animals. These animals were then domesticated together with planting of seeds. However, this theory has little support amongst archaeologists today because subsequent climate data suggests that the region was getting wetter rather than drier.

- The Hilly Flanks hypothesis, proposed by Robert Braidwood in 1948, suggests that agriculture began in the hilly flanks of the Taurus and Zagros mountains, where the climate was not drier, as Childe had believed, and that fertile land supported a variety of plants and animals amenable to domestication.

- The Feasting model by Brian Hayden suggests that agriculture was driven by ostentatious displays of power, such as giving feasts, to exert dominance. This system required assembling large quantities of food, a demand which drove agricultural technology.

- The Demographic theories proposed by Carl Sauer and adapted by Lewis Binford and Kent Flannery posit that an increasingly sedentary population outgrew the resources in the local environment and required more food than could be gathered. Various social and economic factors helped drive the need for food.

- The Evolutionary/Intentionality theory, developed by David Rindos and others, views agriculture as an evolutionary adaptation of plants and humans. Starting with domestication by protection of wild plants, it led to specialization of location and then full-fledged domestication.

Effects of the Neolithic Revolution on Society

The traditional view is that the shift to agricultural food production supported a denser population, which in turn supported larger sedentary communities, the accumulation of goods and tools, and specialization in diverse forms of new labor. Overall a population could increase its size more rapidly when resources were more available. The resulting larger societies led to the development of different means of decision making and governmental organization. Food surpluses made possible the development of a social elite freed from labor, who dominated their communities and monopolized decision-making. There were deep social divisions and inequality between the sexes, with women's status declining as men took on greater roles as leaders and warriors. Social class was determined by occupation, with farmers and craftsmen at the lower end, and priests and warriors at the higher.

Effects of the Neolithic Revolution on Health

Neolithic populations generally had poorer nutrition, shorter life expectancies, and a more labor-intensive lifestyle than hunter-gatherers. Diseases jumped from animals to humans, and agriculturalists suffered from more anemia, vitamin deficiencies, spinal deformations, and dental pathologies.

Overall Impact of the Neolithic Revolution on Modern Life

The way we live today is directly related to the advances made in the Neolithic Revolution. From the governments we live under, to the specialized work laborers do, to the trade of goods and food, humans were irrevocably changed by the switch to sedentary agriculture and domestication of animals. Human population swelled from five million to seven billion today.

Sources

Boundless vets and curates high-quality, openly licensed content from around the Internet. This particular resource used the following sources:

"Neolithic Revolution."

http://en.wikipedia.org/wiki/Neolithic_Revolution
Wikipedia
CC BY-SA.

"Neolithic Revolution."

http://en.wikipedia.org/wiki/Neolithic%20Revolution
Wikipedia
CC BY-SA 3.0.

"Civilization makes its début (8000 – 3000 BC)."

http://en.wikibooks.org/wiki/World_History/Ancient_Civilizations%23Civilization_makes_its_d.C3.A9but_.288000_-_3000_BC.29
Wikibooks
CC BY-SA 3.0.

"Before the Rise of Civilization."

http://en.wikibooks.org/wiki/World_History/Ancient_Civilizations%23Before_the_Rise_of_Civilization
Wikibooks
CC BY-SA 3.0.

"Paleolithic."

http://en.wikipedia.org/wiki/Paleolithic
Wikipedia
CC BY-SA.

"Boundless."

http://www.boundless.com//sociology/definition/hunter-gatherer–2
Boundless Learning
CC BY-SA 3.0.

"The Neolithic Revolution and Sumer."

http://globaleconomics.wikispaces.com/The+Neolithic+Revolution+and+Sumer
Global Economics
CC BY 3.0.

"Paleolithic."

http://en.wikipedia.org/wiki/Paleolithic_period
Wikipedia
CC BY-SA.

Attributions

2. Ancient Mesopotamian Civilizations and Other Early Civilizations

The Sumerians

Learning Objective

- To understand the history and accomplishments of the Sumerian people

Key Points

- The Sumerians were a people living in Mesopotamia from the 27th-20th century BCE.

- The major periods in Sumerian history were the Ubaid period (6500-4100 BCE), the Uruk period (4100-2900 BCE), the Early Dynastic period (2900-2334 BCE), the Akkadian Empire period (2334 – 2218 BCE), the Gutian period (2218-2047 BCE), Sumerian Renaissance/Third Dynasty of Ur (2047-1940 BCE), and then decline.

- Many Sumerian clay tablets have been found with writing. Initially, pictograms were used, followed by cuneiform and then ideograms.

- Sumerians believed in anthropomorphic polytheism, or of many gods in human form that were specific to each city-state.

- Sumerians invented or perfected many forms of technology, including the wheel, mathematics, and cuneiform script.

Terms

City-states

A city that with its surrounding territory forms an independent state.

cuneiform script

Wedge-shaped characters used in the ancient writing systems of Mesopotamia, surviving mainly on clay tablets.

ideograms

Written characters symbolizing an idea or entity without indicating the sounds used to say it.

pictograms

A pictorial symbol for a word or phrase. They are the earliest known forms of writing.

pantheon

The collective gods of a people or religion.

Epic of Gilgamesh

An epic poem from the Third Dynasty of Ur (circa 2100 BCE), which is seen as the earliest surviving great work of literature.

anthropomorphic

Having human characteristics.

"Sumerian" is the name given by the Semitic-speaking Akkadians to non-Semitic speaking people living in Mespotamia. City-states in the region, which were organized by canals and boundary stones and dedicated to a patron god or goddess, first rose to power during the prehistoric Ubaid and Uruk periods. Sumerian written history began in the 27th century BCE, but the first intelligible writing began in the 23rd century BCE. Classical Sumer ends with the rise of the Akkadian Empire in the 23rd century BCE, and only enjoys a brief renaissance in the 21st century BCE. The Sumerians were eventually absorbed into the Akkadian/ Babylonian population.

Periods in Sumerian History

The Ubaid period (6500-4100 BCE) saw the first settlement in southern Mesopotamia by farmers who brought irrigation agriculture. Distinctive, finely painted pottery was evident during this time.

The Uruk period (4100-2900 BCE) saw several transitions. First, pottery began to be mass-produced. Second, trade goods began to flow down waterways in southern Mespotamia, and large, temple-centered cities (most likely theocratic and run by priests-kings) rose up to facilitate this trade. Slave labor was also utilized.

The Early Dynastic period (2900-2334 BCE) saw writing, in contrast to pictograms, become commonplace and decipherable. The Epic of Gilgamesh mentions several leaders, including Gilgamesh himself, who were likely historical kings. The first dynastic king was Etana, the 13th king of the first dynasty of Kish. War was on the increase, and cities erected walls for self-preservation. Sumerian culture began to spread from southern Mesopotamia into surrounding areas.

Sumerian Necklaces and Headgear Sumerian necklaces and headgear discovered in the royal (and individual) graves, showing the way they may have been worn.

During the Akkadian Empire period (2334-2218 BCE), many in the region became bilingual in both Sumerian and Akkadian. Toward the end of the empire, though, Sumerian became increasingly a literary language.

The Gutian period (2218-2047 BCE) was marked by a period of chaos and decline, as Guti barbarians defeated the Akkadian military but were unable to support the civilizations in place.

The Sumerian Renaissance/Third Dynasty of Ur (2047-1940 BCE) saw the rulers Ur-Nammu and Shulgi, whose power extended into southern Assyria. However, the region was becoming more Semitic, and the Sumerian language became a religious language.

The Sumerian Renaissance ended with invasion by the Amorites, whose dynasty of Isin continued until 1700 BCE, at which point Mesopotamia came under Babylonian rule.

Language and Writing

Many Sumerian clay tablets written in cuneiform script have been discovered. They are not the oldest example of writing, but nevertheless represent a great advance in the human ability to write down history and create literature. Initially, pictograms were used, followed by cuneiform, and then ideograms. Letters, receipts, hymns, prayers, and stories have all been found on clay tablets.

Bill of Sale on a Clay Tablet. This clay tablet shows a bill of sale for a male slave and building, circa 2600 BCE.

Religion

Sumerians believed in anthropomorphic polytheism, or of many gods in human form, which were specific to each city-state. The core pantheon consisted of An (heaven), Enki (a healer and friend to humans), Enlil (gave spells spirits must obey), Inanna (love and war), Utu (sun-god), and Sin (moon-god).

Technology

Sumerians invented or improved a wide range of technology, including the wheel, cuneiform script, arithmetic, geometry, irrigation, saws and other tools, sandals, chariots, harpoons, and beer.

Sources

Attributions

CC licensed content, Specific attribution

- Boundless World History. **Authored by**: Boundless. **Located at**: https://courses.lumenlearning.com/boundless-worldhistory/. **License**: *CC BY-SA: Attribution-ShareAlike*

The Akkadian Empire

Learning Objective

- Describe the key political characteristics of the Akkadian Empire

Key Points

- The Akkadian Empire was an ancient Semitic empire centered in the city of Akkad and its surrounding region in ancient Mesopotamia, which united all the indigenous Akkadian speaking Semites and the Sumerian speakers under one rule within a multilingual empire.

- King Sargon, the founder of the empire, conquered several regions in Mesopotamia and consolidated his power by instating Akaddian officials in new territories. He extended trade across Mesopotamia and strengthened the economy through rain-fed agriculture in northern Mesopotamia.

- The Akkadian Empire experienced a period of successful conquest under Naram-Sin due to benign climatic conditions, huge agricultural surpluses, and the confiscation of wealth.

- The empire collapsed after the invasion of the Gutians. Changing climatic conditions also contributed to internal rivalries and fragmentation, and the empire eventually split into the Assyrian Empire in the north and the Babylonian empire in the south.

Terms

Gutians

A group of barbarians from the Zagros Mountains who invaded the Akkadian Empire and contributed to its collapse.

Sargon

The first king of the Akkadians. He conquered many of the surrounding regions to establish the massive multilingual empire.

Akkadian Empire

An ancient Semitic empire centered in the city of Akkad and its surrounding region in ancient Mesopotamia.

Cuneiform

One of the earliest known systems of writing, distinguished by its wedge-shaped marks on clay tablets, and made by means of a blunt reed for a stylus.

Semites

Today, the word "Semite" may be used to refer to any member of any of a number of peoples of ancient Southwest Asian descent, including the Akkadians, Phoenicians, Hebrews (Jews), Arabs, and their descendants.

Naram-Sin

An Akkadian king who conquered Ebla, Armum, and Magan, and built a royal residence at Tell Brak.

The Akkadian Empire was an ancient Semitic empire centered in the city of Akkad, which united all the indigenous Akkadian speaking Semites and Sumerian speakers under one rule. The Empire controlled Mesopotamia, the Levant, and parts of Iran.

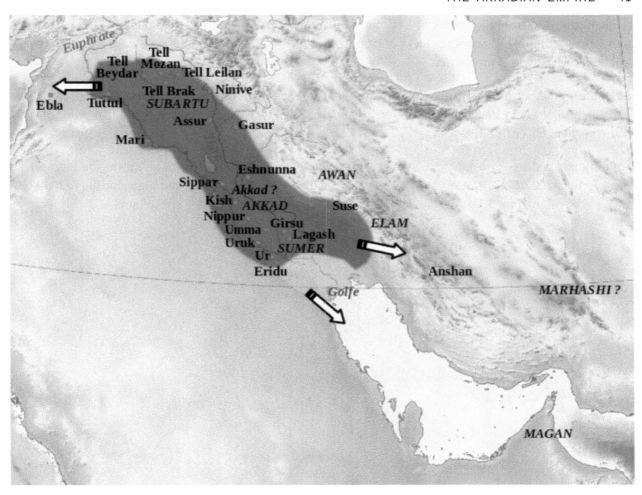

Map of the Akkadian Empire. The Akkadian Empire is pictured in brown. The directions of the military campaigns are shown as yellow arrows.

Its founder was Sargon of Akkad (2334–2279 BCE). Under Sargon and his successors, the Akkadian Empire reached its political peak between the 24th and 22nd centuries BCE. Akkad is sometimes regarded as the first empire in history.

Sargon and His Dynasty

Sargon claimed to be the son of La'ibum or Itti-Bel, a humble gardener, and possibly a *hierodule*, or priestess to Ishtar or Inanna. Some later claimed that his mother was an "entu" priestess (high priestess). Originally a cupbearer to king Ur-Zababa of Kish, Sargon became a gardener, which gave him access to a disciplined corps of workers who also may have served as his first soldiers. Displacing Ur-Zababa, Sargon was crowned king and began a career of foreign conquest. He invaded Syria and Canaan on four different campaigns, and spent three years subduing the countries of "the west" to unite them with Mesopotamia "into a single empire."

Sargon's empire reached westward as far as the Mediterranean Sea and perhaps Cyprus (Kaptara); northward as far as the mountains; eastward over Elam; and as far south as Magan (Oman)—a region over which he purportedly reigned for 56 years, though only four "year-names" survive. He replaced rulers with noble citizens of Akkad. Trade extended from the silver mines of Anatolia to the lapis lazuli mines in

Afghanistan, and from the cedars of Lebanon to the copper of Magan. The empire's breadbasket was the rain-fed agricultural system of northern Mesopotamia (Assyria), and a chain of fortresses was built to control the imperial wheat production.

Sargon, throughout his long life, showed special deference to the Sumerian deities, particularly Inanna (Ishtar), his patroness, and Zababa, the warrior god of Kish. He called himself "the anointed priest of Anu" and "the great ensi of Enlil".

Sargon managed to crush his opposition even in old age. Difficulties also broke out in the reign of his sons, Rimush (2278–2270 BCE), who was assassinated by his own courtiers, and Manishtushu (2269–2255 BCE), who reigned for 15 years. He, too, was likely assassinated in a palace conspiracy.

Bronze head of a king. Bronze head of a king, most likely Sargon of Akkad but possibly Naram-Sin. Unearthed in Nineveh (now in Iraq).

Naram-Sin

Manishtushu's son and successor, Naram-Sin (called, Beloved of Sin) (2254–2218 BCE), assumed the imperial title "King Naram-Sin, King of the Four Quarters." He was also, for the first time in Sumerian culture, addressed as "the god of Agade (Akkad)." This represents a marked shift away from the previous religious belief that kings were only representatives of the people toward the gods.

Naram-Sin conquered Ebla and Armum, and built a royal residence at Tell Brak, a crossroads at the heart of the Khabur River basin of the Jezirah. Naram-Sin also conquered Magan and created garrisons to protect the main roads. This productive period of Akkadian conquest may have been based upon benign climatic conditions, huge agricultural surpluses, and the confiscation of the wealth of other peoples.

Stele of Naram-Sin. This stele commemorates Naram-Sin's victory against the Lullubi from Zagros in 2260 BCE. Naram-Sin is depicted to be wearing a horned helmet, a symbol of divinity, and is also portrayed in a larger scale in comparison to others to emphasize his superiority.

Living in the Akkadian Empire

Future Mesopotamian states compared themselves to the Akkadian Empire, which they saw as a classical standard in governance. The economy was dependent on irrigated farmlands of southern Iraq, and rain-fed agriculture of Northern Iraq. There was often a surplus of agriculture but shortages of other goods, like metal ore, timber, and building stone. Art of the period often focused on kings, and depicted somber and grim conflict and subjugation to divinities. Sumerians and Akkadians were bilingual in each other's languages, but Akkadian gradually replaced Sumerian. The empire had a postal service, and a library featuring astronomical observations.

Collapse of the Akkadian Empire

The Empire of Akkad collapsed in 2154 BCE, within 180 years of its founding. The collapse ushered in a Dark Age period of regional decline that lasted until the rise of the Third Dynasty of Ur in 2112 BCE. By the end of the reign of Naram-Sin's son, Shar-kali-sharri (2217-2193 BCE), the empire had weakened significantly. There was a period of anarchy between 2192 BC and 2168 BCE. Some centralized authority may have been restored under Shu-Durul (2168-2154 BCE), but he was unable to prevent the empire collapsing outright from the invasion of barbarian peoples, known as the Gutians, from the Zagros Mountains.

Little is known about the Gutian period or for how long it lasted. Cuneiform sources suggest that the Gutians' administration showed little concern for maintaining agriculture, written records, or public safety; they reputedly released all farm animals to roam about Mesopotamia freely, and soon brought about famine and rocketing grain prices. The Sumerian king Ur-Nammu (2112-2095 BCE) later cleared the Gutians from Mesopotamia during his reign.

The collapse of rain-fed agriculture in the Upper Country due to drought meant the loss of the agrarian subsidies which had kept the Akkadian Empire solvent in southern Mesopotamia. Rivalries between pastoralists and farmers increased. Attempts to control access to water led to increased political instability; meanwhile, severe depopulation occurred.

After the fall of the Akkadian Empire, the Akkadian people coalesced into two major Akkadian speaking nations: Assyria in the north, and, a few centuries later, Babylonia in the south.

Sources

Attributions

CC licensed content, Specific attribution

Babylon

- Describe key characteristics of the Babylonian Empire under Hammurabi

Key Points

- A series of conflicts between the Amorites and the Assyrians followed the collapse of the Akkadian Empire, out of which Babylon arose as a powerful city-state c. 1894 BCE.

- Babylon remained a minor territory for a century after it was founded, until the reign of its sixth Amorite ruler, Hammurabi (1792-1750 BCE), an extremely efficient ruler who established a bureaucracy with taxation and centralized government.

- Hammurabi also enjoyed various military successes over the whole of southern Mesopotamia, modern-day Iran and Syria, and the old Assyrian Empire in Asian Minor.

- After the death of Hammurabi, the First Babylonian Dynasty eventually fell due to attacks from outside its borders.

Terms

Marduk

The south Mesopotamian god that rose to supremacy in the pantheon over the previous god, Enlil.

Hammurabi

The sixth king of Babylon, who, under his rule, saw Babylonian advancements, both militarily and bureaucratically.

Code of Hammurabi

A code of law that echoed and improved upon earlier written laws of Sumer, Akkad, and Assyria.

Amorites

An ancient Semitic-speaking people from ancient Syria who also occupied large parts of Mesopotamia in the 21st Century BCE.

The Rise of the First Babylonian Dynasty

Following the disintegration of the Akkadian Empire, the Sumerians rose up with the Third Dynasty of Ur in the late 22nd century BCE, and ejected the barbarian Gutians from southern Mesopotamia. The Sumerian "Ur-III" dynasty eventually collapsed at the hands of the Elamites, another Semitic people, in 2002 BCE. Conflicts between the Amorites (Western Semitic nomads) and the Assyrians continued until Sargon I (1920-1881 BCE) succeeded as king in Assyria and withdrew Assyria from the region, leaving the Amorites in control (the Amorite period).

One of these Amorite dynasties founded the city-state of Babylon circa 1894 BCE, which would ultimately take over the others and form the short-lived first Babylonian empire, also called the Old Babylonian Period.

A chieftain named Sumuabum appropriated the then relatively small city of Babylon from the neighboring Mesopotamian city state of Kazallu, turning it into a state in its own right. Sumuabum appears never to have been given the title of King, however.

The Babylonians Under Hammurabi

Babylon remained a minor territory for a century after it was founded, until the reign of its sixth Amorite ruler, Hammurabi (1792-1750 BCE). He was an efficient ruler, establishing a centralized bureaucracy with taxation. Hammurabi freed Babylon from Elamite dominance, and then conquered the whole of southern Mesopotamia, bringing stability and the name of Babylonia to the region.

The armies of Babylonia under Hammurabi were well-disciplined, and he was able to invade modern-day Iran to the east and conquer the pre-Iranic Elamites, Gutians and Kassites. To the west, Hammurabi enjoyed military success against the Semitic states of the Levant (modern Syria), including the powerful kingdom of Mari. Hammurabi also entered into a protracted war with the Old Assyrian Empire for control of Mesopotamia and the Near East. Assyria had extended control over parts of Asia Minor from the 21st century BCE, and from the latter part of the 19th century BCE had asserted itself over northeast Syria and central Mesopotamia as well. After a protracted, unresolved struggle over decades with the Assyrian king Ishme-Dagan, Hammurabi forced his successor, Mut-Ashkur, to pay tribute to Babylon c. 1751 BCE, thus giving Babylonia control over Assyria's centuries-old Hattian and Hurrian colonies in Asia Minor.

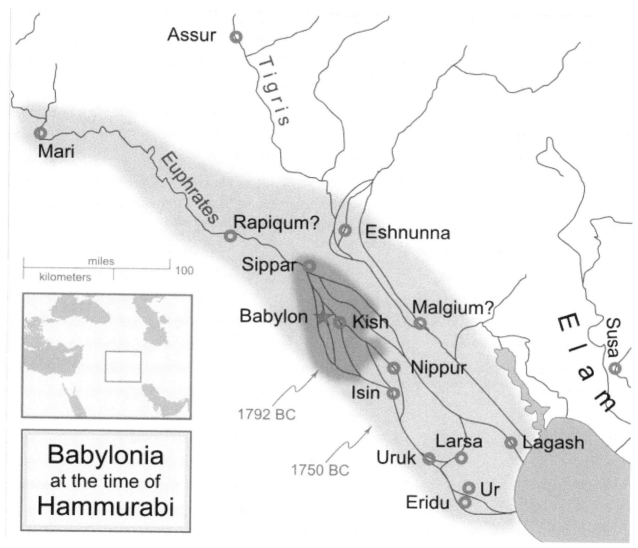

Babylonia under Hammurabi. The extent of the Babylonian Empire at the start and end of Hammurabi's reign.

One of the most important works of this First Dynasty of Babylon was the compilation in about 1754 BCE of a code of laws, called the Code of Hammurabi, which echoed and improved upon the earlier written laws of Sumer, Akkad, and Assyria. It is one of the oldest deciphered writings of significant length in the world. The Code consists of 282 laws, with scaled punishments depending on social status, adjusting "an eye for an eye, a tooth for a tooth." Nearly one-half of the Code deals with matters of contract. A third of the code addresses issues concerning household and family relationships.

From before 3000 BC until the reign of Hammurabi, the major cultural and religious center of southern Mesopotamia had been the ancient city of Nippur, where the god Enlil reigned supreme. However, with the rise of Hammurabi, this honor was transferred to Babylon, and the god Marduk rose to supremacy (with the god Ashur remaining the dominant deity in Assyria). The city of Babylon became known as a "holy city," where any legitimate ruler of southern Mesopotamia had to be crowned. Hammurabi turned what had previously been a minor administrative town into a major city, increasing its size and population dramatically, and conducting a number of impressive architectural works.

The Decline of the First Babylonian Dynasty

Despite Hammurabi's various military successes, southern Mesopotamia had no natural, defensible boundaries, which made it vulnerable to attack. After the death of Hammurabi, his empire began to disintegrate rapidly. Under his successor Samsu-iluna (1749-1712 BCE), the far south of Mesopotamia was lost to a native Akkadian king, called Ilum-ma-ili, and became the Sealand Dynasty; it remained free of Babylon for the next 272 years.

Both the Babylonians and their Amorite rulers were driven from Assyria to the north by an Assyrian-Akkadian governor named Puzur-Sin, c. 1740 BCE. Amorite rule survived in a much-reduced Babylon, Samshu-iluna's successor, Abi-Eshuh, made a vain attempt to recapture the Sealand Dynasty for Babylon, but met defeat at the hands of king Damqi-ilishu II. By the end of his reign, Babylonia had shrunk to the small and relatively weak nation it had been upon its foundation.

Sources

Attributions

CC licensed content, Specific attribution

- Boundless World History. **Authored by**: Boundless. **Located at**: https://courses.lumenlearning.com/boundless-worldhistory/. **License**: *CC BY-SA: Attribution-ShareAlike*

Babylonian Culture

Learning Objective

- Evaluate the extent and influence of Babylonian culture

Key Points

- Babylonian temples were massive structures of crude brick, supported by buttresses. Such uses of brick led to the early development of the pilaster and column, and of frescoes and enameled tiles.

- Certain pieces of Babylonian art featured crude three-dimensional statues, and gem-cutting was considered a high-perfection art.

- The Babylonians produced extensive compendiums of astronomical records containing catalogues of stars and constellations, as well as schemes for calculating various astronomical coordinates and phenomena.

- Medicinally, the Babylonians introduced basic medical processes, such as diagnosis and prognosis, and also catalogued a variety of illnesses with their symptoms.

- Both Babylonian men and women learned to read and write, and much of Babylonian literature is translated from ancient Sumerian texts, such as the Epic of Gilgamesh.

Terms

Epic of Gilgamesh

One of the most famous Babylonian works, a twelve-book saga translated from the original Sumerian.

pilaster

An architectural element in classical architecture used to give the appearance of a supporting column and to articulate an extent of wall, with only an ornamental function.

etiology

Causation. In medicine, cause or origin of disease or condition.

mudbrick

A brick mixture of loam, mud, sand, and water mixed with a binding material, such as rice husks or straw.

Enūma Anu Enlil

A series of cuneiform tablets containing centuries of Babylonian observations of celestial phenomena.

Diagnostic Handbook

The most extensive Babylonian medical text, written by Esagil-kin-apli of Borsippa.

Art and Architecture

In Babylonia, an abundance of clay and lack of stone led to greater use of mudbrick. Babylonian temples were thus massive structures of crude brick, supported by buttresses. The use of brick led to the early development of the pilaster and column, and of frescoes and enameled tiles. The walls were brilliantly colored, and sometimes plated with zinc or gold, as well as with tiles. Painted terracotta cones for torches were also embedded in the plaster. In Babylonia, in place of the bas-relief, there was a preponderance of three-dimensional figures—the earliest examples being the Statues of Gudea—that were realistic, if also somewhat clumsy. The paucity of stone in Babylonia made every pebble a commodity and led to a high perfection in the art of gem-cutting.

Astronomy

During the 8th and 7th centuries BCE, Babylonian astronomers developed a new empirical approach to astronomy. They began studying philosophy dealing with the ideal nature of the universe and began employing an internal logic within their predictive planetary systems. This was an important contribution to astronomy and the philosophy of science, and some scholars have thus referred to this new approach as the first scientific revolution. Tablets dating back to the Old Babylonian period document the application of mathematics to variations in the length of daylight over a solar year. Centuries of Babylonian observations of celestial phenomena are recorded in a series of cuneiform tablets known as the "Enūma Anu Enlil." In fact, the oldest significant astronomical text known to mankind is Tablet 63 of the Enūma Anu Enlil, the

Venus tablet of Ammi-saduqa, which lists the first and last visible risings of Venus over a period of about 21 years. This record is the earliest evidence that planets were recognized as periodic phenomena. The oldest rectangular astrolabe dates back to Babylonia c. 1100 BCE. The MUL.APIN contains catalogues of stars and constellations as well as schemes for predicting heliacal risings and the settings of the planets, as well as lengths of daylight measured by a water-clock, gnomon, shadows, and intercalations. The Babylonian GU text arranges stars in "strings" that lie along declination circles (thus measuring right-ascensions or time-intervals), and also employs the stars of the zenith, which are also separated by given right-ascensional differences.

Medicine

The oldest Babylonian texts on medicine date back to the First Babylonian Dynasty in the first half of the 2nd millennium BCE. The most extensive Babylonian medical text, however, is the Diagnostic Handbook written by the ummânū, or chief scholar, Esagil-kin-apli of Borsippa.

The Babylonians introduced the concepts of diagnosis, prognosis, physical examination, and prescriptions. The Diagnostic Handbook additionally introduced the methods of therapy and etiology outlining the use of empiricism, logic, and rationality in diagnosis, prognosis and treatment. For example, the text contains a list of medical symptoms and often detailed empirical observations along with logical rules used in combining observed symptoms on the body of a patient with its diagnosis and prognosis. In particular, Esagil-kin-apli discovered a variety of illnesses and diseases and described their symptoms in his Diagnostic Handbook, including those of many varieties of epilepsy and related ailments.

Literature

Libraries existed in most towns and temples. Women as well as men learned to read and write, and had knowledge of the extinct Sumerian language, along with a complicated and extensive syllabary.

A considerable amount of Babylonian literature was translated from Sumerian originals, and the language of religion and law long continued to be written in the old agglutinative language of Sumer. Vocabularies, grammars, and interlinear translations were compiled for the use of students, as well as commentaries on the older texts and explanations of obscure words and phrases. The characters of the syllabary were organized and named, and elaborate lists of them were drawn up.

There are many Babylonian literary works whose titles have come down to us. One of the most famous of these was the Epic of Gilgamesh, in twelve books, translated from the original Sumerian by a certain Sin-liqi-unninni, and arranged upon an astronomical principle. Each division contains the story of a single adventure in the career of King Gilgamesh. The whole story is a composite product, and it is probable that some of the stories are artificially attached to the central figure.

A Tablet from the Epic of Gilgamesh. The Deluge tablet of the Gilgamesh epic in Akkadian.

Philosophy

The origins of Babylonian philosophy can be traced back to early Mesopotamian wisdom literature, which embodied certain philosophies of life, particularly ethics, in the forms of dialectic, dialogs, epic poetry, folklore, hymns, lyrics, prose, and proverbs. Babylonian reasoning and rationality developed beyond empirical observation. It is possible that Babylonian philosophy had an influence on Greek philosophy, particularly Hellenistic philosophy. The Babylonian text Dialogue of Pessimism contains similarities to the agonistic thought of the sophists, the Heraclitean doctrine of contrasts, and the dialogs of Plato, as well as a precursor to the maieutic Socratic method of Socrates.

Neo-Babylonian Culture

The resurgence of Babylonian culture in the 7th and 6th century BCE resulted in a number of developments. In astronomy, a new approach was developed, based on the philosophy of the ideal nature of the early universe, and an internal logic within their predictive planetary systems. Some scholars have called this the first scientific revolution, and it was later adopted by Greek astronomers. The Babylonian astronomer Seleucus of Seleucia (b. 190 BCE) supported a heliocentric model of planetary motion. In mathematics, the Babylonians devised the base 60 numeral system, determined the square root of two correctly to seven places, and demonstrated knowledge of the Pythagorean theorem before Pythagoras.

Sources

Attributions

CC licensed content, Specific attribution

- Boundless World History. **Authored by**: Boundless. **Located at**: https://courses.lumenlearning.com/boundless-worldhistory/. **License**: *CC BY-SA: Attribution-ShareAlike*

The Phoenicians

- Describe key aspects of Phoenician culture

Key Points

- Phoenicia was an ancient Semitic maritime trading culture situated on the western, coastal part of the Fertile Crescent and centered on the coastline of modern Lebanon and Tartus Governorate in Syria from 1550 to 300 BCE.

- The Phoenicians used the galley, a man-powered sailing vessel, and are credited with the invention of the bireme.

- Each Phoenician city-state was a politically independent unit. City-states often came into conflict with others of its kind, or formed leagues and alliances.

- A league of independent city-state ports, with others on the islands and along other coasts of the Mediterranean Sea, was ideally suited for trade between the Levant area (which was rich in natural resources) and the rest of the ancient world.

- Cyrus the Great of Persia conquered Phoenicia in 539 BCE, and divided Phoenicia into four vassal kingdoms: Sidon, Tyre, Arwad, and Byblos.

- Alexander the Great conquered Phoenicia beginning with Tyre in 332 BCE. The rise of Hellenistic Greece gradually ousted the remnants of Phoenicia's former dominance over the Eastern Mediterranean trade routes.

Terms

city-state

An independent or autonomous entity, not administered as a part of another local government, whose territory consists of a city and possibly its surrounding territory.

bireme

An ancient oared warship (galley) with two decks of oars, probably invented by the Phoenicians.

Phoenicia

An ancient Semitic maritime trading culture situated on the western, coastal part of the Fertile Crescent.

Cyrus the Great

Also known as Cyrus II of Persia, Cyrus the Elder. Founder of the Achaemenid Empire.

Alexander the Great

Also known as Alexander III of Macedon. His military was extremely successful, and he created one of the largest empires in history.

Phoenicia was an ancient Semitic civilization situated on the western, coastal part of the Fertile Crescent near modern-day Lebanon, Israel, Jordan, Palestine, and Syria. All major Phoenician cities were on the coastline of the Mediterranean. It was an enterprising maritime trading culture that spread across the Mediterranean from 1550 BCE to 300 BCE. The Phoenicians used the galley, a man-powered sailing vessel, and are credited with the invention of the bireme oared ship. They were famed in Classical Greece and Rome as "traders in purple," which refers to their monopoly on the precious purple dye of the Murex snail, used for royal clothing, among other things.

Assyrian Warship. Assyrian warship (probably built by Phoenicians) with two rows of oars, relief from Nineveh, c. 700 BCE.

Phoenician became one of the most widely used writing systems. It was spread by Phoenician merchants across the Mediterranean world, where it evolved and was assimilated by many other cultures. The Aramaic alphabet, a modified form of Phoenician, was the ancestor of modern Arabic script, while Hebrew script is a stylistic variant of the Aramaic script. The Greek alphabet (and by extension its descendants, such as the Latin, the Cyrillic, and the Coptic) was a direct successor of Phoenician, though certain letter values were changed to represent vowels.

Phoenicians are widely thought to have originated from the earlier Canaanite inhabitants of the region. Although Egyptian seafaring expeditions had already been made to Byblos to bring back "cedars of Lebanon" as early as the 3rd millennium BCE, continuous contact only occurred in the Egyptian New Empire period.

It is important to note that Phoenicia is a Classical Greek term used to refer to the region of the major Canaanite port towns, and does not correspond exactly to a cultural identity that would have been recognized by the Phoenicians themselves. It is uncertain to what extent the Phoenicians viewed themselves as a single ethnicity and nationality. Their civilization was organized in city-states, similar to that of ancient Greece. However, in terms of archaeology, language, life style and religion, there is little to set the Phoenicians apart as markedly different from other Semitic cultures of Canaan. As Canaanites, they were unique in their remarkable seafaring achievements.

Each Phoenician city-state was a politically independent unit. City-states often came into conflict with one another, with the result that one may dominate another. City-states were also inclined to collaborate in leagues and alliances. Though ancient boundaries of city-centered cultures fluctuated, the city of Tyre held the southernmost border of Phoenician territory.

Phoenician Sarcophagus. A Phoenician sarcophagus at the burial grounds of Antarados, northern Lebanon, 480-450 BCE. Made from Greek marble.

Rise and Decline

The high point of Phoenician culture and sea power is usually placed c. 1200-800 BCE, though many of the most important Phoenician settlements had been established long before this period. Archeology has identified cultural elements of the Phoenician zenith as early as the 3rd millennium BCE. The league of independent city-state ports, with others on the islands and along other coasts of the Mediterranean Sea, was ideally suited for trade between the Levant area (which was rich in natural resources) and the rest of the ancient world. During the early Iron Age, around 1200 BCE, Sea Peoples appeared in the area from the north, which weakened and destroyed the Egyptians and Hittites, respectively. In the resulting power vacuum, a number of Phoenician cities rose as significant maritime powers.

These societies rested on three power-bases: the king; the temple and its priests; and the councils of elders. Byblos first became the predominant center from where the Phoenicians dominated the Mediterranean and Erythraean (Red) Sea routes. It was here that the first inscription in the Phoenician alphabet was found, on the sarcophagus of Ahiram (c. 1200 BCE). Tyre rose to power several hundred years later. One of its kings, the priest Ithobaal (887–856 BCE), ruled Phoenicia as far north as Beirut and Cyprus. Carthage was founded in 814 BCE, under Pygmalion of Tyre (820–774 BCE). The collection of city-states constituting Phoenicia came to be characterized by outsiders and the Phoenicians as Sidonia or Tyria. Phoenicians and Canaanites alike were called Sidonians or Tyrians, as one Phoenician city came to prominence after another.

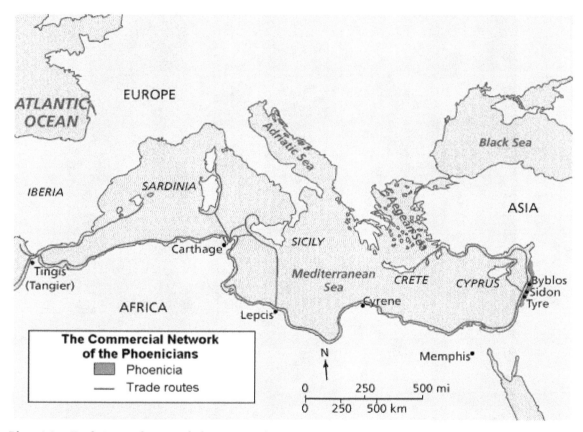

Phoenician Trade Network. Map of Phoenicia and its trade routes.

Persian Rule

Cyrus the Great of Persia conquered Phoenicia in 539 BCE. The Persians divided Phoenicia into four vassal kingdoms: Sidon, Tyre, Arwad, and Byblos. Though these vassal kingdoms prospered and furnished fleets for the Persian kings, Phoenician influence declined after this period. It is likely that much of the Phoenician population migrated to Carthage and other colonies following the Persian conquest. In 350 or 345 BCE, a rebellion in Sidon was crushed by Artaxerxes III.

Hellenistic Rule

Alexander the Great took Tyre in 332 BCE after the Siege of Tyre, and kept the existing king in power. He gained control of the other Phoenician cities peacefully, and the rise of Hellenistic Greece gradually ousted the remnants of Phoenicia's former dominance over the Eastern Mediterranean trade routes. Phoenician culture disappeared entirely in the motherland. Carthage continued to flourish in North Africa. It oversaw the mining of iron and precious metals from Iberia, and used its considerable naval power and mercenary armies to protect commercial interests. It was finally destroyed by Rome in 146 BC, at the end of the Punic Wars.

Sources

Attributions

CC licensed content, Specific attribution

- Boundless World History. **Authored by**: Boundless. **Located at**: https://courses.lumenlearning.com/boundless-worldhistory/. **License**: *CC BY-SA: Attribution-ShareAlike*

The Minoans

- Evaluate the impact of Minoan culture on other cultures and empires of the time

Key Points

- The Minoan civilization was an Aegean Bronze Age civilization that arose on the island of Crete, and flourished from approximately the 27th century to the 15th century BCE.

- The term "Minoan" was coined after the mythic "king" Minos, who was associated in Greek myth with the labyrinth identified with the site at Knossos.

- The Bronze Age allowed upper Minoan classes to practice leadership activities and to expand their influence, eventually replacing the original hierarchies of the local elites with monarchist power structures.

- The apex of Minoan civilization occurred during a period of large building projects, as palaces were rebuilt and settlements sprung up throughout Crete.

- Evidence of the influence of Minoan civilization outside Crete can be seen in Minoan handicraft on the Greek mainland, likely the result of a connection between Mycene and Minoan trade networks. The Minoans were also connected to Egypt and the Canaanite civilization.

- The Minoan civilization declined due to natural catastrophe, but the Dynasty of Knossos was able to spread its influence over Crete until it was overrun by the Mycenaean Greeks.

Terms

Linear B

A syllabic script that was used for writing Mycenaean Greek— the earliest attested form of Greek.

Minoan civilization

An Aegean Bronze Age civilization that arose on the island of Crete and flourished from approximately the 27th century to the 15th century BCE.

Knossos

A syllabic script that was used for writing Mycenaean Greek, the earliest attested form of Greek.

Neopalatial period

The period of the new or second palaces of Minoan Crete, corresponding roughly with 17th and 16th centuries BCE.

Linear A

The primary script used in palace and religious writings of the Minoan civilization, one of two currently undeciphered writing systems used in ancient Crete.

The Minoan civilization was an Aegean Bronze Age civilization that arose on the island of Crete, and flourished from approximately the 27th century to the 15th century BCE.

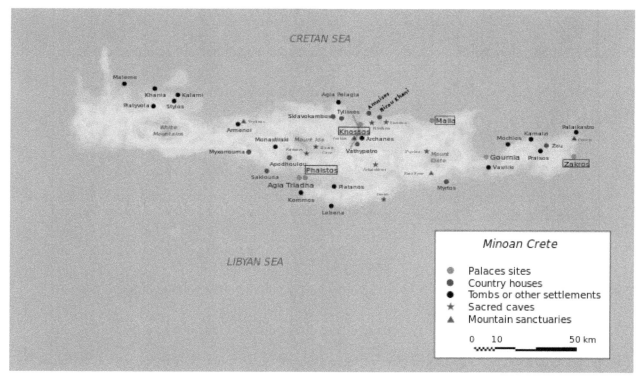

Minoan Crete. A map of Minoan Crete.

The early inhabitants of Crete settled as early as 128,000 BCE, during the Middle Paleolithic Age. It was not until 5000 BCE that the first signs of advanced agriculture appeared, marking the beginning of civilization. The term "Minoan" was coined by Arthur Evans after the mythic "king" Minos. Minos was associated in Greek myth with the labyrinth, which is identified with the site at Knossos.

The Bronze Age began in Crete around 2700 BCE, when several localities on the island developed into centers of commerce and handwork. This development enabled the upper classes to continuously practice leadership activities and to expand their influence. It is likely that the original hierarchies of the local elites were replaced by monarchist power structures— a precondition for the creation of the great palaces.

Around 1700 BCE, there was a large disturbance in Crete, possibly an earthquake or an invasion from Anatolia. The palaces at Knossos, Phaistos, Malia, and Kato Zakros were destroyed. But with the start of the Neopalatial period (the 17th and 16th centuries BCE), population increased again, palaces were rebuilt on a larger scale, and new settlements sprung up all over the island. This period represents the apex of the Minoan civilization.

Knossos – North Portico. Restored North Entrance of the Knossos palace complex, with the charging bull fresco.

The influence of the Minoan civilization outside Crete has been seen in the evidence of valuable Minoan handicraft items on the Greek mainland. It is likely that the ruling house of Mycene was connected to the Minoan trade network. After c. 1700 BCE, the material culture on the Greek mainland achieved a new level due to Minoan influence. Connections between Egypt and Crete are also prominent. Minoan ceramics are found in Egyptian cities, and the Minoans imported several items from Egypt, especially papyrus, as well as architectural and artistic ideas. The Egyptian hieroglyphs served as a model for Minoan pictographic writing, from which the famous Linear A and Linear B writing systems later developed. There has also been evidence of Minoan influence among Canaanite artifacts.

The Minoan culture began to decline c. 1450 BCE, following an earthquake, the eruption of the Thera volcano, or another possible natural catastrophe. Several important palaces in locations such as Mallia, Tylissos, Phaistos, Hagia Triade, as well as the living quarters of Knossos were destroyed, but the palace in Knossos seems to have remained largely intact. The preservation of this palace resulted in the Dynasty in Knossos spreading its influence over large parts of Crete until it was overrun by Mycenaean Greeks.

Society and Culture

Pottery

The best surviving examples of Minoan art are its pottery and palace architecture with frescos that include landscapes, stone carvings, and intricately carved seal stones. Ceramics from the Early Minoan period are characterized by linear patterns of spirals, triangles, curved lines, crosses, and fishbone motifs. In the Middle Minoan period, naturalistic designs such as fish, squid, birds, and lilies were common. In the Late Minoan period, flowers and animals were still the most characteristic, but the variability had increased. The "palace style" of the region around Knossos is characterized by a strong geometric simplification of naturalistic shapes and monochromatic paintings. The similarities between Late Minoan and Mycenaean art are notable. Frescoes were the main form of art during the period of Late Minoan culture.

Religion

The Minoans seem to have worshiped primarily goddesses, and can be described as a "matriarchal religion." Although there is some evidence of male gods, depictions of Minoan goddesses vastly outnumber depictions of anything that could be considered a Minoan god. While some of these depictions of women are speculated to be images of worshippers and priestesses officiating at religious ceremonies, as opposed to the deity, several goddesses appear to be portrayed. These include a mother goddess of fertility, a mistress of the animals, a protectress of cities, the household, the harvest, and the underworld, to name a few. The goddesses are often depicted with serpents, birds, or poppies, and are often shown with a figure of an animal upon her head.

Sources

Attributions

CC licensed content, Specific attribution

3. Ancient Egypt

The Old Kingdom

Learning Objective

- Explain the reasons for the rise and fall of the Old Kingdom

Key Points

- The Old Kingdom is the name commonly given to the period when Egypt gained in complexity and achievement, spanning from the Third Dynasty through the Sixth Dynasty (2686-2181 BCE).

- The royal capital of Egypt during the Old Kingdom was located at Memphis, where the first notable king of the Old Kingdom, Djoser, established his court.

- In the Third Dynasty, formerly independent ancient Egyptian states became known as Nomes, which were ruled solely by the pharaoh. The former rulers of these states were subsequently forced to assume the role of governors, or otherwise work in tax collection.

- Egyptians during this Dynasty worshipped their pharaoh as a god, and believed that he ensured the stability of the cycles that were responsible for the annual flooding of the Nile. This flooding was necessary for their crops.

- The Fourth Dynasty saw multiple large-scale construction projects under pharaohs Sneferu, Khufu, and Khufu's sons Djedefra and Khafra, including the famous pyramid and Sphinx at Giza.

- The Fifth Dynasty saw changes in religious beliefs, including the rise of the cult of the sun god Ra, and the deity Osiris.

Terms

Ra

The sun god, or the supreme Egyptian deity, worshipped as the creator of all life, and usually portrayed with a falcon's head bearing a solar disc.

Osiris

The Egyptian god of the underworld, and husband and brother of Isis.

Nomes

Subnational, administrative division of Ancient Egypt.

nomarchs

Semi-feudal rulers of Ancient Egyptian provinces.

Old Kingdom

Encompassing the Third to Eighth Dynasties, the name commonly given to the period in the 3rd millennium BCE, when Egypt attained its first continuous peak of complexity and achievement.

Djoser

An ancient Egyptian pharaoh of the Third Dynasty, and the founder of the Old Kingdom.

necropolis

A cemetery, especially a large one belonging to an ancient city.

Sneferu

A king of the Fourth Dynasty, who used the greatest mass of stones in building pyramids.

The Old Kingdom is the name commonly given to the period from the Third Dynasty through the Sixth Dynasty (2686-2181 BCE), when Egypt gained in complexity and achievement. The Old Kingdom is the first of three so-called "Kingdom" periods that mark the high points of civilization in the Nile Valley. During this time, a new type of pyramid (the step) was created, as well as many other massive building projects, including the Sphinx. Additionally, trade became more widespread, new religious ideas were born, and the strong centralized government was subtly weakened and finally collapsed.

The king (not yet called Pharaoh) of Egypt during this period resided in the new royal capital, Memphis. He was considered a living god, and was believed to ensure the annual flooding of the Nile. This flooding was necessary for crop growth. The Old Kingdom is perhaps best known for a large number of pyramids, which were constructed as royal burial places. Thus, the period of the Old Kingdom is often called "The Age of the Pyramids."

Egypt's Old Kingdom was also a dynamic period in the development of Egyptian art. Sculptors created early portraits, the first life-size statues, and perfected the art of carving intricate relief decoration. These had two principal functions: to ensure an ordered existence, and to defeat death by preserving life in the next world.

The Beginning: Third Dynasty (c. 2650-2613 BCE)

The first notable king of the Old Kingdom was Djoser (reigned from 2691-2625 BCE) of the Third Dynasty, who ordered the construction of the step pyramid in Memphis' necropolis, Saqqara. It was in this era that formerly independent ancient Egyptian states became known as nomes, and were ruled solely by the king. The former rulers of these states were forced to assume the role of governors or tax collectors.

Golden Age: Fourth Dynasty (2613-2494 BCE)

The Old Kingdom and its royal power reached a zenith under the Fourth Dynasty, which began with Sneferu (2613-2589 BCE). Using a greater mass of stones than any other king, he built three pyramids: Meidum, the Bent Pyramid, and the Red Pyramid. He also sent his military into Sinai, Nubia and Libya, and began to trade with Lebanon for cedar.

Sneferu was succeeded by his (in)famous son, Khufu (2589-2566 BCE), who built the Great Pyramid of Giza. After Khufu's death, one of his sons built the second pyramid, and the Sphinx in Giza. Creating these massive projects required a centralized government with strong powers, sophistication and prosperity. Builders of the pyramids were not slaves but peasants, working in the farming off-season, along with specialists like stone cutters, mathematicians, and priests. Each household needed to provide a worker for these projects, although the wealthy could have a substitute.

The Pyramid of Khufu at Giza. The Great Pyramid of Giza was built c. 2560 BCE, by Khufu during the Fourth Dynasty. It was built as a tomb for Khufu and constructed over a 20-year period. Modern estimates place construction efforts to require an average workforce of 14,567 people and a peak workforce of 40,000.

Great Sphinx of Giza and the pyramid of Khafre. The Sphinx is a limestone statue of a reclining mythical creature with a lion's body and a human head that stands on the Giza Plateau on the west bank of the Nile in Giza, Egypt. The face is generally believed to represent the face of King Khafra.

The later kings of the Fourth Dynasty were king Menkaura (2532-2504 BCE), who built the smallest pyramid in Giza, Shepseskaf (2504-2498 BCE), and perhaps Djedefptah (2498-2496 BCE). During this period, there were military expeditions into Canaan and Nubia, spreading Egyptian influence along the Nile into modern-day Sudan.

Religious Changes: Fifth Dynasty (2494-2345 BCE)

The Fifth Dynasty began with Userkaf (2494-2487 BCE), and with several religious changes. The cult of the sun god Ra, and temples built for him, began to grow in importance during the Fifth Dynasty. This lessened efforts to build pyramids. Funerary prayers on royal tombs (called Pyramid Texts) appeared, and the cult of the deity Osiris ascended in importance.

Egyptians began to build ships to trade across maritime routes. Goods included ebony, incense, gold, and copper. They traded with Lebanon for cedar, and perhaps with modern-day Somalia for other goods. Ships were held together by tightly tied ropes.

Decline and Collapse: The Sixth Dynasty (2345-2181 BCE)

The power of the king and central government declined during this period, while that of nomarchs (regional governors) increased. These nomarchs were not part of the royal family. They passed down the title through their lineage, thus creating local dynasties that were not under the control of the king. Internal disorder resulted during and after the long reign of Pepi II (2278-2184 BCE), due to succession struggles, and eventually led to civil war. The final blow was a severe drought between 2200-2150 BCE, which prevented Nile flooding. Famine, conflict, and collapse beset the Old Kingdom for decades.

Sources

Attributions

CC licensed content, Specific attribution

The First Intermediate Period

Learning Objective

- Describe the processes by which the First Intermediate Period occurred, and then transitioned into the Middle Kingdom

Key Points

- The First Intermediate Period was a dynamic time in history, when rule of Egypt was roughly divided between two competing power bases. One of those bases resided at Heracleopolis in Lower Egypt, a city just south of the Faiyum region. The other resided at Thebes in Upper Egypt.

- The Old Kingdom fell due to problems with succession from the Sixth Dynasty, the rising power of provincial monarchs, and a drier climate that resulted in widespread famine.

- Little is known about the Seventh and Eighth Dynasties due to a lack of evidence, but the Seventh Dynasty was most likely an oligarchy, while Eighth Dynasty rulers claimed to be the descendants of the Sixth Dynasty kings. Both ruled from Memphis.

- The Heracleopolitan Kings saw periods of both violence and peace under their rule, and eventually brought peace and order to the Nile Delta region.

- Siut princes to the south of the Heracleopolitan Kingdom became wealthy from a variety of agricultural and economic activities, and acted as a buffer during times of conflict between the northern and southern parts of Egypt.

- The Theban Kings enjoyed a string of military successes, the last of which was a victory against the Heracleopolitan Kings that unified Egypt under the Twelfth Dynasty.

Terms

First Intermediate Period

A period of political conflict and instability lasting approximately 100 years and spanning the Seventh to Eleventh Dynasties.

Mentuhotep II

A pharaoh of the Eleventh Dynasty, who defeated the Heracleopolitan Kings and unified Egypt. Often considered the first pharaoh of the Middle Kingdom.

nomarchs

Ancient Egyptian administration officials responsible for governing the provinces.

oligarchy

A form of power structure in which power effectively rests with a small number of people who are distinguished by royalty, wealth, family ties, education, corporate, or military control.

The First Intermediate Period (c. 2181-2055 BCE), often described as a "dark period" in ancient Egyptian history after the end of the Old Kingdom, spanned approximately 100 years. It included the Seventh, Eighth, Ninth, Tenth, and part of the Eleventh dynasties.

The First Intermediate Period was a dynamic time in history when rule of Egypt was roughly divided between two competing power bases: Heracleopolis in Lower Egypt, and Thebes in Upper Egypt. It is believed that political chaos during this time resulted in temples being pillaged, artwork vandalized, and statues of kings destroyed. These two kingdoms eventually came into military conflict. The Theban kings conquered the north, which resulted in the reunification of Egypt under a single ruler during the second part of the Eleventh dynasty.

Events Leading to the First Intermediate Period

The Old Kingdom, which preceded this period, fell for numerous reasons. One was the extremely long reign of Pepi II (the last major king of the Sixth Dynasty), and the resulting succession issues. Another major problem was the rise in power of the provincial nomarchs. Toward the end of the Old Kingdom, the positions of the nomarchs had become hereditary, creating family legacies independent from the king. They erected tombs in their own domains and often raised armies, and engaged in local rivalries. A third reason for the dissolution of centralized kingship was the low level of the Nile inundation, which may have resulted in a drier climate, lower crop yields, and famine.

The Seventh and Eighth Dynasties at Memphis

The Seventh and Eighth dynasties are often overlooked because very little is known about the rulers of these two periods. The Seventh Dynasty was most likely an oligarchy based in Memphis that attempted to retain control of the country. The Eighth Dynasty rulers, claiming to be the descendants of the Sixth Dynasty kings, also ruled from Memphis.

The Heracleopolitan Kings

After the obscure reign of the Seventh and Eighth dynasty kings, a group of rulers rose out of Heracleopolis in Lower Egypt, and ruled for approximately 94 years. These kings comprise the Ninth and Tenth Dynasties, each with 19 rulers.

The founder of the Ninth Dynasty, Wahkare Khety I, is often described as an evil and violent ruler who caused much harm to the inhabitants of Egypt. He was seized with madness, and, as legend would have it, was eventually killed by a crocodile. Kheti I was succeeded by Kheti II, also known as Meryibre, whose reign was essentially peaceful but experienced problems in the Nile Delta. His successor, Kheti III, brought some degree of order to the Delta, although the power and influence of these Ninth Dynasty kings were still insignificant compared to that of the Old Kingdom kings.

A distinguished line of nomarchs rose out of Siut (or Asyut), which was a powerful and wealthy province in the south of the Heracleopolitan kingdom. These warrior princes maintained a close relationship with the kings of the Heracleopolitan royal household, as is evidenced by the inscriptions in their tombs. These inscriptions provide a glimpse at the political situation that was present during their reigns, and describe the Siut nomarchs digging canals, reducing taxation, reaping rich harvests, raising cattle herds, and maintaining an army and fleet. The Siut province acted as a buffer state between the northern and southern rulers and bore the brunt of the attacks from the Theban kings.

The Theban Kings

The Theban kings are believed to have been descendants of Intef or Inyotef, the nomarch of Thebes, often called the "Keeper of the Door of the South. " He is credited with organizing Upper Egypt into an independent ruling body in the south, although he himself did not appear to have tried to claim the title of king. Intef II began the Theban assault on northern Egypt, and his successor, Intef III, completed the attack and moved into Middle Egypt against the Heracleopolitan kings. The first three kings of the Eleventh Dynasty (all named Intef) were, therefore, also the last three kings of the First Intermediate Period. They were succeeded by a line of kings who were all called Mentuhotep. Mentuhotep II, also known as Nebhepetra, would eventually defeat the Heracleopolitan kings around 2033 BCE, and unify the country to continue the Eleventh Dynasty and bring Egypt into the Middle Kingdom.

Mentuhotep II. Painted sandstone seated statue of Nebhepetre Mentuhotep II, Egyptian Museum, Cairo.

Sources

Attributions

CC licensed content, Specific attribution

The Second Intermediate Period

Learning Objective

- Explain the dynamics between the various groups of people vying for power during the Second Intermediate Period

Key Points

- The brilliant Twelfth Dynasty was succeeded by a weaker Thirteenth Dynasty, which experienced a splintering of power.

- The Hyksos made their first appearance during the reign of Sobekhotep IV, and overran Egypt at the end of the Fourteenth Dynasty. They ruled through the Fifteenth and Sixteenth Dynasties.

- The Abydos Dynasty was a short-lived Dynasty that ruled over part of Upper Egypt, and was contemporaneous with the Fifteenth and Sixteenth Dynasties.

- The Seventeeth Dynasty established itself in Thebes around the time that the Hyksos took power in Egypt, and co-existed with the Hyksos through trade for a period of time. However, rulers from the Seventeenth Dynasty undertook several wars of liberation that eventually once again unified Egypt in the Eighteenth Dynasty.

Terms

Hyksos

An Asiatic people from West Asia who took over the eastern Nile Delta, ending the Thirteenth dynasty of Egypt and initiating the Second Intermediate Period.

Abydos Dynasty

A short-lived local dynasty ruling over parts of Upper Egypt during the Second Intermediate Period in Ancient Egypt.

Baal

The native storm god of the Hyksos.

Second Intermediate Period

Spanning the Fourteenth to Seventeenth Dynasties, a period of Egyptian history where power was split between the Hyksos and a Theban-based dynasty in Upper Egypt.

The Second Intermediate Period (c. 1782-1550 BCE) marks a time when Ancient Egypt once again fell into disarray between the end of the Middle Kingdom, and the start of the New Kingdom. It is best known as the period when the Hyksos, who reigned during the Fifteenth and Sixteenth Dynasties, made their appearance in Egypt.

The Thirteenth Dynasty (1803 – 1649 BCE)

The brilliant Egyptian Twelfth Dynasty—and the Golden Age of the Middle Kingdom— came to an end around 1800 BCE with the death of Queen Sobekneferu (1806-1802 BCE), and was succeeded by the much weaker Thirteenth Dynasty (1803-1649 BCE). Pharoahs ruled from Memphis until the Hyksos conquered the capital in 1650 BCE.

The Fourteenth Dynasty (c. 1725-1650 BCE)

The Thirteenth Dynasty proved unable to hold onto the long land of Egypt, and the provincial ruling family in Xois, located in the marshes of the western Delta, broke away from the central authority to form the Fourteenth Dynasty. The capital of this dynasty was likely Avaris. It existed concurrently with the Thirteenth Dynasty, and its rulers seemed to be of Canaanite or West Semitic descent.

Fourteenth Dynasty Territory. The area in orange is the territory possibly under control of the Fourteenth Dynasty.

The Fifteenth Dynasty (c. 1650-1550 BCE)

The Hyksos made their first appearance in 1650 BCE and took control of the town of Avaris. They would also conquer the Sixteenth Dynasty in Thebes and a local dynasty in Abydos (see below). The Hyksos were of mixed Asiatic origin with mainly Semitic components, and their native storm god, Baal, became associated with the Egyptian storm god Seth. They brought technological innovation to Egypt, including bronze and pottery techniques, new breeds of animals and new crops, the horse and chariot, composite bow, battle-axes, and fortification techniques for warfare. These advances helped Egypt later rise to prominence.

Luxor Temple. Thebes was the capital of many of the Sixteenth Dynasty pharaohs.

The Sixteenth Dynasty

This dynasty ruled the Theban region in Upper Egypt for 70 years, while the armies of the Fifteenth Dynasty advanced against southern enemies and encroached on Sixteenth territory. Famine was an issue during this period, most notably during the reign of Neferhotep III.

The Abydos Dynasty

The Abydos Dynasty was a short-lived local dynasty that ruled over part of Upper Egypt and was contemporaneous with the Fifteenth and Sixteenth Dynasties c. 1650-1600 BCE. The royal necropolis of the Abydos Dynasty was found in the southern part of Abydos, in an area called Anubis Mountain in ancient times, adjacent to the tombs of the Middle Kingdom rulers.

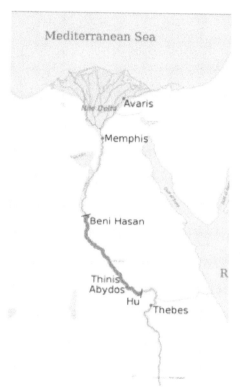

The Abydos Dynasty. This map shows the possible extent of power of the Abydos Dynasty (in red).

The Seventeenth Dynasty (c. 1580-1550 BCE)

Around the time Memphis and Itj-tawy fell to the Hyksos, the native Egyptian ruling house in Thebes declared its independence from Itj-tawy and became the Seventeenth Dynasty. This dynasty would eventually lead the war of liberation that drove the Hyksos back into Asia. The Theban-based Seventeenth Dynasty restored numerous temples throughout Upper Egypt while maintaining peaceful trading relations with the Hyksos kingdom in the north. Indeed, Senakhtenre Ahmose, the first king in the line of Ahmoside kings, even imported white limestone from the Hyksos-controlled region of Tura to make a granary door at the Temple of Karnak. However, his successors—the final two kings of this dynasty—,Seqenenre Tao and Kamose, defeated the Hyksos through several wars of liberation. With the creation of the Eighteenth Dynasty around 1550 BCE, the New Kingdom period of Egyptian history began with Ahmose I, its first pharaoh, who completed the expulsion of the Hyksos from Egypt and placed the country, once again, under centralized administrative control.

Sources

Attributions

CC licensed content, Specific attribution

- Boundless World History. **Authored by**: Boundless. **Located at**: https://courses.lumenlearning.com/boundless-worldhistory/. **License**: *CC BY-SA: Attribution-ShareAlike*

The New Kingdom

Learning Objective

- Explain the reasons for the collapse of the New Kingdom

Key Points

- The New Kingdom saw Egypt attempt to create a buffer against the Levant and by attaining its greatest territorial by extending into Nubia and the Near East. This was possibly a result of the foreign rule of the Hyksos during the Second Intermediate Period,

- The Eighteenth Dynasty contained some of Egypt's most famous pharaohs, including Hatshepsut, Akhenaten, Thutmose III, and Tutankhamun. Hatshepsut concentrated on expanding Egyptian trade, while Thutmose III consolidated power.

- Akhenaten's devotion to Aten defined his reign with religious fervor, while art flourished under his rule and attained an unprecedented level of realism.

- Due to Akenaten's lack of interest in international affairs, the Hittites gradually extended their influence into Phoenicia and Canaan.

- Ramesses II attempted war against the Hittites, but eventually agreed to a peace treaty after an indecisive result.

- The heavy cost of military efforts in addition to climatic changes resulted in a loss of centralized power at the end of the Twentieth Dynasty, leading to the Third Intermediate Period.

Terms

Hyksos

An Asiatic people from West Asia who took over the eastern Nile Delta, ending the Thirteenth dynasty of Egypt and initiating the Second Intermediate Period.

Abydos Dynasty

A short-lived local dynasty ruling over parts of Upper Egypt during the Second Intermediate Period in Ancient Egypt.

Baal

The native storm god of the Hyksos.

Second Intermediate Period

Spanning the Fourteenth to Seventeenth Dynasties, a period of Egyptian history where power was split between the Hyksos and a Theban-based dynasty in Upper Egypt.

The New Kingdom of Egypt, also referred to as the Egyptian Empire, is the period in ancient Egyptian history between 1550-1070 BCE, covering the Eighteenth, Nineteenth, and Twentieth Dynasties of Egypt. The New Kingdom followed the Second Intermediate Period, and was succeeded by the Third Intermediate Period. It was Egypt's most prosperous time and marked the peak of its power.

The Nineteenth and Twentieth Dynasties (1292-1069 BCE) are also known as the Ramesside period, after the eleven pharaohs that took the name of Ramesses. The New Kingdom saw Egypt attempt to create a buffer against the Levant and attain its greatest territorial extent. This was possibly a result of the foreign rule of the Hyksos during the Second Intermediate Period.

The Eighteenth Dynasty (c. 1543-1292 BCE)

The Eighteenth Dynasty, also known as the Thutmosid Dynasty, contained some of Egypt's most famous pharaohs, including Ahmose I, Hatshepsut, Thutmose III, Amenhotep III, Akhenaten (c. 1353-1336 BCE) and his queen Nefertiti, and Tutankhamun. Queen Hatshepsut (c. 1479 – 1458 BCE) concentrated on expanding Egypt's external trade by sending a commercial expedition to the land of Punt, and was the longest-reigning woman pharaoh of an indigenous dynasty. Thutmose III, who would become known as the greatest military pharaoh, expanded Egypt's army and wielded it with great success to consolidate the empire created by his predecessors. These victories maximized Egyptian power and wealth during the reign of Amenhotep III. It was also during the reign of Thutmose III that the term "pharaoh," originally referring to the king's palace, became a form of address for the king.

One of the best-known Eighteenth Dynasty pharaohs is Amenhotep IV (c. 1353-1336 BCE), who changed his name to Akhenaten in honor of Aten and whose exclusive worship of the deity is often interpreted as the first instance of monotheism. Under his reign Egyptian art flourished and attained an unprecedented level of realism. Toward the end of this dynasty, the Hittites had expanded their influence into Phoenicia and Canaan, the outcome of which would be inherited by the rulers of the Nineteenth Dynasty.

Bust of Akhenaten. Akhenaten, born Amenhotep IV, was the son of Queen Tiye. He rejected the old Egyptian religion and promoted the Aten as a supreme deity.

The Nineteenth Dynasty (c. 1292-1187 BCE)

New Kingdom Egypt would reach the height of its power under Seti I and Ramesses II, who fought against the Libyans and Hittites. The city of Kadesh was a flashpoint, captured first by Seti I and then used as a peace bargain with the Hatti, and later attacked again by Ramesses II. Eventually, the Egyptians and Hittites signed a lasting peace treaty.

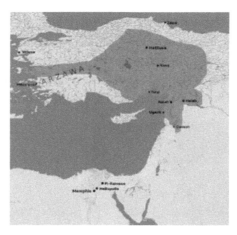

*Egyptian and Hittite Empires. This map
shows the Egyptian (green) and Hittite (red)
Empires around 1274 BCE.*

Ramesses II had a large number of children, and he built a massive funerary complex for his sons in the Valley of the Kings. The Nineteenth Dynasty ended in a revolt led by Setnakhte, the founder of the Twentieth Dynasty.

*Temple of Ramesses II. Detail of the Temple
of Ramesses II.*

The Twentieth Dynasty (c. 1187-1064 BCE)

The last "great" pharaoh from the New Kingdom is widely regarded to be Ramesses III. In the eighth year of his reign, the Sea Peoples invaded Egypt by land and sea, but were defeated by Ramesses III.

The heavy cost of warfare slowly drained Egypt's treasury and contributed to the gradual decline of the Egyptian Empire in Asia. The severity of the difficulties is indicated by the fact that the first known labor strike in recorded history occurred during the 29th year of Ramesses III's reign, over food rations. Despite a palace conspiracy which may have killed Ramesses III, three of his sons ascended the throne successively as Ramesses IV, Ramesses VI and Ramesses VIII. Egypt was increasingly beset by droughts, below-normal flooding of the Nile, famine, civil unrest, and official corruption. The power of the last pharaoh of the dynasty, Ramesses XI, grew so weak that, in the south, the High Priests of Amun at Thebes became the de facto rulers of Upper Egypt. The Smendes controlled Lower Egypt even before Ramesses XI's death. Menes eventually founded the Twenty-first Dynasty at Tanis.

Sources

Attributions

CC licensed content, Specific attribution

- Boundless World History. **Authored by**: Boundless. **Located at**: https://courses.lumenlearning.com/boundless-worldhistory/. **License**: *CC BY-SA: Attribution-ShareAlike*

Hatshepsut

Learning Objective

- Describe the achievements of Hatshepsut in Ancient Egypt

Key Points

- Hatshepsut reigned Egypt from 1478-1458 BCE, during the Eighteenth Dynasty. She ruled longer than any other woman of an indigenous Egyptian dynasty.

- Hatshepsut established trade networks that helped build the wealth of the Eighteenth Dynasty.

- Hundreds of construction projects and statuary were commissioned by Hatshepsut, including obelisks and monuments at the Temple of Karnak.

- While not the first female ruler of Egypt, Hatshepsut's reign was longer and more prosperous; she oversaw a peaceful, wealthy era.

- The average woman in Egypt was quite liberated for the time, and had a variety of property and other rights.

- Hatshepsut died in 1458 BCE in middle age, possibly of diabetes and bone cancer. Her mummy was discovered in 1903 and identified in 2007.

Terms

kohl

A black powder used as eye makeup.

obelisks

Stone pillars, typically having a square or rectangular cross section and a pyramidal tip, used as a monument.

co-regent

The situation wherein a monarchical position, normally held by one person, is held by two.

Hatshepsut reigned in Egypt from 1478-1458 BCE, during the Eighteenth Dynasty, longer than any other woman of an indigenous Egyptian dynasty. According to Egyptologist James Henry Breasted, she was "the first great woman in history of whom we are informed." She was the daughter of Thutmose I and his wife Ahmes. Hatshepsut's husband, Thutmose II, was also a child of Thutmose I, but was conceived with a different wife. Hatshepsut had a daughter named Neferure with her husband, Thutmose II. Thutmose II also fathered Thutmose III with Iset, a secondary wife. Hatshepsut ascended to the throne as co-regent with Thutmose III, who came to the throne as a two-year old child.

Statue of Hatshepsut. This statue of Hatshepsut is housed at the Metropolitan Museum of Art in New York City.

Trade Networks

Hatshepsut established trade networks that helped build the wealth of the Eighteenth Dynasty. This included a successful mission to the Land of Punt in the ninth year of her reign, which brought live myrrh trees and frankincense (which Hatshepsut used as kohl eyeliner) to Egypt. She also sent raiding expeditions to Byblos and Sinai, and may have led military campaigns against Nubia and Canaan.

Building Projects

Hatshepsut was a prolific builder, commissioning hundreds of construction projects and statuary. She had monuments constructed at the Temple of Karnak, and restored the original Precinct of Mut at Karnak, which had been ravaged during the Hyksos occupation of Egypt. She installed twin obelisks (the tallest in the world at that time) at the entrance to this temple, one of which still stands. Karnak's Red Chapel was intended as a shrine to her life, and may have stood with these obelisks.

The Temple of Pakhet was a monument to Bast and Sekhmet, lioness war goddesses. Later in the Nineteenth Dynasty, King Seti I attempted to take credit for this monument. However, Hatshepsut's masterpiece was a mortuary temple at Deir el-Bahri; the focal point was the Djeser-Djeseru ("the Sublime of Sublimes"), a colonnaded structure built 1,000 years before the Greek Parthenon. The Hatshepsut needle, a granite obelisk, is considered another great accomplishment.

Hatshepsut Temple. The colonnaded design is evident in this temple.

Female Rule

Hatshepsut was not the first female ruler of Egypt. She had been preceded by Merneith of the First Dynasty, Nimaathap of the Third Dynasty, Nitocris of the Sixth Dynasty, Sobekneferu of the Twelfth Dynasty,

Ahhotep I of the Seventeenth Dynasty, Ahmose-Nefertari, and others. However, Hatshepsut's reign was longer and more prosperous; she oversaw a peaceful, wealthy era. She was also proficient at self-promotion, which was enabled by her wealth.

Hieroglyphs of Thutmose III and Hatshepsut. Hatshepsut, on the right, is shown having the trappings of a greater role.

The word "king" was considered gender-neutral, and women could take the title. During her father's reign, she held the powerful office of God's Wife, and as wife to her husband, Thutmose II, she took an active role in administration of the kingdom. As pharaoh, she faced few challenges, even from her co-regent, who headed up the powerful Egyptian army and could have unseated her, had he chosen to do so.

Women's Status in Egypt

The average woman in Egypt was quite liberated for the time period. While her foremost role was as mother and wife, an average woman might have worked in weaving, perfume making, or entertainment. Women could own their own businesses, own and sell property, serve as witnesses in court cases, be in the company of men, divorce and remarry, and have access to one-third of their husband's property.

Hatshepsut's Death

Hatshepsut died in 1458 BCE in middle age; no cause of death is known, although she may have had diabetes and bone cancer, likely from a carcinogenic skin lotion. Her mummy was discovered in the Valley of the Kings by Howard Carer in 1903, although at the time, the mummy's identity was not known. In 2007, the mummy was found to be a match to a missing tooth known to have belonged to Hatshepsut.

Osirian Statues of Hatshepsut. These statues of Hatshepsut at her tomb show her holding the crook and flail associated with Osiris.

After her death, mostly during Thutmose III's reign, haphazard attempts were made to remove Hatshepsut from certain historical and pharaonic records. Amenhotep II, the son of Thutmose III, may have been responsible. The Tyldesley hypothesis states that Thutmose III may have decided to attempt to scale back Hatshepsut's role to that of regent rather than king.

Sources

Attributions

CC licensed content, Specific attribution

- Boundless World History. **Authored by**: Boundless. **Located at**: https://courses.lumenlearning.com/boundless-worldhistory/. **License**: *CC BY-SA: Attribution-ShareAlike*

The Decline of Ancient Egypt

Learning Objective

- Explain why Ancient Egypt declined as an economic and political force

Key Points

- After a renaissance in the 25th Dynasty, ancient Egypt was occupied by Assyrians, initiating the Late Period.

- In 525 BCE, Egypt was conquered by Persia, and incorporated into the Achaemenid Persian Empire.

- In 332 BCE, Egypt was given to Macedonia and Alexander the Great. During this period, the new capital of Alexandria flourished.

- Egypt became a Roman province after the defeat of Marc Antony and Queen Cleopatra VII in 30 BCE. During this period, religious and other traditions slowly declined.

Terms

Hellenistic

Relating to Greek history, language, and culture, during the time between the death of Alexander the Great and the defeat of Mark Antony and Cleopatra in 31 BCE.

hieroglyphics

A formal writing system used by ancient Egyptians, consisting of pictograms.

pagan

A person holding religious beliefs other than those of the main world religions, Christianity, Judaism, and Islam.

Ancient Egypt went through a series of occupations and suffered a slow decline over a long period of time. First occupied by the Assyrians, then the Persians, and later the Macedonians and Romans, Egyptians would never again reach the glorious heights of self-rule they achieved during previous periods.

Third Intermediate Period (1069-653 BCE)

After a renaissance in the Twenty-fifth dynasty, when religion, arts, and architecture (including pyramids) were restored, struggles against the Assyrians led to eventual conquest of Egypt by Esarhaddon in 671 BCE. Native Egyptian rulers were installed but could not retain control of the area, and former Pharaoh Taharqa seized control of southern Egypt for a time, until he was defeated again by the Assyrians. Taharqa's successor, Tanutamun, also made a failed attempt to regain Egypt, but was defeated.

Late Period (672-332 BCE)

Having been victorious in Egypt, the Assyrians installed a series of vassals known as the Saite kings of the Twenty-sixth Dynasty. In 653 BCE, one of these kings, Psamtik I, was able to achieve a peaceful separation from the Assyrians with the help of Lydian and Greek mercenaries. In 609 BCE, the Egyptians attempted to save the Assyrians, who were losing their war with the Babylonians, Chaldeans, Medians, and Scythians. However, they were unsuccessful.

In 525 BCE, the Persians, led by Cambyses II, invaded Egypt, capturing the Pharaoh Psamtik III. Egypt was joined with Cyprus and Phoenicia in the sixth satrapy of the Achaemenid Persian Empire, also called the Twenty-seventh Dynasty. This ended in 402 BCE, and the last native royal house of dynastic Egypt, known as the Thirtieth Dynasty, was ruled by Nectanebo II. Persian rule was restored briefly in 343 BCE, known as the Thirty-first Dynasty, but in 332 BCE, Egypt was handed over peacefully to the Macedonian ruler, Alexander the Great.

Macedonian and Ptolemaic Period (332-30 BCE)

Alexander the Great was welcomed into Egypt as a deliverer, and the new capital city of Alexandria was a showcase of Hellenistic rule, capped by the famous Library of Alexandria. Native Egyptian traditions were honored, but eventually local revolts, plus interest in Egyptian goods by the Romans, caused the Romans to wrest Egypt from the Macedonians.

Roman Period (30 BCE-641CE)

Egypt became a Roman province after the defeat of Marc Antony and Queen Cleopatra VII in 30 BCE. Some Egyptian traditions, including mummification and worship of local gods, continued, but local administration was handled exclusively by Romans. The spread of Christianity proved to be too powerful, and pagan rites were banned and temples closed. Egyptians continued to speak their language, but the ability to read hieroglyphics disappeared as temple priests diminished.

Sources

Attributions

CC licensed content, Specific attribution

- Boundless World History. **Authored by**: Boundless. **Located at**: https://courses.lumenlearning.com/boundless-worldhistory/. **License**: *CC BY-SA: Attribution-ShareAlike*

Ancient Egyptian Religion

Learning Objective

- Describe the religious beliefs and practices of Ancient Egypt

Key Points

- The religion of Ancient Egypt lasted for more than 3,000 years, and was polytheistic, meaning there were a multitude of deities, who were believed to reside within and control the forces of nature.

- Formal religious practice centered on the pharaoh, or ruler, of Egypt, who was believed to be divine, and acted as intermediary between the people and the gods. His role was to sustain the gods so that they could maintain order in the universe.

- The Egyptian universe centered on Ma'at, which has several meanings in English, including truth, justice and order. It was fixed and eternal; without it the world would fall apart.

- The most important myth was of Osiris and Isis. The divine ruler Osiris was murdered by Set (god of chaos), then resurrected by his sister and wife Isis to conceive an heir, Horus. Osiris then became the ruler of the dead, while Horus eventually avenged his father and became king.

- Egyptians were very concerned about the fate of their souls after death. They believed ka (life-force) left the body upon death and needed to be fed. Ba, or personal spirituality, remained in the body. The goal was to unite ka and ba to create akh.

- Artistic depictions of gods were not literal representations, as their true nature was considered mysterious. However, symbolic imagery was used to indicate this nature.

- Temples were the state's method of sustaining the gods, since their physical images were housed and cared for; temples were not a place for the average person to worship.

- Certain animals were worshipped and mummified as representatives of gods.

- Oracles were used by all classes.

Terms

Ma'at

The Egyptian universe.

heka

The ability to use natural forces to create "magic."

pantheon

The core actors of a religion.

polytheistic

A religion with more than one worshipped god.

ka

The spiritual part of an individual human being or god that survived after death.

Duat

The realm of the dead; residence of Osiris.

ba

The spiritual characteristics of an individual person that remained in the body after death. Ba could unite with the ka.

akh

The combination of the ka and ba living in the afterlife.

The religion of Ancient Egypt lasted for more than 3,000 years, and was polytheistic, meaning there were a multitude of deities, who were believed to reside within and control the forces of nature. Religious practices were deeply embedded in the lives of Egyptians, as they attempted to provide for their gods and win their favor. The complexity of the religion was evident as some deities existed in different manifestations and had multiple mythological roles. The pantheon included gods with major roles in the universe, minor deities (or "demons"), foreign gods, and sometimes humans, including deceased Pharaohs.

Formal religious practice centered on the pharaoh, or ruler, of Egypt, who was believed to be divine, and acted as intermediary between the people and the gods. His role was to sustain the gods so that they could maintain order in the universe, and the state spent its resources generously to build temples and provide for rituals. The pharaoh was associated with Horus (and later Amun) and seen as the son of Ra. Upon death, the pharaoh was fully deified, directly identified with Ra and associated with Osiris, the god of death and rebirth. However, individuals could appeal directly to the gods for personal purposes through prayer or requests for magic; as the pharaoh's power declined, this personal form of practice became stronger. Popular religious practice also involved ceremonies around birth and naming. The people also invoked "magic" (called heka) to make things happen using natural forces.

Gods of the Pantheon. This wall painting shows, from left to right, the gods Osiris, Anubis and Horus.

Cosmology

The Egyptian universe centered on Ma'at, which has several meanings in English, including truth, justice and order. It was fixed and eternal (without it the world would fall apart), and there were constant threats of disorder requiring society to work to maintain it. Inhabitants of the cosmos included the gods, the spirits of deceased humans, and living humans, the most important of which was the pharaoh. Humans should cooperate to achieve this, and gods should function in balance. Ma'at was renewed by periodic events, such as the annual Nile flood, which echoed the original creation. Most important of these was the daily journey of the sun god Ra.

Egyptians saw the earth as flat land (the god Geb), over which arched the sky (goddess Nut); they were separated by Shu, the god of air. Underneath the earth was a parallel underworld and undersky, and beyond the skies lay Nu, the chaos before creation. Duat was a mysterious area associated with death and rebirth, and each day Ra passed through Duat after traveling over the earth during the day.

Egyptian Cosmology. In this artwork, the air god Shu is assisted by other gods in holding up Nut, the sky, as Geb, the earth, lies beneath.

Myths

Egyptian myths are mainly known from hymns, ritual and magical texts, funerary texts, and the writings of Greeks and Romans. The creation myth saw the world as emerging as a dry space in the primordial ocean of chaos, marked by the first rising of Ra. Other forms of the myth saw the primordial god Atum transforming into the elements of the world, and the creative speech of the intellectual god Ptah.

The most important myth was of Osiris and Isis. The divine ruler Osiris was murdered by Set (god of chaos), then resurrected by his sister and wife Isis to conceive an heir, Horus. Osiris then became the ruler of the dead, while Horus eventually avenged his father and became king. This myth set the Pharaohs, and their succession, as orderliness against chaos.

The Afterlife

Egyptians were very concerned about the fate of their souls after death, and built tombs, created grave goods and gave offerings to preserve the bodies and spirits of the dead. They believed humans possessed ka, or life-force, which left the body at death. To endure after death, the ka must continue to receive offerings of food; it could consume the spiritual essence of it. Humans also possessed a ba, a set of spiritual characteristics unique to each person, which remained in the body after death. Funeral rites were meant to release the ba so it could move, rejoin with the ka, and live on as an akh. However, the ba returned to the body at night, so the body must be preserved.

Mummification involved elaborate embalming practices, and wrapping in cloth, along with various rites, including the Opening of the Mouth ceremony. Tombs were originally mastabas (rectangular brick structures), and then pyramids.

However, this originally did not apply to the common person: they passed into a dark, bleak realm that was the opposite of life. Nobles did receive tombs and grave gifts from the pharaoh. Eventually, by about 2181 BCE, Egyptians began to believe every person had a ba and could access the afterlife. By the New Kingdom, the soul had to face dangers in the Duat before having a final judgment, called the Weighing of the Heart, where the gods compared the actions of the deceased while alive to Ma'at, to see if they were worthy. If so, the ka and ba were united into an akh, which then either traveled to the lush underworld, or traveled with Ra on his daily journey, or even returned to the world of the living to carry out magic.

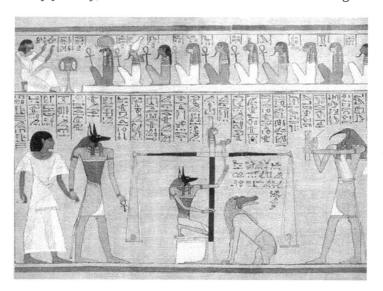

Funerary Text. In this section from the Book of the Dead for the scribe Hunefer, the Weighing of the Heart is shown.

Rise and Fall of Gods

Certain gods gained a primary status over time, and then fell as other gods overtook them. These included the sun god Ra, the creator god Amun, and the mother goddess Isis. There was even a period of time where Egypt was monotheistic, under Pharaoh Akhenaten, and his patron god Aten.

The Relationships of Deities

Just as the forces of nature had complex interrelationships, so did Egyptian deities. Minor deities might be linked, or deities might come together based on the meaning of numbers in Egyptian mythology (i.e., pairs represented duality). Deities might also be linked through syncretism, creating a composite deity.

Artistic Depictions of Gods

Artistic depictions of gods were not literal representations, since their true nature was considered mysterious. However, symbolic imagery was used to indicate this nature. An example was Anubis, a funerary god, who was shown as a jackal to counter its traditional meaning as a scavenger, and create protection for the mummy.

Temples

Temples were the state's method of sustaining the gods, as their physical images were housed and cared for; they were not a place for the average person to worship. They were both mortuary temples to serve deceased pharaohs and temples for patron gods. Starting as simple structures, they grew more elaborate, and were increasingly built from stone, with a common plan. Ritual duties were normally carried out by priests, or government officials serving in the role. In the New Kingdom, professional priesthood became common, and their wealth rivaled that of the pharaoh.

Rituals and Festivals

Aside from numerous temple rituals, including the morning offering ceremony and re-enactments of myths, there were coronation ceremonies and the sed festival, a renewal of the pharaoh's strength during his reign. The Opet Festival at Karnak involved a procession carrying the god's image to visit other significant sites.

Animal Worship

At many sites, Egyptians worshipped specific animals that they believed to be manifestations of deities. Examples include the Apis bull (of the god Ptah), and mummified cats and other animals.

Use of Oracles

Commoners and pharaohs asked questions of oracles, and answers could even be used during the New Kingdom to settle legal disputes. This might involve asking a question while a divine image was being carried, and interpreting movement, or drawing lots.

Sources

Attributions

CC licensed content, Specific attribution

Ancient Egyptian Art

- Examine the development of Egyptian Art under the Old Kingdom

Key Points

- Ancient Egyptian art includes painting, sculpture, architecture, and other forms of art, such as drawings on papyrus, created between 3000 BCE and 100 CE.
- Most of this art was highly stylized and symbolic. Much of the surviving forms come from tombs and monuments, and thus have a focus on life after death and preservation of knowledge.
- Symbolism meant order, shown through the pharaoh's regalia, or through the use of certain colors.
- In Egyptian art, the size of a figure indicates its relative importance.
- Paintings were often done on stone, and portrayed pleasant scenes of the afterlife in tombs.
- Ancient Egyptians created both monumental and smaller sculptures, using the technique of sunk relief.
- Ka statues, which were meant to provide a resting place for the ka part of the soul, were often made of wood and placed in tombs.
- Faience was sintered-quartz ceramic with surface vitrification, used to create relatively cheap small objects in many colors. Glass was originally a luxury item but became more common, and was used to make small jars, for perfume and other liquids, to be placed in tombs. Carvings of vases, amulets, and images of deities and animals were made of steatite. Pottery was sometimes covered with enamel, particularly in the color blue.
- Papyrus was used for writing and painting, and and was used to record every aspect of Egyptian life.

- Architects carefully planned buildings, aligning them with astronomically significant events, such as solstices and equinoxes. They used mainly sun-baked mud brick, limestone, sandstone, and granite.

- The Amarna period (1353-1336 BCE) represents an interruption in ancient Egyptian art style, subjects were represented more realistically, and scenes included portrayals of affection among the royal family.

Terms

scarabs

Ancient Egyptian gem cut in the form of a scarab beetle.

Faience

Glazed ceramic ware.

ushabti

Ancient Egyptian funerary figure.

Ka

The supposed spiritual part of an individual human being or god that survived after death, and could reside in a statue of the person.

sunk relief

Sculptural technique in which the outlines of modeled forms are incised in a plane surface beyond which the forms do not project.

regalia

The emblems or insignia of royalty.

papyrus

A material prepared in ancient Egypt from the stem of a water plant, used in sheets for writing or painting on.

Ancient Egyptian art includes painting, sculpture, architecture, and other forms of art, such as drawings on papyrus, created between 3000 BCE and 100 AD. Most of this art was highly stylized and symbolic. Many of the surviving forms come from tombs and monuments, and thus have a focus on life after death and preservation of knowledge.

Symbolism

Symbolism in ancient Egyptian art conveyed a sense of order and the influence of natural elements. The regalia of the pharaoh symbolized his or her power to rule and maintain the order of the universe. Blue and gold indicated divinity because they were rare and were associated with precious materials, while black expressed the fertility of the Nile River.

Hierarchical Scale

In Egyptian art, the size of a figure indicates its relative importance. This meant gods or the pharaoh were usually bigger than other figures, followed by figures of high officials or the tomb owner; the smallest figures were servants, entertainers, animals, trees and architectural details.

Painting

Before painting a stone surface, it was whitewashed and sometimes covered with mud plaster. Pigments were made of mineral and able to stand up to strong sunlight with minimal fade. The binding medium is unknown; the paint was applied to dried plaster in the "fresco a secco" style. A varnish or resin was then applied as a protective coating, which, along with the dry climate of Egypt, protected the painting very well. The purpose of tomb paintings was to create a pleasant afterlife for the dead person, with themes such as journeying through the afterworld, or deities providing protection. The side view of the person or animal was generally shown, and paintings were often done in red, blue, green, gold, black and yellow.

Wall Painting of Nefertari. In this wall painting of Nefertari, the side view is apparent.

Sculpture

Ancient Egyptians created both monumental and smaller sculptures, using the technique of sunk relief. In this technique, the image is made by cutting the relief sculpture into a flat surface, set within a sunken area shaped around the image. In strong sunlight, this technique is very visible, emphasizing the outlines and forms by shadow. Figures are shown with the torso facing front, the head in side view, and the legs parted, with males sometimes darker than females. Large statues of deities (other than the pharaoh) were not common, although deities were often shown in paintings and reliefs.

Colossal sculpture on the scale of the Great Sphinx of Giza was not repeated, but smaller sphinxes and animals were found in temple complexes. The most sacred cult image of a temple's god was supposedly held in the naos in small boats, carved out of precious metal, but none have survived.

Ka statues, which were meant to provide a resting place for the ka part of the soul, were present in tombs as of Dynasty IV (2680-2565 BCE). These were often made of wood, and were called reserve heads, which were plain, hairless and naturalistic. Early tombs had small models of slaves, animals, buildings, and objects to provide life for the deceased in the afterworld. Later, ushabti figures were present as funerary figures to act as servants for the deceased, should he or she be called upon to do manual labor in the afterlife.

Ka Statue. The ka statue was placed in the tomb to provide a physical place for the ka to manifest. This statue is found at the Egyptian Museum of Cairo.

Many small carved objects have been discovered, from toys to utensils, and alabaster was used for the more expensive objects. In creating any statuary, strict conventions, accompanied by a rating system, were followed. This resulted in a rather timeless quality, as few changes were instituted over thousands of years.

Faience, Pottery, and Glass

Faience was sintered-quartz ceramic with surface vitrification used to create relatively cheap, small objects in many colors, but most commonly blue-green. It was often used for jewelry, scarabs, and figurines. Glass was originally a luxury item, but became more common, and was to used to make small jars, of perfume and other liquids, to be placed in tombs. Carvings of vases, amulets, and images of deities and animals were made of steatite. Pottery was sometimes covered with enamel, particularly in the color blue. In tombs, pottery was used to represent organs of the body removed during embalming, or to create cones, about ten inches tall, engraved with legends of the deceased.

Papyrus

Papyrus is very delicate and was used for writing and painting; it has only survived for long periods when buried in tombs. Every aspect of Egyptian life is found recorded on papyrus, from literary to administrative documents.

Architecture

Architects carefully planned buildings, aligning them with astronomically significant events, such as solstices and equinoxes, and used mainly sun-baked mud brick, limestone, sandstone, and granite. Stone was reserved for tombs and temples, while other buildings, such as palaces and fortresses, were made of bricks. Houses were made of mud from the Nile River that hardened in the sun. Many of these houses were destroyed in flooding or dismantled; examples of preserved structures include the village Deir al-Madinah and the fortress at Buhen.

The Giza Necropolis, built in the Fourth Dynasty, includes the Pyramid of Khufu (also known as the Great Pyramid or the Pyramid of Cheops), the Pyramid of Khafre, and the Pyramid of Menkaure, along with smaller "queen" pyramids and the Great Sphinx.

The Pyramids of Giza. The Pyramid of Khufu (Great Pyramid) is the largest of the pyramids pictured here.

The Temple of Karnak was first built in the 16th century BCE. About 30 pharaohs contributed to the buildings, creating an extremely large and diverse complex. It includes the Precincts of Amon-Re, Montu and Mut, and the Temple of Amehotep IV (dismantled).

*The Temple of Karnak. Shown here is the hypostyle hall of the
Temple of Karnak.*

The Luxor Temple was constructed in the 14th century BCE by Amenhotep III in the ancient city of
Thebes, now Luxor, with a major expansion by Ramesses II in the 13th century BCE. It includes the
79-foot high First Pylon, friezes, statues, and columns.

The Amarna Period (1353-1336 BCE)

During this period, which represents an interruption in ancient Egyptian art style, subjects were represented
more realistically, and scenes included portrayals of affection among the royal family. There was a sense of
movement in the images, with overlapping figures and large crowds. The style reflects Akhenaten's move
to monotheism, but it disappeared after his death.

Sources

Attributions

CC licensed content, Specific attribution

- Boundless World History. **Authored by**: Boundless. **Located at**: https://courses.lumenlearning.com/boundless-worldhistory/.
  License: *CC BY-SA: Attribution-ShareAlike*

Ancient Egyptian Monuments

Key Points

- Ancient Egyptian architects carefully planned buildings, aligning them with astronomically significant events, such as solstices and equinoxes, and used mainly sun-baked mud brick, limestone, sandstone, and granite.

- Egyptian pyramids were highly reflective, referenced the sun, and were usually placed on the West side of the Nile River.

- About 135 pyramids have been discovered in Egypt, with the largest (in Egypt and the world) being the Great Pyramid of Giza.

- The Great Sphinx of Giza is a reclining sphinx (a mythical creature with a lion's body and a human head); its face is meant to represent the Pharaoh Khafra. It is the world's oldest and largest monolith.

- Egyptian temples were used for official, formal worship of the gods by the state, and to commemorate pharaohs. The temple was the house of a particular god, and Egyptians would perform rituals, give offerings, re-enact myths, and keep order in the universe (ma'at).

- The Temple of Karnak was first built in the 16th century BCE. About 30 pharaohs contributed to the buildings, creating an extremely large and diverse complex.

- The Luxor Temple was constructed in the 14th century BCE by Amenhotep III in the ancient city of Thebes, now Luxor. It later received a major expansion by Ramesses II in the 13th century BCE.

Terms

monolith

A large single upright block of stone, especially one shaped into, or serving as, a pillar or monument.

friezes

Broad, horizontal bands of sculpted or painted decoration.

pylon

In ancient Egypt, two tapering towers with a less elevated section between them, forming a gateway.

peristyle courts

In ancient Egypt, courts that open to the sky.

Hypostyle halls

In ancient Egypt, covered rooms with columns.

equinoxes

Either of the two times in the year when the sun crosses the celestial equator, and day and night are of equal length.

solstices

Either of the two times in the year (summer and winter) when the sun reaches its highest or lowest point in the sky at noon.

ma'at

The ancient Egyptian concept of truth, balance, order, harmony, law, morality and justice.

obelisks

Stone pillars, typically having a square or rectangular cross section and pyramidal top, used as monuments or landmarks.

Ancient Egyptian architects carefully planned buildings, aligning them with astronomically significant events, such as solstices and equinoxes. They used mainly sun-baked mud brick, limestone, sandstone, and granite. Stone was reserved for tombs and temples, while other buildings, such as palaces and fortresses, were made of bricks.

Pyramids

Egyptian pyramids referenced the rays of the sun, and appeared highly polished and reflective, with a capstone that was generally a hard stone like granite, sometimes plated with gold, silver or electrum. Most were placed west of the Nile, to allow the pharaoh's soul to join with the sun during its descent.

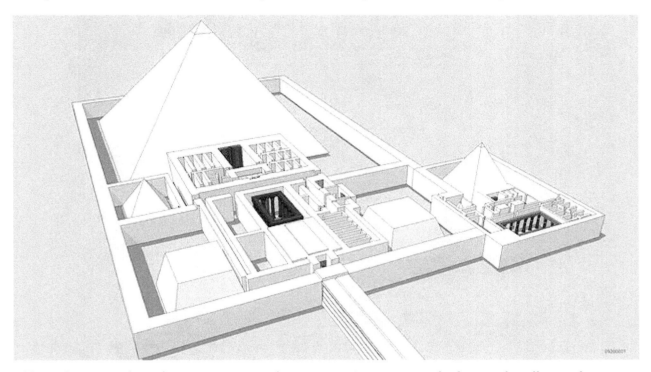

Old Kingdom Pyramid Temple Reconstruction. In this reconstruction, a causeway leads out to the valley temple.

About 135 pyramids have been discovered in Egypt, with the largest (in Egypt and the world) being the Great Pyramid of Giza. Its base is over 566,000 square feet in area, and was one of the Seven Wonders of the Ancient World. The Giza Necropolis, built in the Fourth Dynasty, includes the Pyramid of Khufu (also known as the Great Pyramid or the Pyramid of Cheops), the Pyramid of Khafre and the Pyramid of Menkaure, along with smaller "queens" pyramids and the Great Sphinx.

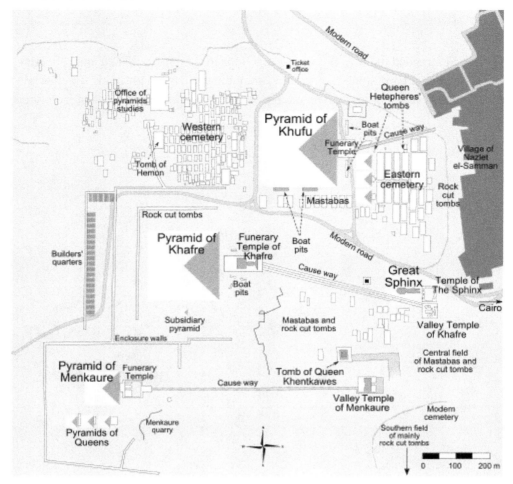

Map of Giza Pyramid Complex. A map showing the layout of the Giza Pyramid area, including the Pyramids of Khufu, Khafre, Menkaure, and the Great Sphinx.

The Great Sphinx of Giza

This limestone statue of a reclining sphinx (a mythical creature with a lion's body and a human head) is located on the Giza Plateau to the west of the Nile. It is believed the face is meant to represent the Pharaoh Khafra. It is the largest and oldest monolith statue in the world, at 241 feet long, 63 feet wide, and 66.34 feet tall. It is believed to have been built during the reign of Pharaoh Khafra (2558-2532 BCE). It was probably a focus of solar worship, as the lion is a symbol associated with the sun.

The Great Sphinx of Giza. Here the Great Sphinx is shown against the Pyramid of Kahfre.

Temples

Egyptian temples were used for official, formal worship of the gods by the state, and to commemorate pharaohs. The temple was the house dedicated to a particular god, and Egyptians would perform rituals there, give offerings, re-enact myths and keep order in the universe (ma'at). Pharaohs were in charge of caring for the gods, and they dedicated massive resources to this task. Priests assisted in this effort. The average citizen was not allowed into the inner sanctum of the temple, but might still go there to pray, give offerings, or ask questions of the gods.

The inner sanctuary had a cult image of the temple's god, as well as a series of surrounding rooms that became large and elaborate over time, evolving into massive stone edifices during the New Kingdom. Temples also often owned surrounding land and employed thousands of people to support its activities, creating a powerful institution. The designs emphasized order, symmetry and monumentality. Hypostyle halls (covered rooms filled with columns) led to peristyle courts (open courts), where the public could meet with priests. At the front of each court was a pylon (broad, flat towers) that held flagpoles. Outside the temple building was the temple enclosure, with a brick wall to symbolically protect from outside disorder; often a sacred lake would be found here. Decoration included reliefs (bas relief and sunken relief) of images and hieroglyphic text and sculpture, including obelisks, figures of gods (sometimes in sphinx form), and votive figures. Egyptian religions faced persecution by Christians, and the last temple was closed in 550 AD.

The Temple of Karnak was first built in the 16th century BCE. About 30 pharaohs contributed to the buildings, creating an extremely large and diverse complex. It includes the Precincts of Amon-Re, Montu and Mut, and the Temple of Amehotep IV (dismantled).

Temple of KarnakThis view of the Temple of Karnak shows they hypostyle hall, with massive columns.

The Luxor Temple was constructed in the 14th century BCE by Amenhotep III in the ancient city of Thebes, now Luxor, with a major expansion by Ramesses II in the 13th century BCE. It includes the 79-foot high First Pylon, friezes, statues, and columns.

Luxor Temple. Shown here is the entrance pylon of Luxor Temple, one of the major New Kingdom temples.

Sources

Attributions

CC licensed content, Specific attribution

- Boundless World History. **Authored by**: Boundless. **Located at**: https://courses.lumenlearning.com/boundless-worldhistory/. **License**: *CC BY-SA: Attribution-ShareAlike*

Ancient Egyptian Trade

Key Points

- Trade was occurring in the 5th century BCE onwards, especially with Canaan, Lebanon, Nubia and Punt.
- Just before the First Dynasty, Egypt had a colony in southern Canaan that produced Egyptian pottery for export to Egypt.
- In the Second Dynasty, Byblos provided quality timber that could not be found in Egypt.
- By the Fifth Dynasty, trade with Punt gave Egyptians gold, aromatic resins, ebony, ivory, and wild animals.
- A well-traveled land route from the Nile to the Red Sea crossed through the Wadi Hammamat. Another route, the Darb el-Arbain, was used from the time of the Old Kingdom of Egypt.
- Egyptians built ships as early as 3000 BCE by lashing planks of wood together and stuffing the gaps with reeds. They used them to import goods from Lebanon and Punt.

Terms

papyrus

A material prepared in ancient Egypt from the stem of a water plant, used in sheets for writing, painting, or making rope, sandals, and boats.

obsidian

A hard, dark, glasslike volcanic rock.

electrum

A natural or artifical alloy of gold, with at least 20% silver, used for jewelry.

myrrh

A fragrant gum resin obtained from certain trees, often used in perfumery, medicine and incense.

malachite

A bright green mineral consisting of copper hydroxyl carbonate.

Early examples of ancient Egyptian trade included contact with Syria in the 5th century BCE, and importation of pottery and construction ideas from Canaan in the 4th century BCE. By this time, shipping was common, and the donkey, camel, and horse were domesticated and used for transportation. Lebanese cedar has been found in the tombs of Nekhen, dated to the Naqada I and II periods. Egyptians during this period also imported obsidian from Ethiopia, gold and incense from Nubia in the south, oil jugs from Palestine, and other goods from the oases of the western desert and the cultures of the eastern Mediterranean. Egyptian artifacts from this era have been found in Canaan and parts of the former Mesopotamia. In the latter half of the 4th century BCE, the gemstone lapis lazuli was being imported from Badakhshan (modern-day Afghanistan).

Just before the First Dynasty, Egypt had a colony in southern Canaan that produced Egyptian pottery for export to Egypt. In the Second Dynasty, Byblos provided quality timber that could not be found in Egypt. By the Fifth Dynasty, trade with Punt gave Egyptians gold, aromatic resins, ebony, ivory, and wild animals. Egypt also traded with Anatolia for tin and copper in order to make bronze. Mediterranean trading partners provided olive oil and other fine goods.

Egypt commonly exported grain, gold, linen, papyrus, and finished goods, such as glass and stone objects.

Depiction of Queen Hatshepsut's Expedition to Punt. This painting shows Queen Hatshepsut's expedition to Punt.

Land Trade Routes

A well-traveled land route from the Nile to the Red Sea crossed through the Wadi Hammamat, and was known from predynastic times. This route allowed travelers to move from Thebes to the Red Sea port of Elim, and led to the rise of ancient cities.

Another route, the Darb el-Arbain, was used from the time of the Old Kingdom of Egypt to trade gold, ivory, spices, wheat, animals, and plants. This route passed through Kharga in the south and Asyut in the north, and was a major route between Nubia and Egypt.

Maritime Trade Routes

Egyptians built ships as early as 3000 BCE by lashing planks of wood together and stuffing the gaps with reeds.

Egyptian Sailing Ship. This painting depicts an Egyptian ship from c. 1420 BCE.

Pharaoh Sahure, of the Fifth Dynasty, is known to have sent ships to Lebanon to import cedar, and to the Land of Punt for myrrh, malachite, and electrum. Queen Hatshepsut sent ships for myrrh in Punt, and extended Egyptian trade into modern-day Somalia and the Mediterranean.

Queen Hatshepsut. Queen Hatshepsut expanded trade into modern-day Somalia and the Mediterranean.

An ancient form of the Suez Canal is believed to have been started by Pharaoh Senusret II or III of the Twelfth Dynasty, in order to connect the Nile River with the Red Sea.

Sources

Attributions

CC licensed content, Specific attribution

- Boundless World History. **Authored by**: Boundless. **Located at**: https://courses.lumenlearning.com/boundless-worldhistory/. **License**: *CC BY-SA: Attribution-ShareAlike*

Ancient Egyptian Culture

Learning Objective

- Examine the artistic and social developments of the Middle Kingdom

Key Points

- The Middle Kingdom (2134-1690 BCE) was a time of prosperity and stability, as well as a resurgence of art, literature, and architecture.Block statue was a new type of sculpture invented in the Middle Kingdom, and was often used as a funerary monument.
- Literature had new uses during the Middle Kingdom, and many classics were written during the period.

Terms

funerary monuments

Sculpture meant to decorate a tomb within a pyramid.

The Middle Kingdom (2134-1690 BCE) was a time of prosperity and stability, as well as a resurgence of art, literature, and architecture. Two major innovations of the time were the block statue and new forms of literature.

The Block Statue

The block statue came into use during this period. This type of sculpture depicts a squatting man with knees drawn close to the chest and arms folded on top of the knees. The body may be adorned with a cloak, which makes the body appear to be a block shape. The feet may be covered by the cloak, or left uncovered. The head was often carved in great detail, and reflected Egyptian beauty ideals, including large ears and small breasts. The block statue became more popular over the years, with its high point in the Late Period, and was often used as funerary monuments of important, non-royal individuals. They may have been intended as guardians, and were often fully inscribed.

Example of Block Statue. An example of a block statue from the Late Period, c. 650-633 BCE.

Literature

In the Middle Kingdom period, due to growth of middle class and scribes, literature began to be written to entertain and provide intellectual stimulation. Previously, literature served the purposes of maintaining divine cults, preserving souls in the afterlife, and documenting practical activities. However, some Middle Kingdom literature may have been transcriptions of the oral literature and poetry of the Old Kingdom. Future generations of Egyptians often considered Middle Kingdom literature to be "classic," with the ultimate example being the Story of Sinuhe.

Sources

Attributions

CC licensed content, Specific attribution

4. Ancient Greece and the Hellenistic World

Archaic Greece

Key Points

- The Archaic period saw significant urbanization, and the development of the concept of the *polis*, as it was used in classical Greece.

- Archaic Greece, from the mid-seventh century onward, has been referred to as an "age of tyrants."

- The Homeric Question concerns the doubts and consequent debate over the historicity of the *Iliad* and the *Odyssey,* as well as the identity of their author, Homer.

Terms

synoecism

The amalgamation of several small settlements into a single urban center.

polis

The literal translation of this word from Greek is "city." It typically refers to the Greek city-states of the Archaic and Classical periods.

Archaic Greece

The Archaic period of Greek history lasted from the 8th century BCE to the second Persian invasion of Greece in 480 BCE. The period began with a massive increase in the Greek population and a structural revolution that established the Greek city-states, or *polis*. The Archaic period saw developments in Greek politics, economics, international relations, warfare, and culture. It also laid the groundwork for the classical period, both politically and culturally. During this time, the Greek alphabet developed, and the earliest surviving Greek literature was composed. Monumental sculpture and red-figure pottery also developed in Greece, and in Athens, the earliest institutions of democracy were implemented.

Some written accounts of life exist from this time period in the form of poetry, law codes, inscriptions on votive offerings, and epigrams inscribed on tombs. However, thorough written histories, such as those that exist from the Greek classical period, are lacking. Historians do have access to rich archaeological evidence from this period, however, that informs our understanding of Greek life during the Archaic period.

View from Philopappos, Acropolis Hill. The Acropolis of Athens, a noted polis of classical Greece.

Development of the *Polis*

The Archaic period saw significant urbanization and the development of the concept of the *polis* as it was used in classical Greece. However, the polis did not become the dominant form of sociopolitical organization throughout Greece during the Archaic period, and in the north and west of the country it did not become dominant until later in the classical period. The process of urbanization known as "synoecism" (or the amalgamation of several small settlements into a single urban center), took place in much of Greece during the 8th century. Both Athens and Argos, for example, coalesced into single settlements near the end of that century. In some settlements, physical unification was marked by the construction of defensive city walls. The increase in population, and evolution of the *polis* as a sociopolitical structure, necessitated a new form of political organization.

Age of Tyranny

Archaic Greece from the mid-7th century onward has been referred to as an "age of tyrants." Various explanations have been provided for the rise of tyranny in the 7th century. The most popular explanation dates back to Aristotle, who argued that tyrants were set up by the people in response to the nobility becoming less tolerable. Because there is no evidence from this time period demonstrating this to be the case, historians have looked for alternate explanations. Some argue that tyrannies were set up by individuals who controlled privates armies, and that early tyrants did not need the support of the people at all. Others suggest that tyrannies were established as a consequence of in-fighting between rival oligarchs, rather than as a result of fighting between oligarchs and the people.

Other historians question the existence of a 7th century "age of tyrants" altogether. In the Archaic period, the Greek word *tyrannos* did not have the negative connotations it had later in the classical period. Often the word could be used as synonymous with "king." As a result, many historians argue that Greek tyrants were not considered illegitimate rulers, and cannot be distinguished from any other rulers during the same period.

The Homeric Question

The Homeric Question concerns the doubts and consequent debate over the identity of Homer, the author of the *Iliad* and the *Odyssey*; it also questions the historicity of the two books. Many scholars agree that regardless of who authored Homer's works, it is highly likely that the poems attributed to him were part of a generations-old oral tradition, with many scholars believing the works to be transcribed some time in the 6th century BCE or earlier. Many estimates place the events of Homer's Trojan War as preceding the Greek Dark Ages, of approximately 1250 to 750 BCE. The *Iliad*, however, has been placed immediately following the Greek Dark Age period.

Sources

Attributions

CC licensed content, Specific attribution

The Rise of Classical Greece

Learning Objective

- Understand the significance of Cleisthenes' reforms to the rise of Classical Greece

Key Points

- The classical period followed the Archaic period, and was succeeded by the Hellenistic period.
- Much of modern Western politics, artistic and scientific thought, literature, and philosophy derives from this period of Greek history.
- Through Cleisthenes' reforms, the people endowed their city with isonomic institutions, and established ostracism.
- A corpus of reforms made to Athenian political administration during this time led to the emergence of a wider democracy in the 460s and 450s BCE.

Terms

Classical Greece

A 200 year period in Greek culture, lasting from the 5th through 4th centuries BCE.

Cleisthenes

A noble Athenian of the Alcmaeonid family, credited with reforming the constitution of ancient Athens, and setting it on a democratic footing in 508/7 BCE.

isonomic

A word used by ancient Greek writers to refer to various kinds of popular government with the general goal of "equal rights."

ostracism

A procedure under Athenian democracy by which any citizen could be expelled from the city-state of Athens for ten years.

trittyes

Population divisions in ancient Attica, established by the reforms of Cleisthenes in 508 BCE.

Classical Greece was a 200-year period in Greek culture lasting from the 5th to the 4th centuries BCE. This period saw the annexation of much of modern-day Greece by the Persian Empire, as well as its subsequent independence. Classical Greece also had a powerful influence on the Roman Empire, and greatly influenced the foundations of Western civilization. Much of modern Western politics, artistic and scientific thought, literature, and philosophy derives from this period of Greek history. The classical period was preceded by the Archaic period, and was succeeded by the Hellenistic period.

Rise of the City-States

The term "city-state," which is English in origin, does not fully translate the Greek term for these same entities, *polis*. *Poleis* were different from ancient city-states in that they were ruled by bodies of the citizens who lived there. Many were initially established, as in Sparta, via a network of villages, with a governance center being established in a central urban center. As notions of citizenship rose to prominence among landowners, *polis* came to embody an entire body of citizens and the term could be used to describe the populace of a place, rather than the physical location itself. Basic elements of a *polis* often included the following:

- Self-governance, autonomy, and independence
- A social hub and financial marketplace, called an *agora*
- Urban planning and architecture
- Temples, altars, and other sacred precincts, many of which would be dedicated to the patron deity of the city
- Public spaces, such as gymnasia and theaters
- Defensive walls to protect against invasion
- Coinage minted by the city

Polis were established and expanded by synoecism, or the absorption of nearby villages and tribes. Most cities were composed of several tribes that were in turn composed of groups sharing common ancestry, and their extended families. Territory was a less helpful means of thinking about the shape of a *polis* than regions of shared religious and political associations.

Dwellers of a *polis* were typically divided into four separate social classes, with an individual's status usually being determined at birth. Free adult men born of legitimate citizens were considered citizens with full legal and political rights, including the right to vote, be elected into office, and bear arms, with the obligation to serve in the army during wartime. The female relatives and underage children of full citizens were also considered citizens, but they had no formal political rights. They were typically represented within society by their adult male relatives. Citizens of other *poleis* who chose to reside in a different *polis* possessed full rights in their place of origin, but had no political rights in their new place of residence. Otherwise, such citizens had full personal and property rights subject to taxation. Finally, slaves were considered possessions of their owner and had no rights or privileges other than those granted by their owner.

Greco-Persian Wars

The Greco-Persian Wars, also referred to as the Persian Wars, were a series of conflicts that began in 499 BCE and lasted until 449 BCE, between the Achaemenid Empire of Persia (modern-day Iran) and Greek city-states. The conflict began when Cyrus the Great conquered the Greek-inhabited region of Ionia in 547 BCE. After struggling to control the cities of Ionia, the Persians appointed tyrants to rule each of them. When the tyrant of Miletus embarked on an unsuccessful expedition to conquer the island of Naxos with Persian support, however, a rebellion was incited throughout Hellenic Asia Minor against the Persians. This rebellion, known as the Ionian Revolt, lasted until 493 BCE, and drew increasingly more regions throughout Asia Minor into the conflict.

Eventually the Ionians suffered a decisive defeat and the rebellion collapsed. Subsequently, Darius the Great, the Persian ruler, sought to secure his empire from further revolts and interference from the mainland Greeks, and embarked upon a scheme to conquer all of Greece. The first Persian invasion of Greece began in 492 BCE, and was successful in conquering Macedon and re-subjugating Thrace. In 490 BCE, a second force was sent to Greece across the Aegean Sea, successfully subjugating the Cyclades. However, the Persians were defeated by the Athenians at the Battle of Marathon, putting a halt to Darius's plan until his death in 486 BCE.

In 480 BCE, Darius's son, Xerxes, personally led the second Persian invasion of Greece with one of the largest ancient armies ever assembled. His invasion was successful and Athens was burned. However, the following year, the Allied Greek states went on the offensive, defeating the Persian army at the Battle of Plataea and ending the invasion of Greece. The Greeks continued to expel Persian forces from Greece and surrounding areas, but the actions of Spartan General Pausanias at the siege of Byzantium alienated many of the Greek states from the Spartans, causing the anti-Persian alliance to be reconstituted around Athenian leadership in what became known as the Delian League. The Delian League continued the campaign against the Persians for the next three decades. Some historical sources suggest the end of hostilities between the Greeks and the Persians was marked by a peace treaty between Athens and Persia, called the Peace of Callias.

Athenian Democracy

Athenian democracy developed around the 5th century BCE, in the Greek city-state of Athens. It is the first known democracy in the world. Other Greek cities set up democracies, most following the Athenian model, but none are as well documented as Athens. Athenian democracy was a system of direct democracy, in which participating citizens voted directly on legislation and executive bills. Participation was open to adult, land-owning men, which historians estimate numbered between 30,000 and 50,000 individuals, out of a total population of approximately 250,000 to 300,000.

Before the first attempt at democratic government, Athens was ruled by a series of *archons*, or chief magistrates, and the Areopagus, which was made up of ex-*archons*. *Archons* were typically aristocrats who ruled to their own advantage. Additionally, a series of laws codified by Draco in 621 BCE reinforced the power of the aristocracy over all other citizens. A mediator called Solon reshaped the city-state by restructuring the way citizenship was defined in order to absorb the traditional aristocracy within it, and established the right of every Athenian to participate in meetings of governing assemblies. The Areopagus, however, retained ultimate lawmaking authorities.

Cleisthenes

In 510 BCE, Spartan troops helped the Athenians overthrow their king, the tyrant Hippias, son of Peisistratos. Cleomenes I, king of Sparta, put in place a pro-Spartan oligarchy headed by Isagoras. But his rival, Cleisthenes, with the support of the middle class and aided by democrats, managed to take over. Cleomenes intervened in 508 and 506 BCE, but could not stop Cleisthenes, who was then supported by the Athenians. Through his reforms, the people endowed their city with institutions furnished with equal rights (i.e., isonomic institutions), and established ostracism, a procedure by which any citizen could be expelled from the city-state of Athens for ten years.

Bust of Cleisthenes. Modern bust of Cleisthenes, known as "the father of Athenian democracy," on view at the Ohio Statehouse, Columbus, Ohio. Cleisthenes, the father of Greek democracy, reformed traditional Athenian government controlled by ruling tribes into the first government "of the people" (a demos, or democracy).

The isonomic and isegoric democracy was first organized into about 130 demes— political subdivisions created throughout Attica. Ten thousand citizens exercised their power via an assembly (the *ekklesia*, in Greek), of which they all were a part, that was headed by a council of 500 citizens chosen at random. The city's administrative geography was reworked, the goal being to have mixed political groups—not federated by local interests linked to the sea, the city, or farming—whose decisions (declaration of war, etc.) would depend on their geographical situations. The territory of the city was subsequently divided into 30 trittyes. It was this corpus of reforms that would allow the emergence of a wider democracy in the 460s and 450s BCE.

Sources

Attributions

CC licensed content, Specific attribution

- Boundless World History. **Authored by**: Boundless. **Located at**: https://courses.lumenlearning.com/boundless-worldhistory/. **License**: *CC BY-SA: Attribution-ShareAlike*

Sparta

Key Points

- Sparta was a prominent city-state in ancient Greece, situated on the banks of the Eurotas River in Laconia in southeastern Peloponnese.

- Given its military preeminence, Sparta was recognized as the overall leader of the combined Greek forces during the Greco-Persian Wars, and defeated Athens during the Peloponnesian War.

- Sparta's defeat by Thebes in the Battle of Leuctra in 371 BCE ended Sparta's prominent role in Greece, but it maintained its political independence until the Roman conquest of Greece in 146 BCE.

- Sparta functioned under an oligarchy of two hereditary kings.

- Unique in ancient Greece for its social system and constitution, Spartan society focused heavily on military training and excellence.

- Spartan women enjoyed status, power, and respect that was unequaled in the rest of the classical world.

Terms

Sparta

A prominent city-state in ancient Greece situated on the banks of the Eurotas River in Laconia. The dominant military power in ancient Greece.

agoge

The rigorous education and training regimen mandated for all male Spartan citizens, except for the firstborn sons of the ruling houses Eurypontid and Agiad.

Sparta was a prominent city-state in ancient Greece situated on the banks of the Eurotas River in Laconia in southeastern Peloponnese. It emerged as a political entity around the 10th century BCE, when the invading Dorians subjugated the local, non-Dorian population. Around 650 BCE, it rose to become the dominant military power in ancient Greece. Given its military preeminence, Sparta was recognized as the overall leader of the combined Greek forces during the Greco-Persian Wars. Between 431 and 404 BCE, Sparta was the principal enemy of Athens during the Peloponnesian War, from which it emerged victorious, though at great cost. Sparta's defeat by Thebes in the Battle of Leuctra in 371 BCE ended Sparta's prominent role in Greece. However, it maintained its political independence until the Roman conquest of Greece in 146 BCE.

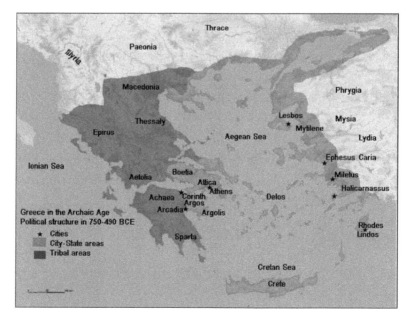

Political geography of ancient Greece. The map shows the political structure of Greece in the Archaic Age.

The Rise of Classical Sparta

The Spartans were already considered a land-fighting force to be reckoned with when, in 480 BCE, a small force of Spartans, Thespians, and Thebans made a legendary final stand at the Battle of Thermopylae against the massive Persian army during the Greco-Persian Wars. The Greek forces suffered very high casualties before finally being encircled and defeated. One year later, Sparta led a Greek alliance against the Persians at the Battle of Plataea where their superior weaponry, strategy, and bronze armor proved a huge asset in achieving a resounding victory. This decisive victory put an end to the Greco-Persian War, as well as Persian ambitions of spreading into Europe. Despite being fought as part of a alliance, the victory was credited to Sparta, which had been the de facto leader of the entire Greek expedition.

In the later classical period, Sparta fought amongst Athens, Thebes, and Persia for supremacy within the region. As a result of the Peloponnesian War, Sparta developed formidable naval power, enabling it to subdue many key Greek states and even overpower the elite Athenian navy. A period of Spartan Hegemony was inaugurated at the end of the 5th century BCE, when Sparta defeated the Athenian Empire and invaded Persian provinces in Anatolia.

Spartan Culture and Government

Sparta functioned under an oligarchy. The state was ruled by two hereditary kings of the Agiad and Eurypontid families, both supposedly descendants of Heracles, and equal in authority so that one could not act against the power and political enactments of his colleague. Unique in ancient Greece for its social system and constitution, Spartan society was completely focused on military training and excellence. Its inhabitants were classified as Spartiates (Spartan citizens who enjoyed full rights), Mothakes (non-Spartan, free men raised as Spartans), Perioikoi (freed men), and Helots (state-owned serfs, part of the enslaved, non-Spartan, local population).

Male Spartans began military training at age seven. The training was designed to encourage discipline and physical toughness, as well as emphasize the importance of the Spartan state. Boys lived in communal messes and, according to Xenophon, whose sons attended the *agoge*, the boys were fed "just the right amount for them never to become sluggish through being too full, while also giving them a taste of what it is not to have enough." Besides physical and weapons training, boys studied reading, writing, music, and dancing. Special punishments were imposed if boys failed to answer questions sufficiently laconically (i.e., briefly and wittily).

Spartan Hoplite. Marble statue of a helmed hoplite (5th century BCE), Archaeological Museum of Sparta, Greece.

At age 20, the Spartan citizen began his membership in one of the *syssitia* (dining messes or clubs), which were composed of about 15 members each, and were compulsory. Here each group learned how to bond and rely on one another. The Spartans were not eligible for election to public office until the age of 30. Only native Spartans were considered full citizens, and were obliged to undergo military training as prescribed by law, as well as participate in, and contribute financially to, one of the *syssitia*.

Spartan Women

Female Spartan citizens enjoyed status, power, and respect that was unequaled in the rest of the classical world. The higher status of females in Spartan society started at birth. Unlike in Athens, Spartan girls were fed the same food as their brothers. Nor were they confined to their father's house or prevented from exercising or getting fresh air. Spartan women even competed in sports. Most important, rather than being married at the age of 12 or 13, Spartan law forbade the marriage of a girl until she was in her late teens or early 20s. The reasons for delaying marriage were to ensure the birth of healthy children, but the effect was to spare Spartan women the hazards and lasting health damage associated with pregnancy among adolescents.

Spartan women, better fed from childhood and fit from exercise, stood a far better chance of reaching old age than their sisters in other Greek cities, where the median life expectancy was 34.6 years, or roughly ten years below that of men. Unlike Athenian women, who wore heavy, concealing clothes and were rarely seen outside the house, Spartan women wore dresses (*peplos*) slit up the side to allow freer movement, and moved freely about the city, either walking or driving chariots.

Sources

Attributions

CC licensed content, Specific attribution

- Boundless World History. **Authored by**: Boundless. **Located at**: https://courses.lumenlearning.com/boundless-worldhistory/. **License**: *CC BY-SA: Attribution-ShareAlike*

Culture in Classical Sparta

Learning Objective
• Understand the key characteristics of Sparta's society

Key Points
• Sparta was an oligarchic city-state, ruled by two hereditary kings equal in authority. • Spartan society was largely structured around the military, and around military training. • Inhabitants were classified as Spartiates (Spartan citizens, who enjoyed full rights), Mothakes (non-Spartan, free men raised as Spartans), Perioikoi (free, but non-citizen inhabitants), and Helots (state-owned serfs, part of the enslaved non-Spartan, local population). • Spartiates began military training at the age of seven. • At the age of 20, Spartiates were initiated into full citizenship and joined a *syssitia*. • Helots were granted many privileges, in comparison to enslaved populations in other Greek city-states. • The Helot population outnumbered the Spartiate population, and grew over time, causing societal tensions. • Female Spartans enjoyed status, power, and respect that was unequaled in the rest of the classical world.

Terms

ephors

Ephors were ancient Spartan officials who shared power with the hereditary kings. Five individuals were elected annually to swear on behalf of the city, whereas kings served for a lifetime and swore only on their own behalf.

gerousia

The gerousia were a council of Spartan elders comprised of men over the age of 60, who were elected for life, and usually were members of one of the two kings' households.

Delphi

A famous ancient sanctuary that served as the seat of an oracle, who consulted on important decisions throughout the ancient classical world.

The Spartan Political System

Sparta functioned under an oligarchy. The state was ruled by two hereditary kings of the Agiad and Eurypontid families, both supposedly descendants of Heracles, and equal in authority so that one could not act against the power and political enactments of his colleague. The duties of the kings were religious, judicial, and military in nature. They were the chief priests of the state, and maintained contact with Delphi, the sanctuary that exercised great authority in Spartan politics.

By 450 BCE, the kings' judicial authority was restricted to cases dealing with heiresses, adoptions, and public roads. Over time, royal prerogatives were curtailed further until, aside from their service as military generals, the kings became mere figureheads. For example, from the time of the Greco-Persian Wars, the kings lost the right to declare war and were shadowed in the field by two officials, known as *ephors*. The *ephors* also supplanted the kings' leadership in the realm of foreign policy. Civil and criminal cases were also decided by *ephors*, as well as a council of 28 elders over the age of 60, called the *gerousia*. The *gerousia* were elected for life, and usually were members of one of the two kings' households. The *gerousia* discussed high state policy decisions, then proposed action alternatives to the *damos*—a collective body of Spartan citizenry, who would then select one of the options by voting.

Spartan Citizenship

Unique in ancient Greece for its social system, Spartan society was completely focused on military training and excellence. Its inhabitants were classified as Spartiates (Spartan citizens, who enjoyed full rights), Mothakes (non-Spartan, free men raised as Spartans), Perioikoi (free, but non-citizen inhabitants), and Helots (state-owned serfs, part of the enslaved, non-Spartan, local population).

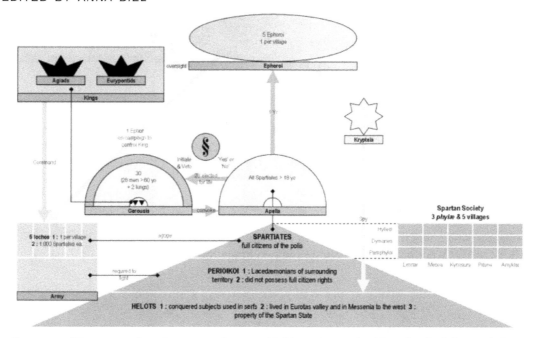

Structure of Spartan society. Spartan society was highly regimented, with a clearly delineated class system.

Male Spartans began military training at age seven. The training was designed to encourage discipline and physical toughness, as well as emphasize the importance of the Spartan state. Typically only men who were to become Spartiates underwent military training, although two exceptions existed to this rule. *Trophimoi*, or "foster sons," from other Greek city-states were allowed to attend training as foreign students. For example, the Athenian general Xenophon sent his two sons to Sparta as *trophimoi*. Additionally, sons of a Helot could enroll as a *syntrophos* if a Spartiate formally adopted him and paid his way. If a *syntrophos* did exceptionally well in training, he could be sponsored to become a Spartiate. Likewise, if a Spartan could not afford to pay the expenses associated with military training, they potentially could lose their right to citizenship.

Boys who underwent training lived in communal messes and, according to Xenophon, whose sons attended the *agoge*, the boys were fed "just the right amount for them never to become sluggish through being too full, while also giving them a taste of what it is not to have enough." Besides physical and weapons training, boys studied reading, writing, music, and dancing. Special punishments were imposed if boys failed to answer questions sufficiently laconically (i.e., briefly and wittily).

At age 20, the Spartan citizen began his membership in one of the *syssitia* (dining messes or clubs), which were composed of about 15 members each, and were compulsory. Here each group learned how to bond and rely on one another. The Spartans were not eligible for election to public office until the age of 30. Only native Spartans were considered full citizens, and were obliged to undergo military training as prescribed by law, as well as participate in, and contribute financially to, one of the *syssitia*.

Helots

Spartiates were actually a minority within Sparta, and Helots made up the largest class of inhabitants of the city-state. Helots were originally free Greeks that the Spartans had defeated in battle, and subsequently enslaved. In contrast to populations conquered by other Greek cities, the male Helot population was not exterminated, and women and children were not treated as chattel. Instead, Helots were given a subordinate position within Spartan society more comparable to the serfs of medieval Europe. Although Helots did not have voting rights, they otherwise enjoyed a relatively privileged position, in comparison to slave populations in other Greek city-states.

The Spartan poet, Tyrtaios, gives account that Helots were permitted to marry and retain half the fruits of their labor. They were also allowed religious freedoms and could own a limited amount of personal property. Up to 6,000 Helots even accumulated enough wealth to buy their own freedom in 227 BCE.

Since Spartiates were full-time soldiers, manual labor fell to the Helot population who worked as unskilled serfs, tilling the Spartan land or accompanying the Spartan army as non-combatants. Helot women were often used as wet nurses.

Relations between Helots and their Spartan masters were often strained, and there is evidence that at least one Helot revolt occurred circa 465-460 BCE. Many historians argue that because the Helots were permitted such privileges as the maintenance of family and kinship groups and ownership of property, they were better able to retain their identity as a conquered people and thus were more effective at organizing rebellions. Over time, the Spartiate population continued to decline and the Helot population grew, and the imbalance in power exasperated tensions that already existed.

Spartan Women

Female Spartans enjoyed status, power, and respect that was unequaled in the rest of the classical world. The higher status of females in Spartan society started at birth. Unlike in Athens, Spartan girls were fed the same food as their brothers. Nor were they confined to their father's house or prevented from exercising or getting fresh air. Spartan women even competed in sports. Most important, rather than being married at the age of 12 or 13, Spartan law forbade the marriage of a girl until she was in her late teens or early 20s. The reasons for delaying marriage were to ensure the birth of healthy children, but the effect was to spare Spartan women the hazards and lasting health damage associated with pregnancy among adolescents.

Spartan women, better fed from childhood and fit from exercise, stood a far better chance of reaching old age than their sisters in other Greek cities where the median life expectancy was 34.6 years, or roughly ten years below that of men. Unlike Athenian women who wore heavy, concealing clothes and were rarely seen outside the house, Spartan women wore dresses (*peplos*) slit up the side to allow freer movement, and moved freely about the city, either walking or driving chariots.

Sources

Attributions

CC licensed content, Specific attribution

- Boundless World History. **Authored by**: Boundless. **Located at**: https://courses.lumenlearning.com/boundless-worldhistory/. **License**: *CC BY-SA: Attribution-ShareAlike*

The Persian Wars

Learning Objective

- Explain the consequences of the Persian Wars.

Key Points

- The Persian Wars began in 499 BCE, when Greeks in the Persian-controlled territory rose in the Ionian Revolt.
- Athens, and other Greek cities, sent aid, but were quickly forced to back down after defeat in 494 BCE.
- Subsequently, the Persians suffered many defeats at the hands of the Greeks, led by the Athenians.
- Silver mining contributed to the funding of a massive Greek army that was able to rebuke Persian assaults and eventually defeat the Persians entirely.
- The end of the Persian Wars led to the rise of Athens as the leader of the Delian League.

Terms

Persian Wars

A series of conflicts, from 499-449 BCE, between the Achaemenid Empire of Persia and city-states of the Hellenic world.

> ### hoplites
>
> A citizen-soldier of one of the ancient Greek city-states, armed primarily with spears and a shield.

The Persian Wars (499-449 BCE) were fought between the Achaemenid Empire and the Hellenic world during the Greek classical period. The conflict saw the rise of Athens, and led to its Golden Age.

Origins of the Conflict

Greeks of the classical period believed, and historians generally agree, that in the aftermath of the fall of Mycenaean civilization, many Greek tribes emigrated and settled in Asia Minor. These settlers were from three tribal groups: the Aeolians, Dorians, and Ionians. The Ionians settled along the coasts of Lydia and Caria, and founded 12 towns that remained politically separate from one another, although they did recognize a shared cultural heritage. This formed the basis for an exclusive Ionian "cultural league." The Lydians of western Asia Minor conquered the cities of Ionia, which put the region at conflict with the Median Empire, the precursor to the Achaemenid Empire of the Persian Wars, and a power that the Lydians opposed.

In 553 through 550 BCE, the Persian prince Cyrus led a successful revolt against the last Median king Astyages, and founded the Achaemenid Empire. Seeing an opportunity in the upheaval, the famous Lydian king Croesus asked the oracle at Delphi whether he should attack the Persians in order to extend his realm. According to Herodotus, he received the ambiguous answer that "if Croesus was to cross the Halys [River] he would destroy a great empire." Croesus chose to attack, and in the process he destroyed his own empire, with Lydia falling to Prince Cyrus. The Ionians sought to maintain autonomy under the Persians as they had under the Lydians, and resisted the Persians militarily for some time. However, due to their unwillingness to rise against the Lydians during previous conflicts, they were not granted special terms. Finding the Ionians difficult to rule, the Persians installed tyrants in every city, as a means of control.

Achaemenid Empire Map. The Achaemenid Empire at its greatest extent.

The Ionian Revolt

In 499 BCE, Greeks in the region rose up against Persian rule in the Ionian Revolt. At the heart of the rebellion lay a deep dissatisfaction with the tyrants who were appointed by the Persians to rule the local Greek communities. Specifically, the riot was incited by the Milesian tyrant Aristagoras, who in the wake of a failed expedition to conquer Naxos, utilized Greek unrest against Persian king Darius the Great to his own political purposes.

Athens and other Greek cities sent aid, but were quickly forced to back down after defeat in 494 BCE, at the Battle of Lade. As a result, Asia Minor returned to Persian control. Nonetheless, the Ionian Revolt remains significant as the first major conflict between Greece and the Persian Empire, as well as the first phase of the Persian Wars. Darius vowed to exact revenge against Athens, and developed a plan to conquer all Greeks in an attempt to secure the stability of his empire.

First Persian Invasion of Greece

In 492 BCE, the Persian general, Mardonius, led a campaign through Thrace and Macedonia. During this campaign, Mardonius re-subjugated Thrace and forced Macedonia to become a fully submissive client of the Persian Empire, whereas before they had maintained a broad degree of autonomy. While victorious, he was wounded and forced to retreat back into Asia Minor. Additionally, he lost his 1200-ship naval fleet to a storm off the coast of Mount Athos. Darius sent ambassadors to all Greek cities to demand full submission in light of the recent Persian victory, and all cities submitted, with the exceptions of Athens and Sparta, both of which executed their respective ambassadors. These actions signaled Athens' continued defiance and brought Sparta into the conflict.

In 490 BCE, approximately 100,000 Persians landed in Attica intending to conquer Athens, but were defeated at the Battle of Marathon by a Greek army of 9,000 Athenian hoplites and 1,000 Plateans, led by the Athenian general, Miltiades. The Persian fleet continued to sail to Athens but, seeing it garrisoned, decided not to attempt an assault. The Battle of Marathon was a watershed moment in the Persian Wars, in that it demonstrated to the Greeks that the Persians could be defeated. It also demonstrated the superiority of the more heavily armed Greek hoplites.

Greek-Persian duel. Depiction of a Greek hoplite and a Persian warrior fighting each other on an ancient kylix.

Interbellum (490-480 BCE)

After the failure of the first Persian invasion, Darius raised a large army with the intent of invading Greece again. However, in 486 BCE, Darius's Egyptian subjects revolted, postponing any advancement against Greece. During preparations to march on Egypt, Darius died and his son, Xerxes I, inherited the throne. Xerxes quickly crushed the Egyptians and resumed preparations to invade Greece.

Second Invasion of Greece

In 480 BCE, Xerxes sent a much more powerful force of 300,000 soldiers by land, with 1,207 ships in support, across a double pontoon bridge over the Hellespont. This army took Thrace before descending on Thessaly and Boetia, whilst the Persian navy skirted the coast and resupplied the ground troops. The Greek fleet, meanwhile, dashed to block Cape Artemision. After being delayed by Leonidas I, the Spartan king of the Agiad Dynasty, at the Battle of Thermopylae (a battle made famous due to the sheer imbalance of forces, with 300 Spartans facing the entire Persian Army), Xerxes advanced into Attica, where he captured and burned Athens. But the Athenians had evacuated the city by sea, and under the command of Themistocles, defeated the Persian fleet at the Battle of Salamis.

In 483 BCE, during the period of peace between the two Persian invasions, a vein of silver ore had been discovered in the Laurion (a small mountain range near Athens), and the ore that was mined there paid for the construction of 200 warships to combat Aeginetan piracy. A year later, the Greeks, under the Spartan Pausanias, defeated the Persian army at Plataea. Meanwhile, the allied Greek navy won a decisive victory at the Battle of Mycale, destroying the Persian fleet, crippling Xerxe's sea power, and marking the ascendency of the Greek fleet. Following the Battle of Plataea and the Battle of Mycale, the Persians began withdrawing from Greece and never attempted an invasion again.

Greek Counterattack

The Battle of Mycale was in many ways a turning point, after which the Greeks went on the offensive against the Persian fleet. The Athenian fleet turned to chasing the Persians from the Aegean Sea, and in 478 BCE, the fleet then proceeded to capture Byzantium. In the course of doing so, Athens enrolled all the island states, and some mainland states, into an alliance called the Delian League— so named because its treasury was kept on the sacred island of Delos, whose purpose was to continue fighting the Persian Empire, prepare for future invasions, and organize a means of dividing the spoils of war. The Spartans, although they had taken part in the war, withdrew into isolation afterwards. The Spartans believed that the war's purpose had already been reached through the liberation of mainland Greece and the Greek cities of Asia Minor. Historians also speculate that Sparta was unconvinced of the ability of the Delian League to secure long-term security for Asian Greeks. The Spartan withdrawal from the League allowed Athens to establish unchallenged naval and commercial power within the Hellenic world.

Sources

Attributions

Effects of the Persian Wars

Learning Objective

- Understand the effect the Persian Wars had on the balance of power throughout the classical world

Key Points

- After the second Persian invasion of Greece was halted, Sparta withdrew from the Delian League and reformed the Peloponnesian League with its original allies.

- Many Greek city-states had been alienated from Sparta following the violent actions of Spartan leader Pausanias during the siege of Byzantium.

- Following Sparta's departure from the Delian League, Athens was able to use the resources of the League to its own ends, which led it into conflict with less powerful members of the League.

- The Persian Empire adopted a divide-and-rule strategy in relation to the Greek city-states in the wake of the Persian Wars, stoking already simmering conflicts, including the rivalry between Athens and Sparta, to protect the Persian Empire against further Greek attacks.

Terms

Peloponnesian League

An alliance formed around Sparta in the Peloponnesus, from the 6th to 4th centuries BCE.

> *Delian League*
>
> An association of Greek city-states under the leadership of Athens, the purpose of which was to continue fighting the Persian Empire after the Greek victories at the end of the Second Persian invasion of Greece.
>
> *hegemony*
>
> The political, economic, or military predominance or control of one state over others.

Aftermath of the Persian Wars

As a result of the allied Greek success, a large contingent of the Persian fleet was destroyed and all Persian garrisons were expelled from Europe, marking an end of Persia's advance westward into the continent. The cities of Ionia were also liberated from Persian control. Despite their successes, however, the spoils of war caused greater inner conflict within the Hellenic world. The violent actions of Spartan leader Pausanias at the siege of Byzantium, for instance, alienated many of the Greek states from Sparta, and led to a shift in the military command of the Delian League from Sparta to Athens. This set the stage for Sparta's eventual withdrawal from the Delian League.

Two Leagues

Following the two Persian invasions of Greece, and during the Greek counterattacks that commenced after the Battles of Plataea and Mycale, Athens enrolled all island and some mainland city-states into an alliance, called the Delian League, the purpose of which was to pursue conflict with the Persian Empire, prepare for future invasions, and organize a means of dividing the spoils of war. The Spartans, although they had taken part in the war, withdrew from the Delian League early on, believing that the war's initial purpose had been met with the liberation of mainland Greece and the Greek cities of Asia Minor. Historians also speculate that Sparta decided to leave the League for pragmatic reasons, remaining unconvinced that it was possible to secure long-term security for Greeks residing in Asia Minor, and as a result of their unease with Athenian efforts to increase their power. Once Sparta withdrew from the Delian League after the Persian Wars, it reformed the Peloponnesian League, which had originally been formed in the 6th century and provided the blueprint for what was now the Delian League. The Spartan withdrawal from the League had the effect, however, of allowing Athens to establish unchallenged naval and commercial power, unrivaled throughout the Hellenic world. In fact, shortly after the League's inception, Athens began to use the League's navy for its own purposes, which frequently led it into conflict with other, less powerful League members.

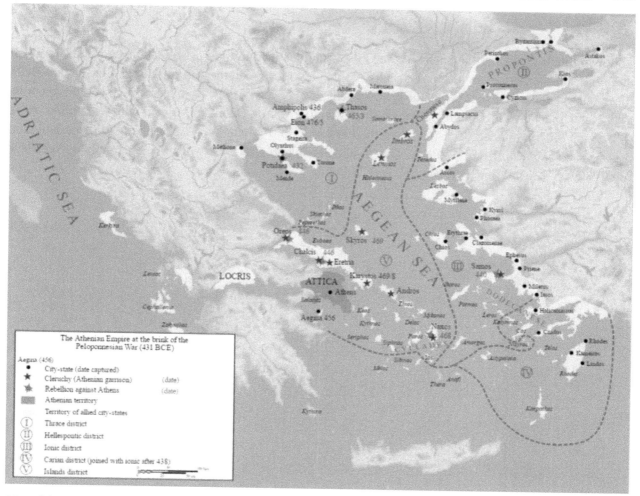

Map of the Athenian Empire c. 431 BCE. The Delian League was the basis for the Athenian Empire, shown here on the brink of the Peloponnesian War (c. 431 BCE).

Delian League Rebellions

A series of rebellions occurred between Athens and the smaller city-states that were members of the League. For example, Naxos was the first member of the League to attempt to secede, in approximately 471 BCE. It was later defeated and forced to tear down its defensive city walls, surrender its fleet, and lost voting privileges in the League. Thasos, another League member, also defected when, in 465 BCE, Athens founded the colony of Amphipolis on the Strymon River, which threatened Thasos' interests in the mines of Mt Pangaion. Thasos allied with Persia and petitioned Sparta for assistance, but Sparta was unable to help because it was facing the largest helot revolution in its history. Nonetheless, relations between Athens and Sparta were soured by the situation. After a three-year long siege, Thasos was recaptured and forced back into the Delian League, though it also lost its defensive walls and fleet, its mines were turned over to Athens, and the city-state was forced to pay yearly tribute and fines. According to Thucydides, the siege of Thasos marked the transformation of the League from an alliance into a hegemony.

Persia

Following their defeats at the hands of the Greeks, and plagued by internal rebellions that hindered their ability to fight foreign enemies, the Persians adopted a policy of divide-and-rule. Beginning in 449 BCE, the Persians attempted to aggravate the growing tensions between Athens and Sparta, and would even bribe politicians to achieve these aims. Their strategy was to keep the Greeks distracted with in-fighting, so as to stop the tide of counterattacks reaching the Persian Empire. Their strategy was largely successful, and there was no open conflict between the Greeks and Persia until 396 BCE, when the Spartan king Agesilaus briefly invaded Asia Minor.

Sources

Attributions

CC licensed content, Specific attribution

- Boundless World History. **Authored by**: Boundless. **Located at**: https://courses.lumenlearning.com/boundless-worldhistory/. **License**: *CC BY-SA: Attribution-ShareAlike*

Athens

Key Points

- Cleisthenes overthrew the dictator Hippias in 511/510 BCE in order to establish democracy at Athens.

- Athens entered its Golden Age in the 5th century BCE, when it abandoned the pretense of parity and relocated the treasury of the Delian League from Delos to Athens. This money funded the building of the Athenian Acropolis, put half the Athenian population on the public payroll, and allowed Athens to build and maintain the dominant naval power in the Greek world.

- With the empire's funds, military dominance, and its political fortunes as guided by statesman and orator Pericles, Athens produced some of the most influential and enduring cultural artifacts of the Western tradition.

- Tensions within the Delian League brought about the Peloponnesian War (431-404 BCE), during which Athens was defeated by its rival, Sparta. Athens lost further power when the armies of Philip II defeated an alliance of Greek city-states.

Terms

Acropolis

A settlement, especially a citadel, built upon an area of elevated ground, frequently a hill with precipitous sides, chosen for purposes of defense. Often the nuclei of large cities of classical antiquity.

Pericles

A prominent and influential Greek statesman, orator, and general of Athens during its Golden Age, in the time between the Persian and Peloponnesian wars.

Delian League

Founded in 478 BCE, an association of Greek city-states under the leadership of Athens, whose purpose was to fight the Persian Empire during the Greco-Persian Wars.

The Rise of Athens (508-448 BCE)

In 514 BCE, the dictator Hippias established stability and prosperity with his rule of Athens, but remained very unpopular as a ruler. With the help of an army from Sparta in 511/510 BCE, he was overthrown by Cleisthenes, a radical politician of aristocratic background who established democracy in Athens.

Prior to the rise of Athens, Sparta, a city-state with a militaristic culture, considered itself the leader of the Greeks, and enforced an hegemony. In 499 BCE, Athens sent troops to aid the Ionian Greeks of Asia Minor, who were rebelling against the Persian Empire during the Ionian Revolt. This provoked two Persian invasions of Greece, both of which were repelled under the leadership of the soldier-statesmen Miltiades and Themistocles, during the Persian Wars. In the decades that followed, the Athenians, with the help of the Spartans and other allied Greek city-states, managed to rout the Persians. These victories enabled Athens to bring most of the Aegean, and many other parts of Greece, together in the Delian League, creating an Athenian-dominated alliance from which Sparta and its allies withdrew.

Greek-Persian Duel.

Athenian Hegemony and the Age of Pericles

The 5th century BCE was a period of Athenian political hegemony, economic growth, and cultural flourishing that is sometimes referred to as the Golden Age of Athens. The latter part of this time period is often called The Age of Pericles. After peace was made with Persia in the 5th century BCE, what started as an alliance of independent city-states became an Athenian empire. Athens moved to abandon the pretense of parity among its allies, and relocated the Delian League treasury from Delos to Athens, where it funded the building of the Athenian Acropolis, put half its population on the public payroll, and maintained the dominant naval power in the Greek world. With the empire's funds, military dominance, and its political fortunes as guided by statesman and orator Pericles, Athens produced some of the most influential and enduring cultural artifacts of Western tradition, during what became known as the Golden Age of Athenian democracy, or the Age of Pericles. The playwrights Aeschylus, Sophocles, and Euripides all lived and worked in Athens during this time, as did historians Herodotus and Thucydides, the physician Hippocrates, and the philosopher Socrates.

Caryatid Statues. The caryatid statues of the Erechtheion on the Acropolis.

Pericles was arguably the most prominent and influential Greek statesman, orator, and general of Athens during its Golden Age. One of his most popular reforms while in power was to allow *thetes* (Athenians without wealth) to occupy public office. Another success of his administration was the creation of the *misthophoria*, a special salary for the citizens that attended the courts as jurors. As Athens' ruler, he helped the city to prosper with a resplendent culture and democratic institutions.

5th century Athenian Political Institutions

The administration of the Athenian state was managed by a group of people referred to as magistrates, who were submitted to rigorous public control and chosen by lot. Only two magistrates were directly elected by the Popular Assembly: *strategos (*or generals), and magistrates of finance. All magistrates served for a year or less, with the exception of Pericles, who was elected year after year to public office. At the end of their service, magistrates were required to give an account of their administration and use of public finances.

The most elite posts in the Athenian political system belonged to archons. In ages past, they served as heads of the Athenian state, but in the Age of Pericles they lost much of their influence and power, though they still presided over tribunals. The Assembly of the People was the first organ of democracy in Athens. In theory, it was composed of all the citizens of Athens. However, it is estimated that the maximum number of participants it witnessed was 6,000. The Assembly met in front of the Acropolis and decided on laws and decrees. Once the Assembly gave its decision in a certain matter, the issue was raised to the Council, or *Boule,* to provide definitive approval.

The Council consisted of 500 members, 50 from each tribe, and functioned as an extension of the Assembly. Council members were chosen by lot in a similar manner to magistrates and supervised the work of the magistrates in addition to other legal projects and administrative details. They also oversaw the city-state's external affairs.

Athenian Defeat and Conquest By Macedon

Originally intended as an association of Greek city-states to continue the fight against the Persians, the Delian League soon turned into a vehicle for Athens's own imperial ambitions and empire-building. The resulting tensions brought about the Peloponnesian War (431-404 BCE), in which Athens was defeated by its rival, Sparta. By the mid-4th century BCE, the northern Greek kingdom of Macedon was becoming dominant in Athenian affairs. In 338 BCE, the armies of Philip II of Macedon defeated an alliance of some of the Greek city-states, including Athens and Thebes, at the Battle of Chaeronea, effectively ending Athenian independence.

Sources

Attributions

CC licensed content, Specific attribution

- Boundless World History. **Authored by**: Boundless. **Located at**: https://courses.lumenlearning.com/boundless-worldhistory/. **License**: *CC BY-SA: Attribution-ShareAlike*

Athenian Society

Learning Objective

- Understand the structures of Athenian society in the classical period

Key Points

- The citizens of Athens decided matters of state in the Assembly of the People, the principle organ of Athen's democracy.
- The Athenian democracy provided a number of governmental resources to its population in order to encourage participation in the democratic process.
- Many governmental posts in classical Athens were chosen by lot, in an attempt to discourage corruption and patronage.
- The Athenian elite lived relatively modestly, and wealth and land were not concentrated in the hands of the few, but rather distributed fairly evenly across the upper classes.
- *Thetes* occupied the lowest rung of Athenian society, but were granted the right to hold public office during the reforms of Ephialtes and Pericles.
- Athenian society was a patriarchy; men held all rights and advantages, such as access to education and power.
- Athenian women were dedicated to the care and upkeep of the family home.

Terms

thetes

The lowest social class of citizens in ancient Athens.

Assembly of the People

The democratic congregation of classical Athens, which, in theory, brought together all citizens to decide upon proposed laws and decrees.

Structure of the Athenian Government

In the Assembly of the People, Athenian citizens decided matters of state. In theory, it was composed of all the citizens of Athens; however, it is estimated that the maximum number of participants it included was 6,000. Since many citizens were incapable of exercising political rights, due to their poverty or ignorance, a number of governmental resources existed to encourage inclusivity. For example, the Athenian democracy provided the following to its population:

- Concession of salaries to public functionaries
- Help finding work for the poor
- Land grants for dispossessed villagers
- Public assistance for war widows, invalids, orphans, and indigents

In order to discourage corruption and patronage, most public offices that did not require specialized expertise were appointed by lot rather than by election. Offices were also rotated so that members could serve in all capacities in turn, in order to ensure that political functions were instituted as smoothly as possible regardless of each individual official's capacity.

When the Assembly of the People reached decisions on laws and decrees, the issue was raised to a body called the Council, or *Boule*, to provide definitive approval. The Council consisted of 500 members, 50 from each tribe, and functioned as an extension of the Assembly. Council members, who were chosen by lot, supervised the work of other government officials, legal projects, and other administrative details. They also oversaw the city-state's external affairs.

The Acropolis. View of the Acropolis in Athens, Greece.

Athenians in the Age of Pericles

The Athenian elite lived modestly and without great luxuries compared to the elites of other ancient societies. Wealth and land ownership was not typically concentrated in the hands of a few people. In fact, 71-73% of the citizen population owned 60-65% of the land. By contrast, *thetes* occupied the lowest social class of citizens in Athens. *Thetes* worked for wages or had less than 200 *medimnoi* as yearly income. Many held crucial roles in the Athenian navy as rowers, due to the preference of many ancient navies to rely on free men to row their galleys. During the reforms of Ephialtes and Pericles around 460-450 BCE, *thetes* were granted the right to hold public office.

Boys were educated at home until the age of seven, at which time they began formal schooling. Subjects included reading, writing, mathematics, and music, as well as physical education classes that were intended to prepare students for future military service. At the age of 18, service in the army was compulsory.

Athenian women were dedicated to the care and upkeep of the family home. Athenian society was a patriarchy; men held all rights and advantages, such as access to education and power. Nonetheless, some women, known as *hetaeras*, did receive an education with the specific purpose of entertaining men, similar to the Japanese geisha tradition. *Hetaeras* were considered higher in status than other women, but lower in status than men. One famous example of a *hetaera* is Pericles' mistress, Aspasia of Miletus, who is said to have debated with prominent writers and thinkers, including Socrates.

Sources

Attributions

CC licensed content, Specific attribution

Introduction to the Peloponnesian War

Learning Objective
• Describe the events of the Peloponnesian War

Key Points
• The Peloponnesian War (431-404 BCE) was fought between Athens and its empire, known as the Delian League, and the Peloponnesian League, led by Sparta. • During this conflict, Greek warfare evolved from an originally limited and formalized form of conflict, to all-out struggles between city-states, with large-scale atrocities. • During the first phase, known as the Archidamian War, Sparta launched repeated invasions of Attica while Athens took advantage of its naval supremacy to raid the Peloponnese coast. • Initially Athens' strategy, as guided by Pericles, was to avoid open battle with the more numerous and better trained Spartan hoplites, and to instead rely on Athens' superior naval fleet. • In the aftermath of a devastating plague, Athenians turned against Pericles's defensive strategy in favor of a more aggressive one that would bring war directly to Sparta and its allies. • The Peace of Nicias was signed in 421 BCE, and concluded the first phase of the war. The treaty was undermined, however, by continued fighting and calls for revolt throughout the Peloponnese. • The destruction of Athens' fleet at Aegospotami during the Decelean War effectively ended the Peloponnesian War. Athens surrendered a year later in 404 BCE.

Terms
hoplites Hoplites were citizen-soldiers of Ancient Greek city-states who were primarily armed with spears and shields. *helot* Helots were a subjugated population group that formed the main population of Laconia and Messenia, the territories controlled by Sparta.

The Peloponnesian War (431-404 BCE) was fought between Athens and its empire, known as the Delian League, and the Peloponnesian League, led by Sparta. During this conflict, Greek warfare evolved from an originally limited and formalized form of conflict, to all-out struggles between city-states, complete with large-scale atrocities. The Peloponnesian War provided a dramatic end to the 5th century BCE, shattering religious and cultural taboos, devastating vast swathes of countryside, and destroying whole cities. Historians have traditionally divided the war into several different phases.

The Archidamian War

During the first phase, known as the Archidamian War, Sparta launched repeated invasions of Attica while Athens took advantage of its naval supremacy to raid the Peloponnese coast. Sparta and its allies, with the exception of Corinth, were almost exclusively land-based powers, whereas the Athens empire, though based on a peninsula, had developed impressive naval power. As a result, the two powers were relatively unable to fight decisive battles. The Spartan strategy during the Archidamian War was to invade the land surrounding Athens, depriving Athenians of the productive land around their city. However, Athens maintained access to the sea and did not suffer much from this strategy, though many citizens of Attica abandoned their farms and moved inside the long walls connecting Athens to port Piraeus.

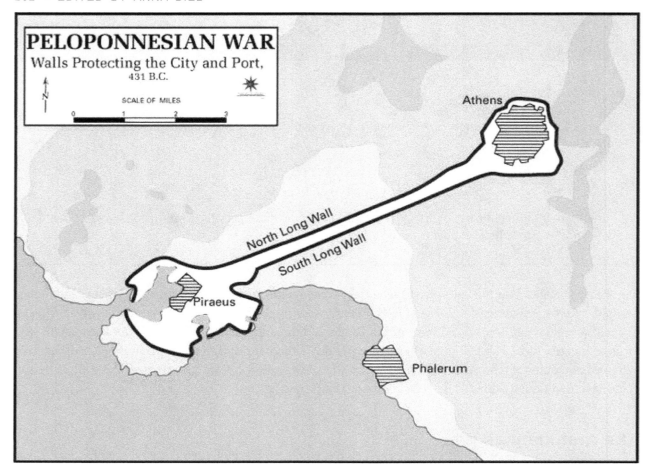

The Walls Protecting Athens. The walls protecting Athens during the Peloponnesian War.

Initially Athens' strategy, as guided by Pericles, was to avoid open battle with the more numerous, and better trained Spartan hoplites, and to instead rely on Athens' superior fleet. As a result, Athens' fleet went on the offensive, winning a victory at Naupactus. Their victory was short-lived, however, because in 430 BCE, an outbreak of plague hit Athens, ravaging the densely packed city and wiping out over 30,000 citizens, sailors, and soldiers, which amounted to roughly one-third to two-thirds of the Athenian population. As a result, Athenian manpower was drastically reduced, and due to widespread fears of plague, foreign mercenaries refused to hire themselves out to Athens. Sparta also abandoned its invasion of Attica during this time, unwilling to risk contact with their diseased enemy.

Pericles and his sons perished as a result of plague, and in the aftermath, Athenians turned against Pericles's defensive strategy in favor of a more aggressive one that would bring war directly to Sparta and its allies. Initially this strategy met with some success as Athens pursued naval raids throughout the Peloponnese. Their successes allowed them to fortify posts throughout the Peloponnese. One such post was near Pylos, on a tiny island called Sphacteria. It began attracting helot runaways from Sparta, which in turn raised Spartan fears that Athenian activities throughout the Peloponnese would incite a mass helot revolt. As a result, the Spartans were driven into action. During the ensuing conflicts, 300 to 400 Spartans were taken hostage, providing Athens with a bargaining chip.

In return, the Spartans raised an army of allies and helots and marched the length of Greece to the Athenian colony of Amphipolis, which controlled several nearby silver mines. These mines were particularly important because they provided much of the money that financed the Athenian war effort. The capture of this colony provided Sparta a bargaining chip as well, and the two rival city-states agreed to sign a truce, exchanging the Spartan hostages for Amphipolis and its silver mines.

Peace of Nicias

The Peace of Nicias was signed in 421 BCE, concluding the first phase of the war. Due to the loss of war hawks in both city-states during the previous conflict, the peace endured for approximately six years. The treaty was undermined, however, by continued fighting and calls for revolt throughout the Peloponnese. Although the Spartans refrained from such actions themselves, their allies remained vocal, particularly Argos. The Athenians supported the Argives and encouraged them to form a coalition of democratic states within the Peloponnese and separate from Sparta. Early Spartan attempts to thwart such a coalition ultimately failed, and the Argives, their allies, and a small Athenian force moved to seize the city of Tegea, near Sparta.

The Battle of Mantinea was the largest land battle fought within Greece during the Peloponnesian War. The Argive allied coalition initially utilized the sheer strength of their combined forces to score early successes, but failed to capitalize on them, providing the elite Spartan forces opportunities to defeat the coalition and save their city from a strategic defeat. The Argive democratic alliance was broken up, and most members were reincorporated into Sparta's Peloponnesian League, reestablishing Spartan hegemony throughout the region.

The Sicilian Expedition

During the 17th year of war, Athens received news that one of their distant allies in Sicily was under attack from Syracuse. The people of Syracuse were ethnically Dorian like the Spartans, and Sicily and their allies, the Athenians, were ethnically Ionian. In 415 BCE, Athens dispatched a massive expeditionary force to attack Syracuse in Sicily. The Athenian force consisted of more than 100 ships, approximately 5,000 infantry, and lightly armored troops. However, their cavalry was limited to about 30 horses, which proved to be no match for the large and highly trained Syracusan cavalry.

Meanwhile, the Syracusans petitioned Sparta for assistance in the matter, and Sparta sent their general, Gylippus, to Sicily with reinforcements. Subsequent Athenian attacks failed and Athens' entire force was destroyed by 413 BCE.

The Second War

This ushered in the final phase of the war, known as the Decelean War, or the Ionian War. By this time, Sparta was receiving support from Persia, and Sparta bolstered rebellions in Athens' Aegean Sea and Ionian subject states, in order to undermine Athens empire. This eventually led to the erosion of Athens' naval supremacy. The Lacedaemonians were no longer content with simply sending aid to Sicily as a means of supporting their ally. Instead, their focus shifted to an offensive strategy against Athens. As a result, Decelea, a town near Athens, was fortified in order to prevent the Athenians from making use of their land year-round, and to thwart overland shipments of supplies. Nearby silver mines were also disrupted, with Spartan hoplites freeing as many as 20,000 Athenian slaves in the vicinity. Due to this disruption in finance, Athens was forced to demand increased tribute from its subject allies, further increasing tension and the threat of rebellion throughout the Athenian empire.

Members of the Peloponnesian League continued to send reinforcements to Syracuse in hopes of driving off the Athenians, but instead, Athens sent another 100 ships and 5,000 troops to Sicily. Gylippus's forces, combined with those of the Syracusans, defeated the Athenians on land. The destruction of Athens' fleet at Aegospotami effectively ended the war, and Athens surrendered a year later in 404 BCE. Corinth and Thebes demanded that Athens be destroyed and all its citizens enslaved, but Sparta refused to destroy a city that had done good service at a time of great danger to Greece, and took Athens into their own alliance system.

Sources

Attributions

CC licensed content, Specific attribution

- Boundless World History. **Authored by**: Boundless. **Located at**: https://courses.lumenlearning.com/boundless-worldhistory/. **License**: *CC BY-SA: Attribution-ShareAlike*

Effects of the Peloponnesian War

Learning Objective

- Understand the effects of the Peloponnesian War on the Greek city-states

Key Points

- The Peloponnesian War ended in victory for Sparta and its allies, but signaled the demise of Athenian naval and political hegemony throughout the Mediterranean.

- Democracy in Athens was briefly overthrown in 411 BCE as a result of its poor handling of the Peloponnesian War. Lysander, the Spartan admiral who commanded the Spartan fleet at Aegospotami in 405 BCE, helped to organize the Thirty Tyrants as Athens' government for the 13 months they maintained power.

- Lysander established many pro-Spartan governments throughout the Aegean, where the ruling classes were more loyal to him than to Sparta as a whole. Eventually Spartan kings, Agis and Pausanias, abolished these Aegean decarchies, curbing Lysander's political influence.

- Agesilaus II was one of two Spartan kings during the period of Spartan hegemony, and is remembered for his multiple campaigns in the eastern Aegean and Persian territories.

- Agesilaus's loss at the Battle of Leuctra effectively ended Spartan hegemony throughout the region.

Terms

hegemony

The political, economic, or military predominance or control of one state over others.

harmosts

A Spartan term for a military governor.

oligarchy

A form of power structure in which a small group of people hold all power and influence in a state.

The Peloponnesian War ended in victory for Sparta and its allies, and led directly to the rising naval power of Sparta. However, it marked the demise of Athenian naval and political hegemony throughout the Mediterranean. The destruction from the Peloponnesian War weakened and divided the Greeks for years to come, eventually allowing the Macedonians an opportunity to conquer them in the mid-4th century BCE.

Athens

Democracy in Athens was briefly overthrown in 411 BCE as a result of its poor handling of the Peloponnesian War. Citizens reacted against Athens' defeat, blaming democratic politicians, such as Cleon and Cleophon. The Spartan army encouraged revolt, installing a pro-Spartan oligarchy within Athens, called the Thirty Tyrants, in 404 BCE. Lysander, the Spartan admiral who commanded the Spartan fleet at Aegospotami in 405 BCE, helped to organize the Thirty Tyrants as a government for the 13 months they maintained power.

During the Thirty Tyrants' rule, five percent of the Athenian population was killed, private property was confiscated, and democratic supporters were exiled. The Thirty appointed a council of 500 to serve the judicial functions that had formerly belonged to all citizens. Despite all this, not all Athenian men had their rights removed. In fact, 3,000 such men were chosen by the Thirty to share in the government of Athens. These men were permitted to carry weapons, entitled to jury trial, and allowed to reside with the city limits. This list of men was constantly being revised, and selection was most likely a reflection of loyalty to the regime, with the majority of Athenians not supporting the Thirty Tyrants' rule.

Nonetheless, the Thirty's regime was not met with much overt opposition for the majority of their rule, as a result of the harsh penalties placed on dissenters. Eventually, the level of violence and brutality carried out by the Thirty in Athens led to increased opposition, stemming primarily from a rebel group of exiles led by Thrasybulus, a former trierarch in the Athenian navy. The increased opposition culminated in a revolution that ultimately overthrew the Thirty's regime. In the aftermath, Athens gave amnesty to the 3,000 men who were given special treatment under the regime, with the exception of those who comprised the governing Thirty and their associated governmental officials. Athens struggled to recover from the upheaval caused by the Thirty Tyrants in the years that followed.

Sparta

As a result of the Peloponnesian War, Sparta, which had primarily been a continental culture, became a naval power. At its peak, Sparta overpowered many key Greek states, including the elite Athenian navy. By the end of the 5th century BCE, Sparta's successes against the Athenian Empire and ability to invade Persian provinces in Anatolia ushered in a period of Spartan hegemony. This hegemonic period was to be short-lived, however.

Lysander

After the end of the Peloponnesian War, Lysander established many pro-Spartan governments throughout the Aegean. Most of the ruling systems set up by Lysander were ten-man oligarchies, called decarchies, in which harmosts, Spartan military governors, were the heads of the government. Because Lysander appointed from within the ruling classes of these governments, the men were more loyal to Lysander than Sparta, making these Aegean outposts similar to a private empire.

Lysander and Spartan king Agis were in agreement with Corinth and Thebes that Athens should be totally destroyed in the aftermath of the Peloponnesian War, but they were opposed by a more moderate faction, headed by Pausanias. Eventually, Pausanias' moderate faction gained the upper hand and Athens was spared, though its defensive walls and port fortifications at Piraeus were demolished. Lysander also managed to require Athens to recall its exiles, causing political instability within the city-state, of which Lysander took advantage to establish the oligarchy that came to be known as the Thirty Tyrants. Because Lysander was also directly involved in the selection of the Thirty, these men were loyal to him over Sparta, causing King Agis and King Pausanias to agree to the abolishment of his Aegean decarchies, and eventually the restoration of democracy in Athens, which quickly curbed Lysander's political influence.

Lysander. A 16th century engraving of Lysander

Agesilaus and His Campaigns

Agesilaus II was one of two Spartan kings during the period of Spartan hegemony. Lysander was one of Agesilaus's biggest supporters, and was even a mentor. During his kingship, Agesilaus embarked on a number of military campaigns in the eastern Aegean and Persian territories. During these campaigns, the Spartans under Agesilaus's command met with numerous rebelling Greek poleis, including the Thebans. The Thebans, Argives, Corinthians, and Athenians had rebelled during the Corinthian War from 395-386 BCE, and the Persians aided the Thebans, Corinthians, and Athenians against the Spartans.

During the winter of 379/378 BCE, a group of Theban exiles snuck into Thebes and succeeded in liberating it, despite resistance from a 1,500-strong Spartan garrison. This led to a number of Spartan expeditions against Thebes, known as The Boeotian War. The Greek city-states eventually attempted to broker peace, but Theban diplomat Epaminondas angered Agesilaus by arguing for the freedom of non-Spartan citizens within Laconia. As a result, Agesilaus excluded the Thebans from the treaty, and the Battle of Leuctra broke out in 371 BCE; the Spartans eventually lost. Sparta's international political influence precipitated quickly after their defeat.

Sources

Attributions

CC licensed content, Specific attribution

- Boundless World History. **Authored by**: Boundless. **Located at**: https://courses.lumenlearning.com/boundless-worldhistory/. **License**: *CC BY-SA: Attribution-ShareAlike*

The Rise of the Macedon

Learning Objective

- Describe Philip II's achievements and how he built up Macedon

Key Points

- The military skills Philip II learned while in Thebes, coupled with his expansionist vision of Macedonian greatness, brought him early successes when he ascended to the throne in 359 BCE.

- Philip earned immense prestige, and secured Macedon's position in the Hellenic world during his involvement in the Third Sacred War, which began in Greece in 356 BCE.

- War with Athens would arise intermittently for the duration of Philip's campaigns, due to conflicts over land, and/or with allies.

- In 337 BCE, Philip created and led the League of Corinth, a federation of Greek states that aimed to invade the Persian Empire.

- In 336 BCE, Philip was assassinated during the earliest stages of the League of Corinth's Persian venture.

- Many Macedonian institutions and demonstrations of power mirrored established Achaemenid conventions.

TermS

sarissas

A long spear or pike about 13-20 feet in length, used in ancient Greek and Hellenistic warfare, that was initially introduced by
Philip II of Macedon.

Macedon rose from a small kingdom on the periphery of classical Greek affairs, to a dominant player in the Hellenic world and beyond, within the span of 25 years between 359 and 336 BCE. Macedon's rise is largely attributable to the policies during Philip II's rule.

Background

In the aftermath of the Peloponnesian War, Sparta rose as a hegemonic power in classical Greece. Sparta's dominance was challenged by many Greek city-states who had traditionally been independent during the Corinthian War of 395-387 BCE. Sparta prevailed in the conflict, but only because Persia intervened on their behalf, demonstrating the fragility with which Sparta held its power over the other Greek city-states. In the next decade, the Thebans revolted against Sparta, successfully liberating their city-state, and later defeating the Spartans at the Battle of Leuctra (371 BCE). Theban general Epaminondas then led an invasion of the Peloponnesus in 370 BCE, invaded Messenia, and liberated the helots, permanently crippling Sparta.

These series of events allowed the Thebans to replace Spartan hegemonic power with their own. For the next nine years, Epaminondas and Theban general Pelopidas further extended Theban power and influence via a series of campaigns throughout Greece, bringing almost every city-state in Greece into the conflict. These years of war ultimately left Greece war-weary and depleted, and during Epaminondas's fourth invasion of the Peloponnesus in 362 BCE, Epaminondas was killed at the Battle of Mantinea. Although Thebes emerged victorious, their losses were heavy, and the Thebans returned to a defensive policy, allowing Athens to reclaim its position at the center of the Greek political system for the first time since the Peloponnesian War. The Athenians' second confederacy would be Macedon's main rivals for control of the lands of the north Aegean.

Philip II's Accession

Philip II of Macedon. Bust of Philip II.

While Philip was young, he was held hostage in Thebes, and received a military and diplomatic education from Epaminondas. By 364 BCE, Philip returned to Macedon, and the skills he learned while in Thebes, coupled with his expansionist vision of Macedonian greatness, brought him early successes when he ascended to the throne in 359 BCE. When he assumed the throne, the eastern regions of Macedonia had been sacked and invaded by the Paionians, and the Thracians and the Athenians had landed a contingent on the coast at Methoni. Philip pushed the Paionians and Thracians back, promising them tributes, and defeated the 3,000 Athenian hoplites at Methoni. In the interim between conflicts, Philip focused on strengthening his army and his overall position domestically, introducing the phalanx infantry corps and arming them with long spears, called sarissas.

A Macedonian Phalanx. Depiction of a Macedonian phalanx armed with sarissas.

In 358 BCE, Philip marched against the Illyrians, establishing his authority inland as far as Lake Ohrid. Subsequently, he agreed to lease the gold mines of Mount Pangaion to the Athenians in exchange for the return of the city of Pydna to Macedon. Ultimately, after conquering Amphipolis in 357 BCE, he reneged on his agreement, which led to war with Athens. During that conflict, Philip conquered Potidaea, but ceded it to the Chalkidian League of Olynthus, with which he was allied. A year later, he also conquered Crenides and changed its name to Philippi, using the gold from the mines there to finance subsequent campaigns.

Third Sacred War

Philip earned immense prestige and secured Macedon's position in the Hellenic world during his involvement in the Third Sacred War, which began in Greece in 356 BCE. Early in the war, Philip defeated the Thessalians at the Battle of Crocus Field, allowing him to acquire Pherae and Magnesia, which was the location of an important harbor, Pagasae. He did not attempt to advance further into central Greece, however, because the Athenians occupied Thermopylae. Although there were no open hostilities between the Athenians and Macedonians at the time, tensions had arisen as a result of Philip's recent land and resource acquisitions. Instead, Philip focused on subjugating the Balkan hill-country in the west and north, and attacking Greek coastal cities, many of which Philip maintained friendly relations with, until he had conquered their surrounding territories. Nonetheless, war with Athens would arise intermittently for the duration of Philip's campaigns, due to conflicts over land and/or with allies.

Persian Influences

For many Macedonian rulers, the Achaemenid Empire in Persia was a major sociopolitical influence, and Philip II was no exception. Many institutions and demonstrations of his power mirrored established Achaemenid conventions. For example, Philip established a Royal Secretary and Archive, as well as the institution of Royal Pages, which would mount the king on his horse in a manner very similar to the way in which Persian kings were mounted. He also aimed to make his power both political and religious in nature, utilizing a special throne stylized after those of the Achaemenid court, to demonstrate his elevated rank. Achaemenid administrative practices were also utilized in Macedonia rule of conquered lands, such as Thrace in 342-334 BCE.

In 337 BCE, Philip created and led the League of Corinth. Members of the league agreed not to engage in conflict with one another unless their aim was to suppress revolution. Another stated aim of the league was to invade the Persian Empire. Ironically, in 336 BCE, Philip was assassinated during the earliest stages of the Persian venture, during the marriage of his daughter Cleopatra to Alexander I of Epirus.

Sources

Attributions

CC licensed content, Specific attribution

- Boundless World History. **Authored by**: Boundless. **Located at**: https://courses.lumenlearning.com/boundless-worldhistory/. **License**: *CC BY-SA: Attribution-ShareAlike*

Alexander the Great

Learning Objective

- Examine Alexander the Great's successes and failures

Key Points

- Alexander the Great spent most of his ruling years on an unprecedented military campaign through Asia and northeast Africa. By the age of 30, he created an empire that stretched from Greece to Egypt, and into present-day Pakistan.

- Alexander inherited a strong kingdom and experienced army, both of which contributed to his successes.

- Alexander's legacy includes the cultural diffusion his engendered conquests, and the rise of Hellenistic culture as a result of his military campaigns.

- Alexander's impressive record was largely due to his smart use of terrain, phalanx and cavalry tactics, bold and adaptive strategy, and the fierce loyalty of his troops.

Terms

Philip II

A king of the Greek kingdom of Macedon from 359 BCE until his assassination in 336 BCE. He was the father of Alexander the Great.

Alexander the Great

Formally Alexander III of Macedon, a Macedonian king who was undefeated in battle and is considered one of history's most successful commanders.

phalanx

A rectangular mass military formation, usually composed entirely of heavy infantry armed with spears, pikes, sarissas, or similar weapons.

Following the decline of the Greek city-states, the Greek kingdom of Macedon rose to power under Philip II. Alexander III, commonly known as Alexander the Great, was born to Philip II in Pella in 356 BCE, and succeeded his father to the throne at the age of 20. He spent most of his ruling years on an unprecedented military campaign through Asia and northeast Africa, and by the age of 30, had created one of the largest empires of the ancient world, which stretched from Greece to Egypt and into present-day Pakistan. He was undefeated in battle and is considered one of history's most successful commanders.

*Alexander the Great. Bust of a young Alexander the Great
from the Hellenistic era, now at the British Museum.*

During his youth, Alexander was tutored by the philosopher Aristotle, until the age of 16. When he succeeded his father to the throne in 336 BCE, after Philip was assassinated, Alexander inherited a strong kingdom and an experienced army. He had been awarded the generalship of Greece, and used this authority to launch his father's military expansion plans. In 334 BCE, he invaded the Achaemenid Empire, ruled Asia Minor, and began a series of campaigns that lasted ten years. Alexander broke the power of Persia in a series of decisive battles, most notably the battles of Issus and Gaugamela. He overthrew the Persian King Darius III, and conquered the entirety of the Persian Empire. At that point, his empire stretched from the Adriatic Sea to the Indus River.

Seeking to reach the "ends of the world and the Great Outer Sea," he invaded India in 326 BCE, but was eventually forced to turn back at the demand of his troops. Alexander died in Babylon in 323 BCE, the city he planned to establish as his capital, without executing a series of planned campaigns that would have begun with an invasion of Arabia. In the years following his death, a series of civil wars tore his empire apart, resulting in several states ruled by the Diadochi, Alexander's surviving generals and heirs. Alexander's legacy includes the cultural diffusion his engendered conquests. He founded some 20 cities that bore his name, the most notable being Alexandria in Egypt. Alexander's settlement of Greek colonists, and the spread of Greek culture in the east, resulted in a new Hellenistic civilization, aspects of which were still evident in the traditions of the Byzantine Empire in the mid-15th century. Alexander became legendary as a classical hero in the mold of Achilles, and he features prominently in the history and myth of Greek and non-Greek cultures. He became the measure against which military leaders compared themselves, and military academies throughout the world still teach his tactics.

Military Generalship

Alexander earned the honorific epithet "the Great" due to his unparalleled success as a military commander. He never lost a battle, despite typically being outnumbered. His impressive record was largely due to his smart use of terrain, phalanx and cavalry tactics, bold strategy, and the fierce loyalty of his troops. The Macedonian phalanx, armed with the *sarissa*, a spear up to 20 feet long, had been developed and perfected by Alexander's father, Philip II. Alexander used its speed and maneuverability to great effect against larger, but more disparate, Persian forces. Alexander also recognized the potential for disunity among his diverse army, due to the various languages, cultures, and preferred weapons individual soldiers wielded. He overcame the possibility of unrest among his troops by being personally involved in battles, as was common among Macedonian kings.

In his first battle in Asia, at Granicus, Alexander used only a small part of his forces—perhaps 13,000 infantry, with 5,000 cavalry—against a much larger Persian force of 40,000. Alexander placed the phalanx at the center, and cavalry and archers on the wings, so that his line matched the length of the Persian cavalry line. By contrast, the Persian infantry was stationed behind its cavalry. Alexander's military positioning ensured that his troops would not be outflanked; further, his phalanx, armed with long pikes, had a considerable advantage over the Persians' scimitars and javelins. Macedonian losses were negligible compared to those of the Persians.

At Issus in 333 BCE, his first confrontation with Darius, he used the same deployment, and again the central phalanx pushed through. Alexander personally led the charge in the center and routed the opposing army. At the decisive encounter with Alexander at Gaugamela, Darius equipped his chariots with scythes on the wheels to break up the phalanx and equipped his cavalry with pikes. Alexander in turn arranged a double phalanx, with the center advancing at an angle, which parted when the chariots bore down and reformed once they had passed. The advance proved successful and broke Darius's center, and Darius was forced to retreat once again.

When faced with opponents who used unfamiliar fighting techniques, such as in Central Asia and India, Alexander adapted his forces to his opponents' style. For example, in Bactria and Sogdiana, Alexander successfully used his javelin throwers and archers to prevent outflanking movements, while massing his cavalry at the center. In India, confronted by Porus's elephant corps, the Macedonians opened their ranks to envelop the elephants, and used their sarissas to strike upwards and dislodge the elephants' handlers.

Sources

Attributions

CC licensed content, Specific attribution

- Boundless World History. **Authored by**: Boundless. **Located at**: https://courses.lumenlearning.com/boundless-worldhistory/. **License**: *CC BY-SA: Attribution-ShareAlike*

5. Early Roman Civilization and the Roman Republic

The Origins of Etruria

Learning Objective

- Explain the relationship between the Etruscan and Roman civilizations

Key Points

- The prevailing view is that Rome was founded by Italics who later merged with Etruscans. Rome was likely a small settlement until the arrival of the Etruscans, who then established Rome's urban infrastructure.

- The Etruscans were indigenous to the Mediterranean area, probably stemming from the Villanovan culture.

- The mining and commerce of metal, especially copper and iron, led to an enrichment of the Etruscans, and to the expansion of their influence in the Italian Peninsula and the western Mediterranean Sea. Conflicts with the Greeks led the Etruscans to ally themselves with the Carthaginians.

- The Etruscans governed within a state system, with only remnants of the chiefdom or tribal forms. The Etruscan state government was essentially a theocracy.

- Aristocratic families were important within Etruscan society, and women enjoyed, comparatively, many freedoms within society.

- The Etruscan system of belief was an immanent polytheism that incorporated indigenous, Indo-European, and Greek influences.

- It is believed that the Etruscans spoke a non-Indo-European language, probably related to what is called the Tyrsenian language family, which is itself an isolate family, or in other words, unrelated directly to other known language groups.

Terms

Etruscan

The modern name given to a civilization of ancient Italy in the area corresponding roughly to Tuscany, western Umbria, and northern Latium.

theocracy

A form of government in which a deity is officially recognized as the civil ruler, and official policy is governed by officials regarded as divinely guided, or is pursuant to the doctrine of a particular religion or religious group.

oligarchic

A form of power structure in which power effectively rests with a small number of people. These people could be distinguished by royalty, wealth, family ties, education, corporate, or military control. Such states are often controlled by a few prominent families who typically pass their influence from one generation to the next; however, inheritance is not a necessary condition for the application of this term.

Those who subscribe to an Italic (a diverse group of people who inhabited pre-Roman Italy) foundation of Rome, followed by an Etruscan invasion, typically speak of an Etruscan "influence" on Roman culture; that is, cultural objects that were adopted by Rome from neighboring Etruria. The prevailing view is that Rome was founded by Italics who later merged with Etruscans. In that case, Etruscan cultural objects are not a heritage but are, instead, influences. Rome was likely a small settlement until the arrival of the Etruscans, who then established its initial urban infrastructure.

Origins

The origins of the Etruscans are mostly lost in prehistory. Historians have no literature, and no original texts of religion or philosophy. Therefore, much of what is known about this civilization is derived from grave goods and tomb findings. The main hypotheses state that the Etruscans were indigenous to the region, probably stemming from the Villanovan culture or from the Near East. Etruscan expansion was focused both to the north, beyond the Apennines, and into Campania. The mining and commerce of metal, especially copper and iron, led to an enrichment of the Etruscans, and to the expansion of their influence in the Italian Peninsula and the western Mediterranean Sea. Here, their interests collided with those of the Greeks, especially in the 6t[h] century BCE, when Phoceans of Italy founded colonies along the coast of Sardinia, Spain, and Corsica. This led the Etruscans to ally themselves with the Carthaginians, whose interests also collided with the Greeks.

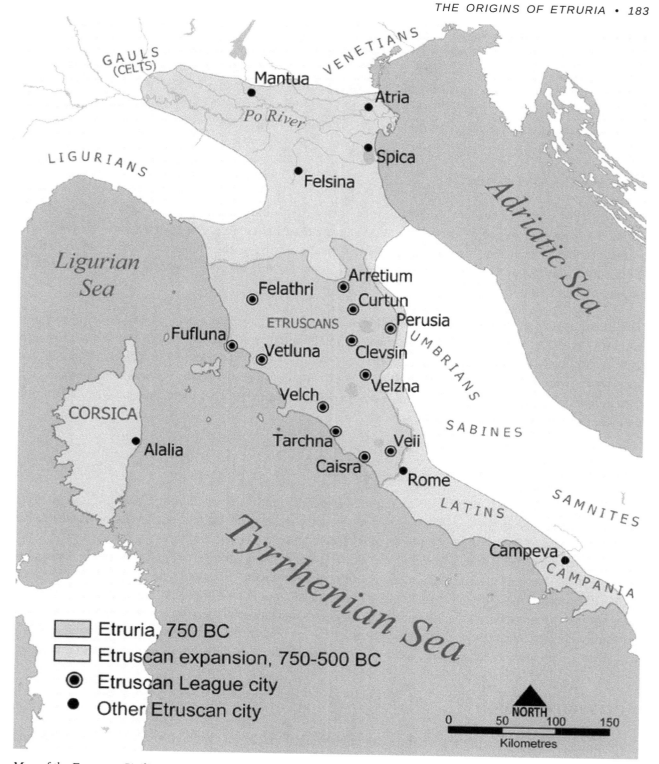

Map of the Etruscan Civilization. Extent of Etruscan civilization and the 12 Etruscan League cities.

Around 540 BCE, the Battle of Alalia led to a new distribution of power in the western Mediterranean Sea. Though the battle had no clear winner, Carthage managed to expand its sphere of influence at the expense of the Greeks, and Etruria saw itself relegated to the northern Tyrrhenian Sea with full ownership of Corsica. From the first half of the 5th century BCE, the new international political situation signaled the beginning of Etruscan decline after they had lost their southern provinces. In 480 BCE, Etruria's ally,

Carthage, was defeated by a coalition of Magna Graecia cities led by Syracuse. A few years later, in 474 BCE, Syracuse's tyrant, Hiero, defeated the Etruscans at the Battle of Cumae. Etruria's influence over the cities of Latium and Campania weakened, and it was taken over by the Romans and Samnites. In the 4th century, Etruria saw a Gallic invasion end its influence over the Po valley and the Adriatic coast. Meanwhile, Rome had started annexing Etruscan cities. These events led to the loss of the Northern Etruscan provinces. Etruria was conquered by Rome in the 3rd century BCE.

Etruscan Government

The Etruscans governed using a state system of society, with only remnants of the chiefdom and tribal forms. In this way, they were different from the surrounding Italics. Rome was, in a sense, the first Italic state, but it began as an Etruscan one. It is believed that the Etruscan government style changed from total monarchy to an oligarchic republic (as the Roman Republic did) in the 6th century BCE, although it is important to note this did not happen to all city-states.

The Etruscan state government was essentially a theocracy. The government was viewed as being a central authority over all tribal and clan organizations. It retained the power of life and death; in fact, the gorgon, an ancient symbol of that power, appears as a motif in Etruscan decoration. The adherents to this state power were united by a common religion. Political unity in Etruscan society was the city-state, and Etruscan texts name quite a number of magistrates without explanation of their function (the camthi, the parnich, the purth, the tamera, the macstrev, etc.).

Etruscan Families

According to inscriptional evidence from tombs, aristocratic families were important within Etruscan society. Most likely, aristocratic families rose to prominence over time through the accumulation of wealth via trade, with many of the wealthiest Etruscan cities located near the coast.
The Etruscan name for family was *lautn*, and at the center of the *lautn* was the married couple. Etruscans were monogamous, and the lids of large numbers of sarcophagi were decorated with images of smiling couples in the prime of their life, often reclining next to each other or in an embrace. Many tombs also included funerary inscriptions naming the parents of the deceased, indicating the importance of the mother's side of the family in Etruscan society. Additionally, Etruscan women were allowed considerable freedoms in comparison to Greek and Roman women, and mixed-sex socialization outside the domestic realm occurred.

Etruscan Religion

The Etruscan system of belief was an immanent polytheism; that is, all visible phenomena were considered to be a manifestation of divine power, and that power was subdivided into deities that acted continually on the world of man and could be dissuaded or persuaded in favor of human affairs. Three layers of deities are evident in the extensive Etruscan art motifs. One appears to be divinities of an indigenous nature: Catha and Usil, the sun; Tivr, the moon; Selvans, a civil god; Turan, the goddess of love; Laran, the god of war; Leinth, the goddess of death; Maris; Thalna; Turms; and the ever-popular Fufluns, whose name is related in an unknown way to the city of Populonia and the *populus Romanus,* the Roman people.

Ruling over this pantheon of lesser deities were higher ones that seem to reflect the Indo-European system: Tin or Tinia, the sky; Uni, his wife (Juno); and Cel, the earth goddess. In addition the Greek gods were taken into the Etruscan system: Aritimi (Artemis), Menrva (Minerva), and Pacha (Bacchus). The Greek heroes taken from Homer also appear extensively in art motifs.

The Greek polytheistic approach was similar to the Etruscan religious and cultural base. As the Romans emerged from the legacy created by both of these groups, it shared in a belief system of many gods and deities.

Etruscan Language and Etymology

Knowledge of the Etruscan language is still far from complete. It is believed that the Etruscans spoke a non-Indo-European language, probably related to what is called the Tyrsenian language family, which is itself an isolate family, or in other words, unrelated directly to other known language groups. No etymology exists for *Rasna*, the Etruscans' name for themselves, though Italian historic linguist, Massimo Pittau, has proposed that it meant "shaved" or "beardless." The hypothesized etymology for *Tusci*, a root for "Tuscan" or "Etruscan," suggests a connection to the Latin and Greek words for "tower," illustrating the *Tusci* people as those who built towers. This was possibly based upon the Etruscan preference for building hill towns on high precipices that were enhanced by walls. The word may also be related to the city of Troy, which was also a city of towers, suggesting large numbers of migrants from that region into Etruria.

Sources

Attributions

Etruscan Artifacts

Learning Objective

- Explain the importance of Etruscan artifacts to our understanding of their history

Key Points

- Princely tombs did not house individuals, but families who were interred over long periods.

- Although many Etruscan cities were later assimilated by Italic, Celtic, or Roman ethnic groups, the Etruscan names and inscriptions that survive within the ruins provide historic evidence as to the range of settlements that the Etruscans constructed.

- It is unclear whether Etruscan cultural objects are influences upon Roman culture or part of native Roman heritage. The criterion for deciding whether or not an object originated in Rome or descended to the Romans from the Etruscans is the date of the object and the opinion of ancient sources regarding the provenance of the object's style.

- Although Diodorus of Sicily wrote, in the 1st century, of the great achievements of the Etruscans, little survives or is known of it.

Terms

oligarchic

A form of power structure in which power effectively rests with a small number of people. These people could be distinguished by royalty, wealth, family ties, education, corporate, or military control. Such states are often controlled by a few prominent families who typically pass their influence from one generation to the next, but inheritance is not a necessary condition for the application of this term.

sarcophagi

A box-like funeral receptacle for a corpse, most commonly carved in stone and displayed above ground.

Historians have no literature or original Etruscan religious or philosophical texts on which to base knowledge of their civilization, so much of what is known is derived from grave goods and tomb findings. Princely tombs did not house individuals, but families who were interred over long periods. The decorations and objects included at these sites paint a picture of Etruscan social and political life. For instance, wealth from trade seems to have supported the rise of aristocratic families who, in turn, were likely foundational to the Etruscan oligarchic system of governance. Indeed, at some Etruscan tombs, physical evidence of trade has been found in the form of grave goods, including fine faience ware cups, which was likely the result of trade with Egypt. Additionally, the depiction of married couples on many sarcophagi provide insight into the respect and freedoms granted to women within Etruscan society, as well as the emphasis placed on romantic love as a basis for marriage pairings.

Sarcophagus of the Spouses. Sarcophagus of an Etruscan couple in the Louvre, Room 18.

Although many Etruscan cities were later assimilated by Italic, Celtic, or Roman ethnic groups, the Etruscan names and inscriptions that survive within the ruins provide historic evidence of the range of settlements constructed by the Etruscans. Etruscan cities flourished over most of Italy during the Roman Iron Age. According to ancient sources, some cities were founded by the Etruscans in prehistoric times, and bore entirely Etruscan names. Others were later colonized by the Etruscans from Italic groups.

Nonetheless, relatively little is known about the architecture of the ancient Etruscans. What is known is that they adapted the native Italic styles with influence from the external appearance of Greek architecture. Etruscan architecture is not generally considered part of the body of Greco-Roman classical architecture. Though the houses of the wealthy were evidently very large and comfortable, the burial chambers of tombs, and the grave-goods that filled them, survived in greater numbers. In the southern Etruscan area, tombs contain large, rock-cut chambers under a tumulus in large necropoli.

There is some debate among historians as to whether Rome was founded by Italic cultures and then invaded by the Etruscans, or whether Etruscan cultural objects were adopted subsequently by Roman peoples. In other words, it is unclear whether Etruscan cultural objects are influences upon Roman culture, or part of native Roman heritage. Among archaeologists, the main criteria for deciding whether or not an object originated in Rome, or descended to the Romans from the Etruscans, is the date of the object, which is often determined by process of carbon dating. After this process, the opinion of ancient sources is consulted.

Although Diodorus of Sicily wrote in the 1st century of the great achievements of the Etruscans, little survives or is known of it. Most Etruscan script that does survive are fragments of religious and funeral texts. However, it is evident, from Etruscan visual art, that Greek myths were well known.

Sources

Attributions

CC licensed content, Specific attribution

- Boundless World History. **Authored by**: Boundless. **Located at**: https://courses.lumenlearning.com/boundless-worldhistory/. **License**: *CC BY-SA: Attribution-ShareAlike*

Etruscan Religion

Learning Objective

- Describe some of the key characteristics of the Etruscan belief system

Key Points

- The Etruscan system of belief was an immanent polytheism, meaning all visible phenomena were considered to be a manifestation of divine power, and that power was subdivided into deities that acted continually on the world of man.

- The Etruscan scriptures were a corpus of texts termed the *Etrusca Disciplina*, a set of rules for the conduct of all divination.

- Three layers of deities are evident in the extensive Etruscan art motifs: indigenous, Indo-European, and Greek.

- Etruscan beliefs concerning the afterlife were influenced by a number of sources, particularly those of the early Mediterranean region.

Terms

polytheism

The worship of, or belief in, multiple deities, usually assembled into a pantheon of gods and goddesses, each with their own specific religions and rituals.

Etrusca Disciplina

A corpus of texts that comprised the Etruscan scriptures, which essentially provided a systematic guide to divination.

The Etruscan system of belief was an immanent polytheism; that is, all visible phenomena were considered to be a manifestation of divine power and that power was subdivided into deities that acted continually on the world of man, and could be dissuaded or persuaded in favor of human affairs. The Greek polytheistic approach was similar to the Etruscan religious and cultural base. As the Romans emerged from the legacy created by both of these groups, it shared in a belief system of many gods and deities.

Etrusca Disciplina

The Etruscan scriptures were a corpus of texts, termed the *Etrusca Disciplina*. These texts were not scriptures in the typical sense, and foretold no prophecies. The Etruscans did not appear to have a systematic rubric for ethics or morals. Instead, they concerned themselves with the problem of understanding the will of the gods, which the Etruscans considered inscrutable. The Etruscans did not attempt to rationalize or explain divine actions or intentions, but to simply divine what the gods' wills were through an elaborate system of divination. Therefore, the *Etrusca Disciplina* is mainly a set of rules for the conduct of all sorts of divination. It does not dictate what laws shall be made or how humans are to behave, but instead elaborates rules for how to ask the gods these questions and receive their answers.

Divinations were conducted by priests, who the Romans called *haruspices* or *sacerdotes*. A special magistrate was designated to look after sacred items, but every man had religious responsibilities. In this way, the Etruscans placed special emphasis upon intimate contact with divinity, consulting with the gods and seeking signs from them before embarking upon a task.

Spirits and Deities

Three layers of deities are evident in the extensive Etruscan art motifs. One appears to be divinities of an indigenous nature: Catha and Usil, the sun; Tivr, the moon; Selvans, a civil god; Turan, the goddess of love; Laran, the god of war; Leinth, the goddess of death; Maris; Thalna; Turms; and the ever-popular Fufluns, whose name is related in some unknown way to the city of Populonia and the *populus Romanus* (the Roman people). Ruling over this pantheon of lesser deities were higher ones that seem to reflect the Indo-European system: Tin or Tinia, the sky; Uni, his wife (Juno); and Cel, the earth goddess. In addition, the Greek gods were taken into the Etruscan system: Aritimi (Artemis), Menrva (Minerva), and Pacha (Bacchus). The Greek heroes taken from Homer also appear extensively in art motifs.

Mars of Todi. The Mars of Todi, a life-sized Etruscan bronze sculpture of a soldier making a votive offering, most likely to Laran, the Etruscan god of war; late 5th to early 4th century BCE.

The Afterlife

Etruscan beliefs concerning the afterlife seem to be influenced by a number of sources. The Etruscans shared in general early Mediterranean beliefs. For instance, much like the Egyptians, the Etruscans believed that survival and prosperity in the afterlife depended on the treatment of the deceased's remains. Souls of ancestors are found depicted around Etruscan tombs, and after the 5th century BCE, the deceased are depicted in iconography as traveling to the underworld. In several instances, spirits of the dead are referred to as *hinthial*, or one who is underneath. The transmigrational world beyond the grave was patterned after the Greek Hades and ruled by Aita. The deceased were guided there by Charun, the equivalent of Death, who was blue and wielded a hammer. The Etruscan version of Hades was populated by Greek mythological figures, some of which were of composite appearance to those in Greek mythology.

Etruscan tombs imitated domestic structures, contained wall paintings and even furniture, and were spacious. The deceased was depicted in the tomb at the prime of their life, and often with a spouse. Not everyone had a sarcophagus, however. Some deceased individuals were laid out on stone benches, and depending on the proportion of inhumation, versus cremation, rites followed, cremated ashes and bones might be put into an urn in the shape of a house, or in a representation of the deceased.

Reconstruction of an Etruscan Temple. 19th century reconstruction of an Etruscan temple, in the courtyard of the Villa Giulia Museum in Rome, Italy.

Sources

Attributions

CC licensed content, Specific attribution

- Boundless World History. **Authored by**: Boundless. **Located at**: https://courses.lumenlearning.com/boundless-worldhistory/. **License**: *CC BY-SA: Attribution-ShareAlike*

The Founding of Rome

- Explain how the founding of Rome is rooted in mythology

- The national epic poem of mythical Rome, the *Aeneid* by Virgil, tells the story of how the Trojan prince, Aeneas, came to Italy. The *Aeneid* was written under the emperor Augustus, who, through Julius Caesar, claimed ancestry from Aeneas.

- The Alba Longan line, begun by Iulus, Aeneas's son, extends to King Procas, who fathered two sons, Numitor and Amulius.
  According to the myth of Romulus and Remus, Amulius captured Numitor, sent him to prison, and forced the daughter of Numitor, Rhea Silvia, to become a virgin priestess among the Vestals.

- Despite Amulius' best efforts, Rhea Silvia had twin boys, Romulus and Remus, by Mars. Romulus and Remus eventually overthrew Amulius, and restored Numitor.

- In the course of a dispute during the founding of the city of Rome, Romulus killed Remus. Thus Rome began with a fratricide, a story that was later taken to represent the city's history of internecine political strife and bloodshed.

- According to the archaeological record of the region, the development of Rome itself is presumed to have coalesced around the migrations of various Italic tribes, who originally inhabited the Alban Hills as they moved into the agriculturally-superior valley near the Tiber River.

- The discovery of a series of fortification walls on the north slope of Palatine Hill, most likely dating to the middle of the 8th century BCE, provide the strongest evidence of the original site and date of the founding of the city of Rome.

Terms

Romulus

The founder of Rome, and one of two twin sons of Rhea Silvia and Mars.

Aeneas

A Trojan survivor of the Trojan War who, according to legend, journeyed to Italy and founded the bloodline that would eventually lead to the Julio-Claudian emperors.

Rome

An Italic civilization that began on the Italian Peninsula as early as the 8th century BCE. Located along the Mediterranean Sea, and centered on one city, it expanded to become one of the largest empires in the ancient world.

The founding of Rome can be investigated through archaeology, but traditional stories, handed down by the ancient Romans themselves, explain the earliest history of their city in terms of legend and myth. The most familiar of these myths, and perhaps the most famous of all Roman myths, is the story of Romulus and Remus, the twins who were suckled by a she-wolf. This story had to be reconciled with a dual tradition, set earlier in time.

Romulus and the Founding of Rome

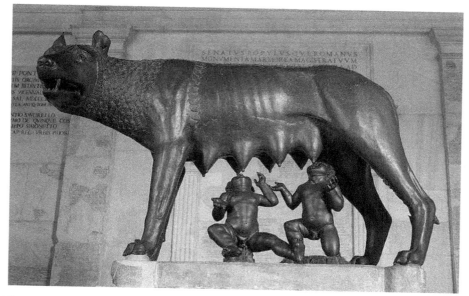

The Capitoline Wolf. The iconic sculpture of Romulus and Remus being suckled by the she-wolf who raised them. Traditional scholarship says the wolf-figure is Etruscan, 5th century BCE, with figures of Romulus and Remus added in the 15th century CE by Antonio Pollaiuolo. Recent studies suggest that the wolf may be a medieval sculpture dating from the 13th century CE.

Romulus and Remus were purported to be sons of Rhea Silvia and Mars, the god of war. Because of a prophecy that they would overthrow their great-uncle Amulius, who had overthrown Silvia's father, Numitor, they were, in the manner of many mythological heroes, abandoned at birth. Both sons were left to die on the Tiber River, but were saved by a number of miraculous interventions. After being carried to safety by the river itself, the twins were nurtured by a she-wolf and fed by a woodpecker, until a shepherd, named Faustulus, found them and took them as his sons.

When Remus and Romulus became adults and learned the truth about their birth and upbringing, they killed Amulius and restored Numitor to the throne. Rather than wait to inherit Alba Longa, the city of their birth, the twins decided to establish their own city. They quarreled, however, over where to locate the new city, and in the process of their dispute, Romulus killed his brother. Thus Rome began with a fratricide, a story that was later taken to represent the city's history of internecine political strife and bloodshed.

Aeneas and the Aeneid

The national epic of mythical Rome, the *Aeneid* by Virgil, tells the story of how the Trojan prince, Aeneas, came to Italy. Although the Aeneid was written under the emperor Augustus between 29 and 19 BCE, it tells the story of the founding of Rome centuries before Augustus's time. The hero, Aeneas, was already well known within Greco-Roman legend and myth, having been a character in the *Iliad*. But Virgil took the disconnected tales of Aeneas's wanderings, and his vague association with the foundation of Rome, and fashioned it into a compelling foundation myth or national epic. The story tied Rome to the legends of Troy, explained the Punic Wars, glorified traditional Roman virtues, and legitimized the Julio-Claudian dynasty as descendants of the founders, heroes, and gods of Rome and Troy.

Virgil makes use of symbolism to draw comparisons between the emperor Augustus and Aeneas, painting them both as founders of Rome. The Aeneid also contains prophecies about Rome's future, the deeds of Augustus, his ancestors, and other famous Romans. The shield of Aeneas even depicts Augustus's victory at Actium in 31 BCE. Virgil wrote the Aeneid during a time of major political and social change in Rome, with the fall of the republic and the Final War of the Roman Republic tearing through society and causing many to question Rome's inherent greatness. In this context, Augustus instituted a new era of prosperity and peace through the reintroduction of traditional Roman moral values. The Aeneid was seen as reflecting this aim by depicting Aeneas as a man devoted and loyal to his country and its greatness, rather than being concerned with his own personal gains. The *Aeneid* also gives mythic legitimization to the rule of Julius Caesar, and by extension, to his adopted son, Augustus, by immortalizing the tradition that renamed Aeneas's son Iulus, making him an ancestor to the family of Julius Caesar.

According to the *Aeneid,* the survivors from the fallen city of Troy banded together under Aeneas, underwent a series of adventures around the Mediterranean Sea, including a stop at newly founded Carthage under the rule of Queen Dido, and eventually reached the Italian coast. The Trojans were thought to have landed in an area between modern Anzio and Fiumicino, southwest of Rome, probably at Laurentum, or in other versions, at Lavinium, a place named for Lavinia, the daughter of King Latinus, who Aeneas married. Aeneas' arrival started a series of armed conflicts with Turnus over the marriage of Lavinia. Before the arrival of Aeneas, Turnus was engaged to Lavinia, who then married Aeneas, which began the conflict. Aeneas eventually won the war and killed Turnus, which granted the Trojans the right to stay and to assimilate with the local peoples. The young son of Aeneas, Ascanius, also known as Iulus, went on to found Alba Longa and the line of Alban kings who filled the chronological gap between the Trojan saga and the traditional founding of Rome in the 8th century BCE.

Toward the end of this line, King Procas appears as the father of Numitor and Amulius. At Procas' death, Numitor became king of Alba Longa, but Amulius captured him and sent him to prison. He also forced the daughter of Numitor, Rhea Silvia, to become a virgin priestess among the Vestals. For many years, Amulius was the king. The tortuous nature of the chronology is indicated by Rhea Silvia's ordination among the Vestals, whose order was traditionally said to have been founded by the successor of Romulus, Numa Pompilius.

The Archaeological Record

According to the archaeological record of the region, the Italic tribes who originally inhabited the Alban Hills moved down into the valleys, which provided better land for agriculture. The area around the Tiber River was particularly advantageous and offered many strategic resources. For instance, the river itself provided a natural border on one side of the settlement, and the hills on the other side provided another defensive position for the townspeople. A settlement in this area would have also allowed for control of the river, including commercial and military traffic, as well as a natural observation point at Isola Tiberina. This was especially important, since Rome was at the intersection of the principal roads to the sea from Sabinum and Etruria, and traffic from those roads could not be as easily controlled.

The development of Rome itself is presumed to have coalesced around the migrations of these various tribes into the valley, as evidenced by differences in pottery and burial techniques. The discovery of a series of fortification walls on the north slope of Palatine Hill, most likely dating to the middle of the 8th century BCE, provide the strongest evidence for the original site and date of the founding of the city of Rome.

Sources

Attributions

CC licensed content, Specific attribution

- Boundless World History. **Authored by**: Boundless. **Located at**: https://courses.lumenlearning.com/boundless-worldhistory/. **License**: *CC BY-SA: Attribution-ShareAlike*

The Seven Kings

- Explain the significance of the Seven Kings of Rome to Roman culture

Key Points

- Romulus was Rome's first king and the city's founder. He is best known for the Rape of the Sabine Women and the establishment of the Senate, as well as various voting practices.

- Numa Pompilius was a just, pious king who established the cult of the Vestal Virgins at Rome, and the position of Pontifex Maximus. His reign was characterized by peace.

- Tullus Hostilius had little regard for the Roman gods, and focused entirely on military expansion. He constructed the home of the Roman Senate, the *Curia Hostilia*.

- Ancus Marcius ruled peacefully and only fought wars when Roman territories needed defending.

- Lucius Tarquinius Priscus increased the size of the Senate and began major construction works, including the Temple to Jupiter Optimus Maximus, and the Circus Maximus.

- Servius Tullius built the first *pomerium*—walls that fully encircled the Seven Hills of Rome. He also made organizational changes to the Roman army, and implemented a new constitution for the Romans, further developing the citizen classes.

- Lucius Tarquinius Superbus's reign is remembered for his use of violence and intimidation, as well as his disrespect of Roman custom and the Roman Senate. He was eventually overthrown, thus leading to the establishment of the Roman Republic.

Terms

absolute monarchy

A monarchical form of government in which the monarch has absolute power among his or her people. This amounts to unrestricted political power over a sovereign state and its people.

patrician

A group of elite families in ancient Rome.

The first 200 years of Roman history occurred under a monarchy. Rome was ruled by seven kings over this period of time, and each of their reigns were characterized by the personality of the ruler in question. Each of these kings is credited either with establishing a key Roman tradition, or constructing an important building. None of the seven kings were known to be dynasts, and no reference is made to the hereditary nature of kingdom until after the fifth king, Tarquinius Priscus.

The king of Rome possessed absolute power over the people, and the Senate provided only a weak, oligarchic counterbalance to his power, primarily exercising only minor administrative powers. For these reasons, the kingdom of Rome is considered an absolute monarchy. Despite this, Roman kings, with the exception of Romulus, were elected by citizens of Rome who occupied the Curiate Assembly. There, members would vote on candidates that had been nominated by a chosen member of the Senate, called an inter-rex. Candidates could be chosen from any source.

Romulus

Romulus was Rome's legendary first king and the city's founder. In 753 BCE, Romulus began building the city upon the Palatine Hill. After founding and naming Rome, as the story goes, he permitted men of all classes to come to Rome as citizens, including slaves and freemen, without distinction. To provide his citizens with wives, Romulus invited the neighboring tribes to a festival in Rome where he abducted the young women amongst them (this is known as The Rape of the Sabine Women). After the ensuing war with the Sabines, Romulus shared the kingship with the Sabine king, Titus Tatius. Romulus selected 100 of the most noble men to form the Roman Senate as an advisory council to the king. These men were called *patres* (from *pater:* father, head), and their descendants became the patricians. He also established voting, and class structures that would define sociopolitical proceedings throughout the Roman Republic and Empire.

Numa Pompilius

After the death of Romulus, there was an *interregnum* for one year, during which ten men chosen from the senate governed Rome as successive *interreges*. Numa Pompilius, a Sabine, was eventually chosen by the senate to succeed Romulus because of his reputation for justice and piety. Numa's reign was marked by peace and religious reform. Numa constructed a new temple to Janus and, after establishing peace with Rome's neighbors, shut the doors of the temple to indicate a state of peace. The doors of the temple remained closed for the balance of his reign. He established the cult of the Vestal Virgins at Rome, as well as the "leaping priests," known as the Salii, and three flamines, or priests, assigned to Jupiter, Mars, and Quirinus. He also established the office and duties of Pontifex Maximus, the head priest of the Roman state religion.

Tullus Hostilius

Tullus Hostilius was much like Romulus in his warlike behavior, and completely unlike Numa in his lack of respect for the gods. Tullus waged war against Alba Longa, Fidenae and Veii, and the Sabines. It was during Tullus' reign that the city of Alba Longa was completely destroyed, after which Tullus integrated its population into Rome. According to the Roman historian Livy, Tullus neglected the worship of the gods until, towards the end of his reign, he fell ill and became superstitious. However, when Tullus called upon Jupiter and begged assistance, Jupiter responded with a bolt of lightning that burned the king and his house to ashes. Tullus is attributed with constructing a new home for the Senate, the *Curia Hostilia*, which survived for 562 years after his death.

Ancus Marcius

Following the death of Tullus, the Romans elected a peaceful and religious king in his place—Numa's grandson, Ancus Marcius. Much like his grandfather, Ancus did little to expand the borders of Rome, and only fought war when his territories needed defending.

Lucius Tarquinius Priscus

Lucius Tarquinius Priscus was the fifth king of Rome and the first of Etruscan birth. After immigrating to Rome, he gained favor with Ancus, who later adopted him as his son. Upon ascending the throne, he waged wars against the Sabines and Etruscans, doubling the size of Rome and bringing great treasures to the city.One of his first reforms was to add 100 new members to the Senate from the conquered Etruscan tribes, bringing the total number of senators to 200. He used the treasures Rome had acquired from conquests to build great monuments for Rome, including the Roman Forum, the temple to Jupiter on the Capitoline Hill, and the Circus Maximus. His reign is best remembered for the introduction of Etruscan symbols of military distinction and civilian authority
into the Roman tradition, including the scepter of the king, the rings
worn by senators, and the use of the tuba for military purposes.

The Temple of Jupiter Optimus Maximus. 19th century illustration depicting the Temple of Jupiter Optimus Maximus above the Tiber River during the Roman Republic.

Servius Tullus

Following Priscus's death, his son-in-law, Servius Tullius, succeeded him to the throne. Like his father-in-law before him, Servius fought successful wars against the Etruscans. He used the treasure from his campaigns to build the first *pomerium*—walls that fully encircled the Seven Hills of Rome. He also made organizational changes to the Roman army, and was renowned for implementing a new constitution for the Romans and further developing the citizen classes. Servius's reforms brought about a major change in Roman life—voting rights were now based on socioeconomic status, transferring much of the power into the hands of the Roman elite. The 44-year reign of Servius came to an abrupt end when he was assassinated in a conspiracy led by his own daughter, Tullia, and her husband, Lucius Tarquinius Superbus.

Lucius Tarquinius Superbus

While in power, Tarquinius conducted a number of wars against Rome's neighbors, including the Volsci, Gabii, and the Rutuli. Tarquinius also engaged in a series of public works, notably the completion of the Temple of Jupiter Optimus Maximus on the Capitoline Hill. Tarquin's reign, however, is best remembered for his use of violence and intimidation in his attempts to maintain control over Rome, as well as his disrespect of Roman custom and the Roman Senate. Tensions came to a head when the king's son, Sextus Tarquinius, raped Lucretia, wife and daughter to powerful Roman nobles. Lucretia then told her relatives about the attack and subsequently committed suicide to avoid the dishonor of the episode. Four men, led by Lucius Junius Brutus, incited a revolution, and as a result, Tarquinius and his family were deposed and expelled from Rome in 509 BCE. Because of his actions and the way they were viewed by the people, the word for King, *rex*, held a negative connotation in Roman culture until the fall of the Roman Empire. Brutus and Collatinus became Rome's first consuls, marking the beginning of the Roman Republic. This new government would survive for the next 500 years, until the rise of Julius Caesar and Caesar Augustus, and cover a period in which Rome's authority and area of control extended to cover great areas of Europe, North Africa, and the Middle East.

Sources

Attributions

CC licensed content, Specific attribution

- Boundless World History. **Authored by**: Boundless. **Located at**: https://courses.lumenlearning.com/boundless-worldhistory/. **License**: *CC BY-SA: Attribution-ShareAlike*

Early Roman Society

Learning Objective

- Describe what Roman society was like in its early years

Key Points

- Roman society was extremely patriarchal and hierarchical. The adult male head of a household had special legal powers and privileges that gave him jurisdiction over all the members of his family.

- The status of freeborn Romans was established by their ancestry, census ranking, and citizenship.

- The most important division within Roman society was between patricians, a small elite who monopolized political power, and plebeians, who comprised the majority of Roman society.

- The Roman census divided citizens into six complex classes based on property holdings.

- Most adult, free-born men within the city limits of Rome held Roman citizenship. Classes of non-citizens existed and held different legal rights.

Terms

tax farming

A technique of financial management in which future, uncertain revenue streams are fixed into periodic rents via assignment by legal contract to a third party.

> *plebeians*
>
> A general body of free Roman citizens who were part of the lower strata of society.
>
> *patricians*
>
> A group of ruling class families in ancient Rome.

Roman society was extremely patriarchal and hierarchical. The adult male head of a household had special legal powers and privileges that gave him jurisdiction over all the members of his family, including his wife, adult sons, adult married daughters, and slaves, but there were multiple, overlapping hierarchies at play within society at large. An individual's relative position in one hierarchy might have been higher or lower than it was in another. The status of freeborn Romans was established by the following:

- Their ancestry
- Their census rank, which in turn was determined by the individual's wealth and political privilege
- Citizenship, of which there were grades with varying rights and privileges

Ancestry

The most important division within Roman society was between patricians, a small elite who monopolized political power, and plebeians, who comprised the majority of Roman society. These designations were established at birth, with patricians tracing their ancestry back to the first Senate established under Romulus. Adult, male non-citizens fell outside the realms of these divisions, but women and children, who were also not considered formal citizens, took the social status of their father or husband. Originally, all public offices were only open to patricians and the classes could not intermarry, but, over time, the differentiation between patrician and plebeian statuses became less pronounced, particularly after the establishment of the Roman republic.

Census Rankings

The Roman census divided citizens into six complex classes based on property holdings. The richest class was called the senatorial class, with wealth based on ownership of large agricultural estates, since members of the highest social classes did not traditionally engage in commercial activity. Below the senatorial class was the equestrian order, comprised of members who held the same volume of wealth as the senatorial classes, but who engaged in commerce, making them an influential early business class. Certain political and quasi-political positions were filled by members of the equestrian order, including tax farming and leadership of the Praetorian Guard. Three additional property-owning classes occupied the rungs beneath the equestrian order. Finally, the *proletarii* occupied the bottom rung with the lowest property values in the kingdom.

Citizenship

Citizenship in ancient Rome afforded political and legal privileges to free individuals with respect to laws, property, and governance. Most adult, free-born men within the city limits of Rome held Roman citizenship. Men who lived in towns outside of Rome might also hold citizenship, but some lacked the right to vote. Free-born, foreign subjects during this period were known as *peregrini*, and special laws existed to govern their conduct and disputes, though they were not considered Roman citizens during the Roman kingdom period. Free-born women in ancient Rome were considered citizens, but they could not vote or hold political office. The status of woman's citizenship affected the citizenship of her offspring. For example, in a type of Roman marriage called *conubium*, both spouses must be citizens in order to marry. Additionally, the phrase *ex duobus civibus Romanis natos*, translated to mean "children born of two Roman citizens," reinforces the importance of both parents' legal status in determining that of their offspring.

*Roman citizenship. The toga, shown here on
a statue restored with the head of Nerva,
was the distinctive garb of Roman citizens*

Classes of non-citizens existed and held different legal rights. Under Roman law, slaves were considered property and held no rights. However, certain laws did regulate the institution of slavery, and extended protections to slaves that were not granted to other forms of property. Slaves who had been manumitted became freedmen and enjoyed largely the same rights and protections as free-born citizens. Many slaves descended from debtors or prisoners of war, especially women and children who were captured during foreign military campaigns and sieges.

Ironically, many slaves originated from Rome's conquest of Greece, and yet Greek culture was considered, in some respects by the Romans, to be superior to their own. In this way, it seems Romans regarded slavery as a circumstance of birth, misfortune, or war, rather than being limited to, or defined by, ethnicity or race. Because it was defined mainly in terms of a lack of legal rights and status, it was also not considered a permanent or inescapable position. Some who had received educations or learned skills that allowed them to earn their own living were manumitted upon the death of their owner, or allowed to earn money to buy their freedom during their owner's lifetime. Some slave owners also freed slaves who they believed to be their natural children. Nonetheless, many worked under harsh conditions, and/or suffered inhumanely under their owners during their enslavement.

Most freed slaves joined the lower plebeian classes, and worked as farmers or tradesmen, though as time progressed and their numbers increased, many were also accepted into the equestrian class. Some went on to populate the civil service, whereas others engaged in commerce, amassing vast fortunes that were rivaled only by those in the wealthiest classes.

Sources

Attributions

The Establishment of the Roman Republic

Learning Objective
• Explain why and how Rome transitioned from a monarchy to a republic

Key Points
• The Roman monarchy was overthrown around 509 BCE, during a political revolution that resulted in the expulsion of Lucius Tarquinius Superbus, the last king of Rome.   • Despite waging a number of successful campaigns against Rome's neighbors, securing Rome's position as head of the Latin cities, and engaging in a series of public works, Tarquinius was a very unpopular king, due to his violence and abuses of power.   • When word spread that Tarquinius's son raped Lucretia, the wife of the governor of Collatia, an uprising occurred in which a number of prominent patricians argued for a change in government.   • A general election was held during a legal assembly, and participants voted in favor of the establishment of a Roman republic.   • Subsequently, all Tarquins were exiled from Rome and an interrex and two consuls were established to lead the new republic.

Terms

interrex

Literally, this translates to mean a ruler that presides over the period between the rule of two separate kings; or, in other words, a short-term regent.

plebeians

A general body of free Roman citizens who were part of the lower strata of society.

patricians

A group of ruling class families in ancient Rome.

The Roman monarchy was overthrown around 509 BCE, during a political revolution that resulted in the expulsion of Lucius Tarquinius Superbus, the last king of Rome. Subsequently, the Roman Republic was established.

Background

Tarquinius was the son of Lucius Tarquinius Priscus, the fifth king of Rome's Seven Kings period. Tarquinius was married to Tullia Minor, the daughter of Servius Tullius, the sixth king of Rome's Seven Kings period. Around 535 BCE, Tarquinius and his wife, Tullia Minor, arranged for the murder of his father-in-law. Tarquinius became king following Servius Tullius's death.

Tarquinius waged a number of successful campaigns against Rome's neighbors, including the Volsci, Gabii, and the Rutuli. He also secured Rome's position as head of the Latin cities, and engaged in a series of public works, such as the completion of the Temple of Jupiter Optimus Maximus. However, Tarquinius remained an unpopular king for a number of reasons. He refused to bury his predecessor and executed a number of leading senators whom he suspected remained loyal to Servius. Following these actions, he refused to replace the senators he executed and refused to consult the Senate in matters of government going forward, thus diminishing the size and influence of the Senate greatly. He also went on to judge capital criminal cases without the advice of his counselors, stoking fear among his political opponents that they would be unfairly targeted.

The Rape of Lucretia and An Uprising

Tarquin and Lucretia. Titian's Tarquin and Lucretia (1571).

During Tarquinius's war with the Rutuli, his son, Sextus Tarquinius, was sent on a military errand to Colla-tia, where he was received with great hospitality at the governor's mansion. The governor's wife, Lucretia, hosted Sextus while the governor was away at war. During the night, Sextus entered her bedroom and raped her. The next day, Lucretia traveled to her father, Spurius Lucretius, a distinguished prefect in Rome, and, before witnesses, informed him of what had happened. Because her father was a chief magistrate of Rome, her pleas for justice and vengeance could not be ignored. At the end of her pleas, she stabbed herself in the heart with a dagger, ultimately dying in her own father's arms. The scene struck those who had witnessed it with such horror that they collectively vowed to publicly defend their liberty against the outrages of such tyrants.

Lucius Junius Brutus, a leading citizen and the grandson of Rome's fifth king, Tarquinius Priscus, publicly opened a debate on the form of government that Rome should have in place of the existing monarchy. A number of patricians attended the debate, in which Brutus proposed the banishment of the Tarquins from all territories of Rome, and the appointment of an interrex to nominate new magistrates and to oversee an election of ratification. It was decided that a republican form of government should temporarily replace the monarchy, with two consuls replacing the king and executing the will of a patrician senate. Spurius Lucretius was elected interrex, and he proposed Brutus, and Lucius Tarquinius Collatinus, a leading citizen who was also related to Tarquinius Priscus, as the first two consuls. His choice was ratified by the *comitia curiata*, an organization of patrician families who primarily ratified decrees of the king.

In order to rally the plebeians to their cause, all were summoned to a legal assembly in the forum, and Lucretia's body was paraded through the streets. Brutus gave a speech and a general election was held. The results were in favor of a republic. Brutus left Lucretius in command of the city as interrex, and pursued the king in Ardea where he had been positioned with his army on campaign. Tarquinius, however, who had heard of developments in Rome, fled the camp before Brutus arrived, and the army received Brutus favorably, expelling the king's sons from their encampment. Tarquinius was subsequently refused entry into Rome and lived as an exile with his family.

The Establishment of the Republic

Brutus and Lucretia. The statue shows Brutus holding the knife and swearing the oath, with Lucretia.

Although there is no scholarly agreement as to whether or not it actually took place, Plutarch and Appian both claim that Brutus's first act as consul was to initiate an oath for the people, swearing never again to allow a king to rule Rome. What is known for certain is that he replenished the Senate to its original number of 300 senators, recruiting men from among the equestrian class. The new consuls also created a separate office, called the rex sacrorum, to carry out and oversee religious duties, a task that had previously fallen to the king.

The two consuls continued to be elected annually by Roman citizens and advised by the senate. Both consuls were elected for one-year terms and could veto each other's actions. Initially, they were endowed with all the powers of kings past, though over time these were broken down further by the addition of magistrates to the governmental system. The first magistrate added was the praetor, an office that assumed judicial authority from the consuls. After the praetor, the censor was established, who assumed the power to conduct the Roman census.

Sources

Attributions

CC licensed content, Specific attribution

- Boundless World History. **Authored by**: Boundless. **Located at**: https://courses.lumenlearning.com/boundless-worldhistory/. **License**: *CC BY-SA: Attribution-ShareAlike*

Structure of the Republic

- Describe the political structure of the Roman Republic

Key Points

- The Constitution of the Roman Republic was a set of guidelines and principles passed down, mainly through precedent. The constitution was largely unwritten and uncodified, and evolved over time.

- Roman citizenship was a vital prerequisite to possessing many important legal rights.The Senate passed decrees that were called *senatus consulta*, ostensibly "advice" from the senate to a magistrate. The focus of the Roman Senate was usually foreign policy.

- There were two types of legislative assemblies. The first was the *comitia* ("committees"), which were assemblies of all Roman citizens. The second was the *concilia* ("councils"), which were assemblies of specific groups of citizens.

- The *comitia centuriata* was the assembly of the centuries (soldiers), and they elected magistrates who had imperium powers (consuls and praetors). The *comitia tributa*, or assembly of the tribes (the citizens of Rome), was presided over by a consul and composed of 35 tribes. They elected quaestors, curule aediles, and military tribunes.

- Dictators were sometimes elected during times of military emergency, during which the constitutional government would be disbanded.

Terms

patricians

A group of ruling class families in ancient Rome.

plebeian

A general body of free Roman citizens who were part of the lower strata of society.

Roman Senate

A political institution in the ancient Roman Republic. It was not an elected body, but one whose members were appointed by the consuls, and later by the censors.

The Constitution of the Roman Republic was a set of guidelines and principles passed down, mainly through precedent. The constitution was largely unwritten and uncodified, and evolved over time. Rather than creating a government that was primarily a democracy (as was ancient Athens), an aristocracy (as was ancient Sparta), or a monarchy (as was Rome before, and in many respects after, the Republic), the Roman constitution mixed these three elements of governance into their overall political system. The democratic element took the form of legislative assemblies; the aristocratic element took the form of the Senate; and the monarchical element took the form of the many term-limited consuls.

The Roman SPQR Banner. "SPQR" (senatus populusque romanus) was the Roman motto, which stood for "the Senate and people of Rome."

The Roman Senate

The Senate's ultimate authority derived from the esteem and prestige of the senators, and was based on both precedent and custom. The Senate passed decrees, which were called *senatus consulta*, ostensibly "advice" handed down from the senate to a magistrate. In practice, the magistrates usually followed the *senatus consulta*. The focus of the Roman Senate was usually foreign policy. However, the power of the Senate expanded over time as the power of the legislative assemblies declined, and eventually the Senate took a greater role in civil law-making. Senators were usually appointed by Roman censors, but during times of military emergency, such as the civil wars of the 1st century BCE, this practice became less prevalent, and the Roman dictator, triumvir, or the Senate itself would select its members.

Curia Iulia—the Roman Senate House. The Curia Julia in the Roman Forum, the seat of the imperial Senate.

Legislative Assemblies

Roman citizenship was a vital prerequisite to possessing many important legal rights, such as the rights to trial and appeal, marriage, suffrage, to hold office, to enter binding contracts, and to enjoy special tax exemptions. An adult male citizen with full legal and political rights was called *optimo jure*. The *optimo jure* elected assemblies, and the assemblies elected magistrates, enacted legislation, presided over trials in capital cases, declared war and peace, and forged or dissolved treaties. There were two types of legislative assemblies. The first was the *comitia* ("committees"), which were assemblies of all *optimo jure*. The second was the *concilia* ("councils"), which were assemblies of specific groups of *optimo jure*.

Citizens on these assemblies were organized further on the basis of curiae (familial groupings), centuries (for military purposes), and tribes (for civil purposes), and each would each gather into their own assemblies. The Curiate Assembly served only a symbolic purpose in the late Republic, though the assembly was used to ratify the powers of newly elected magistrates by passing laws known as *leges curiatae*. The *comitia centuriata* was the assembly of the centuries (soldiers). The president of the *comitia centuriata* was usually a consul, and the *comitia centuriata* would elect magistrates who had imperium powers (consuls and praetors). It also elected censors. Only the *comitia centuriata* could declare war and ratify the results of a census. It also served as the highest court of appeal in certain judicial cases.

The assembly of the tribes, the *comitia tributa*, was presided over by a consul, and was composed of 35 tribes. The tribes were not ethnic or kinship groups, but rather geographical subdivisions. While it did not pass many laws, the *comitia tributa* did elect quaestors, curule aediles, and military tribunes. The Plebeian Council was identical to the assembly of the tribes, but excluded the patricians. They elected their own officers, plebeian tribunes, and plebeian aediles. Usually a plebeian tribune would preside over the assembly. This assembly passed most laws, and could also act as a court of appeal.

Since the tribunes were considered to be the embodiment of the plebeians, they were sacrosanct. Their sacrosanctness was enforced by a pledge, taken by the plebeians, to kill any person who harmed or interfered with a tribune during his term of office. As such, it was considered a capital offense to harm a tribune, to disregard his veto, or to interfere with his actions. In times of military emergency, a dictator would be appointed for a term of six months. The constitutional government would be dissolved, and the dictator would be the absolute master of the state. When the dictator's term ended, constitutional government would be restored.

Executive Magistrates

Magistrates were the elected officials of the Roman republic. Each magistrate was vested with a degree of power, and the dictator, when there was one, had the highest level of power. Below the dictator was the censor (when they existed), and the consuls, the highest ranking ordinary magistrates. Two were elected every year and wielded supreme power in both civil and military powers. The ranking among both consuls flipped every month, with one outranking the other.

Below the consuls were the praetors, who administered civil law, presided over the courts, and commanded provincial armies. Censors conducted the Roman census, during which time they could appoint people to the Senate. Curule aediles were officers elected to conduct domestic affairs in Rome, who were vested with powers over the markets, public games, and shows. Finally, at the bottom of magistrate rankings were the quaestors, who usually assisted the consuls in Rome and the governors in the provinces with financial tasks. Plebeian tribunes and plebeian aediles were considered representatives of the people, and acted as a popular check over the Senate through use of their veto powers, thus safeguarding the civil liberties of all Roman citizens.

Each magistrate could only veto an action that was taken by an equal or lower ranked magistrate. The most significant constitutional power a magistrate could hold was that of imperium or command, which was held only by consuls and praetors. This gave the magistrate in question the constitutional authority to issue commands, military or otherwise.

Election to a magisterial office resulted in automatic membership in the Senate for life, unless impeached. Once a magistrate's annual term in office expired, he had to wait at least ten years before serving in that office again. Occasionally, however, a magistrate would have his command powers extended through prorogation, which effectively allowed him to retain the powers of his office as a promagistrate.

Sources

Attributions

CC licensed content, Specific attribution

- Boundless World History. **Authored by**: Boundless. **Located at**: https://courses.lumenlearning.com/boundless-worldhistory/. **License**: *CC BY-SA: Attribution-ShareAlike*

Roman Society Under the Republic

Learning Objective

- Describe the relationship between the government and the people in the time of the Roman Republic

Key Points

- A number of developments affected the relationship between Rome's republican government and society, particularly in regard to how that relationship differed among patricians and plebeians.

- In 494 BCE, plebeian soldiers refused to march against a wartime enemy, in order to demand the right to elect their own officials.

- The passage of Lex Trebonia forbade the co-opting of colleagues to fill vacant positions on tribunes in order to sway voting in favor of patrician blocs over plebeians.

- Throughout the 4th century BCE, a series of reforms were passed that required all laws passed by the plebeian council to have the full force of law over the entire population. This gave the plebeian tribunes a positive political impact over the entire population for the first time in Roman history.

- In 445 BCE, the plebeians demanded the right to stand for election as consul. Ultimately, a compromise was reached in which consular command authority was granted to a select number of military tribunes.

- The Licinio-Sextian law was passed in 367 BCE; it addressed the economic plight of the plebeians and prevented the election of further patrician magistrates.

- In the decades following the passage of the Licinio-Sextian law, further legislation was enacted that granted political equality to the plebeians. Nonetheless, it remained difficult for a plebeian from an unknown family to enter the Senate, due to the rise of a new patricio-plebeian aristocracy that was less interested in the plight of the average plebeian.

Terms

plebeian

A general body of free Roman citizens who were part of the lower strata of society.

patricians

A group of ruling class families in ancient Rome.

In the first few centuries of the Roman Republic, a number of developments affected the relationship between the government and the Roman people, particularly in regard to how that relationship differed across the separate strata of society.

The Patrician Era (509-367 BCE)

The last king of Rome, Lucius Tarquinius Superbus, was overthrown in 509 BCE. One of the biggest changes that occurred as a result was the establishment of two chief magistrates, called consuls, who were elected by the citizens of Rome for an annual term. This stood in stark contrast to the previous system, in which a king was elected by senators, for life. Built in to the consul system were checks on authority, since each consul could provide balance to the decisions made by his colleague. Their limited terms of office also opened them up to the possibility of prosecution in the event of abuses of power. However, when consuls exercised their political powers in tandem, the magnitude and influence they wielded was hardly different from that of the old kings.

In 494 BCE, Rome was at war with two neighboring tribes, and plebeian soldiers refused to march against the enemy, instead seceding to the Aventine Hill. There, the plebeian soldiers took advantage of the situation to demand the right to elect their own officials. The patricians assented to their demands, and the plebeian soldiers returned to battle. The new offices that were created as a result came to be known as "plebeian tribunes," and they were to be assisted by "plebeian aediles."

In the early years of the republic, plebeians were not permitted to hold magisterial office. Tribunes and aediles were technically not magistrates, since they were only elected by fellow plebeians, as opposed to the unified population of plebeians and patricians. Although plebeian tribunes regularly attempted to block legislation they considered unfavorable, patricians could still override their veto with the support of one or more other tribunes. Tension over this imbalance of power led to the passage of Lex Trebonia, which forbade the co-opting of colleagues to fill vacant positions on tribunes in order to sway voting in favor of one or another bloc. Throughout the 4th century BCE, a series of reforms were passed that required all laws passed by the plebeian council to have equal force over the entire population, regardless of status as patrician or plebeian. This gave the plebeian tribunes a positive political impact over the entire population for the first time in Roman history.

Gaius Gracchus. This 18th century drawing shows Gaius Gracchus, tribune of the people, presiding over the plebeian council.

In 445 BCE, the plebeians demanded the right to stand for election as consul. The Roman Senate initially refused them this right, but ultimately a compromise was reached in which consular command authority was granted to a select number of military tribunes, who, in turn, were elected by the centuriate assembly with veto power being retained by the senate.

Around 400 BCE, during a series of wars that were fought against neighboring tribes, the plebeians demanded concessions for the disenfranchisement they experienced as foot soldiers fighting for spoils of war that they were never to see. As a result, the Licinio-Sextian law was eventually passed in 367 BCE, which addressed the economic plight of the plebeians and prevented the election of further patrician magistrates.

The Conflict of the Orders Ends (367-287 BCE)

In the decades following the passage of the Licinio-Sextian law, further legislation was enacted that granted political equality to the plebeians. Nonetheless, it remained difficult for a plebeian from an unknown family to enter the Senate. In fact, the very presence of a long-standing nobility, and the Roman population's deep respect for it, made it very difficult for individuals from unknown families to be elected to high office.

Additionally, elections could be expensive, neither senators nor magistrates were paid for their services, and the Senate usually did not reimburse magistrates for expenses incurred during their official duties, providing many barriers to the entry of high political office by the non-affluent.

Ultimately, a new patricio-plebeian aristocracy emerged and replaced the old patrician nobility. Whereas the old patrician nobility existed simply on the basis of being able to run for office, the new aristocracy existed on the basis of affluence. Although a small number of plebeians had achieved the same standing as the patrician families of the past, new plebeian aristocrats were less interested in the plight of the average plebeian than were the old patrician aristocrats. For a time, the plebeian plight was mitigated, due higher employment, income, and patriotism that was wrought by a series of wars in which Rome was engaged; these things eliminated the threat of plebeian unrest. But by 287 BCE, the economic conditions of the plebeians deteriorated as a result of widespread indebtedness, and the plebeians sought relief. Roman senators, most of whom were also creditors, refused to give in to the plebeians' demands, resulting in the first plebeian secession to Janiculum Hill.

In order to end the plebeian secession, a dictator, Quintus Hortensius, was appointed. Hortensius, who was himself a plebeian, passed a law known as the "Hortensian Law." This law ended the requirement that an *auctoritas patrum* be passed before a bill could be considered by either the plebeian council or the tribal assembly, thus removing the final patrician senatorial check on the plebeian council. The requirement was not changed, however, in the centuriate assembly. This provided a loophole through which the patrician senate could still deter plebeian legislative influence.

Sources

Attributions

CC licensed content, Specific attribution

- Boundless World History. **Authored by**: Boundless. **Located at**: https://courses.lumenlearning.com/boundless-worldhistory/. **License**: *CC BY-SA: Attribution-ShareAlike*

Republican Wars and Conquest

Key Points

- Early Roman Republican wars were wars of both expansion and defense, aimed at protecting Rome from neighboring cities and nations, and establishing its territory within the region.

- The Samnite Wars were fought against the Etruscans and effectively finished off all vestiges of Etruscan power by 282 BCE.

- By the middle of the 3rd century and the end of the Pyrrhic War, Rome had effectively dominated the Italian peninsula and won an international military reputation.

- Over the course of the three Punic Wars, Rome completely defeated Hannibal and razed Carthage to the ground, thereby acquiring all of Carthage's North African and Spanish territories.

- After four Macedonian Wars, Rome had established its first permanent foothold in the Greek world, and divided the Macedonian Kingdom into four client republics.

Terms

Punic Wars

A series of three wars fought between Rome and Carthage, from 264 BCE to 146 BCE, that resulted in the complete destruction of Carthage.

Pyrrhus

Greek general and statesman of the Hellenistic era. Later he became king of Epirus (r. 306-302, 297-272 BCE) and Macedon (r. 288-284, 273-272 BCE). He was one of the strongest opponents of early Rome. Some of his battles, though successful, cost him heavy losses, from which the term "Pyrrhic victory" was coined.

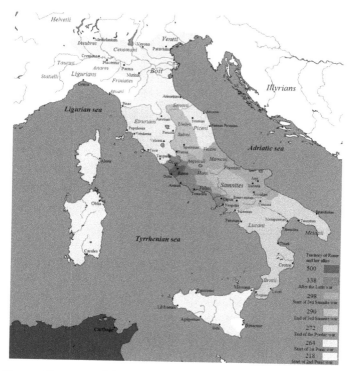

Roman Conquest of the Italian Peninsula. This map shows the expansion of Roman territory through the various wars fought during the Republican period.

Early Republic

Early Campaigns (458-396 BCE)

The first Roman Republican wars were wars of both expansion and defense, aimed at protecting Rome from neighboring cities and nations, as well as establishing its territory in the region. Initially, Rome's immediate neighbors were either Latin towns and villages or tribal Sabines from the Apennine hills beyond. One by one, Rome defeated both the persistent Sabines and the nearby Etruscan and Latin cities. By the end of this period, Rome had effectively secured its position against all immediate threats.

Expansion into Italy and the Samnite Wars (343-282 BCE)

The First Samnite War, of 343 BCE-341 BCE, was a relatively short affair. The Romans beat the Samnites in two battles, but were forced to withdraw from the war before they could pursue the conflict further, due to the revolt of several of their Latin allies in the Latin War. The Second Samnite War, from 327 BCE-304 BCE, was much longer and more serious for both the Romans and Samnites, but by 304 BCE the Romans had effectively annexed the greater part of the Samnite territory and founded several colonies therein. Seven years after their defeat, with Roman dominance of the area seemingly assured, the Samnites rose again and defeated a Roman army in 298 BCE, to open the Third Samnite War. With this success in hand, they managed to bring together a coalition of several of Rome's enemies, but by 282 BCE, Rome finished off the last vestiges of Etruscan power in the region.

Pyrrhic War (280-275 BCE)

By the beginning of the 3rd century BCE, Rome had established itself as a major power on the Italian Peninsula, but had not yet come into conflict with the dominant military powers in the Mediterranean Basin at the time: the Carthage and Greek kingdoms. When a diplomatic dispute between Rome and a Greek colony erupted into a naval confrontation, the Greek colony appealed for military aid to Pyrrhus, ruler of the northwestern Greek kingdom of Epirus. Motivated by a personal desire for military accomplishment, Pyrrhus landed a Greek army of approximately 25,000 men on Italian soil in 280 BCE. Despite early victories, Pyrrhus found his position in Italy untenable. Rome steadfastly refused to negotiate with Pyrrhus as long as his army remained in Italy. Facing unacceptably heavy losses with each encounter with the Roman army, Pyrrhus withdrew from the peninsula (thus giving rise to the term "pyrrhic victory").

In 275 BCE, Pyrrhus again met the Roman army at the Battle of Beneventum. While Beneventum's outcome was indecisive, it led to Pyrrhus's complete withdrawal from Italy, due to the decimation of his army following years of foreign campaigns, and the diminishing likelihood of further material gains. These conflicts with Pyrrhus would have a positive effect on Rome. Rome had shown it was capable of pitting its armies successfully against the dominant military powers of the Mediterranean, and that the Greek kingdoms were incapable of defending their colonies in Italy and abroad. Rome quickly moved into southern Italia, subjugating and dividing the Greek colonies. By the middle of the 3rd century, Rome effectively dominated the Italian peninsula, and had won an international military reputation.

Mid-Republic

Punic Wars

The First Punic War began in 264 BCE, when Rome and Carthage became interested in using settlements within Sicily to solve their own internal conflicts. The war saw land battles in Sicily early on, but focus soon shifted to naval battles around Sicily and Africa. Before the First Punic War, there was essentially no Roman navy. The new war in Sicily against Carthage, a great naval power, forced Rome to quickly build a fleet and train sailors. Though the first few naval battles of the First Punic War were catastrophic disasters for Rome, Rome was eventually able to beat the Carthaginians and leave them without a fleet or sufficient funds to raise another. For a maritime power, the loss of Carthage's access to the Mediterranean stung financially and psychologically, leading the Carthaginians to sue for peace.

Continuing distrust led to the renewal of hostilities in the Second Punic War, when, in 218 BCE, Carthaginian commander Hannibal attacked a Spanish town with diplomatic ties to Rome. Hannibal then crossed the Italian Alps to invade Italy. Hannibal's successes in Italy began immediately, but his brother, Hasdrubal, was defeated after he crossed the Alps on the Metaurus River. Unable to defeat Hannibal on Italian soil, the Romans boldly sent an army to Africa under Scipio Africanus, with the intention of threatening the Carthaginian capital. As a result, Hannibal was recalled to Africa, and defeated at the Battle of Zama.

Carthage never managed to recover after the Second Punic War, and the Third Punic War that followed was, in reality, a simple punitive mission to raze the city of Carthage to the ground. Carthage was almost defenseless, and when besieged offered immediate surrender, conceding to a string of outrageous Roman demands. The Romans refused the surrender and the city was stormed and completely destroyed after a short siege. Ultimately, all of Carthage's North African and Spanish territories were acquired by Rome.

Hannibal's Famous Crossing of the Alps. Depiction of Hannibal and his army crossing the Alps during the Second Punic War.

Macedon and Greece

Rome's preoccupation with its war in Carthage provided an opportunity for Philip V of the kingdom of Macedonia, located in the northern part of the Greek peninsula, to attempt to extend his power westward. Over the next several decades, Rome clashed with Macedon to protect their Greek allies throughout the First, Second, and Third Macedonian Wars. By 168 BCE, the Macedonians had been thoroughly defeated, and Rome divided the Macedonian Kingdom into four client republics. After a Fourth Macedonian War, and nearly a century of constant crisis management in Greece (which almost always was a result of internal instability when Rome pulled out), Rome decided to divide Macedonia into two new Roman provinces, Achaea and Epirus.

Sources

Attributions

CC licensed content, Specific attribution

- Boundless World History. **Authored by**: Boundless. **Located at**: https://courses.lumenlearning.com/boundless-worldhistory/. **License**: *CC BY-SA: Attribution-ShareAlike*

Crises of the Republic

Learning Objective

- Explain how crises in the 1st century BCE further destabilized the Roman Republic

Key Points

- Though the causes and attributes of individual crises varied throughout the decades, an underlying theme of conflict between the aristocracy and ordinary citizens drove the majority of actions.

- The Gracchi brothers, Tiberius and Gaius, introduced a number of populist agrarian and land reforms in the 130s and 120s BCE that were heavily opposed by the patrician Senate. Both brothers were murdered by mob violence after political stalemates.

- Political instability continued, as populist Marius and optimate Sulla engaged in a series of conflicts that culminated in Sulla seizing power and marching to Asia Minor against the decrees of the Senate, and Marius seizing power in a coup back at Rome.

- The Catilinarian Conspiracy discredited the populist party, in turn repairing the image of the Senate, which had come to be seen as weak and not worthy of such violent attack.

- Under the terms of the First Triumvirate, Pompey's arrangements would be ratified and Caesar would be elected consul in 59 BCE; he subsequently served as governor of Gaul for five years. Crassus was promised the consulship later.

- The triumvirate crumbled in the wake of growing political violence and Crassus and Caesar's daughter's death.

- A resolution was passed by the Senate that declared that if Caesar did not lay down his arms by July 49 BCE, he would be considered an enemy of the Republic. Meanwhile, Pompey was granted dictatorial powers over the Republic.

- On January 10, 49 BCE, Caesar crossed the Rubicon and marched towards Rome. Pompey, the consuls, and the Senate all abandoned Rome for Greece, and Caesar entered the city unopposed.

Terms

Gracchi Brothers

Brothers Tiberius and Gaius, Roman plebeian nobiles who both served as tribunes in the late 2nd century BCE. They attempted to pass land reform legislation that would redistribute the major patrician landholdings among the plebeians.

plebeian

A general body of free Roman citizens who were part of the lower strata of society.

patrician

A group of ruling class families in ancient Rome.

The Crises of the Roman Republic refers to an extended period of political instability and social unrest that culminated in the demise of the Roman Republic, and the advent of the Roman Empire from about 134 BCE-44 BCE. The exact dates of this period of crisis are unclear or are in dispute from scholar to scholar. Though the causes and attributes of individual crises varied throughout the decades, an underlying theme of conflict between the aristocracy and ordinary citizens drove the majority of actions.

Optimates were a traditionalist majority of the late Roman Republic. They wished to limit the power of the popular assemblies and the Tribune of the Plebeians, and to extend the power of the Senate, which was viewed as more dedicated to the interests of the aristocrats. In particular, they were concerned with the rise of individual generals, who, backed by the tribunate, the assemblies, and their own soldiers, could shift power from the Senate and aristocracy. Many members of this faction were so-classified because they used the backing of the aristocracy and the Senate to achieve personal goals, not necessarily because they favored the aristocracy over the lower classes. Similarly, the populists did not necessarily champion the lower classes, but often used their support to achieve personal goals.

Following a period of great military successes and economic failures of the early Republican period, many plebeian calls for reform among the classes had been quieted. However, many new slaves were being imported from abroad, causing an unemployment crisis among the lower classes. A flood of unemployed citizens entered Rome, giving rise to populist ideas throughout the city.

The Gracchi Brothers

Tiberius Gracchus took office as a tribune of the plebeians in late 134 BCE. At the time, Roman society was a highly stratified class system with tensions bubbling below the surface. This system consisted of noble families of the senatorial rank (patricians), the knight or equestrian class, citizens (grouped into two or three classes of self-governing allies of Rome: landowners; and plebs, or tenant freemen, depending on the time period), non-citizens who lived outside of southwestern Italy, and at the bottom, slaves. The government owned large tracts of farm land that it had gained through invasion or escheat. This land was rented out to either large landowners whose slaves tilled the land, or small tenant farmers who occupied the property on the basis of a sub-lease. Beginning in 133 BCE, Tiberius tried to redress the grievances of displaced small tenant farmers. He bypassed the Roman Senate, and passed a law limiting the amount of land belonging to the state that any individual could farm, which resulted in the dissolution of large plantations maintained by rich landowners on public land.

A political back-and-forth ensued in the Senate as the other tribune, Octavius, blocked Tiberius's initiatives, and the Senate denied funds needed for land reform. When Tiberius sought re-election to his one-year term (an unprecedented action), the oligarchic nobles responded by murdering Tiberius, and mass riots broke out in the city in reaction to the assassination. About nine years later, Tiberius Gracchus's younger brother, Gaius, passed more radical reforms in favor of the poorer plebeians. Once again, the situation ended in violence and murder as Gaius fled Rome and was either murdered by oligarchs or committed suicide. The deaths of the Gracchi brothers marked the beginning of a late Republic trend in which tensions and conflicts erupted in violence.

Gaius Gracchus Addressing the People. Silvestre David Mirys' rendition of the the tribune, Gaius Gracchus, addressing the people of Rome.

Marius and Sulla

The next major reformer of the time was Gaius Marius, who like the Gracchi, was a populist who championed the lower classes. He was a general who abolished the property requirement for becoming a soldier, which allowed the poor to enlist in large numbers. Lucius Cornelius Sulla was appointed as Marius's quaestor (supervisor of the financial affairs of the state) in 107 BCE, and later competed with Marius for supreme power. Over the next few decades, he and Marius engaged in a series of conflicts that culminated in Sulla seizing power and marching to Asia Minor against the decrees of the Senate. Marius launched a coup in Sulla's absence, putting to death some of his enemies and instituting a populist regime, but died soon after.

Bust of Sulla. The bust of Lucius Cornelius Sulla, an optimate who marched against Rome and installed himself as dictator in 82-81 BCE.

Pompey, Crassus, and the Catilinarian Conspiracy

In 77 BCE, two of Sulla's former lieutenants, Gnaeus Pompeius Magnus ("Pompey the Great") and Marcus Licinius Crassus, had left Rome to put down uprisings and found the populist party, attacking Sulla's constitution upon their return. In an attempt to forge an agreement with the populist party, both lieutenants promised to dismantle components of Sulla's constitution that the populists found disagreeable, in return for being elected consul. The two were elected in 70 BCE and held true to their word. Four years later, in

66 BCE, a movement to use peaceful means to address the plights of the various classes arose; however, after several failures in achieving their goals, the movement, headed by Lucius Sergius Catilina and based in Faesulae, a hotbed of agrarian agitation, decided to march to Rome and instigate an uprising. Marcus Tullius Cicero, the consul at the time, intercepted messages regarding recruitment and plans, leading the Senate to authorize the assassination of many Catilinarian conspirators in Rome, an action that was seen as stemming from dubious authority. This effectively disrupted the conspiracy and discredited the populist party, in turn repairing the image of the Senate, which had come to be seen as weak and not worthy of such violent attack.

First Triumvirate

In 62 BCE, Pompey returned from campaigning in Asia to find that the Senate, elated by its successes against the Catiline conspirators, was unwilling to ratify any of Pompey's arrangements, leaving Pompey powerless. Julius Caesar returned from his governorship in Spain a year later and, along with Crassus, established a private agreement with Pompey known as the First Triumvirate. Under the terms of this agreement, Pompey's arrangements would be ratified and Caesar would be elected consul in 59 BCE, subsequently serving as governor of Gaul for five years. Crassus was promised the consulship later.

When Caesar became consul, he saw the passage of Pompey's arrangements through the Senate, at times using violent means to ensure their passage. Caesar also facilitated the election of patrician Publius Clodius Pulcher to the tribunate in 58 BCE, and Clodius sidelined Caesar's senatorial opponents, Cato and Cicero. Clodius eventually formed armed gangs that terrorized Rome and began to attack Pompey's followers, who formed counter-gangs in response, marking the end of the political alliance between Pompey and Caeser. Though the triumvirate was briefly renewed in the face of political opposition for the consulship from Domitius Ahenobarbus, Crassus's death during an expedition against the Kingdom of Parthia, and the death of Pompey's wife, Julia, who was also Caesar's daughter, severed any remaining bonds between Pompey and Caesar.

Beginning in the summer of 54 BCE, a wave of political corruption and violence swept Rome, reaching a climax in January 52 BCE, when Clodius was murdered in a gang war. Caesar presented an ultimatum to the Senate on January 1, 49 BCE, which was ultimately rejected. Subsequently, a resolution was passed that declared that if Caesar did not lay down his arms by July, he would be considered an enemy of the Republic. The senators adopted Pompey as their champion, and on January 7, Pompey was granted dictatorial powers over the Republic by the Senate. Pompey's army, however, was composed mainly of untested conscripts, and on January 10, Caesar crossed the Rubicon with his more experienced forces in defiance of Roman laws, and marched towards Rome. Pompey, the consuls, and the Senate all abandoned Rome for Greece, in the face of Caeser's rapidly advancing forces, and Caesar entered the city unopposed.

Sources

Attributions

CC licensed content, Specific attribution

- Boundless World History. **Authored by**: Boundless. **Located at**: https://courses.lumenlearning.com/boundless-worldhistory/. **License**: *CC BY-SA: Attribution-ShareAlike*

6. The Roman Empire

Julius Caesar

Learning Objective

- Explain the rise of Julius Caesar and his various successes

Key Points

- In 60 BCE, Julius Caesar, Marcus Licinius Crassus, and Gnaeus Pompeius Magnus (Pompey the Great) formed a political alliance, known as the First Triumvirate, that was to dominate Roman politics for several years, though their populist tactics were opposed by the conservative Senate.

- Caesar enjoyed great success as commander in the Gallic Wars. Upon conclusion of the wars, he refused to return to Rome as ordered by the Senate, and instead, crossed the Rubicon in 49 BCE with a legion, entering Roman territory under arms.

- Caesar fought in a civil war against his old colleague, Pompey, who had aligned himself with conservative interests in the Senate. Caesar quickly defeated his rival and many other Senate conservatives who had previously opposed him.

- With most of his enemies gone, Caesar installed himself as dictator in perpetuity. As dictator, he instituted a series of reforms and, most notably, created the Julian calendar.

- Caesar was assassinated in 44 BCE by his remaining enemies in the Senate, throwing Rome into another period of chaos and civil war.

Terms

dictator

During Caesar's time, in the late Roman Republic, ruler for life. In the early Republic, by contrast, a dictator was a general appointed by the Senate, who served temporarily during a national emergency.

Julius Caesar

A Roman general, statesman, consul, and author, who played a critical role in the events that led to the demise of the Roman Republic and the rise of the Roman Empire.

Pompey

A military and political leader of the late Roman Republic, who represented the Roman Senate in a civil war against Julius Caesar.

Gaius Julius Caesar was a Roman general, statesman, consul, and notable author of Latin prose. He played a critical role in the events that led to the demise of the Roman Republic and the rise of the Roman Empire. In 60 BCE, Caesar, Marcus Licinius Crassus, and Gnaeus Pompeius Magnus (Pompey the Great) formed a political alliance, known as the First Triumvirate, that was to dominate Roman politics for several years. Caesar made the initial overtures that led to the informal alliance. An acclaimed military commander who had also served in a variety of political offices, Caesar sought election as consul in 59 BCE, along with two other candidates. The election was particularly contentious, with corruption occurring on all sides. Caesar won, as well as conservative Marcus Bibulus, but saw that he could further his political influence with Crassus and Pompey. Their attempts to amass power through populist tactics were opposed by the conservative ruling class within the Roman Senate, among them Cato the Younger and Cicero. Meanwhile, Caesar's victories in the Gallic Wars, completed by 51 BCE, extended Rome's territory to the English Channel and the Rhine River. Caesar became the first Roman general to cross both when he built a bridge across the Rhine and conducted the first invasion of Britain.

These achievements granted Caesar unmatched military power and threatened to eclipse the standing of his colleague, Pompey, who had realigned himself with the Senate after the death of Crassus in 53 BCE. With the Gallic Wars concluded, the Senate ordered Caesar to step down from his military command and return to Rome. Caesar refused and marked his defiance in 49 BCE by crossing the Rubicon (shallow river in northern Italy) with a legion. In doing so, he deliberately broke the law on imperium and engaged in an open act of insurrection and treason. Civil War ensued, with Pompey representing the Roman Senate forces against Caesar, but Caesar quickly defeated Pompey in 48 BCE, and dispatched Pompey's supporters in the following year. During this time, many staunch Senate conservatives, such as Cato the Younger, were either killed or committed suicide, thereby greatly decreasing the number of optimates in Rome.

Caesar as Dictator

Bust of Julius Caesar. Gaius Julius Caesar was a Roman general, statesman, consul, and notable author of Latin prose.

After assuming control of the government upon the defeat of his enemies in 45 BCE, Caesar began a program of social and governmental reforms that included the creation of the Julian calendar. He centralized the bureaucracy of the Republic and eventually proclaimed himself "dictator in perpetuity." It is important to note that Caesar did not declare himself *rex* (king), but instead, claimed the title of dictator. Contrary to the negative connotations that the modern use of the word evokes, the Roman dictator was appointed by the Senate during times of emergency as a unilateral decision-maker who could act more quickly than the usual bureaucratic processes that the Republican government would allow. Upon bringing the Roman state out of trouble, the dictator would then resign and restore power back to the Senate. Thus, Caesar's declaration ostensibly remained within the Republican framework of power, though the huge amounts of power he had gathered for himself in practice set him up similar to a monarch.

Caesar used his powers to fill the Senate with his own partisans. He also increased the number of magistrates who were elected each year, which created a large pool of experienced magistrates and allowed Caesar to reward his supporters. He used his powers to appoint many new senators, which eventually raised the Senate's membership to 900. All the appointments were of his own partisans, which robbed the senatorial aristocracy of its prestige and made the Senate increasingly subservient to him. To minimize the risk that another general might attempt to challenge him, Caesar passed a law that subjected governors to term limits. All of these changes watered down the power of the Senate, which infuriated those used to aristocratic privilege. Such anger proved to be fuel for Caesar's eventual assassination.

Despite the defeat of most of his conservative enemies, however, underlying political conflicts had not been resolved. On the Ides of March (March 15) 44 BCE, Caesar was scheduled to appear at a session of the Senate, and a group of senators led by Marcus Junius Brutus and Gaius Cassius Longinus conspired to assassinate him. Though some of his assassins may have had ulterior personal vendettas against Caesar, Brutus is said to have acted out of concern for the Republic in the face of what he considered to be a monarchical tyrant. Mark Antony, one of Caesar's generals and administrator of Italy during Caesar's campaigns abroad, learned such a plan existed the night before, and attempted to intercept Caesar, but the plotters anticipated this and arranged to meet him outside the site of the session and detain him him there. Caesar was stabbed 23 times and lay dead on the ground for some time before officials removed his body.

A new series of civil wars broke out following Caesar's assassination, and the constitutional government of the Republic was never restored. Caesar's adopted heir, Octavian, later known as Augustus, rose to sole power, and the era of the Roman Empire began.

Sources

Attributions

CC licensed content, Specific attribution

- Boundless World History. **Authored by**: Boundless. **Located at**: https://courses.lumenlearning.com/boundless-worldhistory/. **License**: *CC BY-SA: Attribution-ShareAlike*

Founding of the Roman Empire

Learning Objective

- Explain the key features of Augustus's reign and the reasons for its successes

Key Points

- Following the assassination of his maternal great-uncle Julius Caesar in 44 BCE, Caesar's will named Octavian as his adopted son and heir when Octavian was only 19 years old.

- By ingratiating himself with his father's legions, Octavian was able to fulfill the military demands of the Roman Senate. He quickly gained both power and prestige and formed the Second Triumvirate with Antony and Lepidus in 43 BCE.

- By 31 BCE, Octavian had emerged as the sole ruler of Rome, upon the political and military defeat of the two other triumvirs.

Terms

Mark Antony

Julius Caesar's right hand man, and a member of the Second Triumvirate. He was eventually defeated by Octavian at the Battle of Actium in 31 BCE.

Augustus

The founder of the Roman Empire, known as Octavian during his early years and during his rise to power.

Augustus is regarded by many scholars as the founder and first emperor of the Roman Empire. He ruled from 27 BCE until his death in 14 CE.

Rise to Power

Augustus was born Gaius Octavius, and in his early years was known as Octavian. He was from an old and wealthy equestrian branch of the plebeian Octavii family. Following the assassination of his maternal great-uncle, Julius Caesar, in 44 BCE, Caesar's will named Octavian as his adopted son and heir when Octavian was only 19 years old. The young Octavian quickly took advantage of the situation and ingratiated himself with both the Roman people and his adoptive father's legions, thereby elevating his status and importance within Rome. Octavian found Mark Antony, Julius Caesar's former colleague and the current consul of Rome, in an uneasy truce with Caesar's assassins, who had been granted general amnesty for their part in the plot. Nonetheless, Antony eventually succeeded in driving most of them out of Rome, using Caesar's eulogy as an opportunity to mount public opinion against the assassins.

Mark Antony began amassing political support, and Octavian set about rivaling it. Eventually, many Caesarian sympathizers began to view Octavian as the lesser evil of the two. Octavian allied himself with optimate factions, despite their opposition to Caesar when he was alive. The optimate orator, Marcus Tullius Cicero, began attacking Antony in a series of speeches, portraying him as a threat to the republican order of Rome. As public opinion against him mounted, Antony fled to Cisalpine Gaul at the end of his consular year.

Octavian further established himself both politically and militarily in the following months. He was declared a senator and granted the power of military command, *imperium*, in 43 BCE, and was further able to leverage his successes to obtain the vacant consulships left by the two defeated consuls of that year.

Octavian eventually reached an uneasy truce with Mark Antony and Marcus Lepidus in October 43 BCE, and together, the three formed the Second Triumvirate to defeat the assassins of Caesar. Following their victory against Brutus at Phillipi, the Triumvirate divided the Roman Republic among themselves and ruled as military dictators. Relations within the Triumvirate were strained as the various members sought greater political power. Civil war between Antony and Octavian was averted in 40 BCE, when Antony married Octavian's sister, Octavia Minor. Despite his marriage, Antony continued a love affair with Cleopatra, the former lover of Caesar and queen of Egypt, further straining political ties to Rome. Octavian used Antony's relationship with Cleopatra to his own advantage, portraying Antony as less committed to Rome. With Lepidus expelled in 36 BCE, the Triumvirate finally disintegrated in the year 33. Finally, disagreements between Octavian and Antony erupted into civil war in the year 31 BCE.

The Roman Senate, at Octavian's direction, declared war on Cleopatra's regime in Egypt and proclaimed Antony a traitor. Antony was defeated by Octavian at the naval Battle of Actium the same year. Defeated, Antony fled with Cleopatra to Alexandria where they both committed suicide. With Antony dead, Octavian was left as the undisputed master of the Roman world. Octavian would assume the title Augustus, and reign as the first Roman Emperor.

Augustus of Prima Porta. The statue of Augustus of Prima Porta is perhaps one of the best known images of the Emperor Augustus. It portrays the emperor as perpetually youthful, and depicts many of the key propaganda messages that Augustus put forth during his time as emperor.

Sources

Attributions

CC licensed content, Specific attribution

- Boundless World History. **Authored by**: Boundless. **Located at**: https://courses.lumenlearning.com/boundless-worldhistory/. **License**: *CC BY-SA: Attribution-ShareAlike*

The Pax Romana

Learning Objective

- Describe the key reasons for and characteristics of the Pax Romana

Key Points

- The Pax Romana was established under Augustus, and for that reason it is sometimes referred to as the Pax Augusta.
- Augustus closed the Gates of Janus three times to signify the onset of peace: in 29 BCE, 25 BCE, and 13 BCE, likely in conjunction with the Ara Pacis ceremony.
- The Romans regarded peace not as an absence of war, but as the rare situation that existed when all opponents had been beaten down and lost the ability to resist. Thus, Augustus had to persuade Romans that the prosperity they could achieve in the absence of warfare was better for the Empire than the potential wealth and honor acquired when fighting a risky war.
- The Ara Pacis is a prime example of the propaganda Augustus employed to promote the Pax Romana, and depicts images of Roman gods and the city of Rome personified amidst wealth and prosperity.

Terms

Pax Romana

The long period of relative peace and minimal expansion by military force experienced by the Roman Empire in the 1st and 2nd centuries CE. Also sometimes known as the Pax Augusta.

Ara Pacis Augustae

The Altar of Augustan Peace, a sacrificial altar that displays imagery of the peace and prosperity Augustus achieved during the Pax Romana.

Augustus's Constitutional Reforms

After the demise of the Second Triumvirate, Augustus restored the outward facade of the free Republic with governmental power vested in the Roman Senate, the executive magistrates, and the legislative assemblies. In reality, however, he retained his autocratic power over the Republic as a military dictator. By law, Augustus held powers granted to him for life by the Senate, including supreme military command and those of tribune and censor. It took several years for Augustus to develop the framework within which a formally republican state could be led under his sole rule.

Augustus passed a series of laws between the years 30 and 2 BCE that transformed the constitution of the Roman Republic into the constitution of the Roman Empire. During this time, Augustus reformed the Roman system of taxation, developed networks of roads with an official courier system, established a standing army, established the Praetorian Guard, created official police and fire-fighting services for Rome, and rebuilt much of the city during his reign.

First Settlement

During the First Settlement, Augustus modified the Roman political system to make it more palatable to the senatorial classes, eschewing the open authoritarianism exhibited by Julius Caesar and Mark Anthony. In 28 BCE, in a calculated move, Augustus eradicated the emergency powers he held as dictator and returned all powers and provinces to the Senate and the Roman people. Members of the Senate were unhappy with this prospect, and in order to appease them, Augustus agreed to a ten-year extension of responsibilities over disorderly provinces. As a result of this, Augustus retained *imperium* over the provinces where the majority of Rome's soldiers were stationed. Augustus also rejected monarchical titles, instead calling himself *princeps civitatis* ("First Citizen"). The resulting constitutional framework became known as the Principate, the first phase of the Roman Empire.

At this time, Augustus was given honorifics that made his full name *Imperator Caesar divi filius Augustus*. *Imperator* stressed military power and victory and emphasized his role as commander-in-chief. *Divi filius* roughly translates to "son of the divine," enhancing his legitimacy as ruler without deifying him completely. The use of Caesar provided a link between himself and Julius Caesar, who was still very popular among lower classes. Finally, the name Augustus raised associations to Rome's illustrious and majestic traditions, without creating heavy authoritarian overtones.

By the end of the first settlement, Augustus was in an ideal political position. Although he no longer held dictatorial powers, he had created an identity of such influence that authority followed naturally.

Second Settlement

In the wake of Augustus's poor health, a second settlement was announced in 23 BCE. During this time, Augustus outwardly appeared to rein in his constitutional powers, but really continued to extend his dominion throughout the Empire. Augustus renounced his ten-year consulship, but in return, secured the following concessions for himself.

- A seat on the consuls's platform at the front of the Curia

- The right to speak first in a Senate meeting, or *ius primae relationis*

- The right to summon a meeting of the Senate, which was a useful tool for policy making

- Care of Rome's grain supply, or *cura annonae*, which gave him sweeping patronage powers over the plebs

Augustus was also granted the role of *tribunicia potestas*, which enabled him to act as the guardian of the citizens of Rome. This position came with a number of benefits, including the right to propose laws to the Senate whenever he wanted, veto power of laws, and the ability to grant amnesty to any citizen accused of a crime. Though the role of *tribunicia potestas* effectively gave Augustus legislative supremacy, it also had many positive connotations hearkening back to the Republic, making Augustus's position less offensive to the aristocracy. Beyond Rome, Augustus was granted *maius imperium*, meaning greater (proconsular) power. This position enabled him to effectively override the orders of any other provincial governor in the Roman Empire, in addition to governing his own provinces and armies.

Augustus and the Pax Romana

The *Pax Romana* (Latin for "Roman peace") was a long period of relative peace and minimal expansion by military forces experienced by the Roman Empire in the 1st and 2nd centuries CE. Since this period was initiated during Augustus's reign, it is sometimes called Pax Augusta. Its span was approximately 206 years (27 BCE to 180 CE).

The Pax Romana started after Augustus, then Octavian, met and defeated Mark Antony in the Battle of Actium in 31 BCE. Augustus created a junta of the greatest military magnates and gave himself the titular honor. By binding together these leading magnates into a single title, he eliminated the prospect of civil war. The Pax Romana was not immediate, despite the end of the civil war, because fighting continued in Hispania and in the Alps. Despite continuous wars of imperial expansion on the Empire's frontiers and one year-long civil war over the imperial succession, the Roman world was largely free from large-scale conflict for more than two centuries. Augustus dramatically enlarged the Empire, annexing Egypt, Dalmatia, Pannonia, Noricum, and Raetia, expanded possessions in Africa as well as into Germania, and completed the conquest of Hispania. Beyond Rome's frontiers, he secured the Empire with a buffer region of client states, and made peace with the troublesome Parthian Empire through diplomacy.

Augustus closed the Gates of Janus (the set of gates to the Temple of Janus, which was closed in times of peace and opened in times of war) three times. The first time was in 29 BCE and the second in 25 BCE. The third closure is undocumented, but scholars have persuasively dated the event to 13 BCE during the Ara Pacis ceremony, which was held after Augustus and Agrippa jointly returned from pacifying the provinces.

Augustus faced some trouble making peace an acceptable mode of life for the Romans, who had been at war with one power or another continuously for 200 years prior to this period. The Romans regarded peace not as an absence of war, but the rare situation that existed when all opponents had been beaten down and lost the ability to resist. Augustus's challenge was to persuade Romans that the prosperity they could achieve in the absence of war was better for the Empire than the potential wealth and honor acquired from fighting. Augustus succeeded by means of skillful propaganda. Subsequent emperors followed his lead, sometimes producing lavish ceremonies to close the Gates of Janus, issuing coins with Pax on the reverse, and patronizing literature extolling the benefits of the Pax Romana.

The Ara Pacis Augustae

The Ara Pacis Augustae, or Altar of Augustan Peace, is one of the best examples of Augustan artistic propaganda and the prime symbol of the new Pax Romana. It was commissioned by the Senate in 13 BCE to honor the peace and bounty established by Augustus following his return from Spain and Gaul. The theme of peace is seen most notably in the east and west walls of the Ara Pacis, each of which had two panels, although only small fragments remain for one panel on each side. On the east side sits an unidentified goddess presumed by scholars to be Tellus, Venus, or Peace within an allegorical scene of prosperity and fertility. Twins sit on her lap along with a cornucopia of fruits. Personifications of the wind and sea surround her, each riding on a bird or a sea monster. Beneath the women rests a bull and lamb, both sacrificial animals, and flowering plants fill the empty space. The nearly incomplete second eastern panel appears to depict a female warrior, possibly Roma, amid the spoils of conquest.

The Tellus Mater Panel of the Ara Pacis. The eastern wall of the Ara Pacis, which depicts the Tellus Mater surrounded by symbols of fertility and prosperity.

Augustus died in 14 CE at the age of 75. He may have died from natural causes, although unconfirmed rumors swirled that his wife Livia poisoned him. His adopted son (also stepson and former son-in-law), Tiberius, succeeded him to the throne.

Sources

Attributions

CC licensed content, Specific attribution

- Boundless World History. **Authored by**: Boundless. **Located at**: https://courses.lumenlearning.com/boundless-worldhistory/. **License**: *CC BY-SA: Attribution-ShareAlike*

The Julio-Claudian Emperors

Learning Objective

- Describe the reigns of the emperors who followed Augustus

Key Points

- Tiberius was the second emperor of the Roman Empire, and was considered one of Rome's greatest generals.

- Tiberius conquered Pannonia, Dalmatia, Raetia, and temporarily, parts of Germania. His conquests laid the foundations for the northern frontier.

- When Tiberius died on March 16, 37 CE, his estate and titles were left to Caligula and Tiberius's grandson, Gemellus. However, Caligula's first act as Princeps was to to void Tiberius's will and have Gemellus executed.

- Although Caligula is described as a noble and moderate ruler during the first six months of his reign, sources portray him as a cruel and sadistic tyrant, immediately thereafter.

- In 38 CE, Caligula focused his attention on political and public reform; however, by 39 CE, a financial crisis had emerged as a result of Caligula's use of political payments, which had overextended the state's treasury. Despite financial difficulties, Caligula began a number of construction projects during this time.

- In 41 CE, Caligula was assassinated as part of a conspiracy by officers of the Paretorian Guard, senators, and courtiers.

- Claudius, the fourth emperor of the Roman Empire, was the first Roman Emperor to be born outside of Italy.

- Despite his lack of experience, Claudius was an able and efficient administrator, as well as an ambitious builder. He constructed many roads, aqueducts, and canals across the Empire.

- Claudius's appointment as emperor by the Praetorian Guard damaged his reputation.

This was amplified when Claudius became the first emperor to resort to bribery as a means to secure army loyalty. Claudius also rewarded the Praetorian Guard that had named him emperor with 15,000 sesterces.

Terms

Julio-Claudian dynasty

The first five Roman emperors who ruled the Roman Empire, including Augustus, Tiberius, Caligula, Claudius, and Nero.

Praetorian Guard

A force of bodyguards used by the Roman emperors. They also served as secret police, and participated in wars.

Tiberius

Tiberius was the second emperor of the Roman Empire and reigned from 14 to 37 CE. The previous emperor, Augustus, was his stepfather; this officially made him a Julian. However, his biological father was Tiberius Claudius Nero, making him a Claudian by birth. Subsequent emperors would continue the blended dynasty of both families for the next 30 years, leading historians to name it the Julio-Claudian Dynasty. Tiberius is also the grand-uncle of Caligula, his successor, the paternal uncle of Claudius, and the great-grand uncle of Nero.

Tiberius is considered one of Rome's greatest generals. During his reign, he conquered Pannonia, Dalmatia, Raetia, and temporarily, parts of Germania. His conquests laid the foundations for the northern frontier. However, he was known by contemporaries to be dark, reclusive, and somber—a ruler who never really wanted to be emperor. The tone was set early in his reign when the Senate convened to validate his position as Princeps. During the proceedings, Tiberius attempted to play the part of the reluctant public servant, but came across as derisive and obstructive. His direct orders appeared vague, inspiring more debate than action and leaving the Senate to act on its own. After the death of Tiberius's son in 23 CE, the emperor became even more reclusive, leaving the administration largely in the hands of his unscrupulous Praetorian Prefects.

Tiberius, Romisch-Germanisches Museum, Cologne

Caligula

When Tiberius died on March 16, 37 CE, his estate and titles were left to Caligula and Tiberius's grandson, Gemellus, with the intention that they would rule as joint heirs. However, Caligula's first act as Princeps was to to void Tiberius's will and have Gemellus executed. When Tiberius died, he had not been well liked. Caligula, on the other hand, was almost universally heralded upon his assumption of the throne. There are few surviving sources on Caligula's reign. Caligula's first acts as emperor were generous in spirit, but political in nature. He granted bonuses to the military, including the Praetorian Guard, city troops, and the army outside of Italy. He destroyed Tiberius's treason papers and declared that treason trials would no longer continue as a practice, even going so far as to recall those who had already been sent into exile for treason. He also helped those who had been adversely affected by the imperial tax system, banished certain sexual deviants, and put on large public spectacles, such as gladiatorial games, for the common people.

Although he is described as a noble and moderate ruler during the first six months of his reign, sources portray him as a cruel and sadistic tyrant immediately thereafter. The transitional point seems to center around an illness Caligula experienced in October of 37 CE. It is unclear whether the incident was merely an illness, or if Caligula had been poisoned. Either way, following the incident, the young emperor began dealing with what he considered to be serious threats, by killing or exiling those who were close to him. During the remainder of his reign, he worked to increase the personal power of the emperor during his short reign, and devoted much of his attention to ambitious construction projects and luxurious dwellings for himself.

In 38 CE, Caligula focused his attention on political and public reform. He published the accounts of public funds, which had not been done under Tiberius's reign, provided aid to those who lost property in fires, and abolished certain taxes. He also allowed new members into the equestrian and senatorial orders. Perhaps most significantly, he restored the practice of democratic elections, which delighted much of the public but was a cause for concern among the aristocracy.

By 39 CE, a financial crisis had emerged as a result of Caligula's use of political payments, which had overextended the state's treasury. In order to to restock the treasury, Caligula began falsely accusing, fining, and even killing individuals in order to seize their estates. He also asked the public to lend the state money, and raised taxes on lawsuits, weddings, and prostitution, as well as auctioning the lives of gladiators at shows. Wills that left items to Tiberius were also reinterpreted as having left said items to Caligula. Centurions who had acquired property by plunder were also forced to turn over their spoils to the state, and highway commissioners were accused of incompetence and embezzlement and forced to repay money that they might not have taken in the first place. Around the same time, a brief famine occurred, possibly as a result of the financial crisis, though its causes remain unclear.

Despite financial difficulties, Caligula began a number of construction projects during this time. He initiated the construction of two aqueducts in Rome, Awua Claudia and Anio Novus, which were considered contemporary engineering marvels. In 39 CE, he ordered the construction of a temporary floating bridge between the resort of Baiae and the port of Puteoli, which rivaled the bridge Persian king Xerxes had constructed across the Hellespont. Caligula had two large ships constructed for himself that were among the largest constructed in the ancient world. The larger of the two was essentially an elaborate floating palace with marble floors and plumbing. He also improved the harbors at Rhegium and Sicily, which allowed for increased grain imports from Egypt, possibly in response to the famine Rome experienced.

During his reign, the Empire annexed the Kingdom of Mauretania as a province. Mauretania had previously been a client kingdom ruled by Ptolemy of Mauretania. Details on how and why Mauretania was ultimately annexed remain unclear. Ptolemy was had been invited to Rome by Caligula and suddenly executed in what was seemingly a personal political move, rather than a calculated response to military of economic needs. However, Roman possession of Mauretania ultimately proved to be a boon to the territory, as the subsequent rebellion of Tacfarinas demonstrated how exposed the African Proconsularis was on its western borders. There also was a northern campaign to Britannia that was aborted during Caligula's reign, though there is not a cohesive narrative of the event.

In 39 CE, relations between Caligula and the Senate deteriorated. Caligula ordered a new set of treason investigations and trials, replacing the consul and putting a number of senators to death. Many other senators were reportedly treated in a degrading fashion and humiliated by Caligula. In 41 CE, Caligula was assassinated as part of a conspiracy by officers of the Praetorian Guard, senators, and courtiers. The conspirators used the assassination as an opportunity to re-institute the Republic, but were ultimately unsuccessful.

Caligula. Emperor Caligula, Ny Carlsberg Glyptotek.

Claudius

Claudius, the fourth emperor of the Roman Empire, was the first Roman Emperor to be born outside of Italy. He was afflicted with a limp and slight deafness, which caused his family to ostracize him and exclude him from public office until he shared the consulship with his nephew, Caligula, in 37 CE. Due to Claudius's afflictions, it is likely he was spared from the many purges of Tiberius and Caligula's reigns. As a result, Claudius was declared Emperor by the Praetorian Guard after Caligula's assassination, due to his position as the last man in the Julio-Claudian line.

Despite his lack of experience, Claudius was an able and efficient administrator, as well as an ambitious builder; he constructed many roads, aqueducts, and canals across the Empire. His reign also saw the beginning of the conquest of Britain. Additionally, Claudius presided over many public trials, and issued up to 20 edicts a day. However, in spite of his capable rule, Claudius continued to be viewed as vulnerable by the Roman nobility throughout his reign, forcing Claudius to constantly defend his position. He did so by emphasizing his place within the Julio-Claudian family, dropping the cognomen, Nero, from his name, and replacing it with Caesar.

Nonetheless, his appointment as emperor by the Praetorian Guard caused damage to his reputation, and this was amplified when Claudius became the first emperor to resort to bribery as a means to secure army loyalty. Claudius also rewarded the Praetorian Guard that had named him emperor with 15,000 sesterces.

Bust of Emperor Claudius.

Sources

Attributions

CC licensed content, Specific attribution

- Boundless World History. **Authored by**: Boundless. **Located at**: https://courses.lumenlearning.com/boundless-worldhistory/. **License**: *CC BY-SA: Attribution-ShareAlike*

The Last Julio-Claudian Emperors

Learning Objective

- Explain how Nero and other factors contributed to the fall of the Julio-Claudian Dynasty

Key Points

- Nero reigned as Roman Emperor from 54 to 68 CE, and was the last emperor in the Julio-Claudian Dynasty.

- Very early in Nero's rule, problems arose, due to his mother, Agrippina the Younger's competition for influence with Nero's two main advisers, Seneca and Burrus.

- Nero minimized the influence of all of his advisers and effectively eliminating all rivals to his throne. He also slowly removed power from the Senate, despite having promised to grant them with powers equivalent to those they had under republican rule.

- In March 68, Gaius Gulius Vindex, the governor of Gallia Lugdunensis, rebelled against Nero's tax policies and called upon the support of Servius Sulpicius Galba, the governor of Hispania Tarraconensis, who not only joined the rebellion, but also declared himself emperor in opposition to Nero. Galba would become the first emperor in what was known as the Year of the Four Emperors.

- Vespasian was the fourth and final emperor to rule in the year 69 CE, and established the stable Flavian Dynasty, that was to succeed the Julio-Claudians.

Terms

Praetorian Guard

A force of bodyguards used by the Roman emperors. They also served as secret police and participated in wars.

Julio-Claudian dynasty

The first five Roman emperors who ruled the Roman Empire, including Augustus, Tiberius, Caligula, Claudius, and Nero.

Flavian dynasty

A Roman imperial dynasty that ruled the Roman Empire from 69 to 96 CE, encompassing the reigns of Vespasian and his two sons, Titus and Domitian.

Nero

Nero reigned as Roman Emperor from 54 to 68 CE, and was the last emperor in the Julio-Claudian Dynasty. Nero focused on diplomacy, trade, and enhancing the cultural life of the Empire during his rule. He ordered theaters to be built and promoted athletic games. However, according to Tacitus, a historian writing one generation after Nero's rule, Nero was viewed by many Romans as compulsive and corrupt. Suetonius, another historian writing a generation after Nero's rule, claims that Nero began the Great Fire of Rome in 64 CE, in order to clear land for a palatial complex he was planning.

A marble bust of Nero, at the Antiquarium of the Palatine.

Early Rule

When Claudius died in 54, Nero was established as the new emperor. According to some ancient historians, Agrippina the Younger, Nero's mother, poisoned Claudius in order to make Nero the youngest Roman emperor (at the age of 17). Very early in Nero's rule, problems arose due to Agrippina's competition for influence with Nero's two main advisers, Seneca and Burrus. For example, in the year 54, Agrippina caused a scandal by attempting to sit with Nero while he met with the Armenian envoy, an unheard of act, since women were not permitted to be in the same room as men while official business was being conducted. The next year, Agrippina attempted to intervene on behalf of Nero's wife, Octavia, with whom Nero was dissatisfied and cheating on with a former slave. With the help of his adviser, Seneca, Nero managed to resist his mother's interference yet again.

Sensing his resistance to her influence, Agrippina began pushing for Britannicus, Nero's stepbrother, to become emperor. Britannicus was still shy of 14 years old, and legally still a minor, but because he was the son of the previous emperor, Claudius, by blood, Agrippina held hope that he would be accepted as the true heir to the throne. Her efforts were thwarted, however, when Britannicus mysteriously died one day short of becoming a legal adult. Many ancient historians claim that Britannicus was poisoned by his stepbrother, Nero. Shortly thereafter, Agrippina was ordered out of the imperial residence.

Consolidation of Power

Over time, Nero began minimizing the influence of all advisers and effectively eliminating all rivals to his throne. Even Seneca and Burrus were accused of conspiring against, and embezzling from the emperor;

they were eventually acquitted, reducing their roles from careful management of the government to mere moderation of Nero's actions on the throne. In 58 CE, Nero became romantically involved with Poppaea Sabina, the wife of his friend and future emperor, Otho. Because divorcing his current wife and marrying Poppaea did not seem politically feasible with his mother still alive, Nero ordered Agrippina's murder the following year.

Nero's consolidation of power included a slow usurpation of authority from the Senate. Although he had promised the Senate powers equivalent to those it had under republican rule, over the course of the first decade of Nero's rule, the Senate was divested of all its authority, which led directly to the Pisonian Conspiracy of 65. Gaius Calpurnius Piso, a Roman statesman, organized the conspiracy against Nero with the help of Subrius Flavus, a tribune, and Sulpicius Asper, a centurion of the Praetorian Guard, in order to restore the Republic and wrest power from the emperor. However, the conspiracy failed when it was discovered by a freedman, who reported the details to Nero's secretary. This led to the execution of all conspirators. Seneca was also ordered to commit suicide after he admitted to having prior knowledge of the plot.

Vindex and Galba's Revolt

In March 68, Gaius Gulius Vindex, the governor of Gallia Lugdunensis, rebelled against Nero's tax policies and called upon the support of Servius Sulpicius Galba, the governor of Hispania Tarraconensis, who not only joined the rebellion, but also declared himself emperor in opposition to Nero. Two months later, Vindex's forces were defeated at the Battle of Vesontio, and Vindex committed suicide. The legions that defeated Vindex then attempted to proclaim their own commander, Verginius, as emperor, but Verginius refused to act against Nero. Meanwhile, public support for Galba grew despite his being officially declared a public enemy. In response, Nero began to flee Rome only to turn back when the army officers that were with him refused to obey his commands. When Nero returned, he received word that the Senate had declared him a public enemy and intended to beat him to death—although in actuality, the Senate remained open to mediating an end to the conflict, and many senators felt a sense of loyalty to Nero, even if only on account of him being the last of the Julio-Claudian line. However, Nero was unaware of this and convinced his private secretary to help him take his own life.

Year of the Four Emperors

The suicide of Emperor Nero was followed by a brief period of civil war. Then, between June 68 and December 69, four emperors ruled in succession: Galba, Otho, Vitellius, and Vespasian.

Galba was recognized as emperor following Nero's suicide, but he did not remain popular for long. On his march to Rome, he either destroyed or took enormous fines from towns that did not accept him immediately. Once in Rome, Galba made many of Nero's reforms redundant, including ones that benefited important people within Roman society. Galba executed many senators and equites without trial, in a paranoid attempt to consolidate his power, which unsettled many, including the Praetorian Guard. Finally, the legions of Germania Inferior refused to swear allegiance and obedience to Galba, instead proclaiming the governor Vitellius as emperor.

This caused Galba to panic and name Lucius Calpurnius Piso Licinianus, a young senator, as his successor. This upset many people, but especially Marcus Salvius Otho, who had coveted after the title for himself.

Otho bribed the Praetorian Guard to support him and embarked upon a coup d'etat, during which Galba was killed by the Praetorians. Otho was recognized as emperor by the Senate the same day and was expected by many to be a fair ruler. Unfortunately, soon thereafter, Vitellius declared himself Imperator in Germania, and dispatched half his army to march on Italy.

Otho attempted to broker a peace, but Vitellius was uninterested, especially because his legions were some of the finest in the empire, which gave him a great advantage over Otho. Indeed, Otho was eventually defeated at the Battle of Bedriacum, and rather than flee and attempt a counterattack, Otho committed suicide. He had been emperor for little more than three months. Vitellius was recognized as emperor by the Senate. Very quickly thereafter, he proceeded to bankrupt the imperial treasury by throwing a series of feasts, banquets, and triumphal parades. He tortured and executed money lenders who demanded payment and killed any citizens who named him as their heir. He also lured many political rivals to his palace in order to assassinate them.

Meanwhile, many of the legions in the African province of Egypt, and the Middle East provinces of Iudaea and Syria, including the governor of Syria, acclaimed Vespasian as their emperor. A force marched from the Middle East to Rome, and Vespasian traveled to Alexandria, where he was officially named Emperor. From there, Vespasian invaded Italy and won a crushing victory over Vitellius's army at the Second Battle of Bedriacum. Vitellius was found by Vespasian's men at the imperial palace and put to death. The Senate acknowledged Vespasian as emperor the next day, marking the beginning of the Flavian Dynasty, which was to succeed the Julio-Claudian line. Vespasian remained emperor for the rest of his natural life.

A plaster cast of Vespasian in the Pushkin Museum, after an original held in the Louvre.

Sources

Attributions

CC licensed content, Specific attribution

- Boundless World History. **Authored by**: Boundless. **Located at**: https://courses.lumenlearning.com/boundless-worldhistory/. **License**: *CC BY-SA: Attribution-ShareAlike*

The Flavian Dynasty

Learning Objective

- Analyze how Vespasian consolidated control over the empire

Key Points

- Vespasian, a general for the Roman army, founded the Flavian Dynasty, which ruled the Empire for 27 years.

- While Vespasian besieged Jerusalem during the Jewish rebellion, emperor Nero committed suicide and plunged Rome into a year of civil war, known as the Year of the Four Emperors.

- After Galba and Otho perished in quick succession, Vitellius became the third emperor in April 69 CE.

- The Roman legions of Roman Egypt and Judaea reacted by declaring Vespasian, their commander, emperor on July 1, 69 CE.

- In his bid for imperial power, Vespasian joined forces with Mucianus, the governor of Syria, and Primus, a general in Pannonia, leaving his son, Titus, to command the besieging forces at Jerusalem; Primus and Mucianus led the Flavian forces against Vitellius, while Vespasian took control of Egypt.

- On December 20, 69, Vitellius was defeated, and the following day, Vespasian was declared Emperor by the Senate.

- Little information survives about the government during Vespasian's ten-year rule; he reformed the financial system at Rome after the campaign against Judaea ended successfully, and initiated several ambitious construction projects.

Terms

Colosseum

Also known as the Flavian Amphitheater, an oval amphitheater in the center of the city of Rome, Italy, built of concrete and sand. The largest amphitheater ever built, used for gladiatorial contests and public spectacles, such as mock sea battles, animal hunts, executions, re-enactments of famous battles, and dramas based on Classical mythology.

Year of the Four Emperors

A year in the history of the Roman Empire, 69 CE, in which four emperors ruled in succession: Galba, Otho, Vitellius, and Vespasian.

Praetorian Guard

A force of bodyguards used by Roman Emperors, who also served as secret police and participated in wars.

Overview

The Flavian Dynasty was a Roman imperial dynasty that ruled the Roman Empire between 69 CE and 96 CE, encompassing the reigns of Vespasian (69-79 CE), and his two sons Titus (79-81 CE) and Domitian (81-96 CE). The Flavians rose to power during the civil war of 69, known as the Year of the Four Emperors. After Galba and Otho died in quick succession, Vitellius became emperor in mid 69 CE. His claim to the throne was quickly challenged by legions stationed in the Eastern provinces, who declared their commander, Vespasian, emperor in his place. The Second Battle of Bedriacum tilted the balance decisively in favor of the Flavian forces, who entered Rome on December 20. The following day, the Roman Senate officially declared Vespasian emperor of the Roman Empire, thus commencing the Flavian Dynasty. Although the dynasty proved to be short-lived, several significant historic, economic, and military events took place during their reign.

The Flavians initiated economic and cultural reforms. Under Vespasian, new taxes were devised to restore the Empire's finances, while Domitian revalued the Roman coinage by increasing its silver content. A massive building program was enacted to celebrate the ascent of the Flavian Dynasty, leaving multiple enduring landmarks in the city of Rome, the most spectacular of which was the Flavian Amphitheater, better known as the Colosseum.

Rise to Power

On June 9, 68 CE, amidst growing opposition of the Senate and the army, Nero committed suicide, and with him the Julio-Claudian Dynasty came to an end. Chaos ensued, leading to a year of brutal civil war, known as the Year of the Four Emperors, during which the four most influential generals in the Roman Empire—Galba, Otho, Vitellius and Vespasian—successively vied for imperial power. News of Nero's death reached Vespasian as he was preparing to besiege the city of Jerusalem. Almost simultaneously the Senate had declared Galba, then governor of Hispania Tarraconensis (modern Spain), as Emperor of Rome. Rather than continue his campaign, Vespasian decided to await further orders and send Titus to greet the new Emperor. Before reaching Italy however, Titus learned that Galba had been murdered and replaced by Otho, the governor of Lusitania (modern Portugal). At the same time, Vitellius and his armies in Germania had risen in revolt, and prepared to march on Rome, intent on overthrowing Otho. Not wanting to risk being taken hostage by one side or the other, Titus abandoned the journey to Rome and rejoined his father in Judaea.

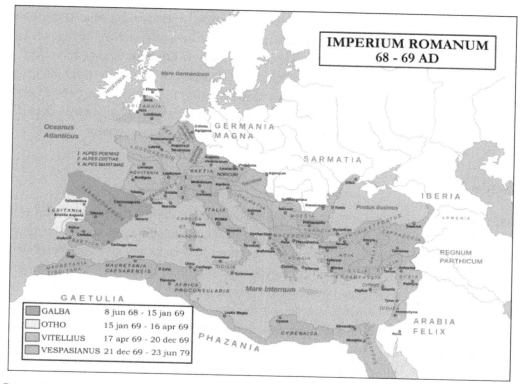

Roman Empire in 69 CE. The Roman Empire during the Year of the Four Emperors (69 CE). Purple areas indicate provinces loyal to Vespasian and Gaius Licinius Mucianus. Green areas indicate provinces loyal to Vitellius.

Otho and Vitellius realized the potential threat posed by the Flavian faction. With four legions at his disposal, Vespasian commanded a strength of nearly 80,000 soldiers. His position in Judaea further granted him the advantage of being nearest to the vital province of Egypt, which controlled the grain supply to Rome. His brother, Titus Flavius Sabinus II, as city prefect, commanded the entire city garrison of Rome. Tensions among the Flavian troops ran high, but as long as Galba and Otho remained in power, Vespasian refused to take action. When Otho was defeated by Vitellius at the First Battle of Bedriacum however, the armies in Judaea and Egypt took matters into their own hands, and declared Vespasian emperor on July 1, 69. Vespasian accepted, and entered an alliance with Gaius Licinius Mucianus, the governor of Syria, against Vitellius. A strong force drawn from the Judaean and Syrian legions marched on Rome under the command of Mucianus, while Vespasian himself travelled to Alexandria, leaving Titus in charge of ending the Jewish rebellion.

Meanwhile in Rome, Domitian was placed under house arrest by Vitellius, as a safeguard against future Flavian aggression. Support for the old emperor was waning however, as more legions throughout the empire pledged their allegiance to Vespasian. On October 24, 69, the forces of Vitellius and Vespasian clashed at the Second Battle of Bedriacum, which ended in a crushing defeat for the armies of Vitellius. In despair, he attempted to negotiate a surrender. Terms of peace, including a voluntary abdication, were agreed upon with Titus Flavius Sabinus II, but the soldiers of the Praetorian Guard—the imperial body-guard—considered such a resignation disgraceful, and prevented Vitellius from carrying out the treaty. After several skirmishes between the factions, eventually Vitellius was killed and on December 21, the Senate proclaimed Vespasian emperor of the Roman Empire.

Although the war had officially ended, a state of anarchy and lawlessness pervaded in the first days fol-lowing the demise of Vitellius. In early 70 AD, order was properly restored by Mucianus, who headed an interim government with Domitian as the representative of the Flavian family in the Senate. Upon receiv-ing the tidings of his rival's defeat and death at Alexandria, the new Emperor at once forwarded supplies of urgently needed grain to Rome, along with an edict or a declaration of policy, in which he gave assurance of an entire reversal of the laws of Nero, especially those relating to treason. However, in early 70, Ves-pasian was still in Egypt, continuing to consolidate support from the Egyptians before departing. By the end of the year, he finally returned to Rome, and was properly installed as Emperor.

Vespasian's Rule

Little factual information survives about Vespasian's government during the ten years he was Emperor. Vespasian spent his first year as a ruler in Egypt, during which the administration of the empire was given to Mucianus, aided by Vespasian's son, Domitian. Modern historians believe that Vespasian remained there, in order to consolidate support from the Egyptians. In mid-70, Vespasian first came to Rome and immediately embarked on a widespread propaganda campaign to consolidate his power and promote the new dynasty. His reign is best known for financial reforms following the demise of the Julio-Claudian Dynasty, such as the institution of the tax on urinals, and the numerous military campaigns fought during the 70s. The most significant of these was the First Jewish-Roman War, which ended in the destruction of the city of Jerusalem by Titus. In addition, Vespasian faced several uprisings in Egypt, Gaul, and Ger-mania, and reportedly survived several conspiracies against him. Vespasian helped rebuild Rome after the civil war, adding a temple of peace, and beginning construction of the Flavian Amphitheater, better known as the Colosseum.

Many modern historians note the increased amount of propaganda that appeared during Vespasian's reign. Stories of a supernatural emperor, who was destined to rule, circulated in the empire. Nearly one-third of all coins minted in Rome under Vespasian celebrated military victory or peace. The word *vindex* was removed from coins so as not to remind the public of rebellious Vindex. Construction projects bore inscriptions praising Vespasian and condemning previous emperors. A temple of peace was constructed in the forum as well. Vespasian approved histories written under his reign, ensuring biases against him were removed.

Vespasian also gave financial rewards to writers. The ancient historians who lived through the period, such as Tacitus, Suetonius, Josephus, and Pliny the Elder, speak suspiciously well of Vespasian, while condemn-ing the emperors who came before him. Tacitus admits that his status was elevated by Vespasian, Josephus identifies Vespasian as a patron and savior, and Pliny dedicated his Natural Histories to Vespasian's son, Titus.

Those who spoke against Vespasian were punished. A number of stoic philosophers were accused of corrupting students with inappropriate teachings and were expelled from Rome. Helvidius Priscus, a pro-republic philosopher, was executed for his teachings.

Vespasian died of natural causes on June 23, 79, and was immediately succeeded by his eldest son, Titus.

Bust of Vespasian. Vespasian founded the Flavian Dynasty, which ruled the Empire for twenty-seven years.

Sources

Attributions

CC licensed content, Specific attribution

- Boundless World History. **Authored by**: Boundless. **Located at**: https://courses.lumenlearning.com/boundless-worldhistory/. **License**: *CC BY-SA: Attribution-ShareAlike*

Crises of the Roman Empire

Learning Objective

- Describe the problems afflicting the Roman Empire during the third century

Key Points

- The situation of the Roman Empire became dire in 235 CE, when emperor Alexander Severus was murdered by his own troops after defeat by Germanic tribes.

- In the years following the emperor's death, generals of the Roman army fought each other for control of the Empire, and neglected their duties of defending the empire from invasion. As a result, various provinces became victims of frequent raids.

- By 268, the Empire had split into three competing states: the Gallic Empire, including the Roman provinces of Gaul, Britannia, and Hispania; the Palmyrene Empire, including the eastern provinces of Syria Palaestina and Aegyptus; and the Italian-centered and independent Roman Empire proper.

- One of the most profound and lasting effects of the Crisis of the Third Century was the disruption of Rome's extensive internal trade network under the Pax Romana.

- The continuing problems of the Empire would be radically addressed by Diocletian, allowing the Empire to continue to survive in the West for over a century, and in the East for over a millennium.

Terms

Pax Romana

The long period of relative peacefulness and minimal expansion by the Roman military force that was experienced by the Roman Empire after the end of the Final War of the Roman Republic, and before the beginning of the Crisis of the Third Century.

coloni

A tenant farmer from the late Roman Empire and Early Middle Ages; sharecroppers.

Crisis of the Third Century

A period in which the Roman Empire nearly collapsed under the combined pressures of invasion, civil war, plague, and economic depression.

Overview

The Crisis of the Third Century, also known as Military Anarchy or the Imperial Crisis, (235-284 CE) was a period in which the Roman Empire nearly collapsed under the combined pressures of invasion, civil war, plague, and economic depression. The Crisis began with the assassination of Emperor Severus Alexander by his own troops in 235, initiating a 50-year period in which there were at least 26 claimants to the title of Emperor, mostly prominent Roman army generals, who assumed imperial power over all or part of the Empire. Twenty-six men were officially accepted by the Roman Senate as emperor during this period, and thus became legitimate emperors.

By 268, the Empire had split into three competing states: the Gallic Empire, including the Roman provinces of Gaul, Britannia, and (briefly) Hispania; the Palmyrene Empire, including the eastern provinces of Syria Palaestina and Aegyptus; and the Italian-centered and independent Roman Empire proper, between them. Later, Aurelian (270-275) reunited the empire; the Crisis ended with the ascension and reforms of Diocletian in 284.

The Crisis resulted in such profound changes in the Empire's institutions, society, economic life, and, eventually, religion, that it is increasingly seen by most historians as defining the transition between the historical periods of classical antiquity and late antiquity.

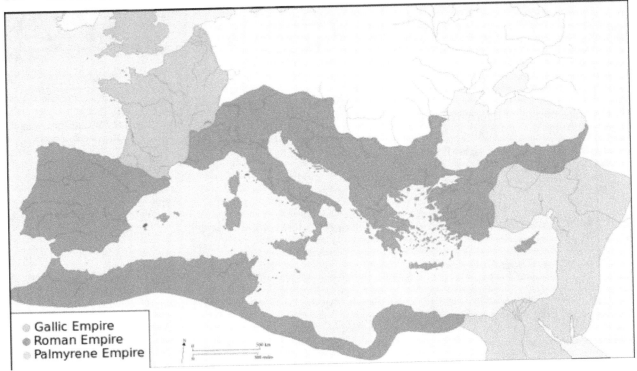

The Roman Empire in 271 CE. The divided Empire during the Crisis of the Third Century.

History of the Crisis

The situation of the Roman Empire became dire in 235 CE, when Emperor Alexander Severus was murdered by his own troops. Many Roman legions had been defeated during a campaign against Germanic peoples raiding across the borders, while the emperor was focused primarily on the dangers from the Sassanid Persian Empire. Leading his troops personally, Alexander Severus resorted to diplomacy and paying tribute, in an attempt to pacify the Germanic chieftains quickly. According to Herodian, this cost him the respect of his troops, who may have felt they should be punishing the tribes who were intruding on Rome's territory.

In the years following the emperor's death, generals of the Roman army fought each other for control of the Empire and neglected their duties of defending the empire from invasion. Provincials became victims of frequent raids along the length of the Rhine and Danube rivers, by such foreign tribes as the Carpians, Goths, Vandals, and Alamanni, and attacks from Sassanids in the east. Climate changes and a rise in sea levels ruined the agriculture of what is now the Low Countries, forcing tribes to migrate. Additionally, in 251, the Plague of Cyprian (possibly smallpox) broke out, causing large-scale death, and possibly weakened the ability of the Empire to defend itself.

After the loss of Valerian in 260, the Roman Empire was beset by usurpers, who broke it up into three competing states. The Roman provinces of Gaul, Britain, and Hispania broke off to form the Gallic Empire. After the death of Odaenathus in 267, the eastern provinces of Syria, Palestine, and Aegyptus became independent as the Palmyrene Empire, leaving the remaining Italian-centered Roman Empire proper in the middle.

An invasion by a vast host of Goths was defeated at the Battle of Naissus in 268 or 269. This victory was significant as the turning point of the crisis, when a series of tough, energetic soldier-emperors took power. Victories by Emperor Claudius II Gothicus over the next two years drove back the Alamanni and recovered Hispania from the Gallic Empire. When Claudius died in 270 of the plague, Aurelian, who had commanded the cavalry at Naissus, succeeded him as the emperor and continued the restoration of the Empire.

Aurelian reigned (270-275) through the worst of the crisis, defeating the Vandals, the Visigoths, the Palmyrenes, the Persians, and then the remainder of the Gallic Empire. By late 274, the Roman Empire was reunited into a single entity, and the frontier troops were back in place. More than a century would pass before Rome again lost military ascendancy over its external enemies. However, dozens of formerly thriving cities, especially in the Western Empire, had been ruined, their populations dispersed and, with the breakdown of the economic system, could not be rebuilt. Major cities and towns, even Rome itself, had not needed fortifications for many centuries; many then surrounded themselves with thick walls.

Finally, although Aurelian had played a significant role in restoring the Empire's borders from external threat, more fundamental problems remained. In particular, the right of succession had never been clearly defined in the Roman Empire, leading to continuous civil wars as competing factions in the military, Senate, and other parties put forward their favored candidate for emperor. Another issue was the sheer size of the Empire, which made it difficult for a single autocratic ruler to effectively manage multiple threats at the same time. These continuing problems would be radically addressed by Diocletian, allowing the Empire to continue to survive in the West for over a century, and in the East for over a millennium.

Impact

One of the most profound and lasting effects of the Crisis of the Third Century was the disruption of Rome's extensive internal trade network. Ever since the Pax Romana, starting with Augustus, the Empire's economy had depended in large part on trade between Mediterranean ports and across the extensive road systems to the Empire's interior. Merchants could travel from one end of the Empire to the other in relative safety within a few weeks, moving agricultural goods produced in the provinces to the cities, and manufactured goods produced by the great cities of the East to the more rural provinces.

With the onset of the Crisis of the Third Century, however, this vast internal trade network broke down. The widespread civil unrest made it no longer safe for merchants to travel as they once had, and the financial crisis that struck made exchange very difficult with the debased currency. This produced profound changes that, in many ways, foreshadowed the very decentralized economic character of the coming Middle Ages.

Large landowners, no longer able to successfully export their crops over long distances, began producing food for subsistence and local barter. Rather than import manufactured goods from the Empire's great urban areas, they began to manufacture many goods locally, often on their own estates, thus beginning the self-sufficient "house economy" that would become commonplace in later centuries, reaching its final form in the Middle Ages' manorialism. The common free people of the Roman cities, meanwhile, began to move out into the countryside in search of food and better protection.

Made desperate by economic necessity, many of these former city dwellers, as well as many small farmers, were forced to give up hard-earned, basic civil rights in order to receive protection from large land-holders.

In doing so, they became a half-free class of Roman citizen known as *coloni*. They were tied to the land, and in later Imperial law their status was made hereditary. This provided an early model for serfdom, the origins of medieval feudal society and of the medieval peasantry.

Sources

Attributions

CC licensed content, Specific attribution

- Boundless World History. **Authored by**: Boundless. **Located at**: https://courses.lumenlearning.com/boundless-worldhistory/. **License**: *CC BY-SA: Attribution-ShareAlike*

Diocletian and the Tetrarchy

Learning Objective

- Describe the change in attitudes towards Christians and their statuses within the Roman Empire

Key Points

- Diocletian secured the empire's borders and purged it of all threats to his power. He separated and enlarged the empire's civil and military services, and reorganized the empire's provincial divisions, establishing the largest and most bureaucratic government in the history of the empire.

- Diocletian also restructured the Roman government by establishing the Tetrarchy, a system of rule in which four men shared rule over the massive Roman Empire. The empire was effectively divided in two, with an Augustus and a subordinate Caesar in each half.

- Diocletian established administrative capitals for each of the Tetrarchs, which were located closer to the empire's borders. Though Rome retained its unique Prefect of the City, it was no longer the administrative capital.

- By 313, therefore, there remained only two emperors: Constantine in the west and Licinius in the east. The tetrarchic system was at an end, although it took until 324 for Constantine to finally defeat Licinius, reunite the two halves of the Roman Empire, and declare himself sole Augustus.

Terms

tetrarchy

A form of government in which power is divided between four individuals. In ancient Rome, a system of government instituted by Diocletian that split power between two rulers in the east, and two rulers in the west.

Diocletian

Roman emperor from 284 to 305 CE. Established the tetrarchy and instituted economic and tax reforms to stabilize the Roman Empire.

Diocletian and the Stabilization of the Roman Empire

Diocletian was Roman emperor from 284 to 305 CE. Born to a family of low status in the Roman province of Dalmatia, Diocletian rose through the ranks of the military to become cavalry commander to the Emperor Carus. After the deaths of Carus and his son Numerian on campaign in Persia, Diocletian was proclaimed emperor. Diocletian's reign stabilized the empire, and marked the end of the Crisis of the Third Century. He appointed fellow officer, Maximian, as Augustus, co-emperor, in 286. Diocletian delegated further in 293, appointing Galerius and Constantius as caesars, junior co-emperors. Under this "tetrarchy," or "rule of four," each emperor would rule over a quarter-division of the empire. Diocletian further secured the empire's borders and purged it of all threats to his power.

He separated and enlarged the empire's civil and military services and reorganized the empire's provincial divisions, establishing the largest and most bureaucratic government in the history of the empire. He established new administrative centers in Nicomedia, Mediolanum, Antioch, and Trier, closer to the empire's frontiers than the traditional capital at Rome had been. Building on third-century trends towards absolutism, he styled himself an autocrat, elevating himself above the empire's masses with imposing forms of court ceremonies and architecture. Bureaucratic and military growth, constant campaigning, and construction projects increased the state's expenditures and necessitated a comprehensive tax reform. From at least 297 on, imperial taxation was standardized, made more equitable, and levied at generally higher rates.

Reconstruction of Diocletian's Palace in its original appearance, upon completion in 305 CE (viewed from the south-west).

The Tetrarchy

The first phase of Diocletian's government restructuring, sometimes referred to as the diarchy ("rule of two"), involved the designation of the general Maximian as co-emperor—first as Caesar (junior emperor) in 285, then Augustus in 286. This reorganization allowed Diocletian to take care of matters in the eastern regions of the empire, while Maximian similarly took charge of the western regions, thereby halving the administrative work required to oversee an empire as large as Rome's. In 293, feeling more focus was needed on both civic and military problems, Diocletian, with Maximian's consent, expanded the imperial college by appointing two Caesars (one responsible to each Augustus)—Galerius and Constantius Chlorus.

In 305, the senior emperors jointly abdicated and retired, allowing Constantius and Galerius to be elevated in rank to Augusti. They in turn appointed two new Caesars—Severus II in the west under Constantius, and Maximinus in the east under Galerius—thereby creating the second tetrarchy.

The four tetrarchs based themselves not at Rome but in other cities closer to the frontiers, mainly intended as headquarters for the defense of the empire against bordering rivals. Although Rome ceased to be an operational capital, it continued to be the nominal capital of the entire Roman Empire, not reduced to the status of a province, but under its own, unique Prefect of the City (*praefectus urbis*).

Zones of Influence in the Roman Tetrarchy. This map shows the four zones of influence under Diocletian's tetrarchy.

In terms of regional jurisdiction, there was no precise division between the four tetrarchs, and this period did not see the Roman state actually split up into four distinct sub-empires. Each emperor had his zone of influence within the Roman Empire, but this influence mainly applied to the theater of war. The tetrarch was himself often in the field, while delegating most of the administration to the hierarchic bureaucracy headed by his respective Praetorian Prefect. The Praetorian Prefect was the title of a high office in the Roman Empire, originating as the commander of the Praetorian Guard, the office gradually acquired extensive legal and administrative functions, with its holders becoming the emperor's chief aides.

Demise of the Tetrarchy

When, in 305, the 20-year term of Diocletian and Maximian ended, both abdicated. Their Caesares, Galerius and Constantius Chlorus, were both raised to the rank of Augustus, and two new Caesares were appointed: Maximinus (Caesar to Galerius) and Flavius Valerius Severus (Caesar to Constantius). These four formed the second tetrarchy.

However, the system broke down very quickly thereafter. When Constantius died in 306, Galerius promoted Severus to Augustus while Constantine, Constantius' son, was proclaimed Augustus by his father's troops. At the same time, Maxentius, the son of Maximian, who also resented being left out of the new arrangements, defeated Severus before forcing him to abdicate and then arranging his murder in 307. Maxentius and Maximian both then declared themselves Augusti. By 308, there were therefore no fewer than four claimants to the rank of Augustus (Galerius, Constantine, Maximian and Maxentius), and only one to that of Caesar (Maximinus).

In 308, Galerius, together with the retired emperor Diocletian and the supposedly retired Maximian, called an imperial "conference" at Carnuntum on the River Danube. The council agreed that Licinius would become Augustus in the West, with Constantine as his Caesar. In the East, Galerius remained Augustus, and Maximinus remained his Caesar. Maximian was to retire, and Maxentius was declared an usurper. This agreement proved disastrous: by 308 Maxentius had become de facto ruler of Italy and Africa even without any imperial rank, and neither Constantine nor Maximinus—who had both been Caesares since 306 and 305, respectively—were prepared to tolerate the promotion of the Augustus Licinius as their superior.

After an abortive attempt to placate both Constantine and Maximinus with the meaningless title *filius Augusti* ("son of the Augustus," essentially an alternative title for Caesar), they both had to be recognized as Augusti in 309. However, four full Augusti all at odds with each other did not bode well for the tetrarchic system.

Between 309 and 313, most of the claimants to the imperial office died or were killed in various civil wars. Constantine forced Maximian's suicide in 310. Galerius died naturally in 311. Maxentius was defeated by Constantine at the Battle of the Milvian Bridge in 312, and subsequently killed. Maximinus committed suicide at Tarsus in 313, after being defeated in battle by Licinius.

By 313, therefore, there remained only two emperors: Constantine in the west and Licinius in the east. The tetrarchic system was at an end, although it took until 324 for Constantine to finally defeat Licinius, reunite the two halves of the Roman Empire, and declare himself sole Augustus.

Sources

Attributions

CC licensed content, Specific attribution

- Boundless World History. **Authored by**: Boundless. **Located at**: https://courses.lumenlearning.com/boundless-worldhistory/. **License**: *CC BY-SA: Attribution-ShareAlike*

The Rise of Christianity

Learning Objective

- Describe the challenges Christians faced in the Roman Empire

Key Points

- Christians suffered from sporadic and localized persecutions over a period of two and a half centuries, as their refusal to participate in Imperial Cult of Rome was considered an act of treason, and was thus punishable by execution.

- The Diocletianic, or Great Persecution, was the last and most severe persecution of Christians in the Roman Empire, which lasted from 302-311 CE. Galerius issued an edict of toleration in 311, which granted Christians the right to practice their religion, but did not restore any taken property back to them.

- The Edict of Milan in 313 made the empire officially neutral with regard to religious worship; it neither made the traditional religions illegal nor made Christianity the state religion.

Terms

the Great Persecution

The last and most severe persecution of Christians in the Roman Empire.

Edict of Milan

An agreement in 313 CE by Constantine and Licinius to treat Christians benevolently within the Roman Empire.

Persecution of Early Christians

Christianity posed a serious threat to the traditional Romans. The idea of monotheism was considered offensive against the polytheistic Roman pantheon, and came into further conflict with the Imperial Cult, in which emperors and some members of their families were worshipped as divine. As such, Christianity was considered criminal and was punished harshly.

The first recorded official persecution of Christians on behalf of the Roman Empire was in 64 CE, when, as reported by the Roman historian Tacitus, Emperor Nero blamed Christians for the Great Fire of Rome. According to Church tradition, it was during the reign of Nero that Peter and Paul were martyred in Rome. However, modern historians debate whether the Roman government distinguished between Christians and Jews prior to Nerva's modification of the Fiscus Judaicus in 96, from which point practicing Jews paid the tax and Christians did not.

The Diocletianic or Great Persecution was the last and most severe persecution of Christians in the Roman Empire, which lasted from 302-311 CE. In 303, the emperors Diocletian, Maximian, Galerius, and Constantius issued a series of edicts rescinding the legal rights of Christians and demanding that they comply with traditional Roman religious practices. Later edicts targeted the clergy and ordered all inhabitants to sacrifice to the Roman gods (a policy known as universal sacrifice). The persecution varied in intensity across the empire—it was weakest in Gaul and Britain, where only the first edict was applied, and strongest in the Eastern provinces. Persecutory laws were nullified by different emperors at different times, but Constantine and Licinius's Edict of Milan (313) has traditionally marked the end of the persecution.

During the Great Persecution, Diocletian ordered Christian buildings and the homes of Christians torn down, and their sacred books collected and burned during the Great Persecution. Christians were arrested, tortured, mutilated, burned, starved, and condemned to gladiatorial contests to amuse spectators. The Great Persecution officially ended in April of 311, when Galerius, senior emperor of the Tetrarchy, issued an edict of toleration which granted Christians the right to practice their religion, though it did not restore any property to them. Constantine, Caesar in the western empire, and Licinius, Caesar in the east, also were signatories to the edict of toleration. It has been speculated that Galerius' reversal of his long-standing policy of Christian persecution has been attributable to one or both of these co-Caesars.

The Rise of Christianity

The Diocletianic persecution was ultimately unsuccessful. As one modern historian has put it, it was simply "too little and too late." Christians were never purged systematically in any part of the empire, and Christian evasion continually undermined the edicts' enforcement. Although the persecution resulted in death, torture, imprisonment, or dislocation for many Christians, the majority of the empire's Christians avoided punishment. Some bribed their way to freedom or fled. In the end, the persecution failed to check the rise of the church. By 324, Constantine was sole ruler of the empire, and Christianity had become his favored religion.

By 324, Constantine, the Christian convert, ruled the entire empire alone. Christianity became the greatest beneficiary of imperial largesse. The persecutors had been routed. As the historian J. Liebeschuetz has written: "The final result of the Great Persecution provided a testimonial to the truth of Christianity, which it could have won in no other way." After Constantine, the Christianization of the Roman empire would continue apace. Under Theodosius I (r. 378-395), Christianity became the state religion. By the 5th century, Christianity was the empire's predominant faith, and filled the same role paganism had at the end of the 3rd century. Because of the persecution, however, a number of Christian communities were riven between those who had complied with imperial authorities (*traditores*) and those who had refused. In Africa, the Donatists, who protested the election of the alleged traditor, Caecilian, to the bishopric of Carthage, continued to resist the authority of the central church until after 411. The Melitians in Egypt left the Egyptian Church similarly divided.

The Edict of Milan

In 313, Constantine and Licinius announced in the Edict of Milan "that it was proper that the Christians and all others should have liberty to follow that mode of religion which to each of them appeared best," thereby granting tolerance to all religions, including Christianity. The Edict of Milan went a step further than the earlier Edict of Toleration by Galerius in 311, and returned confiscated Church property. This edict made the empire officially neutral with regard to religious worship; it neither made the traditional religions illegal, nor made Christianity the state religion (as did the later Edict of Thessalonica in 380 CE). The Edict of Milan did, however, raise the stock of Christianity within the empire, and it reaffirmed the importance of religious worship to the welfare of the state.

Sources

Attributions

CC licensed content, Specific attribution

- Boundless World History. **Authored by**: Boundless. **Located at**: https://courses.lumenlearning.com/boundless-worldhistory/. **License**: *CC BY-SA: Attribution-ShareAlike*

Constantine

Learning Objective

- Evaluate Constantine's rise to power and relationship with Christianity

Key Points

- The age of Constantine marked a distinct epoch in the history of the Roman Empire, both for founding Byzantium in the east, as well as his adoption of Christianity as a state religion.

- As emperor, Constantine enacted many administrative, financial, social, and military reforms to strengthen the empire.

- Constantine experienced a dramatic event in 312 at the Battle of the Milvian Bridge, after which Constantine claimed the emperorship in the west and converted to Christianity.

- According to some sources, on the evening of October 27, with the armies preparing for battle, Constantine had a vision of a cross, which led him to fight under the protection of the Christian god.

- The accession of Constantine was a turning point for early Christianity; after his victory, Constantine took over the role of patron of the Christian faith.

Terms

Battle of the Milvian Bridge

A battle that took place between the Roman Emperors, Constantine I and Maxentius, on October 28, 312, and is often seen as the beginning of Constantine's conversion to Christianity.

Edict of Milan

The February 313 CE agreement to treat Christians benevolently within the Roman Empire, thereby ending years of persecution.

Chi-Rho

One of the earliest forms of christogram, which is used by some Christians, and was used by the Roman emperor, Constantine I (r. 306-337), as part of a military standard.

Constantine the Great was a Roman Emperor from 306-337 CE. Constantine was the son of Flavius Valerius Constantius, a Roman army officer, and his consort, Helena. His father became Caesar, the deputy emperor in the west, in 293 CE. Constantine was sent east, where he rose through the ranks to become a military tribune under the emperors Diocletian and Galerius. In 305, Constantius was raised to the rank of Augustus, senior western emperor, and Constantine was recalled west to campaign under his father in Britannia (modern Great Britain). Acclaimed as emperor by the army at Eboracum (modern-day York) after his father's death in 306 CE, Constantine emerged victorious in a series of civil wars against the emperors Maxentius and Licinius, to become sole ruler of both west and east by 324 CE.

As emperor, Constantine enacted many administrative, financial, social, and military reforms to strengthen the empire. The government was restructured and civil and military authority separated. A new gold coin, the solidus, was introduced to combat inflation. It would become the standard for Byzantine and European currencies for more than a thousand years. As the first Roman emperor to claim conversion to Christianity, Constantine played an influential role in the proclamation of the Edict of Milan in 313, which decreed tolerance for Christianity in the empire. He called the First Council of Nicaea in 325, at which the Nicene Creed was professed by Christians. In military matters, the Roman army was reorganized to consist of mobile field units and garrison soldiers capable of countering internal threats and barbarian invasions. Constantine pursued successful campaigns against the tribes on the Roman frontiers—the Franks, the Alamanni, the Goths, and the Sarmatians—even resettling territories abandoned by his predecessors during the Crisis of the Third Century.

Constantine's reputation flourished during the lifetime of his children and for centuries after his reign. The medieval church upheld him as a paragon of virtue, while secular rulers invoked him as a prototype, a point of reference, and the symbol of imperial legitimacy and identity. One of his major political legacies, aside from moving the capital of the empire to Constantinople, was that, in leaving the empire to his sons, he replaced Diocletian's tetrarchy with the principle of dynastic succession.

The Battle of the Milvian Bridge

Eusebius of Caesarea, and other Christian sources, record that Constantine experienced a dramatic event in 312 at the Battle of the Milvian Bridge, after which Constantine claimed the emperorship in the west, and converted to Christianity. The Battle of the Milvian Bridge took place between the Roman Emperors, Constantine I and Maxentius, on October 28, 312. It takes its name from the Milvian Bridge, an important route over the Tiber. Constantine won the battle and started on the path that led him to end the tetrarchy and become the sole ruler of the Roman Empire. Maxentius drowned in the Tiber during the battle, and his body was later taken from the river and decapitated.

According to chroniclers, such as Eusebius of Caesarea and Lactantius, the battle marked the beginning of Constantine's conversion to Christianity. Eusebius of Caesarea recounts that Constantine looked up to the sun before the battle and saw a cross of light above it, and with it the Greek words Ἐν Τούτῳ Νίκα ("in this sign, conquer!"), often rendered in a Latin version, "*in hoc signo vinces.*" Constantine commanded his troops to adorn their shields with a Christian symbol (the Chi-Rho), and thereafter they were victorious. The Arch of Constantine, erected in celebration of the victory, certainly attributes Constantine's success to divine intervention; however, the monument does not display any overtly Christian symbolism, so there is no scholarly consensus on the events' relation to Constantine's conversion to Christianity.

Missorium depicting Constantine's son Constantius II, accompanied by a guardsman with the Chi Rho monogram depicted on his shield.

Following the battle, Constantine ignored the altars to the gods prepared on the Capitoline, and did not carry out the customary sacrifices to celebrate a general's victorious entry into Rome, instead heading directly to the imperial palace. Most influential people in the empire, however, especially high military officials, had not been converted to Christianity, and still participated in the traditional religions of Rome;

Constantine's rule exhibited at least a willingness to appease these factions. The Roman coins minted up to eight years after the battle still bore the images of Roman gods. The monuments he first commissioned, such as the Arch of Constantine, contained no reference to Christianity.

Constantine and Christianity

While the Roman Emperor Constantine the Great reigned (306-337 CE), Christianity began to transition to the dominant religion of the Roman Empire. Historians remain uncertain about Constantine's reasons for favoring Christianity, and theologians and historians have argued about which form of Early Christianity he subscribed to. There is no consensus among scholars as to whether he adopted his mother Helena's Christianity in his youth, or (as claimed by Eusebius of Caesarea) encouraged her to convert to the faith himself. Some scholars question the extent to which he should be considered a Christian emperor: "Constantine saw himself as an 'emperor of the Christian people.' If this made him a Christian is the subject of debate," although he allegedly received a baptism shortly before his death.

Constantine's decision to cease the persecution of Christians in the Roman Empire was a turning point for early Christianity, sometimes referred to as the Triumph of the Church, the Peace of the Church, or the Constantinian Shift. In 313, Constantine and Licinius issued the Edict of Milan, decriminalizing Christian worship. The emperor became a great patron of the Church and set a precedent for the position of the Christian emperor within the Church, and the notion of orthodoxy, Christendom, ecumenical councils, and the state church of the Roman Empire, declared by edict in 380. He is revered as a saint and isapostolos in the Eastern Orthodox Church and Oriental Orthodox Church for his example as a "Christian monarch."

Sources

Attributions

CC licensed content, Specific attribution

- Boundless World History. **Authored by**: Boundless. **Located at**: https://courses.lumenlearning.com/boundless-worldhistory/. **License**: *CC BY-SA: Attribution-ShareAlike*

The Shift East

Learning Objective

- Explain why Constantine moved the capital of the empire to Constantinople, and the consequences that had for the empire as a whole

Key Points

- After defeating Maxentius and his rebellion, Constantine gradually consolidated his military superiority over his rivals in the crumbling Tetrarchy, in particular Licinius.

- Eventually, Constantine defeated Licinius, making him the sole emperor of the empire, thereby ending the tetrarchy.

- Licinius' defeat came to represent the defeat of a rival center of Pagan and Greek-speaking political activity in the east, and it was proposed that a new eastern capital should represent the integration of the east into the Roman Empire as a whole; Constantine chose Byzantium.

- The city was thus founded in 324, dedicated on May 11, 330, and renamed Constantinople.

- The Byzantine Empire considered Constantine its founder, and the Holy Roman Empire reckoned him among the venerable figures of its tradition.

Terms

Byzantium

An ancient Greek colony on the site that later became Constantinople, and eventually Istanbul.

Byzantine Empire

Also referred to as the Eastern Roman Empire, was the continuation of the Roman Empire in the east during Late Antiquity and the Middle Ages, when the empire's capital city was Constantinople.

The age of Constantine marked a distinct epoch in the history of the Roman Empire. He built a new imperial residence at Byzantium, and renamed the city Constantinople after himself (the laudatory epithet of "New Rome" came later, and was never an official title). It would later become the capital of the empire for over one thousand years; for this reason the later Eastern Empire would come to be known as the Byzantine Empire.

Background: War With Licinius

After defeating Maxentius, Constantine gradually consolidated his military superiority over his rivals in the crumbling tetrarchy. In 313, he met Licinius in Milan to secure their alliance by the marriage of Licinius and Constantine's half-sister, Constantia. During this meeting, the emperors agreed on the so-called Edict of Milan, officially granting full tolerance to Christianity and all religions in the Empire. In the year 320, Licinius allegedly reneged on the religious freedom promised by the Edict of Milan in 313, and began to oppress Christians anew, generally without bloodshed, but resorting to confiscations and sacking of Christian office-holders.

This dubious arrangement eventually became a challenge to Constantine in the west, climaxing in the great civil war of 324. Licinius, aided by Goth mercenaries, represented the past and the ancient Pagan faiths. Constantine and his Franks marched under the standard of the *labarum* Chi-Rho, and both sides saw the battle in religious terms. Outnumbered, but fired by their zeal, Constantine's army emerged victorious in the Battle of Adrianople. Licinius fled across the Bosphorus and appointed Martius Martinianus, the commander of his bodyguard, as Caesar, but Constantine next won the Battle of the Hellespont, and finally the Battle of Chrysopolis on September 18, 324. Licinius and Martinianus surrendered to Constantine at Nicomedia on the promise their lives would be spared: they were sent to live as private citizens in Thessalonica and Cappadocia, respectively, but in 325, Constantine accused Licinius of plotting against him and had them both arrested and hanged. Licinius's son (the son of Constantine's half-sister) was also killed. Thus, Constantine became the sole emperor of the Roman Empire.

Foundation of Constantinople

Licinius' defeat came to represent the defeat of a rival center of Pagan and Greek-speaking political activity in the east, as opposed to the Christian and Latin-speaking Rome, and it was proposed that a new eastern capital should represent the integration of the east into the Roman Empire as a whole, as a center of learning, prosperity, and cultural preservation for the whole of the eastern Roman Empire. Among the various locations proposed for this alternative capital, Constantine appears to have toyed earlier with Serdica (present-day Sofia), as he was reported saying that "Serdica is my Rome." Sirmium and Thessalonica were also considered. Eventually, however, Constantine decided to work on the Greek city of Byzantium, which offered the advantage of having already been extensively rebuilt on Roman patterns of urbanism, during the preceding century, by Septimius Severus and Caracalla, who had already acknowledged its strategic importance.

The city was thus founded in 324, dedicated on May 11, 330, and renamed *Constantinopolis* ("Constantine's City" or Constantinople in English). Special commemorative coins were issued in 330 to honor the event. The new city was protected by the relics of the True Cross, the Rod of Moses, and other holy relics, though a cameo now at the Hermitage Museum also represented Constantine crowned by the tyche of the new city. The figures of old gods were either replaced or assimilated into a framework of Christian symbolism. Constantine built the new Church of the Holy Apostles on the site of a temple to Aphrodite. Generations later there was the story that a divine vision led Constantine to this spot, and an angel no one else could see led him on a circuit of the new walls. The capital would often be compared to the 'old' Rome as *Nova Roma Constantinopolitana*, the "New Rome of Constantinople." Constantinople was a superb base from which to guard the Danube River, and it was reasonably close to the eastern frontiers. Constantine also began the building of the great fortified walls, which were expanded and rebuilt in subsequent ages.

Constantinopolis Coin. Coin struck by Constantine I to commemorate the founding of Constantinople.

Legacy

Historian J.B. Bury asserts that "the foundation of Constantinople [...] inaugurated a permanent division between the Eastern and Western, the Greek and the Latin, halves of the empire—a division to which events had already pointed—and affected decisively the whole subsequent history of Europe."

The Byzantine Empire considered Constantine its founder, and the Holy Roman Empire reckoned him among the venerable figures of its tradition. In the later Byzantine state, it had become a great honor for an emperor to be hailed as a "new Constantine." Ten emperors, including the last emperor of the Eastern Roman Empire, carried the name. Monumental Constantinian forms were used at the court of Charlemagne to suggest that he was Constantine's successor and equal. Constantine acquired a mythic role as a warrior against "heathens."

Sources

Attributions

CC licensed content, Specific attribution

- Boundless World History. **Authored by**: Boundless. **Located at**: https://courses.lumenlearning.com/boundless-worldhistory/. **License**: *CC BY-SA: Attribution-ShareAlike*

The Decline and Fall of the Roman Empire

Learning Objective

- Analyze, broadly, the causes of the fall of the Roman Empire

Key Points

- Throughout the 5th century, the empire's territories in western Europe and northwestern Africa, including Italy, fell to various invading or indigenous peoples, in what is sometimes called the Migration Period.

- By the late 3rd century, the city of Rome no longer served as an effective capital for the emperor, and various cities were used as new administrative capitals. Successive emperors, starting with Constantine, privileged the eastern city of Byzantium, which he had entirely rebuilt after a siege.

- In 476, after being refused lands in Italy, Odacer and his Germanic mercenaries took Ravenna, the Western Roman capital at the time, and deposed Western Emperor Romulus Augustus. The whole of Italy was quickly conquered, and Odoacer's rule became recognized in the Eastern Empire.

- Four broad schools of thought exist on the decline and fall of the Roman Empire: decay owing to general malaise, monocausal decay, catastrophic collapse, and transformation.

Terms

Migration Period

Also known as the period of the Barbarian Invasions, it was a period of intensified human migration in Europe from about 400 to 800 CE, during the transition from Late Antiquity to the Early Middle Ages.

Odoacer

A soldier, who came to power in the Western Roman Empire in 476 CE. His reign is commonly seen as marking the end of the Western Roman Empire.

The Fall of the Western Roman Empire was the process of decline during which the empire failed to enforce its rule, and its vast territory was divided into several successor polities. The Roman Empire lost the strengths that had allowed it to exercise effective control; modern historians mention factors including the effectiveness and numbers of the army, the health and numbers of the Roman population, the strength of the economy, the competence of the emperor, the religious changes of the period, and the efficiency of the civil administration. Increasing pressure from barbarians outside Roman culture also contributed greatly to the collapse. The reasons for the collapse are major subjects of the historiography of the ancient world, and they inform much modern discourse on state failure.

By 476 CE, when Odoacer deposed Emperor Romulus, the Western Roman Empire wielded negligible military, political, or financial power and had no effective control over the scattered western domains that could still be described as Roman. Invading "barbarians" had established their own polities on most of the area of the Western Empire. While its legitimacy lasted for centuries longer and its cultural influence remains today, the Western Empire never had the strength to rise again.

It is important to note, however, that the so-called fall of the Roman Empire specifically refers to the fall of the *Western* Roman Empire, since the Eastern Roman Empire, or what became known as the Byzantine Empire, whose capital was founded by Constantine, remained for another 1,000 years. Theodosius was the last emperor who ruled over the whole empire. After his death in 395, he gave the two halves of the empire to his two sons, Arcadius and Honorius; Arcadius became ruler in the east, with his capital in Constantinople, and Honorius became ruler in the west, with his capital in Milan, and later Ravenna.

Rome in the 5th Century CE

Throughout the 5th century, the empire's territories in western Europe and northwestern Africa, including Italy, fell to various invading or indigenous peoples in what is sometimes called the Migration Period, also known as the Barbarian Invasions, from the Roman and South European perspective. The first migrations of peoples were made by Germanic tribes, such as the Goths, Vandals, Angles, Saxons, Lombards, Suebi, Frisii, Jutes and Franks; they were later pushed westwards by the Huns, Avars, Slavs, and Bulgars.

Although the eastern half still survived with borders essentially intact for several centuries (until the Muslim conquests), the Empire as a whole had initiated major cultural and political transformations since the Crisis of the Third Century, with the shift towards a more openly autocratic and ritualized form of government, the adoption of Christianity as the state religion, and a general rejection of the traditions and values of Classical Antiquity.

The reasons for the decline of the Empire are still debated today, and are likely multiple. Historians infer that the population appears to have diminished in many provinces (especially western Europe), judging from the diminishing size of fortifications built to protect the cities from barbarian incursions from the 3rd century on. Some historians even have suggested that parts of the periphery were no longer inhabited, because these fortifications were restricted to the center of the city only. By the late 3rd century, the city of Rome no longer served as an effective capital for the emperor, and various cities were used as new administrative capitals. Successive emperors, starting with Constantine, privileged the eastern city of Byzantium, which he had entirely rebuilt after a siege. Later renamed Constantinople, and protected by formidable walls in the late 4th and early 5th centuries, it was to become the largest and most powerful city of Christian Europe in the Early Middle Ages. Since the Crisis of the Third Century, the empire was intermittently ruled by more than one emperor at once (usually two), presiding over different regions.

The Latin-speaking west, under dreadful demographic crisis, and the wealthier Greek-speaking east, also began to diverge politically and culturally. Although this was a gradual process, still incomplete when Italy came under the rule of barbarian chieftains in the last quarter of the 5th century, it deepened further afterward, and had lasting consequences for the medieval history of Europe.

In 476, after being refused lands in Italy, Orestes' Germanic mercenaries, under the leadership of the chieftain Odoacer, captured and executed Orestes and took Ravenna, the Western Roman capital at the time, deposing Western Emperor Romulus Augustus. The whole of Italy was quickly conquered, and Odoacer's rule became recognized in the Eastern Empire. Meanwhile, much of the rest of the Western provinces were conquered by waves of Germanic invasions, most of them being disconnected politically from the east altogether, and continuing a slow decline. Although Roman political authority in the west was lost, Roman culture would last in most parts of the former western provinces into the 6th century and beyond.

Romulus Augustus Resigns the Crown. Charlotte Mary Yonge's 1880 artist rendition of Romulus Augustus resigning the crown to Odoacer.

Theories on the Decline and Fall

The various theories and explanations for the fall of the Roman Empire in the west may be very broadly classified into four schools of thought (although the classification is not without overlap):

- Decay owing to general malaise
- Monocausal decay
- Catastrophic collapse
- Transformation

The tradition positing general malaise goes back to the historian, Edward Gibbon, who argued that the edifice of the Roman Empire had been built on unsound foundations from the beginning. According to Gibbon, the fall was—in the final analysis—inevitable. On the other hand, Gibbon had assigned a major portion of the responsibility for the decay to the influence of Christianity, and is often, though perhaps unjustly, seen as the founding father of the school of monocausal explanation. On the other hand, the school of catastrophic collapse holds that the fall of the empire had not been a pre-determined event and need not be taken for granted. Rather, it was due to the combined effect of a number of adverse processes, many of them set in motion by the Migration Period, that together applied too much stress to the empire's basically sound structure. Finally, the transformation school challenges the whole notion of the 'fall' of the empire, asking instead to distinguish between the fall into disuse of a particular political dispensation, anyway unworkable towards its end; and the fate of the Roman civilization that under-girded the empire. According to this school, drawing its basic premise from the Pirenne thesis, the Roman world underwent a gradual (though often violent) series of transformations, morphing into the medieval world. The historians belonging to this school often prefer to speak of Late Antiquity, instead of the Fall of the Roman Empire.

The Ostrogothic Kingdom, which rose from the ruins of the Western Roman Empire.

Sources

Attributions

CC licensed content, Specific attribution

- Boundless World History. **Authored by**: Boundless. **Located at**: https://courses.lumenlearning.com/boundless-worldhistory/. **License**: *CC BY-SA: Attribution-ShareAlike*

7. The Byzantine Empire

Justinian and Theodora

Key Points

- Emperor Justinian the Great was responsible for substantial expansion of the Byzantine Empire, and for conquering Africa, Spain, Rome, and most of Italy.

- Justinian was responsible for the construction of the Hagia Sophia, the center of Christianity in Constantinople. Even today, the Hagia Sophia is recognized as one of the greatest buildings in the world.

- Justinian also systematized the Roman legal code that served as the basis for law in the Byzantine Empire.

- After a plague reduced the Byzantine population, they lost Rome and Italy to the Ostrogoths, and several important cities to the Persians.

Terms

Hagia Sophia

A church built by Byzantine Emperor Justinian; the center of Christianity in Constantinople and one of the greatest buildings in the world to this day. It is now a mosque in the Muslim Istanbul.

Nika riots

When angry racing fans, already angry over rising taxes, became enraged at Emperor Justinian for arresting two popular charioteers, and tried to depose him in 532 CE.

Byzantine Empire from Constantine to Justinian

One of Constantine's successors, Theodosius I (379-395), was the last emperor to rule both the Eastern and Western halves of the empire. In 391 and 392, he issued a series of edicts essentially banning pagan religion. Pagan festivals and sacrifices were banned, as was access to all pagan temples and places of worship. The state of the empire in 395 may be described in terms of the outcome of Constantine's work. The dynastic principle was established so firmly that the emperor who died in that year, Theodosius I, could bequeath the imperial office jointly to his sons, Arcadius in the East and Honorius in the West.

The Eastern Empire was largely spared the difficulties faced by the west in the third and fourth centuries, due in part to a more firmly established urban culture and greater financial resources, which allowed it to placate invaders with tribute and pay foreign mercenaries. Throughout the fifth century, various invading armies overran the Western Empire but spared the east. Theodosius II further fortified the walls of Constantinople, leaving the city impervious to most attacks; the walls were not breached until 1204.

To fend off the Huns, Theodosius had to pay an enormous annual tribute to Attila. His successor, Marcian, refused to continue to pay the tribute, but Attila had already diverted his attention to the west. After his death in 453, the Hunnic Empire collapsed, and many of the remaining Huns were often hired as mercenaries by Constantinople.

Leo I succeeded Marcian as emperor, and after the fall of Attila, the true chief in Constantinople was the Alan general, Aspar. Leo I managed to free himself from the influence of the non-Orthodox chief by supporting the rise of the Isaurians, a semi-barbarian tribe living in southern Anatolia. Aspar and his son, Ardabur, were murdered in a riot in 471, and henceforth, Constantinople restored Orthodox leadership for centuries.

When Leo died in 474, Zeno and Ariadne's younger son succeeded to the throne as Leo II, with Zeno as regent. When Leo II died later that year, Zeno became emperor. The end of the Western Empire is sometimes dated to 476, early in Zeno's reign, when the Germanic Roman general, Odoacer, deposed the titular Western Emperor Romulus Augustulus, but declined to replace him with another puppet.

Emperor Justinian I

In 527 CE, Justinian I came to the throne in Constantinople. He dreamed of reconquering the lands of the Western Roman Empire and ruling a single, united Roman Empire from his seat in Constantinople.

Emperor Justinian. Byzantine Emperor Justinian I depicted on one of the famous mosaics of the Basilica of San Vitale, Ravenna.

The western conquests began in 533, as Justinian sent his general, Belisarius, to reclaim the former province of Africa from the Vandals, who had been in control since 429 with their capital at Carthage. Belisarius successfully defeated the Vandals and claimed Africa for Constantinople. Next, Justinian sent him to take Italy from the Ostrogoths in 535 CE. Belisarius defeated the Ostrogoths in a series of battles and reclaimed Rome. By 540 CE, most of Italy was in Justinian's hands. He sent another army to conquer Spain.

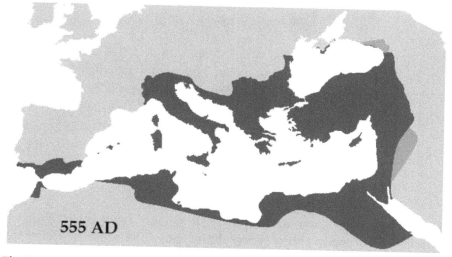

The Byzantine Empire at its greatest extent, in 555 CE under Justinian the Great.

Accomplishments in Byzantium

Justinian also undertook many important projects at home. Much of Constantinople was burned down early in Justinian's reign after a series of riots called the Nika riots, in 532 CE, when angry racing fans became enraged at Justinian for arresting two popular charioteers (though this was really just the last straw for a populace increasingly angry over rising taxes) and tried to depose him. The riots were put down, and Justinian set about rebuilding the city on a grander scale. His greatest accomplishment was the Hagia Sophia, the most important church of the city. The Hagia Sophia was a staggering work of Byzantine architecture, intended to awe all who set foot in the church. It was the largest church in the world for nearly a thousand years, and for the rest of Byzantine history it was the center of Christian worship in Constantinople.

The Hagia Sophia. Byzantine Emperor Justinian built the Greek Orthodox Church of the Holy Wisdom of God, the Hagia Sophia, which was completed in only four and a half years (532 CE-537 CE). Even now, it is universally acknowledged as one of the greatest buildings in the world.

Emperor Justinian's most important contribution, perhaps, was a unified Roman legal code. Prior to his reign, Roman laws had differed from region to region, and many contradicted one another. The Romans had attempted to systematize the legal code in the fifth century but had not completed the effort. Justinian set up a commission of lawyers to put together a single code, listing each law by subject so that it could be easily referenced. This not only served as the basis for law in the Byzantine Empire, but it was the main influence on the Catholic Church's development of canon law, and went on to become the basis of law in many European countries. Justinian's law code continues to have a major influence on public international law to this day.

The impact of a more unified legal code and military conflicts was the increased ability for the Byzantine Empire to establish trade and improve their economic standing. Byzantine merchants traded not only all over the Mediterranean region, but also throughout regions to the east. These included areas around the Black Sea, the Red Sea, and the Indian Ocean.

Theodora

Theodora was empress of the Byzantine Empire and the wife of Emperor Justinian I. She was one of the most influential and powerful of the Byzantine empresses. Some sources mention her as empress regnant, with Justinian I as her co-regent. Along with her husband, she is a saint in the Eastern Orthodox Church, commemorated on November 14.

Theodora participated in Justinian's legal and spiritual reforms, and her involvement in the increase of the rights of women was substantial. She had laws passed that prohibited forced prostitution and closed brothels. She created a convent on the Asian side of the Dardanelles called the Metanoia (Repentance), where the ex-prostitutes could support themselves. She also expanded the rights of women in divorce and property ownership, instituted the death penalty for rape, forbade exposure of unwanted infants, gave mothers some guardianship rights over their children, and forbade the killing of a wife who committed adultery.

Justinian's Difficulties

A terrible plague swept through the empire, killing Theodora and almost killing him. The plague wiped out huge numbers of the empire's population, leaving villages empty and crops unharvested. The army was also afflicted, and the Ostrogoths were able to effectively regain Italy in 546 CE, through guerrilla warfare against the Byzantine occupiers.

With Justinian's army bogged down fighting in Italy, the empire's defenses against the Persians on its eastern frontiers were weakened. In the Roman-Persian Wars, the Persians invaded and destroyed a number of important cities. Justinian was forced to establish a humiliating 50-year peace treaty with them in 561 CE.

Still, Justinian kept the empire from collapse. He sent a new general, Narses, to Italy with a small force. Narses finally defeated the Ostrogoths and drove them back out of Italy. By the time the war was over, Italy, once one of the most prosperous lands in the ancient world, was wrecked. The city of Rome changed hands multiple times, and most of the cities of Italy were abandoned or fell into a long period of decline. The impoverishment of Italy and the weakened Byzantine military made it impossible for the empire to hold the peninsula. Soon a new Germanic tribe, the Lombards, came in and conquered most of Italy, though Rome, Naples, and Ravenna remained isolated pockets of Byzantine control. At the same time, another new barbarian enemy, the Slavs, appeared from north of the Danube. They devastated Greece and the Balkans, and in the absence of strong Byzantine military might, they settled in small communities in these lands.

Sources

Attributions

The Justinian Code

Learning Objective

- Explain the historical significance of Justinian's legal reforms

Key Points

- Shortly after Justinian became emperor in 527, he decided the empire's legal system needed repair.
- Early in his reign, Justinian appointed an official, Tribonian, to oversee this task.
- The project as a whole became known as *Corpus juris civilis*, or the Justinian Code.
- It consists of the *Codex Iustinianus*, the *Digesta*, the *Institutiones*, and the *Novellae*.
- Many of the laws contained in the Codex were aimed at regulating religious practice.
- The *Corpus* formed the basis not only of Roman jurisprudence (including ecclesiastical Canon Law), but also influenced civil law throughout the Middle Ages and into modern nation states.

Terms

Corpus juris civilis

The modern name for a collection of fundamental works in jurisprudence, issued from 529 to 534 by order of Justinian I, Eastern Roman Emperor.

Justinian I

A Byzantine emperor from 527 to 565. During his reign, he sought to revive the empire's greatness and reconquer the lost western half of the historical Roman Empire; he also enacted important legal codes.

Byzantine Emperor Justinian I achieved lasting fame through his judicial reforms, particularly through the complete revision of all Roman law, something that had not previously been attempted. There existed three codices of imperial laws and other individual laws, many of which conflicted or were out of date. The total of Justinian's legislature is known today as the *Corpus juris civilis*.

The work as planned had three parts:

1. *Codex:* a compilation, by selection and extraction, of imperial enactments to date, going back to Hadrian in the 2nd century CE.

2. *Digesta:* an encyclopedia composed of mostly brief extracts from the writings of Roman jurists. Fragments were taken out of various legal treatises and opinions and inserted in the *Digesta*.

3. *Institutiones:* a student textbook, mainly introducing the *Codex*, although it has important conceptual elements that are less developed in the *Codex* or the *Digesta*.

All three parts, even the textbook, were given force of law. They were intended to be, together, the sole source of law; reference to any other source, including the original texts from which the *Codex* and the *Digesta* had been taken, was forbidden. Nonetheless, Justinian found himself having to enact further laws, and today these are counted as a fourth part of the *Corpus*, the *Novellae Constitutiones*. As opposed to the rest of the *Corpus*, the *Novellae* appeared in Greek, the common language of the Eastern Empire.

The work was directed by Tribonian, an official in Justinian's court. His team was authorized to edit what they included. How far they made amendments is not recorded and, in the main, cannot be known because most of the originals have not survived. The text was composed and distributed almost entirely in Latin, which was still the official language of the government of the Byzantine Empire in 529-534, whereas the prevalent language of merchants, farmers, seamen, and other citizens was Greek.

Many of the laws contained in the *Codex* were aimed at regulating religious practice, included numerous provisions served to secure the status of Christianity as the state religion of the empire, uniting church and state, and making anyone who was not connected to the Christian church a non-citizen. It also contained laws forbidding particular pagan practices; for example, all persons present at a pagan sacrifice may be indicted as if for murder. Other laws, some influenced by his wife, Theodora, include those to protect prostitutes from exploitation, and women from being forced into prostitution. Rapists were treated severely. Further, by his policies, women charged with major crimes should be guarded by other women to prevent sexual abuse; if a woman was widowed, her dowry should be returned; and a husband could not take on a major debt without his wife giving her consent twice.

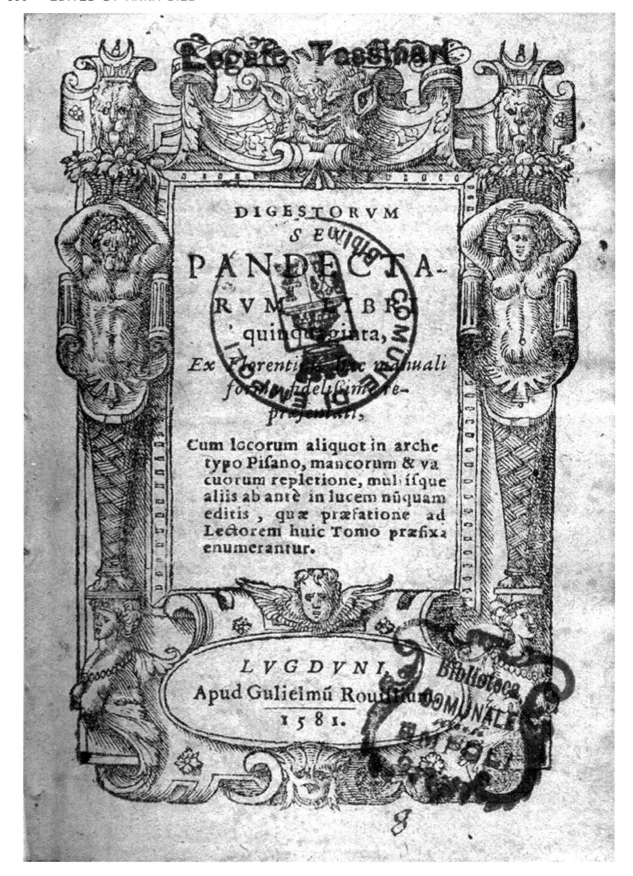

DIGESTORVM

PANDECTA-
RVM LIBR
quinquaginta,

Ex Florentinis ipse manuali
forma fidelissime re-
præsentati;

Cum locorum aliquot in arche
typo Pisano, mancorum & va
cuorum repletione, multisque
aliis ab antè in lucem nûquam
editis , quæ præfatione ad
Lectorem huic Tomo præfixa
enumerantur.

LVGDVNI,
Apud Gulielmû Rouillium
1581.

A later copy of Justinian's Digesta: Digestorum, seu Pandectarum libri quinquaginta. Lugduni apud Gulielmum Rouillium, 1581. From Biblioteca Comunale "Renato Fucini" di Empoli.

Legacy

The *Corpus* forms the basis of Latin jurisprudence (including ecclesiastical Canon Law) and, for historians, provides a valuable insight into the concerns and activities of the later Roman Empire. As a collection, it gathers together the many sources in which the laws and the other rules were expressed or published (proper laws, senatorial consults, imperial decrees, case law, and jurists' opinions and interpretations). It formed the basis of later Byzantine law, as expressed in the *Basilika* of Basil I and Leo VI the Wise. The only western province where the Justinian Code was introduced was Italy, from where it was to pass to western Europe in the 12th century, and become the basis of much European law code. It eventually passed to eastern Europe, where it appeared in Slavic editions, and it also passed on to Russia.

It was not in general use during the Early Middle Ages. After the Early Middle Ages, interest in it revived. It was "received" or imitated as private law, and its public law content was quarried for arguments by both secular and ecclesiastical authorities. The revived Roman law, in turn, became the foundation of law in all civil law jurisdictions. The provisions of the *Corpus Juris Civilis* also influenced the canon law of the Roman Catholic Church; it was said that *ecclesia vivit lege romana*—the church lives by Roman law. Its influence on common law legal systems has been much smaller, although some basic concepts from the *Corpus* have survived through Norman law—such as the contrast, especially in the Institutes, between "law" (statute) and custom. The *Corpus* continues to have a major influence on public international law. Its four parts thus constitute the foundation documents of the western legal tradition.

Sources

Attributions

CC licensed content, Specific attribution

8. The Middle Ages in Europe

The Vikings

- Illustrate how Viking ships were an integral part of Viking culture, influencing trade and warfare

Key Points

- The late 8th to the mid-11th centuries is commonly known as the Viking Age of Scandinavian history.

- Vikings were renowned for their ships, which were an integral part of their culture, facilitating, trade, exploration, and warfare.

- Weapons indicated the social status of a Viking, and warfare and violence were heavily influenced by pagan religious beliefs.

- The Vikings established and engaged in extensive trading networks throughout the known world and had a profound influence on the economic development of Europe and Scandinavia.

- Vikings are often thought of as brutal warriors due to the manner in which they settled in the northeast of England, though in recent years they have been recognized for their technological skills and seamanship.

- Viking culture and stories were written about in the Sagas, stories compiled almost one to three hundred years after Viking raids had mostly ceased.

- When settling land in Greenland and Iceland, Vikings established their form of democratic government which included discussion of rules of law and other issues during Things, assemblies open to all free people.

Terms

Charlemagne

A ruler of the Carolingian Dynasty renowned for his thirty-year military campaign to spread Christianity in Europe and for his interests in education and religion.

longship

A Viking ship intended for warfare and exploration and designed for speed and agility. Longships were equipped with a sail as well as oars, making navigation independent of the wind possible.

Obotrites

A confederation of medieval West Slavic tribes within the territory of modern northern Germany.

Scandinavia

A historical and cultural-linguistic region in northern Europe characterized by a common Germanic heritage and related languages. It includes the three kingdoms of Denmark, Norway, and Sweden.

Constantinople

The capital city of the Roman, Byzantine, Latin, and Ottoman empires. During the 12th century, it was the largest and wealthiest city in Europe.

Vikings were Norse seafarers who originated in Scandinavia and raided, traded, explored, and settled in wide areas of Europe, Asia, and the North Atlantic islands. The period from the earliest recorded raids in the 790s until the Norman conquest of England in 1066 is commonly known as the Viking Age of Scandinavian history. Vikings used the Norwegian Sea and Baltic Sea for sea routes to the south.

Viking Ships

There have been several archaeological finds of Viking ships of all sizes, providing knowledge of the craftsmanship that went into building them. There were many types of Viking ships, built according to their intended uses, though the most iconic type is probably the longship. Longships were intended for warfare and exploration, designed for speed and agility, and equipped with oars to complement the sail, making navigation independent of the wind possible. It was the longship that allowed the Norse to "go Viking" (on an expedition), which might explain why this type of ship has become almost synonymous with the concept of Vikings. Longships were the epitome of Scandinavian naval power at the time, and were highly valued possessions.

Model of a Viking longship
Model of the Gokstad ship. The Gokstad ship is a Viking ship found in a burial mound at Gokstad farm in Sandar,
Sandefjord, Vestfold, Norway. Dendrochronological dating suggests that the ship was built around 890 AD.

Ships were an integral part of Viking culture. They facilitated everyday transportation across seas and waterways, exploration of new lands, raids, conquests, and trade with neighboring cultures. They also held a major religious importance; magnates and people with a high status were sometimes buried in a ship along with animal sacrifices, weapons, provisions, and other items.

Weapons and Warfare

Our knowledge about the arms and armor of the Viking age is based on archaeological finds, pictorial representation, and to some extent on the accounts in the Norse sagas and Norse laws recorded in the 13th century. According to custom, all free Norse men were required to own weapons and were permitted to carry them all the time. Weapons were indicative of a Viking's social status; a wealthy Viking would have a complete ensemble of a helmet, shield, mail shirt, and sword. A typical *bóndi* (freeman) was more likely to fight with a spear and shield, and most also carried a knife and side-arm. Bows were used in the opening stages of land battles and at sea, but they tended to be considered less "honorable" than a weapon that could be used in close combat. Vikings were relatively unusual for the time in their use of axes as a main battle weapon.

The warfare and violence of the Vikings were often motivated and fueled by their belief in Norse religion, focusing on Thor and Odin, the gods of war and death. Apart from two or three representations of (ritual) helmets with protrusions that may be either stylized ravens, snakes, or horns, no depiction of the helmets of Viking warriors, and no preserved helmet, has horns. The stereotypical Viking helmet was thus mainly a fiction of a later romanticized image of the Viking. The formal, close-quarters style of Viking combat (either in shield walls or aboard "ship islands") would have made horned helmets cumbersome and hazardous to the warrior's own side.

The Vikings are believed to have engaged in a disordered style of frenetic, furious fighting, although the brutal perception of the Vikings is largely a misconception, likely attributed to Christian misunderstandings regarding paganism at the time.

Viking Expansion

Facilitated by advanced seafaring skills, Viking activities at times also extended into the Mediterranean littoral, North Africa, the Middle East, and Central Asia. Following extended phases of exploration on seas and rivers, expansion, and settlement, Viking communities and polities were established in diverse areas of northwestern Europe, European Russia, and the North Atlantic islands, and as far as the northeastern coast of North America. During their explorations, Vikings raided and pillaged, but also engaged in trade, settled wide-ranging colonies, and acted as mercenaries. This period of expansion witnessed the wider dissemination of Norse culture while simultaneously introducing strong foreign cultural influences into Scandinavia itself, with profound developmental implications in both directions.

Vikings under Leif Ericsson, the heir to Erik the Red, reached North America and set up a short-lived settlement in present-day L'Anse aux Meadows, Newfoundland and Labrador, Canada. Longer and more-established settlements were formed in Greenland, Iceland, Great Britain, and Normandy.

Viking expansion into continental Europe was limited. Their realm was bordered by powerful cultures to the south. Early on it was the Saxons, who occupied Old Saxony, located in what is now northern Germany. The Saxons were a fierce and powerful people and were often in conflict with the Vikings. To counter the Saxon aggression and solidify their own presence, the Danes constructed the huge defense fortification of Danevirke in and around Hedeby. The Vikings soon witnessed the violent subduing of the Saxons by Charlemagne in the thirty-year Saxon Wars from 772–804. The Saxon defeat resulted in their forced christening and the absorption of Old Saxony into the Carolingian Empire.

Fear of the Franks led the Vikings to further expand Danevirke, and the defense constructions remained in use throughout the Viking Age and even up until 1864. The south coast of the Baltic Sea was ruled by the Obotrites, a federation of Slavic tribes loyal to the Carolingians and later the Frankish empire. The Vikings, led by King Gudfred, destroyed the Obotrite city of Reric on the southern Baltic coast in 808 and transferred the merchants and traders to Hedeby. This secured their supremacy in the Baltic Sea, which endured throughout the Viking Age.

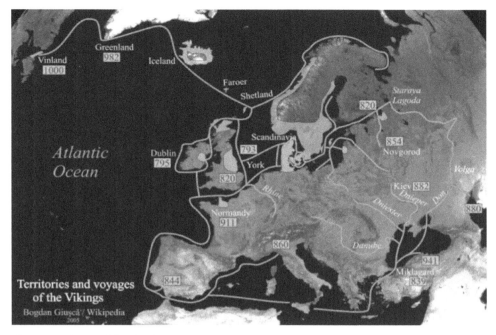

Viking expeditions (blue line)
Light blue: Itineraries of the Vikings, depicting the immense breadth of their voyages through
most of Europe, the Mediterranean Sea, Northern Africa, Asia Minor, the Arctic, and North
America. Light green: main settlement areas, in the first millennium

Legacy

The 200-year Viking influence on European history is filled with tales of plunder and colonization, and the majority of these chronicles came from western witnesses and their descendants. Medieval Christians in Europe were totally unprepared for the Viking incursions and could find no explanation for their arrival and the accompanying suffering they experienced at their hands, save the "Wrath of God." More than any other single event, the attack on Lindisfarne demonized perception of the Vikings for the next twelve centuries. Not until the 1890s did scholars outside Scandinavia begin to seriously reassess the achievements of the Vikings, recognizing their artistry, technological skills, and seamanship.

Studies of genetic diversity have provided scientific confirmation to accompany archaeological evidence of Viking expansion. They additionally indicate patterns of ancestry, imply new migrations, and show the actual flow of individuals between disparate regions. Genetic evidence contradicts the common perception that Vikings were primarily pillagers and raiders. An article by Roger Highfield summarizes recent research and concludes that, as both male and female genetic markers are present, the evidence is indicative of colonization instead of raiding and occupying. However, this is also disputed by unequal ratios of male and female haplotypes, which indicate that more men settled than women, an element of a raiding or occupying population.

Sources

Attributions

- Boundless World History. **Authored by**: Boundless. **Located at**: https://courses.lumenlearning.com/boundless-worldhistory/. **License**: *CC BY-SA: Attribution-ShareAlike*

Charles Martel and Pepin the Short

Learning Objective

- Explain the significance of Charles Martel's victory at the Battle of Tours

Key Points

- Charles Martel was the de facto ruler of Francia (France) who defeated the Umayyad Caliphate in the Battle of Tours.

- The Battle of Tours was historically significant because it stopped the advance of the Muslim empire, which had successfully conquered much of Europe; many historians believe that had Charles failed, no power in Europe would have been able to halt Islamic expansion.

- Charles divided his land between his sons Carloman and Pepin.

- After Carloman retired to religious life, Pepin became the sole ruler of the Franks and continued to consolidate and expand his power to become one of the most powerful and successful rulers of his time.

Terms

Donation of Pepin

Donations bestowed by Pepin the Short that provided a legal basis for the formal organizing of the "Papal States," which inaugurated papal temporal rule over civil authorities.

Battle of Tours

A battle that pitted Frankish and Burgundian forces under Charles Martel against an army of the Umayyad Caliphate led by 'Abdul Rahman Al Ghafiqi, Governor-General of al-Andalus. The latter was defeated, thus ending the expansion of the Muslim empire into Europe.

Umayyad Caliphate

The second of the four major Arab caliphates established after the death of Muhammad; continued the Muslim conquests, incorporating the Caucasus, Transoxiana, Sindh, the Maghreb, and the Iberian Peninsula into the Muslim world, making it the fifth largest empire in history in both area and proportion of the world's population.

Franks

Historically known first as a group of Germanic tribes that inhabited the land between the Lower and Middle Rhine in the 3rd century CE, and second as the people of Gaul who merged with the Gallo-Roman populations during succeeding centuries, passing on their name to modern-day France and becoming part of the heritage of the modern French people.

Charles Martel

Charles Martel (688-741) was a Frankish statesman and military leader who, as Duke and Prince of the Franks and Mayor of the Palace, was de facto ruler of Francia from 718 until his death. The son of the Frankish statesman Pepin of Herstal and a noblewoman named Alpaida, Charles successfully asserted his claims to dominance as successor to his father, who was the power behind the throne in Frankish politics. Continuing and building on his father's work, he restored centralized government in Francia and began the series of military campaigns that re-established the Franks as the undisputed masters of all Gaul.

Apart from his military endeavors, Charles is considered to be a founding figure of the European Middle Ages. Skilled as an administrator as well as a warrior, he is credited with a seminal role in the emerging responsibilities of the knights of courts, and so in the development of the Frankish system of feudalism. Moreover, Charles—a great patron of Saint Boniface—made the first attempt at reconciliation between the Franks and the papacy. Pope Gregory III, whose realm was being menaced by the Lombards, offered Charles the Roman consulship in exchange for becoming the defender of the Holy See, but Charles declined.

Although Charles never assumed the title of king, he divided Francia, as a king would have, between his sons Carloman and Pepin. The latter became the first of the Carolingians, the family of Charles Martel, to become king. Charles's grandson, Charlemagne, extended the Frankish realms to include much of the West, and became the first emperor in the West since the fall of Rome. Therefore, on the basis of his achievements, Charles is seen as laying the groundwork for the Carolingian Empire. In summing up the man, Gibbon wrote that Charles was "the hero of the age," whereas Guerard described him as being the "champion of the Cross against the Crescent."

Battles of Tours

After working to establish a unity in Gaul, Charles's attention was called to foreign conflicts; dealing with the Islamic advance into Western Europe was a foremost concern. Arab and Berber Islamic forces had conquered Spain (711), crossed the Pyrenees (720), seized a major dependency of the Visigoths (721–725), and after intermittent challenges, under Abdul Rahman Al Ghafiqi, Governor-General of al-Andalus, advanced toward Gaul and on Tours, "the holy town of Gaul." In October 732, the army of the Umayyad Caliphate, led by Al Ghafiqi, met Frankish and Burgundian forces under Charles in an area between the cities of Tours and Poitiers (modern north-central France), leading to a decisive, historically important Frankish victory known as the Battle of Tours.

Abdul Rahman Al Ghafiqi was killed, and Charles subsequently extended his authority in the south. Charles further took the offensive after Tours, destroying fortresses at Agde, Béziers, and Maguelonne, and engaging Islamic forces at Nimes, though ultimately failing to recover Narbonne (737) or to fully reclaim the Visigoth's Narbonensis. He thereafter made significant external gains against fellow Christian realms, establishing Frankish control over Bavaria, Alemannia, and Frisia, and compelling some of the Saxon tribes to offer tribute (738). Details of the Battle of Tours, including its exact location and the number of combatants, cannot be determined from accounts that have survived. Notably, the Frankish troops won the battle without cavalry.

Charles's victory is widely believed to have stopped the northward advance of Umayyad forces from the Iberian Peninsula, and to have preserved Christianity in Europe during a period when Muslim rule was overrunning the remains of the old Roman and Persian empires.

Ninth-century chroniclers, who interpreted the outcome of the battle as divine judgment in Charles's favor, gave him the nickname Martellus ("The Hammer"). Later Christian chroniclers and pre-20th-century historians praised Charles Martel as the champion of Christianity, characterizing the battle as the decisive turning point in the struggle against Islam, a struggle which preserved Christianity as the religion of Europe. According to modern military historian Victor Davis Hanson, "most of the 18th and 19th century historians, like Gibbon, saw Poitiers (Tours), as a landmark battle that marked the high tide of the Muslim advance into Europe." Leopold von Ranke felt that "Poitiers (Tours) was the turning point of one of the most important epochs in the history of the world."

There is little dispute that the battle helped lay the foundations of the Carolingian Empire and Frankish domination of Europe for the next century. Most historians agree that "the establishment of Frankish power in western Europe shaped that continent's destiny and the Battle of Tours confirmed that power."

Steuben's Bataille de Poitiers. A painting of the Battle of Tours by Charles de Steuben, 1834–1837.

Pepin the Short

Charles Martel divided his realm between his sons Pepin, called Pepin the Short, and Carloman. Succeeding his father as the Mayor of the Palace in 741, Pepin reigned over Francia jointly with his elder brother Carloman. Pepin ruled in Neustria, Burgundy, and Provence, while Carloman established himself in Austrasia, Alemannia, and Thuringia. The brothers were active in subjugating revolts led by the Bavarians, Aquitanians, Saxons, and Alemanni in the early years of their reign. In 743, they ended the Frankish interregnum by choosing Childeric III, who was to be the last Merovingian monarch, as figurehead king of the Franks.

Being well disposed towards the church and papacy on account of their ecclesiastical upbringing, Pepin and Carloman continued their father's work supporting Saint Boniface in reforming the Frankish church and evangelizing the Saxons. After Carloman, who was an intensely pious man, retired to religious life in 747, Pepin became the sole ruler of the Franks. He suppressed a revolt led by his half-brother Grifo, and succeeded in becoming the undisputed master of all Francia. Giving up pretense, Pepin then forced

Childeric into a monastery and had himself proclaimed king of the Franks with the support of Pope Zachary in 751. The decision was not supported by all members of the Carolingian family, and Pepin had to put down another revolt led by Grifo and by Carloman's son, Drogo.

As king, Pepin embarked on an ambitious program to expand his power. He reformed the legislation of the Franks and continued the ecclesiastical reforms of Boniface. Pepin also intervened in favor of the papacy of Stephen II against the Lombards in Italy. He was able to secure several cities, which he then gave to the pope as part of the Donation of Pepin. This formed the legal basis for the Papal States in the Middle Ages. The Byzantines, keen to make good relations with the growing power of the Frankish empire, gave Pepin the title of Patricius. In wars of expansion, Pepin conquered Septimania from the Islamic Umayyads, and subjugated the southern realms by repeatedly defeating Waifer of Aquitaine and his Basque troops, after which the Basque and Aquitanian lords saw no option but to pledge loyalty to the Franks. Pepin was, however, troubled by the relentless revolts of the Saxons and the Bavarians. He campaigned tirelessly in Germany, but the final subjugation of these tribes was left to his successors.

Pepin died in 768 and was succeeded by his sons Charlemagne and Carloman. Although unquestionably one of the most powerful and successful rulers of his time, Pepin's reign is largely overshadowed by that of his more famous son.

Sources

Attributions

CC licensed content, Specific attribution

- Boundless World History. **Authored by**: Boundless. **Located at**: https://courses.lumenlearning.com/boundless-worldhistory/. **License**: *CC BY-SA: Attribution-ShareAlike*

The Rise of Charlemagne

Learning Objective

- Discuss the political and territorial achievements of Charlemagne

Key Points

- Charlemagne was determined to improve education and religion and bring Europe out of turmoil; to do this he launched a thirty-year military campaign of conquests that united Europe and spread Christianity.

- First he conquered the Lombards in Italy, supporting Pope Adrian I.

- In the Saxon Wars, spanning thirty years and eighteen battles, he conquered Saxony and proceeded to convert the conquered to Christianity.

- By 800 he was the ruler of Western Europe and had control of present-day France, Switzerland, Belgium, the Netherlands, Germany, and parts of Austria and Spain.

Terms

Carolingian Dynasty

An empire during the late medieval realm of the Franks, ruled by the Carolingian family, a Frankish noble family to which Charlemagne belonged.

Frankish state

Territory inhabited and ruled by the Franks, a confederation of Germanic tribes, from the 400s to 800s CE.

Saxons

A group of Germanic tribes first mentioned as living near the North Sea coast of what is now Germany (Old Saxony) in late Roman times.

Lombards

A Germanic people who ruled large parts of the Italian Peninsula from 568 to 774.

Charlemagne's Rise to Power

Charlemagne, also known as Charles the Great or Charles I, was the king of the Franks from 768 and the king of Italy from 774, and from 800 was the first emperor in western Europe since the collapse of the Western Roman Empire three centuries earlier. The expanded Frankish state he founded is called the Carolingian Empire. Charlemagne is considered to be the greatest ruler of the Carolingian Dynasty because of the achievements he made during what seemed like the very middle of the Dark Ages.

Charlemagne was the oldest son of Pepin the Short and Bertrada of Laon. He became king in 768 following the death of his father, and initially was a co-ruler with his brother, Carloman I. Charles received Pepin's original share as Mayor—the outer parts of the kingdom bordering on the sea, namely Neustria, western Aquitaine, and the northern parts of Austrasia—while Carloman was awarded his uncle's former share, the inner parts—southern Austrasia, Septimania, eastern Aquitaine, Burgundy, Provence, and Swabia, lands bordering Italy. Carloman's sudden death in 771 under unexplained circumstances left Charlemagne as the undisputed ruler of the Frankish Kingdom.

Territorial Expansion

Charlemagne was determined to improve education and religion and bring Europe out of turmoil. To do this he launched a thirty-year military campaign from 772–804 of conquests that united Europe and spread Christianity. Charlemagne was engaged in almost constant battle throughout his reign, often at the head of his elite scara bodyguard squadrons, with his legendary sword Joyeuse in hand. The first step that Charlemagne took in building his empire was to conquer new territories.

The first of these conquering campaigns was against the Lombards; Charlemagne came out victorious and won the Lombard lands to the north of Italy. At his succession in 772, Pope Adrian I demanded the return of certain cities in the former exarchate of Ravenna in accordance with a promise at the succession of Desiderius. Instead, Desiderius took over certain papal cities and invaded the Pentapolis, heading for Rome. Adrian sent ambassadors to Charlemagne in the autumn, requesting he enforce the policies of his father, Pepin. Desiderius sent his own ambassadors denying the pope's charges. The ambassadors met at Thionville, and Charlemagne upheld the pope's side. Charlemagne demanded that Desiderius comply with the pope, but Desiderius promptly swore he never would.

Charlemagne and his uncle Bernard crossed the Alps in 773 and chased the Lombards back to Pavia, which they then besieged. The siege lasted until the spring of 774, when Charlemagne visited the pope in Rome. There he confirmed his father's grants of land. Some later chronicles falsely claimed that he also expanded them, granting Tuscany, Emilia, Venice, and Corsica. After the pope granted Charlemagne the title of patrician, he returned to Pavia, where the Lombards were on the verge of surrendering. In return for their lives, the Lombards conceded and opened the gates in early summer.

Charlemagne and Pope Adrian I
The Frankish king Charlemagne was a devout Catholic who maintained a close relationship with the papacy
throughout his life. In 772, when Pope Adrian I was threatened by invaders, the king rushed to Rome to
provide assistance. Shown here, the pope asks Charlemagne for help at a meeting near Rome.

The Saxon Wars and Beyond

In the Saxon Wars, spanning thirty years and eighteen battles, Charlemagne overthrew Saxony and proceeded to convert the conquered to Christianity.

The Germanic Saxons were divided into four subgroups in four regions. Nearest to Austrasia was Westphalia, and furthest away was Eastphalia. Engria was between these two kingdoms, and to the north, at the base of the Jutland peninsula, was Nordalbingia. In his first campaign against the Saxons, in 773, Charlemagne cut down an Irminsul pillar near Paderborn and forced the Engrians to submit. The campaign was cut short by his first expedition to Italy. He returned to Saxony in 775, marching through Westphalia and conquering the Saxon fort at Sigiburg. He then crossed Engria, where he defeated the Saxons again. Finally, in Eastphalia, he defeated a Saxon force and converted its leader, Hessi, to Christianity. Charlemagne returned through Westphalia, leaving encampments at Sigiburg and Eresburg, which had been important Saxon bastions. With the exception of Nordalbingia, Saxony was under his control, but Saxon resistance had not ended.

Following his campaign in Italy to subjugate the dukes of Friuli and Spoleto, Charlemagne returned rapidly to Saxony in 776, where a rebellion had destroyed his fortress at Eresburg. The Saxons were once again brought to heel, but their main leader, Widukind, managed to escape to Denmark, home of his wife. Charlemagne built a new camp at Karlstadt. In 777, he called a national assembly at Paderborn to integrate Saxony fully into the Frankish kingdom. Many Saxons were baptized as Christians.

Outside Charlemagne's Saxon campaigns, he expanded his empire towards southern Germany, southern France, and the island of Corsica. He fought the Avars, adding modern-day Hungary to his empire, and also fought against the Moors of Spain, gaining the northern part of Spain. Through these conquests Charlemagne united Europe and spread Christianity.

By 800 he was the ruler of Western Europe and had control of present-day France, Switzerland, Belgium, the Netherlands, Germany, and parts of Austria and Spain. Charlemagne's successful military campaigns were due to his abilities as a military commander and planner, and to the training of his warriors. He controlled his vast empire by sending agents to supervise its different areas. Charlemagne's accomplishments restored much of the unity of the old Roman Empire and paved the way for the development of modern Europe.

Sources

Attributions

CC licensed content, Specific attribution

- Boundless World History. **Authored by**: Boundless. **Located at**: https://courses.lumenlearning.com/boundless-worldhistory/. **License**: *CC BY-SA: Attribution-ShareAlike*

The Coronation of 800 CE

Learning Objective

- Describe the reasons for Charlemagne receiving the title of Emperor

Key Points

- In 800, Pope Leo III crowned Charlemagne the Emperor of the Romans, thereby extending Charlemagne's power and authority.

- Some historians believe that Charlemagne was surprised by the coronation and would not have gone into the church that day had he known the pope's plan.

- Nonetheless, Charlemagne used these circumstances to claim that he was the renewer of the Roman Empire, which would remain in continuous existence for nearly a millennium, as the Holy Roman Empire.

- Although one of the aims was ostensibly to reunite the entire Roman Empire, given that many at the time (including the pope) did not recognize Empress Irene of the Byzantine Empire as a legitimate ruler, the two empires remained independent and continued to fight for sovereignty throughout the Middle Ages.

- The Pope's motivation for crowning Charlemagne was to give the papacy and the church implicit authority over the empire, since with this act Leo set a precedent for crowning emperors, which subsequent popes would do throughout the reign of the Holy Roman Empire.

Terms

Holy Roman Empire

A multi-ethnic complex of territories in central Europe that developed during the Early Middle Ages and continued until its dissolution in 1806; founded by the coronation of Charlemagne by Pope Leo III.

Empress Irene

A Byzantine empress who ruled from 797–802, during the time of Charlemagne's coronation.

Byzantine Empire

Sometimes referred to as the Eastern Roman Empire, was the continuation of the Roman Empire in the East during Late Antiquity and the Middle Ages, when its capital city was Constantinople.

Coronation

In 799, after Pope Leo III was abused by Romans who tried to put out his eyes and tear out his tongue, he escaped and fled to Charlemagne at Paderborn. Charlemagne, advised by scholar Alcuin of York, travelled to Rome in November 800 and held a council on December 1. On December 23, Leo swore an oath of innocence. At Mass, on Christmas Day (December 25), when Charlemagne knelt at the altar to pray, the pope crowned him *Imperator Romanorum* ("Emperor of the Romans") in Saint Peter's Basilica. In so doing, the pope effectively nullified the legitimacy of Empress Irene of Constantinople. As historian James Bryce writes:

> When Odoacer compelled the abdication of Romulus Augustulus, he did not abolish the Western Empire as a separate power, but caused it to be reunited with or sink into the Eastern, so that from that time there was a single undivided Roman Empire … [Pope Leo III and Charlemagne], like their predecessors, held the Roman Empire to be one and indivisible, and proposed by the coronation of [Charlemagne] not to proclaim a severance of the East and West.

Charlemagne's coronation as emperor, though intended to represent the continuation of the unbroken line of emperors from Augustus to Constantine VI, had the effect of setting up two separate (and often opposing) empires and two separate claims to imperial authority. For centuries to come, the emperors of both West and East would make competing claims of sovereignty over the whole.

In support of Charlemagne's coronation, some argued that the imperial position had actually been vacant, deeming a woman (Irene) unfit to be emperor. However, Charlemagne made no claim to the Byzantine Empire. Whether he actually desired a coronation at all remains controversial—his biographer Einhard related that Charlemagne had been surprised by the pope. Regardless, Byzantium felt its role as the sole heir of the Roman Empire threatened and began to emphasize its superiority and its Roman identity. Relations between the two empires remained difficult. Irene is said to have sought a marriage alliance between herself and Charlemagne, but according to Theophanes the Confessor, who alone mentions it, the scheme was frustrated by Aetios, one of her favorite advisors.

Coronation of Charlemagne
The Coronation of Charlemagne, by assistants of Raphael, c. 1516–1517.

Motivation

For both the pope and Charlemagne, the Roman Empire remained a significant power in European politics at this time, and continued to hold a substantial portion of Italy, with borders not far south of the city of Rome itself. This is the empire that historiography has been labelled the Byzantine Empire, for its capital was Constantinople (ancient Byzantium) and its people and rulers were Greek; it was a thoroughly Hellenic state. Indeed, Charlemagne was usurping the prerogatives of the Roman emperor in Constantinople simply by sitting in judgement over the pope in the first place. Historian John Julius Norwich writes of their motivation:

> By whom, however, could he [the Pope] be tried? In normal circumstances the only conceivable answer to that question would have been the Emperor at Constantinople; but the imperial throne was

at this moment occupied by Irene. That the Empress was notorious for having blinded and murdered her own son was, in the minds of both Leo and Charles, almost immaterial: it was enough that she was a woman. The female sex was known to be incapable of governing, and by the old Salic tradition was debarred from doing so. As far as Western Europe was concerned, the Throne of the Emperors was vacant: Irene's claim to it was merely an additional proof, if any were needed, of the degradation into which the so-called Roman Empire had fallen.

For the pope, then, there was "no living Emperor at the that time." Furthermore, the papacy had since 727 been in conflict with Irene's predecessors in Constantinople over a number of issues, chiefly the continued Byzantine adherence to the doctrine of iconoclasm, the destruction of Christian images. From 750, the secular power of the Byzantine Empire in central Italy had been nullified.

Norwich explains that by bestowing the imperial crown upon Charlemagne, the pope arrogated to himself "the right to appoint the Emperor of the Romans, establishing the imperial crown as his own personal gift but simultaneously granting himself implicit superiority over the Emperor whom he had created." And "because the Byzantines had proved so unsatisfactory from every point of view—political, military and doctrinal—he would select a westerner: the one man who by his wisdom and statesmanship and the vastness of his dominions stood out head and shoulders above his contemporaries."

How realistic either Charlemagne or the pope felt it to be that the people of Constantinople would ever accept the king of the Franks as their emperor, we cannot know; Alcuin speaks hopefully in his letters of an *Imperium Christianum* ("Christian Empire"), wherein, "just as the inhabitants of the [Roman Empire] had been united by a common Roman citizenship," presumably this new empire would be united by a common Christian faith.

Roman Emperor

In any event, Charlemagne used these circumstances to claim that he was the renewer of the Roman Empire, which was perceived to have fallen into degradation under the Byzantines. The title of Emperor remained in the Carolingian family for years to come, but divisions of territory and in-fighting over supremacy of the Frankish state weakened its power and ability to lead. The papacy itself never forgot the title nor abandoned the right to bestow it. When the family of Charlemagne ceased to produce worthy heirs, the pope gladly crowned whichever Italian magnate could best protect him from his local enemies. This devolution led to the dormancy of the title from 924 to 962. The title was revived when Otto I was crowned emperor in 962, fashioning himself as the successor of Charlemagne. The empire would remain in continuous existence for nearly a millennium, as the Holy Roman Empire, a true imperial successor to Charlemagne.

Sources

Attributions

CC licensed content, Specific attribution

- Boundless World History. **Authored by**: Boundless. **Located at**: https://courses.lumenlearning.com/boundless-worldhistory/. **License**: *CC BY-SA: Attribution-ShareAlike*

The End of the Carolingians

Learning Objective

- Identify the reasons for the fall of the Carolingian Dynasty

Key Points

- The Carolingian dynasty was a Frankish noble family with origins in the Arnulfing and Pippinid clans of the 7th century, which saw its reached its peak with the crowning of Charlemagne as the Roman emperor in 800.

- Charlemagne's death in 814 began an extended period of fragmentation and decline of the dynasty that would eventually lead to the evolution of the territories of France and Germany.

- Following the death of Louis the Pious (Charlemagne's son), the surviving adult Carolingians fought a three-year civil war ending only in the Treaty of Verdun, which divided the territory into three separate regions and began the breakup of the empire.

- The Carolingians were displaced in most of the *regna* of the empire in 888, but ruled in East Francia until 911 and held the throne of West Francia intermittently until 987.

- One chronicler dates the end of Carolingian rule with the coronation of Robert II of France as junior co-ruler with his father, Hugh Capet, thus beginning the Capetian dynasty, descendants of which unified France.

- The Carolingian dynasty became extinct in the male line with the death of Eudes, Count of Vermandois. His sister Adelaide, the last Carolingian, died in 1122.

Terms

regna

Territorial regions of independent rule.

Carolingian

Refers to topics concerning or in the time of Charlemagne and his heirs.

Francia

The territory inhabited and ruled by the Franks, a confederation of West Germanic tribes, during Late Antiquity and the Early Middle Ages.

Charlemagne's Death

The Carolingian dynasty began with Charlemagne's grandfather Charles Martel, but began its official reign with Charlemagne's father, Pepin the Short, displacing the Merovingian dynasty. The dynasty reached its peak with the crowning of Charlemagne as the first emperor in the west in over three centuries. Charlemagne's death in 814 began an extended period of fragmentation and decline that would eventually lead to the evolution of the territories of France and Germany.

In 813, Charlemagne called Louis the Pious, king of Aquitaine and his only surviving legitimate son, to his court. There Charlemagne crowned his son with his own hands as co-emperor and sent him back to Aquitaine. He then spent the autumn hunting before returning to Aachen on November 1. In January, he fell ill with pleurisy. He took to his bed on January 21 and as Einhard tells it:

> He died January twenty-eighth, the seventh day from the time that he took to his bed, at nine o'clock in the morning, after partaking of the Holy Communion, in the seventy-second year of his age and the forty-seventh of his reign.

He had a testament of 811, not updated prior to his death, that allocated his assets. He was succeeded by his son, Louis, but his empire lasted only another generation in its entirety; its division, according to custom, between Louis's own sons after their father's death laid the foundation for the modern states of Germany and France.

The Carolingian Dynasty and Its Decline

Charlemagne, who was crowned Emperor by Pope Leo III at Rome in 800, was the greatest Carolingian monarch. His empire, ostensibly a continuation of the Roman Empire, is referred to historiographically as the Carolingian Empire. The traditional Frankish (and Merovingian) practice of dividing inheritances among heirs was not given up by the Carolingian emperors, though the concept of the indivisibility of the Empire was also accepted. The Carolingians had the practice of making their sons minor kings in the various regions (*regna*) of the Empire, which they would inherit on the death of their father.

Following the death of Louis the Pious (Charlemagne's son), the surviving adult Carolingians fought a three-year civil war ending only in the Treaty of Verdun, which divided the empire into three *regna* while according imperial status and a nominal lordship to Lothair I. By this treaty, Lothair received northern Italy and a long stretch of territory from the North Sea to the Mediterranean, essentially along the valleys of the Rhine and the Rhône; this territory includes the regions of Lorraine, Alsace, Burgundy, and Provence. He soon ceded Italy to his eldest son, Louis, and remained in his new kingdom, engaging in alternate quarrels and reconciliations with his brothers and in futile efforts to defend his lands from the attacks of the Northmen (as Vikings were known in Frankish writings) and the Saracens.

The Carolingians differed markedly from the Merovingians in that they disallowed inheritance to illegitimate offspring, possibly in an effort to prevent infighting among heirs and assure a limit to the division of the realm. In the late 9th century, however, the lack of suitable adults among the Carolingians necessitated the rise of Arnulf of Carinthia, an illegitimate child of a legitimate Carolingian king.

The Carolingians were displaced in most of the *regna* of the Empire in 888. They ruled on in East Francia until 911 and held the throne of West Francia intermittently until 987. Carolingian cadet branches continued to rule in Vermandois and Lower Lorraine after the last king died in 987, but they never sought thrones of principalities, and they made peace with the new ruling families. One chronicler dates the end of Carolingian rule with the coronation of Robert II of France as junior co-ruler with his father, Hugh Capet, thus beginning the Capetian dynasty. Capet's descendants—the Capetians, the House of Valois, and the House of Bourbon—progressively unified the country through wars and dynastic inheritance into the Kingdom of France, which was fully declared in 1190 by Philip II Augustus. Thus West Francia of the Carolingian dynasty became France.

Following the breakup of the Frankish Realm, the history of Germany was for 900 years intertwined with the history of the Holy Roman Empire, which subsequently emerged from the eastern portion of Charlemagne's original empire. The territory initially known as East Francia stretched from the Rhine in the west to the Elbe River in the east, and from the North Sea to the Alps. Germany as we know it today did not come into existence until after WWI when the various principalities of the region were united as a modern nation-state.

The Carolingian dynasty became extinct in the male line with the death of Eudes, Count of Vermandois. His sister Adelaide, the last Carolingian, died in 1122.

Carolingian dynasty. Carolingian family tree, from the Chronicon Universale of Ekkehard of Aura, 12th century

Sources

Attributions

CC licensed content, Specific attribution

Rise of the Holy Roman Empire

- Describe the rise of the Holy Roman Empire

Key Points

- In 800, Pope Leo III crowned Charlemagne Emperor of the Romans, reviving the title in Western Europe after more than three centuries, thus creating the Carolingian Empire, whose territory came to be known as the Holy Roman Empire.

- After the dissolution of the Carolingian Dynasty and the breakup of the empire into conflicting territories, Otto I became king of Francia and worked to unify all the German tribes into a single kingdom and greatly expand his powers.

- The title of Emperor was again revived in 962 when Otto I was crowned by Pope John XII, fashioning himself as the successor of Charlemagne and thus establishing the Holy Roman Empire.

Terms

Charlemagne

The first recognized emperor in Western Europe since the fall of the Western Roman Empire three centuries earlier, known for unifying Francia and ushering in a period of cultural renaissance and reform.

Otto I

German king from 936 and emperor of the Holy Roman Empire from 962 until his death in 973; his reign began a continuous existence of the Holy Roman Empire for over eight centuries.

Overview

The Holy Roman Empire was a multi-ethnic complex of territories in central Europe that developed during the Early Middle Ages and continued until its dissolution in 1806. The largest territory of the empire after 962 was Eastern Francia, though it also came to include the Kingdom of Bohemia, the Kingdom of Burgundy, the Kingdom of Italy, and numerous other territories.

In 800, Pope Leo III crowned the Frankish king Charlemagne Emperor of the Romans, reviving the title in Western Europe after more than three centuries. The title continued in the Carolingian family until 888, and from 896 to 899, after which it was contested by the rulers of Italy in a series of civil wars until the death of the last Italian claimant, Berengar, in 924. The title was revived again in 962 when Otto I was crowned emperor, fashioning himself as the successor of Charlemagne and beginning a continuous existence of the empire for over eight centuries. Some historians refer to the coronation of Charlemagne as the origin of the empire, while others prefer the coronation of Otto I as its beginning. Scholars generally concur, however, in relating an evolution of the institutions and principles constituting the empire, describing a gradual assumption of the imperial title and role.

The Rise of the Empire

After Charlemagne died in 814, the imperial crown was disputed among the Carolingian rulers of Western Francia and Eastern Francia, with first the western king (Charles the Bald) and then the eastern (Charles the Fat) attaining the prize. After the death of Charles the Fat in 888, however, the Carolingian Empire broke apart, and was never restored. According to Regino of Prüm, the parts of the realm "spewed forth kinglets," and each part elected a kinglet "from its own bowels." After the death of Charles the Fat, those crowned emperor by the pope controlled only territories in Italy. The last such emperor was Berengar I of Italy, who died in 924.

A few decade earlier, around 900, autonomous stem duchies (Franconia, Bavaria, Swabia, Saxony, and Lotharingia) reemerged in East Francia. After the Carolingian king Louis the Child died without issue in 911, East Francia did not turn to the Carolingian ruler of West Francia to take over the realm, but instead elected one of the dukes, Conrad of Franconia, as *Rex Francorum Orientalium*. On his deathbed, Conrad yielded the crown to his main rival, Henry the Fowler of Saxony, who was elected king at the Diet of Fritzlar in 919. Henry reached a truce with the raiding Magyars, and in 933 he won a first victory against them in the Battle of Riade.

Otto I, Holy Roman Emperor

Henry the Fowler died in 936, but his descendants, the Liudolfing (or Ottonian) dynasty, would continue to rule the eastern kingdom for roughly a century. Upon Henry's death, Otto I, his son and designated successor, was elected King in Aachen in 936. Otto continued his father's work of unifying all German tribes into a single kingdom and greatly expanded the king's powers at the expense of the aristocracy. Through strategic marriages and personal appointments, Otto installed members of his family in the kingdom's most important duchies. This reduced the various dukes, who had previously been co-equals with the king, to royal subjects under his authority. Otto transformed the Roman Catholic Church in Germany to strengthen the royal office and subjected its clergy to his personal control.

After putting down a brief civil war among the rebellious duchies, Otto defeated the Magyars at the Battle of Lechfeld in 955, thus ending the Hungarian invasions of Western Europe. The victory against the pagan Magyars earned Otto a reputation as a savior of Christendom and secured his hold over the kingdom. In 951, Otto came to the aid of Adelaide, the widowed queen of Italy, defeating her enemies, marrying her, and taking control of Italy. By 961, Otto had conquered the Kingdom of Italy and extended his realm's borders to the north, east, and south. Following the example of Charlemagne's coronation as "Emperor of the Romans" in 800, Otto was crowned emperor in 962 by Pope John XII in Rome, thus intertwining the affairs of the German kingdom with those of Italy and the papacy. Otto's coronation as emperor marked the German kings as successors to the empire of Charlemagne, which through the concept of *translatio imperii* also made them consider themselves successors to Ancient Rome.

Otto's later years were marked by conflicts with the papacy and struggles to stabilize his rule over Italy. Reigning from Rome, Otto sought to improve relations with the Byzantine Empire, which opposed his claim to emperorship and his realm's further expansion to the south. To resolve this conflict, the Byzantine princess Theophanu married Otto's son, Otto II, in April 972. Otto finally returned to Germany in August 972 and died at Memleben in 973. Otto II succeeded him as Holy Roman Emperor.

Otto I. Replica of the Magdeburger Reiter, equestrian monument traditionally regarded as portrait of Otto I (Magdeburg, original c. 1240)

Sources

Attributions

CC licensed content, Specific attribution

- Boundless World History. **Authored by**: Boundless. **Located at**: https://courses.lumenlearning.com/boundless-worldhistory/. **License**: *CC BY-SA: Attribution-ShareAlike*

The Norman Invasion of 1066 CE

Learning Objective

- Evaluate the extent to which Harold's loss at the Battle of Hastings was due to the fact that he was ill-prepared for battle and whether it might have been possible to mitigate the circumstances that led to that fact

Key Points

- Harold was crowned king after the death of Edward the Confessor in January 1066. Shortly after he was crowned king, Harold faced invasions by his brother Tostig, the Norwegian King Harald III of Norway, and Duke William II of Normandy.

- Harold defeated Tostig and Harald III at the battle of Stamford Bridge on September 25, 1066.

- Harold's army marched south to confront William at the Battle of Hastings on October 14, 1066. Harold was defeated by the strength of William's attack and because his army was still recovering from Stamford.

Terms

Normans

The Normans, a people descended from Norse Vikings who settled in the territory of Normandy in France after being given land by the French king, conquered other lands and protected the French coast from foreign attacks.

Battle of Hastings

The decisive battle in the Norman Conquest of England fought on October 14, 1066, between the Norman-Fench army of Duke William II of Normandy and the English army under Anglo-Saxon King Harold II.

Background

The Norman conquest of England was the 11th-century invasion and occupation of England by an army of Norman, Breton, and French soldiers led by Duke William II of Normandy, later styled William the Conqueror.

William's claim to the English throne derived from his familial relationship with the childless Anglo-Saxon King Edward the Confessor, who may have encouraged William's hopes for the throne. Edward died in January 1066 and was succeeded by his brother-in-law Harold Godwinson. Harold faced invasions by William, his own brother Tostig, and the Norwegian King Harald Hardrada (Harold III of Norway).

Preparations and Early Battles

The English army was organized along regional lines, with the *fyrd*, or local levy, serving under a local magnate—an earl, bishop, or sheriff. The fyrd was composed of men who owned their own land and were equipped by their community to fulfill the king's demands for military forces. As a whole, England could furnish about 14,000 men for the fyrd when it was called out. The fyrd usually served for two months, except in emergencies. It was rare for the whole national fyrd to be called out; between 1046 and 1065 it was done only three times—in 1051, 1052, and 1065. The king also had a group of personal armsmen known as housecarls, who formed the backbone of the royal forces. The composition, structure, and size of Harold's army contributed to his defeat against William.

Harold had spent mid-1066 on the south coast with a large army and fleet, waiting for William to invade. The bulk of his forces were militia who needed to harvest their crops, so on September 8 Harold dismissed the militia and the fleet. Learning of the Norwegian invasion, he rushed north, gathering forces as he went, and took the Norwegians by surprise, defeating them at the Battle of Stamford Bridge on September 25. Harald of Norway and Tostig were killed, and the Norwegians suffered such great losses that only 24 of the original 300 ships were required to carry away the survivors. The English victory came at great cost, as Harold's army was left in a battered and weakened state.

Meanwhile, William had assembled a large invasion fleet and gathered an army from Normandy and the rest of France, including large contingents from Brittany and Flanders. William spent almost nine months on his preparations, as he had to construct a fleet from nothing. The Normans crossed to England a few days after Harold's victory over the Norwegians, following the dispersal of Harold's naval force, and landed at Pevensey in Sussex on September 28. A few ships were blown off course and landed at Romney, where the Normans fought the local fyrd. After landing, William's forces built a wooden castle at Hastings, from which they raided the surrounding area. More fortifications were erected at Pevensey.

Battle of Hastings

The deaths of Tostig and Hardrada at Stamford left William as Harold's only serious opponent. While Harold and his forces were recovering from Stamford, William landed his invasion forces at Pevensey and established a beachhead for his conquest of the kingdom. Harold was forced to march south swiftly, gathering forces as he went.

Harold's army confronted William's invaders on October 14 at the Battle of Hastings. The battle began at about 9 a.m. and lasted all day, but while a broad outline is known, the exact events are obscured by contradictory accounts in the sources. Although the numbers on each side were probably about equal, William had both cavalry and infantry, including many archers, while Harold had only foot soldiers and few archers. In the morning, the English soldiers formed up as a shield wall along the ridge, and were at first so effective that William's army was thrown back with heavy casualties. Some of William's Breton troops panicked and fled, and some of the English troops appear to have pursued them. Norman cavalry then attacked and killed the pursuing troops. While the Bretons were fleeing, rumors swept the Norman forces that the duke had been killed, but William rallied his troops. Twice more the Normans made feigned withdrawals, tempting the English into pursuit, and allowing the Norman cavalry to attack them repeatedly.

The available sources are more confused about events in the afternoon, but it appears that the decisive event was the death of Harold, about which differing stories are told. William of Jumieges claimed that Harold was killed by William. It has also been claimed that the Bayeux Tapestry shows Harold's death by an arrow to the eye, but this may be a later reworking of the tapestry to conform to 12th-century stories. Other sources stated that no one knew how Harold died because the press of battle was so tight around the king that the soldiers could not see who struck the fatal blow.

The Bayeux Tapestry: The controversial panel depicting Harold II's death. The tapestry depicts the loss of the Anglo-Saxon troops to the Norman forces. Here, a figure some think to be Harold Godwinson is shown falling at the Battle of Hastings. Harold is shown with an arrow to the eye.

Sources

Attributions

CC licensed content, Specific attribution

- Boundless World History. **Authored by**: Boundless. **Located at**: https://courses.lumenlearning.com/boundless-worldhistory/. **License**: *CC BY-SA: Attribution-ShareAlike*

The Magna Carta

Learning Objective

- Explain why the Magna Carta was created and why it is considered a failure of democracy

Key Points

- The Magna Carta was signed by King John in June 1215 and was the first document to impose legal limits on the king's personal powers.

- Clause 61 stated that a committee of twenty five barons could meet and overrule the will of the king—a serious challenge to John's authority as ruling monarch.

- The charter was renounced as soon as the barons left London; the pope annulled the document, saying it impaired the church's authority over the "papal territories" of England and Ireland.

- England moved to civil war, with the barons trying to replace the monarch they disliked with an alternative. They offered the crown to Prince Louis of France, who was declared king in London in May 1216.

- The Magna Carta survived to become a "sacred text," but in practice did not limit the power of kings in the medieval period. Instead, it paved the way for later constitutional documents, including the Constitution of the United States.

> **Terms**
>
> *clause 61*
>
> Section of the Magna Carta that stated a committee of twenty-five barons could at any time meet and overrule the will of the king if he defied the provisions of the charter, and could seize his castles and possessions if it was considered necessary.
>
> *English Civil War*
>
> A series of armed conflicts and political machinations in the period 1642-1651 between Parliamentarians (Roundheads) and Royalists (Cavaliers) in the Kingdom of England, principally over the manner of its government.

Norman Kings after the Conquest

At the death of William the Conqueror in 1087, his lands were divided into two parts. His Norman lands went to his eldest son, Robert Curthose and his English lands to his second son, William Rufus. This presented a dilemma for those nobles who held land on both sides of the English Channel, who decided to unite England and Normandy once more under one ruler. The pursuit of this aim led them to revolt against William in favor of Robert in the Rebellion of 1088. As Robert failed to appear in England to rally his supporters, William won the support of the English lords with silver and promises of better government, and defeated the rebellion. William died while hunting in 1100.

Despite Robert's rival claims to William's land, his younger brother Henry immediately seized power in England. Robert, who invaded in 1101, disputed Henry's control of England. This military campaign ended in a negotiated settlement that confirmed Henry as king. The peace was short lived, and Henry invaded the Duchy of Normandy in 1105 and 1106, finally defeating Robert at the Battle of Tinchebray.

Henry I of England named his daughter Matilda his heir, but when he died in 1135 Matilda was far from England in Anjou or Maine, while her cousin Stephen was closer in Boulogne, giving him the advantage he needed to race to England and have himself crowned and anointed king of England. After Stephen's death in 1154, Henry II succeeded as the first Angevin king of England, so-called because he was also the Count of Anjou in northern France. He therefore added England to his extensive holdings in Normandy and Aquitaine. England became a key part of a loose-knit assemblage of lands spread across Western Europe, later termed the Angevin Empire. Henry was succeeded by his third son, Richard, whose reputation for martial prowess won him the epithet "Lionheart." When Richard died, his brother John—Henry's fifth and only surviving son—took the throne

Magna Carta

Over the course of King John's reign (1199-1216), a combination of higher taxes, unsuccessful wars, and conflict with the pope had made him unpopular with his barons. In 1215 some of the most important barons engaged in open rebellion against their king. King John met with the leaders of the barons, along with their French and Scot allies, to seal the Great Charter (*Magna Carta* in Latin), which imposed legal limits on the king's personal powers. It was sealed under oath by King John at Runnymede, on the bank of the River Thames near Windsor, England, on June 15, 1215. It promised the protection of church rights, protection for the barons from illegal imprisonment, access to swift justice, and limitations on feudal payments to the Crown, to be implemented through a council of twenty-five barons.

Magna Carta. One of four known surviving original copies of the Magna Carta of 1215, written in iron gall ink on parchment in medieval Latin, authenticated with the Great Seal of King John. This document is held at the British Library.

Background

Although the kingdom had a robust administrative system, the nature of government under the Angevin monarchs was ill-defined and uncertain. John and his predecessors had ruled using the principle of *vis et voluntas*, or "force and will," making executive and sometimes arbitrary decisions, often justified on the basis that a king was above the law. Many contemporary writers believed that monarchs should rule in accordance with the custom and the law, with the counsel of the leading members of the realm, but there was no model for what should happen if a king refused to do so.

John had lost most of his ancestral lands in France to King Philip II in 1204 and had struggled to regain them for many years, raising extensive taxes on the barons to accumulate money to fight a war that ultimately ended in expensive failure in 1214. Following the defeat of his allies at the Battle of Bouvines, John had to sue for peace and pay compensation. John was already personally unpopular with a number of the barons, many of whom owed money to the Crown, and little trust existed between the two sides. A triumph would have strengthened his position, but within a few months after his unsuccessful return from France, John found that rebel barons in the north and east of England were organizing resistance to his rule.

John met the rebel leaders at Runnymede, a water-meadow on the south bank of the River Thames, on June 10, 1215. Here the rebels presented John with their draft demands for reform, the "Articles of the Barons." Stephen Langton's pragmatic efforts at mediation over the next ten days turned these incomplete demands into a charter capturing the proposed peace agreement; a few years later, this agreement was renamed Magna Carta, meaning "Great Charter."

Clause 61

The 1215 document contained a large section that is now called clause 61 (the clauses were not originally numbered). This section established a committee of twenty-five barons who could at any time meet and overrule the will of the king if he defied the provisions of the charter, and could seize his castles and possessions if it was considered necessary. It contained a commitment from John that he would "seek to obtain nothing from anyone, in our own person or through someone else, whereby any of these grants or liberties may be revoked or diminished."

Clause 61 was a serious challenge to John's authority as a ruling monarch. He renounced it as soon as the barons left London; Pope Innocent III also annulled the "shameful and demeaning agreement, forced upon the King by violence and fear." The pope rejected any call for restraints on the king, saying it impaired John's dignity. He saw the charter as an affront to the church's authority over the king and the "papal territories" of England and Ireland, and he released John from his oath to obey it. The rebels knew that King John could never be restrained by Magna Carta, and so they sought a new King.

The Magna Carta – Failed Diplomacy That Changed the World. A National History Day group documentary. The theme that year (2011) was Debate and Diplomacy in History: Successes, Failures, and Consequences. As a result, you will notice a great emphasis on these ideas throughout the course of the video.

- https://youtu.be/RBuHH8bK250

The First Barons' War

With the failure of the Magna Carta to achieve peace or restrain John, the barons reverted to the more traditional type of rebellion by trying to replace the monarch they disliked with an alternative. In a measure of some desperation, despite the tenuousness of his claim and despite the fact that he was French, they offered the crown of England to Prince Louis of France, who was proclaimed king in London in May 1216. John travelled around the country to oppose the rebel forces, directing, among other operations, a two-month siege of the rebel-held Rochester Castle. He died of dysentery contracted whilst on campaign in eastern England during late 1216; supporters of his son Henry III went on to achieve victory over Louis and the rebel barons the following year.

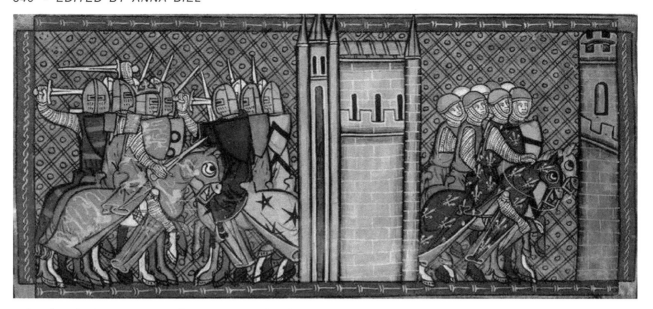

John of England vs Louis VIII of France. Created in the 14th Century; the image King John of England in battle with the Francs (left), Prince Louis VIII of France on the march (right).

Legacy

As a means of preventing war, the Magna Carta was a failure, rejected by most of the barons, and was legally valid for no more than three months. In practice, the Magna Carta did not generally limit the power of kings in the medieval period, but by the time of the English Civil War it had become an important symbol for those who wished to show that the king was bound by the law. The charter is widely known throughout the English-speaking world as having influenced common and constitutional law, as well as political representation and the development of parliament. The text's association with ideals of democracy, limitation of power, equality, and freedom under law led to the rule of constitutional law in England and beyond. It influenced the early settlers in New England and inspired later constitutional documents, including the Constitution of the United States.

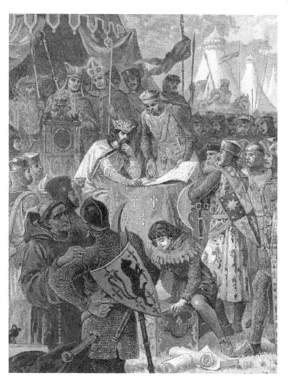

John of England signs the Magna Carta. John of England signs the Magna Carta. Image from Cassell's History of England, Century Edition, published c. 1902. This image depicts the stress under the king and all those in England struggling for power.

Sources

Attributions

CC licensed content, Specific attribution

- Boundless World History. **Authored by**: Boundless. **Located at**: https://courses.lumenlearning.com/boundless-worldhistory/. **License**: *CC BY-SA: Attribution-ShareAlike*

The Hundred Years' War

Learning Objective

- Discuss the three phases of conflict in the Hundred Years' War and Joan of Arc's role in it

Key Points

- The root causes of the conflict can be found in the demographic, economic, and social crises of 14th-century Europe. The outbreak of war was motivated by a gradual rise in tension between the kings of France and England about Guyenne, Flanders, and Scotland. The Hundred Years' War is commonly divided into three phases separated by truces: the Edwardian Era War (1337–1360); the Caroline War (1369–1389); and the Lancastrian War (1415–1453).

- The Edwardian War was driven by Edward III's ambition to maintain sovereignty in Aquitaine and assert his claim as the rightful king of France by unseating his rival, Philip VI of France.

- The Caroline War was named after Charles V of France, who resumed the war after the Treaty of Brétigny.

- The Lancastrian War was the third phase of the Anglo-French Hundred Years' War. It lasted from 1415, when Henry V of England invaded Normandy, to 1453, when the English failed to recover Bordeaux.

- Joan of Arc was a French peasant woman who had visions commanding her to drive out the invaders. She inspired the French troops, and they retook many French cities held by the English. Joan was burned at the stake and, 25 years after her death, declared a martyr.

Terms

the Black Death

One of the most devastating pandemics in human history, resulting in the deaths of an estimated 75 to 200 million people and peaking in Europe in the years 1348–1350.

Treaty of Brétigny

A treaty signed on May 25, 1360, between King Edward III of England and King John II (the Good) of France. It is seen as having marked the end of the first phase of the Hundred Years' War.

the Black Prince

A name used to refer to Edward of Woodstock, used chiefly since the 16th century, and not during Edward's lifetime. The name is thought to stem from his black armor or brutal attitude in battle.

duchy

A territory, fief, or domain ruled by a duke or duchess.

Joan of Arc

Considered a heroine of France for her role during the Lancastrian phase of the Hundred Years' War; canonized as a Roman Catholic saint.

Background

In the 13th century, after the Magna Carta failed to prevent the Baron Wars, King John and his son King Henry III's reigns were characterized by numerous rebellions and civil wars, often provoked by incompetence and mismanagement in government. The reign of Henry III's son Edward I (1272–1307), was rather more successful. Edward enacted numerous laws strengthening the powers of his government, and he summoned the first officially sanctioned Parliaments of England. He conquered Wales and attempted to use a succession dispute to gain control of the Kingdom of Scotland, though this developed into a costly and drawn-out military campaign.

After the disastrous reign of Edward II, which saw military losses and the Great Famine, Edward III reigned from 1327–1377, restoring royal authority and transforming the Kingdom of England into the most efficient military power in Europe. His reign saw vital developments in legislature and government—in particular the evolution of the English parliament—as well as the ravages of the Black Death. After defeating, but not subjugating, the Kingdom of Scotland, he declared himself rightful heir to the French throne in 1338, but his claim was denied. This started what would become known as the Hundred Years' War.

The Hundred Years' War

The Hundred Years' War is the term used to describe a series of conflicts from 1337 to 1453, between the rulers of the Kingdom of England and the House of Valois for control of the French throne. These 116 years saw a great deal of battle on the continent, most of it over disputes as to which family line should rightfully be upon the throne of France. By the end of the Hundred Years' War, the population of France was about half what it had been before the era began.

The root causes of the conflict can be found in the demographic, economic, and social crises of 14th-century Europe. The outbreak of war was motivated by a gradual rise in tension between the kings of France and England about Guyenne, Flanders, and Scotland. The dynastic question, which arose due to an interruption of the direct male line of the Capetians, was the official pretext.

The dispute over Guyenne is even more important than the dynastic question in explaining the outbreak of the war. Guyenne posed a significant problem to the kings of France and England; Edward III was a vassal of Philip VI of France and was required to recognize the sovereignty of the king of France over Guyenne. In practical terms, a judgment in Guyenne might be subject to an appeal to the French royal court. The king of France had the power to revoke all legal decisions made by the king of England in Aquitaine, which was unacceptable to the English. Therefore, sovereignty over Guyenne was a latent conflict between the two monarchies for several generations.

The war owes its historical significance to multiple factors. Although primarily a dynastic conflict, the war gave impetus to ideas of French and English nationalism. By its end, feudal armies had been largely replaced by professional troops, and aristocratic dominance had yielded to a democratization of the manpower and weapons of armies. The wider introduction of weapons and tactics supplanted the feudal armies where heavy cavalry had dominated. The war precipitated the creation of the first standing armies in Western Europe since the time of the Western Roman Empire, composed largely of commoners and thus helping to change their role in warfare. With respect to the belligerents, English political forces over time came to oppose the costly venture. The dissatisfaction of English nobles, resulting from the loss of their continental landholdings, became a factor leading to the civil wars known as the Wars of the Roses (1455–1487). In France, civil wars, deadly epidemics, famines, and bandit free-companies of mercenaries reduced the population drastically. Deprived of its continental possessions, England was left with the sense of being an island nation, which profoundly affected its outlook and development for more than 500 years.

Historians commonly divide the war into three phases separated by truces: 1) the Edwardian Era War (1337–1360); 2) the Caroline War (1369–1389); and 3) the Lancastrian War (1415–1453), which saw the slow decline of English fortunes after the appearance of Joan of Arc in 1429.

The Edwardian Era War

The Edwardian War was the first series of hostilities of the Hundred Years' War. It was a series of punctuated, separate conflicts waged between the kingdoms of England and France and their various allies for control of the French throne. The Edwardian War was driven by Edward III's ambition to maintain sovereignty in Aquitaine and assert his claim as the rightful king of France by unseating his rival, Philip VI of France.

Edward had inherited the duchy of Aquitaine, and as duke of Aquitaine he was a vassal to Philip VI of France. He refused, however, to acknowledge his fealty to Philip, who responded by confiscating the duchy of Aquitaine in 1337; this precipitated war, and soon, in 1340, Edward declared himself king of France. Edward III and his son the Black Prince led their armies on a largely successful campaign across France. Hostilities were paused in the mid-1350s for the deprivations of the Black Death. Then war continued, and the English were victorious at the Battle of Poitiers (1356), where the French king, John II, was captured and held for ransom. The Truce of Bordeaux was signed in 1357 and was followed by two treaties in London in 1358 and 1359.

After the treaties of London failed, Edward launched the Rheims campaign. Though largely unsuccessful, this campaign led to the Treaty of Brétigny (signed 1360), which settled certain lands in France on Edward for renouncing his claim to the French throne. This peace lasted nine years, until a second phase of hostilities known as the Caroline War began.

The Caroline War

The Caroline War was named after Charles V of France, who resumed the war after the Treaty of Brétigny. In May 1369, the Black Prince, son of Edward III of England, refused an illegal summons from the French king demanding he come to Paris, and Charles responded by declaring war. He immediately set out to reverse the territorial losses imposed at Brétigny, but was largely successful. His successor, Charles VI, made peace with Richard II, son of the Black Prince, in 1389. This truce was extended many times until the war was resumed in 1415.

The Lancastrian War

The Lancastrian War was the third phase of the Anglo-French Hundred Years' War. It lasted from 1415, when Henry V of England invaded Normandy, to 1453, when the English failed to recover Bordeaux. It followed a long period of peace from 1389, at end of the Caroline War. This phase was named after the House of Lancaster, the ruling house of the Kingdom of England, to which Henry V belonged. After the invasion of 1419, Henry V and, after his death, his brother John of Lancaster, Duke of Bedford, brought the English to the height of their power in France, with an English king crowned in Paris.

However, by that time, with charismatic leaders such as Joan of Arc, strong French counterattacks had started to win back all English continental territories, except the Pale of Calais, which was finally captured in 1558. Charles VII of France was crowned in Notre-Dame de Reims in 1429. The Battle of Castillon (1453) was the last battle of the Hundred Years' War, but France and England remained formally at war until the Treaty of Picquigny in 1475. English, and later British, monarchs would continue to claim the French throne until 1800.

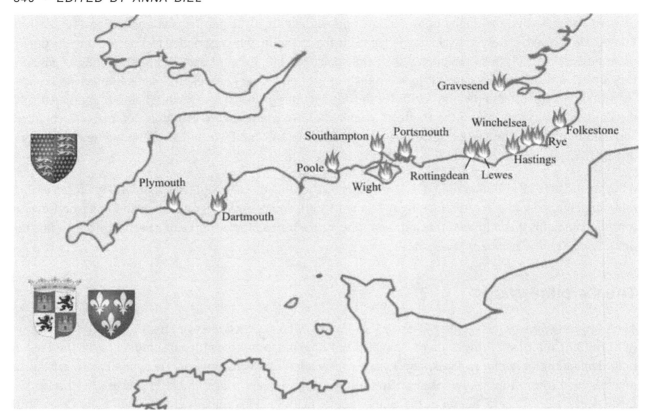

Attacks on England by the Franco-Castilian Navy, 1374-1380. The Franco-Castilian Navy, led by Admirals de Vienne and Tovar, managed to raid the English coasts for the first time since the beginning of the Hundred Years' War.

Joan of Arc

Joan of Arc is considered a heroine of France for her role during the Lancastrian phase of the Hundred Years' War, and was canonized as a Roman Catholic saint. Joan of Arc was born to Jacques d'Arc and Isabelle Romée, a peasant family, at Domrémy, in northeast France. Joan said she received visions of the Archangel Michael, Saint Margaret, and Saint Catherine of Alexandria instructing her to support Charles VII and recover France from English domination late in the Hundred Years' War. The uncrowned King Charles VII sent Joan to the siege of Orléans as part of a relief mission. She gained prominence after the siege was lifted only nine days later. Several additional swift victories led to Charles VII's coronation at Reims. This long-awaited event boosted French morale and paved the way for the final French victory.

On May 23, 1430, Joan was captured at Compiègne by the English-allied Burgundian faction. She was later handed over to the English and then put on trial by the pro-English Bishop of Beauvais Pierre Cauchon on a variety of charges. She was convicted on May 30, 1431, and burned at the stake when she was about nineteen years old.

Joan of Arc. Painting, c. 1485. An artist's interpretation, since the only known direct portrait has not survived.

Twenty-five years after her execution, an inquisitorial court authorized by Pope Callixtus III examined the trial, pronounced her innocent, and declared her a martyr. Joan of Arc was beatified in 1909 and canonized in 1920. She is one of the nine secondary patron saints of France, along with St. Denis, St. Martin of Tours, St. Louis, St. Michael, St. Remi, St. Petronilla, St. Radegund, and St. Thérèse of Lisieux.

Joan of Arc Biography. Joan of Arc (1412–1431) was born a peasant and became a heroine of France.

- https://youtu.be/0q3uAu1EuRc

Attributions

CC licensed content, Specific attribution

- Boundless World History. **Authored by**: Boundless. **Located at**: https://courses.lumenlearning.com/boundless-worldhistory/. **License**: *CC BY-SA: Attribution-ShareAlike*

The Crusades

- Describe the origins of the Crusades

Key Points

- The Crusades were a series of military conflicts conducted by Christian knights to defend Christians and the Christian empire against Muslim forces.

- The Holy Land was part of the Roman Empire until the Islamic conquests of the 7th and 8th centuries. Thereafter, Christians were permitted to visit parts of the Holy Land until 1071, when Christian pilgrimages were stopped by the Seljuq Turks.

- The Seljuq Turks had taken over much of Byzantium after the Byzantine defeat at the Battle of Manzikert in 1071.

- In 1095 at the Council of Piacenza, Byzantine Emperor Alexios I Komnenos requested military aid from Urban II to fight the Turks.

- In July 1095, Urban turned to his homeland of France to recruit men for the expedition. His travels there culminated in the Council of Clermont in November, where he gave speeches combining the idea of pilgrimage to the Holy Land with that of waging a holy war against infidels, which received an enthusiastic response.

Terms

Seljuq Empire

A medieval Turko-Persian Sunni Muslim empire that controlled a vast area stretching from the Hindu Kush to eastern Anatolia and from Central Asia to the Persian Gulf. The Seljuq Turk attack on Byzantium helped spur the crusades.

heretical

Relating to departure from established beliefs or customs.

Byzantine Empire

The predominantly Greek-speaking continuation of the eastern half of the Roman Empire during Late Antiquity and the Middle Ages.

schism

A division or a split, usually between groups belonging to a religious denomination.

The Crusades were a series of military conflicts conducted by Christian knights for the defense of Christians and for the expansion of Christian domains between the 11th and 15th centuries. Generally, the Crusades refer to the campaigns in the Holy Land sponsored by the papacy against Muslim forces. There were other crusades against Islamic forces in southern Spain, southern Italy, and Sicily, as well as campaigns of Teutonic knights against pagan strongholds in Eastern Europe. A few crusades, such as the Fourth Crusade, were waged within Christendom against groups that were considered heretical and schismatic. Crusades were fought for many reasons—to capture Jerusalem, recapture Christian territory, or defend Christians in non-Christian lands; as a means of conflict resolution among Roman Catholics; for political or territorial advantage; and to combat paganism and heresy.

Origin of the Crusades

The origin of the Crusades in general, and particularly of the First Crusade, is widely debated among historians. The confusion is partially due to the numerous armies in the First Crusade, and their lack of direct unity. The similar ideologies held the armies to similar goals, but the connections were rarely strong, and unity broke down often. The Crusades are most commonly linked to the political and social situation in 11th-century Europe, the rise of a reform movement within the papacy, and the political and religious confrontation of Christianity and Islam in Europe and the Middle East. Christianity had spread throughout Europe, Africa, and the Middle East in Late Antiquity, but by the early 8th century Christian rule had become limited to Europe and Anatolia after the Muslim conquests.

Background in Europe

The Holy Land had been part of the Roman Empire, and thus the Byzantine Empire, until the Islamic conquests. In the 7th and 8th centuries, Islam was introduced in the Arabian Peninsula by the Islamic prophet Muhammad and his followers. This formed a unified Muslim polity, which led to a rapid expansion of Arab power, the influence of which stretched from the northwest Indian subcontinent, across Central Asia, the Middle East, North Africa, southern Italy, and the Iberian Peninsula, to the Pyrenees. Tolerance, trade, and political relationships between the Arabs and the Christian states of Europe waxed and waned. For example, the Fatimid caliph al-Hakim bi-Amr Allah destroyed the Church of the Holy Sepulchre, but his successor allowed the Byzantine Empire to rebuild it. Pilgrimages by Catholics to sacred sites were permitted, resident Christians were given certain legal rights and protections under Dhimmi status, and interfaith marriages were not uncommon. Cultures and creeds coexisted and competed, but the frontier conditions became increasingly inhospitable to Catholic pilgrims and merchants.

At the western edge of Europe and of Islamic expansion, the Reconquista (recapture of the Iberian Peninsula from the Muslims) was well underway by the 11th century, reaching its turning point in 1085 when Alfonso VI of León and Castile retook Toledo from Muslim rule. Increasingly in the 11th century, foreign knights, mostly from France, visited Iberia to assist the Christians in their efforts.

The heart of Western Europe had been stabilized after the Christianization of the Saxon, Viking, and Hungarian peoples by the end of the 10th century. However, the breakdown of the Carolingian Empire gave rise to an entire class of warriors who now had little to do but fight among themselves. The random violence of the knightly class was regularly condemned by the church, and so it established the Peace and Truce of God to prohibit fighting on certain days of the year.

At the same time, the reform-minded papacy came into conflict with the Holy Roman Emperors, resulting in the Investiture Controversy. The papacy began to assert its independence from secular rulers, marshaling arguments for the proper use of armed force by Catholics. Popes such as Gregory VII justified the subsequent warfare against the emperor's partisans in theological terms. It became acceptable for the pope to utilize knights in the name of Christendom, not only against political enemies of the papacy, but also against Al-Andalus, or, theoretically, against the Seljuq dynasty in the east. The result was intense piety, an interest in religious affairs, and religious propaganda advocating a just war to reclaim Palestine from the Muslims. Participation in such a war was seen as a form of penance that could counterbalance sin.

Aid to Byzantium

To the east of Europe lay the Byzantine Empire, composed of Christians who had long followed a separate Orthodox rite; the Eastern Orthodox and Roman Catholic churches had been in schism since 1054. Historians have argued that the desire to impose Roman church authority in the east may have been one of the goals of the Crusades, although Urban II, who launched the First Crusade, never refers to such a goal in his letters on crusading. The Seljuq Empire had taken over almost all of Anatolia after the Byzantine defeat at the Battle of Manzikert in 1071; however, their conquests were piecemeal and led by semi-independent warlords, rather than by the sultan. A dramatic collapse of the empire's position on the eve of the Council of Clermont brought Byzantium to the brink of disaster. By the mid-1090s, the Byzantine Empire was largely confined to Balkan Europe and the northwestern fringe of Anatolia, and faced Norman enemies in the west as well as Turks in the east. In response to the defeat at Manzikert and subsequent Byzantine losses in Anatolia in 1074, Pope Gregory VII had called for the *milites Christi* ("soldiers of Christ") to go to Byzantium's aid.

Seljuq Empire. The Great Seljuq Empire at its greatest extent (1092).

While the Crusades had causes deeply rooted in the social and political situations of 11th-century Europe, the event actually triggering the First Crusade was a request for assistance from Byzantine emperor Alexios I Komnenos. Alexios was worried about the advances of the Seljuqs, who had reached as far west as Nicaea, not far from Constantinople. In March 1095, Alexios sent envoys to the Council of Piacenza to ask Pope Urban II for aid against the Turks.

Urban responded favorably, perhaps hoping to heal the Great Schism of forty years earlier, and to reunite the Church under papal primacy by helping the eastern churches in their time of need. Alexios and Urban had previously been in close contact in 1089 and later, and had openly discussed the prospect of the (re)union of the Christian church. There were signs of considerable co-operation between Rome and Constantinople in the years immediately before the Crusade.

In July 1095, Urban turned to his homeland of France to recruit men for the expedition. His travels there culminated in the Council of Clermont in November, where, according to the various speeches attributed to him, he gave an impassioned sermon to a large audience of French nobles and clergy, graphically detailing the fantastical atrocities being committed against pilgrims and eastern Christians. Urban talked about the violence of European society and the necessity of maintaining the Peace of God; about helping the Greeks, who had asked for assistance; about the crimes being committed against Christians in the east; and about a new kind of war, an armed pilgrimage, and of rewards in heaven, where remission of sins was offered to any who might die in the undertaking. Combining the idea of pilgrimage to the Holy Land with that of waging a holy war against infidels, Urban received an enthusiastic response to his speeches and soon after began collecting military forces to begin the First Crusade.

Council of Clermont. Pope Urban II at the Council of Clermont, where he gave speeches in favor of a Crusade.

Sources

Attributions

CC licensed content, Specific attribution

- Boundless World History. **Authored by**: Boundless. **Located at**: https://courses.lumenlearning.com/boundless-worldhistory/. **License**: *CC BY-SA: Attribution-ShareAlike*

The First Crusade

Learning Objective

- Evaluate the events of the First Crusade

Key Points

- The First Crusade (1095–1099), called for by Pope Urban II, was the first of a number of crusades that attempted to recapture the Holy Lands.

- It was launched on November 27, 1095, by Pope Urban II with the primary goal of responding to an appeal from Byzantine Emperor Alexios I Komnenos, who had been defeated by Turkish forces.

- An additional goal soon became the principal objective—the Christian reconquest of the sacred city of Jerusalem and the Holy Land and the freeing of the Eastern Christians from Muslim rule.

- The first object of the campaign was Nicaea, previously a city under Byzantine rule, which the Crusaders captured on June 18, 1097, by defeating the troops of Kilij Arslan.

- After marching through the Mediterranean region, the Crusaders arrived at Jerusalem, launched an assault on the city, and captured it in July 1099, massacring many of the city's Muslim and Jewish inhabitants.

- In the end, they established the crusader states of the Kingdom of Jerusalem, the County of Tripoli, the Principality of Antioch, and the County of Edessa.

Terms

Church of the Holy Sepulchre

A church within the Christian Quarter of the Old City of Jerusalem that contains, according to traditions dating back to at least the 4th century, the two holiest sites in Christendom—the site where Jesus of Nazareth was crucified and Jesus's empty tomb, where he is said to have been buried and resurrected.

Alexios I Komnenos

Byzantine emperor from 1081 to 1118, whose appeals to Western Europe for help against the Turks were also the catalyst that likely contributed to the convoking of the Crusades.

Pope Urban II

Pope from March 12, 1088, to his death in 1099, he is best known for initiating the First Crusade.

People's Crusade

An expedition seen as the prelude to the First Crusade that lasted roughly six months, from April to October 1096, and was led mostly by peasants.

Overview

The First Crusade (1095–1099), called for by Pope Urban II, was the first of a number of crusades intended to recapture the Holy Lands. It started as a widespread pilgrimage in western Christendom and ended as a military expedition by Roman Catholic Europe to regain the Holy Lands taken in the Muslim conquests of the Mediterranean (632–661), ultimately resulting in the recapture of Jerusalem in 1099.

It was launched on November 27, 1095, by Pope Urban II with the primary goal of responding to an appeal from Byzantine Emperor Alexios I Komnenos, who requested that western volunteers come to his aid and help to repel the invading Seljuq Turks from Anatolia (modern-day Turkey). An additional goal soon became the principal objective—the Christian reconquest of the sacred city of Jerusalem and the Holy Land and the freeing of the Eastern Christians from Muslim rule.

During the crusade, knights, peasants, and serfs from many regions of Western Europe travelled over land and by sea, first to Constantinople and then on toward Jerusalem. The Crusaders arrived at Jerusalem, launched an assault on the city, and captured it in July 1099, massacring many of the city's Muslim and Jewish inhabitants. They also established the crusader states of the Kingdom of Jerusalem, the County of Tripoli, the Principality of Antioch, and the County of Edessa.

People's Crusade

Pope Urban II planned the departure of the crusade for August 15, 1096; before this, a number of unexpected bands of peasants and low-ranking knights organized and set off for Jerusalem on their own, on an expedition known as the People's Crusade, led by a monk named Peter the Hermit. The peasant population had been afflicted by drought, famine, and disease for many years before 1096, and some of them seem to have envisioned the crusade as an escape from these hardships. Spurring them on had been a number of meteorological occurrences beginning in 1095 that seemed to be a divine blessing for the movement—a meteor shower, an aurorae, a lunar eclipse, and a comet, among other events. An outbreak of ergotism had also occurred just before the Council of Clermont. Millenarianism, the belief that the end of the world was imminent, widespread in the early 11th century, experienced a resurgence in popularity. The response was beyond expectations; while Urban might have expected a few thousand knights, he ended up with a migration numbering up to 40,000 Crusaders of mostly unskilled fighters, including women and children.

Lacking military discipline in what likely seemed a strange land (Eastern Europe), Peter's fledgling army quickly found itself in trouble despite the fact that they were still in Christian territory. This unruly mob began to attack and pillage outside Constantinople in search of supplies and food, prompting Alexios to hurriedly ferry the gathering across the Bosporus one week later. After crossing into Asia Minor, the crusaders split up and began to plunder the countryside, wandering into Seljuq territory around Nicaea, where they were massacred by an overwhelming group of Turks.

People's Crusade massacre. An illustration showing the defeat of the People's Crusade by the Turks.

The First Crusade

The four main Crusader armies left Europe around the appointed time in August 1096. They took different paths to Constantinople and gathered outside the city walls between November 1096 and April 1097; Hugh of Vermandois arrived first, followed by Godfrey, Raymond, and Bohemond. This time, Emperor Alexios was more prepared for the Crusaders; there were fewer incidents of violence along the way.

The Crusaders may have expected Alexios to become their leader, but he had no interest in joining them, and was mainly concerned with transporting them into Asia Minor as quickly as possible. In return for food and supplies, Alexios requested that the leaders to swear fealty to him and promise to return to the Byzantine Empire any land recovered from the Turks. Before ensuring that the various armies were shuttled across the Bosporus, Alexios advised the leaders on how best to deal with the Seljuq armies they would soon encounter.

Siege of Nicaea and March to Jerusalem

The Crusader armies crossed over into Asia Minor during the first half of 1097, where they were joined by Peter the Hermit and the remainder of his little army. Alexios also sent two of his own generals, Manuel Boutoumites and Tatikios, to assist the Crusaders. The first object of their campaign was Nicaea, previously a city under Byzantine rule, but which had become the capital of the Seljuq Sultanate of Rum under Kilij Arslan I. Arslan was away campaigning against the Danishmends in central Anatolia at the time, and had left behind his treasury and his family, underestimating the strength of these new Crusaders.

Subsequently, upon the Crusaders' arrival, the city was subjected to a lengthy siege, and when Arslan had word of it he rushed back to Nicaea and attacked the Crusader army on May 16. He was driven back by the unexpectedly large Crusader force, with heavy losses suffered on both sides in the ensuing battle. The siege continued, but the Crusaders had little success as they found they could not blockade Lake Iznik, which the city was situated on, and from which it could be provisioned. To break the city, Alexios had the Crusaders' ships rolled over land on logs, and at the sight of them the Turkish garrison finally surrendered, 18 June 18. The city was handed over to the Byzantine troops.

At the end of June, the Crusaders marched on through Anatolia. They were accompanied by some Byzantine troops under Tatikios, and still harbored the hope that Alexios would send a full Byzantine army after them. After a battle with Kilij Arslan, the Crusaders marched through Anatolia unopposed, but the journey was unpleasant, as Arslan had burned and destroyed everything he left behind in his army's flight. It was the middle of summer, and the Crusaders had very little food and water; many men and horses died. Fellow Christians sometimes gave them gifts of food and money, but more often than not the Crusaders simply looted and pillaged whenever the opportunity presented itself.

Proceeding down the Mediterranean coast, the crusaders encountered little resistance, as local rulers preferred to make peace with them and furnish them with supplies rather than fight.

Capture of Jerusalem

On June 7, the Crusaders reached Jerusalem, which had been recaptured from the Seljuqs by the Fatimids only the year before. Many Crusaders wept upon seeing the city they had journeyed so long to reach.

The arrival at Jerusalem revealed an arid countryside, lacking in water or food supplies. Here there was no prospect of relief, even as they feared an imminent attack by the local Fatimid rulers. The Crusaders resolved to take the city by assault. They might have been left with little choice, as it has been estimated that only about 12,000 men, including 1,500 cavalry, remained by the time the army reached Jerusalem.

After the failure of the initial assault, a meeting between the various leaders was organized in which it was agreed upon that a more concerted attack would be required in the future. On June 17, a party of Genoese mariners under Guglielmo Embriaco arrived at Jaffa and provided the Crusaders with skilled engineers, and perhaps more critically, supplies of timber (cannibalized from the ships) with which to build siege engines. The Crusaders' morale was raised when a priest, Peter Desiderius, claimed to have had a divine vision of Bishop Adhemar instructing them to fast and then march in a barefoot procession around the city walls, after which the city would fall, following the Biblical story of Joshua at the siege of Jericho.

The final assault on Jerusalem began on July 13; Raymond's troops attacked the south gate while the other contingents attacked the northern wall. Initially the Provençals at the southern gate made little headway, but the contingents at the northern wall fared better, with a slow but steady attrition of the defense. On July 15, a final push was launched at both ends of the city, and eventually the inner rampart of the northern wall was captured. In the ensuing panic, the defenders abandoned the walls of the city at both ends, allowing the Crusaders to finally enter.

Capture of Jerusalem. A depiction of the capture of Jerusalem in 1099 from a medieval manuscript. The burning buildings of Jerusalem are centered in the image. The various Crusaders are surrounding and besieging the village armed for an attack.

The massacre that followed the capture of Jerusalem has attained particular notoriety, as a "juxtaposition of extreme violence and anguished faith." The eyewitness accounts from the Crusaders themselves leave little doubt that there was a great slaughter in the aftermath of the siege. Nevertheless, some historians propose that the scale of the massacre was exaggerated in later medieval sources. The slaughter lasted a day; Muslims were indiscriminately killed, and Jews who had taken refuge in their synagogue died when it was burnt down by the Crusaders. The following day, Tancred's prisoners in the mosque were slaughtered. Still, it is clear that some Muslims and Jews of the city survived the massacre, either escaping or being taken prisoner to be ransomed. The Eastern Christian population of the city had been expelled before the siege by the governor, and thus escaped the massacre.

On July 22, a council was held in the Church of the Holy Sepulchre to establish a king for the newly created Kingdom of Jerusalem. Raymond IV of Toulouse and Godfrey of Bouillon were recognized as the leaders of the crusade and the siege of Jerusalem. Raymond was the wealthier and more powerful of the two, but at first he refused to become king, perhaps attempting to show his piety and probably hoping that the other nobles would insist upon his election anyway. The more popular Godfrey did not hesitate like Raymond, and accepted a position as secular leader.

Having captured Jerusalem and the Church of the Holy Sepulchre, the Crusaders had fulfilled their vow.

Sources

Attributions

CC licensed content, Specific attribution

- Boundless World History. **Authored by**: Boundless. **Located at**: https://courses.lumenlearning.com/boundless-worldhistory/. **License**: *CC BY-SA: Attribution-ShareAlike*

The Second Crusade

Learning Objective

- Explain the successes and failures of the Second Crusade

Key Points

- The Second Crusade was started in 1147 in response to the fall of the County of Edessa the previous year to the forces of Zengi; Edessa was founded during the First Crusade.
- The Second Crusade was led by two European kings—Louis VII of France and Conrad III of Germany.
- The German and French armies took separate routes to Anatolia, fighting skirmishes along the way, and both were defeated separately by the Seljuq Turks.
- Louis and Conrad and the remnants of their armies eventually reached Jerusalem and participated in an ill-advised attack on Damascus in 1148.
- The Second Crusade was a failure for the Crusaders and a great victory for the Muslims.

Terms

Louis VII

A Capetian king of the Franks from 1137 until his death who led troops in the Second Crusade.

Manuel I Komneno

A Byzantine Emperor of the 12th century who reigned over a crucial turning point in the history of Byzantium and the Mediterranean, including the Second Crusade.

Conrad III

First German king of the Hohenstaufen dynasty, who led troops in the Second Crusade.

Moors

The Muslim inhabitants of the Maghreb, North Africa and the Iberian Peninsula, Sicily, and Malta during the Middle Ages, who initially were Berber and Arab peoples of North African descent.

The Second Crusade

The Second Crusade (1147–1149) was the second major crusade launched from Europe as a Catholic holy war against Islam. The Second Crusade was started in 1147 in response to the fall of the County of Edessa the previous year to the forces of Zengi. The county had been founded during the First Crusade by King Baldwin of Boulogne in 1098. While it was the first Crusader state to be founded, it was also the first to fall.

The Second Crusade was announced by Pope Eugene III, and was the first of the crusades to be led by European kings, namely Louis VII of France and Conrad III of Germany, who had help from a number of other European nobles. The armies of the two kings marched separately across Europe. After crossing Byzantine territory into Anatolia, both armies were separately defeated by the Seljuq Turks. The main Western Christian source, Odo of Deuil, and Syriac Christian sources claim that the Byzantine Emperor Manuel I Komnenos secretly hindered the Crusaders' progress, particularly in Anatolia, where he is alleged to have deliberately ordered Turks to attack them. Louis and Conrad and the remnants of their armies reached Jerusalem and participated in an ill-advised attack on Damascus in 1148. The Crusade in the east was a failure for the Crusaders and a great victory for the Muslims. It would ultimately have a key influence on the fall of Jerusalem and give rise to the Third Crusade at the end of the 12th century.

The only Christian success of the Second Crusade came to a combined force of 13,000 Flemish, Frisian, Norman, English, Scottish, and German Crusaders in 1147. Traveling by ship from England to the Holy Land, the army stopped and helped the smaller (7,000) Portuguese army capture Lisbon, expelling its Moorish occupants.

Crusade in the East

Joscelin II had tried to take back Edessa, but Nur ad-Din defeated him in November 1146. On February 16, 1147, the French Crusaders met to discuss their route. The Germans had already decided to travel overland through Hungary, as the sea route was politically impractical because Roger II, king of Sicily, was an enemy of Conrad. Many of the French nobles distrusted the land route, which would take them through the Byzantine Empire, the reputation of which still suffered from the accounts of the First Crusaders. Nevertheless, it was decided to follow Conrad, and to set out on June 15.

German Route

The German crusaders, accompanied by the papal legate and Cardinal Theodwin, intended to meet the French in Constantinople. Ottokar III of Styria joined Conrad at Vienna, and Conrad's enemy Géza II of Hungary allowed them to pass through unharmed. When the German army of 20,000 men arrived in Byzantine territory, Emperor Manuel I Komnenos feared they were going to attack him, and Byzantine troops were posted to ensure that there was no trouble. On September 10, the Germans arrived at Constantinople, where relations with Manuel were poor. There was a battle, after which the Germans were convinced that they should cross into Asia Minor as quickly as possible.

In Asia Minor, Conrad decided not to wait for the French, and marched towards Iconium, capital of the Seljuq Sultanate of Rûm. Conrad split his army into two divisions. The authority of the Byzantine Empire in the western provinces of Asia Minor was more nominal than real, with much of the provinces being a no-man's land controlled by Turkish nomads. Conrad underestimated the length of the march against Anatolia, and anyhow assumed that the authority of Emperor Manuel was greater in Anatolia than was in fact the case. Conrad took the knights and the best troops with him to march overland and sent the camp followers with Otto of Freising to follow the coastal road. The king's contingent was almost totally destroyed by the Seljuqs on October 25, 1147, at the second Battle of Dorylaeum.

French Route

The French crusaders departed from Metz in June 1147, led by Louis, Thierry of Alsace, Renaut I of Bar, Amadeus III, Count of Savoy and his half-brother William V of Montferrat, William VII of Auvergne, and others, along with armies from Lorraine, Brittany, Burgundy, and Aquitaine. A force from Provence, led by Alphonse of Toulouse, chose to wait until August and cross by sea. At Worms, Louis joined with crusaders from Normandy and England.

They followed Conrad's route fairly peacefully, although Louis came into conflict with King Geza of Hungary when Geza discovered Louis had allowed an attempted Hungarian usurper to join his army. Relations within Byzantine territory were grim, and the Lorrainers, who had marched ahead of the rest of the French, also came into conflict with the slower Germans whom they met on the way.

The French met the remnants of Conrad's army at Lopadion, and Conrad joined Louis's force. They followed Otto of Freising's route, moving closer to the Mediterranean coast, and they arrived at Ephesus in December, where they learned that the Turks were preparing to attack them. Manuel had sent ambassadors complaining about the pillaging and plundering that Louis had done along the way, and there was no guarantee that the Byzantines would assist them against the Turks. Meanwhile, Conrad fell sick and returned to Constantinople, where Manuel attended to him personally, and Louis, paying no attention to the warnings of a Turkish attack, marched out from Ephesus with the French and German survivors. The Turks were indeed waiting to attack, but in a small battle outside Ephesus, the French and Germans were victorious.

They reached Laodicea on the Lycus early in January 1148, around the same time Otto of Freising's army had been destroyed in the same area. After resuming the march, the vanguard under Amadeus of Savoy was separated from the rest of the army at Mount Cadmus, and Louis's troops suffered heavy losses from the Turks. After being delayed for a month by storms, most of the promised ships from Provence did not arrive at all. Louis and his associates claimed the ships that did make it for themselves, while the rest of the army had to resume the long march to Antioch. The army was almost entirely destroyed, either by the Turks or by sickness.

Siege of Damascus

The remains of the German and French armies eventually continued on to Jerusalem, where they planned an attack on the Muslim forces in Damascus. The Crusaders decided to attack Damascus from the west, where orchards would provide them with a constant food supply. They arrived at Daraiya on July 23. The following day, the well-prepared Muslims constantly attacked the army advancing through the orchards outside Damascus. The defenders had sought help from Saif ad-Din Ghazi I of Mosul and Nur ad-Din of Aleppo, who personally led an attack on the Crusader camp. The Crusaders were pushed back from the walls into the orchards, where they were prone to ambushes and guerrilla attacks.

According to William of Tyre, on July 27 the Crusaders decided to move to the plain on the eastern side of the city, which was less heavily fortified, but also had much less food and water. Some records indicate that Unur had bribed the leaders to move to a less defensible position, and that Unur had promised to break off his alliance with Nur ad-Din if the Crusaders went home. Meanwhile, Nur ad-Din and Saif ad-Din had by now arrived. With Nur ad-Din in the field it was impossible for the Crusaders to return to their better position. The local Crusader lords refused to carry on with the siege, and the three kings had no choice but to abandon the city. First Conrad, then the rest of the army, decided to retreat to Jerusalem on July 28, and they were followed the whole way by Turkish archers, who constantly harassed them.

Siege of Damascus. A print of the Siege of Damascus.

Aftermath

Each of the Christian forces felt betrayed by the other. In Germany, the Crusade was seen as a huge debacle, with many monks writing that it could only have been the work of the Devil. Despite the distaste for the memory of the Second Crusade, the experience had notable impact on German literature, with many epic poems of the late 12th century featuring battle scenes clearly inspired by the fighting in the crusade. The cultural impact of the Second Crusade was even greater in France. Unlike Conrad, the Louis's image was improved by the crusade, with many of the French seeing him as a suffering pilgrim king who quietly bore God's punishments.

Relations between the Eastern Roman Empire and the French were badly damaged by the Second Crusade. Louis and other French leaders openly accused Emperor Manuel I of colluding with Turkish attackers during the march across Asia Minor. The memory of the Second Crusade was to color French views of the Byzantines for the rest of the 12th and 13th centuries.

Sources

Attributions

CC licensed content, Specific attribution

- Boundless World History. **Authored by**: Boundless. **Located at**: https://courses.lumenlearning.com/boundless-worldhistory/. **License**: *CC BY-SA: Attribution-ShareAlike*

The Third Crusade

Learning Objective

- Compare and contrast the Third Crusade with the first two

Key Points

- After the failure of the Second Crusade, the Zengid dynasty controlled a unified Syria and engaged in a successful conflict with the Fatimid rulers of Egypt; the Egyptian and Syrian forces were ultimately unified under Saladin, who employed them to reduce the Christian states and recapture Jerusalem in 1187.

- The Crusaders, mainly under the leadership of King Richard of England, captured Acre and Jaffa on their way to Jerusalem.

- Because of conflict with King Richard and to settle succession disputes, the German and French armies left the crusade early, weakening the Christian forces.

- After trying to overtake Jerusalem and having Jaffa change hands several times, Richard and Saladin finalized a treaty granting Muslim control over Jerusalem but allowing unarmed Christian pilgrims and merchants to visit the city.

- The Third Crusade differed from the First Crusade in several ways: kings led the armies into battle, it was in response to European losses, and it resulted in a treaty.

Terms

Richard the Lionheart

King of England from July 6, 1189, until his death; famous for his reputation as a great military leader and warrior.

Saladin

The first sultan of Egypt and Syria and the founder of the Ayyubid dynasty; he led the Muslim military campaign against the Crusader states in the Levant.

Overview

The Third Crusade (1189–1192), also known as The Kings' Crusade, was an attempt by European leaders to reconquer the Holy Land from Saladin. The campaign was largely successful, capturing the important cities of Acre and Jaffa, and reversing most of Saladin's conquests, but it failed to capture Jerusalem, the emotional and spiritual motivation of the crusade.

After the failure of the Second Crusade, the Zengid dynasty controlled a unified Syria and engaged in a conflict with the Fatimid rulers of Egypt. The Egyptian and Syrian forces were ultimately unified under Saladin, who employed them to reduce the Christian states and recapture Jerusalem in 1187. Spurred by religious zeal, King Henry II of England and King Philip II of France (known as Philip Augustus) ended their conflict with each other to lead a new crusade. The death of Henry in 1189, however, meant the English contingent came under the command of his successor, King Richard I of England (known as Richard the Lionheart). The elderly Holy Roman Emperor Frederick Barbarossa also responded to the call to arms, leading a massive army across Anatolia, but he drowned in a river in Asia Minor on June 10, 1190, before reaching the Holy Land. His death caused tremendous grief among the German Crusaders, and most of his troops returned home.

After the Crusaders had driven the Muslims from Acre, Philip and Frederick's successor, Leopold V, Duke of Austria (known as Leopold the Virtuous), left the Holy Land in August 1191. On September 2, 1192, Richard and Saladin finalized a treaty granting Muslim control over Jerusalem but allowing unarmed Christian pilgrims and merchants to visit the city. Richard departed the Holy Land on October 2. The successes of the Third Crusade allowed the Crusaders to maintain considerable states in Cyprus and on the Syrian coast. However, the failure to recapture Jerusalem would lead to the Fourth Crusade.

Background

One of the major differences between the First and Third Crusades is that by the time of the Third Crusade, and to a certain degree during the Second, the Muslim opponents had unified under a single powerful leader. At the time of the First Crusade, the Middle East was severely divided by warring rulers. Without a unified front opposing them, the Christian troops were able to conquer Jerusalem, as well as the other

Crusader states. But under the powerful force of the Seljuq Turks during the Second Crusade and the even more unified power of Saladin during the Third, the Europeans were unable to achieve their ultimate aim of holding Jerusalem.

After the failure of the Second Crusade, Nur ad-Din Zangi had control of Damascus and a unified Syria. Nur ad-Din also took over Egypt through an alliance, and appointed Saladin the sultan of these territories. After Nur ad-Din's death, Saladin also took over Acre and Jerusalem, thereby wresting control of Palestine from the Crusaders, who had conquered the area 88 years earlier. Pope Urban III is said to have collapsed and died upon hearing this news, but it is not actually feasible that tidings of the fall of Jerusalem could have reached him by the time he died, although he did know of the battle of Hattin and the fall of Acre.

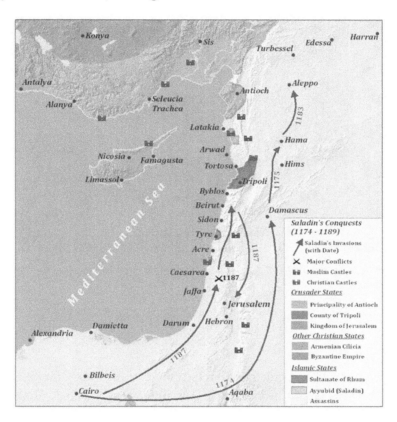

Saladin's Conquest (1174-1189). Map of Saladin's Conquest into the Levant, including invasions routes, major conflicts, strongholds, and occupations.

Siege of Acre

The Siege of Acre was one of the first confrontations of the Third Crusade, and a key victory for the Crusaders but a serious defeat for Saladin, who had hoped to destroy the whole of the Crusader kingdom.

Richard arrived at Acre on June 8, 1191, and immediately began supervising the construction of siege weapons to assault the city, which was captured on July 12. Richard, Philip, and Leopold quarreled over the spoils of the victory. Richard cast down the German flag from the city, slighting Leopold. The rest of the German army returned home.

On July 31, Philip also returned home, to settle the succession in Vermandois and Flanders, and Richard was left in sole charge of the Christian expeditionary forces. As in the Second Crusade, these disagreements and divisions within the European armies led to a weakening of the Christian forces.

Siege of Acre. The Siege of Acre was the first major confrontation of the Third Crusade.

Battle of Arsuf

After the capture of Acre, Richard decided to march to the city of Jaffa. Control of Jaffa was necessary before an attack on Jerusalem could be attempted. On September 7, 1191, however, Saladin attacked Richard's army at Arsuf, thirty miles north of Jaffa. Richard then ordered a general counterattack, which won the battle. Arsuf was an important victory. The Muslim army was not destroyed, despite the considerable casualties it suffered, but it was scattered; this was considered shameful by the Muslims and boosted the morale of the Crusaders. Richard was able to take, defend, and hold Jaffa, a strategically crucial move toward securing Jerusalem. By depriving Saladin of the coast, Richard seriously threatened his hold on Jerusalem.

Advances on Jerusalem and Negotiations

Following his victory at Arsuf, Richard took Jaffa and established his new headquarters there. In November 1191 the Crusader army advanced inland toward Jerusalem. On December 12 Saladin was forced by pressure from his emirs to disband the greater part of his army. Learning this, Richard pushed his army forward, spending Christmas at Latrun. The army then marched to Beit Nuba, only twelve miles from Jerusalem. Muslim morale in Jerusalem was so low that the arrival of the Crusaders would probably have caused the city to fall quickly. Appallingly bad weather—cold with heavy rain and hailstorms—combined with fear that if the Crusader army besieged Jerusalem it might be trapped by a relieving force, led to the decision to retreat back to the coast. In July 1192, Saladin's army suddenly attacked and captured Jaffa with thousands of men.

Richard was intending to return to England when he heard the news that Saladin and his army had captured Jaffa. Richard and a small force of little more than 2,000 men went to Jaffa by sea in a surprise attack. They stormed Jaffa from their ships and the Ayyubids, who had been unprepared for a naval attack, were driven from the city.

On September 2, 1192, following his defeat at Jaffa, Saladin was forced to finalize a treaty with Richard providing that Jerusalem would remain under Muslim control, but allowing unarmed Christian pilgrims and traders to visit the city. The city of Ascalon was a contentious issue, as it threatened communication between Saladin's dominions in Egypt and Syria; it was eventually agreed that Ascalon, with its defenses demolished, be returned to Saladin's control. Richard departed the Holy Land on October 9, 1192.

Aftermath and Comparisons

Neither side was entirely satisfied with the results of the war. Though Richard's victories had deprived the Muslims of important coastal territories and re-established a viable Frankish state in Palestine, many Christians in the Latin West felt disappointed that Richard had elected not to pursue the recapture of Jerusalem. Likewise, many in the Islamic world felt disturbed that Saladin had failed to drive the Christians out of Syria and Palestine. However, trade flourished throughout the Middle East and in port cities along the Mediterranean coastline.

The motivations and results of the Third Crusade differed from those of the First in several ways. Many historians contend that the motivations for the Third Crusade were more political than religious, thereby giving rise to the disagreements between the German, French, and English armies throughout the crusade. By the end, only Richard of England was left, and his small force was unable to finally overtake Saladin, despite successes at Acre and Jaffa. This infighting severely weakened the power of the European forces.

In addition, unlike the First Crusade, in the Second and Third Crusades kings led Crusaders into battle. The presence of European kings in battle set the armies up for instability, for the monarchs had to ensure their own territories were not threatened during their absence. During the Third Crusade, both the German and French armies were forced to return home to settle succession disputes and stabilize their kingdoms.

Furthermore, both the Second and Third Crusades were in response to European losses, first the fall of the Kingdom of Edessa and then the fall of Jerusalem to Saladin. These defensive expeditions could be seen as lacking the religious fervor and initiative of the First Crusade, which was entirely on the terms of the Christian armies.

Finally, the Third Crusade resulted in a treaty that left Jerusalem under Muslim dominion but allowed Christians access for trading and pilgrimage. In the past two crusades, the result had been to conquer and massacre or retreat, with no compromise or middle ground achieved. Despite the agreement in the Third Crusade, the failure to overtake Jerusalem led to still another crusade soon after.

Sources

Attributions

CC licensed content, Specific attribution

- Boundless World History. **Authored by**: Boundless. **Located at**: https://courses.lumenlearning.com/boundless-worldhistory/. **License**: *CC BY-SA: Attribution-ShareAlike*

The Fourth Crusade

Learning Objective

- Describe the failures of the Fourth Crusade

Terms

Crusader states

A number of mostly 12th- and 13th-century feudal states created by Western European crusaders in Asia Minor, Greece, and the Holy Land, and in the eastern Baltic area during the Northern Crusades.

heretics

People who holds beliefs or theories that are strongly at variance with established beliefs or customs, especially those held by the Roman Catholic Church.

Knights Templar

Among the wealthiest and most powerful of the Western Christian military orders; prominent actors in the Crusades.

Great Schism

The break of communion between what are now the Eastern Orthodox and Catholic churches, which has lasted since the 11th century.

Evolution of the Crusades

The Crusades were a series of religious wars undertaken by the Latin church between the 11th and 15th centuries. Crusades were fought for many reasons: to capture Jerusalem, recapture Christian territory, or defend Christians in non-Christian lands; as a means of conflict resolution among Roman Catholics; for political or territorial advantage; and to combat paganism and heresy.

The First Crusade arose after a call to arms in 1095 sermons by Pope Urban II. Urban urged military support for the Byzantine Empire and its Emperor, Alexios I, who needed reinforcements for his conflict with westward-migrating Turks in Anatolia. One of Urban's main aims was to guarantee pilgrims access to the holy sites in the Holy Land that were under Muslim control. Urban's wider strategy may have been to unite the eastern and western branches of Christendom, which had been divided since their split in 1054, and establish himself as head of the unified church. Regardless of the motivation, the response to Urban's preaching by people of many different classes across Western Europe established the precedent for later crusades.

As a result of the First Crusade, four primary Crusader states were created: the Kingdom of Jerusalem, the County of Edessa, the Principality of Antioch, and the County of Tripoli. On a popular level, the First Crusade unleashed a wave of impassioned, pious Catholic fury, which was expressed in the massacres of Jews that accompanied the Crusades and the violent treatment of the "schismatic" Orthodox Christians of the east.

Under the papacies of Calixtus II, Honorius II, Eugenius III, and Innocent II, smaller-scale crusading continued around the Crusader states in the early 12th century. The Knights Templar were recognized, and grants of crusading indulgences to those who opposed papal enemies are seen by some historians as the beginning of politically motivated crusades. The loss of Edessa in 1144 to Imad ad-Din Zengi led to preaching for what subsequently became known as the Second Crusade. King Louis VII and Conrad III led armies from France and Germany to Jerusalem and Damascus without winning any major victories. Bernard of Clairvaux, who had encouraged the Second Crusade in his preachings, was upset with the violence and slaughter directed toward the Jewish population of the Rhineland.

In 1187 Saladin united the enemies of the Crusader states, was victorious at the Battle of Hattin, and retook Jerusalem. According to Benedict of Peterborough, Pope Urban III died of deep sadness on October 19, 1187, upon hearing news of the defeat. His successor, Pope Gregory VIII, issued a papal bull that proposed a third crusade to recapture Jerusalem. This crusade failed to win control of Jerusalem from the Muslims, but did result in a treaty that allowed trading and pilgrimage there for Europeans.

Crusading became increasingly widespread in terms of geography and objectives during the 13th century; crusades were aimed at maintaining political and religious control over Europe and beyond and were not exclusively focused on the Holy Land. In Northern Europe the Catholic church continued to battle peoples whom they considered pagans; Popes such as Celestine III, Innocent III, Honorius III, and Gregory IX preached crusade against the Livonians, Prussians, and Russians. In the early 13th century, Albert of Riga established Riga as the seat of the Bishopric of Riga and formed the Livonian Brothers of the Sword to convert the pagans to Catholicism and protect German commerce.

Fourth Crusade

Innocent III began preaching what became the Fourth Crusade in 1200 in France, England, and Germany, but primarily in France. The Fourth Crusade (1202–1204) was a Western European armed expedition originally intended to conquer Muslim-controlled Jerusalem by means of an invasion through Egypt. Instead, a sequence of events culminated in the Crusaders sacking the city of Constantinople, the capital of the Christian-controlled Byzantine Empire. The Fourth Crusade never came to within 1,000 miles of its objective of Jerusalem, instead conquering Byzantium twice before being routed by the Bulgars at Adrianople.

In January 1203, en route to Jerusalem, the majority of the Crusader leadership entered into an agreement with the Byzantine prince Alexios Angelos to divert to Constantinople and restore his deposed father as emperor. The intention of the Crusaders was then to continue to the Holy Land with promised Byzantine financial and military assistance. On June 23, 1203, the main Crusader fleet reached Constantinople. Smaller contingents continued to Acre.

In August 1203, following clashes outside Constantinople, Alexios Angelos was crowned co-emperor (as Alexios IV Angelos) with Crusader support. However, in January 1204, he was deposed by a popular uprising in Constantinople. The Western Crusaders were no longer able to receive their promised payments, and when Alexios was murdered on February 8, 1204, the Crusaders and Venetians decided on the outright conquest of Constantinople. In April 1204, they captured and brutally sacked the city and set up a new Latin Empire, as well as partitioned other Byzantine territories among themselves.

Byzantine resistance based in unconquered sections of the empire such as Nicaea, Trebizond, and Epirus ultimately recovered Constantinople in 1261.

The Fourth Crusade is considered to be one of the final acts in the Great Schism between the Eastern Orthodox Church and Roman Catholic Church, and a key turning point in the decline of the Byzantine Empire and Christianity in the Near East.

Conquest of Constantinople. A Medieval painting of the Conquest of Constantinople by the Crusaders in 1204.

Later Crusades

After the failure of the Fourth Crusade to hold Constantinople or reach Jerusalem, Innocent III launched the first crusade against heretics, the Albigensian Crusade, against the Cathars in France and the County of Toulouse. Over the early decades of the century the Cathars were driven underground while the French monarchy asserted control over the region. Andrew II of Hungary waged the Bosnian Crusade against the Bosnian church, which was theologically Catholic but in long-term schism with the Roman Catholic Church. The conflict only ended with the Mongol invasion of Hungary in 1241. In the Iberian peninsula, Crusader privileges were given to those aiding the Templars, the Hospitallers, and the Iberian orders that merged with the Order of Calatrava and the Order of Santiago. The papacy declared frequent Iberian crusades, and from 1212 to 1265 the Christian kingdoms drove the Muslims back to the Emirate of Granada, which held out until 1492, when the Muslims and Jews were expelled from the peninsula.

Around this time, popularity and energy for the Crusades declined. One factor in the decline was the disunity and conflict among Latin Christian interests in the eastern Mediterranean. Pope Martin IV compromised the papacy by supporting Charles of Anjou, and tarnished its spiritual luster with botched secular "crusades" against Sicily and Aragon. The collapse of the papacy's moral authority and the rise of nationalism rang the death knell for crusading, ultimately leading to the Avignon Papacy and the Western Schism. The mainland Crusader states were extinguished with the fall of Tripoli in 1289 and the fall of Acre in 1291.

Centuries later, during the middle of the 15th century, the Latin church tried to organize a new crusade aimed at restoring the Eastern Roman or Byzantine Empire, which was gradually being torn down by the advancing Ottoman Turks. The attempt failed, however, as the vast majority of Greek civilians and a growing part of their clergy refused to recognize and accept the short-lived near-union of the churches of East and West signed at the Council of Florence and Ferrara by the Ecumenical patriarch Joseph II of Constantinople. The Greek population, reacting to the Latin conquest, believed that the Byzantine civilization that revolved around the Orthodox faith would be more secure under Ottoman Islamic rule. Overall, religious-observant Greeks preferred to sacrifice their political freedom and political independence in order to preserve their faith's traditions and rituals in separation from the Roman See.

In the late-14th and early-15th centuries, "crusades" on a limited scale were organized by the kingdoms of Hungary, Poland, Wallachia, and Serbia. These were not the traditional expeditions aimed at the recovery of Jerusalem but rather defensive campaigns intended to prevent further expansion to the west by the Ottoman Empire.

Sources

Attributions

Feudalism

Learning Objective

- Recall the structure of the feudal state and the responsibilities and obligations of each level of society

Key Points

- Feudalism flourished in Europe between the 9th and 15th centuries.

- Feudalism in England determined the structure of society around relationships derived from the holding and leasing of land, or *fiefs*.

- In England, the feudal pyramid was made up of the king at the top with the nobles, knights, and vassals below him.

- Before a lord could grant land to a tenant he would have to make him a vassal at a formal ceremony. This ceremony bound the lord and vassal in a contract.

- While modern writers such as Marx point out the negative qualities of feudalism, such as the exploitation and lack of social mobility for the peasants, the French historian Marc Bloch contends that peasants were part of the feudal relationship; while the vassals performed military service in exchange for the fief, the peasants performed physical labour in return for protection, thereby gaining some benefit despite their limited freedom.

- The 11th century in France saw what has been called by historians a "feudal revolution" or "mutation" and a "fragmentation of powers" that increased localized power and autonomy.

Terms

homage

In the Middle Ages this was the ceremony in which a feudal tenant or vassal pledged reverence and submission to his feudal lord, receiving in exchange the symbolic title to his new position.

fealty

An oath, from the Latin fidelitas (faithfulness); a pledge of allegiance of one person to another.

vassals

Persons who entered into a mutual obligation to a lord or monarch in the context of the feudal system in medieval Europe.

fiefs

Heritable property or rights granted by an overlord to a vassal.

mesne tenant

A lord in the feudal system who had vassals who held land from him, but who was himself the vassal of a higher lord.

Overview

Feudalism was a set of legal and military customs in medieval Europe that flourished between the 9th and 15th centuries. It can be broadly defined as a system for structuring society around relationships derived from the holding of land, known as a fiefdom or fief, in exchange for service or labour.

The classic version of feudalism describes a set of reciprocal legal and military obligations among the warrior nobility, revolving around the three key concepts of lords, vassals, and fiefs. A lord was in broad terms a noble who held land, a vassal was a person who was granted possession of the land by the lord, and a fief was what the land was known as. In exchange for the use of the fief and the protection of the lord, the vassal would provide some sort of service to the lord. There were many varieties of feudal land tenure, consisting of military and non-military service. The obligations and corresponding rights between lord and vassal concerning the fief formed the basis of the feudal relationship.

Feudalism, in its various forms, usually emerged as a result of the decentralization of an empire, especially in the Carolingian empires, which lacked the bureaucratic infrastructure necessary to support cavalry without the ability to allocate land to these mounted troops. Mounted soldiers began to secure a system of hereditary rule over their allocated land, and their power over the territory came to encompass the social, political, judicial, and economic spheres.

Many societies in the Middle Ages were characterized by feudal organizations, including England, which was the most structured feudal society, France, Italy, Germany, the Holy Roman Empire, and Portugal. Each of these territories developed feudalism in unique ways, and the way we understand feudalism as a unified concept today is in large part due to critiques after its dissolution. Karl Marx theorized feudalism as a pre-capitalist society, characterized by the power of the ruling class (the aristocracy) in their control of arable land, leading to a class society based upon the exploitation of the peasants who farm these lands, typically under serfdom and principally by means of labour, produce, and money rents.

While modern writers such as Marx point out the negative qualities of feudalism, the French historian Marc Bloch contends that peasants were an integral part of the feudal relationship: while the vassals performed military service in exchange for the fief, the peasants performed physical labour in return for protection, thereby gaining some benefit despite their limited freedom. Feudalism was thus a complex social and economic system defined by inherited ranks, each of which possessed inherent social and economic privileges and obligations. Feudalism allowed societies in the Middle Ages to retain a relatively stable political structure even as the centralized power of empires and kingdoms began to dissolve.

Structure of the Feudal State in England

Feudalism in 12th-century England was among the better structured and established systems in Europe at the time. The king was the absolute "owner" of land in the feudal system, and all nobles, knights, and other tenants, termed vassals, merely "held" land from the king, who was thus at the top of the feudal pyramid.

Below the king in the feudal pyramid was a tenant-in-chief (generally in the form of a baron or knight), who was a vassal of the king. Holding from the tenant-in-chief was a mesne tenant—generally a knight or baron who was sometimes a tenant-in-chief in their capacity as holder of other fiefs. Below the mesne tenant, further mesne tenants could hold from each other in series.

Vassalage

Before a lord could grant land (a fief) to someone, he had to make that person a vassal. This was done at a formal and symbolic ceremony called a commendation ceremony, which was composed of the two-part act of homage and oath of fealty. During homage, the lord and vassal entered into a contract in which the vassal promised to fight for the lord at his command, while the lord agreed to protect the vassal from external forces.

Roland pledges his fealty to Charlemagne. Roland (right) receives the sword, Durandal, from the hands of Charlemagne (left). From a manuscript of a chanson de geste, c. 14th Century.

Once the commendation ceremony was complete, the lord and vassal were in a feudal relationship with agreed obligations to one another. The vassal's principal obligation to the lord was "aid," or military service. Using whatever equipment the vassal could obtain by virtue of the revenues from the fief, he was responsible for answering calls to military service on behalf of the lord. This security of military help was the primary reason the lord entered into the feudal relationship. In addition, the vassal could have other obligations to his lord, such as attendance at his court, whether manorial or baronial, or at the king's court.

The vassal's obligations could also involve providing "counsel," so that if the lord faced a major decision he would summon all his vassals and hold a council. At the level of the manor this might be a fairly mundane matter of agricultural policy, but could also include sentencing by the lord for criminal offenses, including capital punishment in some cases. In the king's feudal court, such deliberation could include the question of declaring war. These are only examples; depending on the period of time and location in Europe, feudal customs and practices varied.

Feudalism in France

In its origin, the feudal grant of land had been seen in terms of a personal bond between lord and vassal, but with time and the transformation of fiefs into hereditary holdings, the nature of the system came to be seen as a form of "politics of land." The 11th century in France saw what has been called by historians a "feudal revolution" or "mutation" and a "fragmentation of powers" that was unlike the development of feudalism in England, Italy, or Germany in the same period or later. In France, counties and duchies began to break down into smaller holdings as castellans and lesser seigneurs took control of local lands, and (as comital families had done before them) lesser lords usurped/privatized a wide range of prerogatives and rights of the state—most importantly the highly profitable rights of justice, but also travel dues, market dues, fees for using woodlands, obligations to use the lord's mill, etc. Power in this period became more personal and decentralized.

Sources

Attributions

CC licensed content, Specific attribution

- Boundless World History. **Authored by**: Boundless. **Located at**: https://courses.lumenlearning.com/boundless-worldhistory/. **License**: *CC BY-SA: Attribution-ShareAlike*

The Manor System

- Illustrate the hierarchy of the manor system by describing the roles of lords, villeins, and serfs

- The lord of a manor was supported by his land holdings and contributions from the peasant population. Serfs who occupied land belonging to the lord were required to work the land, and in return received certain entitlements.

- Serfdom was the status of peasants in the manor system, and villeins were the most common type of serf in the Middle Ages.

- Villeins rented small homes with or without land; as part of their contract with the lord they were expected to spend some time working the land.

- Villeins could not move away without the lord's consent and the acceptance of the new lord whose manor they were to move to. Because of the protection villeins received from the lord's manor, it was generally not favorable to move away unless the landlord proved to be especially tyrannical.

- The manor system was made up of three types of land: demesne, dependent, and free peasant land.

- Manorial structures could be found throughout medieval Western and Eastern Europe: in Italy, Poland, Lithuania, Baltic nations, Holland, Prussia, England, France, and the Germanic kingdoms.

Terms

demesne

All the land, not necessarily all physically connected to the manor house, that was retained by the lord of a manor for his own use and support, under his own management.

serfs

Peasants under feudalism, specifically relating to manorialism. It was a condition of bondage that developed primarily during the High Middle Ages in Europe.

villein

The most common type of serf in the Middle Ages. They had more rights and a higher status than the lowest serf, but existed under a number of legal restrictions that differentiated them from freemen.

freemen

Men who were not serfs in the feudal system.

Manorialism was an essential element of feudal society and was the organizing principle of rural economy that originated in the villa system of the Late Roman Empire. Manorialism was widely practiced in medieval Western Europe and parts of central Europe, and was slowly replaced by the advent of a money-based market economy and new forms of agrarian contract.

Manorialism was characterized by the vesting of legal and economic power in the lord of a manor. The lord was supported economically from his own direct landholding in a manor (sometimes called a *fief*), and from the obligatory contributions of the peasant population who fell under the jurisdiction of the lord and his court. These obligations could be payable in several ways: in labor, in kind, or, on rare occasions, in coin. Manorial structures could be found throughout medieval Western and Eastern Europe: in Italy, Poland, Lithuania, Baltic nations, Holland, Prussia, England, France, and the Germanic kingdoms.

The main reason for the development of the system was perhaps also its greatest strength: the stabilization of society during the destruction of Roman imperial order. With a declining birthrate and population, labor was the key factor of production. Successive administrations tried to stabilize the imperial economy by freezing the social structure into place: sons were to succeed their fathers in their trade, councilors were forbidden to resign, and coloni, the cultivators of land, were not to move from the land they were attached to. The workers of the land were on their way to becoming serfs. As the Germanic kingdoms succeeded Roman authority in the West in the 5th century, Roman landlords were often simply replaced by Gothic or Germanic ones, with little change to the underlying situation or displacement of populations. Thus the system of manorialism became ingrained into medieval societies.

The Manor System

Manors each consisted of three classes of land:

- Demesne, the part directly controlled by the lord and used for the benefit of his household and dependents;

- Dependent (serf or villein) holdings carrying the obligation that the peasant household supply the lord with specified labor services or a part of its output; and

- Free peasant land, without such obligation but otherwise subject to manorial jurisdiction and custom, and owing money rent fixed at the time of the lease.

Additional sources of income for the lord included charges for use of his mill, bakery, or wine-press, or for the right to hunt or to let pigs feed in his woodland, as well as court revenues and single payments on each change of tenant. On the other side of the account, manorial administration involved significant expenses, perhaps a reason why smaller manors tended to rely less on villein tenure.

Serfdom

Serfdom was the status of peasants under feudalism, specifically relating to manorialism. It was a condition of bondage that developed primarily during the Middle Ages in Europe.

Serfs who occupied a plot of land were required to work for the lord of the manor who owned that land, and in return were entitled to protection, justice, and the right to exploit certain fields within the manor to maintain their own subsistence. Serfs were often required to work on not only the lord's fields, but also his mines, forests, and roads. The manor formed the basic unit of feudal society, and the lord of a manor and his serfs were bound legally, economically, and socially. Serfs formed the lowest class of feudal society.

A serf digging the land, c. 1170 CE. "Digging," detail from the Hunterian Psalter, Glasgow University Library MS Hunter.

Many of the negative components of manorialism, and feudalism in general, revolve around the bondage of the serf, his lack of social mobility, and his low position on the social hierarchy. However, a serf had some freedoms within his constraints. Though the common wisdom is that a serf owned "only his belly"—even his clothes were the property, in law, of his lord—he might still accumulate personal property and wealth, and some serfs became wealthier than their free neighbors, although this happened rarely. A well-to-do serf might even be able to buy his freedom. A serf could grow what crops he saw fit on his lands, although a serf's taxes often had to be paid in wheat. The surplus crops he would sell at market.

The landlord could not dispossess his serfs without legal cause, was supposed to protect them from the depredations of robbers or other lords, and was expected to support them by charity in times of famine. Many such rights were enforceable by the serf in the manorial court.

Villeins

A villein (or *villain*) was the most common type of serf in the Middle Ages. Villeins had more rights and a higher status than the lowest serf, but existed under a number of legal restrictions that differentiated them from freemen. Villeins generally rented small homes with or without land. As part of the contract with the landlord, the lord of the manor, they were expected to spend some of their time working on the lord's fields. Contrary to popular belief, the requirement was not often greatly onerous, and was often only seasonal, as was the duty to help at harvest-time, for example. The rest of villeins' time was spent farming their own land for their own profit.

Like other types of serfs, villeins were required to provide other services, possibly in addition to paying rent of money or produce. Villeins were tied to the land and could not move away without their lord's consent and the acceptance of the lord to whose manor they proposed to migrate to. Villeins were generally able to hold their own property, unlike slaves.

Villeinage was not a purely uni-directional exploitative relationship. In the Middle Ages, land within a lord's manor provided sustenance and survival, and being a villein guaranteed access to land and kept crops secure from theft by marauding robbers. Landlords, even where legally entitled to do so, rarely evicted villeins, because of the value of their labour. Villeinage was preferable to being a vagabond, a slave, or an un-landed laborer.

In many medieval countries, a villein could gain freedom by escaping from a manor to a city or borough and living there for more than a year, but this action involved the loss of land rights and agricultural livelihood, a prohibitive price unless the landlord was especially tyrannical or conditions in the village were unusually difficult.

Plowing a French field (French ducal manor in March Les Très Riches Heures du Duc de Berry, c.1410). In the foreground, a farmer plowing a field with a plow pulled by two oxen; man the leader with a long pole. Winemakers prune the vine in a pen and till the soil with a hoe to aerate the soil. On the right, a man leans on a bag, presumably to draw seeds that he will then sow. Finally, in the background, a shepherd takes the dog that keeps his flock. In the background is the castle of Lusignan (Poitou), property of the Duke of Berry. Seen on the right of the picture, above the tower Poitiers, is a winged dragon representing the fairy Melusine.

Sources

Attributions

CC licensed content, Specific attribution

The Black Death

Learning Objective

- Evaluate the impact of the Black Death on European society in the Middle Ages

Key Points

- The Black Death resulted in the deaths of an estimated 75-200 million people—approximately 30% of Europe's population.

- It spread from central Asia on rat fleas living on the black rats that were regular passengers on merchant ships, and traveled towards Europe as people fled from one area to another.

- The Great Famine of 1315-1317 and subsequent malnutrition in the population likely caused weakened immunity and susceptibility to disease.

- Medieval doctors thought the plague was created by air corrupted by humid weather, decaying unburied bodies, and fumes produced by poor sanitation.

- The aftermath of the plague created a series of religious, social, and economic upheavals, which had profound effects on the course of European history.

- As people struggled to understand the causes of the Black Death, renewed religious fervor and fanaticism bloomed in its wake, leading to the widespread persecution of minorities.

- Flagellantism, the practice of self-inflicted pain, especially with a whip, became popular as a radical movement during the time of the Black Death, and was eventually deemed heretical by the church.

- The great population loss wrought by the plague brought favorable results to the surviving peasants in England and Western Europe, such as wage increases and more access to land, and was one of the factors in the ending of the feudal system.

Terms

bubonic plague

Disease circulating mainly in fleas on small rodents. Without treatment, the bacterial infection kills about two thirds of infected humans within four days.

the Silk Road

Series of trade and cultural routes that were central to cultural interaction through regions of the Asian continent, connecting the West and East from China to the Mediterranean Sea.

Flagellant

Practitioners of an extreme form of mortification of their own flesh by whipping it with various instruments.

In the Late Middle Ages (1340–1400) Europe experienced the most deadly disease outbreak in history when the Black Death, the infamous pandemic of bubonic plague, hit in 1347. The Black Death was one of the most devastating pandemics in human history, resulting in the deaths of an estimated 75–200 million people and peaking in Europe in the years 1348–1350.

Path of the Black Death to Europe

The Black Death is thought to have originated in the arid plains of Central Asia, where it then travelled along the Silk Road, reaching the Crimea by 1346. It was most likely carried by Oriental rat fleas living on the black rats that were regular passengers on merchant ships.

Mongol dominance of Eurasian trade routes enabled safe passage through more secured trade routes. Goods were not the only thing being traded; disease also was passed between cultures. From Central Asia the Black Death was carried east and west along the Silk Road by Mongol armies and traders making use of the opportunities of free passage within the Mongol Empire offered by the Pax Mongolica. The epidemic began in Europe with an attack that Mongols launched on the Italian merchants' last trading station in the region, Caffa in the Crimea. In the autumn of 1346, plague broke out among the besiegers and then penetrated into the town. When spring arrived, the Italian merchants fled on their ships, unknowingly carrying the Black Death. The plague initially spread to humans near the Black Sea and then outwards to the rest of Europe as a result of people fleeing from one area to another.

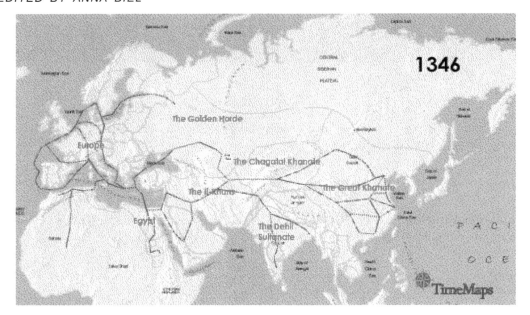

The spread of the Black Death. Animation showing the spread of The Black Death from Central Asia to East Asia and Europe from 1346 to 1351.

Spreading throughout the Mediterranean and Europe, the Black Death is estimated to have killed 30–60% of Europe's total population. While Europe was devastated by the disease, the rest of the world fared much better. In India, populations rose from 91 million in 1300, to 97 million in 1400, to 105 million in 1500. Sub-Saharan Africa also remained largely unaffected by the plagues.

Symptoms and Treatment

The most infamous symptom of bubonic plague is an infection of the lymph glands, which become swollen and painful and are known as *buboes*. *Buboes* associated with the bubonic plague are commonly found in the armpits, groin, and neck region. Gangrene of the fingers, toes, lips, and nose is another common symptom.

Medieval doctors thought the plague was created by air corrupted by humid weather, decaying unburied bodies, and fumes produced by poor sanitation. The recommended treatment for the plague was a good diet, rest, and relocating to a non-infected environment so the individual could get access to clean air. This did help, but not for the reasons the doctors of the time thought. In actuality, because they recommended moving away from unsanitary conditions, people were, in effect, getting away from the rodents that harbored the fleas carrying the infection.

Plague doctors advised walking around with flowers in or around the nose to "ward off the stench and perhaps the evil that afflicted them." Some doctors wore a beak-like mask filled with aromatic items. The masks were designed to protect them from putrid air, which was seen as the cause of infection.

*A plague doctor. Drawing illustrating the clothes and
"beak" of a plague doctor.*

Since people didn't have the knowledge to understand the plague, people believed it was a punishment from God. The thought the only way to be rid of the plague was to be forgiven by God. One method was to carve the symbol of the cross onto the front door of a house with the words "Lord have mercy on us" near it.

Impact of the Black Death on Society and Culture

The aftermath of the plague created a series of religious, social, and economic upheavals, which had profound effects on the course of European history. It took 150 years for Europe's population to recover, and the effects of the plague irrevocably changed the social structure, resulting in widespread persecution of minorities such as Jews, foreigners, beggars, and lepers. The uncertainty of daily survival has been seen as creating a general mood of morbidity, influencing people to "live for the moment."

Because 14th-century healers were at a loss to explain the cause of the plague, Europeans turned to astrological forces, earthquakes, and the poisoning of wells by Jews as possible reasons for the plague's emergence. No one in the 14th century considered rat control a way to ward off the plague, and people began to believe only God's anger could produce such horrific displays. Giovanni Boccaccio, an Italian writer and poet of the 14th century, questioned whether plague was sent by God for human's correction, or if it came through the influence of the heavenly bodies. Christians accused Jews of poisoning public water supplies in an effort to ruin European civilization. The spreading of this rumor led to complete destruction of entire Jewish towns, but it was caused simply by suspicion on the part of the Christians, who noticed that the Jews had lost fewer lives in the Plague due to their hygienic practices. In February 1349, 2,000 Jews were murdered in Strasbourg. In August of the same year, the Jewish communities of Mainz and Cologne were exterminated.

There was a significant impact on religion, as many believed the plague was God's punishment for sinful ways. Church lands and buildings were unaffected, but there were too few priests left to maintain the old schedule of services. Over half the parish priests, who gave the final sacraments to the dying, died themselves. The church moved to recruit replacements, but the process took time. New colleges were opened at established universities, and the training process sped up. The shortage of priests opened new opportunities for lay women to assume more extensive and important service roles in local parishes.

Flagellantism was a 13th and 14th centuries movement involving radicals in the Catholic Church. It began as a militant pilgrimage and was later condemned by the Catholic Church as heretical. The peak of the activity was during the Black Death. Flagellant groups spontaneously arose across Northern and Central Europe in 1349, except in England. The German and Low Countries movement, the Brothers of the Cross, is particularly well documented. They established their camps in fields near towns and held their rituals twice a day. The followers would fall to their knees and scourge themselves, gesturing with their free hands to indicate their sin and striking themselves rhythmically to songs, known as *Geisslerlieder*, until blood flowed. Sometimes the blood was soaked up by rags and treated as a holy relic. Some towns began to notice that sometimes Flagellants brought plague to towns where it had not yet surfaced. Therefore, later they were denied entry. The flagellants responded with increased physical penance.

The Black Death had a profound impact on art and literature. After 1350, European culture in general turned very morbid. The common mood was one of pessimism, and contemporary art turned dark with representations of death. *La Danse Macabre*, or the dance of death, was a contemporary allegory, expressed as art, drama, and printed work. Its theme was the universality of death, expressing the common wisdom of the time that no matter one's station in life, the dance of death united all. It consisted of the personified Death leading a row of dancing figures from all walks of life to the grave—typically with an emperor, king, pope, monk, youngster, and beautiful girl, all in skeleton-state. Such works of art were produced under the impact of the Black Death, reminding people of how fragile their lives and how vain the glories of earthly life were.

Danse Macabre. The Dance of Death (1493) by Michael Wolgemut, from the Liber chronicarum by Hartmann Schedel.

Economic Impact of the Plague

The great population loss wrought by the plague brought favorable results to the surviving peasants in England and Western Europe. There was increased social mobility, as depopulation further eroded the peasants' already weakened obligations to remain on their traditional holdings. Feudalism never recovered. Land was plentiful, wages high, and serfdom had all but disappeared. It was possible to move about and rise higher in life.

The Black Death encouraged innovation of labor-saving technologies, leading to higher productivity. There was a shift from grain farming to animal husbandry. Grain farming was very labor-intensive, but animal husbandry needed only a shepherd, a few dogs, and pastureland.

Since the plague left vast areas of farmland untended, they were made available for pasture and thus put more meat on the market; the consumption of meat and dairy products went up, as did the export of beef and butter from the Low Countries, Scandinavia, and northern Germany. However, the upper classes often attempted to stop these changes, initially in Western Europe, and more forcefully and successfully in Eastern Europe, by instituting sumptuary laws. These regulated what people (particularly of the peasant class) could wear so that nobles could ensure that peasants did not begin to dress and act as higher class members with their increased wealth. Another tactic was to fix prices and wages so that peasants could not demand more with increasing value. In England, the Statute of Labourers of 1351 was enforced, meaning no peasant could ask for more wages than they had in 1346. This was met with varying success depending on the amount of rebellion it inspired; such a law was one of the causes of the 1381 Peasants' Revolt in England.

Plague brought an eventual end of serfdom in Western Europe. The manorial system was already in trouble, but the Black Death assured its demise throughout much of Western and Central Europe by 1500. Severe depopulation and migration of people from village to cities caused an acute shortage of agricultural laborers. In England, more than 1300 villages were deserted between 1350 and 1500.

Black Death ("Hollaback Girl" by Gwen Stefani). It's hard to find a song to parody for such a gruesome subject. Our apologies to Gwen's fans, but it's for the cause of education!

- https://youtu.be/rZy6XilXDZQ

Attributions

CC licensed content, Specific attribution

- Boundless World History. **Authored by**: Boundless. **Located at**: https://courses.lumenlearning.com/boundless-worldhistory/. **License**: *CC BY-SA: Attribution-ShareAlike*

9. The Development of Russia

Rurik and the Foundation of Rus'

Learning Objective

- Understand the key aspects of Rurik's rise to power and the establishment of Kievan Rus'

Key Points

- Rurik and his followers likely originated in Scandinavia and were related to Norse Vikings.
- The Primary Chronicle is one of the few written documents available that tells us how Rurik came to power.
- Local leaders most likely invited Rurik to establish order in the Ladoga region around 862, beginning a powerful legacy of Varangian leaders.
- The capital of Kievan Rus' moved from Novgorod to Kiev after Rurik's successor, Oleg, captured this southern city.

Terms

Primary Chronicle

A text written in the 12th century that relates a detailed history of Rurik's rise to power.

> ### Varangians
>
> Norse Vikings who established trade routes throughout Eurasia and eventually established a powerful dynasty in Russia.
>
> ### Rurik Dynasty
>
> The founders of Kievan Rus' who stayed in power until 1598 and established the first incarnation of a unified Russia.

Rurik

Rurik (also spelled Riurik) was a Varangian chieftain who arrived in the Ladoga region in modern-day Russia in 862. He built the Holmgard settlement near Novgorod in the 860s and founded the first significant dynasty in Russian history called the Rurik Dynasty. Rurik and his heirs also established a significant geographical and political formation known as Kievan Rus', the first incarnation of modern Russia. The Rurik rulers continued to rule Russia into the 16th century and the mythology surrounding the man Rurik is often referred to as the official beginning of Russian history.

Primary Chronicle

The identity of the mythic leader Rurik remains obscure and unknown. His original birthplace, family history, and titles are shrouded in mystery with very few historical clues. Some 19th-century scholars attempted to identify him as Rorik of Dorestad (a Viking-Age trading outpost situated in the northern part of modern-day Germany). However, no concrete evidence exists to confirm this particular origin story.

A page from the Primary Chronicle or The Tale of Bygone Years. This rare written document was created in the 12th century and provides the most promising clues as to the arrival of Rurik in Ladoga.

The debate also continues as to how Rurik came to control the Novgorod region. However, some clues are available from the P*rimary Chronicle.* This document is also known as *The Tale of Bygone Yea*rs and was compiled in Kiev around 1113 by the monk Nestor. It relates the history of Kievan Rus' from 850 to 1110 with various updates and edits made throughout the 12th century by scholarly monks. It is difficult to untangle legend from fact, but this document provides the most promising clues regarding Rurik. *The Primary Chronicle* contends the Varangians were a Viking group, most likely from Sweden or northern Germany, who controlled trade routes across northern Russia and tied together various cultures across Eurasia.

A monument celebrating the millennial anniversary of the arrival of Rurik in Russia. This modern interpretation of Rurik illustrates his powerful place in Russian history and lore.

The various tribal groups, including Chuds, Eastern Slavs, Merias, Veses, and Krivichs, along the northern trade routes near Novgorod often cooperated with the Varangian Rus' leaders. But in the late 850s they rose up in rebellion, according to the P*rimary Chronicle*. However, soon after this rebellion, the local tribes near the Novgorod region began to experience internal disorder and conflict. These events prompted local tribal leaders to invite Rurik and his Varangian leaders back to the region in 862 to reinstate peace and order. This moment in history is known as the *Invitation of the Varangians* and is commonly regarded as the starting point of official Russian history.

Development of Kievan Rus'

According to legend, at the call of the local tribal leaders Rurik, along with his brothers Truvor and Sineus, founded the Holmgard settlement in Ladoga. This settlement is supposed to be at the site of modern-day Novgorod. However, newer archeological evidence suggests that Novgorod was not regularly settled until the 10th century, leading some to speculate that Holmgard refers to a smaller settlement just southeast of the city. The founding of Holmgard signaled a new era in Russian history and the three brothers became the famous founders of the first Rus' ruling dynasty.

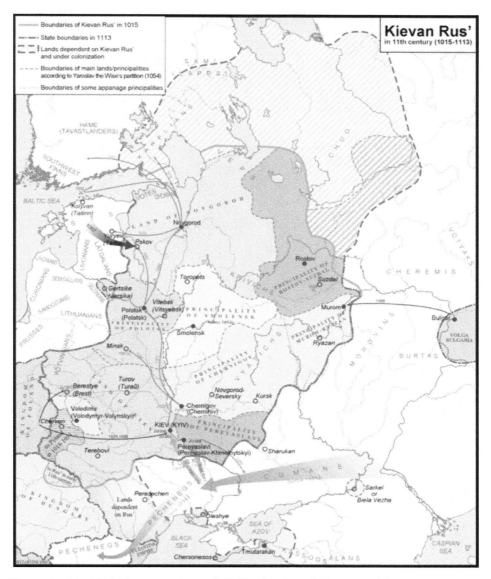

Kievan Rus' in 1015. The expansion and shifting borders of Kievan Rus' become apparent when looking at this map, which includes the two centers of power in Novgorod and Kiev.

Rurik died in 879 and his successor, Oleg, continued the Varangian Rus' expansion in 882 by taking the southern city of Kiev from the Khasars and establishing the medieval state of Kievan Rus'. The capital officially moved to Kiev at this point. With this shift in power, there were two distinct capitals in Kievan Rus', the northern seat of Novgorod and the southern center in Kiev. In Kievan Rus' tradition, the heir apparent would oversee the northern site of Novgorod while the ruling Rus' king stayed in Kiev. Over the next 100 years local tribes consolidated and unified under the Rurik Dynasty, although local fractures and cultural differences continued to play a significant role in the attempt to maintain order under Varangian rule.

Sources

Attributions

CC licensed content, Specific attribution

- Boundless World History. **Authored by**: Boundless. **Located at**: https://courses.lumenlearning.com/boundless-worldhistory/. **License**: *CC BY-SA: Attribution-ShareAlike*

Vladimir I and Christianization

Learning Objective

- Outline the shift from pagan culture to Orthodox Christianity under the rule of Vladimir I

Key Points

- Vladimir I became the ruler of Kievan Rus' after overthrowing his brother Yaropolk in 978.
- Vladimir I formed an alliance with Basil II of the Byzantine Empire and married his sister Anna in 988.
- After his marriage Vladimir I officially changed the state religion to Orthodox Christianity and destroyed pagan temples and icons.
- He built the first stone church in Kiev in 989, called the Church of the Tithes.

Terms

Constantinople

The capital of the Byzantine Empire.

Perun

The pagan thunder god that many locals, and possibly Vladimir I, worshipped before Christianization.

> *Basil II*
>
> The Byzantine emperor who encouraged Vladimir to convert to Christianity and offered a political marriage alliance with his sister, Anna.

Vladimir I

Vladimir I, also known as Vladimir the Great or Vladimir Sviatoslavich the Great, ruled Kievan Rus' from 980 to 1015 and is famous for Christianizing this territory during his reign. Before he gained the throne in 980, he had been the Prince of Novgorod while his father, Sviatoslav of the Rurik Dynasty, ruled over Kiev. During his rule as the Prince of Novgorod in the 970s, and by the time Vladimir claimed power after his father's death, he had consolidated power between modern-day Ukraine and the Baltic Sea. He also successfully bolstered his frontiers against incursions from Bulgarian, Baltic, and Eastern nomads during his reign.

Early Myths of Christianization

The original Rus' territory was comprised of hundreds of small towns and regions, each with its own beliefs and religious practices. Many of these practices were based on pagan and localized traditions. The first mention of any attempts to bring Christianity to Rus' appears around 860. The Byzantine Patriarch Photius penned a letter in the year 867 that described the Rus' region right after the Rus'-Byzantine War of 860. According to Photius, the people of the region appeared enthusiastic about the new religion and he claims to have sent a bishop to convert the population. However, this low-ranking official did not successfully convert the population of Rus' and it would take another twenty years before a significant change in religious practices would come about.

The stories regarding these first Byzantine missions to Rus' during the 860s vary greatly and there is no official record to substantiate the claims of the Byzantine patriarchs. Any local people in small villages who embraced Christian practices would have had to contend with fears of change from their neighbors.

Vladimir I and His Rise to Power

The major player in the Christianization of the Rus' world is traditionally considered Vladimir I. He was born in 958, the youngest of three sons, to the Rus' king Sviatoslav. He ascended to the position of Prince of Novgorod around 969 while his oldest brother, Yaropolk, became the designated heir to the throne in Kiev. Sviatoslav died in 972, leaving behind a fragile political scene among his three sons. Vladimir was forced to flee to Scandinavia in 976 after Yaropolk murdered their brother Oleg and violently took control of Rus'.

Vladimir I. A Christian representation of Vladimir I, who was the first Rus' leader to officially bring Christianity to the region.

Vladimir fled to his kinsman Haakon Sigurdsson, who ruled Norway at the time. Together they gathered an army with the intent to regain control of Rus' and establish Vladimir as the ruler. In 978, Vladimir returned to Kievan Rus' and successfully recaptured the territory. He also slew his brother Yaropolk in Kiev in the name of treason and, in turn, became the ruler of all of Kievan Rus'.

Constantinople and Conversion

Vladimir spent the next decade expanding his holdings, bolstering his military might, and establishing stronger borders against outside invasions. He also remained a practicing pagan during these first years of his rule. He continued to build shrines to pagan gods, traveled with multiple wives and concubines, and most likely continued to promote the worship of the thunder god Perun. However, the *Primary Chronicle* (one of the few written documents about this time) states that in 987 Vladimir decided to send envoys to investigate the various religions neighboring Kievan Rus'.

According to the limited documentation from the time, the envoys that came back from Constantinople reported that the festivities and the presence of God in the Christian Orthodox faith were more beautiful than anything they had ever seen, convincing Vladimir of his future religion.

Another version of events claims that Basil II of Byzantine needed a military and political ally in the face of a local uprising near Constantinople. In this version of the story, Vladimir demanded a royal marriage in return for his military help. He also announced he would Christianize Kievan Rus' if he was offered a desirable marriage tie. In either version of events, Vladimir vied for the hand of Anna, the sister of the ruling Byzantine emperor, Basil II. In order to marry her he was baptized in the Orthodox faith with the name Basil, a nod to his future brother-in-law.

17th-century Church of the Tithes. The original stone Church of the Tithes collapsed from fire and sacking in the 12th century. However, two later versions were erected and destroyed in the 17th and 19th centuries.

He returned to Kiev with his bride in 988 and proceeded to destroy all pagan temples and monuments. He also built the first stone church in Kiev named the Church of the Tithes starting in 989. These moves confirmed a deep political alliance between the Byzantine Empire and Rus' for years to come.

Baptism of Kiev

On his return in 988, Vladimir baptized his twelve sons and many boyars in official recognition of the new faith. He also sent out a message to all residents of Kiev, both rich and poor, to appear at the Dnieper River the following day. The next day the residents of Kiev who appeared were baptized in the river while Orthodox priests prayed. This event became known as the Baptism of Kiev.

Monument of Saint Vladimir in Kiev. This statue sits close to the site of the original Baptism of Kiev.

Pagan uprisings continued throughout Kievan Rus' for at least another century. Many local populations violently rejected the new religion and a particularly brutal uprising occurred in Novgorod in 1071. However, Vladimir became a symbol of the Russian Orthodox religion, and when he died in 1015 his body parts were distributed throughout the country to serve as holy relics.

Sources

Attributions

CC licensed content, Specific attribution

- Boundless World History. **Authored by**: Boundless. **Located at**: https://courses.lumenlearning.com/boundless-worldhistory/. **License**: *CC BY-SA: Attribution-ShareAlike*

Ivan the Terrible

Terms

oprichnina

A state policy enacted by Ivan IV that made him absolute monarch of much of the north and hailed in an era of boyar persecution. Ivan IV successfully grabbed large chunks of land from the nobility and created his own personal guard, the oprichniki, during this era.

Moscow Print Yard

The first publishing house in Russia, which was opened in 1553.

boyar

A member of the feudal ruling elite who was second only to the princes in Russian territories.

Ivan IV

Ivan IV Vasileyevich is widely known as Ivan the Terrible or Ivan the Fearsome. He was the Grand Prince of Moscow from 1533 to 1547 and reigned as the "Tsar of all the Russias" from 1547 until he died in 1584. His complex years in power precipitated military conquests, including Kazan and Astrakhan, that changed the shape and demographic character of Russia forever. He also reshaped the political formation of the Russian state, oversaw a cultural Renaissance in Russia, and shifted power to the head of state, the tsar, a title that had never before been given to a prince in the Rus' lands.

Rise to Power

Ivan IV was born in 1530 to Vasili III and Elena Glinskaya. He was three when he was named the Grand Prince of Moscow after his father's death. Some say his years as the child vice-regent of Moscow under manipulative boyar powers shaped his views for life. In 1547, at the age of sixteen, he was crowned "Tsar of All the Russias" and was the first person to be coronated with that title. This title claimed the heritage of Kievan Rus' while firmly establishing a new unified Russian state. He also married Anastasia Romanovna, which tied him to the powerful Romanov family.

18th-century portrait of Ivan IV. Images of Ivan IV often display a prominent brow and a frowning mouth.

Domestic Innovations and Changes

Despite Ivan IV's reputation as a paranoid and moody ruler, he also contributed to the cultural and political shifts that would shape Russia for centuries. Among these initial changes in relatively peaceful times he:

- Revised the law code, the Sudebnik of 1550, which initiated a standing army, known as the streltsy. This army would help him in future military conquests.

- Developed the Zemsky Sobor, a Russian parliament, along with the council of the nobles, known as the Chosen Council.

- Regulated the Church more effectively with the Council of the Hundred Chapters, which regulated Church traditions and the hierarchy.

- Established the Moscow Print Yard in 1553 and brought the first printing press to Russia.

- Oversaw the construction of St. Basil's Cathedral in Moscow.

St. Basil's Cathedral. This iconic structure was one cultural accomplishment created under Ivan IV's rule.

Oprichnina and Absolute Monarchy

The 1560s were difficult with Russia facing drought and famine, along with a number of Tatar invasions, and a sea-trading blockade from the Swedes and Poles. Ivan IV's wife, Anastasia, was also likely poisoned and died in 1560, leaving Ivan shaken and, some sources say, mentally unstable. Ivan IV threatened to abdicate and fled from Moscow in 1564. However, a group of boyars went to beg Ivan to return in order to keep the peace. Ivan agreed to return with the understanding he would be granted absolute power and then instituted what is known as the oprichnina.

1911 painting by Apollinary Vasnetsov. This painting represents people fleeing from the Oprichniki, the secret service and military oppressors of Ivan IV's reign.

This agreement changed the way the Russian state worked and began an era of oppression, executions, and state surveillance. It split the Russian lands into two distinct spheres, with the northern region around the former Novgorod Republic placed under the absolute power of Ivan IV. The boyar council oversaw the rest of the Russian lands. This new proclamation also started a wave of persecution and against the boyars. Ivan IV executed, exiled, or forcibly removed hundreds of boyars from power, solidifying his legacy as a paranoid and unstable ruler.

Military Conquests and Foreign Relations

Ivan IV established a powerful trade agreement with England and even asked for asylum, should he need it in his fights with the boyars, from Elizabeth I. However, Ivan IV's greatest legacy remains his conquests, which reshaped Russia and pushed back Tatar powers who had been dominating and invading the region for centuries.

His first conquest was the Kazan Khanate, which had been raiding the northeast region of Russia for decades. This territory sits in modern-day Tatarstan. A faction of Russian supporters were already rising up in the region but Ivan IV led his army of 150,000 to battle in June of 1552. After months of siege and blocking Kazan's water supply, the city fell in October. The conquest of the entire Kazan Khanate reshaped relations between the nomadic people and the Russian state. It also created a more diverse population under the fold of the Russian state and the Church.

Ivan IV also embarked on the Livonian War, which lasted 24 years. The war pitted Russia against the Swedish Empire, the Polish-Lithuanian Commonwealth, and Poland. The Polish leader, Stefan Batory, was an ally of the Ottoman Empire in the south, which was also in a tug-of-war with Russia over territory. These two powerful entities on each edge of Russian lands, and the prolonged wars, left the economy in Moscow strained and Russian resources scarce in the 1570s.

Ivan IV also oversaw two decisive territorial victories during his reign. The first was the defeat of the Crimean horde, which meant the southern lands were once again under Russian leadership. The second expansion of Russian territory was headed by Cossack leader Yermak Timofeyevich. He led expeditions into Siberian territories that had never been under Russian rule. Between 1577 and 1580 many new Siberian regions had reached agreements with Russian leaders, allowing Ivan IV to style himself "Tsar of Siberia" in his last years.

Ivan IV's throne. This decadent throne mirrors Ivan the Terrible's love of power and opulence.

Madness and Legacy

Ivan IV left behind a compelling and contradictory legacy. Even his nickname "terrible" is a source for confusion. In Russian the word *grozny* means "awesome," "powerful" or "thundering," rather than "terrible" or "mad." However, Ivan IV often behaved in ruthless and paranoid ways that favors the less flattering interpretation. He persecuted the long-ruling boyars and often accused people of attempting to murder him (which makes some sense when you look at his family's history). His often reckless foreign policies, such as the drawn out Livonian War, left the economy unstable and fertile lands a wreck. Legend also suggests he murdered his son Ivan Ivanovich, whom he had groomed for the throne, in 1581, leaving the throne to his childless son Feodor Ivanovich. However, his dedication to culture and innovation reshaped Russia and solidified its place in the East.

Sources

Attributions

CC licensed content, Specific attribution

- Boundless World History. **Authored by**: Boundless. **Located at**: https://courses.lumenlearning.com/boundless-worldhistory/. **License**: *CC BY-SA: Attribution-ShareAlike*

10. The Renaissance

Introduction to the Renaissance

Learning Objective

- Describe the influences of the Renaissance and historical perspectives by modern-day writers

Key Points

- There is a consensus that the Renaissance began in Florence, Italy, in the 14th century, most likely due to the political structure and the civil and social nature of the city. The Renaissance encompassed the flowering of Latin languages, a change in artistic style, and gradual, widespread educational reform.

- The development of conventions of diplomacy and an increased reliance on observation in science were also markers of the Renaissance.

- The Renaissance is probably best known for its artistic developments and for the development of "Humanism," a movement that emphasized the importance of creating citizens who were able to engage in the civil life of their community.

- Some historians debate the 19th-century glorification of the Renaissance and individual culture heroes as "Renaissance men."

- Some have called into question whether the Renaissance was a cultural "advance" from the Middle Ages, instead seeing it as a period of pessimism and nostalgia for classical antiquity.

Overview

The Renaissance was a period in Europe, from the 14th to the 17th century, regarded as the cultural bridge between the Middle Ages and modern history. It started as a cultural movement in Italy, specifically in Florence, in the late medieval period and later spread to the rest of Europe, marking the beginning of the early modern age.

The intellectual basis of the Renaissance was its own invented version of humanism, derived from the rediscovery of classical Greek philosophy, such as that of Protagoras, who said that "Man is the measure of all things." This new thinking became manifest in art, architecture, politics, science, and literature. Early examples were the development of perspective in oil painting and the recycled knowledge of how to make concrete. Though availability of paper and the invention of metal movable type sped the dissemination of ideas from the later 15th century, the changes of the Renaissance were not uniformly experienced across Europe.

Cultural, Political, and Intellectual Influences

As a cultural movement, the Renaissance encompassed the innovative flowering of Latin and vernacular literatures, beginning with the 14th-century resurgence of learning based on classical sources, which contemporaries credited to Petrarch; the development of linear perspective and other techniques of rendering a more natural reality in painting; and gradual but widespread educational reform.

In politics, the Renaissance contributed the development of the conventions of diplomacy, and in science an increased reliance on observation. Although the Renaissance saw revolutions in many intellectual pursuits, as well as social and political upheaval, it is perhaps best known for its artistic developments and the contributions of such polymaths as Leonardo da Vinci and Michelangelo, who inspired the term "Renaissance man."

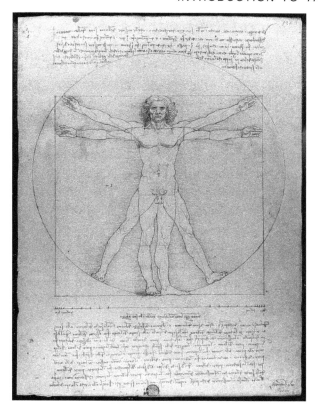

*Leonardo da Vinci's Vitruvian Man Leonardo da Vinci's
Vitruvian Man shows clearly the effect writers of Antiquity
had on Renaissance thinkers. Based on the specifications
in Vitruvius' De architectura (1st century BCE), Leonardo
tried to draw the perfectly proportioned man.*

Beginnings

Various theories have been proposed to account for the origins and characteristics of the Renaissance, focusing on a variety of factors, including the social and civic peculiarities of Florence at the time; its political structure; the patronage of its dominant family, the Medici; and the migration of Greek scholars and texts to Italy following the Fall of Constantinople at the hands of the Ottoman Turks.

Many argue that the ideas characterizing the Renaissance had their origin in late 13th-century Florence, in particular in the writings of Dante Alighieri (1265–1321) and Petrarch (1304–1374), as well as the paintings of Giotto di Bondone (1267–1337). Some writers date the Renaissance quite precisely; one proposed starting point is 1401, when the rival geniuses Lorenzo Ghiberti and Filippo Brunelleschi competed for the contract to build the bronze doors for the Baptistery of the Florence Cathedral (Ghiberti won). Others see more general competition between artists and polymaths such as Brunelleschi, Ghiberti, Donatello, and Masaccio for artistic commissions as sparking the creativity of the Renaissance. Yet it remains much debated why the Renaissance began in Italy, and why it began when it did. Accordingly, several theories have been put forward to explain its origins.

Historical Perspectives on the Renaissance

The Renaissance has a long and complex historiography, and in line with general skepticism of discrete periodizations there has been much debate among historians reacting to the 19th-century glorification of the Renaissance and individual culture heroes as "Renaissance men," questioning the usefulness of "Renaissance" as a term and as a historical delineation.

Some observers have called into question whether the Renaissance was a cultural advance from the Middle Ages, seeing it instead as a period of pessimism and nostalgia for classical antiquity, while social and economic historians, especially of the longue durée (long-term) have focused on the continuity between the two eras, which are linked, as Panofsky observed, "by a thousand ties."

The word "Renaissance," whose literal translation from French into English is "Rebirth," appears in English writing from the 1830s. The word occurs in Jules Michelet's 1855 work, *Histoire de France*. The word "Renaissance" has also been extended to other historical and cultural movements, such as the Carolingian Renaissance and the Renaissance of the 12th century.

The Renaissance: Was it a Thing? – Crash Course World History #22 European learning changed the world in the 15th and 16th centuries, but was it a cultural revolution, or an evolution? We'd argue that any cultural shift that occurs over a couple of hundred years isn't too overwhelming to the people who live through it. In retrospect though, the cultural bloom in Europe during this time was pretty impressive.
Attributions

CC licensed content, Specific attribution

Italian Trade Cities

Learning Objective
• Show how Northern Italy and the wealthy city-states within it became such huge European powers

Key Points
• While Northern Italy was not richer in resources than many other parts of Europe, the level of development, stimulated by trade, allowed it to prosper. In particular, Florence became one of the wealthiest cities in Northern Italy.
• Florence became the center of this financial industry, and the gold florin became the main currency of international trade.
• Luxury goods bought in the Levant, such as spices, dyes, and silks, were imported to Italy and then resold throughout Europe.
• The Italian trade routes that covered the Mediterranean and beyond were also major conduits of culture and knowledge.

Terms

- A rise in population—the population doubled in this period (the demographic explosion)

- An emergence of huge cities (Venice, Florence, and Milan had over 100,000 inhabitants by the 13th century, and many others, such as Genoa, Bologna, and Verona, had over 50,000)

- Rebuilding of the great cathedrals

- Substantial migration from country to city (in Italy the rate of urbanization reached 20%, making it the most urbanized society in the world at that time)

- An agrarian revolution

- Development of commerce

The decline of feudalism and the rise of cities influenced each other; for example, the demand for luxury goods led to an increase in trade, which led to greater numbers of tradesmen becoming wealthy, who, in turn, demanded more luxury goods.

Palazzo della Signoria e Uffizzi, Florence. Florence was one of the most important city-states in Italy.

The Transfer of Culture and Knowledge

The Italian trade routes that covered the Mediterranean and beyond were also major conduits of culture and knowledge. The recovery of lost Greek texts, which had been preserved by Arab scholars, following the Crusader conquest of the Byzantine heartlands revitalized medieval philosophy in the Renaissance of the 12th century. Additionally, Byzantine scholars migrated to Italy during and following the Ottoman conquest of the Byzantines between the 12th and 15th centuries, and were important in sparking the new linguistic studies of the Renaissance, in newly created academies in Florence and Venice. Humanist scholars searched monastic libraries for ancient manuscripts and recovered Tacitus and other Latin authors. The rediscovery of Vitruvius meant that the architectural principles of Antiquity could be observed once more, and Renaissance artists were encouraged, in the atmosphere of humanist optimism, to excel the achievements of the Ancients, like Apelles, of whom they read.

Venice and the Ottoman Empire: Crash Course World History #19 John Green discusses the strange and mutually beneficial relationship between a republic, the city-state of Venice, and an Empire, the Ottomans—and how studying history can help you to be a better boyfriend and/or girlfriend. Together, the Ottoman Empire and Venice grew wealthy by facilitating trade: The Venetians had ships and nautical expertise; the Ottomans had access to many of the most valuable goods in the world, especially pepper and grain. Working together across cultural and religious divides, they both become very rich, and the Ottomans became one of the most powerful political entities in the world.

Sources

Attributions

CC licensed content, Specific attribution

- Boundless World History. **Authored by**: Boundless. **Located at**: https://courses.lumenlearning.com/boundless-worldhistory/. **License**: *CC BY-SA: Attribution-ShareAlike*

Italian Politics

- Describe the intricacies of Italian politics during this time

Key Points

- Northern and Central Italy became prosperous in the late Middle Ages through the growth of international trade and the rise of the merchant class, who eventually gained almost complete control of the governments of the Italian city-states.

- A popular explanation for the Italian Renaissance is the thesis that the primary impetus of the early Renaissance was the long-running series of wars between Florence and Milan, whereby the leading figures of Florence rallied the people by presenting the war as one between the free republic and a despotic monarchy.

- The House of Medici was an Italian banking family, political dynasty, and later royal house in Florence who were the major sponsors of art and architecture in the early and High Renaissance.

Italy in the Late Middle Ages

By the Late Middle Ages (circa 1300 onward), Latium, the former heartland of the Roman Empire, and southern Italy were generally poorer than the north. Rome was a city of ancient ruins, and the Papal States were loosely administered and vulnerable to external interference such as that of France, and later Spain. The papacy was affronted when the Avignon Papacy was created in southern France as a consequence of pressure from King Philip the Fair of France. In the south, Sicily had for some time been under foreign domination, by the Arabs and then the Normans. Sicily had prospered for 150 years during the Emirate of Sicily, and later for two centuries during the Norman Kingdom and the Hohenstaufen Kingdom, but had declined by the late Middle Ages.

The Rise of the Merchant Class

In contrast, Northern and Central Italy had become far more prosperous, and it has been calculated that the region was among the richest in Europe. The new mercantile governing class, who gained their position through financial skill, adapted to their purposes the feudal aristocratic model that had dominated Europe in the Middle Ages. A feature of the High Middle Ages in Northern Italy was the rise of the urban communes, which had broken from the control of bishops and local counts. In much of the region, the landed nobility was poorer than the urban patriarchs in the high medieval money economy, whose inflationary rise left land-holding aristocrats impoverished. The increase in trade during the early Renaissance enhanced these characteristics.

This change also gave the merchants almost complete control of the governments of the Italian city-states, again enhancing trade. One of the most important effects of this political control was security. Those that grew extremely wealthy in a feudal state ran constant risk of running afoul of the monarchy and having their lands confiscated, as famously occurred to Jacques Coeur in France. The northern states also kept many medieval laws that severely hampered commerce, such as those against usury and prohibitions on trading with non-Christians. In the city-states of Italy, these laws were repealed or rewritten.

The 14th century saw a series of catastrophes that caused the European economy to go into recession, including the Hundred Years' War, the Black Death, and numerous famines. It was during this period of instability that the Renaissance authors such as Dante and Petrarch lived, and the first stirrings of Renaissance art were to be seen, notably in the realism of Giotto. Paradoxically, some of these disasters would help establish the Renaissance. The Black Death wiped out a third of Europe's population. The resulting labor shortage increased wages, and the reduced population was therefore much wealthier and better fed, and, significantly, had more surplus money to spend on luxury goods. As incidences of the plague began to decline in the early 15th century, Europe's devastated population once again began to grow. The new demand for products and services also helped create a growing class of bankers, merchants, and skilled artisans.

Warring Italians

Northern Italy and upper Central Italy were divided into a number of warring city-states, the most powerful being Milan, Florence, Pisa, Siena, Genoa, Ferrara, Mantua, Verona, and Venice. High medieval Northern Italy was further divided by the long-running battle for supremacy between the forces of the papacy and of the Holy Roman Empire; each city aligned itself with one faction or the other, yet was divided internally between the two warring parties, Guelfs and Ghibellines. Warfare between the states was common, but invasion from outside Italy was confined to intermittent sorties of Holy Roman emperors. Renaissance politics developed from this background. Since the 13th century, as armies became primarily composed of mercenaries, prosperous city-states could field considerable forces, despite their low populations. In the course of the 15th century, the most powerful city-states annexed their smaller neighbors. Florence took Pisa in 1406, Venice captured Padua and Verona, and the Duchy of Milan annexed a number of nearby areas, including Pavia and Parma.

A popular explanation for the Italian Renaissance is the thesis, first advanced by historian Hans Baron, that the primary impetus of the early Renaissance was the long-running series of wars between Florence and Milan. By the late 14th century, Milan had become a centralized monarchy under the control of the

Visconti family. Giangaleazzo Visconti, who ruled the city from 1378 to 1402, was renowned both for his cruelty and for his abilities, and set about building an empire in Northern Italy. He launched a long series of wars, with Milan steadily conquering neighboring states and defeating the various coalitions led by Florence that sought in vain to halt the advance. This culminated in the 1402 siege of Florence, when it looked as though the city was doomed to fall, before Giangaleazzo suddenly died and his empire collapsed.

Baron's thesis suggests that during these long wars, the leading figures of Florence rallied the people by presenting the war as one between the free republic and a despotic monarchy, between the ideals of the Greek and Roman Republics and those of the Roman Empire and medieval kingdoms. For Baron, the most important figure in crafting this ideology was Leonardo Bruni. This time of crisis in Florence was the period when the most influential figures of the early Renaissance were coming of age, such as Ghiberti, Donatello, Masolino, and Brunelleschi. Inculcated with this republican ideology, they later went on to advocate republican ideas that were to have an enormous impact on the Renaissance.

The Medici Family

The House of Medici was an Italian banking family, political dynasty, and later royal house that first began to gather prominence under Cosimo de' Medici in the Republic of Florence during the first half of the 15th century. The family originated in the Mugello region of the Tuscan countryside, gradually rising until they were able to fund the Medici Bank. The bank was the largest in Europe during the 15th century, which helped the Medici gain political power in Florence—though officially they remained citizens rather than monarchs. The biggest accomplishments of the Medici were in the sponsorship of art and architecture, mainly early and High Renaissance art and architecture. The Medici were responsible for the majority of Florentine art during their reign.

Their wealth and influence initially derived from the textile trade guided by the guild of the *Arte della Lana*. Like other signore families, they dominated their city's government, they were able to bring Florence under their family's power, and they created an environment where art and Humanism could flourish. They, along with other families of Italy, such as the Visconti and Sforza of Milan, the Este of Ferrara, and the Gonzaga of Mantua, fostered and inspired the birth of the Italian Renaissance. The Medici family was connected to most other elite families of the time through marriages of convenience, partnerships, or employment, so the family had a central position in the social network. Several families had systematic access to the rest of the elite families only through the Medici, perhaps similar to banking relationships.

The Medici Bank was one of the most prosperous and most respected institutions in Europe. There are some estimates that the Medici family were the wealthiest family in Europe for a time. From this base, they acquired political power initially in Florence and later in wider Italy and Europe. A notable contribution to the profession of accounting was the improvement of the general ledger system through the development of the double-entry bookkeeping system for tracking credits and debits. The Medici family were among the earliest businesses to use the system.

Cosimo di Giovanni de' Medici was the first of the Medici political dynasty, and had tremendous political power in Florence. Despite his influence, his power was not absolute; Florence's legislative councils at times resisted his proposals, something that would not have been tolerated by the Visconti of Milan, for instance. Throughout his life he was always *primus inter pares*, or first among equals. His power over Florence stemmed from his wealth, which he used to control votes. As Florence was proud of its "democracy,"

Medici pretended to have little political ambition, and did not often hold public office. Aeneas Sylvius, Bishop of Siena and later Pope Pius II, said of him, "Political questions are settled in [Cosimo's] house. The man he chooses holds office… He it is who decides peace and war… He is king in all but name."

Cosimo di Giovanni de' MediciPortrait of Cosimo de' Medici, the found of the House of Medici, by Jacopo Pontormo; the laurel branch (il Broncone) was a symbol used also by his heirs.

Attributions

CC licensed content, Specific attribution

- Boundless World History. **Authored by**: Boundless. **Located at**: https://courses.lumenlearning.com/boundless-worldhistory/. **License**: *CC BY-SA: Attribution-ShareAlike*

The Church During the Italian Renaissance

Learning Objective

- Analyze the church's role in Italy at the time of the Renaissance

Key Points

- The Renaissance began in times of religious turmoil, especially surrounding the papacy, which culminated in the Western Schism, in which three men simultaneously claimed to be the true pope.

- The new engagement with Greek Christian works during the Renaissance, and particularly the return to the original Greek of the New Testament promoted by Humanists Lorenzo Valla and Erasmus, helped pave the way for the Protestant Reformation.

- In addition to being the head of the church, the pope became one of Italy's most important secular rulers, and pontiffs such as Julius II often waged campaigns to protect and expand their temporal domains.

- The Counter-Reformation was a period of Catholic resurgence initiated in response to the Protestant Reformation.

The Church in the Late Middle Ages

The Renaissance began in times of religious turmoil. The late Middle Ages was a period of political intrigue surrounding the papacy, culminating in the Western Schism, in which three men simultaneously claimed to be the true pope. While the schism was resolved by the Council of Constance (1414), a resulting reform movement known as Conciliarism sought to limit the power of the pope. Although the papacy eventually emerged supreme in ecclesiastical matters by the Fifth Council of the Lateran (1511), it was dogged by continued accusations of corruption, most famously in the person of Pope Alexander VI, who was accused variously of simony, nepotism, and fathering four children.

Pope Alexander VIAlexander VI, a Borgia pope infamous for his corruption.

Churchmen such as Erasmus and Luther proposed reform to the church, often based on Humanist textual criticism of the New Testament. In October 1517 Luther published the *Ninety-five Theses*, challenging papal authority and criticizing its perceived corruption, particularly with regard to instances of sold indulgences. The *Ninety-five Theses* led to the Reformation, a break with the Roman Catholic Church that previously claimed hegemony in Western Europe. Humanism and the Renaissance therefore played a direct role in sparking the Reformation, as well as in many other contemporaneous religious debates and conflicts.

Pope Paul III came to the papal throne (1534–1549) after the sack of Rome in 1527, with uncertainties prevalent in the Catholic Church following the Protestant Reformation. Nicolaus Copernicus dedicated *De revolutionibus orbium coelestium* (On the Revolutions of the Celestial Spheres) to Paul III, who became the grandfather of Alessandro Farnese (cardinal), who had paintings by Titian, Michelangelo, and Raphael, as well as an important collection of drawings, and who commissioned the masterpiece of Giulio Clovio, arguably the last major illuminated manuscript, the Farnese Hours.

The Church and the Renaissance

The city of Rome, the papacy, and the Papal States were all affected by the Renaissance. On the one hand, it was a time of great artistic patronage and architectural magnificence, when the church pardoned and even sponsored such artists as Michelangelo, Brunelleschi, Bramante, Raphael, Fra Angelico, Donatello, and da Vinci. On the other hand, wealthy Italian families often secured episcopal offices, including the papacy, for their own members, some of whom were known for immorality.

In the revival of neo-Platonism and other ancient philosophies, Renaissance Humanists did not reject Christianity; quite to the contrary, many of the Renaissance's greatest works were devoted to it, and the church patronized many works of Renaissance art. The new ideals of Humanism, although more secular in some aspects, developed against a Christian backdrop, especially in the Northern Renaissance. In turn, the Renaissance had a profound effect on contemporary theology, particularly in the way people perceived the relationship between man and God.

Michelangelo's Pietà in St. Peter's Basilica, Vatican CityMichelangelo's Pietà exemplifies the character of Renaissance art, combining the classical aesthetic of Greek art with religious imagery, in this case Mother Mary holding the body of Jesus after the crucifixion.

In addition to being the head of the church, the pope became one of Italy's most important secular rulers, and pontiffs such as Julius II often waged campaigns to protect and expand their temporal domains. Furthermore, the popes, in a spirit of refined competition with other Italian lords, spent lavishly both on private luxuries and public works, repairing or building churches, bridges, and a magnificent system of aqueducts in Rome that still function today.

From 1505 to 1626, St. Peter's Basilica, perhaps the most recognized Christian church, was built on the site of the old Constantinian basilica in Rome. This was a time of increased contact with Greek culture, opening up new avenues of learning, especially in the fields of philosophy, poetry, classics, rhetoric, and political science, fostering a spirit of Humanism—all of which would influence the church.

Counter-Reformation

The Counter-Reformation, also called the Catholic Reformation or the Catholic Revival, was the period of Catholic resurgence initiated in response to the Protestant Reformation, beginning with the Council of Trent (1545–1563) and ending at the close of the Thirty Years' War (1648). The Counter-Reformation was a comprehensive effort composed of four major elements—ecclesiastical or structural reconfigurations, new religious orders (such as the Jesuits), spiritual movements, and political reform.

Such reforms included the foundation of seminaries for the proper training of priests in the spiritual life and the theological traditions of the church, the reform of religious life by returning orders to their spiritual foundations, and new spiritual movements focusing on the devotional life and a personal relationship with Christ, including the Spanish mystics and the French school of spirituality. It also involved political activities that included the Roman Inquisition. One primary emphasis of the Counter-Reformation was a mission to reach parts of the world that had been colonized as predominantly Catholic, and also try to reconvert areas, such as Sweden and England, that were at one time Catholic but had been Protestantized during the Reformation.

Attributions

CC licensed content, Specific attribution

- Boundless World History. **Authored by**: Boundless. **Located at**: https://courses.lumenlearning.com/boundless-worldhistory/. **License**: *CC BY-SA: Attribution-ShareAlike*

Petrarch

Learning Objective

- Explain Petrarch's contributions to the Renaissance

Key Points

- Petrarch is traditionally called the "Father of Humanism," both for his influential philosophical attitudes, found in his numerous personal letters, and his discovery and compilation of classical texts.

- Petrarch was born in the Tuscan city of Arezzo in 1304, and spent his early childhood near Florence, but his family moved to Avignon to follow Pope Clement V, who moved there in 1309 to begin the Avignon Papacy.

- He traveled widely in Europe and, during his travels, collected crumbling Latin manuscripts, whose discovery, especially Cicero's letters, helped spark the Renaissance.

- A highly introspective man, he shaped the nascent Humanist movement a great deal because many of the internal conflicts and musings expressed in his writings were seized upon by Renaissance Humanist philosophers and argued continually for the next 200 years.

Overview

Francesco Petrarca (July 20, 1304–July 19, 1374), commonly anglicized as Petrarch, was an Italian scholar and poet in Renaissance Italy, and one of the earliest Humanists. Petrarch's rediscovery of Cicero's letters is often credited for initiating the 14th-century Renaissance. Petrarch is often considered the founder of Humanism. Petrarch's sonnets were admired and imitated throughout Europe during the Renaissance and became a model for lyrical poetry. In the 16th century, Pietro Bembo created the model for the modern Italian language based on Petrarch's works.

Petrarch was born in the Tuscan city of Arezzo in 1304. Petrarch spent his early childhood in the village of Incisa, near Florence. He spent much of his early life at Avignon and nearby Carpentras, where his family moved to follow Pope Clement V, who moved there in 1309 to begin the Avignon Papacy. Petrarch studied law at the University of Montpellier (1316–1320) and the University of Bologna (1320–23); because his father was in the profession of law he insisted that Petrarch and his brother study law also. Petrarch, however, was primarily interested in writing and Latin literature, and considered these seven years wasted.

He traveled widely in Europe, served as an ambassador, and has been called "the first tourist" because he traveled just for pleasure. During his travels, he collected crumbling Latin manuscripts and was a prime mover in the recovery of knowledge from writers of Rome and Greece. He encouraged and advised Leontius Pilatus's translation of Homer from a manuscript purchased by Boccaccio, although he was severely critical of the result. In 1345 he personally discovered a collection of Cicero's letters not previously known to have existed, the collection *ad Atticum.*

Disdaining what he believed to be the ignorance of the centuries preceding the era in which he lived, Petrarch is credited or charged with creating the concept of a historical "Dark Ages."

*Francesco Petrarca Statue of Petrarch
on the Uffizi Palace, in Florence.*

Father Of Humanism

Petrarch is traditionally called the "Father of Humanism," and considered by many to more generally be the "Father of the Renaissance." This honorific is so given both for his influential philosophical attitudes, found in his numerous personal letters, and his discovery and compilation of classical texts.

In his work *Secretum meum* he points out that secular achievements did not necessarily preclude an authentic relationship with God. Petrarch argued instead that God had given humans their vast intellectual and creative potential to be used to their fullest. He inspired Humanist philosophy, which led to the intellectual flowering of the Renaissance. He believed in the immense moral and practical value of the study of ancient history and literature—that is, the study of human thought and action. Petrarch was a devout Catholic and did not see a conflict between realizing humanity's potential and having religious faith.

A highly introspective man, he shaped the nascent Humanist movement a great deal, because many of the internal conflicts and musings expressed in his writings were seized upon by Renaissance Humanist philosophers and argued continually for the next 200 years. For example, Petrarch struggled with the proper relation between the active and contemplative life, and tended to emphasize the importance of solitude and study. In a clear disagreement with Dante, in 1346 Petrarch argued in his *De vita solitaria* that Pope Celestine V's refusal of the papacy in 1294 was a virtuous example of solitary life. Later, the politician and thinker Leonardo Bruni argued for the active life, or "civic humanism." As a result, a number of political, military, and religious leaders during the Renaissance were inculcated with the notion that their pursuit of personal fulfillment should be grounded in classical example and philosophical contemplation.

Attributions

CC licensed content, Specific attribution

- Boundless World History. **Authored by**: Boundless. **Located at**: https://courses.lumenlearning.com/boundless-worldhistory/. **License**: *CC BY-SA: Attribution-ShareAlike*

Humanism

Learning Objective
• Assess how Humanism gave rise to the art of the Renasissance

Key Points
• Humanists reacted against the utilitarian approach to education, seeking to create a citizenry who were able to speak and write with eloquence and thus able to engage the civic life of their communities.
• The movement was largely founded on the ideals of Italian scholar and poet Francesco Petrarca, which were often centered around humanity's potential for achievement.
• While Humanism initially began as a predominantly literary movement, its influence quickly pervaded the general culture of the time, reintroducing classical Greek and Roman art forms and leading to the Renaissance.
• Donatello became renowned as the greatest sculptor of the Early Renaissance, known especially for his Humanist, and unusually erotic, statue of David.
• While medieval society viewed artists as servants and craftspeople, Renaissance artists were trained intellectuals, and their art reflected this newfound point of view.
• In humanist painting, the treatment of the elements of perspective and depiction of light became of particular concern.

Overview

Humanism, also known as Renaissance Humanism, was an intellectual movement embraced by scholars, writers, and civic leaders in 14th- and early-15th-century Italy. The movement developed in response to the medieval scholastic conventions in education at the time, which emphasized practical, pre-professional, and scientific studies engaged in solely for job preparation, and typically by men alone. Humanists reacted against this utilitarian approach, seeking to create a citizenry who were able to speak and write with eloquence and thus able to engage the civic life of their communities. This was to be accomplished through the study of the "*studia humanitatis,*" known today as the humanities: grammar, rhetoric, history, poetry, and moral philosophy. Humanism introduced a program to revive the cultural—and particularly the literary—legacy and moral philosophy of classical antiquity. The movement was largely founded on the ideals of Italian scholar and poet Francesco Petrarca, which were often centered around humanity's potential for achievement.

While Humanism initially began as a predominantly literary movement, its influence quickly pervaded the general culture of the time, re-introducing classical Greek and Roman art forms and contributing to the development of the Renaissance. Humanists considered the ancient world to be the pinnacle of human achievement, and thought its accomplishments should serve as the model for contemporary Europe. There were important centers of Humanism in Florence, Naples, Rome, Venice, Genoa, Mantua, Ferrara, and Urbino.

Humanism was an optimistic philosophy that saw man as a rational and sentient being, with the ability to decide and think for himself. It saw man as inherently good by nature, which was in tension with the Christian view of man as the original sinner needing redemption. It provoked fresh insight into the nature of reality, questioning beyond God and spirituality, and provided knowledge about history beyond Christian history.

Humanist Art

Renaissance Humanists saw no conflict between their study of the Ancients and Christianity. The lack of perceived conflict allowed Early Renaissance artists to combine classical forms, classical themes, and Christian theology freely. Early Renaissance sculpture is a great vehicle to explore the emerging Renaissance style. The leading artists of this medium were Donatello, Filippo Brunelleschi, and Lorenzo Ghiberti. Donatello became renowned as the greatest sculptor of the Early Renaissance, known especially for his classical, and unusually erotic, statue of David, which became one of the icons of the Florentine republic.

Donatello's David is regarded as an iconic Humanist work of art.

Humanism affected the artistic community and how artists were perceived. While medieval society viewed artists as servants and craftspeople, Renaissance artists were trained intellectuals, and their art reflected this newfound point of view. Patronage of the arts became an important activity, and commissions included secular subject matter as well as religious. Important patrons, such as Cosimo de' Medici, emerged and contributed largely to the expanding artistic production of the time.

In painting, the treatment of the elements of perspective and light became of particular concern. Paolo Uccello, for example, who is best known for "The Battle of San Romano," was obsessed by his interest in perspective, and would stay up all night in his study trying to grasp the exact vanishing point. He used perspective in order to create a feeling of depth in his paintings. In addition, the use of oil paint had its beginnings in the early part of the 16th century, and its use continued to be explored extensively throughout the High Renaissance.

"The Battle of San Romano" by Paolo Uccello Italian Humanist paintings were largely concerned with the depiction of perspective and light.

Origins

Some of the first Humanists were great collectors of antique manuscripts, including Petrarch, Giovanni Boccaccio, Coluccio Salutati, and Poggio Bracciolini. Of the three, Petrarch was dubbed the "Father of Humanism" because of his devotion to Greek and Roman scrolls. Many worked for the organized church and were in holy orders (like Petrarch), while others were lawyers and chancellors of Italian cities (such as Petrarch's disciple Salutati, the Chancellor of Florence) and thus had access to book-copying workshops.

In Italy, the Humanist educational program won rapid acceptance and, by the mid-15th century, many of the upper classes had received Humanist educations, possibly in addition to traditional scholastic ones. Some of the highest officials of the church were Humanists with the resources to amass important libraries. Such was Cardinal Basilios Bessarion, a convert to the Latin church from Greek Orthodoxy, who was considered for the papacy and was one of the most learned scholars of his time.

Following the Crusader sacking of Constantinople and the end of the Byzantine Empire in 1453, the migration of Byzantine Greek scholars and émigrés, who had greater familiarity with ancient languages and works, furthered the revival of Greek and Roman literature and science.

Attributions

CC licensed content, Specific attribution

Education and Humanism

- Define Humanism and its goals as a movement in education

Key Points

- The Humanists of the Renaissance created schools to teach their ideas and wrote books all about education.
- One of the most profound and important schools was established and created by Vittorino da Feltre in 1423 in Mantua to provide the children of the ruler of Mantua with a Humanist education.
- Humanists sought to create a citizenry able to speak and write with eloquence and clarity, thus capable of engaging in the civic life of their communities and persuading others to virtuous and prudent actions.
- Humanist schools combined Christianity and classical texts to produce a model of education for all of Europe.

Overview

During the Renaissance, Humanism played a major role in education. Humanists —proponents or practitioners of Humanism during the Renaissance—believed that human beings could be dramatically changed by education. The Humanists of the Renaissance created schools to teach their ideas and wrote books all about education. Humanists sought to create a citizenry able to speak and write with eloquence and clarity, thus capable of engaging in the civic life of their communities and persuading others to virtuous and prudent actions. This was to be accomplished through the study of the humanities: grammar, rhetoric, history, poetry, and moral philosophy.

The Humanists believed that it was important to transcend to the afterlife with a perfect mind and body, which could be attained with education. The purpose of Humanism was to create a universal man whose person combined intellectual and physical excellence and who was capable of functioning honorably in virtually any situation. This ideology was referred to as the *uomo universale,* an ancient Greco-Roman ideal. Education during the Renaissance was mainly composed of ancient literature and history, as it was thought that the classics provided moral instruction and an intensive understanding of human behavior.

The educational curriculum of Humanism spread throughout Europe during the 16th century and became the educational foundation for the schooling of European elites, the functionaries of political administration, the clergy of the various legally recognized churches, and the learned professionals of law and medicine.

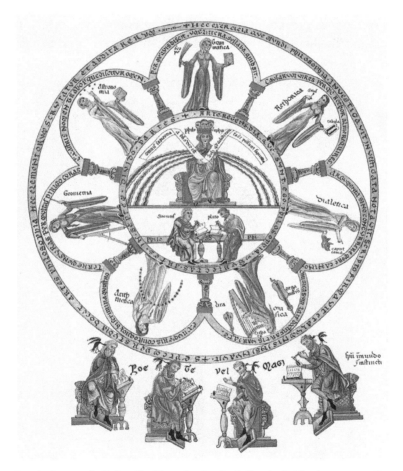

A painting symbolizing the liberal arts, depicting individuals representing the seven areas of liberal arts study, all circling around Plato and Socrates.

Humanist Schools

One of the most important Humanist schools was established by Vittorino da Feltre in 1423. The school was in Mantua, which is a small Italian state. The ruler of Mantua had always wanted to provide a Humanist education for his children, and the school was a way to help him.

Most of Feltre's ideas were based on those of previous classical authors, such as Cicero and Quintilian. The main foundation of the school was liberal studies. Liberal arts were viewed as the key to freedom, which allowed humans to achieve their goals and reach their full potential. Liberal studies included philosophy, history, rhetoric, letters, mathematics, poetry, music, and astronomy. Based on the Greek idea of a "sound mind," the school in Mantua offered physical education as well. This included archery, dance, hunting, and swimming.

The children that attended the schools were generally from upper-class families, though some seats were reserved for poor but talented students. Females were not usually allowed to attend, but were encouraged to know history, learn dance, and appreciate poetry. Some important females that were educated during the Renaissance were Isotta Nogarola, Cassandra Fedele of Venice, and Laura Cereta.

Overall, Humanist education was thought at the time to be an important factor in the preparation of life. Its main goal was to improve the lives of citizens and help their communities. Humanist schools combined Christianity and the classics to produce a model of education for all of Europe.

LAVRA CERETA BRIXIENSIS.
LITERIS ORNATISSIMA.

Laura Cereta (1469–1499) was a Renaissance Humanist and feminist. Most of her writing was in the form of letters to other intellectuals.

Attributions

CC licensed content, Specific attribution

- Boundless World History. **Authored by**: Boundless. **Located at**: https://courses.lumenlearning.com/boundless-worldhistory/.

The Italian Renaissance

Learning Objective

- Describe the art and periodization of the Italian Renaissance

Key Points

- The Florence school of painting became the dominant style during the Renaissance. Renaissance artworks depicted more secular subject matter than previous artistic movements.
- Michelangelo, da Vinci, and Rafael are among the best known painters of the High Renaissance.
- The High Renaissance was followed by the Mannerist movement, known for elongated figures.

The Renaissance began during the 14th century and remained the dominate style in Italy, and in much of Europe, until the 16th century. The term "renaissance" was developed during the 19th century in order to describe this period of time and its accompanying artistic style. However, people who were living during the Renaissance did see themselves as different from their Medieval predecessors. Through a variety of texts that survive, we know that people living during the Renaissance saw themselves as different largely because they were deliberately trying to imitate the Ancients in art and architecture.

Florence And The Renaissance

When you hear the term "Renaissance" and picture a style of art, you are probably picturing the Renaissance style that was developed in Florence, which became the dominate style of art during the Renaissance. During the Middle Ages and the Renaissance, Italy was divided into a number of different city states. Each city state had its own government, culture, economy, and artistic style. There were many different styles of art and architecture that were developed in Italy during the Renaissance. Siena, which was a political ally of France, for example, retained a Gothic element to its art for much of the Renaissance.

Certain conditions aided the development of the Renaissance style in Florence during this time period. In the 15th century, Florence became a major mercantile center. The production of cloth drove their economy and a merchant class emerged. Humanism, which had developed during the 14th century, remained an important intellectual movement that impacted art production as well.

Early Renaissance

During the Early Renaissance, artists began to reject the Byzantine style of religious painting and strove to create realism in their depiction of the human form and space. This aim toward realism began with Cimabue and Giotto, and reached its peak in the art of the "Perfect" artists, such as Andrea Mantegna and Paolo Uccello, who created works that employed one point perspective and played with perspective for their educated, art knowledgeable viewer.

During the Early Renaissance we also see important developments in subject matter, in addition to style. While religion was an important element in the daily life of people living during the Renaissance, and remained a driving factor behind artistic production, we also see a new avenue open to panting—mythological subject matter. Many scholars point to Botticelli's *Birth of Venus* as the very first panel painting of a mythological scene. While the tradition itself likely arose from cassone painting, which typically featured scenes from mythology and romantic texts, the development of mythological panel painting would open a world for artistic patronage, production, and themes.

Botticelli's Birth of Venus was among the most important works of the early Renaissance.

High Renaissance

The period known as the High Renaissance represents the culmination of the goals of the Early Renaissance, namely the realistic representation of figures in space rendered with credible motion and in an appropriately decorous style. The most well known artists from this phase are Leonardo da Vinci, Raphael, Titian, and Michelangelo. Their paintings and frescoes are among the most widely known works of art in the world. Da Vinci's *Last Supper*, Raphael's *The School of Athens* and Michelangelo's Sistine Chapel Ceiling paintings are the masterpieces of this period and embody the elements of the High Renaissance.

Raphael was one of the great artists of the High Renaissance.

Mannerism

High Renaissance painting evolved into Mannerism in Florence. Mannerist artists, who consciously rebelled against the principles of High Renaissance, tended to represent elongated figures in illogical spaces. Modern scholarship has recognized the capacity of Mannerist art to convey strong, often religious, emotion where the High Renaissance failed to do so. Some of the main artists of this period are Pontormo, Bronzino, Rosso Fiorentino, Parmigianino and Raphael's pupil, Giulio Romano.

Attributions

CC licensed content, Specific attribution

- Boundless World History. **Authored by**: Boundless. **Located at**: https://courses.lumenlearning.com/boundless-worldhistory/. **License**: *CC BY-SA: Attribution-ShareAlike*

Art and Patronage

Learning Objective

- Discuss the relationship between art, patronage, and politics during the Renaissance

Key Points

- Although the Renaissance was underway before the Medici family came to power in Florence, their patronage and political support of the arts helped catalyze the Renaissance into a fully fledged cultural movement.

- The Medici wealth and influence initially derived from the textile trade guided by the guild of the Arte della Lana; through financial superiority, the Medici dominated their city's government.

- Medici patronage was responsible for the majority of Florentine art during their reign, as artists generally only made their works when they received commissions in advance.

- Although none of the Medici themselves were scientists, the family is well known to have been the patrons of the famous Galileo Galilei, who tutored multiple generations of Medici children.

Overview

It has long been a matter of debate why the Renaissance began in Florence, and not elsewhere in Italy. Scholars have noted several features unique to Florentine cultural life that may have caused such a cultural movement. Many have emphasized the role played by the Medici, a banking family and later ducal ruling house, in patronizing and stimulating the arts. Lorenzo de' Medici (1449–1492) was the catalyst for an enormous amount of arts patronage, encouraging his countrymen to commission works from the leading artists of Florence, including Leonardo da Vinci, Sandro Botticelli, and Michelangelo Buonarroti. Works by Neri di Bicci, Botticelli, da Vinci, and Filippino Lippi had been commissioned additionally by the convent di San Donato agli Scopeti of the Augustinians order in Florence.

The Medici House Patronage

The House of Medici was an Italian banking family, political dynasty, and later royal house that first began to gather prominence under Cosimo de' Medici in the Republic of Florence during the first half of the 15th century. Their wealth and influence initially derived from the textile trade guided by the guild of the Arte della Lana. Like other signore families, they dominated their city's government, they were able to bring Florence under their family's power, and they created an environment where art and Humanism could flourish. They, along with other families of Italy, such as the Visconti and Sforza of Milan, the Este of Ferrara, and the Gonzaga of Mantua, fostered and inspired the birth of the Italian Renaissance.

The biggest accomplishments of the Medici were in the sponsorship of art and architecture, mainly early and High Renaissance art and architecture. The Medici were responsible for the majority of Florentine art during their reign. Their money was significant because during this period, artists generally only made their works when they received commissions in advance. Giovanni di Bicci de' Medici, the first patron of the arts in the family, aided Masaccio and commissioned Brunelleschi for the reconstruction of the Basilica of San Lorenzo, Florence, in 1419. Cosimo the Elder's notable artistic associates were Donatello and Fra Angelico. The most significant addition to the list over the years was Michelangelo Buonarroti (1475–1564), who produced work for a number of Medici, beginning with Lorenzo the Magnificent, who was said to be extremely fond of the young Michelangelo, inviting him to study the family collection of antique sculpture. Lorenzo also served as patron of Leonardo da Vinci (1452–1519) for seven years. Indeed, Lorenzo was an artist in his own right, and an author of poetry and song; his support of the arts and letters is seen as a high point in Medici patronage.

Medici family members placed allegorically in the entourage of a king from the Three Wise Men in the Tuscan countryside in a Benozzo Gozzoli fresco, c. 1459.

In architecture, the Medici are responsible for some notable features of Florence, including the Uffizi Gallery, the Boboli Gardens, the Belvedere, the Medici Chapel, and the Palazzo Medici. Later, in Rome, the Medici Popes continued in the family tradition by patronizing artists in Rome. Pope Leo X would chiefly commission works from Raphael. Pope Clement VII commissioned Michelangelo to paint the altar wall of the Sistine Chapel just before the pontiff's death in 1534. Eleanor of Toledo, princess of Spain and wife of Cosimo I the Great, purchased the Pitti Palace from Buonaccorso Pitti in 1550. Cosimo in turn patronized Vasari, who erected the Uffizi Gallery in 1560 and founded the Accademia delle Arti del Disegno ("Academy of the Arts of Drawing") in 1563. Marie de' Medici, widow of Henry IV of France and mother of Louis XIII, is the subject of a commissioned cycle of paintings known as the Marie de' Medici cycle, painted for the Luxembourg Palace by court painter Peter Paul Rubens in 1622–1623.

Although none of the Medici themselves were scientists, the family is well known to have been the patrons of the famous Galileo Galilei, who tutored multiple generations of Medici children and was an important figurehead for his patron's quest for power. Galileo's patronage was eventually abandoned by Ferdinando II when the Inquisition accused Galileo of heresy. However, the Medici family did afford the scientist a safe haven for many years. Galileo named the four largest moons of Jupiter after four Medici children he tutored, although the names Galileo used are not the names currently used.

Attributions

CC licensed content, Specific attribution

- Boundless World History. **Authored by**: Boundless. **Located at**: https://courses.lumenlearning.com/boundless-worldhistory/. **License**: *CC BY-SA: Attribution-ShareAlike*

Leonardo da Vinci

Learning Objective

- Describe the works of Leonardo da Vinci that demonstrate his most innovative techniques as an artist

Key Points

- Among the qualities that make da Vinci's work unique are the innovative techniques that he used in laying on the paint, his detailed knowledge of anatomy, his innovative use of the human form in figurative composition, and his use of sfumato.

- Among the most famous works created by da Vinci is the small portrait titled the *Mona Lisa*, known for the elusive smile on the woman's face, brought about by the fact that da Vinci subtly shadowed the corners of the mouth and eyes so that the exact nature of the smile cannot be determined.

- Despite his famous paintings, da Vinci was not a prolific painter; he was a prolific draftsman, keeping journals full of small sketches and detailed drawings recording all manner of things that interested him.

While Leonardo da Vinci is greatly admired as a scientist, an academic, and an inventor, he is most famous for his achievements as the painter of several Renaissance masterpieces. His paintings were groundbreaking for a variety of reasons and his works have been imitated by students and discussed at great length by connoisseurs and critics.

Among the qualities that make da Vinci's work unique are the innovative techniques that he used in laying on the paint, his detailed knowledge of anatomy, his use of the human form in figurative composition, and his use of sfumato. All of these qualities are present in his most celebrated works, the *Mona Lisa*, *The Last Supper*, and the *Virgin of the Rocks*.

The Virgin of the Rocks, Leonardo da Vinci, 1483–1486

The Last Supper

Da Vinci's most celebrated painting of the 1490s is *The Last Supper*, which was painted for the refectory of the Convent of Santa Maria della Grazie in Milan. The painting depicts the last meal shared by Jesus and the 12 Apostles where he announces that one of the them will betray him. When finished, the painting was acclaimed as a masterpiece of design. This work demonstrates something that da Vinci did very well: taking a very traditional subject matter, such as the Last Supper, and completely re-inventing it.

Prior to this moment in art history, every representation of the Last Supper followed the same visual tradition: Jesus and the Apostles seated at a table. Judas is placed on the opposite side of the table of everyone else and is effortlessly identified by the viewer. When da Vinci painted The Last Supper he placed Judas on the same side of the table as Christ and the Apostles, who are shown reacting to Jesus as he announces that one of them will betray him. They are depicted as alarmed, upset, and trying to determine who will commit the act. The viewer also has to determine which figure is Judas, who will betray Christ. By depicting the scene in this manner, da Vinci has infused psychology into the work.

Unfortunately, this masterpiece of the Renaissance began to deteriorate immediately after da Vinci finished painting, due largely to the painting technique that he had chosen. Instead of using the technique of fresco, da Vinci had used tempera over a ground that was mainly gesso in an attempt to bring the subtle effects of oil paint to fresco. His new technique was not successful, and resulted in a surface that was subject to mold and flaking.

Leonardo da Vinci's Last Supper, although much deteriorated, demonstrates the painter's mastery of the human form in figurative composition.

Mona Lisa

Among the works created by da Vinci in the 16th century is the small portrait known as the *Mona Lisa*, or *La Gioconda*, "the laughing one." In the present era it is arguably the most famous painting in the world. Its fame rests, in particular, on the elusive smile on the woman's face—its mysterious quality brought about perhaps by the fact that the artist has subtly shadowed the corners of the mouth and eyes so that the exact nature of the smile cannot be determined.

The shadowy quality for which the work is renowned came to be called sfumato, the application of subtle layers of translucent paint so that there is no visible transition between colors, tones, and often objects. Other characteristics found in this work are the unadorned dress, in which the eyes and hands have no competition from other details; the dramatic landscape background, in which the world seems to be in a state of flux; the subdued coloring; and the extremely smooth nature of the painterly technique, employing oils, but applied much like tempera and blended on the surface so that the brushstrokes are indistinguishable. And again, da Vinci is innovating upon a type of painting here. Portraits were very common in the Renaissance. However, portraits of women were always in profile, which was seen as proper and modest. Here, da Vinci present a portrait of a woman who not only faces the viewer but follows them with her eyes.

Mona LisaIn the Mona Lisa, da Vinci incorporates his sfumato technique to create a shadowy quality.

Virgin And Child With St. Anne

In the painting *Virgin and Child with St. Anne*, da Vinci's composition again picks up the theme of figures in a landscape. What makes this painting unusual is that there are two obliquely set figures superimposed. Mary is seated on the knee of her mother, St. Anne. She leans forward to restrain the Christ Child as he plays roughly with a lamb, the sign of his own impending sacrifice. This painting influenced many contemporaries, including Michelangelo, Raphael, and Andrea del Sarto. The trends in its composition were adopted in particular by the Venetian painters Tintoretto and Veronese.

Virgin and Child with St. Anne (c. 1510) by Leonardo da Vinci, Louvre Museum.

Attributions

CC licensed content, Specific attribution

- Boundless World History. **Authored by**: Boundless. **Located at**: https://courses.lumenlearning.com/boundless-worldhistory/. **License**: *CC BY-SA: Attribution-ShareAlike*

Michelangelo

Learning Objective

- Discuss Michelangelo's achievements in sculpture, painting, and architecture

Key Points

- Michelangelo created his colossal marble statue, the David, out of a single block of marble, which established his prominence as a sculptor of extraordinary technical skill and strength of symbolic imagination.
- In painting, Michelangelo is renowned for the ceiling and *The Last Judgement* of the Sistine Chapel, where he depicted a complex scheme representing Creation, the Downfall of Man, the Salvation of Man, and the Genealogy of Christ.
- Michelangelo's chief contribution to Saint Peter's Basilica was the use of a Greek Cross form and an external masonry of massive proportions, with every corner filled in by a stairwell or small vestry. The effect is a continuous wall-surface that appears fractured or folded at different angles.

Michelangelo was a 16th century Florentine artist renowned for his masterpieces in sculpture, painting, and architectural design. His most well known works are the *David*, the *Last Judgment*, and the *Basilica of Saint Peter's* in the Vatican.

Sculpture: *David*

In 1504, Michelangelo was commissioned to create a colossal marble statue portraying David as a symbol of Florentine freedom. The subsequent masterpiece, *David*, established the artist's prominence as a sculptor of extraordinary technical skill and strength of symbolic imagination. *David* was created out of a single marble block, and stands larger than life, as it was originally intended to adorn the Florence Cathedral.

The work differs from previous representations in that the Biblical hero is not depicted with the head of the slain Goliath, as he is in Donatello's and Verrocchio's statues; both had represented the hero standing victorious over the head of Goliath. No earlier Florentine artist had omitted the giant altogether. Instead of appearing victorious over a foe, David's face looks tense and ready for combat. The tendons in his neck stand out tautly, his brow is furrowed, and his eyes seem to focus intently on something in the distance. Veins bulge out of his lowered right hand, but his body is in a relaxed *contrapposto* pose, and he carries his sling casually thrown over his left shoulder. In the Renaissance, *contrapposto* poses were thought of as a distinctive feature of antique sculpture.

The David by Michelangelo, 1504 Michelangelo's David stands in contrapposto pose.

The sculpture was intended to be placed on the exterior of the Duomo, and has become one of the most recognized works of Renaissance sculpture.

Painting: *The Last Judgement*

In painting, Michelangelo is renowned for his work in the Sistine Chapel. He was originally commissioned to paint tromp-l'oeil coffers after the original ceiling developed a crack. Michelangelo lobbied for a different and more complex scheme, representing Creation, the Downfall of Man, the Promise of Salvation through the prophets, and the Genealogy of Christ. The work is part of a larger scheme of decoration within the chapel that represents much of the doctrine of the Catholic Church.

The composition eventually contained over 300 figures, and had at its center nine episodes from the Book of Genesis, divided into three groups: God's Creation of the Earth, God's Creation of Humankind, and their fall from God's grace, and lastly, the state of Humanity as represented by Noah and his family. Twelve men and women who prophesied the coming of the Jesus are painted on the pendentives supporting the ceiling. Among the most famous paintings on the ceiling are The Creation of Adam, Adam and Eve in the Garden of Eden, the Great Flood, the Prophet Isaiah and the Cumaean Sibyl. The ancestors of Christ are painted around the windows.

The fresco of *The Last Judgment* on the altar wall of the Sistine Chapel was commissioned by Pope Clement VII, and Michelangelo labored on the project from 1536–1541. The work is located on the altar wall of the Sistine Chapel, which is not a traditional placement for the subject. Typically, last judgement scenes were placed on the exit wall of churches as a way to remind the viewer of eternal punishments as they left worship. *The Last Judgment* is a depiction of the second coming of Christ and the apocalypse; where the souls of humanity rise and are assigned to their various fates, as judged by Christ, surrounded by the Saints. In contrast to the earlier figures Michelangelo painted on the ceiling, the figures in *The Last Judgement* are heavily muscled and are in much more artificial poses, demonstrating how this work is in the Mannerist style.

In this work Michelangelo has rejected the orderly depiction of the last judgement as established by Medieval tradition in favor of a swirling scene of chaos as each soul is judged. When the painting was revealed it was heavily criticized for its inclusion of classical imagery as well as for the amount of nude figures in somewhat suggestive poses. The ill reception that the work received may be tied to the Counter Reformation and the Council of Trent, which lead to a preference for more conservative religious art devoid of classical references. Although a number of figures were made more modest with the addition of drapery, the changes were not made until after the death of Michelangelo, demonstrating the respect and admiration that was afforded to him during his lifetime.

The Last Judgement The fresco of The Last Judgment on the altar wall of the Sistine Chapel was commissioned by Pope Clement VII. Michelangelo worked on the project from 1534–1541.

Architecture: St. Peter's Basilica

Finally, although other architects were involved, Michelangelo is given credit for designing St. Peter's Basilica. Michelangelo's chief contribution was the use of a symmetrical plan of a Greek Cross form and an external masonry of massive proportions, with every corner filled in by a stairwell or small vestry. The effect is of a continuous wall surface that is folded or fractured at different angles, lacking the right angles that usually define change of direction at the corners of a building. This exterior is surrounded by a giant order of Corinthian pilasters all set at slightly different angles to each other, in keeping with the ever-changing angles of the wall's surface. Above them the huge cornice ripples in a continuous band, giving the appearance of keeping the whole building in a state of compression.

St. Peter's Basillica Michelangelo designed the dome of St. Peter's Basilica on or before 1564, although it was unfinished when he died.

Attributions

CC licensed content, Specific attribution

- Boundless World History. **Authored by**: Boundless. **Located at**: https://courses.lumenlearning.com/boundless-worldhistory/. **License**: *CC BY-SA: Attribution-ShareAlike*

Christine de Pizan

Learning Objective
• Discuss the significance of Christine de Pizan's work

Key Points
• Christine de Pizan was an Italian-French late medieval author, primarily a court writer, who wrote commissioned works for aristocratic families and addressed literary debates of the era.   • Her work is characterized by a prominent and positive depiction of women who encouraged ethical and judicious conduct in courtly life.   • Much of the impetus for her writing came from her need to earn a living to support her mother, a niece, and her two surviving children after being widowed at the age of 25.   • Christine's participation in a literary debate about Jean de Meun's *Romance of the Rose* allowed her to move beyond the courtly circles, and ultimately to establish her status as a writer concerned with the position of women in society.

Overview

Christine de Pizan (1364–1430) was an Italian-French late medieval author. She served as a court writer for several dukes (Louis of Orleans, Philip the Bold of Burgundy, and John the Fearless of Burgundy) and the French royal court during the reign of Charles VI. She wrote both poetry and prose works such as biographies and books containing practical advice for women. She completed forty-one works during her thirty-year career from 1399 to 1429. She married in 1380 at the age of fifteen, and was widowed ten years later. Much of the impetus for her writing came from her need to earn a living to support her mother, a niece, and her two surviving children. She spent most of her childhood and all of her adult life in Paris and then the abbey at Poissy, and wrote entirely in her adopted language, Middle French.

In recent decades, Christine de Pizan's work has been returned to prominence by the efforts of scholars such as Charity Cannon Willard, Earl Jeffrey Richards, and Simone de Beauvoir. Certain scholars have argued that she should be seen as an early feminist who efficiently used language to convey that women could play an important role within society.

Christine de Pizan. A painting of Christine de Pizan, considered by some scholars to be a proto-feminist, lecturing four men.

Life

Christine de Pizan was born in 1364 in Venice, Italy. Following her birth, her father, Thomas de Pizan, accepted an appointment to the court of Charles V of France, as the king's astrologer, alchemist, and physician. In this atmosphere, Christine was able to pursue her intellectual interests. She successfully educated herself by immersing herself in languages, in the rediscovered classics and Humanism of the early Renaissance, and in Charles V's royal archive, which housed a vast number of manuscripts. But she did not assert her intellectual abilities, or establish her authority as a writer, until she was widowed at the age of 25.

In order to support herself and her family, Christine turned to writing. By 1393, she was writing love ballads, which caught the attention of wealthy patrons within the court. These patrons were intrigued by the novelty of a female writer and had her compose texts about their romantic exploits. Her output during this period was prolific. Between 1393 and 1412 she composed over 300 ballads, and many more shorter poems.

Christine's participation in a literary debate, in 1401–1402, allowed her to move beyond the courtly circles, and ultimately to establish her status as a writer concerned with the position of women in society. During these years, she involved herself in a renowned literary controversy, the "Querelle du Roman de la Rose." She helped to instigate this debate by beginning to question the literary merits of Jean de Meun's The *The Romance of the Rose*. Written in the 13th century, *The Romance of the Rose* satirizes the conventions of courtly love while critically depicting women as nothing more than seducers. Christine specifically objected to the use of vulgar terms in Jean de Meun's allegorical poem. She argued that these terms denigrated the proper and natural function of sexuality, and that such language was inappropriate for female characters such as Madam Reason. According to her, noble women did not use such language. Her critique primarily stemmed from her belief that Jean de Meun was purposely slandering women through the debated text.

The debate itself was extensive, and at its end the principal issue was no longer Jean de Meun's literary capabilities; it had shifted to the unjust slander of women within literary texts. This dispute helped to establish Christine's reputation as a female intellectual who could assert herself effectively and defend her claims in the male-dominated literary realm. She continued to counter abusive literary treatments of women.

Writing

Christine produced a large amount of vernacular works in both prose and verse. Her works include political treatises, mirrors for princes, epistles, and poetry.

Her early courtly poetry is marked by her knowledge of aristocratic custom and fashion of the day, particularly involving women and the practice of chivalry. Her early and later allegorical and didactic treatises reflect both autobiographical information about her life and views and also her own individualized and Humanist approach to the scholastic learned tradition of mythology, legend, and history she inherited from clerical scholars, and to the genres and courtly or scholastic subjects of contemporary French and Italian poets she admired. Supported and encouraged by important royal French and English patrons, she influenced 15th century English poetry.

By 1405, Christine had completed her most famous literary works, *The Book of the City of Ladies* and *The Treasure of the City of Ladies*. The first of these shows the importance of women's past contributions to society, and the second strives to teach women of all estates how to cultivate useful qualities. In *The Treasure of the City of Ladies*, she highlights the persuasive effect of women's speech and actions in everyday life. In this particular text, Christine argues that women must recognize and promote their ability to make peace between people. This ability will allow women to mediate between husband and subjects. She also argues that slanderous speech erodes one's honor and threatens the sisterly bond among women. Christine then argues that "skill in discourse should be a part of every woman's moral repertoire." She believed that a woman's influence is realized when her speech accords value to chastity, virtue, and restraint. She argued that rhetoric is a powerful tool that women could employ to settle differences and to assert themselves. Additionally, *The Treasure of the City of Ladies* provides glimpses into women's lives in 1400, from the great lady in the castle down to the merchant's wife, the servant, and the peasant. She offers advice to governesses, widows, and even prostitutes.

Picture from The Book of the City of Ladies. *The Treasure of the City of Ladies is a manual of education by medieval Italian-French author Christine de Pizan.*

Attributions

CC licensed content, Specific attribution

- Boundless World History. **Authored by**: Boundless. **Located at**: https://courses.lumenlearning.com/boundless-worldhistory/. **License**: *CC BY-SA: Attribution-ShareAlike*

Machiavelli

Learning Objective

- Analyze Machiavelli's impact during his own lifetime and in the modern day

Key Points

- Niccolò Machiavelli was an Italian Renaissance historian, politician, diplomat, philosopher, Humanist, and writer, often called the founder of modern political science.

- His writings were innovative because of his emphasis on practical and pragmatic strategies over philosophical ideals, exemplified by such phrases as "He who neglects what is done for what ought to be done, sooner effects his ruin than his preservation."

- His most famous text, *The Prince*, has been profoundly influential, from the time of his life up to the present day, both on politicians and philosophers.

- *The Prince* describes strategies to be an effective statesman and infamously includes justifications for treachery and violence to retain power.

Overview

Niccolò Machiavelli (May 3, 1469–June 21, 1527) was an Italian Renaissance historian, politician, diplomat, philosopher, Humanist, and writer. He has often been called the founder of modern political science. He was for many years a senior official in the Florentine Republic, with responsibilities in diplomatic and military affairs. He also wrote comedies, carnival songs, and poetry. His personal correspondence is renowned in the Italian language. He was secretary to the Second Chancery of the Republic of Florence from 1498 to 1512, when the Medici were out of power. He wrote his most renowned work, *The Prince* (*Il Principe*) in 1513.

"Machiavellianism" is a widely used negative term to characterize unscrupulous politicians of the sort Machiavelli described most famously in *The Prince*. Machiavelli described immoral behavior, such as dishonesty and killing innocents, as being normal and effective in politics. He even seemed to endorse it in some situations. The book itself gained notoriety when some readers claimed that the author was teaching evil, and providing "evil recommendations to tyrants to help them maintain their power." The term "Machiavellian" is often associated with political deceit, deviousness, and *realpolitik*. On the other hand, many commentators, such as Baruch Spinoza, Jean-Jacques Rousseau, and Denis Diderot, have argued that Machiavelli was actually a republican, even when writing *The Prince*, and his writings were an inspiration to Enlightenment proponents of modern democratic political philosophy.

Portrait of Niccolò Machiavelli. Machiavelli is a political philosopher infamous for his justification of violence in his treatise The Prince.

The Prince

Machiavelli's best-known book, *The Prince*, contains several maxims concerning politics. Instead of the more traditional target audience of a hereditary prince, it concentrates on the possibility of a "new prince." To retain power, the hereditary prince must carefully balance the interests of a variety of institutions to which the people are accustomed. By contrast, a new prince has the more difficult task in ruling: he must first stabilize his newfound power in order to build an enduring political structure. Machiavelli suggests that the social benefits of stability and security can be achieved in the face of moral corruption. Machiavelli believed that a leader had to understand public and private morality as two different things in order to rule well. As a result, a ruler must be concerned not only with reputation, but also must be positively willing to act immorally at the right times.

As a political theorist, Machiavelli emphasized the occasional need for the methodical exercise of brute force or deceit, including extermination of entire noble families to head off any chance of a challenge to the prince's authority. He asserted that violence may be necessary for the successful stabilization of power and introduction of new legal institutions. Further, he believed that force may be used to eliminate political rivals, to coerce resistant populations, and to purge the community of other men of strong enough character to rule, who will inevitably attempt to replace the ruler. Machiavelli has become infamous for such political advice, ensuring that he would be remembered in history through the adjective "Machiavellian."

The Prince is sometimes claimed to be one of the first works of modern philosophy, especially modern political philosophy, in which the effective truth is taken to be more important than any abstract ideal. It was also in direct conflict with the dominant Catholic and scholastic doctrines of the time concerning politics and ethics. In contrast to Plato and Aristotle, Machiavelli insisted that an imaginary ideal society is not a model by which a prince should orient himself.

Influence

Machiavelli's ideas had a profound impact on political leaders throughout the modern west, helped by the new technology of the printing press. During the first generations after Machiavelli, his main influence was in non-Republican governments. One historian noted that *The Prince* was spoken of highly by Thomas Cromwell in England and had influenced Henry VIII in his turn towards Protestantism and in his tactics, for example during the Pilgrimage of Grace. A copy was also possessed by the Catholic king and emperor Charles V. In France, after an initially mixed reaction, Machiavelli came to be associated with Catherine de' Medici and the St. Bartholomew's Day massacre. As one historian reports, in the 16th century, Catholic writers "associated Machiavelli with the Protestants, whereas Protestant authors saw him as Italian and Catholic." In fact, he was apparently influencing both Catholic and Protestant kings.

Modern materialist philosophy developed in the 16th, 17th, and 18th centuries, starting in the generations after Machiavelli. This philosophy tended to be republican, more in the original spirit of Machiavellianism, but as with the Catholic authors, Machiavelli's realism and encouragement of using innovation to try to control one's own fortune were more accepted than his emphasis upon war and politics. Not only were innovative economics and politics results, but also modern science, leading some commentators to say that the 18th century Enlightenment involved a "humanitarian" moderating of Machiavellianism.

Although Jean-Jacques Rousseau is associated with very different political ideas, it is important to view Machiavelli's work from different points of view rather than just the traditional notion. For example, Rousseau viewed Machiavelli's work as a satirical piece in which Machiavelli exposes the faults of one-man rule rather than exalting amorality.

Scholars have argued that Machiavelli was a major indirect and direct influence upon the political thinking of the Founding Fathers of the United States due to his overwhelming favoritism of republicanism and the republic type of government. Benjamin Franklin, James Madison, and Thomas Jefferson followed Machiavelli's republicanism when they opposed what they saw as the emerging aristocracy that they feared Alexander Hamilton was creating with the Federalist Party. Hamilton learned from Machiavelli about the importance of foreign policy for domestic policy, but may have broken from him regarding how rapacious a republic needed to be in order to survive.

Attributions

Erasmus

Key Points

- Erasmus was a Dutch Renaissance Humanist, Catholic priest, social critic, teacher, and theologian known as the "Prince of the Humanists" for his influential scholarship and writings.

- Erasmus lived against the backdrop of the growing European religious Reformation, but while he was critical of the abuses within the Catholic church and called for reform, he kept his distance from Luther and continued to recognize the authority of the pope.

- In *The Handbook of the Christian Soldier*, Erasmus outlines the views of the normal Christian life and critiques formalism—going through the motions of tradition without understanding their basis in the teachings of Christ.

- One of Erasmus's best-known works is *In Praise of Folly,* a satirical attack on superstitions and other traditions of European society in general and the western church in particular.

Overview

Erasmus of Rotterdam, or simply Erasmus, was a Dutch Renaissance Humanist, Catholic priest, social critic, teacher, and theologian.

Erasmus was a classical scholar and wrote in a pure Latin style. Among Humanists he enjoyed the name "Prince of the Humanists," and has been called "the crowning glory of the Christian Humanists." Using Humanist techniques for working on texts, he prepared important new Latin and Greek editions of the New Testament, which raised questions that would be influential in the Protestant Reformation and

Catholic Counter-Reformation. He also wrote *On Free Will, The Praise of Folly, Handbook of a Christian Knight, On Civility in Children, Copia: Foundations of the Abundant Style, Julius Exclusus,* and many other works.

Erasmus lived against the backdrop of the growing European religious Reformation, but while he was critical of the abuses within the Catholic church and called for reform, he kept his distance from Luther and Melanchthon and continued to recognize the authority of the pope, emphasizing a middle path with a deep respect for traditional faith, piety, and grace, rejecting Luther's emphasis on faith alone. Erasmus remained a member of the Roman Catholic church all his life, staying committed to reforming the church and its clerics' abuses from within. He also held to the Catholic doctrine of free will, which some Reformers rejected in favor of the doctrine of predestination. His middle road (*"Via Media"*) approach disappointed and even angered scholars in both camps.

Approach To Scholarship

Erasmus preferred to live the life of an independent scholar and made a conscious effort to avoid any actions or formal ties that might inhibit his freedom of intellect and literary expression. Throughout his life, he was offered many positions of honor and profit throughout the academic world but declined them all, preferring the uncertain but sufficient rewards of independent literary activity.

His residence at Leuven, where he lectured at the university, exposed Erasmus to much criticism from those ascetics, academics, and clerics hostile to the principles of literary and religious reform and the loose norms of the Renaissance adherents to which he was devoting his life.

He tried to free the methods of scholarship from the rigidity and formalism of medieval traditions, but he was not satisfied with this. His revolt against certain forms of Christian monasticism and scholasticism was not based on doubts about the truth of doctrine, nor from hostility to the organization of the church itself, nor from rejection of celibacy or monastic lifestyles. He saw himself as a preacher of righteousness by an appeal to reason, applied frankly and without fear of the magisterium. He always intended to remain faithful to Catholic doctrine, and therefore was convinced he could frankly criticize virtually everyone and everything. Aloof from entangling obligations, Erasmus was the center of the literary movement of his time, corresponding with more than 500 men in the worlds of politics and thought.

Writings

Erasmus wrote both on ecclesiastic subjects and those of general human interest. By the 1530s, the writings of Erasmus accounted for ten to twenty percent of all book sales in Europe.

His serious writings begin early, with the *Enchiridion militis Christiani*—the *Handbook of the Christian Soldier* (1503). In this short work, Erasmus outlines the views of the normal Christian life, which he was to spend the rest of his days elaborating. The chief evil of the day, he says, is formalism—going through the motions of tradition without understanding their basis in the teachings of Christ. Forms can teach the soul how to worship God, or they may hide or quench the spirit. In his examination of the dangers of formalism, Erasmus discusses monasticism, saint worship, war, the spirit of class, and the foibles of "society."

One of Erasmus's best-known works is *In Praise of Folly,* a satirical attack on superstitions and other traditions of European society in general and the western church in particular, written in 1509. *In Praise of Folly* starts off with Folly praising herself, after the manner of the Greek satirist Lucian, whose work Erasmus and Sir Thomas More had recently translated into Latin, a piece of virtuoso foolery; it then takes a darker tone in a series of orations, as Folly praises self-deception and madness and moves to a satirical examination of pious but superstitious abuses of Catholic doctrine and corrupt practices in parts of the Roman Catholic church—to which Erasmus was ever faithful—and the folly of pedants. Erasmus had recently returned disappointed from Rome, where he had turned down offers of advancement in the curia, and Folly increasingly takes on Erasmus's own chastising voice. The essay ends with a straightforward statement of Christian ideals.

Erasmus. Erasmus in 1523 as depicted by Hans Holbein the Younger. The Greek and Latin words on the book translate to "The Herculean Labours of Erasmus of Rotterdam."

Attributions

CC licensed content, Specific attribution

The Printing Revolution

Learning Objective

- Synthesize the impacts of the printing press on distribution of ideas and mass communication

Key Points

- In 1436 Johannes Gutenberg began work on the invention of a new printing press that allowed precise molding of new type blocks from a uniform template and allowed for the creation of high-quality printed books.

- Gutenberg is also credited with the introduction of an oil-based ink that was more durable than the previously used water-based inks. He tested colored inks in his Gutenberg Bible.

- The printing press was a factor in the establishment of a community of scientists who could easily communicate their discoveries through widely disseminated scholarly journals, helping to bring on the scientific revolution.

- Because the printing process ensured that the same information fell on the same pages, page numbering, tables of contents, and indices became common.

- The arrival of mechanical movable type printing introduced the era of mass communication, which permanently altered the structure of society. The relatively unrestricted circulation of information and revolutionary ideas transcended borders.

Overview

The printing press was invented in the Holy Roman Empire by the German Johannes Gutenberg around 1440, based on existing screw presses. Gutenberg, a goldsmith by profession, developed a complete printing system that perfected the printing process through all of its stages by adapting existing technologies to printing purposes, as well as making groundbreaking inventions of his own. His newly devised hand mould made possible for the first time the precise and rapid creation of metal movable type in large quantities, a key element in the profitability of the whole printing enterprise.

The printing press spread within several decades to over 200 cities in a dozen European countries. By 1500, printing presses in operation throughout Western Europe had already produced more than 20 million volumes. In the 16th century, with presses spreading further afield, their output rose tenfold to an estimated 150 to 200 million copies. The operation of a press became so synonymous with the enterprise of printing that it lent its name to an entire new branch of media, the press.

Johannes Gutenberg

Johannes Gutenberg's work on the printing press began in approximately 1436 when he partnered with Andreas Dritzehn—a man he had previously instructed in gem-cutting—and Andreas Heilmann, owner of a paper mill. However, it was not until a 1439 lawsuit against Gutenberg that an official record exists; witnesses' testimony discussed Gutenberg's types, an inventory of metals (including lead), and his type molds.

Early wooden printing press, depicted in 1568. Such presses could produce up to 240 impressions per hour. At the left in the foreground, a "puller" removes a printed sheet from the press. The "beater" to his right is inking the form. In the background, compositors are setting type.

Having previously worked as a professional goldsmith, Gutenberg made skillful use of the knowledge of metals he had learned as a craftsman. He was the first to make type from an alloy of lead, tin, and antimony, which was critical for yielding durable type that produced high-quality printed books and proved to be much better-suited for printing than all other known materials. To create these lead types, Gutenberg used what is considered one of his most ingenious inventions, a special matrix enabling the quick and precise molding of new type blocks from a uniform template. His type case is estimated to have contained around 290 separate letter boxes, most of which were required for special characters, ligatures, punctuation marks, etc.

Mass Communication

In Renaissance Europe, the arrival of mechanical movable type printing introduced the era of mass communication, which permanently altered the structure of society. The relatively unrestricted circulation of information and (revolutionary) ideas transcended borders, captured the masses in the Reformation, and threatened the power of political and religious authorities; the sharp increase in literacy broke the monopoly of the literate elite on education and learning and bolstered the emerging middle class. Across Europe, the increasing cultural self-awareness of its peoples led to the rise of proto-nationalism, accelerated by the flowering of the European vernacular languages to the detriment of Latin's status as *lingua franca*.

As early as 1480 there were printers active in 110 different places in Germany, Italy, France, Spain, the Netherlands, Belgium, Switzerland, England, Bohemia, and Poland. From that time on, it is assumed that "the printed book was in universal use in Europe." By 1500, the printing presses in operation throughout Western Europe had already produced more than 20 million copies. In the following century, their output rose tenfold to an estimated 150 to 200 million copies.

The vast printing capacities meant that individual authors could now become true bestsellers; at least 750,000 copies of Erasmus's works were sold during his lifetime alone (1469–1536). In the period from 1518 to 1524, the publication of books in Germany alone skyrocketed sevenfold; between 1518 and 1520, Luther's tracts were distributed in 300,000 printed copies.

Spread of printing in the 15th century from Mainz, Germany. Printing places showing the spread of incunabula printing in the 15th century. Two hundred seventy-one locations are known; the largest of them are designated by name. The term "incunabula" referred to printed materials and came to denote the printed books themselves in the late 17th century.

Effect On Scholarship And Literacy

The printing press was also a factor in the establishment of a community of scientists who could easily communicate their discoveries through widely disseminated scholarly journals, helping to bring on the scientific revolution. Because of the printing press, authorship became more meaningful and profitable. It was suddenly important who had said or written what, and what the precise formulation and time of composition was. This allowed the exact citing of references, producing the rule, "one author, one work (title), one piece of information." Before, the author was less important, since a copy of Aristotle made in Paris would not be exactly identical to one made in Bologna. For many works prior to the printing press, the name of the author has been entirely lost.

Because the printing process ensured that the same information fell on the same pages, page numbering, tables of contents, and indices became common, though they previously had not been unknown. The process of reading also changed, gradually moving over several centuries from oral readings to silent, private reading. The wider availability of printed materials also led to a drastic rise in the adult literacy rate throughout Europe.

Attributions

CC licensed content, Specific attribution

- Boundless World History. **Authored by**: Boundless. **Located at**: https://courses.lumenlearning.com/boundless-worldhistory/. **License**: *CC BY-SA: Attribution-ShareAlike*

11. The Protestant Reformation

Discontent with the Roman Catholic Church

The Protestant Reformation was the schism within Western Christianity initiated by Martin Luther, John Calvin, and other early Protestants.

Learning Objective
• Explain the main motivating factors behind the Protestant Reformation

Key Points
• The Reformation began as an attempt to reform the Roman Catholic Church, by priests who opposed what they perceived as false doctrines and ecclesiastic malpractice. • Following the breakdown of monastic institutions and scholasticism in late medieval Europe, accentuated by the Avignon Papacy, the Papal Schism, and the failure of the Conciliar movement, the 16th century saw a great cultural debate about religious reforms and later fundamental religious values. John Wycliffe and Jan Hus were early opponents of papal authority, and their work and views paved the way for the Reformation. • Martin Luther was a seminal figure of the Protestant Reformation who strongly disputed the sale of indulgences. His Ninety-Five Theses criticized many of the doctrines and practices of the Catholic Church. • The Roman Catholic Church responded with a Counter-Reformation spearheaded by the new order of the Society of Jesus (Jesuits), specifically organized to counter the Protestant movement.

Terms

The Western Schism

A split within the Catholic Church from 1378 to 1418, when several men simultaneously claimed to be the true pope.

Conciliar movement

A reform movement in the 14th-, 15th-, and 16th-century Catholic Church that held that supreme authority in the church resided with an Ecumenical council, apart from, or even against, the pope. The movement emerged in response to the Western Schism between rival popes in Rome and Avignon.

Indulgences

In Catholic theology, a remission of the punishment that would otherwise be inflicted for a previously forgiven sin as a natural consequence of having sinned. They are granted for specific good works and prayers in proportion to the devotion with which those good works are performed or prayers recited.

Council of Trent

Council of the Roman Catholic Church set up in Trento, Italy, in direct response to the Reformation.

Ecclesiastic

One who adheres to a church-based philosophy.

Doctrine

List of beliefs and teachings by the church.

The Protestant Reformation, often referred to simply as the Reformation, was a schism from the Roman Catholic Church initiated by Martin Luther and continued by other early Protestant reformers in Europe in the 16th century.

Although there had been significant earlier attempts to reform the Roman Catholic Church before Luther—such as those of Jan Hus, Geert Groote, Thomas A Kempis, Peter Waldo, and John Wycliffe—Martin Luther is widely acknowledged to have started the Reformation with his 1517 work The Ninety-Five Theses.

Luther began by criticizing the selling of indulgences, insisting that the pope had no authority over purgatory and that the Catholic doctrine of the merits of the saints had no foundation in the gospel. The Protestant position, however, would come to incorporate doctrinal changes such as *sola scriptura* (by the scripture alone) and *sola fide* (by faith alone). The core motivation behind these changes was theological, though many other factors played a part, including the rise of nationalism, the Western Schism that eroded faith in the papacy, the perceived corruption of the Roman Curia, the impact of humanism, and the new learning of the Renaissance that questioned much traditional thought.

Roots of Unrest

Following the breakdown of monastic institutions and scholasticism in late medieval Europe, accentuated by the Avignon Papacy, the Papal Schism, and the failure of the Conciliar movement, the 16th century saw a great cultural debate about religious reforms and later fundamental religious values. These issues initiated wars between princes, uprisings among peasants, and widespread concern over corruption in the Church, which sparked many reform movement within the church.

These reformist movements occurred in conjunction with economic, political, and demographic forces that contributed to a growing disaffection with the wealth and power of the elite clergy, sensitizing the population to the financial and moral corruption of the secular Renaissance church.

The major individualistic reform movements that revolted against medieval scholasticism and the institutions that underpinned it were humanism, devotionalism, and the observantine tradition. In Germany, "the modern way," or devotionalism, caught on in the universities, requiring a redefinition of God, who was no longer a rational governing principle but an arbitrary, unknowable will that could not be limited. God was now a ruler, and religion would be more fervent and emotional. Thus, the ensuing revival of Augustinian theology, stating that man cannot be saved by his own efforts but only by the grace of God, would erode the legitimacy of the rigid institutions of the church meant to provide a channel for man to do good works and get into heaven.

Humanism, however, was more of an educational reform movement with origins in the Renaissance's revival of classical learning and thought. A revolt against Aristotelian logic, it placed great emphasis on reforming individuals through eloquence as opposed to reason. The European Renaissance laid the foundation for the Northern humanistsin its reinforcement of the traditional use of Latin as the great unifying language of European culture. Since the breakdown of the philosophical foundations of scholasticism, the new nominalism did not bode well for an institutional church legitimized as an intermediary between man and God. New thinking favored the notion that no religious doctrine can be supported by philosophical arguments, eroding the old alliance between reason and faith of the medieval period laid out by Thomas Aquinas.

The great rise of the burghers (merchant class) and their desire to run their new businesses free of institutional barriers or outmoded cultural practices contributed to the appeal of humanist individualism. To many, papal institutions were rigid, especially regarding their views on just price and usury. In the north, burghers and monarchs were united in their frustration for not paying any taxes to the nation, but collecting taxes from subjects and sending the revenues disproportionately to the pope in Italy.

Early Attempts at Reform

The first of a series of disruptive and new perspectives came from John Wycliffe at Oxford University, one of the earliest opponents of papal authority influencing secular power and an early advocate for translation of the Bible into the common language. Jan Hus at the University of Prague was a follower of Wycliffe and similarly objected to some of the practices of the Roman Catholic Church. Hus wanted liturgy in the language of the people (i.e. Czech), married priests, and to eliminate indulgences and the idea of purgatory.

Hus spoke out against indulgences in 1412 when he delivered an address entitled *Quaestio magistri Johannis Hus de indulgentiis*. It was taken literally from the last chapter of Wycliffe's book, *De ecclesia*, and his treatise, *De absolutione a pena et culpa*. Hus asserted that no pope or bishop had the right to take up the sword in the name of the Church; he should pray for his enemies and bless those that curse him; man obtains forgiveness of sins by true repentance, not money. The doctors of the theological faculty replied, but without success. A few days afterward, some of Hus's followers burnt the papal bulls. Hus, they said, should be obeyed rather than the Church, which they considered a fraudulent mob of adulterers and Simonists.

In response, three men from the lower classes who openly called the indulgences a fraud were beheaded. They were later considered the first martyrs of the Hussite Church. In the meantime, the faculty had condemned the forty-five articles and added several other theses, deemed heretical, that had originated with Hus. The king forbade the teaching of these articles, but neither Hus nor the university complied with the ruling, requesting that the articles should first be proven to be un-scriptural. The tumults at Prague had stirred up a sensation; papal legates and Archbishop Albik tried to persuade Hus to give up his opposition to the papal bulls, and the king made an unsuccessful attempt to reconcile the two parties.

Hus was later condemned and burned at the stake despite promise of safe-conduct when he voiced his views to church leaders at the Council of Constance (1414–1418). Wycliffe, who died in 1384, was also declared a heretic by the Council of Constance, and his corpse was exhumed and burned.

Jan Hus burned at the stake

Execution of Jan Hus at the Council of Constance in 1415. His death led to a radicalization of the Bohemian Reformation and to the Hussite Wars in the Crown of Bohemia.

The Creation of New Protestant Churches

The Reformation led to the creation of new national Protestant churches. The largest of the new church's groupings were the Lutherans (mostly in Germany, the Baltics, and Scandinavia) and the Reformed churches (mostly in Germany, France, Switzerland, the Netherlands, and Scotland).

Response from the Catholic Church to the Reformation

The Roman Catholic Church responded with a Counter-Reformation initiated by the Council of Trent and spearheaded by the new order of the Society of Jesus (Jesuits), specifically organized to counter the Protestant movement. In general, Northern Europe, with the exception of most of Ireland, turned Protestant. Southern Europe remained Roman Catholic, while Central Europe was a site of fierce conflict escalating to full-scale war.

Council of Trent by Pasquale Cati

Painting representing the artist's depiction of The Council of Trent. It met for twenty-five sessions between December 13, 1545, and December 4, 1563, in Trento (then the capital of the Prince-Bishopric of Trent in the Holy Roman Empire), apart from the ninth to eleventh sessions held in Bologna during 1547.

Attributions

CC licensed content, Specific attribution

- Boundless World History. **Authored by**: Boundless. **Located at**: https://courses.lumenlearning.com/boundless-worldhistory/. **License**: *CC BY-SA: Attribution-ShareAlike*

Luther and Protestantism

Martin Luther was a seminal figure in the Protestant Reformation; he strongly disputed the claim that freedom from God's punishment for sin could be purchased with money, famously argued in his *Ninety-five Theses* of 1517.

Learning Objectives

- Describe Luther's criticisms of the Catholic Church

Key Points

- Martin Luther was a German professor of theology, composer, priest, monk and seminal figure in the Protestant Reformation.
- Luther strongly disputed the claim that freedom from God's punishment for sin could be purchased with money, called indulgences, which he argued in his *Ninety-five Theses* of 1517.
- When confronted by the church for his critiques, he refused to renounce his writings and was excommunicated by the pope and deemed an outlaw by the emperor.
- Luther's translation of the Bible into the vernacular made it more accessible to the laity, an event that had a tremendous impact on both the church and German culture.

Terms

Ninety-five Theses

A list of propositions for an academic disputation written by Martin Luther in 1517. They advanced Luther's positions against what he saw as abusive practices by preachers selling plenary indulgences, which were certificates that would reduce the temporal punishment for sins committed by the purchaser or their loved ones in purgatory.

Excommunication

An institutional act of religious censure used to deprive, suspend, or limit membership in a religious community or to restrict certain rights within it.

Indulgences

A way to reduce the amount of punishment one has to undergo for sins, usually through the saying of prayers or good works, which during the middle ages included paying for church buildings or other projects.

Overview

Martin Luther (November 10, 1483–February 18, 1546) was a German professor of theology, composer, priest, monk and seminal figure in the Protestant Reformation. Luther came to reject several teachings and practices of the Roman Catholic Church. He strongly disputed the claim that freedom from God's punishment for sin could be purchased with money, proposing an academic discussion of the practice and efficacy of indulgences in his *Ninety-five Theses* of 1517. His refusal to renounce all of his writings at the demand of Pope Leo X in 1520 and the Holy Roman Emperor Charles V at the Diet of Worms in 1521 resulted in his excommunication by the pope and condemnation as an outlaw by the emperor.

Luther taught that salvation and, subsequently, eternal life are not earned by good deeds but are received only as the free gift of God's grace through the believer's faith in Jesus Christ as redeemer from sin. His theology challenged the authority and office of the pope by teaching that the Bible is the only source of divinely revealed knowledge from God, and opposed priestly intervention for the forgiveness of sins by considering all baptized Christians to be a holy priesthood. Those who identify with these, and all of Luther's wider teachings, are called Lutherans, though Luther insisted on Christian or Evangelical as the only acceptable names for individuals who professed Christ.

His translation of the Bible into the vernacular (instead of Latin) made it more accessible to the laity, an event that had a tremendous impact on both the church and German culture. It fostered the development of a standard version of the German language, added several principles to the art of translation, and influenced the writing of an English translation, the Tyndale Bible. His hymns influenced the development of singing in Protestant churches. His marriage to Katharina von Bora, a former nun, set a model for the practice of clerical marriage, allowing Protestant clergy to marry.

In two of his later works, Luther expressed antagonistic views toward Jews, writing that Jewish homes and synagogues should be destroyed, their money confiscated, and their liberty curtailed. Condemned by virtually every Lutheran denomination, these statements and their influence on antisemitism have contributed to his controversial status.

Portrait of Martin Luther

Martin Luther (1528) by Lucas Cranach the Elder.

Portrait of Martin Luther's face.

Personal Life

Martin Luther was born to Hans Luther and his wife Margarethe on November 10, 1483, in Eisleben, Saxony, then part of the Holy Roman Empire. Hans Luther was ambitious for himself and his family, and he was determined to see Martin, his eldest son, become a lawyer.

In 1501, at the age of nineteen, Martin entered the University of Erfurt. In accordance with his father's wishes, he enrolled in law school at the same university that year, but dropped out almost immediately, believing that law represented uncertainty. Luther sought assurances about life and was drawn to theology and philosophy, expressing particular interest in Aristotle, William of Ockham, and Gabriel Biel.

He was deeply influenced by two tutors, Bartholomaeus Arnoldi von Usingen and Jodocus Trutfetter, who taught him to be suspicious of even the greatest thinkers and to test everything himself by experience. Philosophy proved to be unsatisfying, offering assurance about the use of reason but no assurance about loving God, which to Luther was more important. Reason could not lead men to God, he felt, and he thereafter developed a love-hate relationship with Aristotle over the latter's emphasis on reason. For Luther, reason could be used to question men and institutions, but not God. Human beings could learn about God only through divine revelation, he believed, and scripture therefore became increasingly important to him.

Luther dedicated himself to the Augustinian order, devoting himself to fasting, long hours in prayer, pilgrimage, and frequent confession. In 1507, he was ordained to the priesthood, and in 1508, von Staupitz, first dean of the newly founded University of Wittenberg, sent for Luther to teach theology. He was made provincial vicar of Saxony and Thuringia by his religious order in 1515. This meant he was to visit and oversee eleven monasteries in his province.

Start of the Reformation

In 1516, Johann Tetzel, a Dominican friar and papal commissioner for indulgences, was sent to Germany by the Roman Catholic Church to sell indulgences to raise money to rebuild St. Peter's Basilica in Rome. Roman Catholic theology stated that faith alone, whether fiduciary or dogmatic, cannot justify man; justification rather depends only on such faith as is active in charity and good works. The benefits of good works could be obtained by donating money to the church.

On October 31, 1517, Luther wrote to his bishop, Albert of Mainz, protesting the sale of indulgences. He enclosed in his letter a copy of his "Disputation of Martin Luther on the Power and Efficacy of Indulgences," which came to be known as the *Ninety-five Theses*. Historian Hans Hillerbrand writes that Luther had no intention of confronting the church, but saw his disputation as a scholarly objection to church practices, and the tone of the writing is accordingly "searching, rather than doctrinaire." Hillerbrand writes that there is nevertheless an undercurrent of challenge in several of the theses, particularly in Thesis 86, which asks, "Why does the pope, whose wealth today is greater than the wealth of the richest Crassus, build the basilica of St. Peter with the money of poor believers rather than with his own money?"

The first thesis has become famous: "When our Lord and Master Jesus Christ said, 'Repent,' he willed the entire life of believers to be one of repentance." In the first few theses Luther develops the idea of repentance as the Christian's inner struggle with sin rather than the external system of sacramental confession.

In theses 41–47 Luther begins to criticize indulgences on the basis that they discourage works of mercy by those who purchase them. Here he begins to use the phrase, "Christians are to be taught…" to state how he thinks people should be instructed on the value of indulgences. They should be taught that giving to the poor is incomparably more important than buying indulgences, that buying an indulgence rather than giving to the poor invites God's wrath, and that doing good works makes a person better while buying indulgences does not.

Luther objected to a saying attributed to Johann Tetzel that "As soon as the coin in the coffer rings, the soul from purgatory springs." He insisted that, since forgiveness was God's alone to grant, those who claimed that indulgences absolved buyers from all punishments and granted them salvation were in error. Luther closes the *Theses* by exhorting Christians to imitate Christ even if it brings pain and suffering, because enduring punishment and entering heaven is preferable to false security.

It was not until January 1518 that friends of Luther translated the *Ninety-five Theses* from Latin into German and printed and widely copied it, making the controversy one of the first to be aided by the printing press. Within two weeks, copies of the theses had spread throughout Germany; within two months, they had spread throughout Europe.

Ninety-five Theses

1517 Nuremberg printing of the *Ninety-five Theses* as a placard, now in the Berlin State Library.

A photo of a 1517 manuscript of the Luther's Ninety-five Thesis.

Excommunication and Later Life

On June 15, 1520, the pope warned Luther, with the papal bull *Exsurge Domine,* that he risked excommunication unless he recanted forty-one sentences drawn from his writings, including the *Ninety-five Theses,* within sixty days. That autumn, Johann Eck proclaimed the bull in Meissen and other towns. Karl von Miltitz, a papal *nuncio,* attempted to broker a solution, but Luther, who had sent the pope a copy of *On the Freedom of a Christian* in October, publicly set fire to the bull and decretals at Wittenberg on December 10, 1520, an act he defended in *Why the Pope and his Recent Book are Burned and Assertions Concerning All Articles*. As a consequence, Luther was excommunicated by Pope Leo X on January 3, 1521, in the bull *Decet Romanum Pontificem.*

The enforcement of the ban on the *Ninety-five Theses* fell to the secular authorities. On April 18, 1521, Luther appeared as ordered before the Diet of Worms. This was a general assembly of the estates of the Holy Roman Empire that took place in Worms, a town on the Rhine. It was conducted from January 28 to May 25, 1521, with Emperor Charles V presiding. Prince Frederick III, Elector of Saxony, obtained a safe conduct for Luther to and from the meeting.

Johann Eck, speaking on behalf of the empire as assistant of the Archbishop of Trier, presented Luther with copies of his writings laid out on a table and asked him if the books were his, and whether he stood by their contents. Luther confirmed he was their author, but requested time to think about the answer to the second question. He prayed, consulted friends, and gave his response the next day:

> Unless I am convinced by the testimony of the Scriptures or by clear reason (for I do not trust either in the pope or in councils alone, since it is well known that they have often erred and contradicted themselves), I am bound by the Scriptures I have quoted and my conscience is captive to the Word of God. I cannot and will not recant anything, since it is neither safe nor right to go against conscience. May God help me. Amen.

Over the next five days, private conferences were held to determine Luther's fate. The emperor presented the final draft of the Edict of Worms on May 25, 1521, which declared Luther an outlaw, banned his literature, and required his arrest: "We want him to be apprehended and punished as a notorious heretic." It also made it a crime for anyone in Germany to give Luther food or shelter, and permitted anyone to kill Luther without legal consequence.

By 1526, Luther found himself increasingly occupied in organizing a new church, later called the Lutheran Church, and for the rest of his life would continue building the Protestant movement.

An apoplectic stroke on February 18, 1546, deprived him of his speech, and he died shortly afterwards, at 2:45 a.m., aged sixty-two, in Eisleben, the city of his birth. He was buried in the Castle Church in Wittenberg, beneath the pulpit.

Reluctant Revolutionary

PBS Documentary about Martin Luther the "Reluctant Revolutionary." Luther opposed the Catholic Church's practices and in 1517 he wrote his *Ninety-five Theses,* which detailed the church's failings. His actions led to the start of the Protestant Revolution.

Attributions

CC licensed content, Specific attribution

- Boundless World History. **Authored by**: Boundless. **Located at**: https://courses.lumenlearning.com/boundless-worldhistory/. **License**: *CC BY-SA: Attribution-ShareAlike*

Calvinism

Calvinism is a major branch of Protestantism that follows the theological tradition and forms of Christian practice of John Calvin and is characterized by the doctrine of predestination in the salvation of souls.

Learning Objectives

- Compare and contrast Calvinism with Lutheranism

Key Points

- Calvinism is a major branch of Protestantism that follows the theological tradition and forms of Christian practice of John Calvin and other Reformation-era theologians.

- Calvin's theological critiques mostly broke with the Roman Catholic Church, but he differed from Luther on certain theological points, such as the idea that Christ died only for the elect instead of all humanity, like Luther believed.

- Calvin's "Ordinances" of 1541 involved a collaboration of church affairs with the Geneva city council and consistory to bring morality to all areas of life. Geneva became the center of Protestantism.

- Protestantism also spread into France, where the Protestants were derisively nicknamed "Huguenots," and this touched off decades of warfare in France.

- Calvin's *Institutes of the Christian Religion* (1536–1559) was one of the most influential theologies of the era and was written as an introductory textbook on the Protestant faith.

Terms

Predestination

The doctrine that all events have been willed by God, usually with reference to the eventual fate of the individual soul.

Five Points of Calvinism

The basic theological tenets of Calvinism.

Huguenots

A name for French Protestants, originally a derisive term.

Overview

Calvinism is a major branch of Protestantism that follows the theological tradition and forms of Christian practice of John Calvin and other Reformation-era theologians.

Calvinists broke with the Roman Catholic Church but differed from Lutherans on the real presence of Christ in the Eucharist, theories of worship, and the use of God's law for believers, among other things. Calvinism can be a misleading term because the religious tradition it denotes is and has always been diverse, with a wide range of influences rather than a single founder. The movement was first called Calvinism by Lutherans who opposed it, and many within the tradition would prefer to use the word Reformed. While the Reformed theological tradition addresses all of the traditional topics of Christian theology, the word Calvinism is sometimes used to refer to particular Calvinist views on soteriology (the saving of the soul from sin and death) and predestination, which are summarized in part by the Five Points of Calvinism. Some have also argued that Calvinism as a whole stresses the sovereignty or rule of God in all things, including salvation. An important tenet of Calvinism, which differs from Lutheranism, is that God only saves the "elect," a predestined group of individuals, and that these elect are essentially guaranteed salvation, but everyone else is damned.

John Calvin

A portrait of John Calvin, one of the major figures in the Protestant Reformation, by Holbein.

Origins and Rise of Calvinism

First-generation Reformed theologians include Huldrych Zwingli (1484–1531), Martin Bucer (1491–1551), Wolfgang Capito (1478–1541), John Oecolampadius (1482–1531), and Guillaume Farel (1489–1565). These reformers came from diverse academic backgrounds, but later distinctions within

Reformed theology can already be detected in their thought, especially the priority of scripture as a source of authority. Scripture was also viewed as a unified whole, which led to a covenantal theology of the sacraments of baptism and the Lord's Supper as visible signs of the covenant of grace. Another Reformed distinctive present in these theologians was their denial of the bodily presence of Christ in the Lord's Supper. Each of these theologians also understood salvation to be by grace alone, and affirmed a doctrine of particular election (the teaching that some people are chosen by God for salvation). Martin Luther and his successor Philipp Melanchthon were undoubtedly significant influences on these theologians, and to a larger extent later Reformed theologians. The doctrine of justification by faith alone was a direct inheritance from Luther.

Following the excommunication of Luther and condemnation of the Reformation by the pope, the work and writings of John Calvin were influential in establishing a loose consensus among various groups in Switzerland, Scotland, Hungary, Germany, and elsewhere. After the expulsion of Geneva's bishop in 1526, and the unsuccessful attempts of the Berne reformer Guillaume (William) Farel, Calvin was asked to use the organizational skill he had gathered as a student of law to discipline the "fallen city." His "Ordinances" of 1541 involved a collaboration of church affairs with the city council and consistory to bring morality to all areas of life. After the establishment of the Geneva academy in 1559, Geneva became the unofficial capital of the Protestant movement, providing refuge for Protestant exiles from all over Europe and educating them as Calvinist missionaries. These missionaries dispersed Calvinism widely, and formed the French Huguenots in Calvin's own lifetime, as well as caused the conversion of Scotland under the leadership of the cantankerous John Knox in 1560. The faith continued to spread after Calvin's death in 1563, and had reached as far as Constantinople by the start of the 17th century.

Calvin's *Institutes of the Christian Religion* (1536–1559) was one of the most influential theologies of the era. The book was written as an introductory textbook on the Protestant faith for those with some previous knowledge of theology, and covered a broad range of theological topics, from the doctrines of church and sacraments to justification by faith alone and Christian liberty. It vigorously attacked the teachings Calvin considered unorthodox, particularly Roman Catholicism, to which Calvin says he had been "strongly devoted" before his conversion to Protestantism.

Controversies in France

Protestantism spread into France, where the Protestants were derisively nicknamed "Huguenots," and this touched off decades of warfare in France, after initial support by Henry of Navarre was lost due to the "Night of the Placards" affair. Many French Huguenots, however, still contributed to the Protestant movement, including many who emigrated to the English colonies.

Though he was not personally interested in religious reform, Francis I (1515–1547) initially maintained an attitude of tolerance arising from his interest in the humanist movement. This changed in 1534 with the Affair of the Placards. In this act, Protestants denounced the mass in placards that appeared across France, even reaching the royal apartments. The issue of religious faith having been thrown into the arena of politics, Francis was prompted to view the movement as a threat to the kingdom's stability. This led to the first major phase of anti-Protestant persecution in France, in which the *Chambre Ardente* ("Burning Chamber") was established within the Parliament of Paris to handle the rise in prosecutions for heresy. Several thousand French Protestants fled the country during this time, most notably John Calvin, who settled in Geneva.

Calvin continued to take an interest in the religious affairs of his native land and, from his base in Geneva, beyond the reach of the French king, regularly trained pastors to lead congregations in France. Despite heavy persecution by Henry II, the Reformed Church of France, largely Calvinist in direction, made steady progress across large sections of the nation, in the urban bourgeoisie and parts of the aristocracy, appealing to people alienated by the obduracy and the complacency of the Catholic establishment.

Interior of a Calvinist Church

Calvinism has been known at times for its simple, unadorned churches and lifestyles, as depicted in this painting by Emanuel de Witte c.1661.

Painting of the interior of a Calvinist church, which is characterized by large, arching windows and the lack of religious objects or symbols.

Calvinist Theology

The "Five Points of Calvinism" summarize the faith's basic tenets, although some historians contend that it distorts the nuance of Calvin's own theological positions.

The Five Points:

1. "Total depravity" asserts that as a consequence of the fall of man into sin, every person is enslaved to sin. People are not by nature inclined to love God, but rather to serve their own interests and to reject the rule of God. Thus, all people by their own faculties are morally unable to choose to follow God and be saved because they are unwilling to do so out of the necessity of their own natures.

2. "Unconditional election" asserts that God has chosen from eternity those whom he will bring to himself not based on foreseen virtue, merit, or faith in those people; rather, his choice is unconditionally grounded in his mercy alone. God has chosen from eternity to extend mercy to those he has chosen and to withhold mercy from those not chosen. Those chosen receive salvation through Christ alone. Those not chosen receive the just wrath that is warranted for their sins against God.

3. "Limited atonement" asserts that Jesus's substitutionary atonement was definite and certain in its purpose and in what it accomplished. This implies that only the sins of the elect were atoned for by Jesus's death. Calvinists do not believe, however, that the atonement is limited in its value or power, but rather that the atonement is limited in the sense that it is intended for some and not all. All Calvinists would affirm that the blood of Christ was sufficient to pay for every single human being IF it were God's intention to save every single human being.

4. "Irresistible grace" asserts that the saving grace of God is effactually applied to those whom he has determined to save (that is, the elect) and overcomes their resistance to obeying the call of the gospel, bringing them to a saving faith. This means that when God sovereignly purposes to save someone, that individual certainly will be saved. The doctrine holds that this purposeful influence of God's Holy Spirit cannot be resisted.

5. "Perseverance of the saints" asserts that since God is sovereign and his will cannot be frustrated

by humans or anything else, those whom God has called into communion with himself will continue in faith until the end.

SOURCES

Source: Boundless. "Calvinism." *Boundless World History* Boundless, 3 Nov. 2016. Retrieved 23 Jun. 2017 from https://www.boundless.com/world-history/textbooks/boundless-world-history-textbook/the-protestant-reformation-12/protestantism-56/calvinism-1035-17636/

Attributions

CC licensed content, Specific attribution

- Boundless World History. **Authored by**: Boundless. **Located at**: https://courses.lumenlearning.com/boundless-worldhistory/. **License**: *CC BY-SA: Attribution-ShareAlike*

The Anabaptists

The Anabaptists were a group of radical religious reformists formed in Switzerland who suffered violent persecution by both Roman Catholics and Protestants.

Learning Objectives
• Explain why the Anabaptists were ostracized by much of Europe

Key Points
• Anabaptists are Christians who believe in delaying baptism until the candidate confesses his or her faith in Christ, as opposed to being baptized as an infant. • Anabaptists were heavily persecuted during the 16th century and into the 17th century by both Protestants and Roman Catholics, including being drowned and burned at the stake. • Anabaptists were often in conflict with civil society because part of their belief was to follow scripture at all costs, no matter the wishes of secular authority. • Continuing persecution in Europe was largely responsible for the mass emigrations to North America by Amish, Hutterites, and Mennonites, some of the major branches of Anabaptists.

Terms

Magisterial Protestants

A phrase that names the manner in which the Lutheran and Calvinist reformers related to secular authorities, such as princes, magistrates, or city councils; opposed to the Radical Protestants.

Infant baptism

The practice of baptizing infants or young children, sometimes contrasted with what is called "believer's baptism," which is the religious practice of baptizing only individuals who personally confess faith in Jesus.

Ulrich Zwingli

A leader of the Reformation in Switzerland who clashed with the Anabaptists.

Overview

Anabaptism is a Christian movement that traces its origins to the Radical Reformation in Europe. Some consider this movement to be an offshoot of European Protestantism, while others see it as distinct.

Anabaptists are Christians who believe in delaying baptism until the candidate confesses his or her faith in Christ, as opposed to being baptized as an infant. The Amish, Hutterites, and Mennonites are direct descendants of the movement. Schwarzenau Brethren, Bruderhof, and the Apostolic Christian Church are considered later developments among the Anabaptists.

The name *Anabaptist* means "one who baptizes again." Their persecutors named them this, referring to the practice of baptizing persons when they converted or declared their faith in Christ, even if they had been "baptized" as infants. Anabaptists required that baptismal candidates be able to make a confession of faith that was freely chosen, and so rejected baptism of infants. The early members of this movement did not accept the name Anabaptist, claiming that infant baptism was not part of scripture and was therefore null and void. They said that baptizing self-confessed believers was their first true baptism. Balthasar Hubmaier wrote:

> I have never taught Anabaptism…But the right baptism of Christ, which is preceded by teaching and oral confession of faith, I teach, and say that infant baptism is a robbery of the right baptism of Christ.

Anabaptists were heavily persecuted during the 16th century and into the 17th century because of their views on the nature of baptism and other issues, by both Magisterial Protestants and Roman Catholics.

Anabaptists were persecuted largely because of their interpretation of scripture that put them at odds with official state church interpretations and government. Most Anabaptists adhered to a literal interpretation of the Sermon on the Mount, which precluded taking oaths, participating in military actions, and participating in civil government. Some who practiced re-baptism, however, felt otherwise, and complied with these requirements of civil society. They were thus technically Anabaptists, even though conservative Amish, Mennonites, and Hutterites, and some historians, tend to consider them as outside of true Anabaptism.

image

Spread of the Anabaptists 1525–1550 in Central Europe

After starting in Switzerland, Anabaptism spread to Tyrol (modern-day Austria), South Germany, Moravia, the Netherlands, and Belgium.

A map showing the spread of Anabaptists from 1525-1550, mostly within the Holy Roman Empire.

Origins

Anabaptism in Switzerland began as an offshoot of the church reforms instigated by Ulrich Zwingli. As early as 1522 it became evident that Zwingli was on a path of reform preaching when he began to question or criticize such Catholic practices as tithes, the mass, and even infant baptism. Zwingli had gathered a group of reform-minded men around him, with whom he studied classical literature and the scriptures. However, some of these young men began to feel that Zwingli was not moving fast enough in his reform. The division between Zwingli and his more radical disciples became apparent in an October 1523 disputation held in Zurich. When the discussion of the mass was about to be ended without making any actual change in practice, Conrad Grebel stood up and asked "what should be done about the mass?" Zwingli responded by saying the council would make that decision. At this point, Simon Stumpf, a radical priest from Hongg, answered, saying, "The decision has already been made by the Spirit of God."

This incident illustrated clearly that Zwingli and his more radical disciples had different expectations. To Zwingli, the reforms would only go as fast as the city council allowed them. To the radicals, the council had no right to make that decision, but rather the Bible was the final authority on church reform. Feeling frustrated, some of them began to meet on their own for Bible study. As early as 1523, William Reublin began to preach against infant baptism in villages surrounding Zurich, encouraging parents to not baptize their children.

The council ruled in this meeting that all who refused to baptize their infants within one week should be expelled from Zurich. Since Conrad Grebel had refused to baptize his daughter Rachel, born on January 5, 1525, the council decision was extremely personal to him and others who had not baptized their children. Thus, when sixteen of the radicals met on Saturday evening, January 21, 1525, the situation seemed particularly dark.

At that meeting Grebel baptized George Blaurock, and Blaurock in turn baptized several others immediately. These baptisms were the first "re-baptisms" known in the movement. This continues to be the most widely accepted date posited for the establishment of Anabaptism.

Anabaptism then spread to Tyrol (modern-day Austria), South Germany, Moravia, the Netherlands, and Belgium.

Persecutions

Roman Catholics and Protestants alike persecuted the Anabaptists, resorting to torture and execution in attempts to curb the growth of the movement. The Protestants under Zwingli were the first to persecute the Anabaptists, with Felix Manz becoming the first martyr in 1527. On May 20, 1527, Roman Catholic authorities executed Michael Sattler. King Ferdinand declared drowning (called the third baptism) "the best antidote to Anabaptism." The Tudor regime, even the Protestant monarchs (Edward VI of England and Elizabeth I of England), persecuted Anabaptists, as they were deemed too radical and therefore a danger to religious stability. The persecution of Anabaptists was condoned by ancient laws of Theodosius I and Justinian I that were passed against the Donatists, which decreed the death penalty for any who practiced re-baptism. *Martyrs Mirror*, by Thieleman J. van Braght, describes the persecution and execution of thousands of Anabaptists in various parts of Europe between 1525 and 1660. Continuing persecution in Europe was largely responsible for the mass emigrations to North America by Amish, Hutterites, and Mennonites.

image

Burning of an Anabaptist

The burning of a 16th-century Dutch Anabaptist, Anneken Hendriks, who was charged by the Spanish Inquisition with heresy.

Attributions

CC licensed content, Specific attribution

- Boundless World History. **Authored by**: Boundless. **Located at**: https://courses.lumenlearning.com/boundless-worldhistory/. **License**: *CC BY-SA: Attribution-ShareAlike*

The Anglican Church

Beginning with Henry VIII in the 16th century, the Church of England broke away from the authority of the pope and the Catholic Church.

Learning Objectives

- Describe the key developments of the English Reformation, distinguishing it from the wider reformation movement in Europe.

Key Points

- The English Reformation was associated with the wider process of the European Protestant Reformation, though based on Henry VIII's desire for an annulment of his marriage, it was at the outset more of a political affair than a theological dispute.

- Having been refused an annulment by the pope, Henry summoned parliament to deal with annulment, and the breaking with Rome proceeded.

- After Henry's death his son Edward VI was crowned, and the reformation continued with the destruction and removal of decor and religious features, which changed the church forever.

- From 1553, under the reign of Henry's Roman Catholic daughter, Mary I, the Reformation legislation was repealed, and Mary sought to achieve reunion with Rome.

- During Elizabeth I's reign, support for her father's idea of reforming the church continued with some minor adjustments. In this way, Elizabeth and her advisors aimed at a church that found a middle ground.

Terms

Puritans

Group of English Protestants in the 16th and 17th centuries founded by some exiles from the clergy shortly after the accession of Elizabeth I of England.

Annulment

Legal term for declaring a marriage null and void. Unlike divorce, it is usually retroactive, meaning that this kind of marriage is considered to be invalid from the beginning, almost as if it had never taken place. They are closely associated with the Catholic Church, which does not permit divorce, teaching that marriage is a lifelong commitment that cannot be dissolved through divorce.

Nationalism

A belief, creed, or political ideology that involves an individual identifying with, or becoming attached to, one's nation. In Europe, people were generally loyal to the church or to a local king or leader.

Canon Law

The body of laws and regulations made by ecclesiastical authority (church leadership), for the government of a Christian organization or church and its members.

Overview

The English Reformation was a series of events in 16th-century England by which the Church of England broke away from the authority of the pope and the Roman Catholic Church. The English Reformation was, in part, associated with the wider process of the European Protestant Reformation, a religious and political movement that affected the practice of Christianity across most of Europe during this period. Many factors contributed to the process—the decline of feudalism and the rise of nationalism, the rise of the common law, the invention of the printing press and increased circulation of the Bible, and the transmission of new knowledge and ideas among scholars, the upper and middle classes, and readers in general. However, the various phases of the English Reformation, which also covered Wales and Ireland, were largely driven by changes in government policy, to which public opinion gradually accommodated itself.

Role of Henry VIII and Royal Marriages

Henry VIII ascended the English throne in 1509 at the age of seventeen. He made a dynastic marriage with Catherine of Aragon, widow of his brother, Arthur, in June 1509, just before his coronation on Midsummer's Day. Unlike his father, who was secretive and conservative, the young Henry appeared the epitome of chivalry and sociability. An observant Roman Catholic, he heard up to five masses a day (except during the hunting season). Of "powerful but unoriginal mind," he let himself be influenced by his advisors from whom he was never apart, by night or day. He was thus susceptible to whoever had his ear.

This contributed to a state of hostility between his young contemporaries and the Lord Chancellor, Cardinal Thomas Wolsey. As long as Wolsey had his ear, Henry's Roman Catholicism was secure; in 1521, he defended the Roman Catholic Church from Martin Luther's accusations of heresy in a book he wrote—probably with considerable help from the conservative Bishop of Rochester, John Fisher—entitled *The Defence of the Seven Sacraments*, for which he was awarded the title "Defender of the Faith" by Pope Leo X. Wolsey's enemies at court included those who had been influenced by Lutheran ideas, among whom was the attractive, charismatic Anne Boleyn.

Anne arrived at court in 1522 from years in France, where she had been educated by Queen Claude of France. Anne served as maid of honor to Queen Catherine. She was a woman of "charm, style and wit, with will and savagery which made her a match for Henry." By the late 1520s, Henry wanted his marriage to Catherine annulled. She had not produced a male heir who survived into adulthood, and Henry wanted a son to secure the Tudor dynasty.

Henry claimed that this lack of a male heir was because his marriage was "blighted in the eyes of God"; Catherine had been his late brother's wife, and it was therefore against biblical teachings for Henry to have married her—a special dispensation from Pope Julius II had been needed to allow the wedding to take place. Henry argued that this had been wrong and that his marriage had never been valid. In 1527 Henry asked Pope Clement VII to annul the marriage, but the pope refused. According to Canon Law the pope cannot annul a marriage on the basis of a canonical impediment previously dispensed. Clement also feared the wrath of Catherine's nephew, Holy Roman Emperor Charles V, whose troops earlier that year had sacked Rome and briefly taken the pope prisoner.

image

Portrait of Henry VIII (1491–1547)

Portrait by Hans Holbein the Younger, 1539–1540.

In 1529 the king summoned parliament to deal with annulment, thus bringing together those who wanted reform but disagreed what form it should take; it became known as the Reformation Parliament. There were common lawyers who resented the privileges of the clergy to summon laity to their courts, and there were those who had been influenced by Lutheran evangelicalism and were hostile to the theology of Rome; Thomas Cromwell was both.

Cromwell was a lawyer and a member of Parliament—a Protestant who saw how Parliament could be used to advance the Royal Supremacy, which Henry wanted, and to further Protestant beliefs and practices Cromwell and his friends wanted.

The breaking of the power of Rome proceeded little by little starting in 1531. The Act in Restraint of Appeals, drafted by Cromwell, declared that clergy recognized Henry as the "sole protector and Supreme Head of the Church and clergy of England." This declared England an independent country in every respect.

Meanwhile, having taken Anne to France on a pre-nuptial honeymoon, Henry married her in Westminster Abbey in January 1533.

Henry maintained a strong preference for traditional Catholic practices and, during his reign, Protestant reformers were unable to make many changes to the practices of the Church of England. Indeed, this part of Henry's reign saw trials for heresy of Protestants as well as Roman Catholics.

The Reformation during Edward VI

When Henry died in 1547, his nine-year-old son, Edward VI, inherited the throne. Under King Edward VI, more Protestant-influenced forms of worship were adopted. Under the leadership of the Archbishop of Canterbury, Thomas Cranmer, a more radical reformation proceeded. Cranmer introduced a series of religious reforms that revolutionized the English church from one that—while rejecting papal supremacy—remained essentially Catholic to one that was institutionally Protestant. All images in churches were to be dismantled. Stained glass, shrines, and statues were defaced or destroyed. Roods, and often their lofts and screens, were cut down and bells were taken down. Vestments were prohibited and either burned or sold. Chalices were melted down or sold. The requirement of the clergy to be celibate was lifted. Processions were banned and ashes and palms were prohibited.

A new pattern of worship was set out in the Book of Common Prayer (1549 and 1552). These were based on the older liturgy but influenced by Protestant principles. Cranmer's formulation of the reformed religion, finally divesting the communion service of any notion of the real presence of God in the bread and the wine, effectively abolished the mass. The publication of Cranmer's revised prayer book in 1552, supported by a second Act of Uniformity, "marked the arrival of the English Church at protestantism." The prayer book of 1552 remains the foundation of the Church of England's services. However, Cranmer was unable to implement all these reforms once it became clear in the spring of 1553 that King Edward, upon whom the whole Reformation in England depended, was dying.

Catholic Restoration

From 1553, under the reign of Henry's Roman Catholic daughter, Mary I, the Reformation legislation was repealed, and Mary sought to achieve reunion with Rome. Her first Act of Parliament was to retroactively validate Henry's marriage to her mother and so legitimize her claim to the throne.

After 1555, the initial reconciling tone of the regime began to harden. The medieval heresy laws were restored and 283 Protestants were burned at the stake for heresy. Full restoration of the Catholic faith in England to its pre-Reformation state would take time. Consequently, Protestants secretly ministering to underground congregations were planning for a long haul, a ministry of survival. However, Mary died in November 1558, childless and without having made provision for a Catholic to succeed her, undoing her work to restore the Catholic Church in England.

Elizabeth I

Following Mary's death, her half-sister Elizabeth inherited the throne. One of the most important concerns during Elizabeth's early reign was religion. Elizabeth could not be Catholic, as that church considered her illegitimate, being born of Anne Boleyn. At the same time, she had observed the turmoil brought about by Edward's introduction of radical Protestant reforms. Communion with the Catholic Church was again severed by Elizabeth. Chiefly she supported her father's idea of reforming the church, but she made some minor adjustments. In this way, Elizabeth and her advisors aimed at a church that included most opinions.

Elizabeth I and the Church of England

Dr. Tarnya Cooper, the National Portrait Gallery's Chief Curator and Curator of Sixteenth Century Portraits, discusses Elizabeth I's solution to religious turmoil in England.

Two groups were excluded in Elizabeth's Church of England. Roman Catholics who remained loyal to the pope were not tolerated. They were, in fact, regarded as traitors because the pope had refused to accept Elizabeth as Queen of England. Roman Catholics were given the hard choice of being loyal either to their church or their country. For some priests it meant life on the run, and in some cases death for treason.

The other group not tolerated were people who wanted reform to go much further, and who finally gave up on the Church of England. They could no longer see it as a true church. They believed it had refused to obey the Bible, so they formed small groups of convinced believers outside the church. One of the main groups that formed during this time was the Puritans. The government responded with imprisonment and exile to try to crush these "separatists."

Reformation and Division, 1530–1558

Professor Wrightson examines the various stages of the reformation in England, beginning with the legislative, as opposed to doctrinal, reformation begun by Henry VIII in a quest to settle the Tudor succession. Wrightson shows how the jurisdictional transformation of the royal supremacy over the church resulted, gradually, in the introduction of true religious change. The role played by various personalities at Henry's court, and the manner in which the king's own preferences shaped the doctrines of the Church of England, are considered. Doctrinal change, in line with continental Protestant developments, accelerated under Edward VI, but was reversed by Mary I. However, Wrightson suggests that, by this time, many aspects of Protestantism had been internalized by part of the English population, especially the young, and so the reformation could not wholly be undone by Mary's short reign. The lecture ends with the accession of Elizabeth I in 1558, an event which presaged further religious change.

Attributions

The French Wars of Religion

The French Wars of Religion (1562–98) is the name of a period of fighting between French Catholics and Protestants (Huguenots).

Learning Objectives

- Discuss how the patterns of warfare that took place in France affected the Huguenots

Key Points

- Protestant ideas were first introduced to France during the reign of Francis I, who firmly opposed Protestantism, but continued to try and seek a middle course until the later stages of his regime.

- As the Huguenots gained influence and displayed their faith more openly, Roman Catholic hostility to them grew, spurning eight civil wars from 1562 to 1598.

- The wars were interrupted by breaks in peace that only lasted temporarily as the Huguenots' trust in the Catholic throne diminished, and the violence became more severe and Protestant demands became grander.

- One of the most infamous events of the wars was the St. Bartholomew's Day Massacre in 1572, when thousands of Huguenots were killed by Catholics.

- The pattern of warfare followed by brief periods of peace continued for nearly another quarter-century. The proclamation of the Edict of Nantes, and the subsequent protection of Huguenot rights, finally quelled the uprisings.

Terms

Edict of Nantes

Issued on April 13, 1598, by Henry IV of France; granted the Huguenots substantial rights in a nation still considered essentially Catholic.

Huguenots

Members of the Protestant Reformed Church of France during the 16th and 17th centuries; inspired by the writings of John Calvin.

Real Presence

A term used in various Christian traditions to express belief that in the Eucharist, Jesus Christ is really present in what was previously just bread and wine, and not merely present in symbol.

Overview

The French Wars of Religion (1562–1598) is the name of a period of civil infighting and military operations primarily between French Catholics and Protestants (Huguenots). The conflict involved the factional disputes between the aristocratic houses of France, such as the House of Bourbon and the House of Guise, and both sides received assistance from foreign sources.

The exact number of wars and their respective dates are the subject of continued debate by historians; some assert that the Edict of Nantes in 1598 concluded the wars, although a resurgence of rebellious activity following this leads some to believe the Peace of Alais in 1629 is the actual conclusion. However, the Massacre of Vassy in 1562 is agreed to have begun the Wars of Religion; up to a hundred Huguenots were killed in this massacre. During the wars, complex diplomatic negotiations and agreements of peace were followed by renewed conflict and power struggles.

Between 2,000,000 and 4,000,000 people were killed as a result of war, famine, and disease, and at the conclusion of the conflict in 1598, Huguenots were granted substantial rights and freedoms by the Edict of Nantes, though it did not end hostility towards them. The wars weakened the authority of the monarchy, already fragile under the rule of Francis II and then Charles IX, though the monarchy later reaffirmed its role under Henry IV.

Introduction of Protestantism

Protestant ideas were first introduced to France during the reign of Francis I (1515–1547) in the form of Lutheranism, the teachings of Martin Luther, and circulated unimpeded for more than a year around Paris.

Although Francis firmly opposed heresy, the difficulty was initially in recognizing what constituted it; Catholic doctrine and definition of orthodox belief was unclear. Francis I tried to steer a middle course in the developing religious schism in France.

Calvinism, a form of Protestant religion, was introduced by John Calvin, who was born in Noyon, Picardy, in 1509, and fled France in 1536 after the Affair of the Placards. Calvinism in particular appears to have developed with large support from the nobility. It is believed to have started with Louis Bourbon, Prince of Condé, who, while returning home to France from a military campaign, passed through Geneva, Switzerland, and heard a sermon by a Calvinist preacher. Later, Louis Bourbon would become a major figure among the Huguenots of France. In 1560, Jeanne d'Albret, Queen regnant of Navarre, converted to Calvinism possibly due to the influence of Theodore de Beze. She later married Antoine de Bourbon, and their son Henry of Navarre would be a leader among the Huguenots.

Affair of the Placards

Francis I continued his policy of seeking a middle course in the religious rift in France until an incident called the Affair of the Placards. The Affair of the Placards began in 1534 when Protestants started putting up anti-Catholic posters. The posters were extreme in their anti-Catholic content—specifically, the absolute rejection of the Catholic doctrine of "Real Presence." Protestantism became identified as "a religion of rebels," helping the Catholic Church to more easily define Protestantism as heresy. In the wake of the posters, the French monarchy took a harder stand against the protesters. Francis I had been severely criticized for his initial tolerance towards Protestants, and now was encouraged to repress them.

Tensions Mount

King Francis I died on March 31, 1547, and was succeeded to the throne by his son Henry II. Henry II continued the harsh religious policy that his father had followed during the last years of his reign. In 1551, Henry issued the Edict of Châteaubriant, which sharply curtailed Protestant rights to worship, assemble, or even discuss religion at work, in the fields, or over a meal.

An organized influx of Calvinist preachers from Geneva and elsewhere during the 1550s succeeded in setting up hundreds of underground Calvinist congregations in France. This underground Calvinist preaching (which was also seen in the Netherlands and Scotland) allowed for the formation of covert alliances with members of the nobility and quickly led to more direct action to gain political and religious control.

As the Huguenots gained influence and displayed their faith more openly, Roman Catholic hostility to them grew, even though the French crown offered increasingly liberal political concessions and edicts of toleration. However, these measures disguised the growing tensions between Protestants and Catholics.

The Eight Wars of Religion

These tensions spurred eight civil wars, interrupted by periods of relative calm, between 1562 and 1598. With each break in peace, the Huguenots' trust in the Catholic throne diminished, and the violence became more severe and Protestant demands became grander, until a lasting cessation of open hostility finally occurred in 1598.

The wars gradually took on a dynastic character, developing into an extended feud between the Houses of Bourbon and Guise, both of which—in addition to holding rival religious views—staked a claim to the French throne. The crown, occupied by the House of Valois, generally supported the Catholic side, but on occasion switched over to the Protestant cause when it was politically expedient.

St. Bartholomew's Day Massacre

One of the most infamous events of the Wars of Religion was the St. Bartholomew's Day Massacre of 1572, when Catholics killed thousands of Huguenots in Paris. The massacre began on the night of August 23, 1572 (the eve of the feast of Bartholomew the Apostle), two days after the attempted assassination of Admiral Gaspard de Coligny, the military and political leader of the Huguenots. The king ordered the killing of a group of Huguenot leaders, including Coligny, and the slaughter spread throughout Paris and beyond. The exact number of fatalities throughout the country is not known, but estimates are that between about 2,000 and 3,000 Protestants were killed in Paris, and between 3,000 and 7,000 more in the French provinces. Similar massacres took place in other towns in the weeks following. By September 17, almost 25,000 Protestants had been massacred in Paris alone. Outside of Paris, the killings continued until October 3. An amnesty granted in 1573 pardoned the perpetrators.

The massacre also marked a turning point in the French Wars of Religion. The Huguenot political movement was crippled by the loss of many of its prominent aristocratic leaders, as well as many re-conversions by the rank and file, and those who remained were increasingly radicalized.

image

St. Bartholomew Massacre painting by François Dubois, a Huguenot painter

Born circa 1529 in Amiens, Dubois settled in Switzerland. Although Dubois did not witness the massacre, he depicts Admiral Coligny's body hanging out of a window at the rear to the right. To the left rear, Catherine de' Medici is shown emerging from the Château du Louvre to inspect a heap of bodies.

War of the Three Henrys

The War of the Three Henrys (1587–1589) was the eighth and final conflict in the series of civil wars in France known as the Wars of Religion. It was a three-way war fought between:

- King Henry III of France, supported by the royalists and the politiques;
- King Henry of Navarre, leader of the Huguenots and heir-presumptive to the French throne, supported by Elizabeth I of England and the Protestant princes of Germany; and
- Henry of Lorraine, Duke of Guise, leader of the Catholic League, funded and supported by Philip II of Spain.

The war began when the Catholic League convinced King Henry III to issue an edict outlawing Protestantism and annulling Henry of Navarre's right to the throne. For the first part of the war, the royalists and the Catholic League were uneasy allies against their common enemy, the Huguenots. Henry of Navarre sought foreign aid from the German princes and Elizabeth I of England.

Henry III successfully prevented the junction of the German and Swiss armies. The Swiss were his allies, and had come to invade France to free him from subjection, but Henry III insisted that their invasion was not in his favor, but against him, forcing them to return home.

In Paris, the glory of repelling the German and Swiss Protestants all fell to the Duke of Guise. The king's actions were viewed with contempt. People thought that the king had invited the Swiss to invade, paid them for coming, and sent them back again. The king, who had really performed the decisive part in the campaign, and expected to be honored for it, was astounded that public voice should thus declare against him. The Catholic League had put its preachers to good use.

Open war erupted between the royalists and the Catholic League. Charles, Duke of Mayenne, Guise's younger brother, took over the leadership of the league. At the moment it seemed that he could not possibly resist his enemies. His power was effectively limited to Blois, Tours, and the surrounding districts. In these dark times the King of France finally reached out to his cousin and heir, the King of Navarre. Henry III declared that he would no longer allow Protestants to be called heretics, while the Protestants revived the strict principles of royalty and divine right. As on the other side ultra-Catholic and anti-royalist doctrines were closely associated, so on the side of the two kings the principles of tolerance and royalism were united.

In July 1589, in the royal camp at Saint-Cloud, a Dominican monk named Jacques Clément gained an audience with the King and drove a long knife into his spleen. Clément was killed on the spot, taking with him the information of who, if anyone, had hired him. On his deathbed, Henri III called for Henry of Navarre, and begged him, in the name of statecraft, to become a Catholic, citing the brutal warfare that would ensue if he refused. He named Henry Navarre as his heir, who became Henry IV.

Edict of Nantes

Fighting continued between Henry IV and the Catholic League for almost a decade. The warfare was finally quelled in 1598 when Henry IV recanted Protestantism in favor of Roman Catholicism, issued as the Edict of Nantes. The edict established Catholicism as the state religion of France, but granted the Protestants equality with Catholics under the throne and a degree of religious and political freedom within their domains. The edict simultaneously protected Catholic interests by discouraging the founding of new Protestant churches in Catholic-controlled regions. With the proclamation of the Edict of Nantes, and the subsequent protection of Huguenot rights, pressures to leave France abated.

In offering general freedom of conscience to individuals, the edict gave many specific concessions to the Protestants, such as amnesty and the reinstatement of their civil rights, including the right to work in any field or for the state and to bring grievances directly to the king. This marked the end of the religious wars that had afflicted France during the second half of the 16th century.

Attributions

- Boundless World History. **Authored by**: Boundless. **Located at**: https://courses.lumenlearning.com/boundless-worldhistory/. **License**: *CC BY-SA: Attribution-ShareAlike*

Religious Divide in the Holy Roman Empire

The Thirty Years' War was a series of wars between various Protestant and Catholic states in the fragmented Holy Roman Empire between 1618 and 1648.

Learning Objective

- Understand the origins of the Thirty Years' War

Key Points

- The Holy Roman Empire was a fragmented collection of largely independent states, which, after the Protestant Reformation in the 16th century, was divided between Catholic and Protestant rulership.

- The Peace of Augsburg ended early conflict between German Lutherans and Catholics and established a principle in which princes were guaranteed the right to select either Lutheranism or Catholicism within the domains they controlled.

- Although the Peace of Augsburg created a temporary end to hostilities, it did not resolve the underlying religious conflict, which was made yet more complex by the spread of Calvinism throughout Germany in the years that followed.

- The war began when the newly elected Holy Roman Emperor, Ferdinand II, tried to impose religious uniformity on his domains, forcing Roman Catholicism on its peoples, and the Protestant states banded together to revolt against him.

Terms

Ferdinand II

His rule coincided with the Thirty Years' War and his aim, as a zealous Catholic, was to restore Catholicism as the only religion in the empire and suppress Protestantism.

Peace of Augsburg

A treaty between Charles V and the forces of Lutheran princes on September 25, 1555, which officially ended the religious struggle between the two groups and allowed princes in the Holy Roman Empire to choose which religion would reign in their principality.

Overview

The Thirty Years' War was a series of wars in Central Europe between 1618 and 1648. It was one of the longest and most destructive conflicts in European history, resulting in millions of casualties.

Initially a war between various Protestant and Catholic states in the fragmented Holy Roman Empire, it gradually developed into a more general conflict involving most of the great powers. These states employed relatively large mercenary armies, and the war became less about religion and more of a continuation of the France-Habsburg rivalry for European political pre-eminence. In the 17th century, religious beliefs and practices were a much larger influence on an average European. In that era, almost everyone was vested on one side of the dispute or another.

The war began when the newly elected Holy Roman Emperor, Ferdinand II, tried to impose religious uniformity on his domains, forcing Roman Catholicism on its peoples. The northern Protestant states, angered by the violation of their rights to choose granted in the Peace of Augsburg, banded together to form the Protestant Union. Ferdinand II was a devout Roman Catholic and relatively intolerant when compared to his predecessor, Rudolf II. His policies were considered heavily pro-Catholic.

The Holy Roman Empire

The Holy Roman Empire was a fragmented collection of largely independent states. The position of the Holy Roman Emperor was mainly titular, but the emperors, from the House of Habsburg, also directly ruled a large portion of imperial territory (lands of the Archduchy of Austria and the Kingdom of Bohemia), as well as the Kingdom of Hungary. The Austrian domain was thus a major European power in its own right, ruling over some eight million subjects. Another branch of the House of Habsburg ruled over Spain and its empire, which included the Spanish Netherlands, southern Italy, the Philippines, and most of the Americas. In addition to Habsburg lands, the Holy Roman Empire contained several regional powers, such as the Duchy of Bavaria, the Electorate of Saxony, the Margraviate of Brandenburg, the Electorate of the Palatinate, Landgraviate of Hesse, the Archbishopric of Trier, and the Free Imperial City of Nuremberg.

Peace of Augsburg

After the Protestant Reformation, these independent states became divided between Catholic and Protestant rulership, giving rise to conflict. The Peace of Augsburg (1555), signed by Charles V, Holy Roman Emperor, ended the war between German Lutherans and Catholics. The Peace established the principle *Cuius regio, eius religio* ("Whose realm, his religion"), which allowed Holy Roman Empire state princes to select either Lutheranism or Catholicism within the domains they controlled, ultimately reaffirming the independence they had over their states. Subjects, citizens, or residents who did not wish to conform to a prince's choice were given a period in which they were free to emigrate to different regions in which their desired religion had been accepted.

Although the Peace of Augsburg created a temporary end to hostilities, it did not resolve the underlying religious conflict, which was made yet more complex by the spread of Calvinism throughout Germany in the years that followed. This added a third major faith to the region, but its position was not recognized in any way by the Augsburg terms, to which only Catholicism and Lutheranism were parties.

image

Religion in the Holy Roman Empire, 1618

Religion in the Holy Roman Empire on the eve of the Thirty Years' War. Blues indicate Catholic regions and red/orange indicate Protestant (including Lutheran, Calvinist, Hussite, and Reform).

German map of religious demographics in the Holy Roman Empire before the outbreak of the Thirty Years' War.

Tension Mount

Religious tensions remained strong throughout the second half of the 16th century. The Peace of Augsburg began to unravel—some converted bishops refused to give up their bishoprics, and certain Habsburg and other Catholic rulers of the Holy Roman Empire and Spain sought to restore the power of Catholicism in the region. This was evident from the Cologne War (1583–1588), in which a conflict ensued when the prince-archbishop of the city, Gebhard Truchsess von Waldburg, converted to Calvinism. As he was an imperial elector, this could have produced a Protestant majority in the college that elected the Holy Roman Emperor, a position that Catholics had always held.

At the beginning of the 17th century, the Rhine lands and those south to the Danube were largely Catholic, while the north was dominated by Lutherans, and certain other areas, such as west-central Germany, Switzerland, and the Netherlands, were dominated by Calvins. Minorities of each creed existed almost everywhere, however. In some lordships and cities, the numbers of Calvinists, Catholics, and Lutherans were approximately equal.

Much to the consternation of their Spanish ruling cousins, the Habsburg emperors who followed Charles V (especially Ferdinand I and Maximilian II, but also Rudolf II and his successor, Matthias) were content to allow the princes of the empire to choose their own religious policies. These rulers avoided religious wars within the empire by allowing the different Christian faiths to spread without coercion. This angered those who sought religious uniformity. Meanwhile, Sweden and Denmark, both Lutheran kingdoms, sought to assist the Protestant cause in the Empire, and wanted to gain political and economic influence there as well.

By 1617, it was apparent that Matthias, Holy Roman Emperor and King of Bohemia, would die without an heir, with his lands going to his nearest male relative, his cousin Archduke Ferdinand II of Austria, heir-apparent and Crown Prince of Bohemia.

War Breaks Out

Ferdinand II, educated by the Jesuits, was a staunch Catholic who wanted to impose religious uniformity on his lands. This made him highly unpopular in Protestant Bohemia. The population's sentiments notwithstanding, the added insult of the nobility's rejection of Ferdinand, who had been elected Bohemian Crown Prince in 1617, triggered the Thirty Years' War in 1618, when his representatives were thrown out of a window and seriously injured. The so-called Defenestration of Prague provoked open revolt in Bohemia, which had powerful foreign allies. Ferdinand was upset by this calculated insult, but his intolerant policies in his own lands had left him in a weak position. The Habsburg cause in the next few years would seem to suffer unrecoverable reverses. The Protestant cause seemed to wax toward a quick overall victory.

The war can be divided into four major phases: The Bohemian Revolt, the Danish intervention, the Swedish intervention, and the French intervention.

image

Ferdinand II

Ferdinand II, Holy Roman Emperor and King of Bohemia, whose aim, as a zealous Catholic, was to restore Catholicism as the only religion in the empire and suppress Protestantism, and whose actions helped precipitate the Thirty Years' War.

Attributions

Bohemian Period

The Bohemian Revolt (1618–1620) was an uprising of the Bohemian estates against the rule of the Habsburg dynasty, in particular Emperor Ferdinand II, which triggered the Thirty Years' War.

Learning Objective

- Describe the events surrounding the Defenestration of Prague

Key Points

- Since 1526, the Kingdom of Bohemia had been governed by Catholic Habsburg kings who were tolerant of their largely Protestant subjects.

- Toward the end his reign, Emperor Matthias, realizing he would die without an heir, arranged for his lands to go to his nearest male relative, the staunchly Catholic Archduke Ferdinand II of Austria.

- Protestants in Bohemia were wary of Ferdinand reversing the religious tolerance and freedom formerly established by the Peace of Augsburg.

- In 1618, Ferdinand's royal representatives were thrown out of a window and seriously injured in the so-called Defenestration of Prague, which provoked open Protestant revolt in Bohemia.

- The dispute culminated after several battles in the final Battle of White Mountain, where the Protestants suffered a decisive defeat. This started re-Catholicization of the Czech lands, but also triggered the Thirty Years' War, which spread to the rest of Europe and devastated vast areas of central Europe, including the Czech lands.

Terms
Defenestration
The act of throwing someone out of a window.
Bohemian Revolt
An uprising of the Bohemian estates against the rule of the Habsburg dynasty.

Background

In 1555, the Peace of Augsburg had settled religious disputes in the Holy Roman Empire by enshrining the principle of *Cuius regio, eius religio*, allowing a prince to determine the religion of his subjects. Since 1526, the Kingdom of Bohemia had been governed by Habsburg kings who did not force their Catholic religion on their largely Protestant subjects. In 1609, Rudolf II, Holy Roman Emperor and King of Bohemia (1576–1612), increased Protestant rights. He was increasingly viewed as unfit to govern, and other members of the Habsburg dynasty declared his younger brother, Matthias, to be family head in 1606. Upon Rudolf's death, Matthias succeeded in the rule of Bohemia.

Without heirs, Emperor Matthias sought to assure an orderly transition during his lifetime by having his dynastic heir (the fiercely Catholic Ferdinand of Styria, later Ferdinand II, Holy Roman Emperor) elected to the separate royal thrones of Bohemia and Hungary. Ferdinand was a proponent of the Catholic Counter-Reformation, and not well-disposed to Protestantism or Bohemian freedoms. Some of the Protestant leaders of Bohemia feared they would be losing the religious rights granted to them by Emperor Rudolf II in his Letter of Majesty (1609). They preferred the Protestant Frederick V, Elector of the Palatinate (successor of Frederick IV, the creator of the Protestant Union). However, other Protestants supported the stance taken by the Catholics, and in 1617 Ferdinand was duly elected by the Bohemian Estates to become the Crown Prince and, automatically upon the death of Matthias, the next King of Bohemia.

The Defenestration of Prague

The king-elect then sent two Catholic councillors (Vilem Slavata of Chlum and Jaroslav Borzita of Martinice) as his representatives to Hradčany castle in Prague in May 1618. Ferdinand had wanted them to administer the government in his absence. On May 23, 1618, an assembly of Protestants seized them and threw them (and also secretary Philip Fabricius) out of the palace window, which was some sixty-nine feet off the ground. Remarkably, though injured, they survived. This event, known as the Defenestration of Prague, started the Bohemian Revolt. Soon afterward, the Bohemian conflict spread through all of the Bohemian Crown, including Bohemia, Silesia, Upper and Lower Lusatia, and Moravia. Moravia was already embroiled in a conflict between Catholics and Protestants. The religious conflict eventually spread across the whole continent of Europe, involving France, Sweden, and a number of other countries.

image

Defenestration of Prague

A later woodcut of the Defenestration of Prague in 1618, which triggered the Thirty Years' War.

A woodcut of the Defenestrations of Prague, depicting several men tossing another man out of a window to the right and other men around the room pushing others toward the windows.

Aftermath

Immediately after the defenestration, the Protestant estates and Catholic Habsburgs started gathering allies for war. After the death of Matthias in 1619, Ferdinand II was elected Holy Roman Emperor. At the same time, the Bohemian estates deposed Ferdinand as King of Bohemia (Ferdinand remained emperor, since the titles are separate) and replaced him with Frederick V, Elector Palatine, a leading Calvinist and son-in-law of the Protestant James VI and I, King of Scotland, England, and Ireland.

Because they deposed a properly chosen king, the Protestants could not gather the international support they needed for war. Just two years after the Defenestration of Prague, Ferdinand and the Catholics regained power in the Battle of White Mountain on November 8, 1620. This became known as the first battle in the Thirty Years' War.

This was a serious blow to Protestant ambitions in the region. As the rebellion collapsed, the widespread confiscation of property and suppression of the Bohemian nobility ensured the country would return to the Catholic side after more than two centuries of Protestant dissent.

There was plundering and pillaging in Prague for weeks following the battle. Several months later, twenty-seven nobles and citizens were tortured and executed in the Old Town Square. Twelve of their heads were impaled on iron hooks and hung from the Bridge Tower as a warning. This also contributed to catalyzing the Thirty Years' War.

Attributions

Danish Intervention

After the Bohemian Revolt was suppressed by Ferdinand II, the Danish king, Christian IV, fearing that recent Catholic successes threatened his sovereignty as a Protestant nation, led troops against Ferdinand.

Learning Objective

- Analyze the reasons for Denmark getting involved in the war

Key Points

- After the Defenestration of Prague and the ensuing Bohemian Revolt, the Protestants warred with the Catholic League until the former were firmly defeated at the Battle of Stadtlohn in 1623.

- With news of the outcome reaching Frederick V of the Palatinate, the king was forced to sign an armistice with Holy Roman Emperor Ferdinand II, thus ending the "Palatine Phase" of the Thirty Years' War.

- Peace was short lived; the Danish duchy, under the rule of Christian IV, rallied troops to support the Protestants against Ferdinand.

- Ferdinand received support from Albrecht von Wallenstein, who led troops to defeat Christian IV's army.

- With another military success for the Catholics, Ferdinand II took back several Protestant holdings and declared the Edict of Restitution in an attempt to restore the religious and territorial situations reached in the Peace of Augsburg.

Terms

Edict of Restitution

Passed eleven years into the Thirty Years' War, this edict was a belated attempt by Ferdinand II to impose and restore the religious and territorial situations reached in the Peace of Augsburg (1555).

Background

After the Defenestration of Prague and the ensuing Bohemian Revolt, the Protestants warred with the Catholic League until the former were firmly defeated at the Battle of Stadtlohn in 1623. After this catastrophe, Frederick V, already in exile in The Hague, and under growing pressure from his father-in-law, James I, to end his involvement in the war, was forced to abandon any hope of launching further campaigns. The Protestant rebellion had been crushed. Frederick was forced to sign an armistice with Holy Roman Emperor Ferdinand II, thus ending the "Palatine Phase" of the Thirty Years' War.

Dutch Intervention

Peace following the imperial victory at Stadtlohn proved short lived, with conflict resuming at the initiation of Denmark. Danish involvement, referred to as the Low Saxon War, began when Christian IV of Denmark, a Lutheran who also ruled as Duke of Holstein, a duchy within the Holy Roman Empire, helped the Lutheran rulers of neighboring Lower Saxony by leading an army against Ferdinand II's imperial forces in 1625. Denmark had feared that the recent Catholic successes threatened its sovereignty as a Protestant nation.

Christian IV had profited greatly from his policies in northern Germany. For instance, in 1621, Hamburg had been forced to accept Danish sovereignty. Denmark's King Christian IV had obtained for his kingdom a level of stability and wealth that was virtually unmatched elsewhere in Europe. Denmark was funded by tolls on the Oresund and also by extensive war reparations from Sweden.

Denmark's cause was aided by France, which together with Charles I had agreed to help subsidize the war, not the least because Christian was a blood uncle to both the Stuart king and his sister Elizabeth of Bohemia through their mother, Anne of Denmark. Some 13,700 Scottish soldiers under the command of General Robert Maxwell, 1st Earl of Nithsdale, were sent as allies to help Christian IV. Moreover, some 6,000 English troops under Charles Morgan also eventually arrived to bolster the defense of Denmark, though it took longer for them to arrive than Christian had hoped, due partially to the ongoing British campaigns against France and Spain. Thus, Christian, as war-leader of the Lower Saxon Circle, entered the war with an army of only 20,000 mercenaries, some of his allies from England and Scotland, and a national army 15,000 strong, leading them as Duke of Holstein rather than as King of Denmark.

War Ensues

To fight Christian, Ferdinand II employed the military help of Albrecht von Wallenstein, a Bohemian nobleman who had made himself rich from the confiscated estates of his Protestant countrymen. Wallenstein pledged his army, which numbered between 30,000 and 100,000 soldiers, to Ferdinand II in return for the right to plunder the captured territories. Christian, who knew nothing of Wallenstein's forces when he invaded, was forced to retire before the combined forces of Wallenstein and Tilly. Christian's mishaps continued when all of the allies he thought he had were forced aside: France was in the midst of a civil war, Sweden was at war with the Polish–Lithuanian Commonwealth, and neither Brandenburg nor Saxony was interested in changes to the tenuous peace in eastern Germany. Moreover, neither of the substantial British contingents arrived in time to prevent Wallenstein's defeat of Mansfeld's army at the Battle of Dessau Bridge (1626) or Tilly's victory at the Battle of Lutter (1626). Mansfeld died some months later of illness, apparently tuberculosis, in Dalmatia.

Wallenstein's army marched north, occupying Mecklenburg, Pomerania, and Jutland itself, but proved unable to take the Danish capital, Copenhagen, on the island of Zealand. Wallenstein lacked a fleet, and neither the Hanseatic ports nor the Poles would allow the building of an imperial fleet on the Baltic coast. He then laid siege to Stralsund, the only belligerent Baltic port with sufficient facilities to build a large fleet; it soon became clear, however, that the cost of continuing the war would far outweigh any gains from conquering the rest of Denmark. Wallenstein feared losing his northern German gains to a Danish-Swedish alliance, while Christian IV had suffered another defeat in the Battle of Wolgast (1628); both were ready to negotiate.

Negotiations and the Edict of Restitution

Negotiations concluded with the Treaty of Lübeck in 1629, which stated that Christian IV could retain control over Denmark (including the duchies of Sleswick and Holstein) if he would abandon his support for the Protestant German states. Thus, in the following two years, the Catholic powers subjugated more land. At this point, the Catholic League persuaded Ferdinand II to take back the Lutheran holdings that were, according to the Peace of Augsburg, rightfully the possession of the Catholic Church. Enumerated in the Edict of Restitution (1629), these possessions included two archbishoprics, sixteen bishoprics, and hundreds of monasteries. In the same year, Gabriel Bethlen, the Calvinist prince of Transylvania, died. Only the port of Stralsund continued to hold out against Wallenstein and the emperor, having been bolstered by Scottish "volunteers" who arrived from the Swedish army to support their countrymen already there in the service of Denmark.

image

Christian IV of Denmark

Christian IV receives homage from the countries of Europe as mediator in the Thirty Years' War. Painting by Grisaille by Adrian van de Venne, 1643.

Attributions

CC licensed content, Specific attribution

Swedish Intervention

The Swedish intervention in the Thirty Years' War, when King Gustav II Adolf of Sweden ordered a full-scale invasion of the Catholic states, was a major turning point of the war.

Learning Objective

- Discuss why the Swedish were inclined to join in the war

Key Points

- The Swedish intervention in the Thirty Years' War, which took place between 1630 and 1635, was a major turning point of the war, often considered to be an independent conflict.

- The king of Sweden, Gustav Adolph, had been well informed of the war between the Catholics and Protestants in the Holy Roman Empire for some time, but did not get involved because of an ongoing conflict with Poland.

- While Sweden was under a truce with Poland, Gustav reformed the Swedish military, leading to an army that became the model for all of Europe.

- From 1630 to 1634, Swedish-led armies drove the Catholic forces back, regaining much of the lost Protestant territory, especially at the key Battle of Breitenfeld.

- By the spring of 1635, the Catholic and the Protestant sides met for negotiations, producing the Peace of Prague (1635), which entailed a delay in the enforcement of the Edict of Restitution for forty years.

Terms

Gustavus Adolphus

The king of Sweden from 1611 to 1632, credited with founding the Swedish Empire, who led Sweden to military supremacy during the Thirty Years' War.

Pomerania

A region on the southern shore of the Baltic Sea in Central Europe, split between Germany and Poland.

Overview

The Swedish intervention in the Thirty Years' War, which took place between 1630 and 1635, was a major turning point of the war, often considered to be an independent conflict. After several attempts by the Holy Roman Empire to prevent the spread of Protestantism in Europe, King Gustav II Adolf of Sweden ordered a full-scale invasion of the Catholic states. Although he was killed in action, his armies successfully defeated their enemies and gave birth to the Swedish Empire after proving their ability in combat. The new European power would last for a hundred years before being overwhelmed by numerous enemies in the Great Northern War.

Background

The king of Sweden, Gustav II Adolph, had been well informed of the war between the Catholics and Protestants in the Holy Roman Empire for some time, but his hands were tied because of the constant enmity of Poland. The Polish royal family, the primary branch of the House of Vasa, had once claimed the throne of Sweden.

Lutheranism was the primary religion of Sweden, and had by then established a firm grip on the country, but it was not solely the result of religious sentiment that Sweden converted. Notably, one of the reasons that Sweden had so readily embraced it was because converting to Lutheranism allowed the crown to seize all the lands in Sweden that were possessed by the Roman Catholic Church. As a result of this seizure and the money that the crown gained, the crown was greatly empowered.

Gustav was concerned about the growing power of the Holy Roman Empire, and like Christian IV before him, was heavily subsidized by Cardinal Richelieu, the chief minister of Louis XIII of France, and by the Dutch.

Sweden's Army

During this time, and while Sweden was under a truce with Poland, Gustav established a military system that was to become the envy of Europe. He drew up a new military code. The new improvements to Sweden's military order even pervaded the state by fueling fundamental changes in the economy. The military reforms—among which tight discipline was one of the prevailing principles—brought the Swedish military to the highest levels of military readiness and were to become the standard that European states would strive for.

The severity of discipline was not the only change that took place in the army. Soldiers were to be rewarded for meritorious service. Soldiers who had displayed courage and distinguished themselves in the line of duty were paid generously, in addition to being given pensions. The corp of engineers were the most modern of their age, and in the campaigns in Germany the population repeatedly expressed surprise at the extensive nature of the entrenchment and the elaborate nature of the equipment.

Swedish Intervention

From 1630 to 1634, Swedish-led armies drove the Catholic forces back, regaining much of the lost Protestant territory. During the campaign, Sweden managed to conquer half of the imperial kingdoms, making it the continental leader of Protestantism until the Swedish Empire ended in 1721.

Swedish forces entered the Holy Roman Empire via the Duchy of Pomerania, which had served as the Swedish bridgehead since the Treaty of Stettin (1630). After dismissing Wallenstein in 1630, from fear he was planning a revolt, Ferdinand II became dependent on the Catholic League. Gustavus Adolphus allied with France and Bavaria.

At the Battle of Breitenfeld (1631), Gustavus Adolphus's forces defeated the Catholic League led by Tilly. A year later, they met again in another Protestant victory, this time accompanied by the death of Tilly. The upper hand had now switched from the Catholic League to the Protestant Union, led by Sweden.

image

King Gustav of Sweden

The victory of Gustavus Adolphus at the Battle of Breitenfeld (1631).

A painting of Gustav of Sweden riding a horse on a hill overlooking a battlefield and countryside.

With Tilly dead, Ferdinand II returned to the aid of Wallenstein and his large army. Wallenstein marched to the south, threatening Gustavus Adolphus's supply chain. Gustavus Adolphus knew that Wallenstein was waiting for the attack and was prepared, but found no other option. Wallenstein and Gustavus Adolphus clashed in the Battle of Lützen (1632), where the Swedes prevailed, but Gustavus Adolphus was killed.

Ferdinand II's suspicion of Wallenstein resumed in 1633, when Wallenstein attempted to arbitrate the differences between the Catholic and Protestant sides. Ferdinand II may have feared that Wallenstein would switch sides, and arranged for his arrest after removing him from command. One of Wallenstein's soldiers,

Captain Devereux, killed him when he attempted to contact the Swedes in the town hall of Eger (Cheb) on February 25, 1634. The same year, the Protestant forces, lacking Gustav's leadership, were smashed at the First Battle of Nördlingen by the Spanish-Imperial forces commanded by Cardinal-Infante Ferdinand.

Peace of Prague

By the spring of 1635, all Swedish resistance in the south of Germany had ended. After that, the imperialist and the Protestant German sides met for negotiations, producing the Peace of Prague (1635), which entailed a delay in the enforcement of the Edict of Restitution for forty years and allowed Protestant rulers to retain secularized bishoprics held by them in 1627. This protected the Lutheran rulers of northeastern Germany, but not those of the south and west. Initially after the Peace of Prague, the Swedish armies were pushed back by the reinforced imperial army north into Germany.

The treaty also provided for the union of the army of the emperor and the armies of the German states into a single army of the Holy Roman Empire. Finally, German princes were forbidden from establishing alliances amongst themselves or with foreign powers, and amnesty was granted to any ruler who had taken up arms against the emperor after the arrival of the Swedes in 1630.

This treaty failed to satisfy France, however, because of the renewed strength it granted the Habsburgs. France then entered the conflict, beginning the final period of the Thirty Years' War. Sweden did not take part in the Peace of Prague, and it joined with France in continuing the war.

Attributions

Swedish-French Intervention

No longer able to tolerate the encirclement of two major Habsburg powers on its borders, Catholic France entered the Thirty Years' War on the side of the Protestants to counter the Habsburgs and bring the war to an end.

Learning Objective

- Identify the reasons why France was invested in the events of the Thirty Years' War

Key Points

- France, though Roman Catholic, was a rival of the Holy Roman Empire and Spain because they considered the Habsburgs too powerful since they held a number of territories on France's eastern border.

- Cardinal Richelieu, the chief minister of King Louis XIII of France, made the decision to enter into direct war against the Habsburgs in 1634, but France suffered military defeats early on, losing territory to the Holy Roman Empire.

- The tide of the war turned clearly toward France and against Spain in 1640, starting with the siege and capture of the fort at Arras.

- After the Peace of Prague, the Swedes reorganized the Royal Army and reentered the war, winning important battles against the imperial army.

- In 1648, the Swedes and the French defeated the imperial army at the Battle of Zusmarshausen, and the Spanish at Lens, and later won the Battle of Prague, which became the last action of the Thirty Years' War.

Terms

Vulgate Bible

A late 4th century Latin translation of the Bible that became, during the 16th century, the Catholic church's officially promulgated Latin version of the Bible.

Gustavus Adolphus

The king of Sweden from 1611 to 1632, who led Sweden to military supremacy during the Thirty Years' War, helping to determine the political as well as the religious balance of power in Europe.

France's Opposition to the Holy Roman Empire

France, though Roman Catholic, was a rival of the Holy Roman Empire and Spain. Cardinal Richelieu, the chief minister of King Louis XIII of France, considered the Habsburgs too powerful because they held a number of territories on France's eastern border, including portions of the Netherlands. Richelieu had already begun intervening indirectly in the war in January 1631, when the French diplomat Hercule de Charnacé signed the Treaty of Bärwalde with Gustavus Adolphus, by which France agreed to support the Swedes with 1,000,000 livres each year in return for a Swedish promise to maintain an army in Germany against the Habsburgs. The treaty also stipulated that Sweden would not conclude a peace with the Holy Roman Emperor without first receiving France's approval.

France Enters the War

After the Swedish rout at Nördlingen in September 1634 and the Peace of Prague in 1635, in which the Protestant German princes sued for peace with the German emperor, Sweden's ability to continue the war alone appeared doubtful, and Richelieu made the decision to enter into direct war against the Habsburgs. France declared war on Spain in May 1635, and on the Holy Roman Empire in August 1636, opening offensives against the Habsburgs in Germany and the Low Countries. France aligned its strategy with the allied Swedes in Wismar (1636) and Hamburg (1638).

Early French military efforts were met with disaster, and the Spanish counter-attacked, invading French territory. The imperial general Johann von Werth and Spanish commander Cardinal-Infante Ferdinand ravaged the French provinces of Champagne, Burgundy, and Picardy, and even threatened Paris in 1636. Then, the tide began to turn for the French. The Spanish army was repulsed by Bernhard of Saxe-Weimar. Bernhard's victory in the Battle of Compiègne pushed the Habsburg armies back towards the borders of France. Then widespread fighting ensued until 1640, with neither side gaining an advantage.

However, the war reached a climax and the tide of the war turned clearly toward France and against Spain in 1640, starting with the siege and capture of the fort at Arras. The French conquered Arras from the Spanish following a siege that lasted from June 16 to August 9, 1640. When Arras fell, the way was opened for the French to take all of Flanders. The ensuing French campaign against the Spanish forces in Flanders culminated with a decisive French victory at Rocroi in May 1643.

Continued Swedish War Efforts

After the Peace of Prague, the Swedes reorganized the Royal Army under Johan Banér and created a new one, the Army of the Weser, under the command of Alexander Leslie. The two army groups moved south in the spring of 1636, re-establishing alliances on the way, including a revitalized one with Wilhelm of Hesse-Kassel. The two Swedish armies combined and confronted the imperialists at the Battle of Wittstock. Despite the odds being stacked against them, the Swedish army won. This success largely reversed many of the effects of their defeat at Nördlingen, albeit not without creating some tensions between Banér and Leslie.

After the battle of Wittstock, the Swedish army regained the initiative in the German campaign. In the Second Battle of Breitenfeld, in 1642, outside Leipzig, the Swedish Field Marshal Lennart Torstenson defeated an army of the Holy Roman Empire led by Archduke Leopold Wilhelm of Austria and his deputy, Prince-General Ottavio Piccolomini, Duke of Amalfi. The imperial army suffered 20,000 casualties. In addition, the Swedish army took 5,000 prisoners and seized forty-six guns, at a cost to themselves of 4,000 killed or wounded. The battle enabled Sweden to occupy Saxony and impressed on Ferdinand III the need to include Sweden, and not only France, in any peace negotiations.

Final Battles

Over the next four years, fighting continued, but all sides began to prepare for ending the war. In 1648, the Swedes (commanded by Marshal Carl Gustaf Wrangel) and the French (led by Turenne and Condé) defeated the imperial army at the Battle of Zusmarshausen, and the Spanish at Lens. However, an imperial army led by Octavio Piccolomini managed to check the Franco-Swedish army in Bavaria, though their position remained fragile. The Battle of Prague in 1648 became the last action of the Thirty Years' War. The general Hans Christoff von Königsmarck, commanding Sweden's flying column, entered the city and captured Prague Castle (where the event that triggered the war—the Defenestration of Prague—had taken place thirty years before). There, they captured many valuable treasures, including the *Codex Gigas*, which contains the Vulgate Bible as well as many historical documents all written in Latin, and is still today preserved in Stockholm as the largest extant medieval manuscript in the world. However, they failed to conquer the right-bank part of Prague and the old city, which resisted until the end of the war. These results left only the imperial territories of Austria safely in Habsburg hands.

image

The Swedish siege of Prague in 1648

In 1648, the Swedish army entered Prague and captured Prague Castle, where the catalyst of the war, the Defenestration of Prague, had taken place thirty years before.

Attributions

The Peace of Westphalia

The Peace of Westphalia was a series of peace treaties signed between May and October 1648 in the Westphalian cities of Osnabrück and Münster that ended the Thirty Years' War.

Learning Objective

- Describe the terms of the Peace of Westphalia

Key Points

- The end of the Thirty Years' War was not brought about by one treaty, but instead by a group of treaties, collectively named the Peace of Westphalia.

- The treaties did not restore peace throughout Europe, but they did create a basis for national self-determination.

- Along with several territorial adjustments, the terms of the Peace of Westphalia included a return to the principles in the Peace of Augsburg of 1555, in which each prince would have the right to determine the religion of his own state.

- The treaty also extended that tolerance to allow the minority religion of the territory to practice freely.

- The Peace of Westphalia established important political precedents for state sovereignty, inter-state diplomacy, and balance of power in Europe.

Terms

Fief

An estate of land, especially one held on condition of feudal service.

Letters of Marque

A government license authorizing a person (known as a privateer) to attack and capture enemy vessels and bring them before admiralty courts for condemnation and sale.

Imperial Diet

The legislative body of the Holy Roman Empire, theoretically superior to the emperor himself.

Overview

Over a four-year period, the warring parties of the Thirty Years' War (the Holy Roman Empire, France, and Sweden) were actively negotiating at Osnabrück and Münster in Westphalia. The end of the war was not brought about by one treaty, but instead by a group of treaties, collectively named the Peace of Westphalia. The three treaties involved were the Peace of Münster (between the Dutch Republic and the Kingdom of Spain), the Treaty of Münster (between the Holy Roman Emperor and France and their respective allies), and the Treaty of Osnabrück (between the Holy Roman Empire and Sweden and their respective allies).

image

The Ratification of the Treaty of Münster, 1648

The Treaty of Münster between the Holy Roman Emperor and France was one of three treaties that made up the Peace of Westphalia.

Painting of a large group of men overlooking a table containing the Treaty of Münster.

These treaties ended both the Thirty Years' War (1618–1648) in the Holy Roman Empire and the Eighty Years' War (1568–1648) between Spain and the Dutch Republic, with Spain formally recognizing the independence of the Dutch Republic.

The peace negotiations involved a total of 109 delegations representing European powers, including Holy Roman Emperor Ferdinand III, Philip IV of Spain, the Kingdom of France, the Swedish Empire, the Dutch Republic, the princes of the Holy Roman Empire, and sovereigns of the free imperial cities.

The Terms of the Peace Settlement

Along with ending open warfare between the belligerents, the Peace of Westphalia established several important tenets and agreements:

- The power taken by Ferdinand III in contravention of the Holy Roman Empire's constitution was stripped and returned to the rulers of the Imperial States.

- All parties would recognize the Peace of Augsburg of 1555, in which each prince would have the right to determine the religion of his own state, the options being Catholicism, Lutheranism, and now Calvinism. This affirmed the principle of *cuius regio, eius religio* (Whose realm, his religion).

- Christians living in principalities where their denomination was not the established church were guaranteed the right to practice their faith in public during allotted hours and in private at their will.

- General recognition of the exclusive sovereignty of each party over its lands, people, and agents abroad, and responsibility for the warlike acts of any of its citizens or agents. Issuance of unrestricted letters of marque and reprisal to privateers was forbidden.

There were also several territorial adjustments brought about by the peace settlements. For example, the independence of Switzerland from the empire was formally recognized. France came out of the war in a far better position than any of the other participants. France retained the control of the Bishoprics of Metz, Toul, and Verdun near Lorraine, received the cities of the Décapole in Alsace and the city of Pignerol near the Spanish Duchy of Milan. Sweden received Western Pomerania, Wismar, and the Prince-Bishoprics of Bremen and Verden as hereditary fiefs, thus gaining a seat and vote in the Imperial Diet of the Holy Roman Empire. Barriers to trade and commerce erected during the war were also abolished, and a degree of free navigation was guaranteed on the Rhine.

image

The Holy Roman Empire in 1648

After the Peace of Westphalia, each prince of a given Imperial State would have the right to determine the religion of his own state, the options being Catholicism, Lutheranism, and Calvinism.

A map of the Holy Roman Empire in 1648, including all of the Imperial States.

Impact and Legacy

The treaty did not entirely end conflicts arising out of the Thirty Years' War. Fighting continued between France and Spain until the Treaty of the Pyrenees in 1659. Nevertheless, it did settle many outstanding European issues of the time. Some of the principles developed at Westphalia, especially those relating to respecting the boundaries of sovereign states and non-interference in their domestic affairs, became central to the world order that developed over the following centuries, and remain in effect today. Many of the imperial territories established in the Peace of Westphalia later became the sovereign nation-states of modern Europe.

The Peace of Westphalia established the precedent of peaces established by diplomatic congress, and a new system of political order in central Europe, later called Westphalian sovereignty, based upon the concept of co-existing sovereign states. Inter-state aggression was to be held in check by a balance of power. A norm was established against interference in another state's domestic affairs. As European influence spread across the globe, these Westphalian principles, especially the concept of sovereign states, became central to international law and to the prevailing world order.

image

Europe in 1648

A simplified map of Europe in 1648, showing the new borders established after the Peace of Westphalia.

Attributions

CC licensed content, Specific attribution

- Boundless World History. **Authored by**: Boundless. **Located at**: https://courses.lumenlearning.com/boundless-worldhistory/. **License**: *CC BY-SA: Attribution-ShareAlike*

12. The Rise of Nation-States

Introduction to Nation-States

Learning Objective

- Define a nation-state

Key Points

- The concept of a nation-state is notoriously difficult to define. A working and imprecise definition
  is: a type of state that conjoins the political entity of a state to the cultural entity of a nation, from which it aims to derive its political legitimacy to rule and potentially its status as a sovereign state.

- The origins and early history of nation-states are disputed. Two major theoretical questions have been debated. First, "Which came first, the nation or the nation-state?" Second, "Is nation-state a modern or an ancient idea?" Scholars continue to debate a number of possible hypotheses.

- Most commonly, the idea of a nation-state was and is associated with the rise of the modern system of states, often called the "Westphalian system" in reference to the Treaty of Westphalia (1648).

- Nation-states have their own characteristics that today may be taken-for-granted factors shaping a modern state, but that all developed in contrast to pre-national states.

- The most obvious impact of the nation-state is the creation of a uniform national culture through state policy. Its most demonstrative examples are national systems of compulsory primary education that usually popularize a common language and historical narratives.

Terms

declarative theory of statehood

A theory that defines a state as a person in international law if it meets the following criteria: 1) a defined territory; 2) a permanent population; 3) a government; and 4) a capacity to enter into relations with other states. According to it, an entity's statehood is independent of its recognition by other states.

constitutive theory of statehood

A theory that defines a state as a person in international law if, and only if, it is recognized as sovereign by other states. This theory of recognition was developed in the 19th century. Under it, a state was sovereign if another sovereign state recognized it as such.

Westphalian system

A global system based on the principle of international law that each state has sovereignty over its territory and domestic affairs, to the exclusion of all external powers, on the principle of non-interference in another country's domestic affairs, and that each state (no matter how large or small) is equal in international law. The doctrine is named after the Peace of Westphalia, signed in 1648, which ended the Thirty Years' War.

Nation-Station: Challenges of Definition

The concept of a nation-state is notoriously difficult to define. Anthony Smith, one of the most influential scholars of nation-states and nationalism, argued that a state is a nation-state only if and when a single ethnic and cultural population inhabits the boundaries of a state, and the boundaries of that state are coextensive with the boundaries of that ethnic and cultural population. This is a very narrow definition that presumes the existence of the "one nation, one state" model. Consequently, less than 10% of states in the world meet its criteria. The most obvious deviation from this largely ideal model is the presence of minorities, especially ethnic minorities, which ethnic and cultural nationalists exclude from the majority nation. The most illustrative historical examples of groups that have been specifically singled out as outsiders are the Roma and Jews in Europe. In legal terms, many nation-states today accept specific minorities as being part of the nation, which generally implies that members of minorities are citizens of a given nation-state and enjoy the same rights and liberties as members of the majority nation. However, nationalists and, consequently, symbolic narratives of the origins and history of nation-states often continue to exclude minorities from the nation-state and the nation.

According to a wider working definition, a nation-state is a type of state that conjoins the political entity of a state to the cultural entity of a nation, from which it aims to derive its political legitimacy to rule and potentially its status as a sovereign state if one accepts the declarative theory of statehood as opposed to the constitutive theory. A state is specifically a political and geopolitical entity, while a nation is a cultural and ethnic one. The term "nation-state" implies that the two coincide, in that a state has chosen to adopt and endorse a specific cultural group as associated with it. The concept of a nation-state can be compared and contrasted with that of the multinational state, city-state, empire, confederation, and other state formations with which it may overlap. The key distinction is the identification of a people with a polity in the nation-state.

Origins

The origins and early history of nation-states are disputed. Two major theoretical questions have been debated. First, "Which came first, the nation or the nation-state?" Second, "Is nation-state a modern or an ancient idea?" Some scholars have advanced the hypothesis that the nation-state was an inadvertent byproduct of 15th century intellectual discoveries in political economy, capitalism, mercantilism, political geography, and geography combined together with cartography and advances in map-making technologies. For others, the nation existed first, then nationalist movements arose for sovereignty, and the nation-state was created to meet that demand. Some "modernization theories" of nationalism see it as a product of government policies to unify and modernize an already existing state. Most theories see the nation-state as a modern European phenomenon, facilitated by developments such as state-mandated education, mass literacy, and mass media (including print). However, others look for the roots of nation-states in ancient times.

Most commonly, the idea of a nation-state was and is associated with the rise of the modern system of states, often called the "Westphalian system" in reference to the Treaty of Westphalia (1648). The balance of power that characterized that system depended on its effectiveness upon clearly defined, centrally controlled, independent entities, whether empires or nation-states, that recognized each other's sovereignty and territory. The Westphalian system did not create the nation-state, but the nation-state meets the criteria for its component states.

European boundaries set by the Congress of Vienna, 1815. This map of Europe, outlining borders in 1815, demonstrates that still at the beginning of the 19th century, Europe was divided mostly into empires, kingdoms, and confederations. Hardly any of the entities on the map would meet the criteria of the nation-state.

Characteristics

Nation-states have their own characteristics that today may be taken-for-granted factors shaping a modern state, but that all developed in contrast to pre-national states. Their territory is considered semi-sacred and nontransferable. Nation-states use the state as an instrument of national unity, in economic, social, and cultural life. Nation-states typically have a more centralized and uniform public administration than their imperial predecessors because they are smaller and less diverse. After the 19th-century triumph of the nation-state in Europe, regional identity was usually subordinate to national identity. In many cases, the regional administration was also subordinate to central (national) government. This process has been partially reversed from the 1970s onward, with the introduction of various forms of regional autonomy in formerly centralized states (e.g., France).

The most obvious impact of the nation-state, as compared to its non-national predecessors, is the creation of a uniform national culture through state policy. The model of the nation-state implies that its population constitutes a nation, united by a common descent, a common language, and many forms of shared culture. When the implied unity was absent, the nation-state often tried to create it. The creation of national systems of compulsory primary education is usually linked with the popularization of nationalist narratives. Even today, primary and secondary schools around the world often teach a mythologized version of national history.

Bacon's standard map of Europe, 1923. While some European nation-states emerged throughout the 19th century, the end of World War I meant the end of empires on the continent. They all broke down into a number of smaller states. However, not until the tragedy of World War II and the post-war shifts of borders and population resettlement did many European states become more ethnically and culturally homogeneous and thus closer to the ideal nation-state.

Sources

Attributions

CC licensed content, Specific attribution

The Peace of Westphalia and Sovereignty

Learning Objective

- Explain the significance of the Peace of Westphalia on European politics and diplomacy.

Key Points

- The Peace of Westphalia was a series of peace treaties signed between May and October 1648 in the Westphalian cities of Osnabrück and Münster. The treaties ended the Thirty Years' War and the Eighty Years' War.

- The Thirty Years' War was a series of wars in Central Europe between 1618 and 1648. Initially a war between various Protestant and Catholic states in the fragmented Holy Roman Empire, it developed into a conflict involving most of the great powers.

- The Eighty Years' War, or Dutch War of Independence (1568–1648), was a revolt of the Seventeen Provinces against the political and religious hegemony of Philip II of Spain, the sovereign of the Habsburg Netherlands.

- According to the Peace of Westphalia, all parties would recognize the Peace of Augsburg of 1555; Christians of non-dominant denominations were guaranteed the right to practice their faith; and the exclusive sovereignty of each party over its lands, people, and agents abroad was recognized.
Multiple territorial adjustments were also decided.

- The Peace of Westphalia established the precedent of peace reached by diplomatic congress and a new system of political order in Europe based upon the concept of co-existing sovereign states. The Westphalian principle of the recognition of another state's sovereignty and right to decide its own fate rests at the foundations of international law today.

- The European colonization of Asia and Africa in the 19th century and two global wars in the 20th century dramatically undermined the principles established in Westphalia.

Terms

cuius regio, eius religio

A Latin phrase that literally means "Whose realm, his religion," meaning that the religion of the ruler was to dictate the religion of those ruled. At the Peace of Augsburg of 1555 the rulers of the German-speaking states and Charles V, the emperor, agreed to accept this principle.

The Eighty Years' War

A revolt, known also as the Dutch War of Independence (1568–1648), of the Seventeen Provinces against the political and religious hegemony of Philip II of Spain, the sovereign of the Habsburg Netherlands.

The Thirty Years' War

A series of wars in Central Europe between 1618 and 1648. Initially a war between various Protestant and Catholic states in the fragmented Holy Roman Empire, it gradually developed into a more general conflict involving most of the great powers.

The Peace of Westphalia

A series of peace treaties signed between May and October 1648 in the Westphalian cities of Osnabrück and Münster. The treaties ended the Thirty Years' War (1618–1648) in the Holy Roman Empire and the Eighty Years' War (1568–1648) between Spain and the Dutch Republic, with Spain formally recognizing the independence of the Dutch Republic.

Westphalian sovereignty

The principle of international law that each nation-state has sovereignty over its territory and domestic affairs, to the exclusion of all external powers, on the principle of non-interference in another country's domestic affairs, and that each state (no matter how large or small) is equal in international law. The doctrine is named after the Peace of Westphalia, signed in 1648.

Peace of Augsburg of 1555

A treaty between Charles V and the forces of the Schmalkaldic League, an alliance of Lutheran princes, on September 25, 1555, at the imperial city of Augsburg, in present-day Bavaria, Germany. It officially ended the religious struggle between the two groups and made the legal division of Christendom permanent within the Holy Roman Empire.

Introduction

The Peace of Westphalia was a series of peace treaties signed between May and October 1648 in the Westphalian cities of Osnabrück and Münster. The treaties ended the Thirty Years' War (1618–1648) in the Holy Roman Empire and the Eighty Years' War (1568–1648) between Spain and the Dutch Republic, with Spain formally recognizing the independence of the Dutch Republic. The peace negotiations involved a total of 109 delegations representing European powers. The treaties did not restore peace throughout Europe, but they did create a basis for national self-determination.

Background: Wars in Europe

Two destructive wars were the major triggers behind signing the eventual Peace of Westphalia: the Thirty Years' War in the Holy Roman Empire and the Eighty Years' War between Spain and the Dutch Republic.

The Thirty Years' War was a series of wars in Central Europe between 1618 and 1648. Initially a war between various Protestant and Catholic states in the fragmented Holy Roman Empire, it gradually developed into a more general conflict involving most of the great powers. The war began when the newly elected Holy Roman Emperor, Ferdinand II, tried to impose religious uniformity on his domains, forcing Roman Catholicism on its peoples. The northern Protestant states, angered by the violation of their rights to choose granted in the Peace of Augsburg, banded together to form the Protestant Union. These events caused widespread fears throughout northern and Central Europe, and triggered the Protestant Bohemians living in the dominion of Habsburg Austria to revolt against their nominal ruler, Ferdinand II. They ousted the Habsburgs and instead elected Frederick V, Elector of Palatinate, as their monarch. Frederick took the offer without the support of the union. The southern states, mainly Roman Catholic, were angered by this. Led by Bavaria, these states formed the Catholic League to expel Frederick in support of the emperor.

The war became less about religion and more of a continuation of the France–Habsburg rivalry for European political preeminence. Sweden, a major military power in the day, intervened in 1630 under the great general Gustavus Adolphus and started the full-scale great war on the continent. Spain, wishing to finally crush the Dutch rebels in the Netherlands and the Dutch Republic, intervened under the pretext of helping their dynastic Habsburg ally, Austria. No longer able to tolerate the encirclement of two major Habsburg powers on its borders, Catholic France entered the coalition on the side of the Protestants to counter the Habsburgs.

The Thirty Years' War devastated entire regions, with famine and disease significantly decreasing the populations of the German and Italian states, the Crown of Bohemia, and the Southern Netherlands. The war altered the previous political order of European powers. The rise of Bourbon France, the curtailing of Habsburg ambition, and the ascendancy of Sweden as a great power created a new balance of power on the continent, with France emerging from the war strengthened and increasingly dominant in the latter part of the 17th century.

The Eighty Years' War or Dutch War of Independence (1568–1648) was a revolt of the Seventeen Provinces against the political and religious hegemony of Philip II of Spain, the sovereign of the Habsburg Netherlands. After the initial stages, Philip II deployed his armies and regained control over most of the rebelling provinces. However, under the leadership of the exiled William the Silent, the northern provinces continued their resistance. They were eventually able to oust the Habsburg armies, and in 1581 they established the Republic of the Seven United Netherlands. The war continued in other areas, although the heartland of the republic was no longer threatened. After a twelve-year truce, hostilities broke out again around 1619, which coincided with the Thirty Years' War.

The Peace of Westphalia

Since Lutheran Sweden preferred Osnabrück as a conference venue, its peace negotiations with the Holy Roman Empire, including the allies of both sides, took place in Osnabrück. The empire and its opponent France, including the allies of each, as well as the Republic of the Seven United Netherlands and its opponent Spain (and their respective allies), negotiated in Münster. The peace negotiations had no exact beginning and ending, because the participating total of 109 delegations never met in a plenary session, but arrived between 1643 and 1646 and left between 1647 and 1649.

According to the Peace of Westphalia, all parties would recognize the Peace of Augsburg of 1555, in which each prince would have the right to determine the religion of his own state (the principle of *cuius regio, eius religio*). Christians living in principalities where their denomination was *not* the established church were guaranteed the right to practice their faith in public during allotted hours and in private at their will. The delegates also recognized the exclusive sovereignty of each party over its lands, people, and agents abroad, and responsibility for the warlike acts of any of its citizens or agents.

Multiple territorial adjustments were also decided. Among the most important ones was the recognition of the independence of Switzerland from the Holy Roman Empire and the expansion of the territories of France, Sweden, and Brandenburg-Prussia (later Prussia). The independence of the city of Bremen was clarified. Also, barriers to trade and commerce erected during the war were abolished, and "a degree" of free navigation was guaranteed on the Rhine.

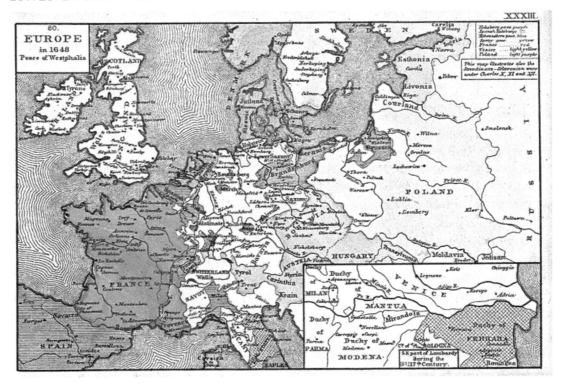

Historical map of Europe after the Peace of Westphalia. From "An Historical Atlas Containing a Chronological Series of One Hundred and Four Maps, at Successive Periods, from the Dawn of History to the Present Day" by Robert H. Labberton, 1884. The map shows the possessions of the two branches of the house of Habsburg [purple]; the possessions of the house of Hohenzollern (union of Prussia with Brandenburg) [blue]; the Swedish empire on both shores of the Baltic and in northern Germany; the Danish monarchy, Denmark, Norway, and Scania; the British isles, with the battlefields of the civil wars; France, with the battlefields of the civil wars [red]; Germany with the battlefields of the Thirty Years' War; the republic of Poland at its greatest extent; the western boundary of Russia.

Legacy

The Peace of Westphalia established the precedent of peace reached by diplomatic congress and a new system of political order in Europe based upon the concept of co-existing sovereign states. Inter-state aggression was to be held in check by a balance of power. A norm was established against interference in another state's domestic affairs, known as the principle of Westphalian sovereignty. This principle of international law presumes that each state has sovereignty over its territory and domestic affairs, to the exclusion of all external powers, on the principle of non-interference in another country's domestic affairs, and that each state (no matter how large or small) is equal in international law. As European influence spread across the globe, these Westphalian principles, especially the concept of sovereign states, became central to international law and to the prevailing world order. However, the European colonization of Asia and Africa in the 19th century and two global wars in the 20th century dramatically undermined the principles established in Westphalia.

After the fall of the Soviet Union, power was seen as unipolar with the United States in absolute control, though nuclear proliferation and the rise of Japan, the European Union, the Middle East, China, and a resurgent Russia have begun to recreate a multipolar political environment. Instead of a traditional balance of power, inter-state aggression may now be checked by the preponderance of power, a sharp contrast to the Westphalian principle.

The Ratification of the Treaty of Münster, 15 May 1648 (1648) by Gerard ter Borch. Two cities, Osnabrück and Münster, were chosen to host the peace talks based on religious divisions between the participating delegations.

Sources

Attributions

CC licensed content, Specific attribution

- Boundless World History. **Authored by**: Boundless. **Located at**: https://courses.lumenlearning.com/boundless-worldhistory/. **License**: *CC BY-SA: Attribution-ShareAlike*

The Reconquista

Learning Objective

- Explain how the Reconquista led to Spain's increasing commitment to Catholicism

Key Points

- The Reconquista is a period in the history of the Iberian Peninsula, spanning approximately 770 years, between the initial Umayyad conquest of Hispania in the 710s and the fall of the Emirate of Granada, the last Islamic state on the peninsula, to expanding Christian kingdoms in 1492.

- By 718 the Muslims were in control of nearly the whole Iberian Peninsula. The advance into Western Europe was only stopped in what is now north-central France by the West Germanic Franks at the Battle of Tours in 732.

- The Kingdom of Asturias became the main base for Christian resistance to Islamic rule in the Iberian Peninsula for several centuries. Medieval Spain was the scene of almost constant warfare between Muslims and Christians.

- By 1250, nearly all of Iberia was back under Christian rule, with the exception of the Muslim kingdom of Granada—the only independent Muslim realm in Spain that would last until 1492.

- Around 1480, Catholic Monarchs Ferdinand II of Aragon and Isabella I of Castile (known as the Catholic Monarchs) established what would be known as the Spanish Inquisition. It was intended to maintain Catholic orthodoxy in their kingdoms.

- In the aftermath of the Reconquista and the Inquisition, Catholicism dominated the politics, social relations, and culture of Spain, shaping Spain as a state and the Spanish as a nation.

Terms

Alhambra Decree

An edict issued on March 31, 1492, by the joint Catholic Monarchs of Spain (Isabella I of Castile and Ferdinand II of Aragon) ordering the expulsion of practicing Jews from the Kingdoms of Castile and Aragon and its territories and possessions by July 31 of that year.

Battle of Covadonga

The first victory by a Christian military force in Iberia following the Islamic conquest of Visigothic Hispania in 711–718. It was fought most likely in 722. The battle was followed by the creation of an independent Christian principality in the mountains of Asturias that became a bastion of Christian resistance to the expansion of Muslim rule. It was from there that the return of Christian rule to the entire Iberian peninsula began.

Visigothic Kingdom

A kingdom that occupied what is now southwestern France and the Iberian Peninsula from the 5th century to the 8th century. One of the Germanic successor states to the Western Roman Empire, the kingdom maintained independence from the Eastern Roman, or Byzantine, Empire. During its existence, Catholicism coalesced in Spain.

Kingdom of Asturias

A kingdom in the Iberian Peninsula founded in 718 by the nobleman Pelagius of Asturias. In 718 or 722, Pelagius defeated an Umayyad patrol at the Battle of Covadonga, in what is usually regarded as the beginning of the Reconquista. It transitioned to the Kingdom of León in 924 and became the main base for Christian resistance to Islamic rule in the Iberian Peninsula for several centuries.

the Catholic Monarchs

The joint title used in history for Queen Isabella I of Castile and King Ferdinand II of Aragon. They were both from the House of Trastámara and were second cousins, both descended from John I of Castile; on marriage they were given a papal dispensation to deal with consanguinity by Sixtus IV. They established the Spanish Inquisition around 1480.

Arianism

A Christian belief that asserts that Jesus Christ is the Son of God who was created by God the Father at a point in time, is distinct from the Father, and is therefore subordinate to the Father. Arian teachings were first attributed to Arius (c. 250–336 CE), a Christian presbyter in Alexandria, Egypt. They gained popularity in the Iberian Peninsula before Catholicism became the predominant religion of the region.

Background

The Reconquista ("reconquest") is a period in the history of the Iberian Peninsula, spanning approximately 770 years, between the initial Umayyad conquest of Hispania in the 710s and the fall of the Emirate of Granada, the last Islamic state on the peninsula, to expanding Christian kingdoms in 1492. Historians traditionally mark the beginning of the Reconquista with the Battle of Covadonga (most likely in 722), and its end is associated with Portuguese and Spanish colonization of the Americas.

The Arab Islamic conquest had dominated most of North Africa by 710 CE. In 711 an Islamic Berber raiding party, led by Tariq ibn Ziyad, was sent to Iberia to intervene in a civil war in the Visigothic Kingdom. Tariq's army crossed the Strait of Gibraltar and won a decisive victory in the summer of 711 when the Visigothic King Roderic was defeated and killed at the Battle of Guadalete. Tariq's commander, Musa, quickly crossed with Arab reinforcements, and by 718 the Muslims were in control of nearly the whole Iberian Peninsula. The advance into Western Europe was only stopped in what is now north-central France by the West Germanic Franks at the Battle of Tours in 732.

A decisive victory for the Christians took place at Covadonga, in the north of the Iberian Peninsula, in the summer of 722. In a minor battle known as the Battle of Covadonga, a Muslim force sent to put down the Christian rebels in the northern mountains was defeated by Pelagius of Asturias, who established the monarchy of the Christian Kingdom of Asturias. In 739, a rebellion in Galicia, assisted by the Asturians, drove out Muslim forces, and it joined the Asturian kingdom. The Kingdom of Asturias became the main base for Christian resistance to Islamic rule in the Iberian Peninsula for several centuries.

Warfare between Muslims and Christians

Muslim interest in the peninsula returned in force around when Al-Mansur sacked Barcelona in 985. Under his son, other Christian cities were subjected to numerous raids. After his son's death, the caliphate plunged into a civil war and splintered into the so-called "Taifa Kingdoms." Medieval Spain was the scene of almost constant warfare between Muslims and Christians. The Almohads, who had taken control of the Almoravids' Maghribi and al-Andalus territories by 1147, surpassed the Almoravides in fundamentalist Islamic outlook, and they treated the non-believer *dhimmis* harshly. Faced with the choice of death, conversion, or emigration, many Jews and Christians left.

The Taifa kingdoms lost ground to the Christian realms in the north. After the loss of Toledo in 1085, the Muslim rulers reluctantly invited the Almoravides, who invaded Al-Andalus from North Africa and established an empire. In the 12th century the Almoravid empire broke up again, only to be taken over by the invasion of the Almohads, who were defeated by an alliance of the Christian kingdoms in the decisive battle of Las Navas de Tolosa in 1212. By 1250, nearly all of Iberia was back under Christian rule, with the exception of the Muslim kingdom of Granada—the only independent Muslim realm in Spain that would last until 1492.

Francisco Pradilla Ortiz, The Capitulation of Granada (1882). The Capitulation of Granada shows Muhammad XII confronting Ferdinand and Isabella.

Despite the decline in Muslim-controlled kingdoms, it is important to note the lasting effects exerted on the peninsula by Muslims in technology, culture, and society.

Spanish Inquisition

Around 1480, Ferdinand II of Aragon and Isabella I of Castile, known as the Catholic Monarchs, established what would be known as the Spanish Inquisition. It was intended to maintain Catholic orthodoxy in their kingdoms and to replace the Medieval Inquisition, which was under Papal control. It covered Spain and all the Spanish colonies and territories, which included the Canary Islands, the Spanish Netherlands, the Kingdom of Naples, and all Spanish possessions in North, Central, and South America.

People who converted to Catholicism were not subject to expulsion, but between 1480 and 1492 hundreds of those who had converted (*conversos* and *moriscos*) were accused of secretly practicing their original religion (crypto-Judaism or crypto-Islam) and arrested, imprisoned, interrogated under torture, and in some cases burned to death, in both Castile and Aragon. In 1492 Ferdinand and Isabella ordered segregation of communities to create closed quarters that became what were later called "ghettos." They also furthered economic pressures upon Jews and other non-Christians by increasing taxes and social restrictions. In 1492 the monarchs issued a decree of expulsion of Jews, known formally as the Alhambra Decree, which gave Jews in Spain four months to either convert to Catholicism or leave Spain. Tens of thousands of Jews emigrated to other lands such as Portugal, North Africa, the Low Countries, Italy, and the Ottoman Empire. Later in 1492, Ferdinand issued a letter addressed to the Jews who had left Castile and Aragon, inviting them back to Spain if they had become Christians. The Inquisition was not definitively abolished until 1834, during the reign of Isabella II, after a period of declining influence in the preceding century.

Most of the descendants of the Muslims who submitted to conversion to Christianity rather than exile during the early periods of the Spanish and Portuguese Inquisition, the Moriscos, were later expelled from Spain after serious social upheaval, when the Inquisition was at its height. The expulsions were carried out more severely in eastern Spain (Valencia and Aragon) due to local animosity towards Muslims and Moriscos perceived as economic rivals; local workers saw them as cheap labor undermining their bargaining position with the landlords. Those that the Spanish Inquisition found to be secretly practicing Islam or Judaism were executed, imprisoned, or expelled. Nevertheless, all those deemed to be "New Christians" were perpetually suspected of various crimes against the Spanish state, including continued practice of Islam or Judaism.

The Inquisition Tribunal as illustrated by Francisco de Goya (1808/1812).

Catholicism

Although the period of rule by the Visigothic Kingdom (c. 5th–8th centuries) saw the brief spread of Arianism, Catholic religion coalesced in Spain at the time. The Councils of Toledo debated creed and liturgy in orthodox Catholicism, and the Council of Lerida in 546 constrained the clergy and extended the power of law over them under the blessings of Rome. In 587, the Visigothic king at Toledo, Reccared, converted to Catholicism and launched a movement in Spain to unify the various religious doctrines that existed in the land. This put an end to dissension on the question of Arianism. The period of Reconquista and the Spanish Inquisition that followed turned Catholicism into the dominant religion of Spain, which has shaped the development of the Spanish state and national identity.

Sources

Attributions

CC licensed content, Specific attribution

• Boundless World History. **Authored by**: Boundless. **Located at**: https://courses.lumenlearning.com/boundless-worldhistory/.

The Spanish Habsburgs

Learning Objective

- Explain why the Spanish Habsburgs grew increasingly feeble as a family

Key Points

- Spain was ruled by the major branch of the Habsburg dynasty over the 16th and 17th centuries. In this period, it dominated Europe politically and militarily, but experienced a gradual decline of influence in the second half of the 17th century under the later Habsburg kings.

- When Spain's first Habsburg ruler, Charles I, became king of Spain in 1516, Spain became central to the dynastic struggles of Europe. Under Charles I, Spain colonized big parts of the Americas and established itself as the first modern global empire.

- Under Philip II, the Spanish empire included territories on every continent then known to Europeans. During his reign, Spain reached the height of its influence and power.

- Under Philip III, a ten-year truce with the Dutch was overshadowed in 1618 by Spain's involvement in the European-wide Thirty Years' War. Additionally, paying for the budget deficits by the mass minting of currency caused an enormous economic crisis.

- Under Philip IV, much of the policy was conducted by the minister Gaspar de Guzmán. Portugal was lost to the crown for good; in Italy and most of Catalonia, French forces were expelled and Catalonia's independence was suppressed.

- Charles' II mental and physical disabilities, caused most likely by the generations of inbreeding among the Spanish Habsburgs, enabled power games on the court and meant that Spain was essentially left leaderless and gradually reduced to a second-rank power.

Terms

Spanish Armada

A Spanish fleet of 130 ships that sailed from A Coruña in August 1588 with the purpose of escorting an army from Flanders to invade England. The strategic aim was to overthrow Queen Elizabeth I of England and the Tudor establishment of Protestantism in England.

consanguinity

The property of being from the same kinship as another person. In that aspect, consanguinity is the quality of being descended from the same ancestor as another person. The laws of many jurisdictions set out degrees of consanguinity in relation to prohibited sexual relations and marriage parties.

Spanish Golden Age

A period of flourishing in arts and literature in Spain, coinciding with the political rise and decline of the Spanish Habsburg dynasty. It does not imply precise dates and is usually considered to have lasted longer than an actual century.

Spain under the Habsburgs

Spain was ruled by the major branch of the Habsburg dynasty over the 16th and 17th centuries. In this period, "Spain" or "the Spains" covered the entire peninsula, politically a confederacy comprising several nominally independent kingdoms in personal union: Aragon, Castile, León, Navarre and, from 1580, Portugal. At the time, the term "Monarchia Catholica" (Catholic Monarchy) remained in use for the monarchy under the Spanish Habsburgs. However, Spain as a unified state came into being by right only after the death of Charles II in 1700, the last ruler of Spain of the Habsburg dynasty.

Under the Habsburgs, Spain dominated Europe politically and militarily, but experienced a gradual decline of influence in the second half of the 17th century under the later Habsburg kings. The Habsburg years were also a Spanish Golden Age of cultural efflorescence.

The Global Power

When Spain's first Habsburg ruler, Charles I, became king of Spain in 1516, Spain became central to the dynastic struggles of Europe. After becoming king of Spain, Charles also became Charles V, Holy Roman Emperor, and because of his widely scattered domains was not often in Spain. As he approached the end of his life he made provision for the division of the Habsburg inheritance into two parts. On the one hand was Spain, its possessions in Europe, North Africa, the Americas, and the Netherlands. On the other hand there was the Holy Roman Empire. This was to create enormous difficulties for his son Philip II of Spain.

The Aztec and Inca Empires were conquered during Charles's reign, from 1519 to 1521 and 1540 to 1558, respectively. Spanish settlements were established in the New World: Mexico City, the most important colonial city established in 1524 to be the primary center of administration in the New World; Florida, colonized in the 1560s; Buenos Aires, established in 1536; and New Granada (modern Colombia), colonized in the 1530s. The Spanish Empire abroad became the source of Spanish wealth and power in Europe. But as precious metal shipments rapidly expanded late in the century this contributed to the general inflation that was affecting the whole of Europe. Instead of fueling the Spanish economy, American silver made the country increasingly dependent on foreign sources of raw materials and manufactured goods.

Philip II became king on Charles I's abdication in 1556. During his reign, there were several separate state bankruptcies, which were partly the cause for the declaration of independence that created the Dutch Republic in 1581. A devout Catholic, Philip organized a huge naval expedition against Protestant England in 1588, known usually as the Spanish Armada, which was unsuccessful, mostly due to storms and grave logistical problems. Despite these problems, the growing inflow of New World silver from the mid-16th century, the justified military reputation of the Spanish infantry, and even the quick recovery of the navy from its Armada disaster made Spain the leading European power, a novel situation of which its citizens were only just becoming aware. The Iberian Union with Portugal in 1580 not only unified the peninsula, but added that country's worldwide resources to the Spanish crown.

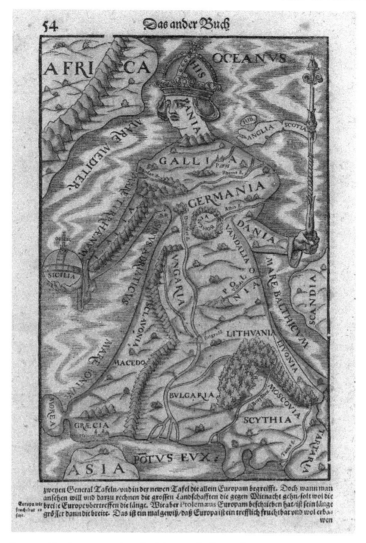

Europa Regina, associated with a Habsburg-dominated Europe under Holy Roman Emperor Charles V of Habsburg (Charles I of Spain). Map of Europe as a queen, printed by Sebastian Munster in Basel in 1570. Europe is shown standing upright with the Iberian Peninsula forming her crowned head.

The Gradual Decline

However, economic and administrative problems multiplied in Castile, and the weakness of the native economy became evident in the following century. Rising inflation, financially draining wars in Europe, the ongoing aftermath of the expulsion of the Jews and Moors from Spain, and Spain's growing dependency on the gold and silver imports combined to cause several bankruptcies that caused an economic crisis in the country, especially in heavily burdened Castile.

Faced with wars against England, France, and the Netherlands, the Spanish government found that neither the New World silver nor steadily increasing taxes were enough to cover their expenses, and went bankrupt again in 1596. Furthermore, the great plague of 1596–1602 killed 600,000 to 700,000 people, or about 10%

of the population. Altogether more than 1,250,000 deaths resulted from the extreme incidence of plague in 17th century Spain. Economically, the plague destroyed the labor force, and created a psychological blow to an already problematic Spain.

Philip II died in 1598, and was succeeded by his son Philip III. In his reign (1598–1621) a ten-year truce with the Dutch was overshadowed in 1618 by Spain's involvement in the European-wide Thirty Years' War. Philip III had no interest in politics or government, preferring to engage in lavish court festivities, religious indulgences, and the theater. His government resorted to a tactic that had been resolutely resisted by Philip II, paying for the budget deficits by the mass minting of increasingly worthless vellones (the currency), causing inflation. In 1607, the government faced another bankruptcy.

Philip III was succeeded in 1621 by his son Philip IV of Spain (reigned 1621–1665). Much of the policy was conducted by the minister Gaspar de Guzmán, Count-Duke of Olivares. In 1640, with the war in Central Europe having no clear winner except the French, both Portugal and Catalonia rebelled. Portugal was lost to the crown for good; in Italy and most of Catalonia, French forces were expelled and Catalonia's independence was suppressed.

Charles II (1665–1700), the last of the Habsburgs in Spain, was three years old when his father, Philip IV, died in 1665. The Council of Castile appointed Philip's second wife and Charles's mother, Mariana of Austria, regent for the minor king. As regent, Mariana managed the country's affairs through a series of favorites ("validos"), whose merits usually amounted to no more than meeting her fancy. Spain was essentially left leaderless and was gradually being reduced to a second-rank power.

Inbreeding

The Spanish branch of the Habsburg royal family was noted for extreme consanguinity. Well aware that they owed their power to fortunate marriages, they married between themselves to protect their gains. Charles's father and his mother, Mariana, were actually uncle and niece. Charles was physically and mentally disabled and infertile, possibly in consequence of this massive inbreeding. Due to the deaths of his half brothers, he was the last member of the male Spanish Habsburg line. He did not learn to speak until the age of four nor to walk until the age of eight, and was treated as virtually an infant until he was ten years old. His jaw was so badly deformed (an extreme example of the so-called Habsburg jaw) that he could barely speak or chew. Fearing the frail child would be overtaxed, his caretakers did not force Charles to attend school.

The Habsburg dynasty became extinct in Spain with Charles II's death in 1700, and the War of the Spanish Succession ensued, in which the other European powers tried to assume power over the Spanish monarchy. The control of Spain was allowed to pass to the Bourbon dynasty.

Sources

Attributions

Philip II and the Spanish Armada

Learning Objective

- Describe Philip II's convictions and how he attempted to carry them out

Key Points

- During the reign of Philip II, Spain reached the height of its influence and power, and remained firmly Roman Catholic. Philip saw himself as a champion of Catholicism, both against the Muslim Ottoman Empire and the Protestants.

- As the Spanish Empire was not a single monarchy with one legal system but a federation of separate realms, Philip often found his authority overruled by local assemblies, and his word less effective than that of local lords.

- When Philip's health began failing, he worked from his quarters in the Palace-Monastery-Pantheon of El Escorial, which he built with Juan Batista de Toledo and which was another expression of Philip's commitments to protect Catholics against the raising influence of Protestantism across Europe.

- Philip's foreign policies were determined by a combination of Catholic fervor and dynastic objectives. He considered himself the chief defender of Catholic Europe, both against the Ottoman Turks and against the forces of the Protestant Reformation.

- Wars with Dutch Provinces, England, France, and the Ottoman Empire all had the under-mining religious aspects of protecting Catholicism in increasingly Protestant Europe or protecting Christianity against Islam.

- Because Philip II was the most powerful European monarch in an era of war and religious conflict, evaluating both his reign and the man himself has become a controversial historical subject.

Terms

Morisco

A term used to refer to former Muslims who converted, or were coerced into converting, to Christianity after Spain outlawed the open practice of Islam by its Mudejar population in the early 16th century. The group was subject to systematic expulsions from Spain's various kingdoms between 1609 and 1614, the most severe of which occurred in the eastern Kingdom of Valencia.

Eighty Years' War

A revolt, known also as the Dutch War of Independence (1568–1648), of the Seventeen Provinces against the political and religious hegemony of Philip II of Spain, the sovereign of the Habsburg Netherlands.

Spanish Armada

A Spanish fleet of 130 ships that sailed from A Coruña in August 1588 with the purpose of escorting an army from Flanders to invade England. The strategic aim was to overthrow Queen Elizabeth I of England and the Tudor establishment of Protestantism in England.

Catholic League

A major participant in the French Wars of Religion, formed by Henry I, Duke of Guise, in 1576. It intended the eradication of Protestants—also known as Calvinists or Huguenots—out of Catholic France during the Protestant Reformation, as well as the replacement of King Henry III. Pope Sixtus V, Philip II of Spain, and the Jesuits were all supporters of this Catholic party.

jure uxoris

A Latin term that means "by right of (his) wife." It is most commonly used to refer to a title of nobility held by a man because his wife holds it *suo jure* ("in her own right"). Similarly, the husband of an heiress could become the legal possessor of her lands *jure uxoris*, "by right of [his] wife." *Jure uxoris* monarchs are not to be confused with kings consort, who were merely consorts of their wives, not co-rulers.

Philip II of Spain

The son of Charles V of the Holy Roman Empire and his wife, Infanta Isabella of Portugal, Philip II of Spain was born in 1527. Known in Spain as "Philip the Prudent," his empire included territories on every continent then known to Europeans, including his namesake the Philippine Islands. During his reign, Spain reached the height of its influence and power, and remained firmly Roman Catholic. Philip saw himself as a champion of Catholicism, both against the Muslim Ottoman Empire and the Protestants. He was the king of Spain from
1556 to 1598.

Philip was married four times and had children with three of his wives. All the marriages had important political implications, as they connected Philip, and thus Spain, with powerful European courts. Philip's first wife was his first cousin Maria Manuela, Princess of Portugal. She was a daughter of Philip's maternal uncle, John III of Portugal, and paternal aunt, Catherine of Austria. Philip's second wife was his first cousin once removed Queen Mary I of England. By this marriage, Philip became *jure uxoris* king of England and Ireland, although the couple was apart more than together as they ruled their respective countries. The marriage produced no children and Mary died in 1558, ending Philip's reign in England and Ireland. Philip's third wife was Elisabeth of Valois, the eldest daughter of Henry II of France and Catherine de' Medici. Philip's fourth and final wife was his niece Anna of Austria.

Domestic Affairs

The Spanish Empire was not a single monarchy with one legal system but a federation of separate realms, each jealously guarding its own rights against those of the House of Habsburg. In practice, Philip often found his authority overruled by local assemblies and his word less effective than that of local lords. He also grappled with the problem of the large Morisco population in Spain, who were forcibly converted to Christianity by his predecessors. In 1569, the Morisco Revolt broke out in the southern province of Granada in defiance of attempts to suppress Moorish customs, and Philip ordered the expulsion of the Moriscos from Granada and their dispersal to other provinces.

Despite its immense dominions, Spain was a country with a sparse population that yielded a limited income to the crown (in contrast to France, for example, which was much more heavily populated). Philip faced major difficulties in raising taxes, the collection of which was largely farmed out to local lords. He was able to finance his military campaigns only by taxing and exploiting the local resources of his empire. The flow of income from the New World proved vital to his militant foreign policy, but nonetheless his exchequer faced bankruptcy several times.
During Philip's reign there were five separate state bankruptcies.

Whereas his father had been forced to an itinerant rule as a medieval king, Philip ruled at a critical turning point toward modernity in European history. He mainly directed state affairs, even when not at court. Indeed, when his health began failing he worked from his quarters in the Palace-Monastery-Pantheon of El Escorial he had built. El Escariol was another expression of Philip's commitment to protect Catholics against the raising influence of Protestantism across Europe. He engaged the Spanish architect Juan Bautista de Toledo to be his collaborator. Together they designed El Escorial as a monument to Spain's role as a center of the Christian world.

Turismo Madrid Consorcio Turístico, Madrid, Spain. A distant view of the Royal Seat of San Lorenzo de El Escorial. In 1984, UNESCO declared The Royal Seat of San Lorenzo of El Escorial a World Heritage Site. It is a popular tourist attraction—more than 500,000 visitors come to El Escorial every year.

Foreign Affairs

Philip's foreign policies were determined by a combination of Catholic fervor and dynastic objectives. He considered himself the chief defender of Catholic Europe, both against the Ottoman Turks and against the forces of the Protestant Reformation. He never relented from his fight against what he saw as heresy, defending the Catholic faith and limiting freedom of worship within his territories. These territories included his patrimony in the Netherlands, where Protestantism had taken deep root. Following the Revolt of the Netherlands in 1568, Philip waged a campaign against Dutch secession. The plans to consolidate control of the Netherlands led to unrest, which gradually led to the Calvinist leadership of the revolt and the Eighty Years' War. This conflict consumed much Spanish expenditure during the later 16th century.

Philip's commitment to restoring Catholicism in the Protestant regions of Europe resulted also in the Anglo-Spanish War (1585–1604). This was an intermittent conflict between the kingdoms of Spain and England that was never formally declared. The war was punctuated by widely separated battles. In 1588, the English defeated Philip's Spanish Armada, thwarting his planned invasion of the country to reinstate Catholicism. But the war continued for the next sixteen years, in a complex series of struggles that included France, Ireland, and the main battle zone, the Low Countries.

Two further Spanish armadas were sent in 1596 and 1597, but were frustrated in their objectives mainly because of adverse weather and poor planning. The war would not end until all the leading protagonists, including Philip, had died.

Philip financed the Catholic League during the French Wars of Religion (primarily fought between French Catholics and French Protestants, known as Huguenots). He directly intervened in the final phases of the wars (1589–1598). His interventions in the fighting—sending the Duke of Parma to end Henry IV's siege of Paris in 1590—and the siege of Rouen in 1592 contributed to saving the French Catholic Leagues's cause against a Protestant monarchy. In 1593, Henry agreed to convert to Catholicism. Weary of war, most French Catholics switched to his side against the hardline core of the Catholic League, who were portrayed by Henry's propagandists as puppets of a foreign monarch, Philip. By the end of 1594 certain league members were still working against Henry across the country, but all relied on the support of Spain. In 1595, therefore, Henry officially declared war on Spain, to show Catholics that Philip was using religion as a cover for an attack on the French state and Protestants that he had not become a puppet of Spain through his conversion, while hoping to take the war to Spain and make territorial gain.

The war was only drawn to an official close with the Peace of Vervins in May 1598; Spanish forces and subsidies were withdrawn. Meanwhile, Henry issued the Edict of Nantes, which offered a high degree of religious toleration for French Protestants. The military interventions in France thus ended in an ironic fashion for Philip: they had failed to oust Henry from the throne or suppress Protestantism in France and yet they had played a decisive part in helping the French Catholic cause gain the conversion of Henry, ensuring that Catholicism would remain France's official and majority faith—matters of paramount importance for the devoutly Catholic Spanish king.

Earlier, after several setbacks in his reign and especially that of his father, Philip had achieved a decisive victory against the Turks at the Lepanto in 1571, with the allied fleet of the Holy League, which he had put under the command of his illegitimate brother, John of Austria. He also successfully secured his succession to the throne of Portugal.

Legacy

Because Philip II was the most powerful European monarch in an era of war and religious conflict, evaluating both his reign and the man himself has become a controversial historical subject. Even in countries that remained Catholic, primarily France and the Italian states, fear and envy of Spanish success and domination created a wide receptiveness for the worst possible descriptions of Philip II. Although some efforts have been made to separate legend from reality, that task has been proven extremely difficult, since many prejudices are rooted in the cultural heritage of European countries. Spanish-speaking historians tend to assess his political and military achievements, sometimes deliberately avoiding issues such as the king's lukewarm attitude (or even support) toward Catholic fanaticism. English-speaking historians tend to show Philip II as a fanatical, despotic, criminal, imperialist monster, minimizing his military victories.

Sources

Attributions

CC licensed content, Specific attribution

- Boundless World History. **Authored by**: Boundless. **Located at**: https://courses.lumenlearning.com/boundless-worldhistory/. **License**: *CC BY-SA: Attribution-ShareAlike*

Elizabeth I and English Patriotism

Key Points

- Elizabeth I (1533–1603) was Queen of England and Ireland from 1558 until her death in 1603. She succeeded her Roman Catholic half-sister, Mary to the throne. Elizabeth never married nor had children and thus was the last monarch of the Tudor dynasty.

- Mary's marriage to Philip II of Spain contributed to the complex relations between England and Spain that after Mary's death dominated Elizabeth's reign in the realm of international relations.

- Elizabeth's efforts led to the Religious Settlement, a legal process by which the Protestant Church of England was restored and the queen took the title of Supreme Governor of the Church of England.

- Elizabeth's foreign policy was largely defensive. While she managed to establish diplomatic relations with some of the most powerful contemporary empires and supported Protestant struggles across Europe, her greatest foreign policy challenge was Catholic Spain and its Armada, over which England eventually triumphed.

- Establishing the Roanoke Colony and chartering the East India Company during Elizabeth's reign was an onset of what would turn into the powerful British Empire.

- The Elizabethan age inspired national pride through classical ideals, international expansion, and naval triumph over the Spanish.

Terms

Spanish Armada

A Spanish fleet of 130 ships that sailed from A Coruña in August 1588 with the purpose of escorting an army from Flanders to invade England. The strategic aim was to overthrow Queen Elizabeth I of England and the Tudor establishment of Protestantism in England.

Religious Settlement

A legal process by which the Protestant Church of England was restored. It was made during the reign of Elizabeth I in response to the religious divisions in England. Described as "The Revolution of 1559," it was set out in two acts of the Parliament of England. The Act of Supremacy of 1558 re-established the Church of England's independence from Rome, while the Act of Uniformity of 1559 outlined what form the English Church should take.

French Catholic League

A major participant in the French Wars of Religion, formed by Henry I, Duke of Guise, in 1576. It intended the eradication of Protestants—also known as Calvinists or Huguenots—out of Catholic France during the Protestant Reformation, as well as the replacement of King Henry III. Pope Sixtus V, Philip II of Spain, and the Jesuits were all supporters of this Catholic party.

Anglo-Spanish War

An intermittent conflict (1585–1604) between the kingdoms of Spain and England that was never formally declared. The war was punctuated by widely separated battles, and began with England's military expedition in 1585 to the Netherlands in support of the resistance of the States General to Spanish Habsburg rule.

Roanoke Colony

A colony established on Roanoke Island, in what is today's Dare County, North Carolina, United States. It was a late 16th-century attempt by Queen Elizabeth I to establish a permanent English settlement. The colony was founded by Sir Walter Raleigh. The colonists disappeared during the Anglo-Spanish War, three years after the last shipment of supplies from England.

Elizabeth I of England

Elizabeth I (1533–1603) was Queen of England and Ireland from 1558 until her death in 1603. She was the daughter of Henry VIII and Anne Boleyn, his second wife, who was executed two and a half years after Elizabeth's birth. Anne's marriage to Henry VIII was annulled and Elizabeth was declared illegitimate. In 1558, Elizabeth succeeded her Roman Catholic half-sister, Mary. She never married nor had children and thus was the last monarch of the Tudor dynasty.

The "Darnley Portrait" of Elizabeth I of England, National Portrait Gallery (c. 1575). The portrait was named after a previous owner. Probably painted from life, it is the source of the face pattern called "The Mask of Youth," which would be used for authorized portraits of Elizabeth for decades to come. Recent research has shown the colors have faded. The oranges and browns would have been crimson red in Elizabeth's time.

Mary I and Philip II of Spain

In 1554, Queen Mary of England married Philip, who only two years later began to rule Spain as Philip II. Under the terms of the Act for the Marriage, Philip was to enjoy Mary I's titles and honors for as long as their marriage should last, and was to co-reign with his wife. Although Elizabeth initially demonstrated solidarity with her sister, the two were sharply divided along religious lines. Mary, a devout Catholic, was determined to crush the Protestant faith, in which Elizabeth had been educated. After Mary married Philip, who saw the protection of Catholicism in Europe as his life's mission, Mary's popularity ebbed away, and many looked to Elizabeth as a focus for their opposition to Mary's religious policies. In 1555, Elizabeth was recalled to court to attend the final stages of Mary's apparent pregnancy. When it became clear that Mary was not pregnant, no one believed any longer that she could have a child. Elizabeth's succession seemed assured.

King Philip acknowledged the new political reality and cultivated his sister-in-law. She was a better ally than the chief alternative, Mary, Queen of Scots, who had grown up in France and was betrothed to the Dauphin of France. When his wife fell ill in 1558, Philip consulted with Elizabeth. By October 1558, Elizabeth was making plans for her government. On November 6, Mary recognized Elizabeth as her heir. On November 17, Mary died and Elizabeth succeeded to the throne.

Religious Settlement

In terms of religious matters, Elizabeth was pragmatic. She and her advisers recognized the threat of a Catholic crusade against England. Elizabeth therefore sought a Protestant solution that would not offend Catholics too greatly while addressing the desires of English Protestants, but she would not tolerate the more radical Puritans, who were pushing for far-reaching reforms. As a result, the parliament of 1559 started to legislate for a church based on the Protestant settlement of Edward VI, with the monarch as its head, but with many Catholic elements. Eventually, Elizabeth was forced to accept the title of Supreme Governor of the Church of England rather than the more contentious title of Supreme Head, which many thought unacceptable for a woman to bear. The new Act of Supremacy became law in 1559. All public officials were to swear an oath of loyalty to the monarch as the supreme governor or risk disqualification from office. The heresy laws were repealed to avoid a repeat of the persecution of dissenters practiced by Mary. At the same time, a new Act of Uniformity was passed, which made attendance at church and the use of an adapted version of the 1552 Book of Common Prayer compulsory, though penalties for those who failed to conform were not extreme.

Foreign Policy

Elizabeth's foreign policy was largely defensive. The exception was the English occupation of Le Havre from October 1562 to June 1563, which ended in failure when Elizabeth's Huguenot (Protestant) allies joined with the Catholics to retake the port. After the occupation and loss of Le Havre, Elizabeth avoided military expeditions on the continent until 1585, when she sent an English army to aid the Protestant Dutch rebels against Philip II. In December 1584, an alliance between Philip II and the French Catholic League undermined the ability of Henry III of France to counter Spanish domination of the Netherlands. It also extended Spanish influence along the channel coast of France, where the Catholic League was strong, and exposed England to invasion. The siege of Antwerp in the summer of 1585 by the Duke of Parma necessitated some reaction on the part of the English and the Dutch. The outcome was the Treaty of Nonsuch of August 1585, in which Elizabeth promised military support to the Dutch. The treaty marked the beginning of the Anglo-Spanish War, which lasted until the Treaty of London in 1604.

After Mary's death, Philip II of Spain had no wish to sever his ties with England, and sent a proposal of marriage to Elizabeth, but was denied. For many years, Philip maintained peace with England and even defended Elizabeth from the pope's threat of excommunication. This was a measure taken to preserve a European balance of power. Ultimately, Elizabeth allied England with the Protestant rebels in the Netherlands (which at the time fought for independence from Spain). Further, English ships began a policy of piracy against Spanish trade and threatened to plunder the great Spanish treasure ships coming from the new world. However, the execution of Mary, Queen of Scots, in 1587 ended Philip's hopes of placing a Catholic on the English throne. He turned instead to more direct plans to invade England, with vague plans to return the country to Catholicism. In 1588 he sent a fleet, the Spanish Armada, across the English Channel. The Spanish were forced into a retreat, and the overwhelming majority of the Armada was destroyed by the harsh weather.

Elizabeth also continued to maintain the diplomatic relations with the Tsardom of Russia originally established by her deceased brother. During her rule, trade and diplomatic relations developed between England and the Barbary states as well. England established a trading relationship with Morocco in opposition to Spain, selling armor, ammunition, timber, and metal in exchange for Moroccan sugar, in spite of a papal ban. Diplomatic relations were also established with the Ottoman Empire with the chartering of the Levant Company and the dispatch of the first English ambassador to the Porte, William Harborne, in 1578.

The Onset of the British Empire

After the travels of Christopher Columbus electrified all of western Europe, England joined in the colonization of the New World. In 1562, Elizabeth sent privateers Hawkins and Drake to seize booty from Spanish and Portuguese ships off the coast of West Africa. Spain was well established in the Americas, while Portugal, in union with Spain from 1580, had an ambitious global empire in Africa, Asia, and South America; France was exploring North America. England was stimulated to create its own colonies, with an emphasis on the West Indies rather than in North America. From 1577 to 1580, Sir Francis Drake circumnavigated the globe. Combined with his daring raids against the Spanish and his great victory over them at Cadiz in 1587, he became a famous hero, but England did not follow up on his claims. In 1583, Humphrey Gilbert sailed to Newfoundland, taking possession of the harbor of St. John's together with all land within two hundred leagues to the north and south of it. In 1584, the queen granted Sir Walter Raleigh a charter for the colonization of Virginia; it was named in her honor. Raleigh sent others to found the Roanoke Colony (it remains a mystery why the settlers there all disappeared). In 1600, the queen chartered the East India Company. It established trading posts that in later centuries evolved into British India, on the coasts of what is now India and Bangladesh. Larger-scale colonization began shortly after Elizabeth's death.

Nationalism

Elizabeth established an English church that helped shape a national identity and remains in place today. Though she followed a largely defensive foreign policy, her reign raised England's status abroad. Under Elizabeth, the nation gained a new self-confidence and sense of sovereignty, as Christendom fragmented. She was the first Tudor to recognize that a monarch ruled by popular consent. She therefore always worked with parliament and advisers she could trust to tell her the truth—a style of government that her Stuart successors failed to follow.

The symbol of Britannia was first used in 1572, and often thereafter, to mark the Elizabethan age as a renaissance that inspired national pride through classical ideals, international expansion, and naval triumph over the Spanish.

Britannia depicted on a half penny of 1936. Britannia was the Greek and Roman term for the geographical region of Great Britain that was inhabited by the Britons and is the name given to the female personification of the island. It was during the reign of Elizabeth I that "Britannia" came to be viewed as a personification of Britain.

Sources

Attributions

The First Stuarts and Catholicism

Learning Objective

- Describe the tensions between the Stuart kings and Parliament over religion

Key Points

- James I and his son and successor, Charles I of England, reigned England in the atmosphere of repeated escalating conflicts with the English Parliament.

- James I believed that he owed his superior authority to God-given right, while Parliament believed the king ruled by contract (an unwritten one, yet fully binding) and that its own rights were equal to those of the king.

- A failed assassination attempt in 1605 against King James I of England and VI of Scotland by a group of provincial English Catholics led by Robert Catesby fueled anti-Catholic sentiments in England. By the 1620s, events on the continent had stirred up anti-Catholic feeling to a new pitch, and James was forced to declare war on Catholic Spain.

- Charles I, married to a Catholic and reluctant to collaborate with or listen to Parliament, reigned in the atmosphere of constant, escalating conflicts with a consistently anti-Catholic Parliament.

- After an eleven-year period of ruling without Parliament, the Long Parliament assembled in 1640 and quickly began proceedings to impeach the king's leading counselors for high treason.

- The escalating conflict between the king and the Parliament resulted in what is known as the English Civil War (1642–1651). A series of armed conflicts and political machinations between Parliamentarians ("Roundheads") and Royalists ("Cavaliers") ended in, among other things, the prosecution of Charles I.

Terms

Thirty Years' War

A series of wars in Central Europe between 1618 and 1648. Initially a war between various Protestant and Catholic states in the fragmented Holy Roman Empire, it gradually developed into a more general conflict involving most of the great powers.

Gunpowder Plot

A failed assassination attempt in 1605 against King James I of England and VI of Scotland by a group of provincial English Catholics led by Robert Catesby. The plan was to blow up the House of Lords during the State Opening of England's Parliament on November 5, 1605, as the prelude to a popular revolt in the Midlands during which James's nine-year-old daughter, Princess Elizabeth, was to be installed as the Catholic head of state.

eleven years' tyranny

The period from 1629 to 1640, when King Charles I of England, Scotland, and Ireland ruled without recourse to Parliament. The king was entitled to do this under the Royal Prerogative. His actions caused discontent among the ruling classes, but the effects were more popular with the common people.

English Civil War

A series of armed conflicts and political machinations between English Parliamentarians ("Roundheads") and Royalists ("Cavaliers") over, principally, the manner of its government. The first (1642–1646) and second (1648–1649) wars pitted the supporters of Charles I against the supporters of the Long Parliament, while the third (1649–1651) saw fighting between supporters of King Charles II and supporters of the Rump Parliament.

Long Parliament

An English Parliament that lasted from 1640 until 1660. It followed the fiasco of the Short Parliament, which had been held for three weeks during the spring of 1640, and which in its turn had followed a parliamentary absence of eleven years.

Background: Reformation in England in Scotland

The separation of the Church of England (or Anglican Church) from Rome under Henry VIII brought England alongside a broad Reformation movement, but the English Reformation differed from its European counterparts. Based on Henry VIII's desire for an annulment of his marriage, it was at the outset more of a political affair than a theological dispute. The break with Rome was effected by a series of acts of Parliament, but Catholic Mary I restored papal jurisdiction in 1553. However, Mary's successor, Elizabeth I, restored the Church of England and reasserted the royal supremacy in 1559. After she died without an heir, James VI, her cousin and King of Scots, succeeded to the throne of England as James I in 1603, thus uniting Scotland and England under one monarch (the Union of the Crowns). He was the first of the Stuart dynasty to rule Scotland and England. He and his son and successor, Charles I of England, reigned England in the atmosphere of repeated escalating conflicts with the English Parliament.

James I and the English Parliament

James developed his political philosophy of the relationship between monarch and parliament in Scotland, and never reconciled himself to the independent stance of the English Parliament and its unwillingness to bow readily to his policies.

The crucial source of concern was that the king and Parliament adhered to two mutually exclusive views about the nature of their relationship. James I believed that he owed his superior authority to God-given right, while Parliament believed the king ruled by contract (an unwritten one, yet fully binding) and that its own rights were equal to those of the king.

On the eve of the state opening of the parliamentary session on November 5, 1605, a soldier called Guy Fawkes was discovered in the cellars of the parliament buildings guarding about twenty barrels of gunpowder with which he intended to blow up Parliament House the following day. A Catholic conspiracy led by a disaffected gentleman called Robert Catesby, the Gunpowder Plot, as it quickly became known, had in fact been discovered in advance of Fawkes's arrest and deliberately allowed to mature in order to catch the culprits red-handed and the plotters unawares.

By the 1620s, events on the continent had stirred up anti-Catholic feeling to a new pitch. A conflict had broken out between the Catholic Holy Roman Empire and the Protestant Bohemians, who had deposed the emperor as their king and elected James's son-in-law, Frederick V, Elector Palatine, in his place, triggering the Thirty Years' War. James reluctantly summoned Parliament as the only means to raise the funds necessary to assist his daughter Elizabeth and Frederick, who had been ousted from Prague by Emperor Ferdinand II in 1620. The Commons on the one hand granted subsidies inadequate to finance serious military operations in aid of Frederick, and on the other called for a war directly against Spain. In November 1621, led by Sir Edward Coke, they framed a petition asking not only for a war with Spain but also for Prince Charles to marry a Protestant, and for enforcement of the anti-Catholic laws. James flatly told them not to interfere in matters of royal prerogative and dissolved Parliament.

The failed attempt to marry Prince Charles with the Catholic Spanish Infanta Maria (known as the Spanish match), which both the Parliament and the public strongly opposed, was followed by even stronger anti-Catholic sentiment in the Commons that was finally echoed in court. The outcome of the Parliament of

1624 was ambiguous; James still refused to declare war, but Charles believed the Commons had committed themselves to financing a war against Spain, a stance which was to contribute to his problems with Parliament in his own reign.

James I of England, Portrait attributed to John de Critz, c. 1605. King of Scotland as James VI from 1567 and King of England and Ireland as James I from the union of the Scottish and English crowns in 1603 until his death.

Charles I and the English Parliament

With the failure of the Spanish match, Charles married French princess Henrietta Maria. Many members of the Commons were opposed to the king's marriage to a Roman Catholic. Although he told Parliament that he would not relax religious restrictions, Charles promised to do exactly that in a secret marriage treaty with Louis XIII of France. Moreover, the treaty placed under French command an English naval force that would be used to suppress the Protestant Huguenots at La Rochelle. Charles was crowned in 1626 at Westminster Abbey without his wife at his side because she refused to participate in a Protestant religious ceremony.

Domestic quarrels between Charles and Henrietta Maria were souring the early years of their marriage. Despite Charles's agreement to provide the French with English ships, in 1627 he launched an attack on the French coast to defend the Huguenots at La Rochelle. The action, led by Buckingham (James and Charles' close collaborator; hated by Parliament), was ultimately unsuccessful. After
Buckingham was assassinated in 1628, Charles's relationship with his Catholic wife dramatically improved.

Although the death of Buckingham effectively ended the war with Spain and eliminated his leadership as an issue, it did not end the conflicts between Charles and Parliament. In January 1629, Charles opened the second session of the English Parliament. Members of the House of Commons began to voice opposition to Charles's policies. Many MPs viewed the imposition of taxes as a breach of the Petition of Right. When Charles ordered a parliamentary adjournment on March 2, members held the Speaker down in his chair so that the ending of the session could be delayed long enough for various resolutions, including Anti-Catholic and tax-regulating laws. The provocation was too much for Charles, who dissolved Parliament. Shortly after the prorogation, without the means in the foreseeable future to raise funds from Parliament for a European war, Charles made peace with France and Spain. The following eleven years, during which Charles ruled England without a Parliament, are referred to as the "personal rule" or the "eleven years' tyranny."

The Long Parliament, which assembled in the aftermath of the personal rule, started in 1640 and quickly began proceedings to impeach the king's leading counselors for high treason. To prevent the king from dissolving it at will, Parliament passed the Triennial Act, which required Parliament to be summoned at least once every three years, and permitted the Lord Keeper of the Great Seal and twelve peers to summon Parliament if the king failed to do so.

Charles I of England, portrait from the studio of Anthony van Dyck, 1636. Studio version of much copied original in the Royal Collection, Windsor Castle. After his succession, Charles quarreled with the Parliament of England, which sought to curb his royal prerogative. Charles believed in the divine right of kings and thought he could govern according to his own conscience. Many of his subjects opposed his policies, in particular the levying of taxes without parliamentary consent, and perceived his actions as those of a tyrannical absolute monarch.

The English Civil War

The escalating conflict between the king and Parliament resulted in what is known as the English Civil War (1642–1651). It was a series of armed conflicts and political machinations between Parliamentarians ("Roundheads") and Royalists ("Cavaliers") over, principally, the manner of its government. The first (1642–1646) and second (1648–1649) wars pitted the supporters of Charles against the supporters of the

Long Parliament, while the third (1649–1651) saw fighting between supporters of King Charles II and supporters of the Rump Parliament. The war ended with the Parliamentarian victory at the Battle of Worcester on September 3, 1651.

The overall outcome of the war was threefold: the trial and execution of Charles I; the exile of his son, Charles II; and the replacement of English monarchy with, at first, the Commonwealth of England (1649–1653), and then the Protectorate (1653–1659) under Oliver Cromwell's personal rule. The monopoly of the Church of England on Christian worship in England ended with the victors consolidating the established Protestant Ascendancy in Ireland. Constitutionally, the wars established the precedent that an English monarch cannot govern without Parliament's consent, although the idea of Parliament as the ruling power of England was legally established as part of the Glorious Revolution in 1688.

Sources

Attributions

CC licensed content, Specific attribution

- Boundless World History. **Authored by**: Boundless. **Located at**: https://courses.lumenlearning.com/boundless-worldhistory/. **License**: *CC BY-SA: Attribution-ShareAlike*

Charles I and the Power to Tax

Learning Objective

- Analyze why the power to determine taxation was so important

Key Points

- Charles I of England continued his father's policy and decided to support Christian IV of Denmark and Frederick V, Elector Palatine, during the Thirty Years' War, which caused major tensions with a Parliament that refused to finance the war.

- After the Commons continued to refuse to provide money and began investigating the Duke of Buckingham, Charles I dissolved Parliament. By 1627, with England still at war, Charles decided to raise "forced loans," or taxes not authorized by Parliament.

- To cope with the ongoing war situation, Charles had introduced martial law, which, as then understood, was not a form of substantive law, but instead a suspension of the rule of law.

- Charles decided that the only way to prosecute the war was to again ask Parliament for money, and Parliament assembled in 1628. As a result, a series of parliamentary declarations establishing a series of personal liberties known as the *Resolutions* were prepared after tense debates.

- In the end, a suggestion to pass the Resolutions as a petition of right won. A committee produced a petition covering discretionary imprisonment, non-Parliamentary taxation, martial law, and forced billeting.

- The 1628 Petition of Right marks the founding of the United Kingdom's modern constitutional monarchy.

Terms

Petition of Right

A major English constitutional document that sets out specific liberties of the subjects that the king is prohibited from infringing. Passed in 1628, it contains restrictions on non-Parliamentary taxation, forced billeting of soldiers, imprisonment without cause, and the use of martial law.

habeas corpus

In medieval Latin it means literally "You may have the body," a recourse in law whereby a person can report an unlawful detention or imprisonment before a court, usually through a prison official.

Thirty Years' War

A series of wars in Central Europe between 1618 and 1648. Initially a war between various Protestant and Catholic states in the fragmented Holy Roman Empire, it gradually developed into a more general conflict involving most of the great powers.

Tonnage and Poundage

Certain duties and taxes first levied in Edward II's reign on every tun (cask) of imported wine, which came mostly from Spain and Portugal, and on every pound weight of merchandise exported or imported. Traditionally it was granted by Parliament to the king for life until the reign of Charles I.

Charles I of England and the English Parliament

In 1625, King James I of England died and was succeeded by his son, who became Charles I. Along with the throne, Charles inherited the Thirty Years' War, in which Christian IV of Denmark and Frederick V, Elector Palatine, who was married to Charles's sister Elizabeth, were attempting to take back their hereditary lands and titles from the Habsburg Monarchy. James had caused significant financial problems with his attempts to support Christian and Frederick, and it was expected that Charles would be more amenable to prosecuting the war responsibly. After he summoned a new Parliament to meet in April 1625, it became clear that he was not. He demanded over £700,000 to assist in prosecuting the war. The House of Commons refused and instead passed two bills granting him only £112,000. In addition, rather than renewing the customs due from Tonnage and Poundage for the entire life of the monarch, which was traditional, the Commons only voted them in for one year. Because of this, the House of Lords rejected the bill, leaving Charles without any money to provide to the war effort.

After the Commons continued to refuse to provide money and began investigating the Duke of Buckingham, Charles's favorite, Charles dissolved Parliament. By 1627, with England still at war, Charles decided to raise "forced loans," or taxes not authorized by Parliament. Anyone who refused to pay would be imprisoned without trial, and if they resisted, would be sent before the Privy Council. Although the judiciary initially refused to endorse these loans, they succumbed to pressure. While Charles continued to demand the loans, more and more wealthy landowners refused to pay, reducing the income from the loans and necessitating a new Parliament being called in 1627.

Martial Law

To cope with the ongoing war situation, Charles had introduced martial law to large swathes of the country, and in 1627 to the entire nation. Crucially, martial law as then understood was not a form of substantive law, but instead a suspension of the rule of law. It was the replacement of normal statutes with a law based on the whims of the local military commander. However, Charles decided that the only way to prosecute the war was to again ask Parliament for money, and Parliament assembled in 1628. As a result, a series of Parliamentary declarations known as the *Resolutions* were prepared after tense debates. They held that imprisonment was illegal, except under law; *habeas corpus* should be granted to anyone, whether they are imprisoned by the king or the Privy Council; defendants could not be remanded in custody until the crime they were charged with was shown; and non-Parliamentary taxation such as the forced loans was illegal (the first three later became the foundations of the Habeas Corpus Act 1679). The *Resolutions* were unanimously accepted by the Commons in April, but they met a mixed reception at the House of Lords, and Charles refused to accept them.

The Petition of Right

The conflict between the king and Parliament escalated. A number of possible alternatives to the *Resolutions* were debated, but finally Sir Edward Coke made a speech suggesting that the Commons join with the House of Lords and pass their four resolutions as a petition of right (although he was not the first to do so). The idea of a petition of right was an established element of Parliamentary procedure, and in addition, had not been expressly prohibited by Charles. A committee produced a petition containing the same elements as the *Resolutions,* covering discretionary imprisonment, non-Parliamentary taxation, martial law, and forced billeting.

The Commons accepted the recommendations on May 8, and after a long debate that attempted to accommodate the hostile king, the House of Lords unanimously voted to join with the Commons on the Petition of Right, while passing their own resolution, assuring the king of their loyalty.

Following the acceptance of the Petition by the House of Lords, Charles sent a message to the Commons "forbidding them to meddle with affairs of state," which produced a furious debate. On June 7, Charles capitulated and accepted the Petition. After setting out a list of individual grievances and statutes that had been broken, the 1628 Petition of Right declares that Englishmen have various "rights and liberties," and provides that no person should be forced to provide a gift, loan, or tax without an Act of Parliament, that no free individual should be imprisoned or detained unless a cause has been shown, and that soldiers or members of the Royal Navy should not be billeted in private houses without the free consent of the owner. It also restricts the use of martial law except in war or direct rebellion and prohibited the formation of commissions.

The Petition of Right, 1628, Parliament of England. The Petition of Right, a major English constitutional document that sets out specific liberties of the subject that the king is prohibited from infringing. Drafted by a committee headed by Sir Edward Coke, it was passed and ratified in 1628.

Significance

Some historians have argued that the passage of the Petition of Right marks the founding of the United Kingdom's modern constitutional monarchy. The Petition of Right also marked a substantial cooperative work between individual parliamentarians and between the Commons and Lords, something that had previously been lacking and that in the end led to the formation of political parties.

Within what is now the Commonwealth of Nations, the Petition was also heavily influential. It remains in force in both New Zealand and Australia, as well as the United Kingdom itself. The Petition also profoundly influenced the rights contained by the Constitution of the United States.

Sources

Attributions

Cromwell and the Roundheads

Learning Objective

- Explain how Cromwell rose to power.

Key Points

- Charles I's belief, inherited from his father, that the power of the crown is God-given and that the king does not have to respect the position of the English Parliament, shaped his reign and led to a political crisis that in the end would cost him his own life.

- After the 1628 Parliament drew up the Petition of Right, Charles I avoided calling a Parliament for the next decade, a period known as the "personal rule" or the "eleven years' tyranny." During this period, Charles's lack of money determined policies.

- Charles finally bowed to pressure and summoned another English Parliament in November 1640. Known as the Long Parliament, it passed laws that strengthened the position of and protected Parliament.

- Charles and his supporters continued to resent Parliament's demands, while Parliamentarians continued to suspect Charles of wanting to impose episcopalianism and unfettered royal rule by military force. After Ireland first descended into chaos, cities and towns declared their sympathies for one faction or the other.

- The English Civil War (1642–1651) pitted the supporters of King Charles I and later his son and successor, Charles II, against the supporters of Parliament. Its outcome was threefold: the trial and execution of Charles I, the exile of Charles II, and the replacement of English monarchy with, at first, the Commonwealth of England (1649–53), and then the Protectorate (1653–59) under Oliver Cromwell's personal rule.

- In 1653, Cromwell was invited by his fellow leaders to rule as Lord Protector of England (which included Wales at the time), Scotland, and Ireland. As a ruler, he executed an aggressive and effective foreign policy.

Terms

New Model Army

An army formed in 1645 by the Parliamentarians in the English Civil War and disbanded in 1660 after the Restoration. It differed from other armies in the series of civil wars referred to as the Wars of the Three Kingdoms in that it was intended as an army liable for service anywhere in the country (including in Scotland and Ireland) rather than being tied to a single area or garrison. Its soldiers became full-time professionals rather than part-time militia.

Roundheads

The name given to the supporters of the Parliament of England during the English Civil War. Also known as Parliamentarians, they fought against Charles I of England and his supporters, the Cavaliers or Royalists, who claimed rule by absolute monarchy and the divine right of kings. Their goal was to give the Parliament supreme control over executive administration.

Long Parliament

An English Parliament that lasted from 1640 until 1660. It followed the fiasco of the Short Parliament, which had been held for three weeks during the spring of 1640, and which in its turn had followed eleven years of parliamentary absence.

eleven years' tyranny

The period from 1629 to 1640, when King Charles I of England, Scotland, and Ireland ruled without recourse to Parliament. The King was entitled to do this under the Royal Prerogative. His actions caused discontent among the ruling classes, but the effects were more popular with the common people.

Cavaliers

A name first used by Roundheads as a term of abuse for the wealthier male Royalist supporters of King Charles I and his son Charles II of England during the English Civil War, the Interregnum, and the Restoration (1642–c. 1679). It was later adopted by the Royalists themselves.

Rump Parliament

The English Parliament after Colonel Thomas Pride purged the Long Parliament on December 6, 1648, of those members hostile to the Grandees' intention to try King Charles I for high treason.

Thirty Years' War

A series of wars in Central Europe between 1618 and 1648. Initially a war between various Protestant and Catholic states in the fragmented Holy Roman Empire, it gradually developed into a more general conflict involving most of the great powers.

tonnage and poundage

Certain duties and taxes first levied in Edward II's reign on every tun (cask) of imported wine, which came mostly from Spain and Portugal, and on every pound weight of merchandise exported or imported. Traditionally it was granted by Parliament to the king for life until the reign of Charles I.

Petition of Right

A major English constitutional document that sets out specific liberties of the subjects that the king is prohibited from infringing. Passed in 1628, it contains restrictions on non-Parliamentary taxation, forced billeting of soldiers, imprisonment without cause, and the use of martial law.

Background: The Stuarts and the English Parliament

Elizabeth I's death in 1603 resulted in the accession of her first cousin twice-removed King James VI of Scotland to the English throne as James I of England, creating the first personal union of the Scottish and English kingdoms. As King of Scots, James had become accustomed to Scotland's weak parliamentary tradition, and the new King of England was genuinely affronted by the constraints the English Parliament attempted to place on him. Despite tensions between the King and Parliament, James's peaceful disposition contributed to relative peace in both England and Scotland. However, his son and successor, Charles I of England, did not share his father's personality, and engaged in even more tense conflicts with Parliament. Charles's belief, inherited from his father, that the power of the crown is God-given and that the king does not have to respect the position of the English Parliament, shaped his reign and led to a political crisis that in the end would cost him his own life.

Having dissolved Parliament in 1627 after it did not meet the king's requirements and threatened his political allies, but unable to raise money without it, Charles assembled a new one in 1628. The new Parliament drew up the Petition of Right, and Charles accepted it as a concession in order to obtain his subsidy. The Petition did not grant him the right of tonnage and poundage, which Charles had been collecting without parliamentary authorization since 1625. Charles I avoided calling a Parliament for the next decade, a period known as the "personal rule" or the "eleven years' tyranny." During this period, Charles's lack of money determined policies. First and foremost, to avoid Parliament, the king needed to avoid war. Charles made peace with France and Spain, effectively ending England's involvement in the Thirty Years' War.

Charles finally bowed to pressure and summoned another English Parliament in November 1640. Known as the Long Parliament, it proved even more hostile to Charles than its predecessor, and passed a law that stated that a new Parliament should convene at least once every three years—without the king's summons, if necessary. Other laws passed by the Parliament made it illegal for the king to impose taxes without parliamentary consent and later gave Parliament control over the king's ministers. Finally, the Parliament passed a law forbidding the king to dissolve it without its consent, even if the three years were up.

Charles and his supporters continued to resent Parliament's demands, while Parliamentarians continued to suspect Charles of wanting to impose episcopalianism and unfettered royal rule by military force. Within months, the Irish Catholics, fearing a resurgence of Protestant power, struck first, and all of Ireland soon descended into chaos. In early January 1642, accompanied by 400 soldiers, Charles attempted to arrest five members of the House of Commons on a charge of treason, but failed to do so.

A few days after this failure, fearing for the safety of his family and retinue, Charles left the London area for the north of the country. Further negotiations by frequent correspondence between the king and the Long Parliament proved fruitless. As the summer progressed, cities and towns declared their sympathies for one faction or the other.

The English Civil War

What followed is know as the English Civil War (1642–1651), which developed into a series of armed conflicts and political machinations between Parliamentarians ("Roundheads") and Royalists ("Cavaliers"). The first (1642–1646) and second (1648–1649) wars pitted the supporters of King Charles I against the supporters of the Long Parliament, while the third (1649–1651) saw fighting between supporters of King Charles II (Charles I's son) and supporters of the Rump Parliament. The war ended with the Parliamentarian victory at the Battle of Worcester on September 3, 1651.

The overall outcome of the war was threefold: the trial and execution of Charles I, the exile of Charles II, and the replacement of English monarchy with, at first, the Commonwealth of England (1649–1653), and then the Protectorate (1653–1659) under Oliver Cromwell's personal rule. The monopoly of the Church of England on Christian worship in England ended with the victors consolidating the established Protestant Ascendancy in Ireland. Constitutionally, the wars established the precedent that an English monarch cannot govern without Parliament's consent, although the idea of Parliament as the ruling power of England was legally established as part of the Glorious Revolution in 1688.

Battle of Naseby, artist unknown. The victory of the Parliamentarian New Model Army over the Royalist Army at the Battle of Naseby on June 14, 1645, marked the decisive turning point in the English Civil War.

Oliver Cromwell's Rise

Oliver Cromwell was relatively obscure for the first forty years of his life. He was an intensely religious man (an Independent Puritan) who entered the English Civil War on the side of the "Roundheads," or Parliamentarians. Nicknamed "Old Ironsides," he was quickly promoted from leading a single cavalry troop to being one of the principal commanders of the New Model Army, playing an important role in the defeat of the royalist forces. Cromwell was one of the signatories of King Charles I's death warrant in 1649, and he dominated the short-lived Commonwealth of England as a member of the Rump Parliament (1649–1653). He was selected to take command of the English campaign in Ireland in 1649–1650. His forces defeated the Confederate and Royalist coalition in Ireland and occupied the country, bringing an end to the Irish Confederate Wars. During this period, a series of Penal Laws were passed against Roman Catholics (a significant minority in England and Scotland but the vast majority in Ireland), and a substantial amount of their land was confiscated. Cromwell also led a campaign against the Scottish army between 1650 and 1651.

In April 1653, he dismissed the Rump Parliament by force, setting up a short-lived nominated assembly known as Barebone's Parliament, before being invited by his fellow leaders to rule as Lord Protector of England (which included Wales at the time), Scotland, and Ireland from December 1653. As a ruler, he executed an aggressive and effective foreign policy. He died from natural causes in 1658 and the Royalists returned to power in 1660, and they had his corpse dug up, hung in chains, and beheaded.

Oliver Cromwell by Samuel Cooper (died 1672), the National Portrait Gallery, London. Cromwell is one of the most controversial figures in the history of the British Isles, considered a regicidal dictator, a military dictator, and a hero of liberty. However, his measures against Catholics in Scotland and Ireland have been characterized as genocidal or near-genocidal, and in Ireland his record is harshly criticized.

Sources

Attributions

CC licensed content, Specific attribution

- Boundless World History. **Authored by**: Boundless. **Located at**: https://courses.lumenlearning.com/boundless-worldhistory/. **License**: *CC BY-SA: Attribution-ShareAlike*

The English Protectorate

Learning Objective

- Describe the English Protectorate, along with its successes and failures

Key Points

- In 1653 Oliver Cromwell was declared Lord Protector of a united Commonwealth of England, Scotland, and Ireland under the terms of the Instrument of Government, inaugurating the period now usually known as the Protectorate.

- Cromwell had two key objectives as Lord Protector: "healing and settling" the nation after the chaos of the civil wars and the regicide, and spiritual and moral reform. While his domestic policies presumed no radical reforms and many focused on protecting public morality through religion, Cromwell followed an aggressive foreign policy.

- Cromwell's over-reliance on the military reopened the wounds of the 1640s and deepened antipathies to the regime.

- Being aware of the contribution the Jewish community made to the economic success of Holland, then England's leading commercial rival, Cromwell encouraged Jews to return to England, 350 years after their banishment by Edward I.

- After Cromwell's death in 1658, his son Richard succeeded as Lord Protector but was unable to manage the Parliament and control the army. In 1660, monarchy was restored.

- Cromwell is one of the most controversial figures in the history of the British Isles, considered a regicidal dictator or a military dictator by some and a hero of liberty by others. His measures against Catholics in Scotland and Ireland, however, have been characterized as genocidal or near-genocidal.

Terms

Rump Parliament

The English Parliament after Colonel Thomas Pride purged the Long Parliament on December 6, 1648, of those members hostile to the Grandees' intention to try King Charles I for high treason.

Interregnum

The period between the execution of Charles I on January 30, 1649, and the arrival of his son Charles II in London on May 29, 1660, which marked the start of the Restoration. During the Interregnum England was under various forms of republican government as the Commonwealth of England.

Barebone's Parliament

Also known as the Little Parliament, the Nominated Assembly, and the Parliament of Saints, was the last attempt of the English Commonwealth (1653) to find a stable political form before the installation of Oliver Cromwell as Lord Protector. It was an assembly nominated entirely by Oliver Cromwell and the Army's Council of Officers.

Third English Civil War

The last of the English Civil Wars (1649–1651), which were a series of armed conflicts and political machinations between Parliamentarians and Royalists. As the Royal army was mostly Scottish, and as the invasion was not accompanied by any major rising or support in England, the war can also be viewed as primarily an Anglo-Scottish War rather than a continuation of the English Civil War.

Instrument of Government

A constitution of the Commonwealth of England, Scotland, and Ireland. Drafted by Major-General John Lambert in 1653, it was the first sovereign codified and written constitution in England.

The Commonwealth of England

The Commonwealth was the period when England, later along with Ireland and Scotland, was ruled as a republic following the end of the Second English Civil War and the trial and execution of Charles I (1649). The republic's existence was declared by the Rump Parliament on May 19, 1649. Power in the early Commonwealth was vested primarily in the Parliament and a Council of State. During this period, fighting continued, particularly in Ireland and Scotland, between the parliamentary forces and those opposed to them, as part of what is now referred to as the Third English Civil War.

In 1653, after the forcible dissolution of the Rump Parliament, Oliver Cromwell was declared Lord Protector of a united Commonwealth of England, Scotland, and Ireland under the terms of the Instrument of Government, inaugurating the period now usually known as the Protectorate. The term "Commonwealth" is sometimes used for the whole of 1649 to 1660—a period referred to by monarchists as the Interregnum—although for other historians, the use of the term is limited to the years prior to Cromwell's formal assumption of power in 1653.

Coat of arms of the Commonwealth of England from 1653 to 1659 during the Protectorate of Oliver Cromwell.

The Protectorate

The Protectorate was the period during the Commonwealth when England (which at that time included Wales), Ireland, and Scotland were governed by a Lord Protector. The Protectorate began in 1653 when, following the dissolution of the Rump Parliament and then Barebone's Parliament, Oliver Cromwell was appointed Lord Protector of the Commonwealth under the terms of the Instrument of Government.

Cromwell had two key objectives as Lord Protector. The first was "healing and settling" the nation after the chaos of the civil wars and the regicide. The social priorities did not, despite the revolutionary nature of the government, include any meaningful attempt to reform the social order. He was also careful in the way he approached overseas colonies. England's American colonies in this period consisted of the New England Confederation, the Providence Plantation, the Virginia Colony, and the Maryland Colony. Cromwell soon secured the submission of these, but largely left them to their own affairs. His second objective was spiritual and moral reform. As a very religious man (Independent Puritan), he aimed to restore liberty of conscience and promote both outward and inward godliness throughout England. The latter translated into rigid religious laws (e.g., compulsory church attendance).

The first Protectorate parliament met in September 1654, and after some initial gestures approving appointments previously made by Cromwell, began to work on a moderate program of constitutional reform. Rather than opposing Parliament's bill, Cromwell dissolved them in January 1655. After a royalist uprising led by Sir John Penruddock, Cromwell divided England into military districts ruled by Army Major-Generals who answered only to him. The fifteen major generals and deputy major generals—called "godly governors"—were central not only to national security, but also to Cromwell's moral crusade. However, the major-generals lasted less than a year. Cromwell's failure to support his men, by sacrificing them to his opponents, caused their demise. Their activities between November 1655 and September 1656 had, nonetheless, reopened the wounds of the 1640s and deepened antipathies to the regime.

During this period Cromwell also faced challenges in foreign policy. The First Anglo-Dutch War, which had broken out in 1652, against the Dutch Republic, was eventually won in 1654. Having negotiated peace with the Dutch, Cromwell proceeded to engage the Spanish in warfare. This involved secret preparations for an attack on the Spanish colonies in the Caribbean and resulted in the invasion of Jamaica, which then became an English colony. The Lord Protector also became aware of the contribution the Jewish community made to the economic success of Holland, then England's leading commercial rival. This led to his encouraging Jews to return to England, 350 years after their banishment by Edward I, in the hope that they would help speed up the recovery of the country after the disruption of the English Civil War.

In 1657, Oliver Cromwell rejected the offer of the Crown presented to him by Parliament and was ceremonially re-installed as Lord Protector, this time with greater powers than had previously been granted him under this title. Most notably, however, the office of Lord Protector was still not to become hereditary, though Cromwell was now able to nominate his own successor. Cromwell's new rights and powers were laid out in the Humble Petition and Advice, a legislative instrument that replaced the Instrument of Government. Despite failing to restore the Crown, this new constitution did set up many of the vestiges of the ancient constitution, including a house of life peers (in place of the House of Lords). In the Humble Petition it was called the "Other House," as the Commons could not agree on a suitable name. Furthermore, Oliver Cromwell increasingly took on more of the trappings of monarchy.

Cromwell's signature before becoming Lord Protector in 1653, and afterwards. "Oliver P," stands for Oliver Protector, similar in style to English monarchs who signed their names as, for example, "Elizabeth R," standing for Elizabeth Regina.

After Cromwell's Death

Cromwell died of natural causes in 1658, and his son Richard succeeded as Lord Protector. Richard sought to expand the basis for the Protectorate beyond the army to civilians. He summoned a Parliament in 1659. However, the republicans assessed his father's rule as "a period of tyranny and economic depression" and attacked the increasingly monarchy-like character of the Protectorate. Richard was unable to manage the Parliament and control the army. In May, a Committee of Safety was formed on the authority of the Rump Parliament, displacing the Protector's Council of State, and was in turn replaced by a new Council of State. A year later monarchy was restored.

Cromwell is one of the most controversial figures in the history of the British Isles, considered a regicidal dictator or a military dictator by some and a hero of liberty by others. His measures against Catholics in Scotland and Ireland have been characterized as genocidal or near-genocidal, and in Ireland his record is harshly criticized.

Following the Irish Rebellion of 1641, most of Ireland came under the control of the Irish Catholic Confederation. In early 1649, the Confederates allied with the English Royalists, who had been defeated by the Parliamentarians in the English Civil War. By May 1652, Cromwell's Parliamentarian army had defeated the Confederate and Royalist coalition in Ireland and occupied the country—bringing an end to the Irish Confederate Wars (or Eleven Years' War). However, guerrilla warfare continued for another year. Cromwell passed a series of Penal Laws against Roman Catholics (the vast majority of the population) and confiscated large amounts of their land. The extent to which Cromwell, who was in direct command for the first year of the campaign, was responsible for brutal atrocities in Ireland is debated to this day.

Sources

Attributions

CC licensed content, Specific attribution

- Boundless World History. **Authored by**: Boundless. **Located at**: https://courses.lumenlearning.com/boundless-worldhistory/. **License**: *CC BY-SA: Attribution-ShareAlike*

Restoration of the Stuarts

Learning Objective

- Evaluate why the Stuarts were brought back and restored to the English throne

Key Points

- Richard Cromwell was Lord Protector of England, Scotland, and Ireland after Oliver Cromwell's death in 1658, but he lacked his father's authority. He proved unable to manage the Parliament and control the army and was removed from his office after several months.

- In the aftermath of Richard's removal, power struggles ensued, with George Monck emerging as a key figure in the restoration of monarchy and bringing Charles II back to England.

- On April 4, 1660, Charles II issued the Declaration of Breda, in which he made several promises in relation to the reclamation of the crown of England. Charles entered London on May 29 and was crowned in 1661.

- The Cavalier Parliament convened for the first time in May 1661, and it would endure for over seventeen years. Like its predecessor, it was overwhelmingly Royalist. It is also known as the Pensionary Parliament for the many pensions it granted to adherents of the king.

- Many Royalist exiles returned and were rewarded. The Indemnity and Oblivion Act, which became law in August 1660, pardoned all past treason against the Crown, but specifically excluded those involved in the trial and execution of Charles I.

Terms

Pride's Purge of 1648

An event that took place in December 1648, during the Second English Civil War, when troops of the New Model Army under the command of Colonel Thomas Pride forcibly removed from the Long Parliament all those who were not supporters of the Grandees in the New Model Army and the Independents. It is arguably the only military *coup d'état* in English history.

Convention Parliament

A parliament in English history which, owing to an abeyance of the Crown, assembled without formal summons by the sovereign.
Its 1660 assembly followed the Long Parliament that had finally voted for its own dissolution in March of that year. Elected as a "free parliament," i.e., with no oath of allegiance to the Commonwealth or to the monarchy, it was predominantly Royalist in its membership.

Indemnity and Oblivion Act

A 1660 act of the Parliament of England that was a general pardon for everyone who had committed crimes during the English Civil War and Interregnum, with the exception of certain crimes such as murder, piracy, buggery, rape, and witchcraft, and people named in the act, such as those involved in the regicide of Charles I.

Declaration of Breda

A proclamation by Charles II of England in which he promised a general pardon for crimes committed during the English Civil War and the Interregnum for all those who recognized Charles as the lawful king; the retention by the current owners of property purchased during the same period; religious toleration; and the payment of pay arrears to members of the army and the recommission of the army into service under the crown. The first three pledges were all subject to amendment by acts of parliament.

Rump Parliament

The English Parliament after Colonel Thomas Pride purged the Long Parliament on December 6, 1648, of those members hostile to the Grandees' intention to try King Charles I for high treason.

Long Parliament

An English Parliament that lasted from 1640 until 1660. It followed the fiasco of the Short Parliament, which had been held for three weeks during the spring of 1640, and which in its turn had followed an eleven-year parliamentary absence.

Committee of Safety

A committee established by the Parliamentarians in July 1642. It was the first of a number of successive committees set up to oversee the English Civil War against King Charles I and the Interregnum. Its last installment was set up in 1659, just before the Restoration, in response to the Rump Parliament, which the day before tried to place the commander of the army Charles Fleetwood as chief of a military council under the authority of the speaker.

Richard Cromwell and the Protectorate

Richard Cromwell (1626–1712) was Lord Protector of England, Scotland, and Ireland after Oliver Cromwell's death in 1658. Richard lacked his father's authority. He attempted to mediate between the army and civil society and allowed a Parliament that contained a large number of disaffected Presbyterians and Royalists. His main weakness was that he did not have the confidence of the army. He summoned a Parliament in 1659, but the republicans assessed Oliver's rule to be "a period of tyranny and economic depression" and attacked the increasingly monarchy-like nature of the Protectorate. Richard proved unable to manage the Parliament and control the army. On May 7, a Committee of Safety was formed on the authority of the Rump Parliament, displacing the Protector's Council of State, and was in turn replaced by a new Council of State on May 19.

BY HIS HIGHNES COUNCIL IN SCOTLAND,

For the GOVERNMENT thereof.

WHEREAS it hath pleaſed the moſt wiſe GOD in His Providence, to take out of this world the moſt Serene and Renowned OLIVER late LORD PROTECTOR of this Commonwealth; And his ſaid Highneſſe, having in his life-time, according to the Humble Petition and Advice, Declared and appointed the moſt Noble and Illuſtrious the Lord RICHARD, eldeſt ſon of his ſaid late Highneſſe, to ſucceed Him in the Government of theſe Nations: we therefore of his Highneſſe Council in Scotland, by direction of the Privy Council in England, do now hereby with one full voice and conſent of tongue and heart, publiſh and declare the ſaid Noble and Illuſtrious Lord RICHARD, to be rightfully PROTECTOR of this Commonwealth of England, Scotland and Ireland, and the Dominions and Territories thereto belonging, to whom we do acknowledge all Fidelity, and conſtant Obedience according to Law and the ſaid Humble Petition and Advice, With all humble and hearty affection; Beſeeching the LORD, by whom Princes rule, to bleſſe Him with long life, and theſe Nations with peace and happineſſe under his Government.

And the ſaid Council do hereby command the Sheriffs of the reſpective Shires, with all poſſible ſpeed, to cauſe theſe Preſents to be publiſhed in all the Market-Towns (except Burghs Royal) in their Sheriffdooms reſpectively; And do likewiſe command the Provoſt and Baylies of the reſpective Burghs Royal in Scotland, with all poſſible ſpeed, to cauſe theſe Preſents to be proclaimed in their reſpective Burghs, with all the Solemnity that is requiſite upon ſuch an occaſion. And the ſaid Sheriffs, Provoſts and Baylies, are hereby required to make reſpective Returns of their Diligence herein to the Council with all expedition.

Given at Edinburgh the Ninth Day of September, 1658.

George Monck, Samuel Disbrowe, Edward Rodes,
John Suintoune, Nathaniel Whetham.

GOD ſave His Highneſſe RICHARD Lord Protector.

EDINBURGH,

Printed by Chriſtopher Higgins, in Harts Cloſe, over againſt the Trone Church, Anno Donini, 1658.

Proclamation announcing the death of Oliver Cromwell and the succession of Richard Cromwell as Lord Protector. Printed in Scotland, 1658. Courtesy of the General Collection, Beinecke Rare Book and Manuscript Library, Yale University, New Haven, Connecticut. In 1660, Richard Cromwell left for France and later traveled around Europe, visiting various European courts. In 1680 or 1681, he returned to England and lodged with the merchant Thomas Pengelly in Cheshunt, Hertfordshire, living off the income from his estate in Hursley. He died in 1712 at the age of 85.

Power Struggles

Charles Fleetwood was appointed a member of the Committee of Safety and of the Council of State, and one of the seven commissioners for the army. On June 9, 1659, he was nominated lord-general (commander-in-chief) of the army. However, his leadership was undermined in Parliament. A royalist uprising was planned for August 1, 1659, and although it never happened, Sir George Booth gained control of

Cheshire. Booth held Cheshire until the end of August, when he was defeated by General John Lambert. On October 26, a Committee of Safety was appointed, of which Fleetwood and Lambert were members. Lambert was appointed major-general of all the forces in England and Scotland, with Fleetwood being general. The Committee of Safety sent Lambert with a large force to meet George Monck, who was in command of the English forces in Scotland, and either negotiate with him or force him to come to terms.

It was into this atmosphere that Monck, the governor of Scotland under the Cromwells, marched south with his army from Scotland. Lambert's army began to desert him, and he returned to London almost alone, though he marched unopposed. The Presbyterian members, excluded in Pride's Purge of 1648, were recalled, and on December 24 the army restored the Long Parliament. Fleetwood was deprived of his command and ordered to appear before Parliament to answer for his conduct. In March 1660, Lambert was sent to the Tower of London, from which he escaped a month later. He tried to rekindle the civil war in favor of the Commonwealth, but he was recaptured by Colonel Richard Ingoldsby, a participant in the regicide of Charles I, who hoped to win a pardon by handing Lambert over to the new regime. Lambert was incarcerated and died in custody in 1684; Ingoldsby was, indeed, pardoned.

Restoration of Charles II

On April 4, 1660, Charles II issued the Declaration of Breda, in which he made several promises in relation to the reclamation of the crown of England. Monck organized the Convention Parliament; on May 8, it proclaimed that King Charles II had been the lawful monarch since the execution of Charles I on January 30, 1649. Charles entered London on May 29, his birthday. To celebrate his Majesty's Return to his Parliament, May 29 was made a public holiday, popularly known as Oak Apple Day. He was crowned at Westminster Abbey on April 23, 1661. The Cavalier Parliament convened for the first time in May 1661, and it would endure for over seventeen years. Like its predecessor, it was overwhelmingly Royalist. It is also known as the Pensionary Parliament for the many pensions it granted to adherents of the king.

Many Royalist exiles returned and were rewarded. The Indemnity and Oblivion Act, which became law in August 1660, pardoned all past treason against the crown, but specifically excluded those involved in the trial and execution of Charles I. Thirty-one of the fifty-nine commissioners (judges) who had signed the death warrant in 1649 were living. In the ensuing trials, twelve were condemned to death. In October 1660, ten were publicly hanged, drawn, and quartered. Oliver Cromwell, Henry Ireton, Judge Thomas Pride, and Judge John Bradshaw were posthumously attained for high treason. In January 1661, the corpses of Cromwell, Ireton, and Bradshaw were exhumed and hanged in chains at Tyburn.

Charles II of England by Peter Lely, 1675, Collection of Euston Hall, Suffolk. King Charles II, the first monarch to rule after the English Restoration.

Sources

Attributions

CC licensed content, Specific attribution

- Boundless World History. **Authored by**: Boundless. **Located at**: https://courses.lumenlearning.com/boundless-worldhistory/. **License**: *CC BY-SA: Attribution-ShareAlike*

The Glorious Revolution

Learning Objective

- Analyze the significant changes the Glorious Revolution made to English government

Key Points

- James II ascended the throne upon the death of his brother, Charles II, in 1685. During his short reign, he became directly involved in the political battles between Catholicism and Protestantism and between the Divine Right of Kings and the political rights of the Parliament of England.

- James's greatest political problem was his Catholicism, which left him alienated from both parties in England. Amidst continuous tensions between the king and Parliament, matters came to a head in June 1688, when James had a son, James. Until then, the throne would have passed to his daughter Mary, a Protestant.

- Mary and her husband, William Henry of Orange, both Protestants, appeared as potential rulers who could lead an anti-James revolution and replace the Catholic king. It is still a matter of controversy whether the initiative for the conspiracy to take over the throne was taken by the English or by William and his wife.

- On June 30, 1688, a group of seven Protestant nobles invited the Prince of Orange to come to England with an army. By September, it became clear that William would invade England. William arrived on November 5.

- In December, James fled the country, and in 1689 William and Mary were appointed monarchs.

- In order to regulate the relationship between the monarch and Parliament, the Bill of Rights was passed in 1689. It lays down limits on the powers of the monarch and sets out the rights of Parliament, including the requirement for regular parliaments, free elections, and freedom of speech in Parliament.

Terms

Divine Right of Kings

A political and religious doctrine of royal and political legitimacy. It asserts that a monarch is subject to no earthly authority, and derives the right to rule directly from the will of God. The king is thus not subject to the will of his people, the aristocracy, or any other estate of the realm, including the Catholic Church.

Penal Laws

A specific series of laws that sought to uphold the establishment of the Church of England against Protestant Nonconformists and Catholicism by imposing various forfeitures, civil penalties, and civil disabilities upon these dissenters. They were repealed in the 19th century during the process of Catholic Emancipation.

Test Act

A series of English penal laws that served as a religious test for public office and imposed various civil disabilities on Roman Catholics and Nonconformists. The principle was that none but people taking communion in the established Church of England were eligible for public employment.

Declaration of Indulgence

A pair of proclamations made by James II of England and VII of Scotland in 1687. It granted broad religious freedom in England by suspending penal laws enforcing conformity to the Church of England and allowing persons to worship in their homes or chapels as they saw fit, and it ended the requirement of affirming religious oaths before gaining employment in government office.

stadtholder

In the Low Countries, a medieval function that during the 16th, 17th, and 18th centuries developed into a rare type of *de facto* hereditary head of state of the thus crowned republic of the Netherlands. Additionally, this position was tasked with maintaining peace and provincial order in the early Dutch Republic.

James II of England

James II of England (VII of Scotland) was the second surviving son of Charles I; he ascended the throne upon the death of his brother, Charles II, in 1685. During his short reign, James became directly involved in the political battles between Catholicism and Protestantism and between the Divine Right of Kings and the political rights of the Parliament of England. James's greatest political problem was his Catholicism, which left him alienated from both parties in England. However, the facts that he had no son and his daughters were Protestants were a "saving grace." James's attempt to relax the Penal Laws alienated Tories, his natural supporters, because they viewed this as tantamount to disestablishment of the Church of England.

Abandoning the Tories, James looked to form a "King's party" as a counterweight to the Anglican Tories, so in 1687 he supported the policy of religious toleration and issued the Declaration of Indulgence. By allying himself with the Catholics, Dissenters, and Nonconformists, James hoped to build a coalition that would advance Catholic emancipation. Matters came to a head in June 1688, when the king had a son, James. Until then, the throne would have passed to his daughter Mary, a Protestant. The prospect of a Catholic dynasty in the kingdoms of England, Scotland, and Ireland was now likely.

James II King of England and VII King of Scots, King of Ireland and Duke of Normandy, painting by Sir Godfrey Kneller, 1683.

Conspiracy: William and Mary

Mary and her husband, her cousin William Henry of Orange, were both Protestants and grandchildren of Charles I of England. William was also stadtholder of the main provinces of the Dutch Republic. He had already acquired the reputation of being the main champion of the Protestant cause against Catholicism and French absolutism. In the developing English crisis, he saw an opportunity to prevent an Anglo-French alliance and bring England to the anti-French side by carrying out a military intervention directed against James. This suited the desires of several English politicians who intended to depose James. It is still a matter of controversy whether the initiative for the conspiracy was taken by the English or by the stadtholder and his wife.

Invasion

On June 30, 1688, a group of seven Protestant nobles invited the Prince of Orange to come to England with an army. By September, it became clear that William would invade England. William arrived on November 5. James refused a French offer to send an expeditionary force, fearing that it would cost him domestic support. He tried to bring the Tories to his side by making concessions, but failed because he still refused to endorse the Test Act. His forward forces had gathered at Salisbury, and James went to join them on November 19 with his main force, having a total strength of about 19,000. Amid anti-Catholic rioting in London, it rapidly became apparent that the troops were not eager to fight, and the loyalty of many of James's commanders was doubtful.

Meanwhile, on November 18, Plymouth had surrendered to William, and on November 21, William began to advance. In December, William's forces met with the king's commissioners to negotiate. James offered free elections and a general amnesty for the rebels. In reality, by that point he was simply playing for time, having already decided to flee the country. James was received in France by his cousin and ally, Louis XIV, who offered him a palace and a pension.

The Bill of Rights

The status of William and Mary in England was unclear while James, though now in France, still had many supporters in the country. In order to avoid James's return to the throne, and facing opposition in Parliament, William let it be known that he was happy for Mary to be queen in name and for preference in the succession given to Princess Anne's (Mary's sister) children over any of William's. Anne declared that she would temporarily waive her right to the crown should Mary die before William, and Mary refused to be made queen without William as king. The Lords accepted the words "abdication" and "vacancy" and Lord Winchester's motion to appoint William and Mary monarchs. The decision was made in light of a great fear that the situation might deteriorate into a civil war.

Although their succession to the English throne was relatively peaceful, much blood would be shed before William's authority was accepted in Ireland and Scotland.

Detail of William and Mary as portrayed on the ceiling of the Greenwich Hospital. Painting: Sir James Thornhill; Photo: James Brittain. William and Mary were co-regents over the Kingdoms of England, Scotland, and Ireland. Parliament offered William and Mary a co-regency, at the couple's behest. After Mary died in 1694, William ruled alone until his death in 1702. William and Mary were childless and were ultimately succeeded by Mary's younger sister, Anne.

The proposal to draw up a statement of rights and liberties and James's invasion of them was first made in January in the Commons, but what would become the Bill of Rights did not pass until December 1689. The Bill was a restatement in statutory form of The Declaration of Rights presented by the Convention Parliament to William and Mary in February 1689, inviting them to become joint sovereigns of England. The Bill of Rights lay down limits on the powers of the monarch and set out the rights of Parliament, including the requirement for regular parliaments, free elections, and freedom of speech in Parliament. It set out certain rights of individuals, including the prohibition of cruel and unusual punishment, and reestablished the liberty of Protestants to have arms for their defense within the rule of law. Furthermore, the Bill of Rights described and condemned several misdeeds of James II of England. These ideas reflected those of the political thinker John Locke, and they quickly became popular in England. It also set out—or, in the view of its drafters, restated—certain constitutional requirements of the Crown to seek the consent of the people, as represented in Parliament.

Significance

The Glorious Revolution of 1688 is considered by some as one of the most important events in the long evolution of the respective powers of Parliament and the Crown in England. The passage of the Bill of Rights stamped out once and for all any possibility of a Catholic monarchy and ended moves towards absolute monarchy in the British kingdoms by circumscribing the monarch's powers. These powers were greatly restricted. He or she could no longer suspend laws, levy taxes, make royal appointments, or maintain a standing army during peacetime without Parliament's permission. Since 1689, government under a system of constitutional monarchy in England, and later the United Kingdom, has been uninterrupted. Also since then, Parliament's power has steadily increased while the Crown's has steadily declined.

Sources

Attributions

CC licensed content, Specific attribution

- Boundless World History. **Authored by**: Boundless. **Located at**: https://courses.lumenlearning.com/boundless-worldhistory/. **License**: *CC BY-SA: Attribution-ShareAlike*

Cardinal Mazarin and the Fronde

- Discuss Cardinal Mazarin's goals during his tenure as regent

- Cardinal Jules Mazarin was an Italian cardinal, diplomat, and politician who served as the Chief Minister to the King of France from 1642 until his death in 1661. He functioned essentially as the co-ruler of France alongside the queen during the regency of Anne, and until his death effectively directed French policy alongside the monarch, Louis XIV.

- Mazarin continued Richelieu's anti-Habsburg policy and laid the foundation for Louis XIV's expansionist policies. He was critical to the negotiations of the Peace of Westphalia, which left France the most powerful state in continental Europe.

- Towards Protestantism at home, Mazarin pursued a policy of promises and calculated delay to defuse armed insurrections and keep the Huguenots disarmed. However, the Huguenots never achieved any protection.

- As the Crown needed to recover from its expenditures in the recent wars, the increase of taxes contributed to already growing social unrest. The attempt to curb existing liberties resulted in a series of civil wars known as the Fronde.

- Although Mazarin and the king confronted the combined opposition of the princes, the nobility, the law courts (parlements), and most of the French people, they won out in the end. The Fronde was divided into two campaigns, that of the parlements and that of the nobles, and its collapse only strengthened the absolute monarchy.

- Mazarin, as the de facto ruler of France, played a crucial role establishing the Westphalian principles that would guide European states' foreign policy and the prevailing world order.

Terms

Edict of Nantes

An edict signed probably in 1598 by King Henry IV of France that granted the Calvinist Protestants of France (also known as Huguenots) substantial rights in the nation, which was, at the time, still considered essentially Catholic. It separated civil from religious unity, treated some Protestants for the first time as more than mere schismatics and heretics, and opened a path for secularism and tolerance. In offering general freedom of conscience to individuals, the Edict offered many specific concessions to the Protestants.

Jansenism

A Catholic theological movement, primarily in France, that emphasized original sin, human depravity, the necessity of divine grace, and predestination. The movement originated from the posthumously published work of the Dutch theologian Cornelius Jansen, who died in 1638. It was opposed by many in the Catholic hierarchy, especially the Jesuits.

Thirty Years' War

A series of wars in Central Europe between 1618 and 1648. Initially a war between various Protestant and Catholic states in the fragmented Holy Roman Empire, it gradually developed into a more general conflict involving most of the great powers.

Peace of Westphalia

A series of peace treaties signed between May and October 1648 in the Westphalian cities of Osnabrück and Münster. These treaties ended the Thirty Years' War (1618–1648) in the Holy Roman Empire, and the Eighty Years' War (1568–1648) between Spain and the Dutch Republic, with Spain formally recognizing the independence of the Dutch Republic.

League of the Rhine

A defensive union of more than fifty German princes and their cities along the River Rhine, formed in August 1658 by Louis XIV of France and negotiated by Cardinal Mazarin (then *de facto* prime minister of France), Hugues de Lionne, and Johann Philipp von Schönborn (Elector of Mainz and Chancellor of the Empire).

The Fronde

A series of civil wars in France between 1648 and 1653, occurring in the midst of the Franco-Spanish War, which had begun in 1635. The king confronted the combined opposition of the princes, the nobility, the law courts (parlements), and most of the French people, yet won out in the end. It was divided into two campaigns, that of the parlements and that of the nobles.

Cardinal Mazarin

Cardinal Jules Mazarin was an Italian cardinal, diplomat, and politician who served as the Chief Minister to the King of France from 1642 until his death in 1661. After serving in the papal army and diplomatic service and at the French court, he entered the service of France and made himself valuable to King Louis XIII's chief minister, Cardinal Richelieu, who brought him into the council of state. After Richelieu's death, Mazarin succeeded him as Chief Minister of France. At the time of King Louis XIII's death in 1643, his successor, Louis XIV, was only five years old, and his mother, Anne of Austria, ruled in his place until he came of age. Mazarin helped Anne expand the limited power her husband had left her. He functioned essentially as the co-ruler of France alongside the queen during the regency of Anne, and until his death Mazarin effectively directed French policy alongside the monarch.

Cardinal Mazarin by Pierre Mignard, 1658-1660. Mazarin succeeded his mentor, Cardinal Richelieu. He was a noted collector of art and jewels, particularly diamonds, and he bequeathed the "Mazarin diamonds" to Louis XIV in 1661, some of which remain in the collection of the Louvre museum in Paris. His personal library was the origin of the Bibliothèque Mazarine in Paris.

Policies

Mazarin continued Richelieu's anti-Habsburg policy and laid the foundation for Louis XIV's expansionist policies. During the negotiations of the Peace of Westphalia, which concluded the Thirty Years' War, Mazarin (together with the queen) represented France with policies that were French rather than Catholic. The terms of the peace treaties ensured Dutch independence from Spain, awarded some autonomy to the various German princes of the Holy Roman Empire, and granted Sweden seats on the Imperial Diet and territories to control the mouths of the Oder, Elbe, and Weser rivers. France, however, profited most from the settlement. Austria, ruled by the Habsburg Emperor Ferdinand III, ceded all Habsburg lands and claims in Alsace to France and acknowledged her *de facto* sovereignty over the Three Bishoprics of Metz, Verdun, and Toul. Moreover, eager to emancipate themselves from Habsburg domination, petty German states sought French protection. This anticipated the formation of the 1658 League of the Rhine, leading to the further diminution of Imperial power.

The League was designed to check the House of Austria in central Germany. In 1659, Mazarin made peace with Habsburg Spain in the Peace of the Pyrenees, which added Roussillon and northern Cerdanya—as French Cerdagne—in the far south, as well as part of the Low Countries, to French territory.

Towards Protestantism at home, Mazarin pursued a policy of promises and calculated delay to defuse armed insurrections and keep the Huguenots disarmed. For six years they believed themselves to be on the eve of recovering the protections of the Edict of Nantes, but in the end they obtained nothing. Mazarin was also more consistently an enemy of Jansenism, more for its political implications than out of theology.

The Fronde

As the Crown needed to recover from its expenditures in the recent wars, the increase of taxes contributed to already growing social unrest. The nobility refused to be taxed, based on their old liberties or privileges, and the brunt fell upon the bourgeoisie. The Fronde began in January 1648, when the Paris mob used children's slings (*frondes*) to hurl stones at the windows of Mazarin's associates. The insurrection did not start with revolutionary goals but aimed to protect the ancient *liberties* from royal encroachments and to defend the established rights of the *parlements*—courts of appeal rather than legislative bodies like the English parliaments. The movement soon degenerated into factions, some of which attempted to overthrow Mazarin and reverse the policies of his predecessor, Cardinal Richelieu, who had taken power for the Crown from great territorial nobles, some of whom became leaders of the Fronde.

In May 1648, a tax levied on judicial officers of the Parlement of Paris provoked not merely a refusal to pay but also a condemnation of earlier financial edicts and a demand for the acceptance of a scheme of constitutional reforms framed by a united committee of the *parlement* (the Chambre Saint-Louis), composed of members of all the sovereign courts of Paris. The military record of what would be known as the First Fronde (the *Fronde Parlementaire*) is almost blank. In August 1648, Mazarin suddenly arrested the leaders of the parlement, whereupon Paris broke into insurrection and barricaded the streets. The royal faction, having no army at its immediate disposal, had to release the prisoners and promise reforms, and on the night of October 22 it fled from Paris. However, France's signing of the Peace of Westphalia allowed the French army to return from the frontiers and put Paris under siege. The two warring parties signed the Peace of Rueil (1649) after little blood had been shed.

The peace lasted until the end of 1649. In January 1650, an armed rebellion (the onset of what would know known known as the Second Fronde or the *Fronde des nobles*) followed the arrests of several nobles by Mazarin. By April 1651, after a series of battles, the rebellion collapsed everywhere. A few months of hollow peace followed and the court returned to Paris. Mazarin, an object of hatred to all the princes, had already retired into exile. His absence left the field free for mutual jealousies, and for the remainder of the year anarchy reigned in France.

In December 1651, Mazarin returned to France with a small army. The war began again, but this time some leaders of the rebellion were pitted against one another. After this campaign the civil war ceased, but in the several other campaigns of the Franco-Spanish War that followed, two great soldiers leading the Fronde were opposed to one another: Henri, Viscount of Turenne, as the defender of France and Louis II, and Prince de Condé as a Spanish invader. In 1652, an insurrectionist government appeared in Paris. Mazarin, feeling that public opinion was solidly against him, left France again. Although in exile, he was not idle, and reached an agreement with Turenne. Turenne's forces pursued Condé's, who in 1653 fled to the Spanish Netherlands. Louis XIV, now of age to claim his throne, re-entered Paris in October 1652 and recalled Mazarin in February 1653. The last vestiges of resistance in Bordeaux fizzled out in the late summer of 1653.

"Louis XIV Crushes the Fronde" by Gilles Guérin, 1654. The Fronde represented the final attempt of the French nobility to battle the king, and they were humiliated. The Fronde facilitated the emergence of absolute monarchy.

Legacy

Following the end of the Thirty Years' War, Mazarin, as the de facto ruler of France, played a crucial role establishing the Westphalian principles that would guide European states' foreign policy and the prevailing world order. Some of these principles, such as nation-state sovereignty over its territory and domestic affairs and the legal equality among states, remain the basis of international law to this day.

The French people suffered terribly in the Fronde, but the wars achieved no constitutional reform. The liberties under attack were feudal, not of individuals, and the Fronde in the end provided an incentive for the establishment of royalist absolutism, since the disorders eventually discredited the feudal concept of liberty. Royal absolutism was reinstalled without any effective limitation. On the death of Mazarin in 1661, Louis XIV assumed personal control of the reins of government and astonished his court by declaring that he would rule without a chief minister.

Sources

Attributions

CC licensed content, Specific attribution

The Sun-King and Authoritarianism

Learning Objective

- Describe Louis XIV's views on royal power and how he expanded his own authority

Key Points

- At the time of King Louis XIII's death in 1643, Louis XIV was only five years old. His mother, Anne of Austria, was named regent, but she entrusted the government to the chief minister, Cardinal Mazarin. Mazarin's policies paved the way for the authoritarian reign of Louis XIV.

- Louis began his personal reign with administrative and fiscal reforms. National debt was quickly reduced through more efficient taxation, although reforms imposing taxes on the aristocracy were late and of limited outcome.

- Louis and his administration also bolstered French commerce and trade by establishing new industries in France and instituted reforms in military administration that curbed the independent spirit of the nobility by imposing order at court and in the army.

- Louis also attempted uniform regulation of civil procedure throughout legally irregular France by issuing a comprehensive legal code, the "Grande Ordonnance de Procédure Civile" of 1667, also known as the Code Louis. One of his most infamous decrees was the Code Noir, which sanctioned slavery in French colonies.

- Louis also attached nobles to his court at Versailles and thus achieved increased control over the French aristocracy. An elaborate court ritual by which the king observed the aristocracy and distributed his favors was created to ensure the aristocracy remained under his scrutiny.

- Following consistent efforts to limit religious tolerance, Louis XIV issued the Edict of

Fontainebleau, which revoked the Edict of Nantes and repealed all the privileges that arose therefrom.

Terms

cuius regio, eius religio

A Latin phrase that literally means "Whose realm, his religion," meaning that the religion of the ruler was to dictate the religion of those ruled. At the Peace of Augsburg of 1555, which ended a period of armed conflict between Roman Catholic and Protestant forces within the Holy Roman Empire, the rulers of the German-speaking states and Charles V, the emperor, agreed to accept this principle.

Declaration of the Clergy of France

A four-article document of the 1681 Assembly of the French clergy promulgated in 1682, which codified the principles of Gallicanism into a system for the first time in an official and definitive formula.

Gallicanism

The belief that popular civil authority—often represented by the monarchs' authority or the state's authority—over the Catholic Church is comparable to the pope's.

Edict of Fontainebleau

A 1685 edict issued by Louis XIV of France, also known as the Revocation of the Edict of Nantes. The Edict of Nantes (1598) had granted the Huguenots the right to practice their religion without persecution from the state.

Code Noir

A decree originally passed by France's King Louis XIV in 1685 that defined the conditions of slavery in the French colonial empire, restricted the activities of free black persons, forbade the exercise of any religion other than Roman Catholicism, and ordered all Jews out of France's colonies.

The Sun King

At the time of King Louis XIII's death in 1643, Louis XIV was only five years old. His mother, Anne of Austria, was named regent in spite of her late husband's wishes. Anne assumed the regency but entrusted the government to the chief minister, Cardinal Mazarin, who helped her expand the limited power her husband had left her. He functioned essentially as the co-ruler of France alongside Queen Anne during her regency, and until his death effectively directed French policy alongside the monarch. In 1651, when Louis

XIV officially came of age, Anne's regency legally ended. However, she kept much power and influence over her son until the death of Mazarin. On the death of Mazarin in 1661, Louis assumed personal control of the reins of government and astonished his court by declaring that he would rule without a chief minister.

Louis XIV, King of France, in 1661 by Charles Le Brun. After Mazarin's death in 1661, Louis assumed personal control of the reins of government and astonished his court by declaring that he would rule without a chief minister: "Up to this moment I have been pleased to entrust the government of my affairs to the late Cardinal. It is now time that I govern them myself. You [he was talking to the secretaries and ministers of state] will assist me with your counsels when I ask for them. I request and order you to seal no orders except by my command ... I order you not to sign anything, not even a passport ... without my command; to render account to me personally each day and to favor no one."

Reforms

Louis began his personal reign with administrative and fiscal reforms. In 1661, the treasury verged on bankruptcy. To rectify the situation, Louis chose Jean-Baptiste Colbert as Controller-General of Finances in 1665. Colbert reduced the national debt through more efficient taxation. Excellent results were achieved, and the deficit of 1661 turned into a surplus in 1666. However, to support the reorganized and enlarged army, the panoply of Versailles, and the growing civil administration, the king needed a good deal of money, but methods of collecting taxes were costly and inefficient. The main weakness of the existing system arose from an old bargain between the French crown and nobility: the king might raise without consent if only he refrained from taxing the nobles. Only towards the close of his reign, under extreme stress of war, was Louis able, for the first time in French history, to impose direct taxes on the aristocracy. This was a step toward equality before the law and toward sound public finance, but so many concessions and exemptions were won by nobles and bourgeois that the reform lost much of its value.

Louis and Colbert also had wide-ranging plans to bolster French commerce and trade. Colbert's administration established new industries, encouraged domestic manufacturers and inventors, and invited manufacturers and artisans from all over Europe to France. This aimed to decrease foreign imports while increasing French exports, hence reducing the net outflow of precious metals from France.

Louis also instituted reforms in military administration and, with the help of his trusted experts, curbed the independent spirit of the nobility by imposing order at court and in the army. Gone were the days when generals protracted war at the frontiers while bickering over precedence and ignoring orders from the capital and the larger politico-diplomatic picture. The old military aristocracy ceased to have a monopoly over senior military positions and rank.

Louis also attempted uniform regulation of civil procedure throughout legally irregular France by issuing a comprehensive legal code, the "Grande Ordonnance de Procédure Civile" of 1667, also known as the Code Louis. Among other things, it prescribed baptismal, marriage, and death records in the state's registers, not the church's, and also strictly regulated the right of the Parlements to remonstrate. The Code Louis played an important part in French legal history as the basis for the Napoleonic code, itself the origin of many modern legal codes.One of Louis's most infamous decrees was the *Grande Ordonnance sur les Colonies* of 1685, also known as the *Code Noir* ("black code"). It sanctioned slavery and limited the ownership of slaves in the colonies to Roman Catholics only. It also required slaves to be baptized.

Centralization of Power

Louis initially supported traditional Gallicanism, which limited papal authority in France, and convened an Assembly of the French clergy in November 1681. Before its dissolution eight months later, the assembly had accepted the Declaration of the Clergy of France, which increased royal authority at the expense of papal power. Without royal approval, bishops could not leave France and appeals could not be made to the pope. Additionally, government officials could not be excommunicated for acts committed in pursuance of their duties. Although the king could not make ecclesiastical law, all papal regulations without royal assent were invalid in France. Unsurprisingly, the pope repudiated the declaration.

Louis also attached nobles to his court at Versailles and thus achieved increased control over the French aristocracy. Apartments were built to house those willing to pay court to the king. However, the pensions and privileges necessary to live in a style appropriate to their rank were only possible by waiting constantly on Louis. For this purpose, an elaborate court ritual was created where the king became the center of attention and was observed throughout the day by the public. With his excellent memory, Louis could see who attended him at court and who was absent, facilitating the subsequent distribution of favors and positions. Another tool Louis used to control his nobility was censorship, which often involved opening letters to discern their author's opinion of the government and king. Moreover, by entertaining, impressing, and domesticating nobles with extravagant luxury and other distractions, Louis not only cultivated public opinion of himself, but also ensured the aristocracy remained under his scrutiny.

This, along with the prohibition of private armies, prevented the aristocracy from passing time on their own estates and in their regional power-bases, from which they historically had waged local wars and plotted resistance to royal authority. Louis thus compelled and seduced the old military aristocracy (the "nobility of the sword") into becoming his ceremonial courtiers, further weakening their power. In their place, he raised commoners or the more recently ennobled bureaucratic aristocracy as presumably easier to control.

Religion

Finally, Louis dramatically limited religious tolerance in France, as he saw the persistence of Protestantism as a disgraceful reminder of royal powerlessness. Responding to petitions, Louis initially excluded Protestants from office, constrained the meeting of synods, closed churches outside Edict of Nantes-stipulated areas, banned Protestant outdoor preachers, and prohibited domestic Protestant migration. He also disallowed Protestant-Catholic intermarriages where third parties objected, encouraged missions to the Protestants, and rewarded converts to Catholicism.

In 1681, Louis dramatically increased his persecution of Protestants. The principle of *cuius regio, eius religio* generally had also meant that subjects who refused to convert could emigrate, but Louis banned emigration and effectively insisted that all Protestants must be converted. In 1685, he issued the Edict of Fontainebleau, which cited the redundancy of privileges for Protestants given their scarcity after the extensive conversions. It revoked the Edict of Nantes and repealed all the privileges that arose therefrom. By his edict, Louis no longer tolerated Protestant groups, pastors, or churches to exist in France. No further churches were to be constructed, and those already existing were to be demolished. Pastors could choose either exile or a secular life. Those Protestants who had resisted conversion were now to be baptized forcibly into the established church.

Sources

Attributions

CC licensed content, Specific attribution

- Boundless World History. **Authored by**: Boundless. **Located at**: https://courses.lumenlearning.com/boundless-worldhistory/. **License**: *CC BY-SA: Attribution-ShareAlike*

Louis XIV and the Huguenots

Key Points

- The Edict of Nantes was issued in 1598 by Henry IV of France. It granted the Calvinist Protestants of France substantial rights in a predominately Catholic nation. The Edict gained a new significance when Louis XIV broke the post-Nantes tradition of relative religious tolerance in France and, in his efforts to fully centralize the royal power, began to persecute the Protestants.

- Louis initially supported traditional Gallicanism, which limited papal authority in France. However, his conflict with the pope did not prevent him from making Catholicism the only legally tolerated religion in France.

- Louis saw the persistence of Protestantism as a disgraceful reminder of royal powerlessness. Responding to petitions, he initially excluded Protestants from office, constrained the meeting of synods, closed churches outside Edict-stipulated areas, banned Protestant outdoor preachers, and prohibited domestic Protestant migration.

- In 1681, Louis dramatically increased the persecution of Protestants. He banned emigration and effectively insisted that all Protestants must be converted. He also began quartering dragoons in Protestant homes.

- In 1685, Louis issued the Edict of Fontainebleau, which cited the redundancy of privileges for Protestants given their scarcity after the extensive conversions. The Edict of Fontainebleau revoked the Edict of Nantes.

- The revocation caused France to suffer a kind of early brain drain, as it lost a large number of skilled craftsmen. Protestants across Europe were horrified at the treatment of their fellow believers, and Louis's public image in most of Europe, especially in Protestant regions, suffered greatly.

Terms

Declaration of the Clergy of France

A four-article document of the 1681 Assembly of the French clergy promulgated in 1682, which codified the principles of Gallicanism into a system for the first time in an official and definitive formula.

Edict of Fontainebleau

A 1685 edict, also known as the Revocation of the Edict of Nantes, issued by Louis XIV of France. The Edict of Nantes (1598) had granted the Huguenots the right to practice their religion without persecution from the state.

cuius regio, eius religio

A Latin phrase that literally means "Whose realm, his religion," meaning that the religion of the ruler was to dictate the religion of those ruled. At the Peace of Augsburg of 1555, which ended a period of armed conflict between Roman Catholic and Protestant forces within the Holy Roman Empire, the rulers of the German-speaking states and Emperor Charles V agreed to accept this principle.

Gallicanism

The belief that popular civil authority—often represented by the monarchs' authority or the State's authority—over the Catholic Church is comparable to the authority of the pope.

Edict of Nantes

An edict signed in 1598 by King Henry IV of France that granted the Calvinist Protestants of France (also known as Huguenots) substantial rights in the nation, which was, at the time, still considered essentially Catholic. In the Edict, Henry aimed primarily to promote civil unity. The document separated civil from religious unity, treated some Protestants for the first time as more than mere schismatics and heretics, and opened a path for secularism and tolerance.

Background: Edict of Nantes

The Edict of Nantes was issued in 1598 by Henry IV of France. It granted the Calvinist Protestants of France, known as Huguenots, substantial rights in a predominately Catholic nation. Through the Edict, Henry aimed to promote civil unity. The Edict treated some, although not all, Protestants with tolerance and opened a path for secularism. It offered general freedom of conscience to individuals and many specific concessions to the Protestants, such as amnesty and the reinstatement of their civil rights, including the right to work in any field or for the state and to bring grievances directly to the king. It marked the end of the religious wars that had afflicted France during the second half of the 16th century. The Edict gained a new significance when Louis XIV, known as the Sun King, broke the post-Nantes tradition of relative religious tolerance in France and, in his efforts to fully centralize the royal power, began to persecute the Protestants.

Louis XIV by Hyacinthe Rigaud (1701). Louis XIV (1638–1715), known as Louis the Great or the Sun King, was a monarch of the House of Bourbon who ruled as King of France from 1643 until his death in 1715. His reign of seventy-two years and 110 days is the longest of any monarch of a major country in European history. In this age of absolutism in Europe, Louis XIV's France was a leader in the growing centralization of power.

Religious Persecution

Louis initially supported traditional Gallicanism, which limited papal authority in France, and convened an Assembly of the French clergy in November 1681. Before its dissolution eight months later, the assembly had accepted the Declaration of the Clergy of France, which increased royal authority at the expense of papal power. Without royal approval, bishops could not leave France and appeals could not be made to the pope. Additionally, government officials could not be excommunicated for acts committed in pursuance of their duties. Although the king could not make ecclesiastical law, all papal regulations without royal assent were invalid in France. Unsurprisingly, the pope repudiated the declaration.

Louis saw the persistence of Protestantism as a disgraceful reminder of royal powerlessness. After all, the Edict of Nantes was the pragmatic concession of his grandfather Henry IV to end the longstanding French Wars of Religion. An additional factor in Louis's thinking was the prevailing contemporary European principle to assure socio-political stability, *cuius regio, eius religio* ("whose realm, his religion"), the idea that the religion of the ruler should be the religion of the realm (the principle originally confirmed in central Europe in the Peace of Augsburg of 1555).

Responding to petitions, Louis initially excluded Protestants from office, constrained the meeting of synods, closed churches outside Edict-stipulated areas, banned Protestant outdoor preachers, and prohibited domestic Protestant migration. He also disallowed Protestant-Catholic intermarriages where third parties objected, encouraged missions to the Protestants, and rewarded converts to Catholicism. An enforced yet steady conversion of Protestants followed, especially among the noble elites.

In 1681, Louis dramatically increased the persecution of Protestants. The principle of *cuius regio, eius religio* had usually meant that subjects who refused to convert could emigrate, but Louis banned emigration and effectively insisted that all Protestants must be converted. Secondly, following the proposal of René de Marillac and the Marquis of Louvois, he began quartering dragoons (mounted infantry) in Protestant homes. Although this was within his legal rights, the policy (known as *dragonnades)* inflicted severe financial strain and atrocious abuse on Protestants. Between 300,000 and 400,000 Huguenots converted, as this entailed financial rewards and exemption from the *dragonnades*.

Edict of Fontainebleau

In 1685, Louis issued the Edict of Fontainebleau, which cited the redundancy of privileges for Protestants given their scarcity after the extensive conversions. The Edict of Fontainebleau revoked the Edict of Nantes, and repealed all the privileges that arose therefrom. By this edict, Louis no longer tolerated Protestant groups, pastors, or churches to exist in France. No further Protestant churches were to be constructed, and those already existing were to be demolished. Pastors could choose either exile or a secular life. Those Protestants who had resisted conversion were to be baptized forcibly into the established church.

The Edict of Fontainebleau is compared by historians with the 1492 Alhambra Decree, ordering the Expulsion of the Jews from Spain, and with Expulsion of the Moriscos during 1609–1614. The three are similar both as outbursts of religious intolerance ending periods of relative tolerance and in their social and economic effects. In practice, the revocation caused France to suffer a kind of early brain drain, as it lost a large number of skilled craftsmen. Some rulers, such as Frederick Wilhelm, Duke of Prussia and Elector of Brandenburg, encouraged the Protestants to seek refuge in their nations. Historians cite the emigration of about 200,000 Huguenots (roughly one-fourth of the Protestant population, or 1% of the French population) who defied royal decrees. However, others view this as an exaggeration. They argue that most of France's preeminent Protestant businessmen and industrialists converted to Catholicism and remained. Protestants across Europe were horrified at the treatment of their fellow believers, and Louis's public image in most of Europe, especially in Protestant regions, suffered greatly. Most Catholics in France, however, applauded the move.

The revocation of the Edict of Nantes created a state of affairs in France similar to that of nearly every other European country of the period (with the brief exception of Great Britain and possibly the Polish-Lithuanian Commonwealth), where only the majority state religion was legally tolerated. The experiment of religious toleration in Europe was effectively ended for the time being. However, French society would sufficiently change by the time of Louis's descendant Louis XVI to welcome toleration in the form of the 1787 Edict of Versailles, also known as the Edict of Tolerance. This restored to non-Catholics their civil rights and the freedom to worship openly.

Sources

Attributions

CC licensed content, Specific attribution

- Boundless World History. **Authored by**: Boundless. **Located at**: https://courses.lumenlearning.com/boundless-worldhistory/. **License**: *CC BY-SA: Attribution-ShareAlike*

Louis XIV's Wars

Learning Objective

- Identify the consequences of Louis XIV's wars

Key Points

- In addition to sweeping domestic reforms, Louis XIV aspired to make France the leading European power. His ambitions pushed other leading European states to form alliances against an increasingly aggressive France.

- The War of Devolution (1667–1668) saw the French forces overrun the Habsburg-controlled Spanish Netherlands and the Franche-Comté. However, a Triple Alliance of England, Sweden, and the Dutch Republic forced France to give most of it back in the Treaty of Aix-la-Chapelle.

- The Franco-Dutch War (1672–1678) pitted France, Sweden, Münster, Cologne, and England against the Dutch Republic, which was later joined by the Austrian Habsburg lands, Brandenburg-Prussia, and Spain to form a Quadruple Alliance. After years of fighting and a series of exhausting battles, the 1678-1679 Treaties of Nijmegen declared the Franche-Comté and the Spanish Netherlands French territories, making France Europe's strongest power.

- The Nine Years' War (1688–1697) once again pitted Louis XIV against a European-wide coalition, the Grand Alliance. By the terms of the Treaty of Ryswick (1697) Louis XIV retained the whole of Alsace but was forced to return Lorraine to its ruler and give up any gains on the right bank of the Rhine. Louis also accepted William III as the rightful King of England.

- All these wars exhausted France financially but turned it into the most powerful state in Europe.

- Louis's expansionist ambitions culminated in the final decisive war of his reign: the War of the Spanish Succession.

Terms

Treaties of Nijmegen

A series of treaties signed in the Dutch city of Nijmegen between August 1678 and December 1679. The treaties ended various interconnected wars among France, the Dutch Republic, Spain, Brandenburg, Sweden, Denmark, the Prince-Bishopric of Münster, and the Holy Roman Empire. The most significant of the treaties was the first, which established peace between France and the Dutch Republic and placed the northern border of France in very nearly its modern position.

Grand Alliance

A European coalition, consisting (at various times) of Austria, Bavaria, Brandenburg, the Dutch Republic, England, the Holy Roman Empire, Ireland, the Palatinate of the Rhine, Portugal, Savoy, Saxony, Scotland, Spain, and Sweden. The organization was founded in 1686 as the League of Augsburg and was originally formed in an attempt to halt Louis XIV of France's expansionist policies.

revocation of the Edict of Nantes

A 1685 edict, also known as the Edict of Fontainebleau, issued by Louis XIV of France, that revoked the right to practice the tolerated forms of Protestantism without persecution from the state granted by the Edict of Nantes (1598).

Truce of Ratisbon

A truce that concluded the War of the Reunions between Spain and France. It was signed in 1684 at the Dominican convent at Ratisbon in Bavaria between Louis XIV of France on the one side and the Holy Roman Emperor, Leopold I, and the Spanish King, Charles II, on the other. The final agreements allowed King Louis to retain Strasbourg, Luxembourg, and other Reunion gains, and returned Kortrijk and Diksmuide, both now in Belgium, to Spain. It was not, however, a definitive peace but only a truce for twenty years.

War of the Reunions

A short conflict (1683–1684) between France and Spain and its allies. It was fueled by the long-running desire of Louis XIV to conquer new lands, many of them comprising part of the Spanish Netherlands, along France's northern and eastern borders. The war was, in some sense, a continuation of the territorial and dynastic aims of Louis XIV as manifested in the War of Devolution and the Franco–Dutch War.

Triple Alliance

A 1668 alliance of England, Sweden, and the Dutch Republic formed to halt the expansion of Louis XIV's France in the War of Devolution. The alliance never engaged in combat against France, but it was enough of a threat to force Louis to halt his offensive and sign the Treaty of Aix-la-Chapelle with Spain.

Introduction

In addition to making sweeping domestic reforms, which completed the process of turning France into the absolute monarchy under the sole authority of the king, Louis XIV aspired to make France the leading European power. His ambitions pushed other leading European states to form alliances against an increasingly aggressive France. Three major wars, the Franco-Dutch War, the Nine Years' War, and the War of the Spanish Succession, as well as two lesser conflicts, the War of Devolution and the War of the Reunions, enabled France to become the most powerful state in Europe. However, this success, which came with the price of massive foreign and military spending, kept France on the continuous verge of bankruptcy. While Louis's detractors argued that the war-related expenditure impoverished France to an extreme extent, his supporters pointed out that while the state was impoverished, France, with all its territorial and political gains, was not.

Louis XIV in 1670, engraved portrait by Robert Nanteuil, Yale University Art Gallery. During Louis's reign, France was the leading European power and fought three major wars: the Franco-Dutch War, the War of the League of Augsburg, and the War of the Spanish Succession. There were also two lesser conflicts: the War of Devolution and the War of the Reunions.

The War of Devolution

In 1665, Louis believed that he had a pretext to go to war with Spain and allow him to claim the Spanish Netherlands (present-day Belgium). However, his claims to the Spanish Netherlands were tenuous; in 1659, France and Spain had concluded the Treaty of the Pyrenees, which ended twenty-four years of war between the two states. With the treaty, King Philip IV of Spain had to cede certain territories and consent to the marriage of his daughter Maria Theresa of Spain to young Louis XIV. With this marriage, Maria Theresa explicitly renounced all rights to her father's inheritance. When Philip IV died in 1665, the French king immediately laid claim to parts of the Spanish Netherlands. He justified this with the fact that the dowry promised at the time of his marriage to Maria Theresa had not been paid and that the French queen's renunciation of her Spanish inheritance was therefore invalid.

The conflict that followed is known as the War of Devolution (1667–1668). It saw the French forces over-run the Habsburg-controlled Spanish Netherlands and the Franche-Comté. However, a Triple Alliance of England, Sweden, and the Dutch Republic forced France to give most of it back in the Treaty of Aix-la-Chapelle. During the negotiations, the Triple Alliance managed to enforce their demands: France abandoned the Franche-Comté and French troops had to withdraw from the Spanish Netherlands. A total of twelve conquered cities remained in the hands of the French king. The most important consequence of the war, however, was the changed attitude of Louis XIV towards the Dutch Republic. The king blamed it, his former close ally, for the creation of the Triple Alliance, whose pressure had put a halt to his conquests. The French foreign policy of the following years was therefore completely geared towards the Dutch Republic's isolation.

The Franco-Dutch War

The Franco-Dutch War (1672–78), called also the Dutch War, was a war that pitted France, Sweden, Münster, Cologne, and England against the Dutch Republic, which was later joined by the Austrian Habsburg lands, Brandenburg-Prussia, and Spain to form a Quadruple Alliance. Continuing his mission to isolate and attack the Dutch Republic, which Louis considered to be a trading rival consisting of seditious republicans and Protestant heretics, the French king made another move on the Spanish Netherlands. His first and primary objective was to gain the support of England. England felt threatened by the Dutch naval power and did not need much encouragement to leave the Triple Alliance. Sweden agreed to indirectly support the invasion of the Republic by threatening Brandenburg-Prussia if that state should intervene.

After years of fighting and a series of exhausting battles, the 1678-1679 Treaties of Nijmegen were signed between France, the Dutch Republic, the Holy Roman Empire, the Spanish Empire, the Prince-Bishopric of Münster, and the Swedish Empire, ending the Franco-Dutch War with the Franche-Comté and the Spanish Netherlands belonging to France, making France Europe's strongest power. The war sparked the rivalry between William III, who later conquered England as part of the Glorious Revolution, and Louis XIV. It also resulted in the decline of the Dutch Republic's dominance in overseas trade.

The Nine Years' War

The Nine Years' War (1688–1697), often called the War of the Grand Alliance or the War of the League of Augsburg, once again pitted Louis XIV against a European-wide coalition, the Grand Alliance, led by the

Anglo-Dutch King William III, Holy Roman Emperor Leopold I, King Charles II of Spain, Victor Amadeus II of Savoy, and several princes of the Holy Roman Empire. It was fought primarily on mainland Europe and its surrounding waters, but it also encompassed a theater in Ireland and in Scotland, where William III and James II struggled for control of Britain and Ireland, and a campaign in colonial North America between French and English settlers and their respective Indian allies (known as King William's War).

Although Louis XIV had emerged from the Franco-Dutch War as the most powerful monarch in Europe, he immediately set about extending his gains to stabilize and strengthen France's frontiers, culminating in the brief War of the Reunions (1683–1684). The resulting Truce of Ratisbon guaranteed France's new borders for twenty years, but Louis' subsequent actions—notably his revocation of the Edict of Nantes in 1685—led to the deterioration of his military and political dominance. His decision to cross the Rhine in September 1688 aimed to extend his influence and pressure the Holy Roman Empire into accepting his territorial and dynastic claims. But when Leopold I and the German princes resolved to resist, and when the States General and William III brought the Dutch and the English into the war against France, the French king at last faced a powerful coalition aimed at curtailing his ambitions.

The main fighting took place around France's borders: in the Spanish Netherlands, the Rhineland, the Duchy of Savoy, and Catalonia. The fighting generally favored Louis XIV's armies, but by 1696 his country was in the grip of an economic crisis. The Maritime Powers (England and the Dutch Republic) were also financially exhausted, and when Savoy defected from the Alliance, all parties were keen for a negotiated settlement. By the terms of the Treaty of Ryswick (1697) Louis XIV retained the whole of Alsace but was forced to return Lorraine to its ruler and give up any gains on the right bank of the Rhine. Louis also accepted William III as the rightful King of England, while the Dutch acquired their barrier fortress system in the Spanish Netherlands to help secure their own borders. However, with the ailing and childless Charles II of Spain approaching his end, a new conflict over the inheritance of the Spanish Empire would soon embroil Louis XIV and the Grand Alliance in a final war—the War of the Spanish Succession.

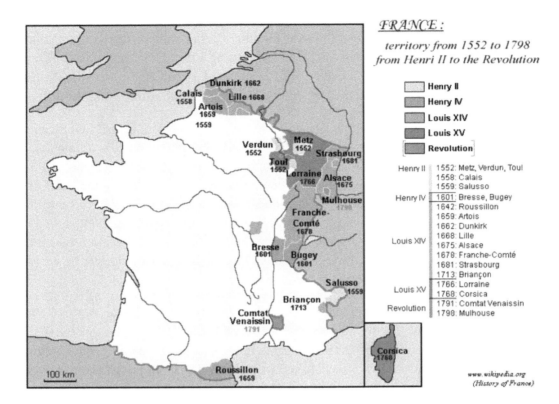

Territorial expansion of France under Louis XIV (1643–1715) is depicted in orange. While Louis's detractors argued that the war-related expenditure impoverished France to an extreme extent, his supporters pointed out that while the state was impoverished, France, with all its territorial and political gains, was not.

Sources

Attributions

CC licensed content, Specific attribution

- Boundless World History. **Authored by**: Boundless. **Located at**: https://courses.lumenlearning.com/boundless-worldhistory/. **License**: *CC BY-SA: Attribution-ShareAlike*

The Question of Spanish Succession

Learning Objective

- Describe the reasons why there was conflict over who should take the Spanish throne

Key Points

- In the late 1690s, the declining health of childless King Charles II of Spain deepened the ongoing dispute over his succession. The main rivals for the Spanish inheritance were the descendants of Louis XIV of France and the Austrian Habsburg Holy Roman Emperor, Leopold I, but the matter was of the utmost importance to Europe as a whole.

- In 1698 and 1700, Louis XIV and William III of England attempted to partition Spain in the effort to avoid a war. Charles II of Spain opposed partition and on his deathbed offered the empire to Philip, Duke of Anjou and Louis's grandson, who became King Philip V Spain.

- Although most European rulers accepted Philip as king, tensions mounted, mostly because of a series of Louis's decisions. Britain, the Dutch Republic, the Holy Roman Emperor, and the petty German states formed another Grand Alliance and declared war on France in 1702.

- With losses, victories, and significant financial costs on both sides, as well as a fragile Grand Alliance, French and British ministers prepared the groundwork for a peace conference, and in 1712 Britain ceased combat operations.

- By the terms of the Treaty of Utrecht (1713) and the Treaty of Rastatt (1714), the Spanish empire was partitioned between the major and minor powers. The Austrians received most of Spain's former European realms, but the Duke of Anjou retained peninsular Spain and Spanish America, where, after renouncing his claim to the French succession, he reigned as King Philip V.

- The partition of the Spanish Monarchy had secured the balance of power and the conditions imposed at Utrecht helped to regulate the relations between the major European powers over the coming century.

Terms

Treaties of Rastatt and Baden

Two peace treaties that in 1714 ended ongoing European conflicts following the War of the Spanish Succession. The first treaty,
signed between France and Austria in the city of Rastatt, followed the earlier Treaty of Utrecht of 1713, which ended hostilities between France and Spain on the one hand, and Britain and the Dutch Republic on the other hand. The second treaty, signed in Baden, was required to end the hostilities between France and the Holy Roman Empire.

Treaty of the Hague

A 1698 treaty, known also as the First Partition Treaty, between England and France. The accord attempted to resolve who would inherit the Spanish throne, proposing that Duke Joseph Ferdinand of Bavaria be the heir. Moreover, the agreement proposed that Louis, le Grand Dauphin, would get Naples, Sicily, and Tuscany, and Archduke Charles, the younger son of Emperor Leopold I, would get the Spanish Netherlands. Leopold, Duke of Lorraine, would take Milan, which in turn ceded Lorraine and Bar to the Dauphin.

Treaty of Utrecht

A series of individual peace treaties, rather than a single document, signed by the belligerents in the War of the Spanish Succession in the Dutch city of Utrecht in 1713. The treaties between several European states, including Spain, Great Britain, France, Portugal, Savoy, and the Dutch Republic, helped end the war.

Treaty of London

A 1700 treaty, known also as the Second Partition Treaty, attempting to restore the Pragmatic Sanction following the death of Duke Joseph Ferdinand of Bavaria. The Pragmatic Sanction had undermined the First Partition Treaty (the Treaty of Hague). Under the new treaty, Archduke Charles (later Charles VI), the second son of Emperor Leopold I, was to become king of Spain when Charles II died, and acquire her oversees colonies.

Grand Alliance

A European coalition consisting (at various times) of Austria, Bavaria, Brandenburg, the Dutch Republic, England, the Holy Roman Empire, Ireland, the Palatinate of the Rhine, Portugal, Savoy, Saxony, Scotland, Spain, and Sweden. The organization was founded in 1686 as the League of Augsburg in an attempt to halt Louis XIV of France's expansionist policies. After the Treaty of Hague was signed in 1701, it went into a second phase as the Alliance of the War of Spanish Succession.

Background

In the late 1690s, the declining health of childless King Charles II of Spain deepened the ongoing dispute over his succession. Spain was no longer a hegemonic power in Europe but the Spanish Empire—a vast confederation that covered the globe and was still
the largest of the European overseas empires—remained resilient. Ultimately, the main rivals for the Spanish inheritance were the heirs and descendants of the Bourbon King Louis XIV of France and the Austrian Habsburg Holy Roman Emperor Leopold I. However, the inheritance was so vast that its transference would dramatically increase either French or Austrian power which, due to the implied threat of European hegemony, was of the utmost importance to Europe as a whole.

Rival Claims and Partitions

The French claim derived from Louis XIV's mother, Anne of Austria (the older sister of Philip IV of Spain), and his wife, Maria Theresa (Philip IV's eldest daughter). France had the stronger claim, as it originated from the eldest daughters in two generations. However, their renunciation of succession rights complicated matters, although in the case of Maria Theresa, the renunciation was considered null and void owing to Spain's breach of her marriage contract with Louis. In contrast, no renunciations tainted the claims of the Emperor Leopold I's son Charles, Archduke of Austria, who was a grandson of Philip III's youngest daughter, Maria Anna. The English and Dutch feared that a French or Austrian-born Spanish king would threaten the balance of power, and thus preferred the Bavarian Prince Joseph Ferdinand, a grandson of Leopold I through his first wife, Margaret Theresa of Spain (the younger daughter of Philip IV).

In an attempt to avoid war, Louis signed the Treaty of the Hague with William III of England in 1698. This agreement divided Spain's Italian territories between Louis's son le Grand Dauphin and the Archduke Charles, with the rest of the empire awarded to Joseph Ferdinand. The signatories, however, omitted to consult Charles II, who was passionately opposed to the dismemberment of his empire. In 1699, he re-confirmed his 1693 will that named Joseph Ferdinand as his sole successor, but the latter died six months later. In 1700, Louis and William III concluded a fresh partitioning agreement, the Treaty of London. It allocated Spain, the Low Countries, and the Spanish colonies to Archduke Charles. The Dauphin would receive all of Spain's Italian territories. On his deathbed in 1700, Charles II unexpectedly offered the entire empire to the Dauphin's second son, Philip, Duke of Anjou, provided it remained undivided. Anjou was not in the direct line of French succession, thus his accession would not cause a Franco-Spanish union. Louis eventually decided to accept Charles II's will, and Philip, Duke of Anjou, became King Philip V of Spain.

Although most European rulers accepted Philip as king, tensions mounted, mostly because of a series of Louis's decisions. Louis's actions enraged Britain and the Dutch Republic. With the Holy Roman Emperor and the petty German states, they formed another Grand Alliance. French diplomacy, however, secured Bavaria, Portugal, and Savoy as Franco-Spanish allies. Around the same time, Louis decided to acknowledge James Stuart, the son of James II, as king of England on the latter's death, infuriating William III. While William died in March 1702, the Austrians, the Dutch, and English allies formally declared war in May 1702.

War of the Spanish Succession

By 1708, the Duke of Marlborough and Prince Eugene of Savoy had secured victory in the Spanish Netherlands and in Italy and defeated Louis XIV's ally Bavaria. The Allies suffered a Pyrrhic victory at the 1709 Battle of Malplaquet, with 21,000 casualties, twice that of the French. French forces elsewhere continued to fight despite their defeats. The Allies were definitively expelled from central Spain by the Franco-Spanish victories at the Battles of Villaviciosa and Brihuega in 1710. France faced invasion, but the unity of the allies broke first. With the Grand Alliance defeated in Spain and its casualties and costs mounting and aims diverging, the Tories came to power in Great Britain in 1710 and resolved to end the war. Eventually, France recovered its military pride with the decisive victory at Denain in 1712. Yet French and British ministers prepared the groundwork for a peace conference, and in 1712 Britain ceased combat operations. The Dutch, Austrians, and German states fought on to strengthen their own negotiating position, but, defeated by Marshal Villars, they were soon compelled to accept Anglo-French mediation.

Battle of Villaviciosa by Jean Alaux, 1836. Philip V of Spain and the Duke of Vendôme pictured after the victory at the 1710.

Peace Treaties

The 1713 Treaty of Utrecht recognized Louis XIV's grandson Philip, Duke of Anjou, as King of Spain (as Philip V), thus confirming the succession stipulated in the will of Charles II. However, Philip was compelled to renounce for himself and his descendants any right to the French throne. The Spanish territories in Europe were apportioned: Savoy received Sicily and parts of the Duchy of Milan, while Charles VI (the Holy Roman Emperor and Archduke of Austria) received the Spanish Netherlands, the Kingdom of Naples, Sardinia, and the bulk of the Duchy of Milan. Portugal had its sovereignty recognized over the lands between the Amazon and Oyapock rivers, in Brazil. In addition, Spain ceded Gibraltar and Minorca to Great Britain and agreed to give to the British the Asiento, a monopoly on the oceanic slave trade to the Spanish colonies in America. In North America, France ceded to Great Britain its claims to Newfoundland, the Hudson's Bay Company, the Acadian colony of Nova Scotia, and the formerly partitioned island of Saint Kitts.

After the signing of the Utrecht treaties, the French continued to be at war with Emperor Charles VI and with the Holy Roman Empire until 1714, when hostilities were ended with the Treaties of Rastatt and

Baden. Spain and Portugal remained formally at war with each other until the Treaty of Madrid of February 1715, while peace between Spain and Emperor Charles VI, unsuccessful claimant to the Spanish crown, came only in 1720 with the signing of the Treaty of The Hague.

The War of the Spanish Succession brought to an end a long period of major conflict in Western Europe. The partition of the Spanish Monarchy had secured the balance of power, and the conditions imposed at Utrecht helped to regulate the relations between the major European powers over the coming century.

Sources

Attributions

CC licensed content, Specific attribution

- Boundless World History. **Authored by**: Boundless. **Located at**: https://courses.lumenlearning.com/boundless-worldhistory/. **License**: *CC BY-SA: Attribution-ShareAlike*

William of Orange and the Grand Alliance

Learning Objective
• Explain William's stake in the War of the Spanish Succession and the goals of the Grand Alliance

Key Points
• As William III's life drew towards its conclusion, he, like many other European rulers, was concerned with the question of succession to the throne of Spain. He sought to prevent the Spanish inheritance from going to the descendants of either Louis XIV or Leopold I, as he feared this would upset the European balance of power.
• Fearing the growing strength of the Holy Roman Empire, Louis XIV turned to William. The two signed two treaties partitioning Spain, but Charles II of Spain's decision to choose Louis's grandson as his successor made Louis ignore his treaty with England.
• While the Tory-dominated House of Commons was keen to prevent further conflict, to William III, France's growing strength made war inevitable. From his perspective, losing the hard-won securities overturned the work of the last twenty years.
• As tensions mounted, Britain and the Dutch Republic grew enraged by Louis's actions and decisions. With the Holy Roman Emperor and the petty German states, they formed another Grand Alliance. Securing the Protestant succession and curbing Louis's ambitions was recognized by the Grand Alliance as one of England's main war aims.
• Before the War of the Spanish Succession was even declared, William died. His successor, Anne, continued William's policies to assure the Protestant succession in England and curb the French hegemony.
• The War of the Spanish Succession resulted in the partition of the Spanish Monarchy,

which secured the balance of power and helped to regulate the relations between the major European powers over the coming century.

Terms

Treaty of Utrecht

A series of individual peace treaties, rather than a single document, signed by the belligerents in the War of the Spanish Succession in the Dutch city of Utrecht in 1713. The treaties between several European states, including Spain, Great Britain, France, Portugal, Savoy, and the Dutch Republic, helped to end the war.

Treaty of Rastatt

A peace treaty between France and Austria, concluded in March 1714 in the Baden city of Rastatt, that put an end to the state of war between them following the War of the Spanish Succession. The treaty followed the earlier Treaty of Utrecht of April 1713, which ended hostilities between France and Spain on the one hand, and Britain and the Dutch Republic on the other hand. A third treaty at Baden was required to end the hostilities between France and the Holy Roman Empire.

Treaty of London

A 1700 treaty, known also as the Second Partition Treaty, attempting to restore the Pragmatic Sanction following the death of Duke Joseph Ferdinand of Bavaria. The Pragmatic Sanction had undermined the First Partition Treaty (the Treaty of Hague). Under the new Treaty, Archduke Charles (later Charles VI), the second son of the Emperor Leopold I, was to become king of Spain when Charles II died, and acquire her oversees colonies.

Grand Alliance

A European coalition, consisting (at various times) of Austria, Bavaria, Brandenburg, the Dutch Republic, England, the Holy Roman Empire, Ireland, the Palatinate of the Rhine, Portugal, Savoy, Saxony, Scotland, Spain, and Sweden. The organization was founded in 1686 as the League of Augsburg in an attempt to halt Louis XIV of France's expansionist policies. After the Treaty of Hague was signed in 1701, it went into a second phase as the Alliance of the War of Spanish Succession.

Treaty of Hague

A 1698 treaty, known also as the First Partition Treaty, between England and France. The accord attempted to resolve who would inherit the Spanish throne, proposing that Duke Joseph Ferdinand of Bavaria be the heir. Moreover, the agreement proposed that Louis, le Grand Dauphin, would get

Naples, Sicily, and Tuscany, and Archduke Charles, the younger son of Emperor Leopold I, would get the Spanish Netherlands. Leopold, Duke of Lorraine, would take Milan, which in turn ceded Lorraine and Bar to the Dauphin.

William III of England and the Spanish Succession

William III (1650–1702) was sovereign Prince of Orange from birth, Dutch Stadtholder (*de facto* hereditary head of state) from 1672, and King of England, Ireland, and Scotland from 1689 until his death. As his life drew towards its conclusion, William, like many other European rulers, was concerned with the question of succession to the throne of Spain, which brought with it vast territories in Italy, the Low Countries, and the New World. The king of Spain, Charles II, had no prospect of having children, and among his closest relatives were Louis XIV and Leopold I, Holy Roman Emperor. William sought to prevent the Spanish inheritance from going to either monarch, as he feared it would upset the balance of power.

King William III of England, portrait by Sir Godfrey Kneller, 1680s, National Galleries, Scotland. A Protestant, William participated in several wars against the powerful Catholic king of France, Louis XIV, in coalition with Protestant and Catholic powers in Europe. Many Protestants heralded him as a champion of their faith.

Partitions

Fearing the growing strength of the Holy Roman Empire, Louis XIV turned to William, his long-standing Protestant rival. England and the Dutch Republic had their own commercial, strategic, and political interests within the Spanish empire, and they were eager to return to peaceful commerce. Louis and William sought to solve the problem of the Spanish inheritance through negotiation based on the principle of partition (at first without prior reference to the Spanish or Austrian courts), to take effect after the death of Charles II.

William and Louis agreed to the First Partition Treaty (Treaty of Hague), which provided for the division of the Spanish Empire: Duke Joseph Ferdinand of Bavaria would obtain Spain, while France and the Holy Roman Emperor would divide the remaining territories between them. However, when Joseph Ferdinand died of smallpox, the issue re-opened. In 1700, the two rulers agreed to the Second Partition Treaty (Treaty of London), under which the territories in Italy would pass to a son of the king of France and the other Spanish territories would be inherited by a son of the Holy Roman Emperor. This arrangement infuriated both the Spanish, who still sought to prevent the dissolution of their empire, and the Holy Roman Emperor, to whom the Italian territories were much more useful than the other lands. Unexpectedly, Charles II willed all Spanish territories to Philip, a grandson of Louis XIV. The French conveniently ignored the Second Partition Treaty and claimed the entire Spanish inheritance.

William III's Stand

The news that Louis XIV had accepted Charles II's will and that the Second Partition Treaty was dead was a personal blow to William III. However, after the exertions of the Nine Years' War, the Tory-dominated House of Commons was keen to prevent further conflict and restore normal commercial activity. Yet to William III, France's growing strength made war inevitable. England also had its own interests in the Spanish Netherlands, and ministers recognized the potential danger posed by an enemy established to the east of the Strait of Dover who, taking advantage of favorable wind and tide, could threaten the British Isles. From William III's perspective, losing the hard-won securities overturned the work of the last twenty years.

Although the French king's ambitions and motives were not fully known, English ministers worked on the assumption that Louis XIV would seek to expand his territory and direct and dominate Spanish affairs. With the threat of a single power dominating Europe and overseas trade, London now undertook to support William III's efforts to reduce the power of France. As tensions mounted, Britain and the Dutch Republic grew enraged by Louis's actions and decisions. With the Holy Roman Emperor and the petty German states, they formed another Grand Alliance. This
European coalition, consisting at various times of various European states, was originally founded in 1686 as the League of Augsburg. It was formed in an attempt to halt Louis XIV's expansionist policies.
In 1701, it went into a second phase.

Even after the formation of the Grand Alliance, the French king continued to antagonize his European rivals. Around the same time as the Alliance was formed, the Catholic James II of England (VII of Scotland)—exiled in Saint-Germain since the Glorious Revolution—died, and Louis XIV recognized James II's Catholic son, James, as King James III of England. The French court insisted that granting James the title of King was a mere formality, but William and English ministers were indignant. Securing the Protestant succession was soon recognized by the Grand Alliance as one of England's main war aims.

The War of the Spanish Succession

However, before the War of the Spanish Succession was even declared, William died. Anne, Mary II's younger sister and William's sister-in-law through his marriage to Mary, ascended to the British throne and at once assured the Privy Council of her two main aims: the maintenance of the Protestant succession and the reduction of the power of France. By the same token, Anne continued William's policies, and many leading statesmen of William's later years remained in office, which turned out fundamental to the success of the Grand Alliance in the early stages of the war.

The Austrians, the Dutch, and English allies formally declared war in May 1702. By 1708 the Duke of Marlborough and Prince Eugene of Savoy had secured victory in the Spanish Netherlands and in Italy, and had defeated Louis XIV's ally Bavaria. France faced invasion, but the unity of the allies broke first. With the Grand Alliance defeated in Spain and its casualties and costs mounting and aims diverging, the Tories came to power in Great Britain in 1710 and resolved to end the war. French and British ministers prepared the groundwork for a peace conference, and in 1712 Britain ceased combat operations. The Dutch, Austrians, and German states fought on to strengthen their own negotiating position, but, defeated by Marshal Villars, they were soon compelled to accept Anglo-French mediation. By the terms of the Treaty of Utrecht (1713) and the Treaty of Rastatt (1714), the Spanish empire was partitioned between the major and minor powers. The Austrians received most of Spain's former European realms, but the Duke of Anjou retained peninsular Spain and Spanish America, where, after renouncing his claim to the French succession, he reigned as King Philip V. The European balance of power was assured.

Sources

Attributions

CC licensed content, Specific attribution

- Boundless World History. **Authored by**: Boundless. **Located at**: https://courses.lumenlearning.com/boundless-worldhistory/. **License**: *CC BY-SA: Attribution-ShareAlike*

The Peace of Utrecht

Learning Objective

- Describe the terms of the Peace of Utrecht and their significance across Europe

Key Points

- The War of the Spanish Succession (1701–1714) was a European conflict triggered by the death of the last Habsburg king of Spain, Charles II, in 1700. As he had reigned over a vast global empire, the question of who would succeed him had long troubled ministers in capitals throughout Europe.

- The balance of victories and losses shifted regularly over the course of the war, with both sides exhausted militarily and financially. As early as 1710, the Tories initiated secret talks with the French, seeking mutual ground whereon Great Britain and France could dictate peace to the rest of Europe.

- The Congress of Utrecht opened in 1712, but it was not accompanied by an armistice. One of the first questions discussed was the nature of the guarantees to be given by France and Spain that their crowns would be kept separate.

- The treaty, which was in fact a series of separate treaties, secured Britain's main war aims: Louis XIV's acknowledgement of the Protestant succession in England, and safeguards to ensure that the French and Spanish thrones remained separate.

- A series of separate treaties signed between 1714 and 1720 ended conflicts that continued in the aftermath of Utrecht between states involved in the War of the Spanish Succession.

- Utrecht marked the rise of Great Britain under Anne and later the House of Hanover and the end of the hegemonic ambitions of France. It also secured the balance of power and helped to regulate the relations between the major European powers over the coming century.

Terms

treaties of Rastatt and Baden

Two peace treaties that in 1714 ended ongoing European conflicts following the War of the Spanish Succession. The first treaty, signed between France and Austria in the city of Rastatt, followed the earlier Treaty of Utrecht of 1713, which ended hostilities between France and Spain on the one hand, and Britain and the Dutch Republic on the other hand. The second treaty, signed in Baden, was required to end the hostilities between France and the Holy Roman Empire.

Grand Alliance

A European coalition consisting (at various times) of Austria, Bavaria, Brandenburg, the Dutch Republic, England, the Holy Roman Empire, Ireland, the Palatinate of the Rhine, Portugal, Savoy, Saxony, Scotland, Spain, and Sweden. The coalition was founded in 1686 as the League of Augsburg in an attempt to halt Louis XIV of France's expansionist policies. After the Treaty of Hague was signed in 1701, it went into a second phase as the Alliance of the War of Spanish Succession.

War of the Spanish Succession

A major European conflict of the early 18th century (1701/2–1714) triggered by the death in 1700 of the last Habsburg king of Spain, Charles II. The Austrians, the Dutch, and English allies formally declared war against France and its allies in May 1702.

Asiento

The permission given by the Spanish government to other countries to sell people as slaves to the Spanish colonies, between 1543 and 1834. In British history, it usually refers to the contract between Spain and Great Britain created in 1713 that dealt with the supply of African slaves for the Spanish territories in the Americas.

Background: The War of the Spanish Succession

The War of the Spanish Succession (1701–1714) was a European conflict triggered by the death of the last Habsburg King of Spain, Charles II, in 1700. He had reigned over a vast global empire and the question of who would succeed him had long troubled ministers in capitals throughout Europe. Attempts to solve the problem by partitioning the empire between the eligible candidates from the royal Houses of France (Bourbon), Austria (Habsburg), and Bavaria (Wittelsbach) ultimately failed, and on his deathbed Charles II fixed the entire Spanish inheritance on Philip, Duke of Anjou, the grandson of King Louis XIV of France. With Philip ruling in Spain, Louis XIV would secure great advantages for his dynasty, but some statesmen regarded a dominant House of Bourbon as a threat to European stability, jeopardizing the balance of power.

To counter Louis XIV's growing dominance, England, the Dutch Republic, and Austria—together with their allies in the Holy Roman Empire—re-formed the Grand Alliance (1701) and supported Emperor Leopold I's claim to the Spanish inheritance for his second son, Archduke Charles. By backing the Habsburg candidate (known to his supporters as King Charles III of Spain) each member of the coalition sought to reduce the power of France, ensure their own territorial and dynastic security, and restore and improve the trade opportunities they had enjoyed under Charles II.

Peace Talks

The balance of victories and losses shifted regularly over the course of the war, with both sides exhausted militarily and financially, also as a result of a series of earlier wars waged in Europe. As early as August 1710, the Tories initiated secret talks with the French, seeking mutual ground whereon Great Britain and France could dictate peace to the rest of Europe.

France and Great Britain had come to terms in October 1711, when the preliminaries of peace had been signed in London. The preliminaries were based on a tacit acceptance of the partition of Spain's European possessions.

The Congress of Utrecht, opened in January 1712, followed, but it was not accompanied by an armistice (only in August did Britain, Savoy, France, and Spain agree to a general suspension of arms).

One of the first questions discussed was the nature of the guarantees to be given by France and Spain that their crowns would be kept separate, but matters did not make much progress until July, when Philip signed a renunciation. With Great Britain and France having agreed upon a truce, the pace of negotiation quickened and the main treaties were finally signed in April 1713.

Treaty of Utrecht

The treaty, which was in fact a series of separate treaties, secured Britain's main war aims: Louis XIV's acknowledgement of the Protestant succession in England and safeguards to ensure that the French and Spanish thrones remained separate. In North America, where the War of the Spanish Succession turned into a war over colonial gains, Louis XIV ceded to Britain the territories of Saint Kitts and Acadia and recognized Britain's sovereignty over Rupert's Land and Newfoundland. In return, Louis XIV kept the major city of Lille on his northern border, but he ceded Furnes, Ypres, Menin, and Tournai to the Spanish Netherlands. He also agreed to the permanent demilitarization of the naval base at Dunkirk. The Dutch received their restricted barrier in the Spanish Netherlands and a share of the trade in the region with Britain. Prussia gained some disputed lands and Portugal won minor concessions in Brazil against encroachments on the Amazon from French Guiana.

In addition, Spain ceded Gibraltar and Minorca to Great Britain and agreed to give to the British the Asiento, a monopoly on the oceanic slave trade to the Spanish colonies in America.Above all, though, Louis XIV had secured for the House of Bourbon the throne of Spain, with his grandson, Philip V, recognized as the rightful king by all signatories.

First edition of the the 1713 Treaty of Utrecht between Great Britain and Spain in Spanish (left), and a later edition in Latin and English. The treaties, signed in the Dutch city of Utrecht, were concluded between the representatives of Louis XIV of France and his grandson Philip V of Spain on one hand, and representatives of Anne of Great Britain, Victor Amadeus II of Sardinia, John V of Portugal, and the United Provinces of the Netherlands on the other.

Aftermath

Utrecht marked the rise of Great Britain under Anne and later the House of Hanover and the end of the hegemonic ambitions of France. The lucrative trading opportunities afforded to the British were gained at the expense of Anne's allies, with the Dutch forgoing a share in the Asiento and the Holy Roman Empire ceding Spain to Philip V and being forced to reinstate the Elector of Bavaria.

After the signing of the Utrecht treaties, the French continued to be at war with the Holy Roman Empire until 1714, when hostilities ended with the treaties of Rastatt and Baden. Spain and Portugal remained formally at war with each other until the Treaty of Madrid of February 1715, while peace between Spain and Emperor Charles VI, unsuccessful claimant to the Spanish crown, came only in 1720 with the signing of the Treaty of The Hague.

Weakened Spain eventually grew in strength under Philip V, and the country would return to the forefront of European politics. With neither Charles VI nor Philip V willing to accept the Spanish partition, and with no treaty existing between Spain and Austria, the two powers would soon clash in order to gain control of Italy, starting with a brief war in 1718. However, the War of the Spanish Succession brought to an end a long period of major conflict in western Europe; the partition of the Spanish Monarchy had secured the balance of power, and the conditions imposed at Utrecht helped to regulate the relations between the major European powers over the coming century.

Sources

Attributions

CC licensed content, Specific attribution

- Boundless World History. **Authored by**: Boundless. **Located at**: https://courses.lumenlearning.com/boundless-worldhistory/. **License**: *CC BY-SA: Attribution-ShareAlike*

Peter the Great

Learning Objective
• Describe Peter the Great's early life

Key Points

- Peter the Great of the House of Romanov ruled the Tsardom of Russia and later the Russian Empire from 1682 until his death. The Romanovs took over Russia in 1613, and the first decades of their reign were marked by attempts to restore peace, both internally and with Russia's rivals.

- After Alexis I's (Peter's father) death, a power struggle between the Miloslavsky family (of Alexis's first wife) and the Naryshkin family (of Alexis's second wife) ensued. Eventually, Peter's half-brother, Ivan V, and ten-year-old Peter became co-tsars, with Sophia Alekseyevna, one of Alexis's daughters from his first marriage, acting as regent.

- Sophia was eventually overthrown, with Peter I and Ivan V continuing to act as co-tsars, yet power was exercised mostly by Peter's mother. It was only when Nataliya died in 1694 that Peter became an independent sovereign, and the sole ruler after Ivan's death in 1696.

- Peter implemented sweeping reforms aimed at modernizing Russia. Heavily influenced by his advisers from Western Europe, he reorganized the Russian army along modern lines and dreamed of making Russia a maritime power.

- Knowing that Russia could not face the Ottoman Empire alone, in 1697 Peter traveled incognito to Europe with the so-called Grand Embassy to seek the aid of the European monarchs. The mission failed, as Europe was at the time preoccupied with the question of the Spanish succession.

- The European trip, although politically a failure, exposed Peter to Western European artists, scientists, craftsmen, and noble families. This broadened his intellectual horizons and convinced him that Russia should follow Western Europe in certain respects.

Terms

boyars

Members of the highest rank of the feudal Bulgarian, Moscovian, Ruthenian (Ukraine and Belarus), Wallachian, and Moldavian aristocracies, second only to the ruling princes (or tsars), from the 10th century to the 17th century.

Grand Embassy

A Russian diplomatic mission sent to Western Europe in 1697–1698 by Peter the Great. The goal of this mission was to strengthen and broaden the Holy League, Russia's alliance with a number of European countries against the Ottoman Empire in its struggle for the northern coastline of the Black Sea.

serfdom

The status of many peasants under feudalism, specifically relating to manorialism. It was a condition of bondage that developed primarily during the High Middle Ages in Europe and lasted in some countries until the mid-19th century.

Political Background

Peter the Great of the House of Romanov (1672–1725) ruled the Tsardom of Russia and later the Russian Empire from 1682 until his death, jointly ruling before 1696 with his elder half-brother, Ivan V. The Romanovs took over Russia in 1613, and the first decades of their reign were marked by attempts to restore peace, both internally and with Russia's rivals, most notably Poland and Sweden.

In order to avoid more civil war, the great nobles, or *boyars,* cooperated with the first Romanovs, enabling them to finish the work of bureaucratic centralization. Thus, the state required service from both the old and the new nobility, primarily in the military. In return, the tsars allowed the *boyars* to complete the process of enserfing the peasants. With the state now fully sanctioning serfdom, peasant rebellions were endemic.

Peter the Great: Early Years

From an early age, Peter's education (commissioned by his father, Tsar Alexis I) was put in the hands of several tutors. In 1676, Tsar Alexis died, leaving the sovereignty to Peter's elder half-brother, Feodor III. Throughout this period, the government was largely run by Artamon Matveev, an enlightened friend of Alexis, the political head of the Naryshkin family (Natalya Naryshkina was Alexis's second wife and Peter's mother) and one of Peter's greatest childhood benefactors. This changed when Feodor died in 1682. As he did not leave any children, a dispute arose between the Miloslavsky family (Maria Miloslavskaya was the first wife of Alexis I) and the Naryshkin family over who should inherit the throne. Peter's other half-brother, Ivan V, was next in line for the throne, but he was chronically ill. Consequently, the Boyar Duma (a council of Russian nobles) chose 10-year-old Peter to become tsar, with his mother as regent.

However, Sophia Alekseyevna, one of Alexis's daughters from his first marriage, led a rebellion of the Streltsy (Russia's elite military corps), which made it possible for her, the Miloslavskys (the clan of Ivan), and their allies to insist that Peter and Ivan be proclaimed joint tsars, with Ivan being acclaimed as the senior. Sophia acted as regent during the minority of the sovereigns and exercised all power. For seven years, she ruled as an autocrat.

Peter the Great as a child, artist unknown. Peter's childhood was marked by power struggles between the families of Alexis I's first and second wives. Although he was named a co-tsar in 1682, at the age of ten, he did not become an independent and sole ruler until 1696.

Taking Over the Power

While Peter was not particularly concerned that others ruled in his name, his mother sought to force him to adopt a more conventional approach. She arranged his marriage to Eudoxia Lopukhina in 1689, but the marriage was a failure. Ten years later Peter forced his wife to become a nun and thus freed himself from the union.

By the summer of 1689, Peter planned to take power from his half-sister Sophia, whose position had been weakened by two unsuccessful Crimean campaigns. After a power struggle, in which the Streltsy was forced to shift its loyalty, Sophia was eventually overthrown, with Peter I and Ivan V continuing to act as co-tsars. Yet Peter could not acquire actual control over Russian affairs. Power was instead exercised by his mother, Natalya Naryshkina. It was only when Nataliya died in 1694 that Peter became an independent sovereign, and the sole ruler after Ivan's death in 1696.

Early Reign

Peter implemented sweeping reforms aimed at modernizing Russia. Heavily influenced by his advisers from Western Europe, he reorganized the Russian army along modern lines and dreamed of making Russia a maritime power. He also implemented social modernization in an absolute manner by introducing French and western dress to his court and requiring courtiers, state officials, and the military to shave their beards and adopt modern clothing styles. One means of achieving this end was the introduction of taxes for long beards and robes in September 1698. The move provoked opposition from the *boyars*.

To improve his nation's position on the seas, Peter sought to gain more maritime outlets and attempted to acquire control of the Black Sea, at the time controlled by the Ottoman Empire. To do so, he would have to expel the Tatars from the surrounding areas, but the initial attempts ended in failure. However, after the 1695 initiative to build a large navy, he officially founded the first Russian Navy base, Taganrog (Sea of Azov).

Peter knew that Russia could not face the Ottoman Empire alone. In 1697 he traveled incognito to Europe on an eighteen-month journey with a large Russian delegatio—the so-called Grand Embassy—to seek the aid of the European monarchs.
The mission failed, as Europe was at the time preoccupied with the question of the Spanish succession. Peter's visit was cut short in 1698, when he was forced to rush home by a rebellion of the Streltsy. The rebellion was easily crushed, but Peter acted ruthlessly towards the mutineers. Over 1,200 of the rebels were tortured and executed, and Peter ordered that their bodies be publicly exhibited as a warning to future conspirators. The Streltsy were disbanded.

Peter's European Education

Although the Grand Embassy failed to complete its political mission of creating an anti-Ottoman alliance, Peter continued the European trip, learning about life in Western Europe. While visiting the Netherlands, he studied shipbuilding and visited with families of art and coin collectors. From Dutch experts, craftsmen, and artists, Peter learned how to draw teeth, catch butterflies, and paint seascapes. In England, he also engaged in painting and navy-related activities, as well as visited Manchester in order to learn the techniques of city building that he would later use to great effect at Saint Petersburg. Furthermore, in 1698 Peter sent a delegation to Malta to observe the training and abilities of the Knights of Malta and their fleet.

Peter's visits to the West impressed upon him the notion that European customs were in several respects superior to Russian traditions. Unlike most of his predecessors and successors, he attempted to follow Western European traditions, fashions, and tastes. He also sought to end arranged marriages, which were the norm among the Russian nobility, because he thought such a practice was barbaric and led to domestic violence, since the partners usually resented each other.

A statue of Peter I working incognito at a Dutch wharf, St. Petersburg. Peter the Great learned the shipbuilding craft in Holland in 1697. It was one of many skills that he acquired during his Western European trip.

Sources

Attributions

CC licensed content, Specific attribution

- Boundless World History. **Authored by**: Boundless. **Located at**: https://courses.lumenlearning.com/boundless-worldhistory/. **License**: *CC BY-SA: Attribution-ShareAlike*

The Westernization of Russia

Learning Objective

- Discuss the reasons why Peter worked so hard to forcibly westernize Russia

Key Points

- In his effort to modernize Russia, the largest state in the world, but one that was economically and socially lagging, Peter introduced autocracy and played a major role in introducing his country to the European state system. His visits to the West impressed upon him the notion that European customs were in several respects superior to Russian traditions.

- Heavily influenced by his advisers from Western Europe, he reorganized the Russian army along modern lines and dreamed of making Russia a maritime power.

- His social reforms included the requirement of Western fashion in his court (including facial hair for men), attempts to end arranged marriages, and the introduction of the Julian Calendar in 1700.

- One of Peter's most audacious goals was reducing the influence of the boyars, or the feudal elite class. He did this by imposing taxes and services on them as well as introducing comprehensive administrative reforms that opened civil service to commoners. However, sharp class divisions, including the already tragic fate of serfs, only deepened.

- Tax and trade reforms enabled the Russian state to expand its treasury almost sixfold between 1680 and 1724.

- Legislation under Peter's rule covered every aspect of life in Russia, and his reform contributed greatly to Russia's military successes and the increase in revenue and productivity. Overall, Peter created a state that further legitimized and strengthened authoritarian rule in Russia.

Terms

boyars

Members of the highest rank of the feudal Bulgarian, Moscovian, Ruthenian, (Ukraine and Belarus), Wallachian, and Moldavian aristocracies, second only to the ruling princes (or tsars), from the 10th century to the 17th century.

Collegia

Government departments in Imperial Russia established in 1717 by Peter the Great. The departments were housed in Saint Petersburg.

serfdom

The status of many peasants under feudalism, specifically relating to manorialism. It was a condition of bondage that developed primarily during the High Middle Ages in Europe and lasted in some countries until the mid-19th century.

kholops

Feudally dependent persons in Russia between the 10th and early 18th centuries. Their legal status was close to that of serfs but in reality closest to that of slaves.

Table of Ranks

A formal list of positions and ranks in the military, government, and court of Imperial Russia. Peter the Great introduced the system in 1722 while engaged in a struggle with the existing hereditary nobility, or boyars. It was formally abolished in 1917 by the newly established Bolshevik government.

Russia at the Turn of the 18th Century

By the time Peter the Great became tsar, Russia was the largest country in the world, stretching from the Baltic Sea to the Pacific Ocean. Much of Russia's expansion had taken place in the 17th century, culminating in the first Russian settlement of the Pacific in the mid-17th century, the reconquest of Kiev, and the pacification of the Siberian tribes. However,
the vast majority of the land was unoccupied, travel was slow, and the majority of the population of 14 million depended on farming. While only a small percentage lived in towns, Russian agriculture, with its short growing season, was ineffective and lagged behind that of Western Europe. The class of kholops, or feudally dependent persons similar to serfs, but whose status was closest to slavery, remained a major institution in Russia until 1723, when Peter converted household kholops into house serfs, thus including them in poll taxation (Russian agricultural kholops were formally converted into serfs in 1679). Russia also remained isolated from the sea trade and its internal trade communications and many manufactures were dependent on the seasonal changes.

Peter and Western Europe

Peter I the Great introduced autocracy in Russia and played a major role in introducing his country to the European state system. His visits to the West impressed upon him the notion that European customs were in several respects superior to Russian traditions. Heavily influenced by his advisers from Western Europe, he reorganized the Russian army along modern lines and dreamed of making Russia a maritime power. He also commanded all of his courtiers and officials to wear European clothing and cut off their long beards, causing great upset among *boyars*, or the feudal elites. Those who sought to retain their beards were required to pay an annual beard tax of one hundred rubles.

Peter also introduced critical social reform. He sought to end arranged marriages, which were the norm among the Russian nobility, seeing the practice as barbaric and leading to domestic violence. In 1699, he changed the date of the celebration of the new year from September 1 to January 1. Traditionally, the years were reckoned from the purported creation of the world, but after Peter's reforms, they were to be counted from the birth of Christ. Thus, in the year 7207 of the old Russian calendar, Peter proclaimed that the Julian Calendar was in effect and the year was 1700.

Peter the Great by Jean-Marc Nattier, 1717.

Administrative Reforms

One of Peter's major goals was reducing the influence of the *boyars*, who stressed Slavic supremacy and opposed European influence. While their clout had declined since the reign of Ivan the Terrible, the Boyar

Duma, an advisory council to the tsar, still wielded considerable political power. Peter saw them as backwards and as obstacles standing in the way of Europeanization and reform. He specifically targeted *boyars* with numerous taxes and obligatory services.

Prior to Peter's rule, Russia's administrative system was relatively antiquated compared to that of many Western European nations. The state was divided into uyezds, which mostly consisted of cities and their immediate surrounding areas. In 1708, Peter abolished these old national subdivisions and established in their place eight governorates. In 1711, a new state body was established: the Governing Senate. All its members were appointed by the tsar from among his own associates, and it originally consisted of ten people. All appointments and resignations of senators occurred by personal imperial decrees. The senate did not interrupt the activity and was the permanent operating state body.Another decree in 1713 established *Landrats* (from the German word for "national council") in each of the governorates, staffed by between eight and twelve professional civil servants, who assisted a royally-appointed governor. In 1719, after the establishment of government departments known as the Collegia, Peter remade Russia's administrative divisions once more. The new provinces were modeled on the Swedish system, in which larger, more politically important areas received more political autonomy, while smaller, more rural areas were controlled more directly by the state.

Peter's distrust of the elitist and anti-reformist *boyars* culminated in 1722 with the creation of the Table of Ranks—a formal list of ranks in the Russian military, government, and royal court. The Table of Ranks established a complex system of titles and honorifics, each classed with a number denoting a specific level of service or loyalty to the tsar; this was among the most audacious of Peter's reforms. Previously, high-ranking state positions were hereditary, but with the establishment of the Table of Ranks, anyone, including a commoner, could work their way up the bureaucratic hierarchy with sufficient hard work and skill. A new generation of technocrats soon supplanted the old *boyar* class and dominated the civil service in Russia. With minimal modifications, the Table of Ranks remained in effect until the Russian Revolution of 1917.

A manuscript copy of the 1722 Table of Ranks.

Finance

Peter's government was constantly in dire need of money, and at first it responded by monopolizing certain strategic industries, such as salt, vodka, oak, and tar. Peter also taxed many Russian cultural customs (such as bathing, fishing, beekeeping, or wearing beards) and issued tax stamps for paper goods. However, with each new tax came new loopholes and new ways to avoid them, and so it became clear that tax reform was simply not enough.

The solution was a sweeping new poll tax, which replaced a household tax on cultivated land. Previously, peasants had skirted the tax by combining several households into one estate. Now, each peasant was assessed individually for a tax paid in cash. This new tax was significantly heavier than the taxes it replaced, and it enabled the Russian state to expand its treasury almost sixfold between 1680 and 1724. Peter also pursued proto-protectionist trade policies, placing heavy tariffs on imports and trade to maintain a favorable environment for Russian-made goods.

Subjugation of the Working Masses

Peter's reign deepened the subjugation of serfs to the will of landowners. He firmly enforced class divisions and his tax code significantly expanded the number of taxable workers, shifting an even heavier burden onto the shoulders of the working class. A handful of Peter's reforms reflected a limited understanding of certain Enlightenment ideals. For example, he created a new class of serfs, known as *state peasants*, who had broader rights than ordinary serfs but still paid dues to the state. He also created state-sanctioned handicraft shops in large cities, inspired by similar shops he had observed in the Netherlands, to provide products for the army. Evidence suggests that Peter's advisers recommended the abolition of serfdom and the creation of a form of "limited freedom," but the gap between slaves and serfs shrank considerably under Peter. By the end of his reign the two were basically indistinguishable.

Outcomes

Peter's reforms set him apart from the tsars that preceded him. In Muscovite Russia, the state's functions were limited mostly to military defense, collection of taxes, and enforcement of class divisions. In contrast, legislation under Peter's rule covered every aspect of life in Russia with exhaustive detail, and it significantly affected the everyday lives of nearly every Russian citizen. The success of reform contributed greatly to Russia's military successes and the increase in revenue and productivity. More importantly, Peter created a state that further legitimized and strengthened authoritarian rule in Russia. Testaments to this lasting influence are the many public institutions in the Soviet Union and the Russian Federation, which trace their origins back to Peter's rule.

Sources

Attributions

CC licensed content, Specific attribution

- Boundless World History. **Authored by**: Boundless. **Located at**: https://courses.lumenlearning.com/boundless-worldhistory/. **License**: *CC BY-SA: Attribution-ShareAlike*

Peter's Foreign Policy

Learning Objective

- Analyze Peter's foreign policy goals and the extent to which he achieved them

Key Points

- To improve his nation's position on the seas, Peter the Great sought to gain more maritime outlets. The goal of making Russia a maritime power shaped Peter's foreign policy.

- Peter's first military efforts were directed against the Ottoman Turks. While his efforts to gain access to the Azov Sea eventually failed, his alliance with the Ottoman Empire against Persia allowed him to access the Caspian Sea.

- Peter's rule was dominated by the Great Northern War, in which he and his allies successfully challenged the dominance of Sweden in the Baltic region. As a result of this war, Russia gained vast Baltic territories and became one of the greatest powers in Europe.

- While during Peter's reign Russia did not formally wage wars with Poland-Lithuania, Peter made the most of the internal chaos and power struggles in the Polish-Lithuanian Commonwealth. He secured formerly Polish-Lithuanian territories in Ukraine and had an impact on internal politics in the Commonwealth.

- Peter's foreign policy turned the Tsardom into the Russian Empire and left Russia one of the most powerful states in Europe and a major player in global politics.

Terms

Treaty of Thorn

A treaty concluded in 1709 between Augustus the Strong of Poland–Lithuania and Peter the Great of Russia during the Great Northern War. The parties revived their alliance, which Charles XII of Sweden had destroyed in the Treaty of Altranstädt (1706), and agreed on restoring the Polish crown to Augustus.

Great Northern War

A 1700–1721 conflict in which a coalition led by the Tsardom of Russia successfully contested the supremacy of the Swedish Empire in Central, Northern, and Eastern Europe. The initial leaders of the anti-Swedish alliance were Peter the Great of Russia, Frederick IV of Denmark–Norway, and Augustus II the Strong of Saxony–Poland.

Treaty of Nystad

The last peace treaty of the Great Northern War of 1700–1721. It was concluded between the Tsardom of Russia and the Swedish Empire in 1721 in the then-Swedish town of Nystad. It shifted the balance of power in the Baltic region from Sweden to Russia.

Eternal Peace Treaty of 1686

A treaty between the Tsardom of Russia and the Polish-Lithuanian Commonwealth signed in 1686 in Moscow. The treaty secured Russia's possession of left-bank Ukraine plus the right-bank city of Kiev. The region of Zaporizhian Sich, Siverian lands, cities of Chernihiv, Starodub, Smolensk, and its outskirts were also ceded to Russia, while Poland retained right-bank Ukraine.

Introduction

Peter the Great became tsar in 1682 upon the death of his elder brother Feodor, but did not become the actual ruler until 1689. He commenced reforming the country, attempting to turn the Russian Tsardom into a modernized empire relying on trade and on a strong, professional army and navy. Heavily influenced by his advisers from Western Europe, he reorganized the Russian army along modern lines and dreamed of making Russia a maritime power. To improve his nation's position on the seas, Peter sought to gain more maritime outlets. His only outlet at the time was the White Sea at Arkhangelsk. The Baltic Sea was controlled by Sweden in the north, while the Black Sea and the Caspian Sea were controlled by the Ottoman Empire and Safavid Empire respectively in the south.

Peter the Great and the Ottoman Empire

Peter's first military efforts were directed against the Ottoman Turks. After the Turkish failure to take Vienna in 1683, Russia joined Austria, Poland, and Venice in the Holy League (1684) to drive the Turks southward. Russia and Poland signed the Eternal Peace Treaty of 1686, in which Poland–Lithuania agreed to recognize the Russian incorporation of Kiev and the left-bank of the Ukraine. The Russo–Turkish War of 1686–1700 followed as part of the joint European effort to confront the Ottoman Empire (the larger European conflict was known as the Great Turkish War). During the war, the Russian army organized the Crimean campaigns of 1687 and 1689, which ended in Russian defeats. Despite these setbacks, Russia launched the Azov campaigns in 1695 and 1696 and successfully occupied Azov (northern extension of the Black Sea) in 1696. However, the gains did not last long. The Russo–Ottoman War of 1710–1711, also known as the Pruth River Campaign, erupted as a consequence of the defeat of Sweden by the Russian Empire in the Battle of Poltava (1709) during the ongoing Great Northern War. The conflict was ended by the 1711 Treaty of the Pruth, which stipulated that Russia return Azov to the Ottomans, and the Russian Azov fleet was destroyed.

Capture of Azov by Russian emperor Peter the Great (on horseback) by Adriaan van Schoonebeek, (1699). While Peter successfully occupied Azov in 1696, the gains did not last long. The Russo-Ottoman War of 1710–1711 was ended by the 1711 Treaty of the Pruth, which stipulated that Russia return Azov to the Ottomans.

However, Peter managed to gain access to the Caspian Sea. In the Russo–Persian War (1722–1723), Russia had managed to conquer swaths of Safavid Irans territories in the North Caucasus, Transcaucasia, and northern mainland Iran, while the Ottoman Turks had invaded and conquered all Iranian territories in the west. The two governments eventually signed a 1724 treaty in Constantinople, dividing a large portion of Iran between them. The annexed Iranian lands located on the east of the conjunction of the rivers Kurosh (Kur) and Aras were given to the Russians, while the lands on the west went to the Ottomans.

Great Northern War

Between the years of 1560 and 1658, Sweden created a Baltic empire centered on the Gulf of Finland. Peter the Great wanted to re-establish a Baltic presence by regaining access to the territories that Russia had lost to Sweden in the first decades of the 17th century. In the late 1690s, the adventurer Johann Patkul managed to ally Russia with Denmark and Saxony by the secret Treaty of Preobrazhenskoye. As Augustus II the Strong, elector of Saxony, gained the Polish crown in 1696, the Polish–Lithuanian Commonwealth, at conflict with Sweden since the mid-17th century, automatically became a member of the alliance.

In 1700, Peter, supported by his allies, declared war on Sweden, which was at the time led by eighteen-year-old King Charles XII. A threefold attack at Swedish Holstein-Gottorp, Swedish Livonia, and Swedish Ingria did not overwhelm the inexperienced Charles XII. Sweden parried the Danish and Russian attacks at Travendal and Narva, and in a counter-offensive pushed Augustus II's forces through the Polish–Lithuanian Commonwealth to Saxony, dethroning Augustus on the way and forcing him to acknowledge defeat in the Treaty of Altranstädt (Augustus was restored in 1709). The treaty also secured the extradition and execution of Patkul, the architect of the anti-Swedish alliance. Peter I had meanwhile recovered and gained ground in Sweden's Baltic provinces. Charles XII moved from Saxony into Russia to confront Peter, but the campaign ended with the destruction of the main Swedish army at the decisive 1709 Battle of Poltava (in present-day Ukraine), and Charles's exile in Ottoman Bender. After Poltava, the anti-Swedish coalition, which by that time had fallen apart twice, was re-established and subsequently joined by Hanover and Prussia. The remaining Swedish forces in plague-stricken areas south and east of the Baltic Sea were evicted, with the last city, Riga, falling in 1710. Sweden proper was invaded from the west by Denmark–Norway and from the east by Russia, which had occupied Finland by 1714. The Danish forces were defeated. Charles XII opened up a Norwegian front, but was killed in Fredriksten in 1718.

The war ended with Sweden's defeat, leaving Russia as the new dominant power in the Baltic region and a major force in European politics. The formal conclusion of the war was marked by the Swedish–Hanoverian and Swedish–Prussian Treaties of Stockholm (1719), the Dano-Swedish Treaty of Frederiksborg (1720), and the Russo–Swedish Treaty of Nystad (1721). In all of them, Sweden ceded some territories to its opponents. In Nystad, King Frederick I of Sweden formally recognized the transfer of Estonia, Livonia, Ingria, and Southeast Finland to Russia, while Russia returned the bulk of Finland to Sweden. As a result, Russia gained vast Baltic territories and became one of the greatest powers in Europe.

VREEDE tekening tuſſchen de Plenipotentiariſſen van den Kyser van Groot Rusland en de Koning van Sweeden, tat Neuſtadt: naar een Oorlog van 21 jaaren. op den 20 Aug. 1721.

PAX inter Magnum Moscovtarum Imper: et Regem Succiae compoſita, ductu Oratorum utriusque cum summa potestate Neoſtadii 20 Augusti die 1721 post bellum 21 annorum.

Per Schenk Exc: Amst: Priv:

Signing of the Treaty of Nystad (1721) by Pieter Schenk (II). Nystad manifested the decisive shift in the European balance of power that the Great Northern War had brought about: the Swedish imperial era ended and Sweden entered the Age of Liberty, while Russia emerged as a new empire.

Polish/Lithuanian–Russian Relations

While during Peter's reign Russia did not formally wage wars with Poland–Lithuania, Peter made the most of the internal chaos and power struggles in the Polish–Lithuanian Commonwealth. After Poltava, the rule of Augustus II was restored thanks to the support of Peter (Treaty of Thorn) and largely against the will of the Polish–Lithuanian nobility. Soon Augustus unsuccessfully wanted to terminate his participation in the Great Northern War and free himself from his dependence on Peter. Attempts at peace with Sweden, which would strengthen Augustus's hand in dealing with Peter, turned elusive. In the end, Saxony-Commonwealth ended up as the only power in the victorious coalition with no territorial gains.

The Polish–Lithuania nobility resisted the Saxon rule and troops in Poland, which led to military resistance. However, the spreading movement, unable to fulfill its mission alone, requested mediation by Peter I. Augustus agreed, and several months of negotiations facilitated by the Russian ambassador followed, with the fighting still intermittently taking place. Eventually Augustus asked for an intervention by Russian forces, the Polish–Lithuanian nobles were defeated by the Saxons in 1716, and a treaty between the king and the Polish–Lithuanian nobility was signed in Warsaw. The Tsardom's mediation and supervision marked a turning point in the Polish/Lithuanian–Russian relations.

Augustus was still able to largely free himself from Peter's protectorate, but in return was excluded from the Treaty of Nystad negotiations. Russia took Livonia, a territory that had been historically contested by Sweden, Russian, and Poland–Lithuania, and the Commonwealth no longer shared a border with Sweden. In real terms, Poland, besides Sweden, was the main victim of the war, because of the damage inflicted on its population, economy, degree of independence, ability to function politically, and potential for self-defense.

Sources

Attributions

CC licensed content, Specific attribution

- Boundless World History. **Authored by**: Boundless. **Located at**: https://courses.lumenlearning.com/boundless-worldhistory/. **License**: *CC BY-SA: Attribution-ShareAlike*

Peter's Domestic Reforms

Learning Objective

- Explain Peter's domestic reforms and what he hoped to accomplish with each of them

Key Points

- Peter the Great recognized the weaknesses of the Russian state and aspired to reform it following Western European models. Seeing the class of *boyars* as obstacles standing in the way of Europeanization and reform, he introduced comprehensive changes into a relatively antiquated system of Russian administration.

- All the administrative reforms, and particularly the introduction of the Table of Ranks, aimed to weaken the position of the old *boyar* class, but they also moved Russia towards the authoritarian rule, where power was largely concentrated in the hand of the head of the state.

- The Orthodox church did not accept Peter's reforms, and Peter refused to accept the power of the patriarch. While the tsar did not abandon Orthodoxy as the main ideological core of the state, he started a process of westernization of the clergy and secular control of the church.

- Peter established Saint Petersburg in 1703. The city was built on the presumption that it would be the most westernized city of Russia. He moved the capital from Moscow to Saint Petersburg in 1712, and the city became the political and cultural center of Russia.

- While Peter died without naming a successor, his manipulations led to the death of his only male heir and the crowning of his second wife, Catherine, the Empress. Catherine was the first woman to rule Imperial Russia, opening the legal path for a century almost entirely dominated by women.

Terms

boyars

Members of the highest rank of the feudal Bulgarian, Moscovian, Ruthenian (Ukraine and Belarus), Wallachian, and Moldavian aristocracies, second only to the ruling princes (or tsars), from the 10th century to the 17th century.

Table of Ranks

A formal list of positions and ranks in the military, government, and court of Imperial Russia. Peter the Great introduced the system in 1722 while engaged in a struggle with the existing hereditary nobility, or boyars. It was formally abolished in 1917 by the newly established Bolshevik government.

Collegia

Government departments in Imperial Russia established in 1717 by Peter the Great. The departments were housed in Saint Petersburg.

Saint Petersburg

Russia's second-largest city after Moscow and an important Russian port on the Baltic Sea. Established by Peter the Great, between 1713–1728 and 1732–1918 it was the imperial capital of Russia. It remains the most westernized city of Russia as well as its cultural capital.

Holy Synod

A congregation of Orthodox church leaders in Russia. It was established by Peter the Great, Stefan Yavorsky, and Feofan Prokopovich in January 1721 to replace the Patriarchate of Moscow. It was abolished following the February Revolution of 1917 and replaced with a restored patriarchate under Tikhon of Moscow.

Peter's Reforms of the Russia State

Unlike most of his predecessors, not only did Peter the Great recognize the weaknesses of the Russian state, which at the time was greatly influenced by the class of *boyars* (feudal elites), but also aspired to reform it following Western European models. Seeing *boyars* as obstacles standing in the way of Europeanization and reform, Peter introduced changes into a relatively antiquated system of Russian administration. In 1708, he established eight governorates and in 1711 the Governing Senate. All its members, originally ten individuals, were appointed by the tsar. The senate did not interrupt the activity and was the permanent operating state body. In 1713, Landrats (from the German word for "national council") were created in each of the governorates. They were staffed by professional civil servants, who assisted a royally-appointed governor. In 1719, after the establishment of government departments known as the Collegia, Peter remade

Russia's administrative divisions once more. The new provinces were modeled on the Swedish system, in which larger, more politically important areas received more political autonomy, while smaller, more rural areas were controlled more directly by the state.

Peter's distrust of the elitist and anti-reformist *boyars* culminated in 1722 with the creation of the Table of Ranks, a formal list of ranks in the Russian military, government, and royal court. The Table of Ranks established a complex system of titles and honorifics, each classed with a number denoting a specific level of service or loyalty to the tsar. Previously, high-ranking state positions were hereditary, but with the establishment of the Table of Ranks, anyone, including a commoner, could work their way up the bureaucratic hierarchy with sufficient hard work and skill. While all these administrative reforms aimed to weaken the position of the old *boyar* class, they also moved Russia towards authoritarian rule, where power was largely concentrated in the hand of the head of the state.

Church Reforms

The Russian tsars traditionally exerted some influence on church operations. However, until Peter's reforms, the church had been relatively free in its internal governance. Peter lost the support of the Russian clergy over his modernizing reforms as local hierarchs became very suspicious of his friendship with foreigners and his alleged Protestant propensities. The tsar did not abandon Orthodoxy as the main ideological core of the state, but attempted to start a process of westernization of the clergy, relying on those with a Western theological education. Simultaneously, Peter remained faithful to the canons of the Eastern Orthodox church. Inviting Ukrainian and Belorussian clergymen, mostly graduates of the highly acclaimed westernized Kiev-Mohyla Academy, unintentionally led to the "Ukrainization" of the Russian church, and by the middle of the 18th century the majority of the Russian Orthodox church was headed by people from Ukraine.

The traditional leader of the church was the Patriarch of Moscow. In 1700, when the office fell vacant, Peter refused to name a replacement and created the position of the custodian of the patriarchal throne, which he controlled by appointing his own candidates. He could not tolerate the thought that a patriarch could have power superior to the tsar, as indeed had happened in the case of Philaret (1619–1633) and Nikon (1652–1666). In 1721, he established the Holy Synod (originally the Ecclesiastical College), which replaced patriarchy altogether. It was administered by a lay director, or Ober-Procurator. The Synod changed in composition over time, but basically it remained a committee of churchmen headed by a lay appointee of the emperor. Furthermore, a new ecclesiastic educational system was begun under Peter. It aimed to improve the usually very poor education of local priests and monks. However, the curriculum was so westernized (emphasis on Latin language and subjects for the price of limited exposure to Greek, the Eastern Church Fathers, and Russian and Slavonic church languages) that monks and priests, while being formally educated, received poor training in preparation for a ministry to a Russian-speaking population steeped in the traditions of Eastern Orthodoxy.

Saint Petersburg

In 1703, during the Great Northern War, Peter the Great established the Peter and Paul fortress on small Hare Island, by the north bank of the Neva River. The fortress was the first brick and stone building of the new projected capital city of Russia and the original citadel of what would eventually be Saint Petersburg. The city was built by conscripted peasants from all over Russia, and tens of thousands of serfs died building it. Peter moved the capital from Moscow to Saint Petersburg in 1712, but referred to Saint Petersburg as the capital (or seat of government) as early as 1704. Western European architects, most notably Swiss Italian Domenico Trezzini and French Jean-Baptiste Alexandre Le Blond, shaped the city in the initial stages of its construction. Such buildings as the Menshikov Palace, Kunstkamera, Peter and Paul Cathedral, and Twelve Collegia became prominent architectural landmarks. In 1724, Peter also established the Academy of Sciences, the University, and the Academic Gymnasium. Saint Petersburg is still the most Westernized city in and the cultural capital of Russia.

Collage of pictures from Saint Petersburg. Clockwise from top left: Peter and Paul Fortress on Zayachy Island, Smolny Cathedral, Bronze Horseman on Senate Square, the Winter Palace, Trinity Cathedral, and the Moyka river with the General Staff Building.

Succession

Peter had two wives, with whom he had fourteen children, but only three survived to adulthood. Upon his return from his European tour in 1698, he sought to end his unhappy arranged marriage to Eudoxia Lopukhina. He divorced the tsaritsa and forced her into joining a convent. Only one child from the marriage, Tsarevich Alexei, survived past his childhood. In 1712, Peter formally married his long-time mistress, Martha Skavronskaya, who upon her conversion to the Russian Orthodox church took the name Catherine.

Peter suspected his eldest child and heir, Alexei, of being involved in a plot to overthrow the emperor. Alexei was tried and confessed under torture during questioning conducted by a secular court. He was convicted and sentenced to be executed. The sentence could be carried out only with Peter's signed authorization, but Alexei died in prison, as Peter hesitated before making the decision. In 1724, Peter had his second wife, Catherine, crowned as empress, although he remained Russia's actual ruler. He died a year later without naming a successor. As Catherine represented the interests of the "new men," commoners who had been brought to positions of great power by Peter based on competence, a successful coup was arranged by her supporters in order to prevent the old elites from controlling the laws of succession.
Catherine was the first woman to rule Imperial Russia (as empress), opening the legal path for a century almost entirely dominated by women, including her daughter Elizabeth and granddaughter-in-law Catherine the Great, all of whom continued Peter the Great's policies in modernizing Russia.

Catherine I of Russia by Jean-Marc Nattier (1716). Catherine, Peter's second wife, was the first woman to rule Imperial Russia (as empress), opening the legal path for a century almost entirely dominated by women.

Sources

Attributions

CC licensed content, Specific attribution

- Boundless World History. **Authored by**: Boundless. **Located at**: https://courses.lumenlearning.com/boundless-worldhistory/. **License**: *CC BY-SA: Attribution-ShareAlike*

9 781641 760133